IMPLOSIONS / EXPLOSIONS

Imprint

Art direction, cover design and editorial coordination
Danika Cooper and Ghazal Jafari
Book design template jovis: Susanne Rösler
Cover Tar sands, Alberta, Canada; photographer Garth Lenz
Proofreading Inez Templeton, Berlin
Lithography Bild1Druck, Berlin
Printing and binding Graspo CZ a.s., Zlín

Bibliographic information published by the Deutsche Nationalbibliothek
The Deutsche Nationalbibliothek lists this publication in the Deutsche
Nationalbibliografie; detailed bibliographic data are available on the Internet
at http://dnb.d-nb.de

jovis Verlag GmbH
Kurfürstenstraße 15/16
10785 Berlin

www.jovis.de

jovis books are available worldwide in selected bookstores. Please contact
your nearest bookseller or visit www.jovis.de for information concerning your
local distribution.

ISBN 978-3-86859-317-4

jovis

IMPLOSIONS / EXPLOSIONS

TOWARDS A STUDY OF PLANETARY URBANIZATION

EDITED BY NEIL BRENNER

PREFACE

This book is a collection of texts connected to a project on planetary urbanization which is being pursued by myself and Christian Schmid of the ETH Zurich in collaboration with researchers at our respective institutions. The book is intended to offer our own collaborators, as well as urban researchers and practitioners elsewhere with allied agendas, some orientation for deciphering the variegated urbanization processes that are presently transforming the planetary socio-ecological landscape. This involves a variety of interlayered forays into concept development, methodological experimentation, historical genealogy, geopolitical economy and cartographic speculation, as well as an immanent critique of inherited and contemporary urban ideologies.

In thus proceeding, we aspire neither to make a definitive statement of the approach under development here, nor do we claim to offer a representative selection of the full diversity of perspectives that are being articulated within the vibrant terrain of contemporary urban theory. Instead, this book is intended simply to draw together some of the core texts associated with an emergent framework that we consider fruitful for deciphering both historical and contemporary urbanization patterns under capitalism. The collection includes several classic texts by pioneering thinkers such as Henri Lefebvre, David Harvey, Edward Soja, Terry McGee, Roberto Luis Monte-Mór and Marcel Meili, as well as a selection of more recent interventions from the last several years—mostly by colleagues and students with whom we are engaged in intensive collaborations and discussions—that advance this approach. The book's contents thus reflect the terrain of a transcontinental dialogue on urbanization and urban theory that has been under way for several years, not only among researchers in Cambridge and Zurich, but also with close colleagues in New York City and Toronto, as well as, among other places, Belo Horizonte, London, Los Angeles, Madrid, Melbourne, Miami, Singapore and Vancouver.

At this stage of our work on the *problematique* of planetary urbanization, only our questions have come into clear focus; the heavy labor of conceptualization, analysis and representation has only just begun. Christian Schmid and I are continuing our work in elaborating and applying our own theory of extended urbanization, both in our joint writing projects and in collaboration with research teams in Cambridge, Zurich and Singapore. We hope that others—scholars, practitioners, activists—will join these developing efforts to reconceptualize the contemporary urban question, not least through critical engagement with the ideas assembled in this volume.

My own perspective on planetary urbanization, as presented in my contributions to this book, has been forged through an intense, long-term dialogue, collaboration and friendship with Christian Schmid. His writings figure crucially throughout this volume, and our collaborative work continues as we wrestle with a variety of thorny epistemological, conceptual, methodological and representational challenges. Our theorization of extended urbanization builds upon and attempts to develop many of the concepts, methods and agendas that are woven through the present volume. While our jointly authored chapters in this volume introduce the broad contours of that theorization, our main statement on the topic is not included here; it will be presented separately as a journal article and, subsequently, as a chapter in our book, *Planetary Urbanization*.[1]

An early version of the theoretical agenda presented in this book was developed during the closing years of my work in the Department of Sociology and Metropolitan Studies Program at New York University, in dialogue with a cluster of brilliant doctoral students in Sociology and American Studies. These include Hillary Angelo, Daniel Aldana Cohen, David J. Madden (now at the London School of Economics), Stuart Schrader and David Wachsmuth. Several chapters in this book originated from those dialogues, and I look forward to future contributions and interventions from this remarkably adventurous generation of critical urbanists.

Andy Merrifield, whose texts likewise occupy a prominent place in this book, has been a long-time friend and comrade, and a persistent interlocutor about the prospects for radical urban theory and practice. His own recent book, *The Politics of the Encounter*, represents a path-breaking foray into the conceptualization of planetary urbanization and the new geographies of political struggle it has provoked.[2] I am hugely grateful for his permission to include several key texts here which are connected to the latter project.

This book is linked closely to my ongoing work as Director of the Urban Theory Lab (UTL) at the Harvard Graduate School of Design (GSD), where I was fortunate to assume a professorship as of summer 2011. I am deeply grateful to Mohsen Mostafavi, Dean of the GSD, for his support of the school's Research Advancement Initiative, which has enabled this and other newly established research/design labs at the GSD to flourish. Additional support for the UTL's ongoing research activities has been generously provided through the Real Estate Academic Initiative (REAI) and the Milton Fund, both of Harvard University. I owe a special note of gratitude to the Weatherhead Center for International Affairs, Harvard University, especially to Executive Director Steven Bloomfield, for a friendly welcome to campus and for generously supporting a variety of UTL research endeavors. The UTL is now gaining momentum in several projects, thanks in no small part to the energetic engagement of its key participants from the GSD's doctoral programs (PhD and Doctor of Design Studies) and Master in Design Studies (MDesS) programs. Particular thanks are due to Ali Fard, Kian Goh, Daniel Ibañez and Nikos Katsikis for their substantial contributions to pushing forward the UTL's developing agenda for theory, research and cartographic experimentation.

The design team for the book consisted of Danika Cooper and Ghazal Jafari of the Harvard GSD's MDesS Program in Urbanism, Landscape, Ecology (ULE); both deserve my deepest thanks for a productive collaboration under a tight deadline. I would also like to extend my thanks to Philipp Sperrle and Susanne Rösler of jovis Verlag in Berlin for their steadfast support for our work on this project. Christine Hwang provided able assistance on various copyediting and administrative tasks.

David Wachsmuth, Christian Schmid, Ingeborg Rocker, Matthew Gandy, Margit Mayer and Ann Yoachim provided invaluable guidance on several crucial editorial and production decisions during various stages of the project's development.

The images used on the book's cover, in the opening pages and in the section introductions offer a striking, if disturbing, lens into the intellectual and political *problematique* we are attempting to open and explore in these pages. We are grateful to photojournalist Garth Lenz for generously collaborating with us to permit their reproduction in this volume.

Many chapters in this book are original contributions, but a number have been published in various scholarly journals since 2010. I would like extend my sincerest thanks to the publishers of these works for their kind cooperation with our requests for permission to include them in this volume. Particular gratitude is due to several friends and colleagues—Bob Catterall, Editor of *CITY*; Julie-Anne Boudreau and Maria Kaika, Editors of the *International Journal of Urban and Regional Research*; and Stuart Elden, Editor of *Environment and Planning D: Society and Space*—for generously supporting and facilitating our use of several key chapters.

—Neil Brenner
Cambridge, USA
August 2013

[1] Neil Brenner and Christian Schmid, *Towards a Theory of Extended Urbanization* (Urban Theory Lab: Harvard-GSD and ETH Zurich, 2013).

[2] Andy Merrifield, *The Politics of the Encounter: Urban Theory and Protest under Planetary Urbanization* (Athens: University of Georgia Press, 2013).

CONTENTS

SEVEN
POLITICAL STRATEGIES, STRUGGLES AND HORIZONS

CODA

1
INTRODUCTION: URBAN THEORY WITHOUT AN OUTSIDE

Neil Brenner

The urban question has long been a flashpoint for intense debate among researchers concerned with the nature of cities and urbanization processes.[1] Despite profound differences of methodology, analytical focus and political orientation, the major twentieth-century approaches to this question have taken an entity commonly labeled as *the city* (or some lexical variation thereof) as their primary unit of analysis and site of investigation.

This foundational epistemological focus was canonized in the 1925 mission statement of urban sociology by Chicago School founders Ernest Burgess and Robert Park, laconically but confidently titled *The City*.[2] It subsequently evolved into a basically self-evident presupposition—so obvious that it did not require explanation or justification—across diverse traditions and terrains of urban research. Indeed, despite their significant epistemological, methodological and political differences from Chicago School urban sociology, the major strands of mid- to late twentieth-century urban studies have likewise focused their analytical gaze primarily, if not exclusively, on "city-like" (nodal, relatively large, densely populated and self-enclosed) sociospatial units. This generalization applies to mainstream quantitative research on city-size distributions, central place systems and urban hierarchies; to the periodizations of capitalist urban development by radical political economists in the 1970s and 1980s; to the influential analyses of post-Fordist cities, global city formation and megacity expansion in the 1990s; and to more recent research forays on neoliberal cities, ordinary cities and postcolonial cities in the late

1990s and into the early 2000s. Whatever their specific methodological orientations, *explananda* and politico-theoretical agendas, each of these influential approaches to the urban question has either (a) documented the replication of city-like settlement types across larger territories; or (b) used a modifying term—mercantile, industrial, Fordist-Keynesian, post-Keynesian, post-Fordist, global, mega, neoliberal, ordinary, postcolonial and so forth—to demarcate its research terrain as a subset of a putatively more general sociospatial form, "the" city.[3]

Of course, there have been many terms on offer for labeling the city-like unit in question—metropolis, conurbation, city-region, metropolitan area, megalopolis, megapolitan zone, and so forth—and these appropriately reflect the changing boundaries, morphologies and scales of human settlement patterns.[4] Concomitantly, across and within each of the aforementioned research traditions, intense debates have long raged regarding the origins, internal dynamics and consequences of city-building, and more generally, regarding the functions of cities in relation to broader political-economic, sociocultural and demographic transformations.[5] But underneath the tumult of disagreement and the relentless series of paradigm shifts that have animated urban theory and research during the last century, a basic consensus has persisted: the urban *problematique* is thought to be embodied, at core, in *cities*—conceived as settlement types characterized by certain indicative features (such as largeness, density and social diversity) that make them qualitatively distinct from a *non-city* social world (suburban, rural and/or "natural") located "beyond" or "outside" them.[6] In effect, as Hillary Angelo and David Wachsmuth explain in their contribution to this volume, the epistemology of urban studies has been characterized by a deeply entrenched *methodological cityism,* which entails "an analytical privileging, isolation and … naturalization of the city in studies of urban processes where the non-city may also be significant."[7]

This book assembles a series of contributions to the urban question that push strongly against the grain of that epistemology. Through diverse modes of engagement (conceptual, methodological, historical, political-economic, representational) and analytical windows (social scientific, cartographic, literary and cinematic), its chapters articulate the elements of a radically different way of understanding the *problematique* of urban theory and research, and more generally, of conceptualizing the imprint and operationality of urban processes on the planetary landscape. In so doing, we aim to advance a hitherto largely subterranean stream of urban research that has, since the mid-twentieth century, cast doubt upon established understandings of the urban as a bounded, nodal and relatively self-enclosed sociospatial condition in favor of more territorially differentiated, morphologically variable, multiscalar and processual conceptualizations.[8] Building upon various concepts, methods and mappings derived from that work, especially Henri Lefebvre's approach, this book aspires to supersede the urban/non-urban divide that has long anchored the epistemology of urban research, and on this basis, to develop a new vision of urban theory *without an outside.*

In so doing, the book's contributors preserve the analytical centrality of agglomeration to the *problematique* of urban theory, but interpret it as only one dimension and morphological expression of the capitalist form of urbanization. In this understanding, the development, intensification and worldwide expansion of capitalism produces a vast, variegated terrain of urban(ized) conditions that include yet progressively extend beyond the zones of agglomeration that have long monopolized the attention of urban researchers. As this erstwhile non-urban realm is increasingly subsumed within and operationalized by a world-encompassing—and, indeed, world-*making*—process of capitalist urbanization, the meaning of the urban must itself be fundamentally reimagined both in theory and in practice.[9]

• • •

Why should the urban/non-urban distinction be transcended, and why now? Clearly, settlement space has long been differentiated by place names, and it seems intuitive to demarcate the terrain of the urban, both historically and today, with reference to the names of the world's great cities—London, New York, Shenzhen, Mumbai, Lagos and so forth. Even amidst the intense volatility associated with accelerated geoeconomic restructuring, such places clearly *do* still exist, and in fact, their size and strategic economic importance appear to be growing, not diminishing. But what, exactly, *are* these places, aside from names on a map that have been institutionalized by governments and branded as investment locations by growth coalitions? What distinguishes them qualitatively from other places within and beyond, say, the South East of England and Western Europe; the US Northeast and North America; the Pearl River Delta and East Asia; Maharashtra and South Asia; or southern Nigeria and West Africa? Do they contain some special quality that makes them unique—their size, perhaps, or their population density? Their infrastructural outlays? Their strategic centrality in global flows of capital and labor? Or, on the other hand, have the sociospatial relations of urbanism that were once apparently contained within these units now exploded haphazardly beyond them, via the ever thickening commodity chains, infrastructural circuits, migration streams and circulatory-logistical networks that today crisscross the planet? But, if this is the case, can any erstwhile city, whatever its size, still be said to have coherent boundaries? Have the everyday social relations, inter-firm networks, labor markets, built environments, infrastructural corridors and socioenvironmental footprints associated with such densified clusters now been extended, thickened, superimposed and interwoven to forge what Jean Gottmann once vividly described as an "irregularly colloidal mixture of rural and suburban landscapes" on national, international, continental and even global scales?[10] And, to the degree that all this is indeed occurring, in a world in which "the city is everywhere and in everything," shouldn't the inherited understanding of the urban as a distinctive settlement type be abandoned, or at least be radically reconceptualized?[11]

This was, of course, precisely the position advanced by Lefebvre over four decades ago, when he opened *La révolution urbaine* with the provocative hypothesis that "society has been completely urbanized."[12] Although he viewed complete urbanization as a virtual object—an emergent condition rather than an actualized reality—Lefebvre suggested that the broad outlines of a complete formation of urbanization were already coming into relief during the 1960s in Western Europe. They were evidenced, he argued, in the fragmentation and destruction of traditional European cities; in the formation of a large-scale territorial megalopolis stretching from England, Paris and the Ruhr region to Scandinavia; in the extension of logistical, commercial and tourist infrastructures deep into previously remote areas; in the construction of major industrial estates and large-scale housing ensembles in formerly peripheral locations in France, Spain and Italy; in the destruction of quasi-autonomous agrarian communities in formerly rural zones; and in wide-ranging processes of environmental degradation across the continent.[13] When actualized on a planetary scale, Lefebvre suggested, such tendencies would entail a relentless, if fragmentary, interweaving of an urban fabric—a "net of uneven mesh"—across the entire world, including terrestrial surfaces, the oceans, the atmosphere and the subterranean, all of which would be ever more directly instrumentalized and operationalized to serve the voracious pursuit of capitalist industrial growth.[14]

In several striking formulations, Lefebvre characterizes the generalization of capitalist urbanization as a process of "implosion-explosion," a phrase he introduced to illuminate the mutually recursive links between capitalist forms of agglomeration and broader transformations of territory, landscape and environment. In some of his initial formulations, Lefebvre uses the metaphor of implosion-explosion in an almost Mumfordesque manner, to characterize the destruction of European mercantile cities (the moment of implosion) and the subsequent growth of megalopolitan territorial formations to support industrialization (the moment of explosion).[15] But Lefebvre subsequently expands his use of the implosion-explosion metaphor to describe some of the wide-ranging territorial transformations that have ensued at various spatial scales during the *longue durée* history of capitalist urbanization. As cities are extended outwards into their surrounding territories and are woven together via thickening long-distance logistics networks, these erstwhile non-city zones are more tightly integrated into large-scale spatial divisions of labor. With the intensification, acceleration and territorial expansion of capitalist forms of growth, precapitalist and mercantile cities and towns are either peripheralized or remade into strategic locations within heavily industrialized landscapes. Subsequently, a further round of sociospatial explosion occurs as urban practices, institutions, infrastructures and built environments are projected aggressively into and across the erstwhile non-urban realm, annihilating any transparent differentiation between city and countryside, and linking local and regional economies more directly to transnational flows of raw material, commodities, labor and capital. In this way, processes of concentration and dispersion, as well as new patterns of core-periphery polarization, are superimposed upon one another across places, territories and scales, creating an almost kaleidoscopic churning of sociospatial arrangements during successive cycles of capitalist development. The notion of implosion-explosion thus comes to describe the production and continual transformation of an industrialized urban fabric in which centers of agglomeration and their operational landscapes are woven together in mutually transformative ways while being co-articulated into a worldwide capitalist system.[16]

In a provocative, widely discussed diagram presented in the opening chapter of *La révolution urbaine*, Lefebvre uses the notion of implosion-explosion to describe the broad constellation of historical-geographical transformations that would, he believed, herald the onset of complete urbanization on a world scale—specifically, "urban concentration, rural exodus, extension of the urban fabric, complete subordination of the agrarian to the urban" (see page 43). When this "critical point" is reached, Lefebvre suggests, the condition of complete urbanization will no longer be hypothetical—a mere "virtual object" whose tendencies are selectively manifested in particular territories, whether in Europe or elsewhere.[17] It will, rather, have become a basic parameter for *planetary* social and environmental relations, imposing new constraints upon the use and transformation of the worldwide built environment, unleashing potentially catastrophic inequalities, conflicts and dangers, but also harboring new opportunities for the democratic appropriation and self-management of space at all scales. In the late 1980s, in one of his final texts, Lefebvre suggested that the critical point of complete urbanization had actually been crossed, and thus that a "planetarization of the urban" was now being realized in practice.[18]

The contributions to this book build upon and extend Lefebvre's hypothesis and subsequent analysis. They suggest various ways in which Lefebvre's virtual object of complete urbanization is today being actualized, albeit unevenly, on a worldwide scale, as well as in specific territories, regions and places; and they explore some of the wide-ranging intellectual, social, political and environmental implications of this state of affairs. As many chapters included here suggest, this newly consolidated, planetary formation of urbanization has blurred, even exploded, long-entrenched sociospatial borders—not only between city and countryside, urban and rural, core and periphery, metropole and colony, society and nature, but also between the urban, regional, national and global scales themselves—thereby creating new formations of a thickly urbanized landscape whose contours are extremely difficult, if not impossible, to theorize, much less to map, on the basis of inherited approaches to urban studies. The present volume assembles some conceptual, methodological, analytical and cartographic tools through which that challenge might be productively confronted. The notion of implosion-explosion is useful in this endeavor not because it offers a finished theory or a fully differentiated cartography of our emergent global-urban moment, but simply because it begins to demarcate the vast, unwieldy *problematique* that opens before us as the legacies of methodological cityism are questioned and tendentially superseded.

●　●　●

In exploring this emergent agenda, our claim in this book is decidedly *not*, as some urbanists have occasionally proposed, that cities (or, more precisely, zones of agglomeration) are dissolving into a placeless society of global flows, borderless connectivity or haphazard spatial dispersal.[19] Nor do we suggest that population density, inter-firm clustering, agglomeration effects or infrastructural concentration—to name just a few of the conditions that are commonly associated with the phenomenon of cityness under modern capitalism—are no longer operationally significant features in contemporary economy and society. On the contrary, the contributors to this volume remain fundamentally concerned with agglomeration processes, their changing role in regimes of capital accumulation, and their variegated expressions in diverse morphological forms and spatial configurations—from large-scale urban regions, polycentric metropolitan territories and linear urban corridors, to inter-urban networks and worldwide urban hierarchies. They simply insist, as Matthew Gandy succinctly proposes, that "cities are just a form of urbanization," and thus that they must be understood as dynamically evolving sites, arenas and outcomes of broader processes of sociospatial and socioecological transformation.[20] David Harvey offers an equally concise formulation of this proposition with his suggestion that "the 'thing' we call a 'city' is the outcome of a 'process' that we call 'urbanization.'"[21]

But how, precisely, to theorize this *process* of urbanization and its variegated geographies? In fact, this task poses considerable challenges because, even though the concept of urbanization may initially appear to connote the dynamic, processual qualities emphasized by Gandy and Harvey, it has actually long been thoroughly mired in the epistemological assumptions of methodological cityism. Along with other meta-concepts such as industrialization, modernization, democratization and rationalization, the concept of urbanization has a long history in the modern social and historical sciences, and has generally been used to invoke one of the putatively all-pervasive "large processes" of modern capitalist social formations.[22] Yet, in most accounts, whether within urban studies, social theory or historical sociology, urbanization refers, *tout court*, to the process of *city* growth: it is circumscribed, by definition, to refer only to the growth of large, and perhaps dense or diverse, settlements, generally in conjunction with some of the other macro-trends of capitalist modernity.

Although its origins may be traced to various strands of nineteenth- and early twentieth-century social theory, such a conceptualization was paradigmatically embodied in American sociologist Kingsley Davis' classic, mid-twentieth-century definition of urbanization as the expansion of the city-based population relative to the total national population. Rather than defining cities in social, morphological or functional terms, Davis famously used numerical population thresholds—generally 20,000 or 100,000—to demarcate their specificity as settlement types.[23] Davis concisely summarized this strictly empirical understanding in the formula: $U = P_c / P_t$ (U = urbanization; P_c = population of cities; and P_t = total national population); and he subsequently devoted several decades of careful empirical research to its international application, eventually producing the first comprehensive worldwide survey of national urbanization levels.[24]

As Christian Schmid and I argue in Ch. 21 below, Davis' mid-century definition is today firmly institutionalized in the data collection systems that are still used by the United Nations (UN) and other global organizations, and it is also still rigidly entrenched within major strands of contemporary social science, urban planning, social policy and public health.[25] Indeed, it is precisely this empiricist, city-centric conceptualization of urbanization that underpins the influential contemporary assertion that an "urban age" has recently dawned due to the putative shift of the majority of the world's population from the countryside to the city. Aside from its empirical blind-spots, which are considerable given the non-standardized definitions of settlement types that are intermixed within the UN's data tables, such a proposition is a deeply misleading basis for understanding the contemporary global urban condition. It presupposes a narrow, ahistorical and population-centric concept of the city, which does not adequately grasp the extraordinary scale and diversity of agglomeration processes that are associated with contemporary forms of urban development around the world. Just as importantly, the urban age concept fails to illuminate the wide-ranging operations and impacts of urbanization processes beyond the large centers of agglomeration, including in zones of resource extraction, agro-industrial enclosure, logistics and communications infrastructure, tourism and waste disposal, which often traverse peripheral, remote and apparently "rural" or "natural" locations.[26]

While such operational landscapes may not contain the population densities, settlement properties, social fabric and infrastructural equipment that are commonly associated with cities, they have long played strategically essential roles in supporting the latter, whether by supplying raw materials, energy, water, food or labor, or through logistics, communications or waste processing functions. More generally, as Marx recognized in his classic analysis of original accumulation (*ursprüngliche Akkumulation*) in *Volume 1* of *Capital*, the enclosure, commodification and ongoing reorganization of such landscapes has figured crucially throughout the history of capitalism in the dispossession, displacement and proletarianization of the very populations that so often cluster within large urban centers.[27] The capitalist form of agglomeration thus presupposes the enclosure and operationalization of large-scale territories located well beyond the city to support its most basic socioeconomic activities, metabolic cycles and growth imperatives.[28] Today, such landscapes are being comprehensively produced, engineered or redesigned through a surge of infrastructural investments, enclosures and large-scale territorial planning strategies intended to support the accelerated growth and expansion of agglomerations around the world. Their developmental rhythms are thus being linked ever more directly to those of the major urban centers via worldwide spatial divisions of labor; and their continuing commodification, enclosure and socioecological degradation is contributing to the forms of mass dispossession and displacement that are uncritically catalogued or even celebrated in contemporary urban age discourse under the rubric of "rural-to-urban" demographic change.[29] Consequently, if a global urban age is indeed currently dawning, this circumstance cannot be understood adequately with reference to the formation of global cities or large-scale megacity regions, but requires systematic consideration of the tendential, if uneven, operationalization of the entire planet—including terrestrial, subterranean, oceanic and atmospheric space—to serve an accelerating, intensifying process of urban industrial development.[30] Insofar as the dominant model of capitalist urbanization continues to be based upon the generalized extraction, production and consumption of fossil fuels, it is directly implicated in a form of global ecological plunder that has permanently altered the earth's climate, while infiltrating the earth's soils, oceans, rivers and atmosphere with unprecedented levels of toxic waste.[31]

From this point of view, then, morphological or population-centric approaches are extremely misleading lenses into the emergent dynamics of global urbanization. This process cannot be understood adequately either with reference to intensified population growth within the world's largest cities, or simply as a replication of city-like settlement types across the earth's surface. Nor, on the other hand, can traditional notions of the hinterland or the rural adequately capture the processes of extended urbanization through which formerly marginalized or remote spaces are being enclosed, operationalized, designed and planned to support the continued agglomeration of capital, labor and infrastructure within the world's large cities and megacity regions. Instead, a new understanding of urbanization is needed, which explicitly theorizes the evolving, mutually recursive relations between agglomeration processes and their operational landscapes, including the forms of land-use intensification, logistical coordination, core-periphery polarization and sociopolitical struggle that accompany the latter at all spatial scales.

Through a variety of methodological strategies and substantive interventions, the contributions to this book offer useful intellectual tools for such an analysis. They replace city- and settlement-centric, population-based models of urbanization with an exploration of the dynamics of implosion-explosion under capitalism, as outlined in general terms above with reference to Lefebvre's provocative metaphor. In such a conceptualization, implosion and explosion are not separate temporal sequences or distinct morphological crystallizations, but represent "moments" in the dialectical sense of the term—mutually interdependent yet intensely conflictual dimensions of a historically constituted, discontinuously evolving totality. As such, processes of implosion-explosion also necessarily involve what Lefebvre aptly termed "the politics of space"—contestation over the political-economic hierarchies and power relations that are inscribed in, and in turn transform, sociospatial arrangements.[32] The key elements of this theorization are summarized schematically in Figure 1.1 (see next page); they are elaborated at length, via diverse avenues of conceptualization, analysis, representation, speculation and critique, in the chapters that follow.

• • •

This book does not provide a definitive statement of the agendas outlined above, but is intended to assemble intellectual resources for elaborating them. The first word of its subtitle, "*towards* a study of planetary urbanization," is meant literally; such a study has

	Methodological cityism	Urban theory without an outside
Unit of analysis	Bounded: the city as a settlement type that is contrasted to other settlement types, usually within a national territory	Open, variegated, multiscalar: the urban as an unevenly developed yet worldwide condition and process of sociospatial transformation
Model of territorial organization	Typological, binary: territory is differentiated among distinct settlement types, with cities contrasted to specific non-city zones—suburbs, towns, villages, rural areas, the countryside and "natural" areas	Processual, dialectical: agglomerations ("cities") relate dialectically to their ("non-city") operational landscapes, which are in turn continually transformed through their roles in supporting agglomerations
Understanding of territorial development	Population-centric: growth of city populations relative to total (national) population size	Mediated through capitalism, state strategies and sociopolitical struggle: worldwide implosion/explosion of capitalist sociospatial organization, encompassing the evolving relations between agglomerations and their operational landscapes within a crisis-prone capitalist world economy
Model of *longue durée* historical- geographical change	Linear, universal: specific cities may grow or decline, but the phenomenon of cityness is increasingly universalized as a settlement type around the world	Discontinuous, uneven: sociospatial configurations (including both agglomerations and their operational landscapes) are creatively destroyed through the crisis-tendencies of capital (mediated through state institutions and sociopolitical struggles), contributing to successive rounds of territorial differentiation and redifferentiation at various spatial scales

1.1 Rethinking the urbanization question

yet to be conducted, but it may be productively informed through some of the concepts, methods, cartographies and political orientations assembled in this book. As Figure 1.2 indicates, the chapters included here fall into three broad categories.

Classic and background texts. This book is not intended to offer a survey either of work on urbanization in general or on the contemporary formation of this process. However, a number of key texts from earlier periods of research on these topics acquire renewed contemporary significance in the context of the wide-ranging intellectual agenda proposed here. Accordingly, several earlier texts have been included that introduce essential analytical tools for our work. The earliest among these is an excerpt from Henri Lefebvre's *La révolution urbaine* (1970), but others range in publication date from the late 1980s to the mid-2000s. They include one of Lefebvre's last publications—a short, rather gloomy essay for *Le Monde* (1989); as well as Terry McGee's pioneering explosion of the urban-rural divide in relation to the *desakota* regions of Asia (1991); an early theorization of extended

Classic and background texts (1970 to 2007)	• Lefebvre, Ch. 2 (1970) • Harvey, Ch. 3 (1996) • Schmid, Ch. 4 (2006) • Meili, Ch. 7 (2006) • Monte-Mór, Ch. 8 (1994) • McGee, Ch. 9 (1991) • Soja and Kanai, Ch. 10 (2007) • Monte- Mór, Ch. 17 (2005) • Schmid, Ch. 18 (2006) • Schmid, Ch. 26 (2006) • Lefebvre, Ch. 34 (1989)
Recent texts (2011-2013)	• Gandy, Ch. 5 (2012) • Schmid, Ch. 6 (2012) • Brenner and Schmid, Ch. 11 (2011) • Merrifield, Ch. 12 (2013) • Brenner, Ch. 13 (2012) • Schmid, Ch. 14 (2012) • Soja, Ch. 19 (2011) • Brenner and Schmid, Ch. 21 (2013) • Gleeson, Ch. 22 (2013) • Wachsmuth, Ch. 23 (2013) • Angelo and Wachsmuth, Ch. 24 (2013) • Brenner and Katsikis, Ch. 27 (2013) • Madden, Ch. 30 (2012) • Merrifield, Ch. 31 (2011)
Newly commissioned texts	• Goonewardena, Ch. 15 • Sevilla-Buitrago, Ch. 16 • Kipfer, Ch. 20 • Merrifield, Ch. 25 • UTL-GSD, Ch. 28 • Katsikis, Ch. 29 • Ajl, Ch. 32 • Friedmann, Ch. 33

1.2 Overview of chapters—period of publication

urbanization by Brazilian planner Roberto Luis Monte-Mór with specific reference to the Amazon (1994) and spatial development in Brazil more generally (2005); a concise, forceful defense of a process-based theorization of urbanization by David Harvey (1996); several excerpts from the pathbreaking, multivolume study of complete urbanization in Switzerland by two members of Studio Basel's research team, Marcel Meili and Christian Schmid (2006); and Ed Soja and J. Miguel Kanai's preliminary yet precise demarcation of the emergent worldwide urban fabric (2006). While these texts were produced prior to the consolidation of the research agenda sketched above, they offer some essential concepts and perspectives that may inform such an investigation.

Recent texts. The bulk of the book is composed of articles and essays on various aspects of planetary urbanization that have been produced during the last several years, mainly by members of my own research group, the Urban Theory Lab (which relocated from New York City to the Harvard GSD during this time), and through an ongoing collaboration with Christian Schmid of the ETH-Zurich. Although not immediately connected either to the Urban Theory Lab or to Christian Schmid's research teams in Zurich and Singapore, our friends and colleagues Matthew Gandy, Brendan Gleeson and Andy Merrifield produced closely aligned interventions during this same period. Their chapters resonate powerfully with the work of our Lab and research network, while extending it in important, original directions. To date, Merrifield's *The Politics of the Encounter* is the only book-length study of planetary urbanization, but the proliferation of articles and essays on this topic during the last two or three years does suggest that a new *problematique*—a set of interconnected explorations and inquiries around a common set of questions—is emerging and gaining some intellectual traction and momentum.[33]

Newly commissioned texts. A final cluster of texts was commissioned specifically for this book, either through projects emerging directly from within the Urban Theory Lab or through dialogues and exchanges with colleagues based elsewhere. These texts broach essential topics that have only partially been addressed in our work to date—including, among others, the historical geographies of enclosure and urbanization (Sevilla-Buitrago, Goonewardena); urbanization, colonization and everyday life (Kipfer, Goonewardena); urbanization and the agrarian question (Sevilla-Buitrago, Ajl); the critique of technoscientific approaches to "world management" (Katsikis); and the politics of spatial organization, urban and otherwise (Kipfer, Goonewardena, Friedmann). Other newly commissioned texts complement themes covered in several sections of the book—these include a chapter by Andy Merrifield on the future of urban studies, and an overview of the problem of visualizing worldwide urbanization by Urban Theory Lab researchers. Taken together, these newly produced chapters reinforce the agendas that have been developed through the Urban Theory Lab's work since 2011, while opening up a range of questions—methodological, historical, contextual, representational and (geo)political—that urgently require sustained attention and elaboration in future work on this *problematique*.

Following this introductory chapter, the book is divided into seven sections followed by a brief Coda. Figure 1.3 surveys the intellectual terrain of the book as a whole by summarizing the key questions around which each of the seven sections, and the Coda, are focused.

Some readers may wish to navigate the book sequentially. Such an approach should prove highly productive insofar as it will offer multiple perspectives on the issues explored within each section, while permitting readers to gain familiarity with the key concepts, methods and arguments upon which successive sections of the book are grounded. However, other approaches to appropriating the book's arguments are also certainly viable, and may open up some illuminating perspectives on the issues at stake. For example, several major threads of argumentation crosscut multiple sections of the book—for instance, on the need to develop new concepts and representations of urbanization processes; on the investigation of the historical geographies of urbanization; on the critique of urban knowledges and

One Foundations— The Urbanization Question	• What is urbanization? How are urbanization processes inscribed in built environments, landscapes and territories, beyond the boundaries of cities? What would a complete or generalized formation of urbanization entail, in experiential, social, spatial and environmental terms?
Two Complete Urbanization— Experience, Site, Process	• Can the spatial boundaries of cities be coherently delineated—whether in theory, analysis or experience? Is a new formation of complete urbanization being consolidated in specific regions and territories? If so, what are its major manifestations—whether in built environments, spatial configurations or infrastructural arrangements, in political discourses, or in everyday life?
Three Planetary Urbanization— Openings	• Is a planetary formation of complete urbanization being consolidated in the early twenty-first century? If so, what are its major experiential, social, spatial and environmental expressions, and what are its sociopolitical implications? What categories of analysis and methods of representation are needed to decipher such trends and transformations?
Four Historical Geographies of Urbanization	• If urbanization includes yet transcends the process of city building, how can the historical geographies of these intertwined processes be conceptualized in relation to ongoing transformations of place, landscape, territory and environment at various spatial scales?
Five Urban Studies and Urban Ideologies	• What are the limitations and blind-spots of inherited and contemporary approaches to the urban question in relation to emergent worldwide urbanization patterns? What is the role of ideological (mis)representations of the city and the urban in historical and contemporary strategies to shape sociospatial and environmental transformations?
Six Visualizations— Ideologies and Experiments	• How to develop appropriately differentiated spatial representations of historical and contemporary urbanization processes? What taxonomies are most effective for mapping a world of generalized urbanization, massive uneven spatial development and continued territorial differentiation? What are the limits and possibilities of inherited mapping strategies and new geospatial data sources for developing a critical cartography of planetary urbanization?
Seven Political Strategies, Struggles and Horizons	• How are worldwide urbanization processes, past and present, mediated through political and institutional strategies? What are their operational elements and targets? What are their implications for spatial organization, resource distribution, power relations and political life? What, if any, alternatives to contemporary urbanization patterns have been envisioned, and/or pursued by theorists, designers, policy makers, citizens, inhabitants and activists?
Coda	• If the traditional city is dissolving, and urbanization is being generalized across the planet, can new forms of citizenship be constructed that empower people collectively to appropriate, transform and reshape the common space of the world?

1.3 Key questions explored in each section of the book

ideologies; on the role of state strategies in mediating urbanization processes at various spatial scales; on the deployment of spatial representations to serve specific strategies of urbanization; and on the question of alternatives to contemporary urbanization patterns. These, and no doubt others, may be accessed quite productively as readers construct their own pathways through the many layers of analysis, experimentation, speculation and debate that are intermeshed across chapters and sections in this volume. A sequential approach to the book's contents may thus be productively complemented through more topical reading strategies that reflect specific research interests, concerns and agendas. The book's organizational structure is intended less to enclose the material within pregiven analytical boxes, than simply as a pragmatic framing device to enhance the accessibility of an otherwise complex, multifaceted and at times quite challenging intellectual terrain.

• • •

The images used on the book's cover and in the section introductions were produced by Garth Lenz, whose photojournalistic work has dramatically documented some of the most horrific industrial scars on the earth's landscape, especially in the Tar Sands of northern Alberta, Canada, as well as in other zones of intensive resource extraction, which have been induced through our fossil fuel-based formation of worldwide urbanization.[34] In recent years, photographic work on colossal landscapes of industrialized resource extraction and environmental destruction—particularly in connection to the large-scale infrastructures required for the production of petrochemicals—has generated considerable attention both in the public sphere and among environmentalists, conservationists, landscape architects and geographers. In many of the most widely circulated images of such landscapes, the specter of worldwide ecological destruction is depicted with such richly aestheticized abstraction that some commentators have described this genre using phrases such as the "toxic sublime" or the "apocalyptic sublime."[35] Lenz's interventions are clearly connected to that genre—there is a surreal, if deeply unsettling, beauty in many of his images of the shockingly degraded landscapes of the Tar Sands. However, his work is quite explicitly linked to a political concern to use his powerful photographic vocabulary to communicate a cautionary message regarding "the true cost of oil" to the public both in Canada and beyond.[36] Lenz's images thus offer a fitting, if extremely grim, provocation for the arguments and perspectives being forged in the present volume: they illustrate one way of visualizing the socially and ecologically disastrous operational landscapes of urbanization— Lefebvre might have described them as a form of "terricide"—that are being forged at a truly colossal scale to support and reproduce urban life under early twenty-first-century capitalism.[37]

While it was, of course, Henri Lefebvre who forecast the situation of complete urbanization, which is today apparently being actualized on a planetary scale, the iconography used in the cover design of his classic text, *The Urban Revolution*—both in its original 1970 version and in its 2003 English translation—is strikingly conventional (Figure 1.4).

In the French version, a classic image of urban density is adopted—a collage of large, iconic buildings pierced by an elevated subway train. In the more recent English translation, a similar, if more readily recognizable, iconography is chosen: one of Haussmann's great Parisian boulevards, forming a knife-like cut through the fabric of a dense urban landscape that stretches endlessly into the horizon. In stark contrast, Lenz's aerial photograph of the Tar Sands on this book's cover takes us far away from the large, dense, vertical landscapes of cityness, into a zone in which the earth's surface has been layered with a viscous sludge, traversed by muddy roads twisting around ponds filled with huge accumulations of toxic waste. As Andy Merrifield proposes in several of his contributions to this book, the Haussmannization of the past, which evicted city dwellers from the center to create a built environment for urbanizing capital, has now been ratcheted up into a worldwide form of neo-Haussmannization. Perhaps Lenz's image of the Tar Sands provides as fitting an iconography for this emergent planetary condition as the image of Haussmann's geometrical boulevard did for an earlier, city-centric formation of urban expansion. The evictions, enclosures and dispossessions continue, but now on the scale of the entire planet, well beyond the inherited built environments of earlier civilizations, leading to unprecedented social devastation and environmental destruction:

> Baron Haussmann tore into central Paris, into its old neighborhoods and poor
> populations, dispatching the latter to the periphery while speculating on the

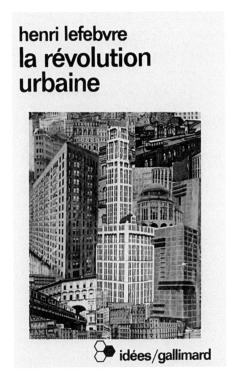

1.4 Iconography of the urban revolution?

center; the built urban form became simultaneously a property machine and a means to divide and rule; today, neo-Haussmannization, in a similar process that integrates financial, corporate and state interests, tears into the globe, sequesters land through forcible slum clearance and eminent domain, valorizing it while banishing former residents to the global hinterlands of post-industrial malaise.[38]

It seems as urgent as ever, under these conditions, to develop theories, analyses and cartographies that situate such operational landscapes—their land-use systems; their labor regimes and property relations; their forms of governance; their ecological impacts; and their rapidly changing social fabrics—quite centrally within our understanding of the contemporary urban condition. This volume is intended to advance that project in the hope that a new understanding of urbanization may prove useful to ongoing struggles—*against* neo-Haussmannization, planetary enclosure, market fundamentalism and global ecological plunder; and *for* a new model of urbanization oriented towards the collective reappropriation and democratic self-management of "planetary space as the work of the human species."[39]

Notes

1   For exemplary overviews of the main lines of debate in twentieth-century urban theory, see Peter Saunders, *Social Theory and the Urban Question*. Second Edition (London: Routledge, 1986); and Mark Gottdiener, *The Social Production of Urban Space* (Austin: University of Texas Press, 1985).

2   Robert Park and Ernest Burgess eds., *The City* (Chicago: University of Chicago Press, 1967 [1925]). See also Neil Brenner and Nikos Katsikis, "Is the Mediterranean Urban?," this book, Ch. 27, Figure 27.1, page 429.

3   Building heavily upon Walter Christaller's central place theory, the quantitative approaches to urban systems of the mid-twentieth century assembled and analyzed diverse indicators on a large number of cities. However, despite its use of "large-N" research designs, this work was still premised upon the same overarching concern with cities as (qualitatively specific, yet increasingly generalized) settlement types that had characterized the earlier work of Burgess, Park and their Chicago School colleagues. For a detailed overview of such quantitative approaches, see Brian J. L. Berry and Frank Horton eds., *Geographic Perspectives on Urban Systems* (Englewood Cliffs: Prentice Hall, 1970). Although periodizations of capitalist urban development within the tradition of radical urban studies productively emphasized the specifically capitalist form of urbanization and the larger spatial divisions of labor in which capitalist cities are embedded, they were still generally grounded upon a generic model of a single city whose morphology was considered to be paradigmatic for the phase of urbanization under investigation. See, for example, the classic distinctions between city-types (mercantile, industrial, Fordist-Keynesian / corporate-monopoly, post-Keynesian) that were developed by David Gordon, "Capitalist Development and the History of American Cities," *Marxism and the Metropolis*, eds. William Tabb and Larry Sawyers (New York: Oxford University Press, 1978) 25-63; and David Harvey, "The Urbanization of Capital," *The Urban Experience* (Baltimore: Johns Hopkins University Press, 1989) 17-58. A similar analytical emphasis on particular types of city—global, mega, post-Fordist, neoliberal, ordinary, post-colonial and so forth—underpins most major strands of contemporary critical urban studies. For overviews of the latter approaches and associated debates see, among other works, Edward Soja, *Postmetropolis: Critical Studies of Cities and Regions* (Cambridge: Blackwell, 2000); Neil Brenner and Roger Keil, eds., *The Global Cities Reader* (New York: Routledge, 2006); and Gary Bridge and Sophie Watson, eds., *The New Blackwell Companion to the City* (Cambridge: Blackwell, 2011).

4   For a useful overview of this terminological proliferation in recent years, see Peter J. Taylor and Robert E. Lang, "The Shock of the New: 100 Concepts Describing Recent Urban Change," *Environment and Planning A* 36 (2004) 951-58.

5   See Saunders, *Social Theory and the Urban Question*; and Gottdiener, *Social Production of Urban Space*.

6   The triad of size, density and heterogeneity was, of course, essential to the classic definition of urbanism proposed by Chicago School sociologist Louis Wirth in 1937. See Wirth, "Urbanism as a Way of Life," *Classic Essays on the Culture of Cities*, ed. Richard Sennett (Englewood Cliffs: Prentice Hall, 1969 [1937]) 143-164. Importantly, however, Wirth's famous triad was not intended to delineate the specificity of cities as settlement types. His goal, rather, was to explain the occurrence of urbanism, an ensemble of social behaviors, interactions and routines that, he predicted, would tend to arise within places containing large, densely settled and socially diverse populations. In fact, from the essay's opening paragraph forwards, Wirth expressed considerable skepticism regarding attempts to define the city based on purely empirical criteria (see Neil Brenner and Christian Schmid, "The 'Urban Age' in Question," this book, Ch. 21). It is ironic, therefore, that Wirth's theory is today so frequently invoked to exemplify precisely the type of empiricist definition of the city that he had so forcefully rejected. Although Wirth's arguments on urbanism have been largely assimilated into the generic, typological understanding of cityness that prevails across the field of urban studies, they actually contain fruitful insights for the development of a more spatially variegated approach. For further discussion, see Neil Brenner, "Louis Wirth's Radiant Urbanism: a Contribution to the Investigation of World Urbanization," Working Paper (Cambridge: Urban Theory Lab, Graduate School of Design, Harvard University, 2013).

7   Hillary Angelo and David Wachsmuth, "Urbanizing Urban Political Ecology: a Critique of Methodological Cityism," this book, Ch. 24, page 377.

8 For a critical evaluation of several such approaches, see Nikos Katsikis, *From Hinterland to Hinterworld: Territorial Organization Beyond Agglomeration* (Doctoral Dissertation, Cambridge: Doctor in Design Studies Program, Graduate School of Design, Harvard University) in progress. Although such approaches have been elaborated in relation to an extremely broad range of substantive themes and concerns, they have been advanced with particular force by, among other authors, Jean Gottmann and Constantinos Doxiadis in the 1960s, Henri Lefebvre in the 1970s, John Friedmann in the 1970s and subsequently, Terry McGee in the 1980s, William Cronon in the 1990s, and Matthew Gandy, Maria Kaika and Erik Swyngedouw in the 2000s. See, for example, Jean Gottmann, *Megalopolis: the Urbanized Northeastern Seaboard of the United States* (Cambridge: MIT Press, 1961); Constantinos Doxiadis, *Ekistics: An Introduction to the Science of Human Settlements* (New York: Oxford University Press, 1968); Henri Lefebvre, "The Right to the City," *Writings on Cities*, eds. and trans. Eleonore Kofman and Elizabeth Lebas (Cambridge: Blackwell, 1996 [1968]) 63-181; Henri Lefebvre, *The Urban Revolution*, trans. Robert Bononno (Minneapolis: University of Minnesota Press, 2003 [1970]); John Friedmann and Clyde Weaver, *Territory and Function* (Berkeley and Los Angeles: University of California Press, 1979); Terry G. McGee, "The Emergence of *Desakota* Regions in Asia: Expanding a Hypothesis," this book, Ch. 9 (originally published in 1991); William Cronon, *Nature's Metropolis: Chicago and the Great West* (New York: Norton, 1991); Matthew Gandy, *Concrete and Clay: Reworking Nature in New York City* (Cambridge: MIT Press, 2005). Maria Kaika, *City of Flows* (New York: Routledge, 2005); and Erik Swyngedouw, "Metabolic Urbanization: the Making of Cyborg Cities," *In the Nature of Cities*, eds. Nik Heynen, Maria Kaika and Erik Swyngedouw (New York: Routledge, 2006) 21-40. There are, obviously, major methodological, conceptual and substantive differences among these works—but they share a systematic concern to supersede city-centric understandings of the urban in favor of territorially variegated and/or metabolic visions of the urban condition. While the influence of Lefebvre's work is omnipresent in the present volume, several chapters critically interrogate the work of other authors who have made major contributions to the development of a territorially variegated or metabolic approach to urban theory. On the work of Kaika, Gandy and Swyngedouw, see Angelo and Wachsmuth, "Urbanizing Urban Political Ecology: a Critique of Methodological Cityism," Ch. 24. On Doxiadis, see Nikos Katsikis, "Two Approaches to 'World Management': R.B. Fuller and C.A. Doxiadis," this book, Ch. 29.

9 On urbanization as a world-making process, see David J. Madden, "City Becoming World: Nancy, Lefebvre and the Global-Urban Imagination," this book, Ch. 30.

10 Gottmann, *Megalopolis*, 5.

11 Ash Amin and Nigel Thrift, *Cities: Reimagining the Urban* (London: Polity, 2002) 1.

12 Henri Lefebvre, "From the City to Urban Society," this book, Ch. 2, page 36.

13 See Henri Lefebvre, "The Right to the City," 69-72; Lefebvre, "From the City to Urban Society," this book, Ch. 2, page 37-38; and Henri Lefebvre, "Reflections on the Politics of Space" and "The Worldwide Experience," *State, Space, World: Selected Essays*, eds. Neil Brenner and Stuart Elden, trans. Gerald Moore, Neil Brenner and Stuart Elden (Minneapolis: University of Minnesota, 2009) 190, 278.

14 Henri Lefebvre, "The Right to the City," 71; Lefebvre, "From the City to Urban Society," this book, Ch. 2, page 37-38.

15 See Lewis Mumford, *The City in History* (New York: Harcourt, Brace and World, 1961).

16 On this reading, Lefebvre's notion of implosion-explosion contains important parallels with David Harvey's account of the contradiction between fixity and motion in the circulation of capital. On the latter, see David Harvey, "The Geopolitics of Capitalism," *Social Relations and Spatial Structures*, eds. Derek Gregory and John Urry (London: Macmillan, 1985) 128-63. For further discussion see Neil Brenner, "Between Fixity and Motion: Accumulation, Territorial Organization and the Historical Geography of Spatial Scales," *Environment and Planning D: Society and Space* 16, 5 (1998) 459-81.

17 Lefebvre, "From the City to Urban Society," this book, Ch. 2, pages 36, 43.

18 Henri Lefebvre, "Dissolving city, Planetary Metamorphosis," this book, Ch. 35, page 569.

19 The *locus classicus* of such arguments is Melvin Webber, "The Post-city Age," *Daedalus* 94, 4 (1968) 1091-110. For a critical review of more recent versions, see Stephen Graham, "The end of Geography or the Explosion of Place: Conceptualizing Space, Place and Information Technology," *Progress in Human Geography* 22, 2 (1998) 165-85.

20 Matthew Gandy, "Where Does the City End?," this book, Ch. 5, page 86.

21 David Harvey, "Cities or Urbanization?," this book, Ch. 3, page 61.

22 On such "big structures" and "large processes," and the history of attempts to understand them in the social and historical sciences, see Charles Tilly, *Big Structures, Large Processes, Huge Comparisons* (New York: Russell Sage Foundation, 1984).

23 Kingsley Davis, "The Origins and Growth of Urbanization in the World," *American Journal of Sociology* 60, 5 (1955) 429-37; Kingsley Davis and Hilda Hertz Golden, "Urbanization and the Development of Pre-industrial Areas," *Economic Development and Cultural Change* 3, 1 (1954) 6-26. For further discussion and critique of Kingsley Davis' approach to urbanization see Brenner and Schmid, "The 'urban age' in question," this book, Ch. 21.

24 Davis and Hertz Golden, "Urbanization and the Development of Pre-industrial Areas," 7; Kingsley Davis, *World Urbanization: 1950–1970, Volume II: Analysis of Trends, Relationships and Development*, Population Series No. 9 (Berkeley: Institute of International Studies, University of California, 1972); Davis, *World Urbanization: 1950–1970, Volume I: Basic Data for Cities, Countries, and Regions*, Population Monograph Series No. 4 (Berkeley: Institute of International Studies, University of California, 1969). For discussion, see also Brenner and Schmid, "The 'Urban Age' in Question," this book, Ch. 21.

25 See Brenner and Schmid, "The 'Urban Age' in Question," this book, Ch. 21.

26 Ibid. The urbanization of the earth's most "remote" places is currently the focus of a collaborative research project in the Urban Theory Lab-GSD on "Extreme Territories of Urbanization." Among other issues, our research team is investigating historical and contemporary patterns of urbanization in the Arctic, the Amazon, the Gobi steppe, the Himalayas and the Sahara desert, as well as in the Pacific Ocean and in the earth's atmosphere.

27 See Álvaro Sevilla-Buitrago, "*Urbs in Rure*: Historical Enclosure and the Extended Urbanization of the Countryside," this book, Ch. 16; and Max Ajl, "The Hypertrophic City Versus the Planet of Fields," this book, Ch. 32.

28 This line of argumentation is developed in an important strand of the urban political ecology literature, especially by authors such as Matthew Gandy, Maria Kaika and Erik Swyngedouw, for whom a Marxian notion of metabolism serves as a key analytical lens for investigating the capitalist form of urbanization (see the works cited in Note 8 above). For critical discussion and evaluation, see Hillary Angelo and David Wachsmuth, "Urbanizing Urban Political Ecology," this book, Ch. 24.

29 This latter point is argued forcefully by Ajl, "The Hypertrophic City," this book, Ch. 32. For a parallel account of such operational landscapes of urbanization, see also Timothy W. Luke, "Global Cities Versus 'Global Cities': Rethinking Contemporary Urbanism as Public Ecology," *Studies in Political Economy* 70 (2003) 11-33.

30 This is one of the core hypotheses currently being explored in the Urban Theory Lab-GSD in our work on "Extreme Territories of Urbanization," and it also lies at the heart of my ongoing collaboration with Christian Schmid on the historical and contemporary geographies of extended urbanization.

31 See Ajl, "The Hypertrophic City"; as well as Luke, "Global Cities Versus 'Global Cities.'"

32 Lefebvre, "Reflections on the Politics of Space"

33 See Andy Merrifield, *The Politics of the Encounter: Urban Theory and Protest under Planetary Urbanization* (Athens: University of Georgia Press, 2013). At recent meetings of the Association of American Geographers (Los Angeles, 2013) and the Research Committee on Urban and Regional Development (RC21) of the International Sociological Association (Berlin, 2013), planetary urbanization was described on several panels as a new "paradigm" for research in urban studies. As I hope the above discussion indicates, I think such labels are extremely premature; we have only just begun to clarify our core questions and to introduce concepts and methodological strategies for confronting them. This book is simply an effort to consolidate and synthesize some of the major intellectual resources that have been produced thus far in relation to this emergent *problematique*.

34 For further examples of Lenz's work, see http://www.garthlenz. com.

35 For a useful overview of such work, with specific reference to the photography of Edward Burtynsky, see Merle Patchett and Andriko Lozowy, "Reframing the Canadian Oil Sands," *Imaginations: Journal of Cross-Cultural Image Studies* 3, 2 (2012) 140-69. Along with the work of Burtynsky, another striking example of this genre is David Maisel, *Black Maps: American Landscape and the Apocalyptic Sublime* (Göttingen: Steidl, 2013).

36 Lenz makes this political agenda quite explicit in his TED talk, "The True Cost of Oil": http://www.ted.com/talks/garth_lenz_ images_of_beauty_and_devastation.html.

37 On Lefebvre's notion of terricide, see Stuart Elden, "Terricide: Lefebvre, Geopolitics and the Killing of the Earth," Department of Politics, University of Warwick, unpublished manuscript, 2013.

38 See Andy Merrifield, "The Right to the City and Beyond: Notes Towards a Lefebvrian Reconceptualization," this book, Ch. 31, page 526.

39 Henri Lefebvre, "The Worldwide and The Planetary," *State, Space, World: Selected Essays*, eds. Neil Brenner and Stuart Elden (Minneapolis: University of Minnesota Press, 2009) 206.

ONE
FOUNDATIONS—
THE URBANIZATION
QUESTION

What is urbanization? How are urbanization processes inscribed in built environments, landscapes and territories, beyond the boundaries of cities? What would a complete or generalized formation of urbanization entail, in experiential, social, spatial and environmental terms?

Henri Lefebvre
David Harvey
Christian Schmid

2
FROM THE CITY TO URBAN SOCIETY

Henri Lefebvre

I'll begin with the following hypothesis: society has been completely urbanized. This hypothesis implies a definition: an *urban society* is a society that results from a process of complete urbanization. This urbanization is virtual today, but will become real in the future.

The above definition resolves any ambiguity in the use of our terms. The words "urban society" are often used to refer to any city or urban agglomeration: the Greek polis, the oriental or medieval city, commercial and industrial cities, small cities, the megalopolis. As a result of the confusion, we have forgotten or overlooked the social relationships (primarily relationships of production) with which each urban type is associated. These so-called urban societies are often compared with one another, even though they have nothing in common. Such a move serves the underlying ideologies of *organicism* (every urban society, viewed on its own, is seen as an organic "whole"), *continuism* (there is a sense of historical continuity or permanence associated with urban society), and *evolutionism* (urban society is characterized by different periods, by the transformation of social relations that fade away or disappear).

Here, I use the term "urban society" to refer to the society that results from industrialization, which is a process of domination that absorbs agricultural production. This urban society cannot take shape conceptually until the end of a process during which the old urban forms, the end result of a series of *discontinuous* transformations, burst apart. An important aspect of the theoretical problem is the ability to situate the discontinuities and continuities with respect to one another. How could any absolute discontinuities exist without an underlying continuity, without support, without some inherent process? Conversely, how can we have continuity without crises, without the appearance of new elements or relationships?

The specialized sciences (sociology, political economy, history, human geography) have proposed a number of ways to characterize "our" society, its reality and deep-seated trends, its actuality and virtuality. Terms such as "industrial and postindustrial society," "the technological society," "the society of abundance," "the leisure society," "consumer society" and so on have been used. Each of these names contains an element of empirical or conceptual truth, as well as an element of exaggeration and extrapolation. Instead of the term "postindustrial society"—the society that is born of industrialization and succeeds it—I will use "urban society"; a term that refers to tendencies, orientations and virtualities, rather than any preordained reality. Such usage in no way precludes a critical examination of contemporary reality, such as the analysis of the "bureaucratic society of controlled consumption."

Science is certainly justified in formulating such theoretical hypotheses and using them as a point of departure. Not only is such a procedure current among the sciences, it is necessary. There can be no science without theoretical hypotheses. My hypothesis, which involves the so-called social sciences, is based on an epistemological and methodological approach. Knowledge is not necessarily a copy or reflection, a simulacrum or simulation of an object that is *already* real. Nor does it necessarily construct its object for the sake of a theory that predates knowledge, a theory of the object or its "models." In my approach, the object is included in the hypothesis; the hypothesis comprehends the object. Even though this "object" is located outside any (empirical) fact, it is not fictional. We can assume the existence of a *virtual object,* urban society; that is, a *possible object,* whose growth and development can be analyzed in relation to a process and a praxis (practical activity). Needless to say, such a hypothesis must be validated. There is, however, no shortage of arguments and proofs to sustain it, from the simplest to the most complex.

For example, agricultural production has lost all its autonomy in the major industrialized nations and as part of a global economy. It is no longer the principal sector of the economy, nor even a sector characterized by any distinctive features (aside from underdevelopment). Even though local and regional features from the time when agricultural production dominated haven't entirely disappeared, it has been changed into a form of industrial production, having become subordinate to its demands, subject to its constraints. Economic growth and industrialization have become self legitimating, extending their effects to entire territories, regions, nations and continents. As a result, the traditional unit typical of peasant life, namely the village, has been transformed. Absorbed or obliterated by larger units, it has become an integral part of industrial production and consumption. The concentration of the population goes hand in hand with that of the mode of production. The *urban fabric* grows, extends its borders, corrodes the residue of agrarian life. This expression, "urban fabric," does not narrowly define the built world of cities but all manifestations of the dominance of the city over the country. In this sense, a vacation home, a highway, a supermarket in the countryside are all part of the urban fabric. Of varying density, thickness and activity, the only regions untouched by it are those that are stagnant or dying, those that are given over to "nature." With the decline of the village life of days gone by, agricultural producers, "farmers," are confronted with the *agricultural town*. Promised by Khrushchev to the Soviet peasants, agricultural towns have appeared in various places around the world. In the United States, aside from certain parts of the South, peasants have virtually disappeared, and we find islands of farm poverty alongside islands of urban poverty. As this global process of industrialization and urbanization was taking place, the large cities exploded, giving rise to growths of dubious value: suburbs, residential conglomerations and industrial complexes, satellite cities that differed little from urbanized towns. Small and midsize cities became dependencies, partial colonies of the metropolis. In this way my hypothesis serves both as a point arrival for existing knowledge and a point of departure for a new study and new projects: complete urbanization. The hypothesis is anticipatory. It prolongs the fundamental tendency of the present. Urban society is gestating in and through the "bureaucratic society of controlled consumption."

A negative argument, proof by the absurd: no other hypothesis will work, no other hypothesis can cover the entire range of problems. Postindustrial society? Then what happens after industrialization? Leisure society? This addresses only part of the question, since we limit our examination of trends and virtualities to "infrastructure," a realist attitude that in no way circumvents the demagoguery inherent in this definition. The indefinite growth of mass consumption? Here, we measure current indices and extrapolate from them, thereby running the risk of reducing reality and virtuality to only one of their aspects. And so on.

The expression "urban society" meets a theoretical need. It is more than simply a literary or pedagogical device, or even the expression of some form of acquired knowledge; it is an elaboration, a search, a conceptual formulation. A movement of thought toward a certain *concrete,* and perhaps toward *the* concrete, assumes shape and detail. This movement, if it proves to be true, will lead to a practice, *urban practice,* that is finally or newly comprehended. Needless to say, a threshold will have to be crossed before entering the concrete, that is, social practice as understood by theory. But there is no empirical recipe for fabricating this product, this urban reality. Isn't this what we so often expect from "urbanism" and what "urbanists" so often promise? Unlike a fact-filled empiricism with its risky extrapolations and fragments of indigestible knowledge, we can build a *theory* from a *theoretical hypothesis.* The development of such a theory is associated with a *methodology.* For example, research involving a virtual object, which attempts to define and realize that object as part of an ongoing project, already has a name: *transduction.* The term reflects an intellectual approach toward a possible object, which we can employ alongside the more conventional activities of deduction and induction. The concept of an urban society, which I introduced above, thus implies a hypothesis and a definition.

Similarly, by "urban revolution" I refer to the transformations that affect contemporary society, ranging from the period when questions of growth and industrialization predominate (models, plans, programs) to the period when the urban problematic becomes predominant, when the search for solutions and modalities unique to urban society are foremost. Some of these transformations are sudden; others are gradual, planned, determined. But which ones? This is a legitimate question. It is by no means certain in advance that the answer will be clear, intellectually satisfying, or unambiguous. The words "urban revolution" do not in themselves refer to actions that are violent. Nor do they exclude them.

But how do we discriminate between the outcome of violent action and the product of rational action before their occurrence? Isn't violence characterized by its ability to spin out of control? Isn't thought characterized by the effort to reduce violence, beginning with the effort to destroy the chains that bind our thought?

There are two aspects of urbanism that we will need to address:

1. For years, scholars have viewed urbanism as a social practice that is fundamentally scientific and technical in nature. In this case, theory can and should address this practice by raising it to a conceptual level and, more specifically, to the level of *epistemology*. However, the absence of any such urban epistemology is striking. Is it worth developing such an epistemology, then? No. In fact, its absence is highly significant. For the *institutional* and *ideological* nature of what is referred to as urbanism has—until a new order comes into being—taken precedence over its scientific nature. If we assume that this procedure can be generalized and that understanding always involves epistemology, then it is clear that it plays no role in contemporary urbanism. It is important to understand why and how.

2. As it currently exists, that is, as a policy (having institutional and ideological components), urbanism can be criticized both from the right and the left. The critique from the right, which is well known, is focused on the past and is frequently humanist. It subsumes and justifies a neoliberal ideology of "free enterprise"; directly or indirectly. It opens a path for the various "private" initiatives of capitalists and capital. The critique from the left, frequently overlooked, is not associated with any so-called leftist group, club, party, apparatus or ideology. Rather, it attempts to open a path to the possible, to explore and delineate a landscape that is not merely part of the "real," the accomplished, occupied by existing social, political and economic forces. It is a *utopian* critique because it steps back from the real without, however, losing sight of it.

We can draw an axis as follows:

$$0 \text{ ———————————————— } 100\%$$

The axis runs from the complete absence of urbanization ("pure nature," the earth abandoned to the elements) on the left to the completion of the process on the right. A signifier for this signified—the *urban* (the urban reality)—this axis is both spatial and temporal: spatial because the process extends through space, which it modifies; temporal because it develops over time. Temporality, initially of secondary importance, eventually becomes the predominant aspect of practice and history. This schema presents no more than an aspect of this history, a division of time that is both abstract and arbitrary and gives rise to operations (periodizations) that have no absolute privilege but are as necessary (relative) as other divisions …

• • •

At one moment in the history of the European West, an event of great importance occurred, but one that remained latent because it went unnoticed. The importance of the city for the social whole became such that the whole seemed to shift. In the relationship between town and country, the emphasis was still on the countryside: real property wealth, the products of the soil, attachment to the land (owners of fiefs or noble titles). Compared with the countryside, the town retained its heterotopic character, marked by its ramparts as well as the transition to suburban areas. At a given moment, these various relationships were reversed; the situation changed. The moment when this shift occurred, this reversal of heterotopy, should be marked along our axis. From this moment on, the city would no longer appear as an urban island in a rural ocean, it would no longer seem a paradox, a monster, a hell or heaven that contrasted sharply with village or country life in a natural environment. It entered people's awareness and understanding as one of the terms in the opposition between town and country. Country? It is now no more than—nothing more than—the town's "environment," its horizon, its limit. Villagers? As far as they were concerned, they no longer worked for the territorial lords, they produced for the city, for the urban market. And even though they realized that the wheat and wood merchants exploited them, they understood that the path to freedom crossed the marketplace.

So what is happening around this crucial moment in history? Thoughtful people no longer see themselves reflected in nature, a shadowy world subject to mysterious forces. Between them and nature, between their home (the focal point of thought, existence) and the world, lies the urban reality, an essential mediating factor. From this moment on, society no longer coincides with the countryside. It no longer coincides with the city, either. The state encompasses them both, joins them in its hegemony by making use of their rivalry. Yet, at the time, the majesty of the state was veiled to its contemporaries. Of whom or what was reason an attribute? Royalty? Divine right? The individual? Yet this is what led to the reform of the city after the destruction of Athens and Rome, after the most important products of those civilizations, logic and law, were lost from view. The logos was reborn, but its rebirth was not attributed to the renaissance of the urban world but to transcendent reason. The rationalism that culminated in Descartes accompanied the reversal that replaced the primacy of the peasantry with the priority of urban life. Although the peasantry didn't see it as such. However, during this period, the *image of the city* came into being.

The city had writing; it had secrets and powers, and clarified the opposition between urbanity (cultured) and rusticity (naive and brutal). After a certain point in time, the city developed its own form of writing: the map or *plan,* the science of *planimetry.* During the sixteenth and seventeenth centuries, when this reversal of meaning took place, maps of European cities began to appear, including the first maps of the city of Paris. These are not yet abstract maps, projections of urban space onto geometric coordinates. A cross between vision and concept, works of art and science, they displayed the city from top to bottom, in perspective, painted, depicted and geometrically described. This perspective, simultaneously idealist and realist—the perspective of thought and power—was situated in the vertical dimension, the dimension of knowledge and reason, and dominated and constituted a totality: the city. This shift of social reality toward the urban, this (relative) discontinuity, can be easily indicated on a space-time axis, whose continuity can be used to situate and date any (relative) breaks. All that is needed is to draw a line between the zero point and the terminal point (which I'll assume to be one hundred).

This reversal of meaning can't be dissociated from the growth of commercial capital and the existence of the market. It was the rise of the mercantile city, which was grafted onto the political city but promoted its own ascendancy, that was primarily responsible. This was soon followed by the appearance of industrial capital and, consequently, the *industrial city.* This requires further explanation. Was industry associated with the city? One would assume it to be associated with the *non-city,* the absence or rupture of urban reality. We know that industry initially developed near the sources of energy (coal and water), raw materials (metals, textiles), and manpower reserves. Industry gradually made its way into the city in search of capital and capitalists, markets, and an abundant supply of low-cost labor. It could locate itself itself anywhere, therefore, but sooner or later made its way into existing cities or created new cities, although it was prepared to move elsewhere if there was an economic advantage in doing so. Just as the political city resisted the conquest—half-pacific, half-violent—of the merchants, exchange and money, similarly the political and mercantile city defended itself from being taken over by a nascent industry, industrial capital and capital itself. But how did it do this? Through corporatism, by establishing relationships.

Historical continuity and evolution mask the effects and ruptures associated with such transitions. Yet something strange and wonderful was also taking place, which helped renew dialectical thought: the non-city and the anti-city would conquer the city, penetrate it, break it apart, and in so doing extend it immeasurably, bringing about the urbanization of society and the growth of the urban fabric that covered what was left of the city prior to the arrival of industry. This extraordinary movement has escaped our attention and has been described in piecemeal fashion because ideologues have tried to eliminate dialectical thought and the analysis of contradictions in favor of logical thought—that is, the identification of coherence and nothing but coherence. Urban reality, simultaneously amplified and exploded, thus loses the features it inherited from the previous period: organic totality, belonging, an uplifting image, a sense of space that was measured and dominated by monumental splendor. It was populated with signs of the urban within the dissolution of urbanity; it became stipulative, repressive, marked by signals, summary codes for circulation (routes), and signage. It was sometimes read as a rough draft, sometimes as an authoritarian message. It was imperious. But none of these descriptive terms completely describes the historical process of implosion-explosion (a metaphor borrowed from nuclear physics) that occurred: the tremendous concentration (of people, activities, wealth, goods, objects, instruments, means and thought) of urban reality and the immense explosion, the projection of numerous, disjunct fragments (peripheries, suburbs, vacation homes, satellite towns) into space.

The *industrial city* (often a shapeless town, a barely urban agglomeration, a conglomerate or conurbation like the Ruhr Valley) serves as a prelude to a *critical zone*. At this moment, the effects of implosion-explosion are most fully felt. The increase in industrial production is superimposed on the growth of commercial exchange and multiplies the number of such exchanges. This growth extends from simple barter to the global market, from the simple exchange between two individuals all the way to the exchange of products, works of art, ideas and human beings. Buying and selling, merchandise and market, money and capital appear to sweep away all obstacles. During this period of generalization, the effect of the process—namely the urban reality—becomes both cause and reason. Induced factors become dominant (inductors). The *urban problematic* becomes a global phenomenon. Can urban reality be defined as a "superstructure" on the surface of the economic structure, whether capitalist or socialist? The simple result of growth and productive forces? Simply a modest marginal reality compared with production? Not at all. Urban reality modifies the relations of production without being sufficient to transform them. It becomes a productive force, like science. Space and the politics of space "express" social relationships but react against them. Obviously, if an urban reality manifests itself and becomes dominant, it does so only through the urban problematic.

What can be done to change this? How can we build cities or "something" that replaces what was formerly the City? How can we reconceptualize the urban phenomenon? How can we formulate, classify and order the innumerable questions that arise—questions that move, although not without considerable resistance, to the forefront of our awareness? Can we achieve significant progress in theory and practice so that our consciousness can comprehend a reality that overflows it and a possible that flees before its grasp?

We can represent this process as follows:

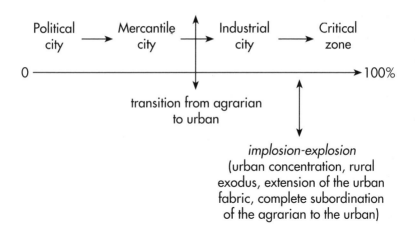

What occurs during the *critical phase?* … Are the theoretical assumptions that enable us to draw an axis such as the one shown above, introduce directed time, and make sense of the critical zone sufficient to help us understand what is taking place? Possibly. In any event, there are several assumptions we can make now. Lacking any proof to the contrary, we can postulate that a second transition occurs, a second reversal of direction and situation. Industrialization, the dominant power and limiting factor, becomes a dominated reality during periods of profound crisis. This results in tremendous confusion, during which the past and the possible, the best and the worst, become intertwined.

In spite of this theoretical hypothesis concerning the possible and its relation to the actual (the "real"), we should not overlook the fact that the onset of urban society and the modalities of urbanization depend on the characteristics of society as it existed during the course of industrialization (neocapitalist or socialist, full economic growth or intense automation). The onset of urban society at different times, the implications and consequences of these initial differences, are part of the problematic associated with the urban phenomenon, or simply the "urban." These terms are preferable to the word "city," which appears to designate a clearly defined, definitive *object,* a scientific object and the immediate goal of action, whereas the theoretical approach requires a critique of this "object" and a more complex notion of the virtual or possible object. Within this perspective there is no science of the city (such as urban sociology or urban economy), but an emerging understanding of the overall process, as well as its term (goal and direction).

The urban (an abbreviated form of urban society) can therefore be defined not as an accomplished reality, situated behind the actual in time, but, on the contrary, as a horizon, an illuminating virtuality. It is the possible, defined by a direction, that moves toward the urban as the culmination of its journey. To reach it—in other words, to realize it— we must first overcome or break through the obstacles that currently make it *impossible.*

Can theoretical knowledge treat this virtual object, the goal of action, as an abstraction? No. From this point on, it is abstract only in the sense that it is a *scientific,* and therefore legitimate, abstraction. Theoretical knowledge can and must reveal the terrain, the foundation on which it resides: an ongoing social practice, an urban practice in the process of formation. It is an aspect of the critical phase that this practice is currently veiled and disjointed, that it possesses only fragments of a reality and a science that are still in the future. It is our job to demonstrate that such an approach has an outcome, that there are solutions to the current problematic. The *virtual object* is nothing but planetary society and the "global city," and it stands outside the global and planetary crisis of reality and thought, outside the old borders that had been drawn when agriculture was dominant and that were maintained during the growth of exchange and industrial production. Nevertheless, the urban problematic can't absorb every problem. There are problems that are unique to agriculture and industry, even though the urban reality modifies them. Moreover, the urban problematic requires that we exercise considerable caution when exploring the realm of the possible. It is the analyst's responsibility to identify and describe the various forms of urbanization and explain what happens to the forms, functions and urban structures that are transformed by the breakup of the ancient city and the process of generalized urbanization.

Until now, the critical phase was perceived as a kind of black box. We know what enters the box, and sometimes we see what comes out, but we don't know what goes on inside. This makes conventional procedures of forecasting and projection useless, since they extrapolate from the actual, from a set of facts. Projections and forecasts have a determined basis only in the fragmentary sciences: demography, for example, or political economy. But what is at stake here, "objectively," is a totality.

● ● ●

The concept developed earlier as a (scientific) hypothesis can now be approached differently. I hope that readers will have a better understanding of it now that it has been freed somewhat of its earlier theoretical status. However, the process is far from complete, and it would be dogmatic to claim that it was. To do so would mean inserting the concept of an "urban society" into a questionable epistemology that we should be wary of because it is premature, because it places the categorical above the problematic, thereby halting, and possibly shifting, the very movement that brought the urban phenomenon to the threshold of awareness in the first place.

The concept of an urban society has freed itself from the myths and ideologies that bind it, whether they arise in the agrarian stages of history and consciousness or in an unwarranted extension of the representations borrowed from the corporate sphere (industrial rationalism). Myths become a part of literature; their poetic and utopian character in no way diminishes their attraction. We also know that ideology has played a large part in the development of a body of doctrine known as urbanism. To continue our exploration of the blind field, we had to jettison that opaque, heavy body: the urban phenomenon in its totality.

The unconscious (the boundary between the misunderstood and the one who misunderstands) appears sometimes as a deceptive and blinding emergence of a rural and industrial past, sometimes as a sense of loss for an urban reality that is slipping away.

In this way, the notion of a critical zone or phase comes into view. Within this zone, the terrain flies before us, the ground is booby-trapped. Although the old concepts no longer work, new concepts are beginning to take shape. Reality isn't the only thing to go; thought itself begins to give way.

Still, we have succeeded in elaborating a coherent discourse that is non-ideological and that is both *of* the urban (inside an emergent urban universe), and *about* the urban (describing it, outlining its contours). This kind of discourse can never be completed. Its incompletion is an essential part of its existence. It is defined as a reflection of the future, implying operations in time as well as space: transduction (construction of a virtual object) and the exploration of the possible-impossible. The temporal dimension, evacuated by epistemology and the philosophy of knowledge, is victoriously reintroduced. Yet transduction is not long-range planning. Like urbanism, it has been called into question; like urbanism it contains a strategy. It mixes ideology and scientificity. Here, as elsewhere, scientificity is an ideology, an excrescence grafted onto real, but fragmentary, knowledge. And like urbanism, long-range planning also extrapolates from a reductive position.

During this exploration, the urban phenomenon appears as something other than, as something more than, a superstructure (of the mode of production). I say this in response to a form of Marxist dogmatism that manifests itself in a variety of ways. The urban problematic is worldwide. The same problems are found in socialism and in capitalism— along with the failure to respond. Urban society can only be defined as global. Virtually, it covers the planet by recreating nature, which has been wiped out by the industrial exploitation of natural resources (material and "human"), by the destruction of so-called natural particularities.

Moreover, the urban phenomenon has had a profound effect on the methods of production: productive forces, relationships of production, and the contradictions between them. It both extends and accentuates, on a new plane, the social character of productive labor and its conflict with the ownership (private) of the means of production. It continues the "socialization of society," which is another way of saying that the urban does not eliminate industrial contradictions. It does not resolve them for the sole reason that it has become dominant. What's more, the conflicts inherent in production (in the relationships of production and capitalist ownership as well as in "socialist" society) hinder the urban phenomenon, prevent urban development, reducing it to growth. This is particularly true of the action of the state under capitalism and state socialism.

To summarize then: society becomes increasingly complex with the transition from the rural to the industrial and from the industrial to the urban. This multifaceted complexification affects space as well as time, for the complexification of space and the objects that occupy space cannot occur without a complexification of time and the activities that occur over time.

This space is occupied by interrelated networks, relationships that are defined by interference. Its homogeneity corresponds to intentions, unified strategies, and systematized logics, on the one hand, and reductive, and consequently simplifying, representations, on the other. At the same time, differences become more pronounced in populating this space, which tends, like any abstract space, toward homogeneity (quantitative, geometric, and logical space). This, in turn, results in conflict and a strange sense of unease. For this space tends toward a unique code, an absolute system, that of exchange and exchange value, of the logical thing and the logic of things. At the same time, it is filled with subsystems, partial codes, messages, and signifiers that do not become part of the unitary procedure that the space stipulates, prescribes, and inscribes in various ways …

The concept of complexification continues to be of service. It is theoretically based on the distinction between growth and development, a distinction imposed by the period, by experience, by a consideration of results. Marx distinguished growth and development only because he wanted to avoid any confusion between quantity and quality. But for Marx the growth (quantitative) and development (qualitative) of society could and must occur simultaneously. Unfortunately, history shows that this is not the case. Growth can occur without development and sometimes development can occur without growth. For half a century, growth has been at work just about everywhere, while rigid social and political relations have been maintained. Although the Soviet Union underwent a period of intense development between 1920 and 1935, objective "factors," namely the productive forces that were left behind by this "superstructure" explosion and the growth targets used as strategic objectives—means construed as ends—soon took their revenge. Wasn't the same true of France after the explosion of May 1968? The law of unequal development (Lenin) should be extended, expanded and formulated in such a way that it can account for the conflict between growth and development that was revealed during the course of the twentieth century.

The theory of complexification anticipates the revenge of development over growth. The same is true for the theory of urban society. This revenge is only just beginning. The basic proposition, that growth cannot continue indefinitely and that the means can remain an end without a catastrophe occurring, still seems paradoxical.

These considerations evoke the prodigious extension of the urban to the entire planet—that is, urban society, its virtualities and potential. It goes without saying that this extension-expansion is not going to be problem-free. Indeed, it has been shown that the urban phenomenon tends to overflow borders, while commercial exchange and industrial and financial organizations, which once seemed to abolish those territorial limits (through the global market, through multinationals), now appear to reaffirm them. In any event, the effects of a possible rupture in industry and finance (a crisis of overproduction, a monetary crisis) would be accentuated by an extension of the urban phenomenon and the formation of urban society …

Part of my analysis may appear at first glance to correspond to the so-called Maoist interpretation of the "global city"; but this interpretation raises a number of objections. There is nothing that prevents emerging centers of power from encountering obstacles and failing. What's more, any contradictions that occur no longer take place between city and country. The principal contradiction is shifted to the urban phenomenon itself: between the centrality of power and other forms of centrality, between the "wealth-power" center and the periphery, between integration and segregation.

A complete examination of the critical phase would far exceed the scope of this text. As an example, what remains of the classic notions of history and historicity? The critical phase can leave neither these concepts nor the corresponding reality intact. Does the extension of the urban phenomenon, the formation of a time-space differential on a global scale, have any relationship to what is still called "historicity"?

This phase is accompanied by the emergence of complex entities, new functions and structures, but this does not mean that the old ones necessarily disappear. For this reason, what is called for is a repeated, and repeatedly refined, analysis of the relations between form and content. Here I've limited myself to the barest outline, consisting of a handful of markers and directional arrows. What is most important is to demonstrate that the dialectical method can exercise its revenge. And why not? Swept aside by the strategy (ideological and institutional) of the industrial period and corporate rationalism, replaced by an advocacy of the operational, deprecated by procedures that are reductive and generalizing (primarily structuralism), dialectical thought reasserts its rights. As I stated earlier, the key issue, in the fullest and most accurate sense of the word, that of centrality, demands a dialectical analysis. The study of the logic of space leads to the study of its contradictions (and those of space-time). Without that analysis, the solutions to the problem are merely dissimulated strategies, hidden beneath an apparent scientificity. On the theoretical level, one of the severest critiques of urbanism as a body of doctrine (not altogether successful) is that it harbors a sociologic and a strategy, while it evacuates dialectical thought in general and the dialectical movements specific to urbanism in particular—in other words, words, internal contradictions, both old and new (one aggravating and masking the other).

Is the urban phenomenon the *total social phenomenon* long sought for by sociologists? Yes and no. Yes, in the sense that it tends toward totality without ever achieving it, that it is essentially totalizing (centrality) but that this totality is never effected. Yes, in the sense that no partial determinism, no fragmentary knowledge can exhaust it; it is simultaneously historical, demographic, geographic, economic, sociologic, psychologic, semiologic and so on. It "is" that and more (thing or non-thing) besides: *form*, for example. In other words, a void, but one that demands or calls forth a content. If the urban is total, it is not total in the way a thing can be, as content that has been amassed, but in the way that thought is, which continues its activity of concentration endlessly but can never hold or maintain that state of concentration, which assembles elements continuously and discovers what it has assembled through a new and different form of concentration. Centrality defines the u-topic (that which has no place and searches for it). The u-topic defines centrality.

But neither the separation of fragment and content nor their confused union can define (and therefore express) the urban phenomenon. For it incorporates a *total reading,* combining the vocabularies (partial readings) of geographers, demographers, economists, sociologists, semiologists and others. These readings take place on different levels. The phenomenon cannot be defined by their sum or synthesis or superposition. In this sense, it is not a totality …

The urban is not produced like agriculture or industry. Yet, as an act that assembles and distributes, it does create. Similarly, manufacturing at one time became a productive force and economic category simply because it brought together labor and tools (technology), which were formerly dispersed. In this sense, the urban phenomenon contains a praxis (urban practice). Its form, as such, cannot be reduced to other forms (it is not isomorphous with other forms and structures), but it absorbs and transforms them …

Although the urban consolidates differences and engenders difference within the things it brings together, it cannot be defined as a system of differences. Either the word "system" implies fulfillment and closure, intelligibility through completion, or it implies nothing more than a certain kind of coherence. But the urban phenomenon is made manifest as movement. Therefore, it cannot achieve closure. The centrality and the dialectical contradiction it implies exclude closure, that is to say, immobility. Even if language appears to be a closed system, the use of language and the production of discourse shatter this perception. Consequently, we cannot define the urban by means of a system (definite); for example, as a series of deviations around invariant points. In fact, the very concept precludes our ability to mandate anything that reduces or suppresses differences. Rather, it would imply the freedom to produce differences (to differ and invent that which differs).

The urban consolidates. As a form, the urban transforms what it brings together (concentrates). It consciously creates difference where no awareness of difference existed: what was only distinct, what was once attached to particularities in the field. It consolidates everything, including determinisms, heterogeneous materials and contents, prior order and disorder, conflict, preexisting communications and forms of communication. As a transforming form, the urban destructures and restructures its elements: the messages and codes that arise in the industrial and agrarian domains …

There is no model for determining the urban through its elements or conditions (what it brings together—contents and activities). Models borrowed from the fields of energy (devices that capture finite, but considerable, quantities of energy) and information (which uses minute amounts of energy) are also inappropriate here. In other words, if we want to find a model, an analytic study of the urban can supply them. But in practice, this has more to do with a path (sense and direction, orientation and horizon) than a model.

This means that there is nothing harmonious about the urban as form and reality, for it also incorporates conflict, including class conflict. What is more, it can only be conceptualized in opposition to segregation, which attempts to resolve conflicts by separating the elements in space. This segregation produces a disaggregation of material and social life. To avoid contradiction, to achieve a purported sense of harmony, a certain form of urbanism prefers the disaggregation of the social bond. The urban presents itself as a place of conflict and confrontation, a unity of contradictions …

We can now identify and formulate a number of *urban laws*. These are not positive laws, the laws associated with an "order of orders," or a model of equilibrium or growth that should be followed or imitated, the laws of an initial affirmation from which consequences can be deduced, or some final analysis that would result in various propositions. No, these are primarily, essentially, negative laws and precepts.

1. We must break down the barriers that block the path and maintain the urban field in thrall to the blinding-blinded (especially in terms of the quantitative aspects of growth).

2. We must put an end to separation, to the separation between people and things, which brings about multiform segregations, the separation between messages, information, codes, and subcodes (in short, the forms of separation that block qualitative development). But in the existing order, what separates imagines itself to be solid; what dissociates is conscious of its power; what divides judges itself to be positive.

3. We must overcome the obstacles that enhance the opacity of relationships and the contrasts between transparency and opacity, that relegate differences to distinct (separate) particularities, that restrict them to a prefabricated space, that mask the polyvalence of ways of living in urban society (modalities and modulations of the everyday and habiting), that outlaw the transgression of norms that stipulate separations.

These negative laws in turn imply a number of positive laws.

1. The urban (urban life, the life of urban society) already implies the substitution of custom for contract. Contract law determines the frameworks of exchange and of reciprocity in exchange. This law comes into being in agrarian societies once they begin to exchange their relative surpluses and (once the world of commodities is in place) achieves its highest expression in logic and language. However, use, in the urban, comprises custom and privileges custom over contract. The use of urban objects (this sidewalk, this street, this crosswalk, this light fixture) is customary, not contractual, unless we wish to postulate the existence of a permanent quasi-contract or pseudocontract for sharing those objects and reducing violence to a minimum. This does not, however, imply that the contract system cannot be improved or transformed.

2. The conception of the urban also strives for the *reappropriation* by human beings of their conditions in time, in space, and in objects—conditions that were, and continue to be, taken away from them so that their recovery will be deferred until after buying and selling have taken place.

    (Is it reasonable to assume that time (the place of values) and space (the medium of exchange) can be reunited in a higher unity, the urban? Yes, providing we clearly point out what everyone already knows: that this unity is a u-topia, a non-place, a possible-impossible, but one that gives meaning to the possible, to action. The space of exchange and the time of values, the space of goods and the supreme good, namely time, cannot be articulated and go their own way, reflecting the incoherence of so-called industrial society. Creating space-time unity would be a possible definition, one among many, of the urban and urban society.)

3. Politically, this perspective cannot be conceived without extensive self-management of production and the enterprise within territorial units. A difficult proposition. The term "politically" is a source of confusion because generalized self-management implies the withering away of the state and the end of politics as such. In this sense, the incompatibility between the state and the urban is radical in nature. The state can only prevent the urban from taking shape. The state has to control the urban phenomenon, not to bring it to fruition but to retard its development, to push it in the direction of institutions that extend to society as a whole, through exchange and the market, the types of organization and management found in the enterprise, institutions developed during periods of growth, where the emphasis is given to quantitative (quantifiable) objectives. But the urban can only establish and serve "habiting" by reversing the state order and the strategy that organizes space globally, through constraint and homogenization, thereby absorbing the subordinate levels of the urban and habiting.

As I have tried to show, urbanism is a mask and a tool: a mask for the state and political action, a tool of interests that are dissimulated within a strategy and a sociologic. Urbanism does not try to model space as a work of art. It does not even try to do so in keeping with its technological imperatives, as it claims. The space it creates is political.

3
CITIES OR URBANIZATION?

David Harvey

The way we see our cities affects the policies and actions we undertake. Is our way of seeing dominated and limited by an obsession with "the city" as a thing, one that marginalizes our sense of urbanization as a process? What is the nature of an understanding of urbanization that can contribute to emancipatory politics?

At the beginning of this century, there were no more than a dozen or so cities in the world with more than a million people. They were all in the advanced capitalist countries and London, by far the largest of them all, had just under seven million. At the beginning of this century, too, no more than 7 percent of the world's population could reasonably be classified as "urban." By the year 2000, there may well be as many as 500 cities with more than a million inhabitants, while the largest of them, Tokyo, São Paulo, Bombay and possibly Shanghai, will boast populations of more than 20 million, trailed by a score of cities, mostly in the so-called developing countries, with upwards of 10 million. Some time early in the twenty-first century, if present trends continue, more than half of the world's population will be classified as urban rather than rural.

The twentieth century has been, then, *the* century of urbanization. Before 1800, the size and numbers of urban concentrations in all social formations seem to have been strictly limited. The nineteenth century saw the breach of those barriers in a few advanced capitalist countries, but the latter half of the twentieth century has seen that localized breach turned into a universal flood of massive urbanization. The future of most of humanity now lies, for the first time in history, fundamentally in urbanizing areas. The qualities of urban living in the twenty-first century will define the qualities of civilization itself.

But judging superficially by the present state of the world's cities, future generations will not find that civilization particularly congenial. Every city has its share (often increasing and in some instances predominant) of concentrated impoverishment and human hopelessness, of malnourishment and chronic diseases, of crumbling or stressed out infrastructures, of senseless and wasteful consumerism, of ecological degradation and excessive pollution, of congestion, of seemingly stymied economic and human development, and of sometimes bitter social strife, varying from individualized violence on the streets to organized crime (often an alternative form of urban governance), through police-state exercises in social control to massive civic protest movements (sometimes spontaneous) demanding political-economic change. For many, then, to talk of the city of the twenty-first century is to conjure up a dystopian nightmare in which all that is judged worst in the fatally flawed character of humanity collects together in some hellhole of despair.

In some of the advanced capitalist countries, that dystopian vision has been strongly associated with the long-cultivated habit on the part of those with power and privilege of running as far from the city centers as possible. Fueled by a permissive car culture, the urge to get some money and get out has taken command. Liverpool's population fell by 40 percent between 1961 and 1991, for example, and Baltimore City's fell from close to a million to under 700,000 in the same three decades. But the upshot has been not only to create endless suburbanization, so-called edge cities, and sprawling megalopoli, but also to make every village and every rural retreat in the advanced capitalist world part of a complex web of urbanization that defies any simple categorization of populations into "urban" and "rural" in that sense that once upon a time could reasonably be accorded to those terms.

The hemorrhaging of wealth, population and power from central cities has left many of them languishing in limbo. Needy populations have been left behind as the rich and influential have moved out. Add to this the devastating loss of jobs (particularly in manufacturing) in recent years and the parlous state of the older cities becomes all too clear. Nearly 250,000 manufacturing jobs have been lost in Manchester in two decades while 40,000 disappeared from Sheffield's steel industry alone in just three short catastrophic years in the mid 1980s. Baltimore likewise lost nearly 200,000 manufacturing jobs from the late 1960s onwards, and there is hardly a single city in the United States that has not been the scene of similar devastation through deindustrialization.

The subsequent train of events has been tragic for many. Communities built to service now defunct manufacturing industries have been left high and dry, wracked with long-term structural unemployment. Disenchantment, dropping out, and quasi-legal means to make ends meet follow. Those in power rush to blame the victims, the police powers move in (often insensitively) and the politico-media complex has a field day stigmatizing and stereotyping an underclass of idle wrongdoers, irresponsible single parents and feckless fathers, debasement of family values, welfare junkies, and much worse. If those marginalized happen to be an ethnic or racially marked minority, as is all too often the case, then the stigmatization amounts to barely concealed racial bigotry. The only rational response on the part of those left marginalized is urban rage, making the actual state of social and, even more emphatically, race relations (for all the campus rhetoric on political correctness) far worse now than it has been for several decades.

But is this a universal tale of urban woe I tell? Or is it something rather more confined to the specific legacies of old-style capitalist industrialization and the cultural predilections of the anti-urban Anglo-Saxon way of life? Central cities throughout continental Europe are, for example, undergoing a singular revival. And such a trend is not merely confined to a few centers, like Paris with its longstanding process of embourgeoisement accelerated by all the *grands projets* for which the French are justly famous. From Barcelona to Hamburg to Turin to Lille, the flow of population and affluence back into the city centers is marked. But, on inspection, all this really signifies is that the same problematic divisions get geographically reversed. It is the periphery that is hurting, and the soulless *banlieu* of Paris and Lyon that have become the centers of riot and disaffection, of racial discrimination and harassment, of deindustrialization and social decay. And if we look more closely at what has been happening in the Anglo-Saxon world, the evidence suggests a dissolution of that simple "doughnut" urban form of inner city decay surrounded by suburban affluence (made so much of in the late 1960s), and its replacement by a complex checkerboard of segregated and protected wealth in an urban soup of equally segregated impoverishment and decay. The unjustly infamous "outer estates" of Glasgow are interspersed with affluent commuter suburbs and the now emerging socioeconomic problems of the inner suburbs in many US cities have forced the wealthy seeking security either further out (the urbanization of the remotest countryside then follows) or into segregated and often highly protected zones wherever they can best be set up …

But all of these problems of the advanced capitalist world pale into insignificance compared to the extraordinary dilemmas of developing countries, with the wildly uncontrolled pace of urbanization in São Paulo, Mexico City, Cairo, Lagos, Bombay, Calcutta and now Shanghai and Beijing. On the surface, there seems to be something different going on here, even more than just that qualitative shift that comes with the quantitative rapidity and mass of urban growth that has Mexico City or São Paulo experiencing in just one generation what London went through in ten and Chicago in three.

Air pollution and localized environmental problems, for example, assume a far more chronic character in developing country cities than they ever did even at the most appalling states of threats to public health in the nineteenth-century cities of Europe and North America. Experts believe that "the present situation in Third World large cities is quite different from the one experienced in the course of fast urbanization in Europe and the United States" and I am inclined to bow to that opinion.[1] But I do so with an important caveat: it is vital for us to understand how, why and in what ways these differences have arisen. For it is, I believe, only in such terms that we will better understand the prospects of urban living in the twenty-first century in *both* the advanced capitalist and the developing world. Sachs is absolutely right, of course, to maintain that "the only progressive interpretation of historical experience is to consider past experiences as anti-models that can be surpassed."[2] But surpassing is not a matter of simple inversion or antidote. It is a matter of dealing with the complex passages from the forces that construct future possibilities and thus make the city, as always, a figure of utopian desire and excitement at the same time as we understand the dystopian complement to the wealth of new possibilities that such social processes create.

Cities Limited and Unlimited

We can best get some sort of purchase on these questions by returning to the historical-geographical issue of how cities did or did not grow in the past. What, for example, were the constraints to urban growth that kept cities so limited in size and number in the past, and what happened sometime before and after 1800 that released urbanization from those limitations?

The answer is relatively simply in its basics. Up until the sixteenth or seventeenth centuries, urbanization was limited by a very specific metabolic relation between cities and their productive hinterlands coupled with the surplus extraction possibilities (grounded in specific class relations) that sustained them. No matter that certain towns and cities were centers of long-distance trade in luxuries or that even some basic goods, like grains, salt, hides and timber could be moved over long distances, the basic provisioning (feeding, watering and energy supply) of the city was always limited by the restricted productive capacity of a relatively confined hinterland. Cities were forced to be "sustainable," to use a currently much-favored word, because they had to be. The recycling of city nightsoils and other urban wastes into the hinterland was a major element in that sustainable pattern of urbanization, making medieval cities seem somewhat of a virtuous bioregionalist form of organization for many contemporary ecologists (though what now looks virtuous must have smelled putrid at the time—"the worse a city smelled," notes Guillerme, "the richer it was").[3] From time to time, the hinterlands of cities were extended by forced trade and conquest (one thinks of North African wheat supply to imperial Rome), and of course localized productivity gains in agriculture or forestry (sometimes a short-run phenomenon that lasted until such time as soil exhaustion set in), and the variable social capacity to squeeze surpluses from a reluctant rural population typically made the constraints on urban growth elastic rather than rigid. But the security of the city economy depended crucially upon the qualities of its localized metabolic support system, in which local environmental qualities (the breeding grounds of pestilences, plagues and diseases of all sorts that periodically decimated urban populations) as well as food, water and energy supply—particularly firewood—figured large. It is worth remembering in this regard, that in 1830 most of the supply of fresh dairy products and vegetables to a city like Paris came from within a relatively restricted suburban zone if not from within the city confines itself. Before 1800, the "footprint" (again to use a currently favored term) of urbanization on the surface of the earth was relatively light (for all the significance cities may have had in the history of politics, science, and civilization): cities trod relatively lightly on the ecosystems that sustained them and were bioregionally defined.

What changed all this, of course, was the wave of new technologies (understood as both hardware and the software of organizational forms) generated by the military-industrial complex of early capitalism. For reasons that I have elsewhere elaborated on at length, capitalism as a mode of production has necessarily targeted the breaking down of spatial barriers and the acceleration of turnover time as fundamental to its agenda of relentless capital accumulation.[4] The overcoming of spatial barriers and the restraints of particularity of location through the production of a particular space of transport and communications (and the consequent "annihilation of space through time" to use Marx's felicitous phrase) has been of enormous significance within the historical dynamic of capitalism, turning that dynamic into a very geographical affair. Many, if not all, of the major waves of innovation that have shaped the world since the sixteenth century have been built around revolutions in transport and communications: the canals, bridges and turnpikes of the early nineteenth century; the railroad, steamboat and telegraph of the mid nineteenth century; the mass transit systems of the late nineteenth century; the automobile, the radio and telephone of the early twentieth century; the jet aircraft and television of the 1950s and 1960s; and most recently, the revolution in telecommunications. Each bundle of innovations has allowed a radical shift in the way that space is organized, and therefore opened up radically new possibilities for the urban process. Breaking with the dependency upon relatively confined bioregions opened up totally new vistas of possibilities for urban growth. Cronon's study of Chicago, *Nature's Metropolis*, tells in this regard an exemplary tale of how the rapid urbanization of that city in the nineteenth century was precisely geared to the human realization of these new possibilities with the effect that the footprint of the city across the whole of the American Midwest and West became ever larger as its metabolic-ecological relations changed and as it itself grew in a few years into one of the largest cities in the world.[5] And internally, as Platt so brilliantly shows in his Chicago-based study of *The Electric City*, the progress of electrification allowed the construction of radically new and dispersed urban forms.[6]

Each round of innovation breaking the barriers of space and time has provided new possibilities. The steam engine, to take just one highly significant historical example, liberated the energy supply of cities from relatively inefficient and highly localized constraints, at the same time as it freed local hinterlands from a chronic conflict over whether to use the land for food or firewood (contemporary students now find it very odd, for example, that one of the closer rings of production with which von Thünen surrounded his city in *The Isolated State* of the early nineteenth century is given over to forestry).[7] But the steam engine could only accomplish its revolutionary role to the degree that it was in turn applied to a field of transport and communications: the coal had to be shunted around. It was and is, therefore, the total bundle of innovations and the synergism that binds them together that is really crucial in opening up new possibilities.

And in this, seemingly quite small things can figure large in what created possibilities for city growth. The military engineers and mathematicians of the eighteenth century, for example, in using water flow as a form of fortification learned that networks were far more efficient in moving water than direct pipes and channels; this recognition (and the study of the mathematics of networks that went with it) had immense significance once it was applied to cities in the nineteenth century: a given head of water flowing down one pipe can provision no more than 5,000 people but that same head of water when flowed around a network can provision twenty times that. This is a useful general metaphor for urban growth possibilities: the development of an interrelated network of cities drawing upon a variety of hinterlands permits an aggregate urban growth process radically greater than that achievable for each in isolation.

Since the mid-1960s, to take another example of a phase in which innumerable innovations (including the necessary mathematical knowledges) have bundled together to create a new synergism of urbanizing possibilities, we have witnessed a reorganization in spatial configurations and urban forms under conditions of yet another intense round in the reduction of spatial barriers and speedup in turnover time. The "global village" of which Marshall McLuhan speculatively wrote in the 1960s has become, at least in some senses, a reality. McLuhan thought that television would be the vehicle, but in truth it was probably the launching of Sputnik that presaged the break, ushering in as it did a new age of satellite communication. But, as in other areas, it is less a single innovation than the total bundle that counts. Containerization, jet-cargo systems, roll-on-roll-off ferries, truck design and, just as important, highway design to support greater weights, have all helped to reduce the cost and time of moving goods over space, while automatic information processing, optimization and control systems, satellite communication, cellular phones and computer technologies, all facilitate the almost instantaneous communication, collation and analysis of information, making the microchip as important as the satellite in understanding the forces that now shape urban life.

Capitalist Urbanization

These new technological and organizational possibilities have all been produced under the impulsions of a capitalist mode of production with its hegemonic military-industrial-financed interests. For this reason, I believe it is not only useful to think of but also important to recognize that we are all embroiled in a *global process of capitalist urbanization* even in those countries that have nominally at least sought a non-capitalistic path of development and a non-capitalistic urban form. The manner and particular style of urbanization varies greatly, of course, depending upon how these capitalist possibilities are proposed, opposed and ultimately realized. But the context of possibilities is very definitely a capitalist production. And the sense of new possibilities continually opening up gives rise to that modernist style of Utopian thinking about technopoles, multifunctionopolises, and the like, which parallels that dystopian imagery about the city I began by invoking.

There are, it seems to me, two basic perspectives from which now to view the conflicting ways such possibilities are being taken up. Firstly, we can look upon urbanization (and the lures of city construction and destruction) in terms of the forces of capital accumulation. Capital realizes its own agenda of "accumulation for accumulation's sake, production for production's sake," against a background of the technological possibilities it has itself created. Urbanization in the advanced capitalist countries, for example, has not in recent history been about sustaining bioregions, ecological complexes, or anything other than sustaining the accumulation of capital.

In the United States, to take the paradigmatic case, capital accumulation through suburbanization and all that this entailed (from the vast associated water projects of the American West, the highway systems, the construction complexes, to say nothing about the automobile, the oil and rubber industries, etc.) was central to the postwar economic success of the United States, even though it produced its nether side in the form of derelict and deserted central cities. The point to emphasize here is not so much the technological mix but the active realization of opportunities for direct capital accumulation by way of that technological complex of possibilities. The exhaustion of these possibilities (for example, the relative saturation of the market for new automobiles) makes capital accumulation more difficult, as every large multinational auto producer now recognizes.

The auto industry now looks, therefore, upon those unsaturated markets in China, India, Latin America, and the deliberately "under-urbanized" world of the former Soviet bloc as its primary realm of future accumulation. But that means reshaping the urban process in those regions to the not particularly environmentally friendly (or even economically feasible) system that for several decades supported economic growth in the United States. While that prospect may send shivers down every mildly ecologically conscious spine, any inability to pursue it will produce even worse *frissons* of horror in the boardrooms of every transnational automobile company, if not the whole capitalist class.

The particular dialectic of attraction and repulsion that capital accumulation exhibits for different sites within the web of urbanization varies spatio-temporally as well as with the fiction of capital concerned. Financial (money) capital, merchant capital, industrial-manufacturing capital, property and landed capital, statist capital, and agro-business capital—to take the most familiar factional breakdown of the capitalist class configuration (the other being local, national and multinational capitals)—have radically different needs as well as radically different ways to explore the possibilities of exploiting the web of urbanization for purposes of capital accumulation. Tensions arise between the factions because they each have quite different capabilities for and interest in geographical movement, varying from the relatively fixed-in-space capital of property, landed and "local" small-scale capital and the instantaneous capacities for movement of transnational finance. Much of the creative destruction we are now witnessing within the urban process has to be understood in terms of such internal contradictions within the dynamics of overall capital accumulation. But the other part of it comes from the increasingly ruinous competition between places (be they nation states, regions, cities or even smaller local jurisdictions) as they find themselves forced to sell themselves at the lowest cost to lure highly mobile capital to earth.

Alternative Urbanization

But the other perspective from which to view the recent history of urbanization is in terms of popular (if not "populist") seizure of the possibilities that capitalist technologies have created. To some degree, this is about the vast historical migrations of labor in response to capital, from one region to another if not from one continent to another. That formulation basically made most sense in the nineteenth and even the early twentieth centuries (though there were always exceptions such as the flood of Irish overseas in the wake of the potato famine, which may have been prompted by conditions of imposed agrarian capitalism but was hardly a "normal" migration of rural population in search of urban liberties and waged labor). But the flood of people into developing country cities is not fundamentally tied to the pulls of employment attached to capital accumulation, or even to the pushes of a reorganizing agrarian capitalism destructive of traditional peasantries (though there are many segments of the world where that process is very strongly in evidence). It is a far more populist search to take advantage of capitalist produced possibilities no matter whether capital accumulation is going on or not, and often in the face of economic conditions that are just as, if not more appalling than, those left behind. And, while one of the effects may be to create vast "informal economies" that operate both as protocapitalist sectors and as feeding grounds for more conventional forms of capitalist exploitation and accumulation, the explanation of the movement in itself can hardly be attributed to the machinations of some organized capitalist class action.[8]

The continuing flow of Asian and African populations into European countries and the Asian and Latino flows into North America exhibit similar qualities producing some wonderfully instructive contrasts right in the heart of capitalist cities. Within earshot of Bow Bells in London, for example, one finds the extraordinary power of international finance capital moving funds almost instantaneously round the world cheek by jowl with a substantial Bengali population (largely unemployed in any conventional sense), which has built a strong migratory bridge into the heart of capitalist society in search of new possibilities in spite of rampant racism and increasingly low wage, informal and temporary working possibilities. Here, too, the industrial reserve army that such migratory movements create may become an active vehicle for capital accumulation by lowering wages but the migratory movement itself, while it may indeed have been initiated by capital looking for labor reserves (as with guest workers and migrant streams from the European periphery), has surely taken on a life of its own.

The massive forced and unforced migrations of peoples now taking place in the world, a movement that seems unstoppable no matter how hard countries strive to enact stringent immigration controls, will have as much if not greater significance in shaping urbanization in the twenty-first century as the powerful dynamic of unrestrained capital mobility and accumulation. And the politics that flow from such migratory movements, while not necessarily antagonistic to continued capital accumulation, are not necessarily consistent with it either, posing serious questions as to whether urbanization by capital accumulation will be anywhere near as hegemonic in the future as it has been in the past, even in the absence of any major organizing force, such as a powerful socialist or pan-religious … movement, that seeks to counteract the manifest injustices and marginalizations of the capitalist form of urbanization by the construction of some alternative urban world.

An Adequate Language

But in all of this I am struck again and again by the difficulty of designing an adequate language, an adequate conceptual apparatus to grasp the nature of the problem we seem to be faced with. I worry that last year's conceptual tools and goals will be used to fight next year's issues in a dynamic situation that more and more requires proactive rather than remedial action. I am not alone in this worry. Nor is this an entirely new dilemma. As Sachs observes of urban politics and policies in the past:

> Urbanists, like economists and generals, were ready for the last battle they won ... the social rhetoric of the charter of Athens served more as a screen to hide their fascination with new building materials, industrialized construction methods, and spatial and architectural aestheticism rather than as a pointer to look at the real person in the streets... In their conceptions of society and human needs, most postwar urbanists demonstrated the same mix of naiveté, dogmatism, and lack of interest in empirical evidence about people's lifestyles as the protagonist of the discussions held in the Soviet Union in the early 1920s.[9]

Are we, then, in danger of repeating the error that Keynes long ago pointed to when he remarked on how we have a strong penchant for organizing our present lives in accordance with the defunct vision of some long dead economist?

In thinking through this problem, I think it important first to recognize that, as a physical artifact, the contemporary city has many layers. It forms what we might call a *palimpsest*, a composite landscape made up of different built forms superimposed upon each other with the passing of time. In some cases, the earliest layers are of truly ancient origin, rooted in the oldest civilizations whose imprints can be discerned beneath today's urban fabric. But even cities of relatively recent date comprise distinctive layers accumulated at different phases in the hurly burly of chaotic urban growth engendered by industrialization, colonial conquest, neocolonial domination, wave after wave of migration, as well as of real estate speculation and modernization. Think, for example, of how the migratory layers that occupy even the rapidly expanding shantytowns of cities in developing countries quickly spawn identifiable physical layers of more and more permanent and solid occupancy.

In the last two hundred years or so, the layers in most cities have accumulated ever thicker and faster in relation to burgeoning population growth, massive voluntary and forced relocations of populations, strong but contradictory paths of economic development, and the powerful technological changes that liberated urban growth from former constraints. But it is nevertheless, as Jencks points out, one of the oddities of cities that they become more and more fixed with time, more and more sclerotic, precisely because of the way they incrementally add things on rather than totally shedding their skins and beginning all over again.[10] Planners, architects, urban designers—"urbanists," in short—all face one common problem: how to plan the construction of the next layers in the urban palimpsest in ways that match future wants and needs without doing too much violence to all that has gone before. What has gone before is important precisely because it is the locus of collective memory, of political identity, and of powerful symbolic meanings at the same time as it constitutes a bundle of resources constituting possibilities as well as barriers in the built environment for creative social change. There is never now a *tabula rasa* upon which new urban forms can be freely constructed. But the general charge of searching for a future while respecting the past all too frequently internalizes the sclerotic tendencies in urban forms into even more sclerotic ways of thinking …

• • •

The "thing" we call a "city" is the outcome of a "process" that we call "urbanization." But in examining the relationship between processes and things, there is a prior epistemological and ontological problem of whether we prioritize the process or the thing and whether or not it is even possible to separate the process from the things embodied in it.

The stance I shall adopt in what follows is largely governed by a dialectical way of thinking in which (a) processes are regarded as in some ways more fundamental than things, and (b) processes are always mediated through the things they produce, sustain and dissolve. Here is, I would suggest, the first point of a radical break that must be made with late nineteenth-century thinking. For at that time, the predominant conclusion, in spite of all the emphasis upon social relations and processes, was that the city was a thing that could be engineered successfully in such a way as to control, contain, modify or enhance social processes. Olmstead, Geddes, Howard, Burnham, Sitte, Wagner, Unwin, all steadily reduced the problem of intricate social processes to a matter of finding the right spatial form. And in this way they set the dominant twentieth-century tone for either a mechanistic approach to urban form, as in the case of Le Corbusier, or the more organic approach of Frank Lloyd Wright.

The difficulty with so-called high modernism and urbanization was not, I submit, its "totalizing" vision, but its persistent habit of privileging things and spatial forms over social processes, and so adopting a metaphysical approach that presumed that social engineering could be accomplished through the engineering of physical form. The antidote is not to abandon all talk of the city as a whole, as is the penchant of postmodernist critique, but to return to the level of social processes as being fundamental to the construction of the things that contain them …

Urbanization must then be understood not in terms of some socio-organizational entity called "the city" (the theoretical object that so many geographers, demographers and sociologists erroneously presume), but as the production of specific and quite heterogeneous spatio-temporal forms embedded within different kinds of social action. Urbanization, understood in this manner, is necessarily constitutive of as well as constituted by social processes. It loses its passive qualities and becomes a dynamic moment in overall processes of social differentiation and social change. For those of us who have abandoned the Newtonian-Cartesian-Kantian conception of spatio-temporality …, the production of space and of spatio-temporality becomes a fundamental moment within social processes, inseparable as a relational attribute of it, rather than as something constituted with absolute qualities *a priori*.

This is, I recognize, a somewhat difficult argument. So let me illustrate the importance of the idea in very general terms. Under the absolute conception of space and time, it would be perfectly reasonable to look upon the massive urbanization in the developing world as a direct product of, say, population growth. If there are urban problems, the argument would then follow, that it is the population issue that must first be resolved. To be sure, there may be feedback effects as the demographic and reproductive characteristics of urban populations begin to diverge from their rural counterparts. But the basic issue here can still reasonably be thought of, given the absolute view of space, as one of population growth. Under the relational view, however, population growth cannot be considered separately at all from the organizational and spatio-temporal conditions embedded in population dynamics as a social process. The capacity to produce space and to construct entirely new forms of spatio-temporality is necessarily a constitutive moment in processes of population change rather than a merely passive site for that change. If that is the case, then it is just as meaningful to argue that it was the liberation of urban growth from its former spatio-temporal and metabolic constraints that permitted aggregate populations to grow at the fast rates they recently have. Had the metabolic barriers to urbanization that prevailed in the past continued to hold, then population growth would most certainly have been of an entirely different sort and order. To put it this way sounds, however, as if I am merely reversing the direction of the causal arrow. But in effect I am arguing that the production of spatio-temporalities within social processes is perpetually changing the horizon of social possibilities. Shifting spatio-temporal horizons for social action become as important to understanding population growth as population growth becomes for understanding the particular spatio-temporal forms of contemporary cities. Above all, it is then clear why attempts to engineer social processes through the imposition of spatial form are doomed from the very outset …

The issue for us is then not gazing into some misty crystal ball to make those always risky and usually erroneous predictions of what the future will look like, but enlisting in the struggle to advance a certain mix of spatio-temporal production processes rather than others in pursuit of certain interests and goals rather than others. In more raw political terms, this says that the production of spatio-temporalities that define the urban are the object of all manner of struggles (class, ethnic, racial, gender, religious, symbolic, etc.) and that hegemonic powers (from finance capital to the World Bank) can secretly impose their agendas by imposing their own particular spatio-temporal orderings. But, though they may seem to deny agency to excluded and marginalized others, such hegemonic institutions can never entirely control the production of space and it is, therefore, in the interstices of that lack of control that all sorts of liberatory and emancipatory possibilities can hide …

Conclusions

Perhaps the chief sin of the twentieth century was that urbanization happened and nobody much either cared or noticed in relation to the other issues of the day judged more important. It would be an egregious error to enter upon the twenty-first century making the same mistake. It is, furthermore, vital to understand that what half-worked for the 1950s will not be adequate for the qualitatively different issues to be fought over the nature of civilization in the twenty-first century. And it is equally vital that the language in which the urban problematic is embedded be transformed, if only to liberate a whole raft of conceptual possibilities that may otherwise remain hidden. Imagine, for example, a world in which we confine our thinking to an absolute conception of space where entities called communities endowed with causal powers address the issue of ecological crisis. This is in fact a very prevalent mode of thought even in "progressive" political circles. It soon leads to what Dobson calls "repressive tribalism and exclusion," citing Edward Goldsmith (editor of *The Ecologist*) as saying "a certain number of 'foreigners' would be allowed to settle" in a community, but that "they would not, thereby partake in the running of the community until such time as the citizens elected them to be of their number."[11] Counterpose the "ecofascism" that arises out of this framework of thought with the relational idea that spatio-temporalities are heterogeneous and actively produced by multiple social processes (varying from capital accumulation to religious worship, or from sexual acts to construction of monuments) and that the "public" ranges across a great (variety of communicative spheres within and between which all sorts of negotiations and conflicts are possible. Add in, furthermore, the vision that environmental-ecological transformations (including the construction of built environments) are potentially just as productive of new environmental niches and social differentiation as they are productive of the homogeneity of ecological crises. The range of possibilities that attaches to this second mode of thought looks to me radically different—and much more enticing for the play of all sorts of emancipatory politics.

Coming to terms with what urban living might be about in the twenty-first century poses, then, a series of key problems to be simultaneously worked on with a set of parallel myths that deserve to be exploded:

The first myth is that the problems posed by urbanization are essentially a consequence of deeper rooted social processes that can and need to be addressed independently of their geographical setting or spatio-temporal ordering. This view should be strenuously opposed with a vision that sees the production of different spatio-temporal orderings and structures as active moments within the social process, the appreciation of which will better reveal how what we conventionally understand by urbanization and urban forms might be redefined and factored in as moments of transformation, and consequently possible points of intervention within that social process.

The second myth is that it is merely a matter of finding the right technologies to get a better fix on how to accommodate burgeoning populations within the urban frame. Opposed to this is a recognition that the new technologies produced by the military-industrial complex of capitalism have again and again opened up new and broadly capitalist-oriented possibilities for urbanization, but that these possibilities ought nevertheless to be distinguished from the predominant forces (such as capital accumulation or populist appropriation) that realize their own agendas.

The third myth is that coming up with the resources to confront urban problems depends on the prior solution of economic development and population growth problems. Opposed to this is the idea that cities have always been fundamentally about wealth creation and wealth consumption, and that getting things right in cities is the only real path towards economic improvement for the mass of the population. And in that, I think we should also include fundamental redefinitions of wealth, well-being and values (including those that affect population growth) in ways that are more conducive to the development of human potentialities as opposed to mere capital accumulation for the selected few.

The fourth myth is that social problems in urbanizing areas are curable only to the degree that the forces of the market are given freer play. Opposed to this is the idea that wealth creation (and redefinition) depends on social collaboration, on cooperation (even between businesses), rather than on some individualized competitive Darwinian struggle for existence. The pursuit of social justice is therefore one important means to achieve improved economic performance and here, at least, communitarian thinking and values do have a potentially creative role to play.

The fifth myth is that community solidarity can provide the stability and power needed to control, manage and alleviate urban problems and that "community" can substitute for public politics. Opposed to this is the recognition that "community," insofar as it exists, is an unstable configuration relative to the conflictual processes that generate, sustain and eventually undermine it, and that insofar as it does acquire permanence, it is frequently an exclusionary and oppressive social form (that becomes particularly dangerous when romanticized), which can be as much at the root of urban conflict and urban degeneration as it can be a panacea for political-economic difficulties.

The sixth myth is that any radical transformation in social relations in urbanizing areas must await some sort of socialist or communist revolution that will then put our cities in sufficiently good order to allow the new social relations to flourish. Opposed to this is the idea that the transformation of social relations in urban settings has to be a continuous process of socioenvironmental change, a long revolution that should have the construction of an alternative society as its long-term goal.

The seventh myth is that strong order, authority and centralized control—be it moral, political, communitarian, religious, physical or militaristic—must be reasserted over our disintegrating and strife-prone cities without, however, interfering in the fundamental liberty of the market. Opposed to this is the understanding that the contemporary form of "market Stalinism" is self-contradictory and the recognition that urbanization has always been about creative forms of opposition, tension and conflict (including those registered through market exchange). The tensions born of heterogeneity cannot and should not be repressed, but liberated in socially exciting ways, even if this means more rather than less conflict, including contestations over socially necessary socialization of market processes for collective ends.

The eighth myth is that diversity and difference, heterogeneity of values, life-style oppositions and chaotic migrations, are to be feared as sources of disorder and that "others" should be kept out to defend the "purity" of place. Opposed to this is the view that cities that cannot accommodate to diversity, to migratory movements, to new lifestyles and to economic, political, religious and value heterogeneity will die either through ossification and stagnation or because they will fall apart in violent conflict. Defining a politics that can bridge the multiple heterogeneities without repressing difference is one of the biggest challenges of twenty-first-century urbanization.

The ninth myth is that cities are anti-ecological. Opposing this is the view that high density urbanized living and inspired forms of urban design are the only paths to a more ecologically sensitive form of civilization in the twenty-first century. We must recognize that the distinction between *environment* as commonly understood and the *built environment* is artificial, and that the urban and everything that goes into it is as much a part of the solution as it is a contributing factor to ecological difficulties. The tangible recognition that the mass of humanity will be located in living environments designated as urban says that the environmental politics must pay as much if not more attention to the qualities of those built and social environments as it now typically does to a fictitiously separated and imagined "natural" environment.

It will take imagination and political guts, a surge of revolutionary fervor and revolutionary change (in thinking as well as in politics) to address these questions adequately. In this regard, at least, there is much to learn from our predecessors for their political and intellectual courage cannot be doubted. But if the rhetoric about handing on a decent living environment to future generations is to have even one iota of meaning, a radically different collective thought process of some sort has to be instituted. A crucial preliminary is to find an adequate language in which to discuss possible futures in a rapidly urbanizing world, a language that actively recognizes that urbanization is both constitutive of, as well as constituted by, the ways such possibilities might potentially be grasped.

Notes

1 Sachs, "Vulnerability of Giant Cities and the Life Lottery," *The Metropolis Era: Volume 1, A World of Giant Cities*, eds. Mattéi Dogan and John D. Kasarda (Newbury: Sage, 1988) 341.

2 Ibid.

3 André Guillerme, *The Age of Water: the Urban Environment in the North of France* (College Station: Texas A & M University Press, 1988) 171.

4 David Harvey, *The Limits to Capital* (Oxford: Blackwell, 1982); David Harvey, *The Condition of Postmodernity* (Oxford: Blackwell, 1989); and David Harvey, *The Urban Experience* (Baltimore: Johns Hopkins University Press, 1989).

5 William Cronon, *Nature's Metropolis: Chicago and the Great West* (New York: Norton, 1991).

6 Harold L. Platt, *The Electric City: Energy and Growth of the Chicago Area, 1880–1930* (Chicago: Chicago University Press, 1991).

7 Johan Heinrich von Thünen, *The Isolated State*, trans. Carla M. Wartenberg (Oxford and New York, Pergamon Press, 1966).

8 See Alejandro Portes, Manuel Castells, and Lauren A. Benton, *The Informal Economy: Studies in Advanced and Less Developed Countries* (Baltimore: Johns Hopkins University Press, 1989).

9 Sachs, "Vulnerability of Giant Cities and the Life Lottery," 343.

10 Charles Jencks, *Heteropolis: Los Angeles, the Riots, and the Strange Beauty of Hetero-Architecture* (London: Academy Editions, 1993).

11 Andrew Dobson, *Green Political Thought* (London: Harper Collins, 1990) 96.

4
NETWORKS, BORDERS, DIFFERENCES: TOWARDS A THEORY OF THE URBAN

Christian Schmid

The process of urbanization has changed fundamentally in recent years. For more than a century, the dominant form of urbanization was concentric, with suburbs arranged like belts around an urban core. This is how the large agglomerations of the twentieth century emerged. Around the end of the century, however, urban growth patterns began to change, as manifested in a wide variety of places: the process of urbanization has become undirected; existing urban forms are beginning to dissolve; centrality is becoming polymorphous; and eccentric urban configurations are evolving. Overarching, polycentric urban regions are taking shape. Extremely heterogeneous in structure, they include old city centers as well as once-peripheral areas.

In this process, new urban configurations are constantly evolving. Lightly settled, once rural areas are caught up in various forms of "peri-urbanization." Urbanists have coined a number of terms to describe the new forms of centrality that are emerging in former peripheral areas: "edge city," "technoburb" or "in-between cities."[1] However, most of these terms, and the concepts behind them, are no more than generalizations of spectacular special cases. A general description of the new form of urbanization led Edward Soja to coin the term "exopolis." By that, he refers to the improbable city orbiting beyond the old agglomeration cores that turns the metropolis inside-out and outside-in at the same time, and has a gravitational center as empty as a "doughnut"—that is, those places lying outside of the center, right on the edge, but still in the middle of things.

Centrality is virtually ubiquitous, and the solid familiarity of what we once knew as urban melts into air.[2] Similarly, Rem Koolhaas tries to pinpoint this phenomenon by speaking about the "generic city": a characterless city that ruthlessly evacuates everything authentic, dispenses with everything that lacks a function, and escapes the chokehold of the center, the "straitjacket of identity."[3]

Such generalizations overlook the fact that contrary trends can be observed as well: in parallel with the reconfiguration of centrality on the urban periphery in recent years, there has also been a "rediscovery of the urban." There have been numerous examples of the restructuring, regeneration and redevelopment of inner cities. Multinational corporations and the urban elites have monopolized areas near the center and turned them into privileged spaces for production, residence and consumption, while less privileged social groups have been pushed out to peripheral areas with poor acess to urban life.[4]

The result has been a complex interplay of peripheralization and centralization. Frequently used expressions such as "de-urbanization" and "re-urbanization" convey only a blurry impression of these changes. The new feature of urbanization is that centrality is becoming general, omnipresent and yet ephemeral. The city can no longer be perceived as a unit because it now consists of overlapping urban realities with indistinct borders. The old models of the city are becoming obsolete. The complex processes involved in restructuring urban regions have not yet received adequate theoretical attention. Current scholarly debate is dominated by partial approaches that examine individual aspects and processes or generalize isolated cases. A new language and new theoretical approaches must be developed in order to understand present-day urbanization processes. The city and urbanization should be understood as general phenomena and should be mutually linked in one overarching theory.

One of the few theories that does exist in this field is that of the French philosopher Henri Lefebvre. Developed more than 40 years ago, it long found little recognition so that its influence is only now achieving its full potential.[5] This pioneering theory is so important because it integrates the categories of the "urban" and of "space" systematically into an overarching social theory, thus making it possible to reflect upon and analyze spatial processes and phenomena on any scale, from the private to the global.[6] In recent years, the theory has enjoyed a remarkable renaissance. It has increasingly been taken up and discussed in a variety of disciplines, in the social sciences as well as in architecture, but it has yet to be applied empirically and further developed.

This chapter reconstructs several of Lefebvre's central arguments and develops a new theoretical framework for empirical analysis, based on three concepts: networks, borders and differences. These three terms guided the empirical research of the project *Switzerland— An Urban Portrait.*[7]

The Thesis of Complete Urbanization

The point of departure for Lefebvre's theory is his thesis of the complete urbanization of society. It states that, with few exceptions, the whole world is caught up in a comprehensive process of urbanization. Today's reality can no longer be grasped using the categories "city" and "country," but must be analyzed using the concepts of urban society.

For Lefebvre, the process of urbanization is closely linked to industrialization. The Industrial Revolution initiated a long, sustained migration from the country into the cities that caused urban areas to spread. Industrialization and urbanization form a highly complex and conflict-laden unity: industrialization provides the conditions and means for urbanization, and urbanization is the consequence of industrialization and of industrial production that is spreading across the globe. Operating from this definition, Lefebvre sees urbanization as a process that is reshaping and colonizing rural areas and at the same time fundamentally transforming and partly destroying historical cities.[8]

Urbanization, Lefebvre argues, is a process that is breaking up agrarian society and robbing it of the elements that had constituted rural life: trades, handicrafts and small local centers. The traditional community—the village—is losing its distinctive character as the hub of rural life. An urban fabric (*tissu urbain*) is spreading across the country. This term refers not only to built-up areas but to the totality of phenomena that result from the dominance of the city over the country. Hence a second home, a freeway, or a supermarket are also part of the urban fabric. This plexus forms the material basis for an entire urban system that ranges from the media and recreational activities to fashion, and it entails a fundamental transformation of daily life, with far-reaching implications. The urban fabric is more or less densely woven—all that remains in the mesh of the weave are rural islands of varying sizes: hamlets, villages, and even entire regions stagnate or decline and are abandoned to "nature."[9]

This worldwide process of urbanization not only alters traditional forms of agrarian society but also leads to a fundamental transformation of cities. From the opposite perspective, the phenomenon of urbanization is manifested in an enormous expansion of urban agglomerations and the spread of urban networks. The metropolis is exploding, scattering countless urban fragments throughout its surroundings. Small and medium-sized cities become dependent; they become virtual colonies of the metropolis.

Lefebvre borrows a powerful metaphor from atomic physics to describe this double process of urbanization: implosion—explosion. By this, he means a "the tremendous concentration (of people, activities, wealth, goods, objects, instruments, means, and thought) of urban reality and the immense explosion, the projection of numerous, disjunct fragments (peripheries, suburbs, vacation homes, satellite towns)."[10]

The City in Urban Society

Lefebvre's theory represents a radical break from the traditional Western understanding of the urban. The city can no longer be grasped as an object, as a definable unity. It is instead a historical category that is breaking down in the process of urbanization. This shifts the focus of interest to the analysis of a process of transformation and its inherent potential: the creation of an urban society.

Nevertheless, urbanization does not mean that all urbanized regions will ultimately become uniform and homogeneous. Nor does it mean that the city is disappearing as a built form and a social reality. How can the new urban forms be understood? What processes are characteristic of them? What is "the city" in urban society?

In order to grasp the specific character of the urbanized world, a fundamental reorientation of analysis is required: the city has to be embedded in the context of society as a whole and its content redefined. Three aspects are particularly significant in Lefebvre's theory: mediation, centrality, and difference.

Mediation

In a first approximation, Lefebvre identifies the urban as a specific level or order of social reality. It is a middle or mediating level situated between two others: that of the private level, of the nearby order, of everyday life, of dwelling, on the one hand, and that of the general level, of the distant order, of the global market, of the state, of knowledge, of institutions, and of ideologies, on the other. This intermediate level takes on crucial significance: it serves as a relay, as mediation, as communication between the general and private levels.

In urbanized society, however, the urban level is at risk of being eroded between the general and private levels. On the one hand, technology and industrialization have led to a universal rationalism, which is undermining the particularities, the specifics, of a given place or location. On the other hand, space is parceled up and subjected to the individualist logic of private enterprise. When a society has been completely urbanized, it is precisely the level of mediation that is lost.[11]

Only the most extreme thesis on the disappearance of the city can, however, reveal the significance of the urban: the city should be understood as a social resource. It represents an essential device for organizing society; it brings widely disparate elements of society together and is therefore productive. This also explains why cities display an astonishing ability to rebuild themselves. The specific quality of the urban lies in the historical cycle of breaking up and reconstituting.[12]

Proceeding from these reflections, Lefebvre arrives at a new definition of the city: the city is a center. It is defined by its centrality. For him, "city" means exchange, rapprochement, convergence, collection, meeting. The city creates a situation in which different things no longer exist separately from one another. As a place of encounter, communication and information, it is also a place where constraints and normality break down and the playful aspect and the unpredictable join in: "The urban is defined as the place where people walk around, find themselves standing before and inside piles of objects, experience the intertwining of the threads of their activities until they become unrecognizable, entangle situations in such a way that they engender unexpected situations."[13]

For Lefebvre, this definition of urban space contains a virtual zero vector: in urban space the space-time vector approaches zero; any point can become a focus toward which everything moves, a privileged space on which everything converges. The city is virtual annulment, the negation of distances in space and time: "the cancellation of distance haunts the occupants of urban space. It is their dream, their symbolized imaginary, represented in a multiplicity of ways."[14]

For Lefebvre, centrality is defined by the association and encounter of whatever exists together in one space at the same time. Thus, it corresponds to a logical form: the point of encounter, the place of coming together. This form has no specific content. Its logic stands for the simultaneity contained within it and from which it results: the simultaneity of everything that can be brought together at or around one point. This form of centrality is constituted both as an act of thinking and as a social act. In mental terms, it is the simultaneity of events, of perceptions, of elements of a whole in the "real." In social terms, it means the coming together and combining of assets and products, of wealth and activities. Centrality can thus also be understood as a totality of differences.[15]

Difference

From this results the third definition of the urban: the city is a place of differences. It is a differential space, in which differences come to light. Space-time distances are replaced by contradictions, contrasts, superimpositions and juxtapositions of different realities. The city can be defined as a place in which differences know, recognize, test, confirm or offset one another.

Differences must be clearly distinguished from particularities: they are elements of active connection, while particularities remain mutually isolated. Particularities come from nature, from the site, from natural resources. They are tied to local conditions and thus still relate to rural society. They are isolated, external and can easily turn into antagonism toward other particularities. Over the course of history, however, they come into contact with one another. Their confrontation evolves into mutual "understanding," and hence into difference. The moment of confrontation always implies an element of conflict. Transformed by this clash, the elements that survive no longer assert themselves separately from one another. Instead, they can only present and re-present themselves within their reciprocal relationships. This is where the concept of difference comes in: a concept obtains its content not only by means of logical thought but also along a variety of paths, that of history and those of the manifold dramas of everyday life. In this way, and under these circumstances, particularities become differences and produce difference.[16]

The Right to the City

Following Lefebvre's theory, the city can be defined in three ways: first, it is a specific level of social reality, the level of mediation; second, it is a social form, centrality; third, it is a specific place, the place of difference. These are formal definitions. The theory does not define the content of the urban, which can only be determined empirically. It originates from the respective social conditions and is the result of involvement with the city. When historical conditions change, the content of urban society is redefined as well.

What is the specific character of the urban in our present globalized society? For Lefebvre, centrality takes on a new quality in this society through the technologies of information and data processing: knowledge and information from all over the world are consolidated and processed at one spot. As a result, the capacities of encounter and association increase; simultaneity is intensified and condensed. Urban centers are taking over the task of accelerating the intellectualization of the global production process. All of these developments result in a renewed centrality based on information. Centrality eliminates peripheral elements and condenses wealth, means of action, knowledge, information and culture. Ultimately, it produces the highest power, the concentration of powers: the decision.[17]

Lefebvre locates the new definition of the urban in the decision center. Today's cities are centers of conception and information, of organization and institutional decision-making on a global scale. They are centers of decision and power that unite all the constitutive elements of society in a limited territory.

The transformation of cities into centers of decision-making and information does not, however, proceed uncontested. Centrality becomes a political question; cities become contested terrain. That is why Lefebvre programmatically calls for a "right to the city": the right not to be forced into a space that was produced solely for the purpose of discrimination. Lefebvre places this right alongside the other rights that define urban civilization: the rights to work, education, health, dwelling, leisure time and life. The right to the city refers not to the city of earlier times but to urban life, to a renewed centrality, to the places of meeting and exchange, to life rhythms and a use of time that enable a full and complete use of these places. This right cannot be simply interpreted as the right to visit or to return to traditional cities. It can only be formulated as the right to a transformed, renewed urban life.[18]

The grand theoretical and practical project that Lefebvre envisions consists in discovering a possible path to this urban world in which unity is no longer opposed to difference, where the homogeneous no longer conflicts with the heterogeneous, and gatherings, encounters, and meetings—not without conflicts—will replace the struggle of individual urban elements that have become antinomies as a result of divisions. This urban space would provide the social basis for a transformed daily life that is open to a wide variety of possibilities.

Perceived, Conceived and Lived Space

That raises the question of how such an urban space can be produced or, to put it another way, how the "city" can be produced under present conditions. This question also leads to the radical transformation of analytical perspective. Both concept and theory must be generalized so that different aspects can be combined with one another as illustrated in the concept of space and the theory of the production of space that Lefebvre elaborated in his 1974 book *The Production of Space*.[19]

Producing space—that may sound strange, as Lefebvre himself admits. Nevertheless, he employs the term deliberately and provocatively to counteract the still widespread notion that space exists prior to the "things" that occupy and fill it. For Lefebvre, space is a social product.

At the center of Lefebvre's theory is the notion that the production of space can be split analytically into three dialectically related dimensions or processes. These dimensions— Lefebvre calls them "formants" or "moments" of the production of space—are doubly defined and consequently doubly named as well. On the one hand, there is the triad of "spatial practice," "representation of space," and "spaces of representation" and, on the other, "perceived," "conceived," and "lived" space. These two sets of terms emphasize a dual approach to space: phenomenological, on the one hand; linguistic and semiotic, on the other.[20]

Three Dimensions of the Production of Space

"Space" has, first of all, a perceptible aspect that can be grasped with the five senses. This perceived space (*espace perçu*) refers directly to the materiality of the elements that constitute a space. Spatial practice (*pratique spatiale*) combines these elements into a spatial order, an order of the simultaneous. Concretely, perceived space refers to networks of interaction of the sort that emerge in daily life (for example, the connection between residence and workplace) or in the production process (networks of production and exchange). These networks are based in turn on materiality: on networks of streets and paths, on houses and production sites.

A space cannot, however, be perceived without first having been conceived in the mind. It is a mental achievement to treat individual elements as a whole, which is then considered a space. This is the source of conceived space (*espace conçu*). Constructions or conceptions of space rest on social conventions that establish which elements are related to one another and which are precluded. These conventions are learned but they are not unalterable; they are, in fact, frequently disputed, contested and negotiated in a discursive (political) context. This is a social process of production that is connected to the production of knowledge and linked to power structures. A conceived space therefore displays and defines a space by representing it (*représentation de l'espace*). Representations of space emerge on the level of discourse, of language as such. In a narrow sense, they comprise verbalized forms such as descriptions, definitions and above all (scientific) theories of space, but also maps and plans, that is, information provided by images and signs. Broadly speaking, representations of space comprise social rules and ethics as well.

Lefebvre calls the third dimension of the production of space "spaces of representation" (*espaces de représentation*). These are spaces that describe "something." Spaces of representation do not refer to space itself but to something else, a third thing: a divine power, logos, the state, the male or female principle. This dimension of the production of space refers to the process of signification, which attaches to a (material) symbolism: the production of meaning gives spaces a symbolic content and thereby makes them spaces of representation. The symbols of space can be taken from nature—like trees or striking natural formations. They can be pure artifacts, like buildings or monuments, or they can also result from a combination of the two, like cultural landscapes, for example. This aspect of space is experienced by people in their everyday lives, and that is why Lefebvre calls it lived space (*espace vécu*). Practical, lived experience cannot be exhausted by theoretical analysis. There is always a surplus that remains: an ineffable and unanalyzable residue that can only be expressed by means of art.

The theory of the production of space thus has at its core a three-level process of production: first, material production; second, the production of knowledge; and third, the production of meaning. Clearly, the subject matter of Lefebvre's theory is neither "space as such" nor the arrangement of (material) objects and artifacts in space but the practical, mental, and symbolic production of relations between these "objects." Space should be understood in an active sense, as a multilayered fabric of connections that are continually produced and reproduced. The object of analysis is active production processes that play out in time.

These three dimensions of the production of space form a conflicting, dialectical unity. It is a threefold determination: space emerges only in the interplay of all three poles.

The Production of the City

How can the city be understood as space? Lefebvre defines the city in three ways. It is the intermediary level of social reality, the site of mediation between the general and the private. The form of the urban is centrality: the city is the site of meeting, encounter, interaction. Finally, the urban is characterized by difference; it is a site where differences collide with one another and thereby produce something new.

At the same time, urban space can be depicted as a three-dimensional production process: the city is a product that only emerges in the conflicting interplay of spatial practice, the representation of space and spaces of representation or of perceived, conceived and lived spaces.

Urban space is, first of all, material, perceivable space. As such, it is a space of material interaction and of physical meeting that is opened up by networks and information flows. Thus the city can be understood as a specific spatial praxis located above the practical-sensory realm and below the abstract one: a praxis of linking and hence of potential meeting, from which something new can emerge. This practical aspect of centrality can be found in a wide range of areas, at intersections or nodes of production networks and communication channels, as connections of social networks in daily life, as sites of encounter and exchange that are open to surprises and innovations.

Second, the city is also a conceived space or a representation of space. What we understand as a city is dependent on the social definition of the urban and thus on the image of the city, on the blueprint or the map, but also on the plan that tries to define and pin down the urban. As a representation of space, the urban always remains initially undefined in an urbanized world. Because the city no longer represents a distinct social unit, an independent manner of production and living, there are many possible ways to define and demarcate a city. This is also why there are so many different definitions of the city today. Depending on one's perspective—scientific, planning, media or political—the city is understood to mean different units. All these various definitions are specific representations of space. They describe discursive demarcations of the content of the urban and entail corresponding strategies of inclusion and exclusion. Definitions of the city become a field in which a variety of strategies and interests are employed.

Third, the city is always a lived space as well, a place of residents who use it and appropriate it for their practices. The urban identifies the place of difference: the specific quality of urban space results from the simultaneous presence of quite distinct worlds and concepts of value, of ethnic, cultural and social groups, of activities, functions and knowledge. Urban space establishes the possibility of bringing all these diverse elements together and making them productive. At the same time, however, there is also a tendency for the elements to cut themselves off and separate. How these differences are experienced and lived in actual daily life is thus crucial.

Urban Space: Networks, Borders, Differences

Lefebvre's general theory of the production of space can be applied empirically in very different ways. It offers no precise methodology, but instead forms a conceptual backdrop that must be put in concrete terms for empirical analysis. Depending on the research question and the goal of analysis, it can be effected and employed in quite varied ways. The theory should not be schematically adopted but rather appropriated, plunged into reality, and creatively implemented.

For our analysis, the primary task is to find simple and imaginative concepts that can productively guide our research and enable us to outline the physiognomy of the urban. We first have to appropriate and translate Lefebvre's complex theory. In the process, we have developed three concepts to guide our investigation: networks, borders, differences.

Networks

Urban space is a space of material interaction, exchange, meeting and encounter. It is permeated by all kinds of networks that connect it to the inside and outside, and whose extension is either local or global depending on its function: networks of trade, production, capital, daily routine, communication and migration.

Urban space can thus be understood by means of the networks that run through it and determine it. Every urban area is affected by a characteristic set of networks that has evolved over the course of its historical development. These networks of interaction describe the material side of urban space; they relate to spatial praxis and thus to the perceivable aspect of space.

They are in turn based on a material infrastructure—on streets, airports, or fiber-optic cables—and they determine the qualities of urban space and its orientation. One central aspect of urbanization is that this material infrastructure is constantly being improved, and so it becomes possible to network the world with ever greater density. Urbanization is, in a sense, the flip-side of globalization, its material basis. In this context, the thesis of complete urbanization also means that networks of interaction are constantly expanding and becoming linked with increasing density.

The observation that the whole world has been networked with the help of satellites and mobile phones to create a global village is almost a truism. But closer examination shows that there is great variance not only in the degree to which urban regions have access to these technologies, but in the networks themselves. These networks are not distributed homogeneously in space; there are holes and gaps in the mesh but also knots or nodes— that is, zones of intense interaction. Center and periphery are no longer determined entirely by geographic position in space, but by relational positioning within global networks.

The crisscrossing networks that are strung out through urban space can be differentiated according to various qualities or features, such as their intensity or density, expansion or range, and their complexity. The first feature is the *intensity* of interaction. To what degree is an urban area integrated into networks? Does it cultivate intense exchange and a variety of connections, or does it tend to be more self-contained? Traditional rural areas are largely distinguished by an absence of networks or of far-reaching connections for exchange; they are self-referential and produce most of what they need themselves.

The second feature is related to the first. The *extension* or range of the networks into which social processes of interaction are integrated can also vary widely. The scale ranges from local to global areas of integration. Two levels are particularly significant in determining urban character: the ties to the region and the links to the world. Through the process of urbanization, the classical morphological form of the urban—a core city and its regional surroundings—has undergone fundamental change. Even though local networks, neighborhoods and communes continue to play an important role in everyday life, the framework of urban interaction has expanded to the regional level, where complex, polycentric networks of production, consumption and leisure are emerging. These networks, each with its own scale, overlap and produce complex patterns. The new forms of the city are correspondingly multifarious and extremely difficult to demarcate. At the same time, the connection to the overarching, global level has also intensified. Global processes have a direct effect on the local level. Today's urban regions can be understood as differentiated nodes of global and regional networks.

Finally, the third feature, the *heterogeneity* of networks, plays a crucial role. The overlapping of various networks can produce surprising connections. The resulting complexity is an important resource for processes of social innovation. Great heterogeneity is thus a central feature of metropolitan regions.

In short, every urban region is characterized by a specific set of networks, but since these networks may differ substantially, it is possible to discover ever new urban configurations.

Borders

The material space of interaction and networks is discontinuous, structured, and bordered. Urban regions are crisscrossed by many borders that cut territories off from the continual flow of network interaction.

Urbanization is a process that transcends borders and can scarcely be stopped by administrative and politically defined territorial borders. It follows that borders are not a primary urban characteristic. On the contrary, the process of urbanization began when the borders between city and country dissolved, and the external barriers that once protected the city and cut it off from its surroundings—walls, ramparts, and moats—fell away. The greenbelts that also served as a symbolic border between cities and the country have since become—where they still exist at all—inner city parks and open spaces. Urban spaces can no longer be geographically defined and delimited. This is a fundamental consequence of the complete urbanization of society. Nevertheless, borders still represent an essential criterion for distinguishing rural and urban areas. A rural area begins the process of urbanization when its boundaries lose their status as separations between discrete units. Urbanization transforms borders from factors of limitation, of closing off, of silence, of inactive difference into zones of exchange, of the interlocking of difference, of overlapping movements.

That is why the meaning of borders is ambivalent. In essence, every border can be considered, following Lefebvre, as "incision-suture": borders are cuts in the continual flow of interaction; they enclose more or less coherent territorial units with their own rules, regulations, laws, customs, traditions, languages, cultures and identities.[21] They are instruments of structuring, of control, of order. But they also mark transitions and differences: two worlds, two different orders, collide at a border. Hence, the border obtains a potential: it can link the separated units. New orders, new concepts, new images and new urban configurations emerge from the urban transformation of borders. These borders have a history; they represent the sedimentation of historical constellations of power that have become inscribed in the terrain like a palimpsest. In the course of urbanization, they are overwritten, but they continue to have an effect—often under the surface—and they acquire new meaning. Thus, it is not the lifting of borders that is an indication of urbanism, but their transformation into productive aspects of urban culture.

The development and quality of borders is a decisive criterion for the kind of urbanism that dominates a given region. A variety of aspects comes into play here. On the one hand, there is the question of the differences between neighboring regions and hence the *potential* that is generated by their connection. On the other hand, the *permeability* of borders plays an important role. It essentially decides whether different territories in an urban region are mutually receptive or whether they cut themselves off from one another.

This also raises the question of the new borders that are created in order to frame and define urban spaces. They are, first and foremost, representations of space, images and proposals that are also invariably influenced by particular interests. Any attempt to define the external borders of an urban region is therefore a political project, whose quality is determined not least by the way it frames regions. Does the framing encourage potentials and the connection of differences or does it opt for homogeneity and separation?

Differences are the third fundamental criterion of the urban: the city is where social differences collide and become productive. The "urban promise" lies in being able to choose one's way of life.[22] Urban lifestyles or cultures differ from villages or rural areas in that they can be described not by their particularities but by their differences.

The presence of different cultures and contexts for action in itself does not make for urban culture. Far more crucial is the way they interlock. Only through the interplay of differences can the energies be released that enable the city to keep reinventing itself. In that respect, difference represents a potential.

Differences may be based on material circumstances, networks and processes of interaction, but in daily life they have to be continuously confirmed or disproved. Differences are tied to lived experience; they characterize lived space, the space of representation. Distinctions like heterotopia, interaction and dynamics are useful in characterizing urban space.

The first distinction addresses the presence of difference—that is, the heterogeneity that is present in urban space. Following Lefebvre, a space dominated by sameness is called an isotopic space. Such a space contrasts with one that unites different things: a *heterotopic* space.[23]

A second distinction concerns the relationships between elements of urban space. Are they *active* and thus also productive, or are they inert, irresponsive and mired in indifference? Through marginalization, segregation and ghettoization, the manifold characteristics of difference are isolated and made unproductive, whereas a developed urban form transforms the juxtaposition of different things into reactive opportunities. The extent of the reaction and the variety of its effects are thus crucial in defining the nature of any prevailing urbanism.

This results in a third distinction between *dynamic* and static differences. Are conflicts played out in the open or behind closed doors? The city allows the differences within it to become potentials of its own dynamic. Differences must therefore be understood dynamically: they aren't something that a city "has" but rather something it is constantly producing and reproducing.

A New Understanding of the Urban

The combination of three criteria—networks, borders and differences—enables us to define different qualities of the urban. Every urban region is distinguished by a specific, inimitable urban culture that is dependent on many factors. In keeping with Lefebvre's theory, a new, relational and dynamic approach can be applied to understanding the urban.

This understanding differs in many respects from classical conceptions, which are no longer capable of grasping and understanding today's urban reality. The size, density or heterogeneity of a city no longer provide fruitful criteria in analyzing the urban reality of today.[24] The size of a city can no longer be determined with certainty, and in any case it has only very limited validity, as smaller cities can also achieve a high degree of urbanity. Nor can many conclusions about the quality of everyday life be drawn from the density of a city. Finally, heterogeneity is a necessary condition of urban life but that alone does not suffice. The crucial point is whether heterogeneous elements yield productive differences. Hence it is not size, density, or heterogeneity that makes a city, but the quality of dynamic, everyday processes of interaction.

The complete urbanization of society makes it possible constantly to recreate the urban. The city becomes omnipresent in a virtual sense; any point has the potential to become central, a place of negotiation, difference, and creativity. New urban situations are possible in a wide variety of places. Hence one-dimensional definitions are no longer worthy of pursuit. The point is rather to identify different forms and manifestations of the urban.

Notes

1   Robert Fishman, *Bourgeois Utopias: The Rise and Fall of Suburbia* (New York: Basic Books, 1987); Joel Garreau, *Edge City: Life on the New Frontier* (New York: Doubleday, 1991); and Thomas Sieverts, *Cities without Cities: Between Place and World, Space, and Time, Town and Country* (London: Routledge, 2002).

2   Edward Soja, "Inside Exopolis: Scenes from Orange Country," *Variations on a Theme Park*, ed. Michael Sorkin (New York: Noonday Press, 1992) 94-122.

3   Rem Koolhaas, "The Generic City," *S, M, L, XL*, eds. Office for Metropolitan Architecture, Rem Koolhaas, and Bruce Mau (Rotterdam: 010 Publishers / New York: Monacelli Press, 1995) 1238-68.

4   See, for example, Neil Smith, *The New Urban Frontier: Gentrification and the Revanchist City* (London: Routledge, 1996).

5   Henri Lefebvre, *The Production of Space*, trans. Donald Nicholson-Smith (Oxford: Blackwell, 1991); Henri Lefebvre, "The Right to the City," *Writings on Cities*, eds. Eleonore Kofman and Elizabeth Lebas (Oxford: Blackwell, 1996); and Henri Lefebvre, *The Urban Revolution*, trans. Robert Bononno (Minneapolis: University of Minnesota Press, 2003).

6   Christian Schmid, *Stadt, Raum und Gesellschaft: Henri Lefebvre und die Theorie der Produktion des Raumes* (Stuttgart: Steiner, 2005).

7   Roger Diener, Jacques Herzog, Marcel Meili, Pierre de Meuron and Christian Schmid, *Switzerland—An Urban Portrait*, ed. ETH Studio Basel (Basel: Birkhäuser, 2006).

8   Lefebvre, *Right to the City*, 70; Lefebvre, *Urban Revolution*, 152.

9   Lefebvre, *Right to the City*, 71; Lefebvre, *Urban Revolution*, 3.

10 Lefebvre, *Urban Revolution*, 14.

11 Lefebvre, *Right to the City*, 141; Lefebvre, *Urban Revolution*, 89, 100.

12 Lefebvre, *Production of Space*, 386.

13 Lefebvre, *Urban Revolution*, 39.

14 Ibid.

15 Lefebvre, *Right to the City*, 118; Lefebvre, *Urban Revolution*, 332.

16 Henri Lefebvre, *Le manifeste différentialiste* (Paris: Gallimard, 1970) 63ff.

17 Lefebvre, *Production of Space*, 332.

18 Lefebvre, *Right to the City*, 158, 179.

19 Lefebvre, *Production of Space*.

20 Schmid, *Stadt, Raum und Gesellschaft*; and Christian Schmid, "Henri Lefebvre's Theory of the Production of Space: Towards a Three-dimensional Dialectic," *Space, Difference, Everyday Life: Reading Henri Lefebvre*, eds. Kanishka Goonewardena, Stefan Kipfer, Richard Milgrom and Christian Schmid (New York: Routledge, 2008).

21 Lefebvre, *Urban Revolution*, 37.

22 Rudolf M. Lüscher and Michael Makropoulos, "Vermutungen zu den Jugendrevolten 1980 / 81, vor allem zu denen in der Schweiz," *Einbruch in den gewöhnlichen Ablauf der Ereignisse*, ed. Rudolf Lüscher (Zurich: Limmat Verlag, 1984) 123–39.

23 Ibid.

24 Louis Wirth, "Urbanism as a Way of Life," *The American Journal of Sociology* 44, 1 (1938) 1–24.

TWO
COMPLETE URBANIZATION—EXPERIENCE, SITE, PROCESS

Can the spatial boundaries
of cities be coherently
delineated—whether in theory,
analysis or experience? Is a
new formation of complete
urbanization being consolidated
in specific regions and
territories? If so, what are its
major manifestations—whether
in built environments, spatial
configurations or infrastructural
arrangements, in political
discourses, or in everyday life?

Matthew Gandy
Christian Schmid
Marcel Meili
Roberto Luis Monte-Mór
Terry G. McGee

5
WHERE DOES
THE CITY END?

Matthew Gandy

How do we know we have reached the edge of the city? Is it an aluminium sign? Is it a thinning out of buildings until there is little but woods and fields? Or is it an abrupt shift to small towns and villages dotted across the landscape? Perhaps it is really none of these things since the city, or at least "urbanization," is now practically everywhere. In his book *The Urban Revolution*, first published in 1970, the French urbanist Henri Lefebvre makes a clear distinction between "city" and "urbanization." "Society has become completely urbanized," writes Lefebvre, "This urbanization is virtual today, but will become real in the future."[1] In the 40 years since Lefebvre wrote these words, the pace and scale of urban growth has accelerated and so has the more ubiquitous dynamic of "urbanization" as infrastructure and ideas have spread into the remotest locales. The urban and the rural have become increasingly difficult to differentiate despite the powerful cultural resonance of this distinction. We can never really understand cities as simply "things in themselves" since they are manifestations of broader processes of change, connection and re-combination. Cities are just a particular form of urbanization.

If we consider London, the current metropolitan boundaries were created in 1965. For the purposes of data collection, planning and service provision, these administrative boundaries are extremely significant, but they only reveal part of the story of what London is as a cultural and geographical entity. If we look within these "lines on the map" where London's outer boroughs meet the ring of counties stretching from Kent in the South East, through the affluent commuter belt of Surrey, Buckinghamshire and Hertfordshire, to Essex in the North East, we find that the distinction between London and "not London" is hazy in terms of identity and topography. A closer look at the 1:25,000 Ordnance Survey map of where the outer London borough of Enfield meets the county of Hertfordshire reveals the complexity of the northern edge of the city: a jumble of archaeological sites, allotments, copses, farms, golf courses, housing estates, playing fields, infrastructure installations and other features (Figure 5.1). And just a few hundred meters further north of the London boundary is the constant rumble of the M25 motorway that Iain Sinclair followed as his walking route around the city in *London Orbital*. For Sinclair, the "amphetamine buzz" of this multilane highway, which has encircled London since 1986, marks both the material and symbolic limit to the contemporary metropolis.[2]

At or beyond the urban fringe, especially in the east of London, we find spaces of intense marginalization, which alter the more familiar map of inner-city deprivation. Poorly connected communities, with limited service provision, are criss-crossed by lines of electricity pylons, busy roads and high-speed rail connections. In Andrea Arnold's extraordinary film *Fishtank* (2009), for example, we encounter the working-class landscapes of Rainham on the London/Essex border. Arnold not only reveals a profound sense of social and cultural claustrophobia, but also the striking significance of "edge" landscapes that veer between an oppressive sense of utilitarian functionality and moments of striking revelation through encounters with "wild urban nature."

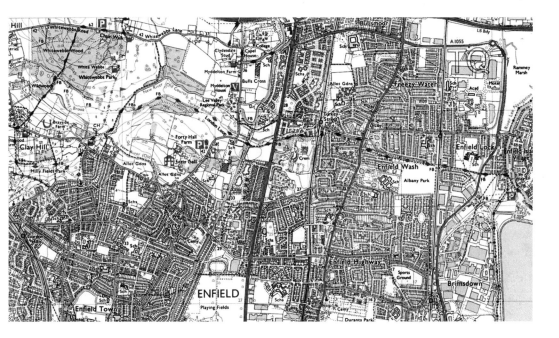

5.1 Detail from Ordnance Survey Explorer Map 173, London North, 1: 25,000 scale, revised 2010, showing the northern boundary of the London borough of Enfield where it meets the County of Hertfordshire

The green-tinged edge of London is artificially sustained, however, by the "greenbelt," a planning device that was first mooted in the mid-1930s and then introduced in the early 1960s in order to prevent ribbon development, sprawl and the drift towards total urbanization in which only pockets of open space might have remained.[3] More recently, the greenbelt has come under intense development pressure from all directions: it is threatened by the ideological assault on strategic planning as a restrictive anachronism but is also challenged as an impediment to the production of new homes that further inflates the London housing market. The real relationship, however, between regional planning, housing and development across London is more complex than these polarized debates would suggest but there remains intense local resistance to any widespread modification of the greenbelt. Spaces beyond London's greenbelt are now being drawn into "zones of intensification" through the extension of transport infrastructure—such as the Crossrail behemoth under construction, or the earmarking of immense areas such as the so-called Thames Gateway to the east as an arena for accelerated state-facilitated development in spite of its remoteness and vulnerability to future flooding.

In addition to roads and other transport infrastructure such as airports, the physical reach of London is also marked by more complex, distant and less widely understood networks. These range from the "soft landscapes" of communications to the vast technological systems that provide energy and water for the city. In the case of water supply, London has an extensive network of pipes, pumping stations, reservoirs, treatment plants, and other infrastructure that is largely unseen and unnoticed to most of the city's inhabitants: only in moments of crisis or failure do these complex and vulnerable systems come sharply into public view.

And what of London's global imprint? Much effort has gone into measuring the impact of cities through concepts such as the "ecological footprint" and other indicators of the environmental effects of urban consumption. In the case of London, the aggregate impact of the city is immense yet per capita contributions reveal local differences and anomalies: poorer parts of the city, for example, have a significantly lower environmental impact because of less car ownership, as well as lower levels of consumption, long-haul travel and other factors. Evidence suggests that these intra-urban differences in wealth and consumption are now deepening in London to an even greater extent than comparable cities like New York.[4] Similarly, if we explore per capita environmental impact at a regional or national level there are affluent rural or semirural communities that blur the conceptual utility of the "city" as a focus for environmental anxiety. The use of footprints and other similar heuristic devices ultimately tell us little about the organizational or political dimensions to production. The analytical scope of environmental psychology, behavioural algorithms, and other atomistic fields of knowledge leaves the phenomenon of contemporary urbanization in a state of epistemological limbo despite its increasing global reach. If we disentangle the metaphorical and ideological aspects to the environmental critique of cities, it becomes possible to focus on the urban process as a socioenvironmental dynamic that transcends the often arbitrary distinctions between the city and the "non-city." And if we move our attention from the material dimensions of urban space to less tangible or visible threads of connection such as cultural networks, financial transactions and other elements, then what we understand London to be becomes immeasurably more complex, diffuse and pervasive.

Notes

1   Henri Lefebvre, *The Urban Revolution*, trans. Robert Bononno (Minneapolis: University of Minnesota Press, 2003 [1970]); and Henri Lefebvre, "From the City to Urban Society," this book, Ch. 2.
2   Iain Sinclair, *London Orbital* (London: Granta, 2002) 64.
3   David Thomas, "London's Green Belt: The Evolution of an Idea," *The Geographical Journal* 129, 1 (March 1963) 14-24.
4   See John Authers, "London Property Prices Now a Cause for Alarm," *The Financial Times* (July 27/28, 2013).

Figure Credits

5.1   Courtesy of the Ordinance Survey.

6
TRAVELING WARRIOR AND COMPLETE URBANIZATION IN SWITZERLAND: LANDSCAPE AS LIVED SPACE

Christian Schmid

The point of departure for this text is a film by Christian Schocher, produced in 1979 and which had its premiere in 1981. At the time, the film was a sensation—at least for the few who saw it. The limited audience and showings were not surprising for a black-and-white film over three hours long, in which a man drives through the country and not much else happens. Yet this is a historic film because it captured, for the first time, an essential trend of contemporary Switzerland: the complete urbanization of society.

This expression draws on one of the most famous hypotheses in urban studies, the opening line of French philosopher and theoretician Henri Lefebvre's groundbreaking 1970 book *La révolution urbaine*.[1] This thesis formulates a tendency, at the time apparent only on a distant horizon, which would soon become a defining reality. Lefebvre understands urbanization in a double sense: on the one hand, urbanization increasingly encompasses broad areas of society; on the other, the urban fabric continues to extend itself into new territories, transforming both historical cities and previously rural areas.

The film is a particular form of semidocumentary. The central character is an actor who takes us on a journey through Switzerland. The scenes he experiences are partly staged, but also determined by real-life settings and coincidences. The character has the family name of "Krieger," that is, "Warrior," and is a traveling salesman who sells perfume. We see him one morning as he leaves his apartment in an anonymous, banal modern suburban housing estate near Zurich and makes his way by car through the hairdressers and beauty salons of Switzerland. The movie title sets the pace: *Traveling Warrior* (*Reisender Krieger*, Christian Schocher, CH 1981).

The warrior throws himself into the fray of everyday urban life, stylish in a Citroën CX, the typical non-conformist car of those years and the successor to the famous Citroën DS. For three hours, we watch as he crisscrosses the whole of Switzerland driving on the highway, through towns and villages. Through the windshield we see the landscape pass by; we also see the houses and the interiors of hotels, restaurants and lounges from the 1970s, which, from today's perspective, lack flair. We experience the atmosphere of the morning, as the owner of a hair salon waits for the first customer of the day. We can almost smell this salon—the stale air, still filled with the scents of the previous day; we hear the typical morning radio broadcast, with its affected cheerfulness seeking in vain to lift the depressive fog of daily existence. In the evening, we see our exhausted warrior check into a cheap hotel, somewhere in Switzerland, perhaps going to a local pub for some variety.

Some of these images are staged, others "documentary," such as when our warrior comes to Zurich, gets drunk in a bar and almost starts a fight. The film also documents images of historical value, such as the Zurich Shopville, the shopping mall beneath the main station, where we see homeless people sleeping in phone booths—for the orderly and clean Zurich of the time this was both an unusual and shocking picture.

The most telling aspects of this film include not only the landscapes through which the traveling warrior passes, but the manner in which they are filmed: the high-voltage power lines along the highway, the commercial buildings lined up beneath the mountains, the multistory parking garages in the villages. The warrior drives through the Swiss Plateau and all the way up the St. Gotthard Pass and back—and yet we see as the backdrop one thing only: urban landscapes.

Town and Country

Why is this the first film that shows the complete urbanization of Switzerland? Although the image of Switzerland is often associated with rural idylls, the portrayal of the city is nothing new in Swiss cinema. Kurt Früh, one of the leading figures of the "old" Swiss cinema, created a cinematic monument to the city of Zurich, and the "New Swiss Film," which emerged from the social and cultural upheavals of the 1960s, is by and large an urban genre: it shows cities and city dwellers; it explores the urban periphery, the suburbs, and urban sprawl; and it focuses on large cities, in particular Geneva—where Alain Tanner, Claude Goretta and Michel Soutter, three of the most famous representatives of the New Swiss Cinema lived and worked—but also Zurich, and later Bern.[2]

The following photo panels are stills from the film *Reisender Krieger* (*Traveling Warrior*, Christian Schocher, CH 1981).

The critique of urbanization is not new either. In Switzerland since the late 1960s, there has been an increasingly vocal and insistent critique of capitalist urban development, which is also reflected in early Swiss documentary films. *Zur Wohnungsfrage (The Housing Question,* Hans and Nina Stürm, 1972), *Die Grünen Kinder (The Green Children,* Kurt Gloor, 1972), *Der Bucheggplatz zum Beispiel* (*The Example of Buchegg Square*, Sebastian C. Schröder, 1973), and *Beton-Fluss (Concrete River,* Hans-Ulrich Schlumpf, 1974) are all documentaries from the first half of the 1970s, which present and criticize various aspects of urbanization: housing shortages in urban centers, large-scale construction of pre-fabricated dwellings in the suburbs, the destruction of existing urban structures through the construction of urban highways, and the expansion of office areas in the inner cities. These films were followed by many others extending well into the 1990s dealing with the same questions. Although many of these films relate to Zurich, where urban conflict was most intense, similar films exist for other parts of Switzerland, in particular Bern. At the same time, there was also the cultural critique of these developments: a characteristic film was *Grauzone* (Fredi Murer, 1979), the title of which was to become iconic: *Gray Zone*. It was not a documentary but a fiction film, and, like *Reisender Krieger*, it was shot in black and white.

What distinguishes *Reisender Krieger* from other films of its time is not its relationship to the city, but rather its relationship to the countryside. In most other films and for most other filmmakers, the city is always seen in contrast to the countryside. For example, though with *Grauzone* Fredi Murer produced an almost paradigmatic film about contemporary urban life, he had previously also created the film *Wir Bergler in den Bergen sind eigentlich nicht schuld, dass wir da sind* (*We mountain men in the mountains are actually not to blame that we are there,* 1974) an immensely important documentary about the life of mountain farmers in Schächental, and then the acclaimed fiction film *Höhenfeuer* (*Alpine Fire,* 1985), which ascribes an almost archetypal universal reality to the mountains. Even today, the polarity between the urban and the rural is still constitutive for the representation of the city in Swiss film. The city is the antithesis of the countryside; it is almost never portrayed as self-evident, but as something to be explained or justified.

The countryside is always close, present in the foreground or background, often evoked in grandiose images. The countryside is the origin, the historical and geographic reference point of the city. It is threatened by modernization, perhaps even doomed, but still it exists, even if only as an alternative, as a vanishing point, and even when it leads only to a dead end, as it does in *Messidor* by Alain Tanner (1979). Like no other film, *Messidor* marks the end to the decade after 1968 and its hope for social change. Like *Reisender Krieger*, *Messidor* is also a road movie through Switzerland, in which two protagonists—one from Geneva, the other from Moudon, and thus from the "countryside"—travel together throughout Switzerland and finally arrive at a tragic end somewhere in a remote village. Here, the "countryside" no longer brings any form of salvation. Schocher, by contrast, arrives at a different conclusion: in *Reisender Krieger* the countryside is itself urbanized. Laconically, Schocher shows what it means to take a sober look at a regular day in Switzerland in all its quotidian banality. This country is urbanized, all the way through to its most remote valleys, but it is not really urban. It is provincial, upstanding, narrow-minded, and boring.

Shortly before *Reisender Krieger* arrived in the cinemas, urban riots broke out in Swiss cities: first, in May 1980, in Zurich; then in Lausanne, Winterthur, Bern and Basel; as well as in other European cities, such as Berlin, Freiburg im Breisgau and Amsterdam.[3] These revolts called for a renewed urban life, namely the opportunity to realize alternative lifestyles, to lead a different, urban life, to access urban culture—and a world outside provincial narrow-mindedness.[4]

In these conflicts, film also played an important role.[5] In particular, a new video movement emerged, which used video as a medium for documentation, for critique and — above all — as a form of political intervention, and in so doing, developed an aesthetic that was entirely new. The most famous film of the Zurich movement was a semidocumentary in black and white, *Züri brännt* (Videoladen Zürich, 1981), the title alluding to the famous song "London's Burning" by The Clash. A dramatic and polemical montage of documentary material accompanied by haunting commentary, the film shows the fight for "another

city" on an epic scale. This was also the moment when, for an instant, the "countryside" disappeared from view, when the city became dangerous and exciting and a part of Switzerland clearly defined itself as urban.

And then *Reisender Krieger* arrived in cinemas in 1981, showing Switzerland in a completely new light: for the first time, we see the mountain regions and the putatively rural areas as part of the urbanized world. At this time, films had a different meaning than today—an entire generation grew up with critical films; they were our "school of life." When I left the cinema after seeing *Reisender Krieger* in 1981, I really saw the Swiss landscape quite differently. At the time, I had just started my studies on urban theory and urbanization, together with my friends from the Ssenter for Applied Urbanism (SAU), a group of students of geography that organized all sorts of urban interventions. One year later, we read Lefebvre's *La révolution urbaine*. Twenty years later, with the team of ETH Studio Basel, I worked on the book *Switzerland—An Urban Portrait*, in which we took Lefebvre's thesis of complete urbanization as the point of departure for our analysis.[6] We were finally able to describe Switzerland as a completely urbanized territory, and to analyze it in exclusively urban terms, without needing to use the word "rural" any longer. At the beginning of this project, we showed our students the movie *Reisender Krieger*.

The Theory of the Production of Space

What can we learn from this film? It shows us some crucial aspects of urbanization that are difficult to identify through academic analysis. To understand them, it makes sense to return to the theory of Henri Lefebvre.

After his landmark books on the city and on urbanization, he published another highly important book in 1974, *La production de l'espace* (*The Production of Space*).[7] The production of space? Why is space produced and not just a given? In this term, we see a far-reaching paradigm shift in the understanding of space, from something that is preexistent to

something that is socially produced, reproduced and transformed. Lefebvre's theory is at once elegant, broad and intricate—challenging to work with in practical applications. Its basis is in three dialectically interconnected dimensions through which Lefebvre develops a theory on the production of space.[8]

The first dimension Lefebvre calls "spatial practice," by which he means how space is produced by daily actions. The most impactful daily action in the urbanized world is commuting. Today, people live in one place and work in another, necessitating travel between them. This type of movement and linkage of different places has become commonplace throughout the urban world; it no longer concerns just working and living, but all areas of everyday life. The experience of driving thus counts as a constitutive element of urban life.

What *Reisender Krieger* shows extremely well is the way in which the urban landscape is produced through quotidian routine. This traveling warrior is a symbol for an urban man who, through his travel, produces and reproduces the urban by establishing networks in urban space. Urbanization means integration into networks of interaction, whether private networks, networks of information, of production, of capital circulation or many others. The film makes clear how rural areas are tied into and changed by these networks. Urbanization is not only the construction of roads and houses, but first and foremost everyday practices, in which, for example, perfume surely plays a key role. "This is how Switzerland smells this winter" is an expression that the traveling warrior uses often to promote his perfume "Blue Dream." Urbanization cannot only be seen, but also heard— and smelled. Urbanization is also the diffusion and alignment of styles and fashions, and precisely in this sense the traveling warrior is an agent of urbanization, spreading its characteristics to the farthest corners of Switzerland.

This spatial practice is the first dimension of the production of space, which Lefebvre calls "perceived space," because it is the aspect of space that we perceive with our five senses.

We can see it, we can smell it, we can taste it, we have a direct physical relationship to the space, which is at the same time the framework and the result of our daily activities. If we imagine that millions of people simultaneously produce their everyday space, and that the urban space emerges from these linkages and overlaps of individual actions, we can imagine that this first dimension of space is not as simple as it at first seems.

Spatial practices alone do not create an urban space. Urban space is not only tangible, but also created in our minds and characterized by images, concepts and maps. We thus arrive at the second dimension in the production of space, which Lefebvre terms "conceived space." As he remarks, we cannot see a space without having already conceived it mentally. Space is not an object, but a relationship among different objects that are linked together through an action—and brought together intellectually through thought processes. This connection to new entities and units that can then be called "spaces," requires a set of rules and definitions that specify what elements constitute which space. The way we see a space is therefore not something that derives directly from intuition, but instead is always mediated through concepts and conventions. This second dimension of the production of space is closely related to specific professions: architects and planners design all kinds of spaces; geographers and sociologists develop concepts and theories; and photographers and film makers produce images of the urban landscape.

With his film, Schocher put forward a new representation of urban space in his era, just as, 25 years later, the ETH Studio Basel has done with its *Urban Portrait*.[9] These representations have an impact, and this is precisely why they are produced. Their aim, if not always openly stated and more often obscured, is to change the collective imagination of space. These representations are meant to cause people to see certain spaces differently, to speak differently about them, and ultimately to act differently. Representations of space are therefore never innocent, but always politically implicated. The rules that are contained in the representations of space, and which emerge from them, ultimately lead, directly or indirectly, to action.

These two dimensions, spatial practice and the representation of space, enable the process of the production of space to be analyzed conclusively, and indeed most scientific analyses do exactly that. But Lefebvre went an important step further—he saw another, third dimension, which is crucial for the production of space: "lived space" (*espace vécu*). This notion of the *vécu* is deeply rooted in French philosophy and difficult to convey in other philosophical traditions. There is no direct translation for the term in either English or German.

The fundamental idea of this "lived" space, or the "lived experience" in a more general sense, lies in its direct connection to our experiences—both personal and social experiences. For instance, for two lovers, the place of their first kiss will always be special. This can be a romantic place along the shore of a lake or a dark corner buried in an underground parking garage, but this place will always have a distinctive imprint, connected to this particular event, this feeling, and this experience. And every time one of the two passes by the place, he or she will be reminded of the event. For these lovers, the place's meaning, or rather its symbolic content, has been fundamentally altered.

This is obviously a highly personal experience that cannot be generalized. But the "lived space" is also a social space, and its production is a social process. For this reason, Lefebvre also uses the expression "spaces of representation," as these are spaces that have specific meaning, that refer to something else, a divine being, a state power—or a revolution. The Bastille was stormed more than two centuries ago, but even today the place where it once stood evokes feelings, emotions and symbolism and holds a special meaning for many people in Paris and throughout France. Spaces of representation are always linked with experiences that can be communicated to later generations, and these experiences, because associated with a specific, concrete space, may reverberate for a long time.

If we try to grasp this third dimension with scientific methods, we encounter considerable difficulties. Henri Lefebvre himself said that this lived space cannot fully be explained

through analytical tools. We need other means: poetry, music—or film. Perhaps the most important aspect in the production of space that a film can convey to us, then, is the experience of a lived space.

The Experience of Complete Urbanization

The end of the 1970s is in some ways a historic moment in the urbanization of Switzerland; for the first time, complete urbanization can be seen and experienced. How does the film *Reisender Krieger* now try to convey this specific experience?

There is one moment in which the traveling warrior stops at a highway rest stop and calls his company from a phone booth. He has an obviously heated argument with his boss, and gets right back into the car, driving a long distance until he finally arrives at his office to resume the discussion with his boss face to face. At this point, the experience of the region he traverses changes immediately. The landscape is reduced to the space between two stages in his work, overlaid by the emotional moments caused by the conflict, and which have nothing to do with the landscape he is passing through. A sort of division of different realities occurs; the real life of the traveling salesman is almost completely detached from the physical experience of the landscape. This kind of overlapping of detached realities has since become an everyday experience. With the Internet and mobile phones, we can continue our work or the conflicts in our relationships even at the beach, dragging our entire everyday existence along with us wherever we go. Space shrinks, distances no longer have the same meaning they had 20 years ago, and different life worlds begin to merge. It is thus an essential part of the urban experience that is made evident in this scene.

The film also makes use of a specific aesthetic to express the experience of urbanization. A crucial element is the mood—the atmosphere the film is able to evoke—causing certain experiences to resonate within us. Driving through the landscape, the highly mobile camera, the slow rhythm of the film, and the sound, which is primarily traffic noises, all

amplify the monotony of the landscape. One aspect of the aesthetic of the film is strongly characteristic of a specific historic representation of urban space, and this is one of the reasons the film's impact is less powerful now than it was at the time it was released. Although only 30 years old, the film presents what seems like an entirely different urban world. *Reisender Krieger* was shot on 16mm film, and while *Grauzone* was produced in 35mm and *Züri brännt* was shot on video, the films achieve very similar forms of aesthetic expression in their use of black and white. The gray that dominates these films serves as a way of expressing a certain experience and inducing a specific feeling. This is not the clear and contrasting black and white we know from movie classics, nor is it the gloom of film noir. It is a foggy, blurry black and white used to show a kind of blurred urban gray zone conquering the whole landscape and transforming it. It is more a kind of gray-on-gray, an absence of color and thus also of life. "Living," it seems, has fallen prey to urbanization, and it must be won back.

Of course, technology is also partly to blame for this aesthetic. *Züri brännt* was produced with the semiprofessional mobile video equipment available at the time—relatively heavy, but still portable equipment with black-and-white cameras; affordable color cameras were only just arriving on the market. The characteristics of the tube cameras, the low resolution and technical shortcomings of recording techniques and postproduction caused the ultimately sluggish, blurry images that flicker across the screen—very typical of the aesthetics of the video movement at the time. In *Reisender Krieger*, the high exposure tolerance of black-and-white film, in contrast to color, undoubtedly also played an important role in the choice of this film stock. The new 16mm black-and-white film was relatively sensitive to light, and even enabled some night filming without additional lighting, but it was relatively coarse-grained, contributing further to the gray effect. In *Grauzone*, on the other hand, there was no technical reason for the choice of black and white; as a 35mm production, it had a full spectrum of technical means available to it. Here, the decision was made purely on the basis of aesthetic criteria.

These films were stylistically influential, establishing a new representation of urban space in which "gray" and "concrete" became verbal and visual metaphors for an inhospitable urban world. The "urban gray zone" became the symbol of the aesthetic, emotional and practical devastation brought about by the process of urbanization itself. These images evoke a very specific experience, hardly comprehensible today. This offers us an important insight: such experiences are not universal but specific, and they change over time.

The Bright Lights of the City

If one looks at how processes of urbanization within Switzerland are represented today, one can identify a fundamental and altogether astonishing transformation. This change is manifested, for example, in *Siedlungen, Agglomerationen (Settlements, Agglomerations)*, the photo series produced by Peter Fischli and David Weiss.[10] In contrast to the "urban gray zone" aesthetic of the 1980s films, their suburban landscapes are in color, perfectly sharp, often with flowers and blue sky—a completely different kind of representation of urban space. Yet this does not mean that these urban landscapes have become harmless. On the contrary, these images express a subtle danger lurking behind the blooms of the yellow forsythia and the cotoneaster. In the photography of Fischli and Weiss, this peril is depicted less in the totalizing and homogenizing tendency of urbanization, than in the fact that these backward-looking images of a long-lost rurality are obscuring the possibilities and potentials of urbanization. Some of the installations of Pipilotti Rist perform a similar experience.[11]

This change in the aesthetics of representations of urbanization is not accidental. Rather, it reflects a change in the urban world itself. "The urban" now has widely positive connotations; this is the result of a long and complex process of "rediscovery of the urban", which has taken place in many places since the 1970s.[12] The gray is no longer an appropriate expression for the experience of urbanization, as the concrete walls, those paradigmatic examples of the horrors of urbanization, have been imbued with new meaning. This is most evident in *Züri brännt*, which begins with a ride on the Hardbrücke, the famous highway flyover leading through Zürich West, the former industrial area of Zurich. This scene is overlaid with an emotional and polemical text about the brutal bleakness of this city. The traveling warrior traverses exactly the same route in the second sequence of the film. The choice of this location corresponded to the spirit of that time in which the Hardbrücke was seen as a memorial to the destruction of the city and the unlivability of urban reality—the most terrible urban place imaginable. Undoubtedly, the Hardbrücke could also be used to represent something else at the time. As early as 1982, SAU had, in its critical multimedia show on the urban development of Zurich, *The Zurich Connection*, shown the same Hardbrücke lit up in bright colors and accompanied ironically by the music of an Italo-Western movie.

Twenty years after the urban revolt, Zürich West has become a part of the fancy urban landscape of Zurich, and the Hardbrücke is now a new and positive symbol for urban vitality. This transformation cannot be understood as an arbitrary development or even as an invention. On the contrary, it was again the experience of the city itself that caused this aesthetic transformation—and in a surprisingly short amount of time. The metaphors, the images, and the representations of space are changing. They do not change only because filmmakers portray them differently, but also because they are experienced in new ways. Yet filmmakers surely belong to those who illuminate these changes and communicate them to wider audiences.

We cannot see a space without having mentally conceived it before, and we cannot conceive it without having experienced it before. This connection makes the three-dimensional dialectic of Lefebvre clearly apparent: at the root of this aesthetic reinterpretation of the urban in Zurich lies a new experience—the urban revolt of 1980, which introduced a new, freer, and more creative use of the existing urban fabric, and in particular made possible a variety of processes of appropriation that were previously inconceivable in cities like Zurich. New experiences suddenly became possible in industrial buildings and between concrete walls: urban experiences in the most fundamental sense, characterized by experiments, spontaneity, legal and illegal parties, surprising meetings, happy and less happy encounters. At the outset, many had to be persuaded to come to the former industrial area of Zürich West where the Hardbrücke is located, for instance to go to a party or to the theater, since it was seen as very uncool. But this changed quickly and a sort of collective learning process took place that in time reached an ever-wider population. Suddenly, the sharp-edged, large-scale, concrete-dominated urban landscape no longer appeared as hostile and alien, but as symbol of the possible and of the urban. The perception and the representation of Zürich West also shifted into what came to be connoted by the term "trendy neighborhood," as this area was soon touted in the media. This was followed by the usual progression of media hype, commercialization and massive investment, finally leading to the familiar process of gentrification. Through this process, these urban spaces became part of the mainstream, as in many other cities.[13] It is an evident consequence that such areas are seen in a completely different light today—and new images are necessary to convey this new experience. These images are often night images: the "bright lights of the city" announce the urban transformation of these areas into the metropolitan mainstream.

The gray concrete no longer expresses the urban experience, and thus gray is no longer appropriate for the representation of complete urbanization. Today, the urban is marked by an enormous differentiation that cannot be reduced to a universal experience. Since the differences are no longer those between town and country, there can no longer be any totalizing representation of urban life—heaven or hell, urban culture or urban nightmare. If the whole of society and the entirety of a territory are urbanized, differences must be identified within the urban sphere itself, and they then give rise to a broad field of new opportunities for cinematic and photographic examination and experimentation. Seen from this perspective, *Reisender Krieger* marks a historic moment in the urban development of Switzerland, which was related to a specific urban experience. In a dialectical movement, the urban practice, the lived experience and the representations of urban space developed into a next round of the production of space. Urbanization has to be understood as a process, and it always opens up to new, unexpected urban constellations, experiences, and struggles.

Notes

1 Henri Lefebvre, *The Urban Revolution*, trans. Robert Bononno (Minneapolis: University of Minnesota Press, 2003).

2 Pierre Lachat, "Der Schweizer Spielfilm vor 1970," *Zwischen Heimat und Niemandsland: Zum Bild der Stadt im Schweizer Spielfilm von 1970–1990, Bericht 17 des NFP "Stadt und Verkehr,"* eds. Margret Bürgisser and Pierre Lachat (Zurich: Natonales Forschungsprogramm Stadt und Verkehr, 1992).

3 Heinz Nigg, ed., *Wir wollen alles, und zwar subito! Die Achtziger Jugendunruhen in der Schweiz und ihre Folgen* (Zurich: Limmat Verlag, 2001); Thomas Stahel, *Wo-Wo-Wonige: Stadt- und wohnpolitische Bewegungen in Zürich nach 1968* (Zurich: Paranoia City, 2006); Christian Schmid, "The Dialectics of Urbanisation in Zurich: Global City Formation and Urban Social Movements," *Possible Urban Worlds: Urban Strategies at the End of the 20th Century*, ed. INURA (Basel: Birkhäuser, 1998) 216-25.

4 Rudolf M. Lüscher and Michael Makropoulos, "Vermutungen zu den Jugendrevolten 1980/81, vor allem zu denen in der Schweiz," *Einbruch in den gewöhnlichen Ablauf der Ereignisse*, ed. Rudolf Lüscher (Zürich: Limmat, 1984) 123-39.

5 Dominique Rudin, "Subversive Ästhetik? Videos der Schweizer Protestbewegung der 1980er-Jahre," *Ästhetisierung des Sozialen—Reklame, Kunst und Politik im Zeitalter visueller Medien*, eds. Lutz Hieber and Stephan Moebius (Bielefeld: Transcript, 2011) 87-114.

6 Roger Diener, Jacques Herzog, Marcel Meili, Pierre de Meuron and Christian Schmid, *Switzerland—An Urban Portrait*, ed. ETH Studio Basel (Basel: Birkhäuser, 2006). See also Christian Schmid, "The Urbanization of Switzerland," this book, Ch.18.

7 Henri Lefebvre, *The Production of Space*, trans. Donald Nicholson Smith (Oxford: Wiley-Blackwell, 1991).

8 Christian Schmid, "Henri Lefebvre's Theory of the Production of Space: Towards a Three-dimensional Dialectic," *Space, Difference, Everyday Life: Reading Henri Lefebvre*, eds. Kanishka Goonewardena, Stefan Kipfer, Richard Milgrom and Christian Schmid (New York: Routledge, 2008) 27-45; Christian Schmid, *Stadt, Raum und Gesellschaft: Henri Lefebvre und die Theorie der Produktion des Raumes* (Stuttgart: Franz Steiner, 2005).

9 See Christian Schmid, "A Typology of Urban Switzerland," this book, Ch.26.

10 Peter Fischli and David Weiss, *Siedlungen, Agglomerationen* (Zurich: Patrick Frey, 1993).

11 See Stephanie Rosenthal, ed., *Pipilotti Rist: Eyeball Massage* (London: Hayward Gallery Publishing, 2012).

12 Christian Schmid, "Henri Lefebvre, the Right to the City, and the New Metropolitan Mainstream," *Cities for People, not for Profit: Critical Urban Theory and the Right to the City*, eds. Neil Brenner, Peter Marcuse and Margit Mayer (New York: Routledge, 2012) 42-62.

13 Christian Schmid and Daniel Weiss, "The New Metropolitan Mainstream," *The Contested Metropolis: Six Cities at the Beginning of the 21st Century*, eds. INURA and Raffaele Paloscia (Basel: Birkhäuser, 2004) 252-60.

Figure Credits

All photographs are stills from the film *Reisender Krieger* (Christian Schocher, 1981).

7
IS THE MATTERHORN CITY?

Marcel Meili

Switzerland is blanketed uniformly by an urban topography. No region, no locality in the country can be described today without noting its close dependence on or connection to every other place in the country. If that is the case, then all the regions that we once categorized as "nature" have ultimately become part of the city. Are the Alps themselves no longer "landscape"? Is the Matterhorn an urban mountain?

In terms of the world of the mountains as an antithesis to the city, the initial situation in Switzerland is paradoxical: the country's remote alpine regions have by no means always been the ones most distant from the city—indeed even 100 years ago that was not the case. Alpine transit routes, international trade in cattle and cheese since the sixteenth century, large emigration and repatriation movements, early industry based on hydropower, and tourism have long since tied the alpine periphery of Switzerland more closely to Europe than the remote regions of the plateau. For example, for a long time the Engadine Valley, upper Ticino, and the Bern Alps were closer to Paris or Milan than either Stammheim or Langenthal. Zuoz became more international than Realp not because its tourists came from the large centers, but because the Engadine Valley had long since been reimporting a continental culture into the Alps along a number of paths. Displacing the centers to the mountains had been part of the history of these areas for centuries—and that is true even though towns have long marketed their rural-alpine features to the city as a trademark to attract tourism. At what point did they themselves become urban?

Differences

One central property of the city is that its body—that is to say, its buildings, streets, and nature zones—is multipurpose, and not just in terms of use but also in terms of symbolism. The same places or buildings are appropriated by a variety of cultures for different functions and different requirements, which are sometimes contradictory, sometimes simultaneous and silent. There are constant clashes not only over use of the same elements but also over control of the same symbols.

In the Alps, by contrast, various forms of appropriation existed side by side for a long time, usually without engaging with one another and often without even coming into contact: tourism, transit traffic, military, agriculture and water management laid claim to parts of the mountains for their own purposes without excessive conflict arising between them. The transformation of the alpine regions—in a sense their internal consolidation—becomes evident from the degree to which the various uses of the mountains are today piled on top of and wedged into one another. Most of the forms for utilizing alpine space that have meanwhile been employed to organize it are thus, paradoxically, simultaneously in competition with and allied to one another. For example, tourism with its access roads and crowded housing is undermining the very landscape on which it depends; the army is a burden on the very nature of the mountains that it is supposed to protect. Alpine agriculture is being driven into a corner because it takes itself seriously as an economic form and not just as a way of maintaining parks for tourists. Cities, nature conservation and tourism engage in heated debate over hydropower, presenting arguments based on economics, ecology, and safety, but all those involved employ the same arguments. The Alps are marketed as a variation of the city within a different context but also as icons of compensation. Moreover, the debate over expansion of the national park—once Europe's largest, now nearly its smallest—is indistinguishable from the embittered struggles over the zoning of any given green space in any given medium-sized Swiss city. This illustrates how many interests have, invisibly but with real consequences, piled on top of one another on the stony alpine meadows.

The intensely competitive occupation of the mountains has both symbolic and physical consequences. Over the decades, the seemingly isolated Swiss Alps have been all but buried under a blanket of material traces and signs. Inescapably invasive, this growth has reached the point that the Alps can no longer possibly embody the mysteries of nature as an alternative to urban living. Roads, handrails, signs, garbage cans, climbing hooks, memorial plaques and triangulation pyramids are among the smaller military installations; larger installations satisfy such needs as hydropower, transportation, sport, agriculture and research. They reflect the near total knowledge of the mountains in this country: they are not only mapped out in minute detail, but registered in all manner of plans and registers for geology, topography, ecology, water, rights, risks, the military and sports. All these maps contain information about one and the same terrain, which is no less comprehensive than the information about the building sites of industrial fallow land; the sophistication of these strands of information and uses acquires urban complexity.

The most ambiguous and far-reaching demands made on the mountains are probably a consequence of the development of tourism. Over the last 30 years tourism seems to have abandoned the tacit agreement long shared by nearly all of the activities in the mountains: the pathos of alpine nature as an alternative world to the city. This transformation is demonstrated by new types of sports that, along with classical alpinism, have appropriated the mountains. Today's hikers pursue mountain sports as if they were indoor athletics, conduct competitions as if they were an urban celebration, and treat mountain roads and waterways as if they were primarily dangerous obstacle courses; for them, the mountains are just another piece of particularly large athletic equipment.

At the same time, there are now tourist services that export almost unmodified variations on everyday urban life to the resorts. The kinds of housing, provisions for consumers and the cultural programs aim increasingly at minimizing the difference from the city, offering just a touch of alpine atmosphere. The decline of the hotels has an almost programmatic dimension to it: the year-round availability of a private (vacation) home requires no significant change from everyday life; there is no need to adapt to the mountains themselves nor to any other social structure.

The appropriation of the Alps by tourism has been an urban enterprise since the eighteenth century. Now, however, the romantic construction of an "expedition" into the alternative world of alpine nature has been abandoned in favor of the expansion of the city by other means. The traces of the "sublime" in the perception of nature have given way to the pleasure of sheer topography or sculpture: the framed valleys and basins convey to the visitor from the flatlands the impressive, even pathos-laden dimensions of spacious nature and the immensity of its sometimes bizarre constructions—but now no longer steeped in the evocative, metaphysical atmosphere that once characterized city dwellers' descriptions. Valley topographies have become the mountainous setting of an oversized, urban scale: a kind of metropolitan staffage, comparable to the silhouette of Manhattan, the nocturnal sea of lights in Los Angeles, or Lake Zurich on a crystal-clear evening.

Both the overlapping of different things as well as the multiplication of the functional and symbolic meaning of the Alps give much of this region a complexity that is equivalent to the urban context.

Networks

A second level of alpine transformation describes a kind of relocation. Of course, consolidated and shortened travel routes have noticeably increased the accessibility of such places. Nearly all of the important cities in the Swiss Alps can be reached by car or train from large urban centers in considerably less than three hours. In a qualitative sense, this shortening of distances has not shifted the mountains on the map; it has essentially relocated them. The distinction between "here" and "there" has become less significant, because the resorts are no longer a different goal but merely one among many that appear on the map of daily peregrinations.

With journeys to the mountains falling in line with other, everyday movements, the transportation networks to the alpine resorts have adapted accordingly. The expansion and consolidation of these networks are now comparable to the growth of local networks in the cities. Apart from the purpose of the journey, public alpine transportation systems no longer differ significantly from a metropolitan transportation system: they are similar in structure, scope, internal organization, economic structure, capacity and even in marketing. Buses travel to the alpine centers on roads that use the same system of traffic lights and parking meters to fight overcrowding that are found in Geneva or Winterthur, a development that is, admittedly, less than 30 years old.

The vanishing point of similarity and density also influences efforts to develop all the other networks in the Alps. However, the fact that virtually all information is available at the same time as it is in the centers is a circumstance that is probably less than 10 years old. Larger resorts are now concentrating on creating cultural, social and economic networks that meet the standards of the urban regions, and they are no longer very far from achieving this. At certain times of year, it has already become more important or more profitable— economically or culturally—to be active in alpine centers than in the large cities. On the level of communication in particular, several alpine centers appear to be global nodes, if they could be mapped as such—thanks in part to the conferences, of course.

It probably matters less that the mountains have moved closer to the cities than that they have become more similar. The networks have contributed to creating a topology so similar to that of urban locations that a visit to the Alps—though still distinguishable from other regular activities in urban space—is no longer experienced as an antithesis. A stay in Crans Montana has become just a special form of everyday life in Lyons or Milan.

Borders

How have the borders that once defined and sealed off the alpine areas survived this development? Have they become a potential for alpine transformation or a hindrance?

The most successful re-formation of a border was that of the alpine crest itself. Like the Mediterranean, the Alps have always been a barrier that is difficult to overcome. But like ship travel in the so-called *Mare Nostrum* (our sea), the crossing of the Alps resulted in a special form of bracketing regions. The Alps and the Mediterranean have always been areas of exchange, not despite but rather because of the natural obstacles.

Silvaplana and Piz Corvatsch in the Upper Engadine, Switzerland

The most recent approach to transportation in Europe is to take resolute action to eliminate the Alps as a hindrance to passage. Alpine cantons and communes are making strenuous efforts to counteract the mountain pass both in terms of transportation and the way it is perceived, by creating undisturbed, rapid and unidentifiable movement. This will do away with the last remnants of a centuries-old overlapping of the Alps as a place of transit and a place of discovery and sojourn, for the pathos of "this side" and "the other side" has lost its relevance along with the notion of conquering the mountains themselves. Resorts will perhaps soon be the only surviving form of perceiving the Alps.

This aggressive elimination of the mountains as a physical obstacle is, however, creating another, unexpected level of urbanization in alpine spaces. The breakthrough in passage across the Alps on a European scale has stimulated movement that is uniting areas traditionally separated by the topography. In the sectors of agriculture, tourism and ecology, alpine areas have joined politically across national borders. Even though they have had considerable difficulties pooling forces that have long been separate and distinct, the overcoming of borders has a long-term potential that goes beyond futile citizens' action groups. If the Alps are someday completely stripped of their mythological aura, they will become a purely commercial product—or a raw material. Those in control will also control important resources like water and electricity.

Matterhorn

Is the Matterhorn now an urban locality? It probably is: being Switzerland's most ubiquitous mountain, it has also become a vehicle for a host of different connotations or traits. No other place in the Alps is as symbolically laden and invested with so many different and contradictory interpretations. Its image stands for a mountain world that has taken over all possible urban functions, and its various simultaneous meanings have long since become entangled in conflicts that can no longer be resolved. Its image and its reality have moved close to or right into the centers. Conversely, the mountain is scarcely used or experienced as anything other than an urban monument, an athletic playground, or a nature museum. If someday soon the urban topography of Switzerland, that boundless urban landscape, penetrates not only the everyday lives of its residents but also their consciousness, it will not be the Twin Towers or a cathedral dome that are the icons of this urban structure but presumably the Matterhorn, invisibly transformed. The distances that once separated and isolated the mountain from other regions and cities are at most only transitions now, and the boundlessness ultimately makes it impossible to localize the mountain. The Matterhorn no longer lies elsewhere but somewhere—and that somewhere is quite close.

Figure Credits

Photograph on page 107 courtesy of Marc van Swoll.

8
EXTENDED URBANIZATION AND SETTLEMENT PATTERNS IN BRAZIL: AN ENVIRONMENTAL APPROACH

Roberto Luís Monte-Mór

This chapter uses an environmental perspective to evaluate the relationship between the city and the countryside, the links between the metropolis and the region, as well as the settlement patterns in contemporary Brazilian society. The analysis is guided by the following questions: How have settlement and population patterns changed in Brazil? To what extent are these changes the result of metropolization? At the dawn of the twenty-first century, how should the relations of urban and rural, metropolis and region, be explored? What new patterns of urbanization are emerging?

This text cannot attempt to answer these questions. Instead, it aims to weave together some ideas and reflections that will hopefully lead to new inquiries. It proceeds from the assumption that, first and foremost, we need to develop a different way of conceptualizing the new territorialities (*territorialidades*) that are shaping our contemporary reality in Brazil and beyond.

First, we consider some of the theories that have sought to explain the relationship between industrialization and urbanization, and on this basis we adopt a specific perspective—*that of extended urbanization at the industrial periphery*. Subsequently, we explore the territorial question within the peripheral zones of capitalism—both in industrial centers and fringe areas—vis-à-vis analogous processes that have been identified in the core capitalist countries. We focus on both the similarities and the differences among these zones.

Second, this text investigates the environmental question in its urban and metropolitan dimensions. The goal, once again, is to reconsider the relationship between built space and natural space, and thus to transcend inherited ideas regarding the urban and the rural as well as the city and the countryside. Finally, this chapter revisits and reevaluates the question of citizenship (*cidadania*) from the perspective of extended urbanization.

Industrialization and Extended Urbanization

The main concept used here to understand the social organization of space in contemporary capitalism is that of *extended urbanization*. This term is derived from Henri Lefebvre's notion of the "urban zone."

Lefebvre elaborated the concept of the urban zone by analyzing the urban-rural dichotomy in industrialized countries and by exploring its political implications—the "right to the city"; the right to spaces of power and citizenship; everyday life and political struggles in space; as well as the social production of space and its consequences, including for relations of reproduction. For Lefebvre, the urban zone refers to the historical stage of spatial organization in which industrial capitalism, already firmly established within the city and controlling everything in its sphere of influence, causes the division of the city (successor to the '*polis*' and the '*civitas*') into two related parts—the core, and the urban fabric. The core is the urban center or nucleus that results from the implosion of the *locus of power*; it is the imprint of the old city. The urban fabric corresponds to the regionally extended network of sociospatial relationships produced through the explosion of the inherited city. As Lefebvre argues:

> The *urban fabric* grows, extends its borders, corrodes the residue of agrarian life. This expression, "urban fabric," does not narrowly define the built world of cities but all manifestations of the dominance of the city over the country. In this sense, a vacation home, a highway, a supermarket in the countryside are all part of the urban fabric. Of varying density, thickness, and activity, the only regions untouched by it are those that are stagnant or dying, those that are given over to nature.[1]

What Lefebvre calls the urban zone is, therefore, the expression of a formation of urbanization that extends beyond the limits of the traditional city while simultaneously encompassing and superseding the industrial city. The urban zone spreads across the region as the forces and relations of production create the sociospatial conditions needed for continued accumulation. These conditions are, by necessity, both urban and industrial in their sociospatial forms.

The metropolitan area is the most obvious example of Lefebvre's notion of the urban zone. It is the expression of extended urbanization in its most visible, immediate form.

The center of the metropolis overlaps with the old—and now imploded—industrial city, recreating an urban core. It is here that power is concentrated. Meanwhile, the extended network of the exploded industrial city assumes the form of an urban fabric—equipped for production and collective consumption, industrial districts, isolated mono-industrial zones, commerce, utilities, residential neighborhoods, agricultural belts, spaces of leisure and so forth.

The dialectical unity of *urban center* and *urban fabric* is the spatial expression of late capitalism. It represents the *de facto* extension of industrial forms of organization onto the configuration of an entire territory, now penetrated by the logics of capitalism. Furthermore, this dialectic is the sociospatial expression of historical stage of capitalism in which, as Mandel has argued, consumer goods, capital, raw materials, food, even nature and space itself, are industrially produced:

> Late capitalism, far from representing a "post industrial society," thus appears as the period in which all the branches of the economy are fully industrialized for the first time; to which one could further add the increasing mechanization of the sphere of circulation (with the exception of pure repair services) and the increasing mechanization of the superstructure.[2]

The socioeconomic organization administered by and through what Lefebvre famously termed the "bureaucratic society of controlled consumption" necessarily assumes a spatial form that is both urban and industrial. It is urban, because it is an expression of the different sectors of civil society and of state-sponsored institutionalization. It is industrial, because it is an expression of the present stage of capital accumulation. Taken together, this urban-industrial spatial paradigm articulates the requirements of late capitalism with reference to the "general conditions of production."

Extended urbanization is the dominant sociospatial form of contemporary capitalism; it spreads beyond cities through networks that penetrate every regional space, integrating them into a worldwide fabric. Extended urbanization assumes diverse forms: it includes the dynamic metropolitan centers and, increasingly, distant peripheries that are linked dialectically back to the centers and subcenters of the capitalist system.

Peripheries: Industries and Frontiers

The precariousness of the general conditions of production in the industrial periphery or semiperiphery has generated, in most cases, a metropolitan concentration—a process that has been described during the last two decades in several studies of urban primacy, migration, industrial development and the like.[3] As is the case in the rest of the capitalist world, the metropolitan expansion that emerged with the industrialization of the periphery resulted in the mutual imbrication of the logic of production and the logic of consumption.

Vis-à-vis the capitalist center, the periphery is distinguished by the near total concentration of the conditions for industrial production (including the collective reproduction of the labor force) in the metropolitan area and in the mono-industrial cities that are typical of the first phase of import substitution industrialization (ISI). The recent extension of industrial production to other regional and national spaces, along with the transformation of such industrial zones through the introduction of communications and information technologies (the so-called third technological revolution), have underpinned processes of spatial restructuring in Brazil since the 1970s. Since that time, the metropolis has been spilling over into its surrounding regions and into distant peripheries. This process has created new patterns and externalities, which are imposed and extended across the entire national territory.

This metropolitanization process engenders kaleidoscopic effects even in the most remote places.[4] The state of Rondônia, in the northwest Amazon region bordering Bolivia, is a case in point. Here, urbanization processes differ only in degrees of intensity relative to trends in more centrally located Brazilian cities and in metropolitan areas elsewhere in the industrialized world. As Brazilian Sociologist Chico de Oliveira pointed out in a classic text dealing with the thorny issue of Brazilian urbanization, fragments of the industrial city are spreading throughout the entire national territory.[5] The exclusionary and violent consequences of this intense, rapid process of urbanization are still impacting the entire country.

Through this combined process of metropolization and extended urbanization, new patterns of spatial occupation and settlement have emerged throughout the entire national territory, from the Rio de Janeiro-São Paulo axis to the agricultural and mining frontiers in the Amazon. These developments are unfolding in ways that are increasingly discontinuous and detached from inherited configurations of geographical space, underscoring the continued relevance of the notions of *deterritorialization* or *delocalization* developed by François Perroux several decades ago.[6] Thus, processes of industrial production and associated forms of collective consumption are emerging in ranches in southern Pará and in cities, towns, villages and mining areas in the hinterland of Rondônia.[7] These processes of peripheral industrialization and urbanization also increasingly involve populations that recently migrated from some of the country's largest urban and metropolitan areas.

Since the 1970s, the earlier form of urbanization, which had produced a rigid urban/rural binarism, has been counteracted through the process of extended urbanization. Viewed from the vantage of point of the great cities and metropolises of the industrial periphery, and also from that of the industrial countries, the initial phase of import substitution industrialization from the mid-1930s to the early 1950s had produced "cities of peasants" in which rural practices were superimposed upon a newly consolidated urban and industrial economy.[8] These practices included subsistence-oriented household economies to complement the family wage, kinship ties, strict social controls and nepotistic social relations. In this situation, precapitalist relations of production coexisted with (underpaid) wage labor, leading to a hybrid type of urban economy.

The second phase of import substitution industrialization was, in the Brazilian context, initiated in the late 1950s during Jucelino Kubitschek's administration. Under this regime of attempted peripheral Fordism, the conditions of industrial production began to be extended throughout the entire national territory. This territorial expansion of the urban-industrial fabric created a formation of extended urbanization that today spreads deep into the Amazon rainforest. Prior to the qualitative leap in civil engineering and construction projects under the Kubitschek government—as epitomized by the construction of Brasilia, the country's new modernist national capital—the now-dominant patterns of industrial and spatial development had not penetrated the Amazon region. In 1964, a military regime was consolidated through a coup, and began to promote economic "developmentalism," while encouraging migrants from across Brazil—including the countryside and cities of the Northeast, and the urbanized agricultural spaces and "peasant" metropolises of the South and Southeast—to move into the Amazon.[9] In this way, with its developmentalist strategies to occupy and modernize the Amazon, the military regime produced "forests of urbanites" (Figure 8.1).

In fact, the new urban and proto-urban forms identified in the author's fieldwork in the Amazonian southern frontiers in Rondônia and Southern Pará do not differ essentially from the urban-industrial forms that economic geographer Allen J. Scott identified as

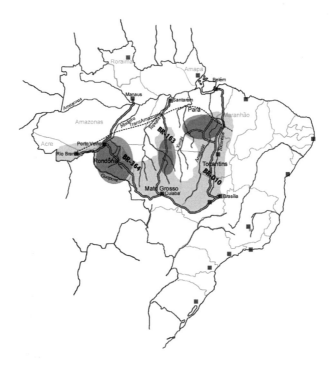

8.1 Major highways and settlement areas in Brazil's southern Amazonian Frontier

proto-urban in Orange County, southern California in the 1980s.[10] Using a slightly different terminology, Edward Soja has described closely analogous processes in his research on Los Angeles.[11] Whether in the technological frontiers of southern California or in the resource extraction frontiers of the Amazon, these proto-urban forms result from the same underlying dynamics that, according to Allen J. Scott, constitute "the very geographical core of the urban process in capitalism … [which is determined by] spatially convergent production processes linked through webs of extended transactional relations."[12] In both southern California and the Amazon, the zones in question are essentially proto-urban insofar as they represent incomplete manifestations of the urban-industrial patterns that are characteristic of contemporary regional and national social formations. In both cases, the essential dualism referenced above between the urban center and the urban fabric has yet to be consolidated. Of course, there are important differences among these regional examples—among other elements, in the intensity of market relations, in the character of urban and territorial networks, and in the quality of the social and natural space that is produced (and destroyed) through both capital and the state. However, these apparently disparate examples contain important parallels insofar as they illustrate the operations of a common logic of extended urbanization.

Fragmentation, expansion, segmentation and involution: these are some of the perspectives that inform our approach to contemporary processes of urbanization. What has produced this fragmentary kaleidoscope of urbanization? Through which concepts and visions can a new approach to the social production of space be elaborated?

The Environmental Question

Consideration of environmental issues will engender profound changes to our understanding of production processes and, more generally, of the spatial and economic organization of contemporary society. Once a mere hypothesis, this proposition may now widely be viewed as an established fact.[13] However, the real impact of this environmental orientation to the built environment still leaves much to be desired, especially in relation to metropolitan centers.

From an ecological standpoint, urban areas have traditionally been conceived as dead spaces. Urban areas have often been the primary focus of contemporary environmental debates due to their role in industrial production or in consumption patterns that significantly erode and waste both human and natural resources. However, the environmental aspect of cities and urban areas themselves has generally been overlooked. Environmental and urban debates have rarely considered issues such as the quality of life and its implications for reclaiming the use-value of urban space and the social meaning of property. This is especially true in times of economic crisis. In fact, the drive to commodify production and spatial organization, especially within urban land markets, is intensified during periods of crisis.

In an economic crisis, real estate is treated as a speculative resource, as a store of value (*reserva de valor*), a mechanism that facilitates the survival of capitalism and the persistence of stratified social relationships.[14] At the same time, the struggle of the urban poor to gain access to housing and, indeed, to the city itself, is the struggle to use urban space as a producer good (*bem de produção*), in order to improve their strategies of social reproduction. The working class strengthens the use value of real estate and of the city itself, for instance, through its use of subsidized public transportation and public services. This access to the city is essential to guarantee the existence of an urban popular economy (*economia popular urbana*) oriented towards social reproduction.[15] Furthermore, among the more affluent sectors of society, whose security in the sphere of social reproduction permits them surplus leisure time, the use value of urban space has also gained relevance as a concept now to be recovered, particularly in light of the restrictions imposed by commodified social spaces.

However, even in the rapidly changing contemporary context, where concerns with the quality of the environment are gaining significance, issues such as the existence and invasion of "natural green spaces," their effects on the quality of urban life, or even questions related to biodiversity, have not engendered consistent analytical efforts or public policy initiatives. Indeed, it appears that ecologists and environmentalists are not equipped at all to deal with the ecology and biodiversity of urban built environments. For instance, the social and ecological sciences appear resistant to urgent questions regarding the preservation of urban and regional biodiversity, for example in relation to the possible impacts of the Tijuca Forest in Rio de Janeiro, the world's largest hand-planted urban rainforest.[16]

There are immense possibilities for both cultural and biological diversity within the metropolis and the fabric of extended urbanization. However, we are so consumed by our urban crises—of culture, knowledge, law and order, democracy, consumption and reproduction, production itself, and so many others in contemporary society—that the integration of natural and human habitats seems unthinkable. Issues such as the integration of the city with the countryside, and relations between the city and the region, still do not have the prominence they deserve on the environmental agenda, even though it is now widely agreed that such questions lie at the heart of the contemporary environmental question.

Academic specialization and fragmentation, a hallmark of the modern period, severely constrain our ability to approach environmental issues coherently. Social scientists think in terms of the built environment, where the logic of reproduction is assumed to be tied to purely social processes. Or, they consider "transformed spaces" in which social processes may change environmental conditions. Ecologists, meanwhile, approach nature and questions of natural reproduction and regeneration solely from the perspective of biological processes.[17] In other words, from the standpoint of environmental and ecological sciences, urban and metropolitan spaces are understood simply as dead spaces. But is this really so? Given the impact of technological advancements in the production of nature, how and when should these spaces be reconstituted? Should we only consider "natural" (re)built environments, such as the Tijuca Forest in Rio de Janeiro, or should we also include preserved spaces such as the Mangabeiras Park in Belo Horizonte?[18] Or, can we imagine another ecology entirely, one that is both urban and metropolitan, at once social and natural? Can we envision an entirely new environment that will have to be conceived, invented or produced from the fragmentation, involution, segmentation and expansion of the urban fabric?

Towards Alternative Metropolitan Ecologies?

Despite increasing awareness of the short- and long-term challenges that urban and metropolitan areas pose to specific ecosystems, as well as to the global environmental balance, the intimate relationship between urban ecology and the environmental question is not yet adequately understood. There is, instead, an *ecological ideology* connected to the *capitalist ecology* that not only transforms social relationships into natural relationships but, following Malthusian notions, ignores the role of local populations and migrants in shaping ecological conditions.[19] This contradictory ideology, which advocates the use of high-rise rooftop gardens in the metropolitan center, while simultaneously adhering to a mythic "return-to-nature" type of ruralism, reifies the divide between built space and natural environment. This interpretation of urban ecology naturalizes the society/nature relation. As a result, this approach ends up confusing the condition of poverty with environmental degradation, equating social and economic crises with the environmental crisis, and usually blames the victims.[20]

How might contemporary approaches inform new ways of thinking about urban and metropolitan ecologies? One of the main elements of such an endeavor concerns the mediation between the micro-level of analysis, which tends to explore issues related to social reproduction and everyday life, and macro-level issues such as housing, food supply, sanitation, urban infrastructure, industrial pollution, consumption patterns and so forth.

At the scale of urban and metropolitan centers, the issue of sanitation is central in countries such as Brazil. Here, the incomplete character of the production and organization of social space generates serious environmental problems in the sphere of collective consumption. Precarious or non-existent sanitary services (water supply, sewers, waste collection) represent a threat to the everyday lives of the urban poor. Moreover, the sewage system affects the entirety of urban and suburban areas and the regional space as well. Traditional solutions have proven to be inefficient and onerous, demanding high levels of investment from a state that has long failed to promote and manage collective well-being. Furthermore, high densities in central urban areas hinder the possibility of alternative solutions. In sum, the search for alternatives, especially those that promote greater permeability or integration among social and natural spaces, demands a reevaluation of traditional urban, metropolitan and territorial models.

Moreover, Brazilian civil society has traditionally been quite weak, and only in recent years has it shown signs of transformation in terms of its capacity to make claims on the state and its ability to play a more active, decisive role in solving immediate collective problems. Several social movements have recently emerged within urban settings and have been extended throughout the urban fabric. Albeit incipiently, these movements have, over enlarging regional territories, begun to articulate new ways of securing autonomy, enhancing sociospatial diversity and establishing more intense connections to the environment. These movements represent a middle-ground between local needs and the global environmental *problematique*.

Across the extended urban fabric, questions are emerging regarding the processes by which natural and transformed space evolves into built space. Assuming a critical orientation towards the hegemonic settlement patterns of the past, this approach focuses on the multiple ways of producing and expanding the urban fabric. Such a research agenda must also consider the impact of these processes on the environmental conditions for the reproduction and conservation of natural space. It would also be useful to identify the different scales and forms through which the urban fabric is being extended. These include, among others, the typical forms of settlement in working class urban peripheries, where the vegetation is destroyed by a dense yet incomplete pattern; the fragmentation of the urban fabric through the parceling of agricultural land and small farms, the construction of industrial areas, commercial nodes and service areas in the urban periphery; and urbanization projects that cater to the elite and seek to conserve nature. An urban analysis that takes the environmental question seriously must also emphasize the relationship between social and biological diversity, and evaluate which forms of ecological conservation are adequate for particular communities.

Against this background, we can return to our central question: does the biodiversity of the built environment matter, or should it simply be ignored and left for dead? If the answer is negative, then the question becomes: at what threshold should the current human environment—that is, urbanized space—be considered "dead"? If, however, the answer is affirmative, then what specific kinds of biodiversity should be taken into consideration? Can social and biological diversity be interconnected through different forms of prioritization and mutual adaptation? With regard to our analysis of transformed natural spaces and social spaces, can we develop different ways to combine social and biological diversity? This line of inquiry returns us to the questions raised above.

Surely, we should no longer think in terms of the old dichotomies associated with the once hegemonic modernism of the recent past. If the environmental question prompts us to reframe the central question regarding the relationship between the city and the countryside, then mediations, articulations, fusions and integrations among these terms represent constitutive parts of the new analytical approach that is beginning to emerge in light of the processes of fragmentation, extension, and splintering that have been identified thus far. The development of new ways to integrate urban and metropolitan centers as well as regions and rural hinterlands seems desirable, inevitable even, if our goal is to improve patterns of settlement and the production of social space. We must confront extended urbanization with *extended naturalization* if we are to deal not only with urban and environmental problems at the micro-level of everyday life, but also with the global aspects of environmental and social crises.

In an economy that is increasingly exclusionary, where power is concentrated in large metropolitan centers, the extraction of surpluses from remote spaces that are subsumed under the logic of industrial production can backfire. The result can be dystopian, as depicted by Ridley Scott in the film *Blade Runner*. There, power has left the city, the metropolis, the urban zone, only to find refuge in nature or beyond planet earth. Only the dispossessed remain in the hyper-degraded Los Angeles, a city of 100 million inhabitants.

This frightening scenario, made worse in the case of Brazil due to its long history of social exclusion, may actually have a silver lining—but only if we succeed in excavating a positive lesson from the present crisis. Brazil is perhaps better positioned than other countries to confront these dangers by reworking the relationship between the city and the countryside, on the one hand, and built space and natural space, on the other. To be sure, extended urbanization poses a direct threat to what little citizenship (*cidadania*) we have been able to establish so far, as noted by Bookchin in his work on the dynamic relationship between increasing urbanization and the decline in citizenship.[21] However, extended urbanization also establishes new territorial arrangements, both environmental and social, that might lead to the resurgence of political-spatial mediations and articulations that were not present under Fordist industrial hegemony. Thus, the integration of the metropolis with the extended urban fabric, the reinvention of urban/rural relations, and the creation of new combinations of natural space and built space—these are issues of highest importance.

Finally, it seems clear that the process of metropolization in Brazil can no longer be considered an isolated phenomenon. Instead, this process has to be understood in relation to its connections to both nearby and remote peripheries. The significance of the metropolitan environmental question—for the understanding of contemporary urban-industrial processes and global ecological challenges more generally—forces us to shift our gaze beyond the city. In other words, it is only by reformulating the meaning of urbanized space, including proto-urban areas, that we might be in a position to reconceptualize the rural question. The monolithic spaces built by hegemonic Fordist industrialism must be opened up to plurality and diversity. This can be attained through the mediation and articulation of the many subspaces that survived the incomplete, partially frustrated process of Fordist modernization. Indeed, perhaps these processes open up the possibility of reinventing contemporary social and political environments, and thus of reinvigorating many of the spatial forms that have been produced through extended urbanization.

The expansion of the urban-industrial fabric is producing new forms of citizenship. This new citizenship has been associated with a new formation of civil society that has emerged vis à vis the failure of the welfare state. These new forms of citizenship—which encompass many sectors of society, including miners, rubber tappers, indigenous groups, as well as professional and neighborhood associations—are being built atop the ruins of the industrial city, the modern state's locus of power. The strength and the expansion of this new citizenship throughout the entire national territory has resulted from the extension of a *polis* over the *rural hinterland* and over the country's different regions. In these spaces where new citizenship practices prevail, a different kind of modernity, one that is characterized by sociobiodiversity (*sócio-bio-diversidades*) might someday emerge.

In this context, one of the tasks ahead is to explore ways to support the creation of a vast *urban* popular economy.[22] This would be a much-needed counterpoint to a global economy centered on exclusion and the consequent destruction of both people and the environment. Furthermore, the new forms of citizenship that are now crystallizing, and which embrace an environmental and ecological consciousness, will only be able to grow and prosper under a different (both old and new) economic base that privileges *collective* social reproduction. This is a necessary precondition if these grassroots movements are to contribute to the creation of new sociospatial and environmental patterns in the world's many centers and peripheries.

Translated by Juan Carlos Cristaldo and Marcio Siwi

Notes

1 Henri Lefebvre, "From the city to urban society," this book, Ch. 2, 37-38.

2 Ernest Mandel, *Late Capitalism* (London: Verso, 1978) 191.

3 To Wallerstein, the semi-periphery is composed of countries occupying a "third structural position" in the international division of labor, meaning that industrial production exceeds 20% of GDP. According to Lipietz, the OECD uses the notion of "newly industrializing countries" (NICs) to label countries in which industrial production represents at least 25% of GDP and 50% of exports. For present purposes, the notion of the industrial periphery refers to countries such as Brazil, which play an increasingly important role as exporters of industrial products for global markets. See Immanuel Wallerstein, "Dependence in an Interdependent World: the Limited Possibilities of Transformation Within the Capitalist World Economy," *African Studies Review* 17, 1 (1974) 1-26; Immanuel Wallerstein, "Semi-Peripheral Countries and the Contemporary World Crisis," *Theory and Society* 3, 4 (1976) 461-83; and Alain Lipietz, 1987. *Mirages and Miracles: the Crisis in Global Fordism* (London: Verso, 1987).

4 On the "kaleidoscopic" character of contemporary urbanization in the industrial core zones, see Edward Soja, Marco Cenzatti and Allan D. Heskin, *Los Angeles: Through the Kaleidoscope of Urban Restructuring* (Los Angeles: University of California Los Angeles, Graduate School of Architecture and Urban Planning, 1985); and Mike Davis, *City of Quartz: Excavating the Future in Los Angeles* (London: Verso, 1990).

5 Francisco Oliveira, "Acumulação Monopolista, Contradições Urbanas e a Nova Qualidade do Conflito de Clases" *Contradições*

Urbanas e Movimentos Sociais, ed. José Álvaro Moisés (Rio De Janeiro: Paz e Terra, 1978).

6 François Perroux, *L'Économie du XX⁰ siècle* (Presses universitaires de Grenoble: Grenoble, 1961).

7 *Translators' note.* Pará is the second largest state in Brazil; the estuary of the Amazon River in the Atlantic Ocean is part of its territory. It is the wealthiest, most populated state in the northeast of North Brazil. The metropolitan area of Belém, the state capital, has a population of over two million. Rondônia is a western Amazonian state bordering Bolivia, created in the 1980s after a former Federal Territory and one of the major targets for agrarian reform in Amazonia during the military dictatorship, in the 1970s.

8 Bryan Roberts, *Cities of Peasants: The Political Economy of Urbanization in the Third World* (London: Arnold, 1978).

9 *Translators' note.* A succession of military generals held power in Brazil between 1964 and 1985. The governments of this period were characterized by an authoritarian approach coupled with a centralized, technocratic agenda for development. In territorial terms, these regimes promoted the occupation of "undeveloped" territories through a series of projects that had both economic and military objectives. A particularly essential initiative, in this context, was the construction of several highways in(to) Amazonia, of which the most famous—albeit not the most important—is the Trans-Amazonian Highway (BR 230). Those highways were intended to promote economic growth and to guarantee effective control of the Amazon region. The Belém Brasília Highway (BR 010), the Cuiabá- Porto Velho—Rio Branco—Manaus Highway (BR 364) and the Cuiabá-Santarém Highway (BR 164) are the main

infrastructural vectors facilitating the formation of the "forests of urbanites" described here.

10　See Roberto Luís Monte-Mór, "Urbanización, Colonización y La Producción Del Espacio Regional En La Región Amazónica Del Brasil," Paper submitted to XVIth Inter-American Planning Congress, San Juan, Puerto Rico: Inter-American Planning Society (SIAP), 1988; Roberto Luís Monte-Mór, "Extended Urbanization in the Industrializing Periphery: Notes on Brazil," Paper submitted to the Annual Meeting of the Association of American Geographers, Baltimore, 1989; and Allen J. Scott, *Metropolis: From the Division of Labor to Urban Form* (Berkeley: University of California Press, 1988).

11　Edward Soja, *Postmodern Geographies: the Reassertion of Space in Critical Social Theory* (London: Verso, 1989).

12　Scott, *Metropolis*, 60.

13　There is a debate regarding the limits and differences within the terms ecology and environment. This is not the place for such a discussion. Here we will merely affirm that the notion of environment is similar in scope to that of social space; it is likewise constituted through society, economy, politics and ecology. Ecology, considered in a transdisciplinary sense, transcends immediate historical or geographical boundaries; like the economy or politics, it is intertwined with multiple environmental and spatial conditions.

14　Henri Lefebvre, *The Survival of Capitalism*, trans. Frank Bryant (New York: St. Martin's Press, 1976).

15　In a first approximation, José Luis Coraggio defines the popular economy as "the set of resources, practices and economic relationships characteristic of the popular economic agents of a society." He argues, "Those agents form reproduction units that depend on their own work fund (formed by the combined capacities of its members)." See José Luis Coraggio, *Ciudades Sin Rumbo: Investigación Urbana y Proyecto Popular* (Quito, Ecuador: Sociedad Interamericana de Planificación: CIUDAD, Centro de Investigaciones, 1991) 335-6.

16　*Translators' note*: This forest is the result of an environmental recuperation project of the late nineteenth century. Under the reign of Emperor Dom Pedro II (1831-1889), coffee farming on the outskirts of Rio de Janeiro intensified deforestation, which in turn compromised the city's water supply. In response, a large reforestation project was carried out, beginning in 1861. Over a period of 13 years 100,000 trees, mostly from native species, were planted.

17　The reference to "natural, transformed and social" spaces is based on the work of Valentín Ibarra, Sergio Puente, and Martha Schteingart, "La Ciudad y El Medio Ambiente," *Demografía y Economía* 18, 1 (1984) 110-43.

18　*Translators' note*: Mangabeiras Park (337 hectares) is the biggest green space in Belo Horizonte, the capital of the State of Minas Gerais, in Southeast Brazil. It is a zone of environmental preservation and research that is open to the public.

19　Fernando Carrion, "Ecología Urbana en Quito Durante la Década de los Setenta," *La Ciudad y El Medio Ambiente En América Latina: Seis Estudios De Caso (Proyecto Ecoville)*, eds. Valentín Ibarra, Sergio Puente, and Fernando Saavedra (México, DF: Colegio de México, Centro de Estudios Demográficos y de Desarrollo Urbano, 1986) 193.

20　Mílton Santos, "A Metrópole: Modernização, Involução e Segmentação," *Reestruturação Urbana: Tendências e Desafios*, eds. Licia do Prado, Edmond Préteceille, Danielle Leborgne, Alain Lipietz (São Paulo: Nobel, 1990).

21　Murray Bookchin, *The Rise of Urbanization and the Decline of Citizenship* (San Francisco: Sierra Club Books, 1987).

22　See Coraggio, *Ciudades Sin Rumbo*.

Figure Credits

8.1　Roberto Luís Monte-Mór, *Modernities in the Jungle: Extended Urbanization in the Brazilian Amazonia* (PhD dissertation, Los Angeles: University of California, 2004).

9
THE EMERGENCE OF *DESAKOTA* REGIONS IN ASIA: EXPANDING A HYPOTHESIS

Terry G. McGee

> The symbiosis of urban and rural in Megalopolis, creating new and interesting patterns of multiple-purpose land use over large areas, gives to the region a rather unique character. Like the downtown business districts with powerful skylines, this aspect of Megalopolis will probably be repeated in slightly different but not too dissimilar versions in many other regions of the rapidly-urbanizing world.
>
> –Jean Gottmann[1]

> Paddy has developed a strikingly similar landscape, broadly similar from the Ganga to the Yangtze … but no other way of life … has led to the evolution of a cultural system so stable and permanent as that associated with the great paddy-plains of Monsoon Asia.
>
> –O. H. K. Spate and A. I. A. Learmonth[2]

This chapter is a preliminary exploration of the emergence or what appear to be new regions of extended urban activity surrounding the core cities of many Asian countries.[3] The ideas to be explored must be placed in the framework of the overall patterns of urbanization at a global and regionalized level, which are predicting a continuing increase in the proportion of the world's urban population. By the year 2020, the UN Centre for Human Settlements predicts that more than 57 percent of the world's population will be living in urban places.[4] This population will be unevenly urbanized, with levels of urbanization at almost 77 percent in developed countries and 53 percent in developing countries. Within the developing countries, the contrast will be even greater, with Latin America 83 percent urbanized, and Africa and Asia close to 50 percent. However, Asia's urban population will account for a very large portion of that of the developing countries. Bangladesh, India, China, Indonesia, and Pakistan together will contain 34 percent of the developing countries' urban population.

These United Nations predictions are largely based on assumptions concerning the growth of population in places defined as urban. The predictions are calculated using growth rates reflecting performance in previous decades. When projected forward, they appear to suggest a successful shift to urbanized societies and a repetition of patterns of the more developed countries. As Ginsburg has commented about urbanization in the United States, "This condition reflects the progression of the ... space-economy to a state of what one might consider 'maturity,' that is, to a condition whereby areas possessed of substantial comparative advantage ... would be drawn effectively, through improved transportation networks, into the national geographic structure."[5] The implication for the urban systems of the largest developing countries is that a continued growth will create immense cities of about 16 million to 30 million. However, this may not be the only possible outcome for Asian urbanization.

The purpose of this chapter is to draw upon earlier ideas put forward by McGee and Ginsburg to challenge this particular view of the urban transition.[6] The Ginsburg-McGee position essentially argued that in the Asian context, the conventional view of the urban transition—which assumes that the widely accepted distinction between rural and urban will persist as the urbanization process advances—needs to be reevaluated. Distinctive areas of agricultural and non-agricultural activity are emerging adjacent to and between urban cores, which are a direct response to preexisting conditions, time-space collapse, economic change, technological developments, and labor force change occurring in a different manner and mix from the operation of these factors in the Western industrialized countries in the nineteenth and early twentieth centuries.

To elaborate further, the conventional view of the urban transition is inadequate in three respects. First, it is too narrow in its view that the widely accepted spatial separation of rural and urban activities will persist as urbanization continues.

Second, it is inadequate in its assumption that the urbanization transition will be inevitable because of the operation of "agglomeration economies" and comparative advantage, which are said to facilitate the concentration of the population in linked urban places. The emergence of such a system was described by Jean Gottmann in 1961 as a "megalopolis" in which, when applied to the northeastern United States, the population was largely concentrated in the urban and suburban areas, but interspersed with areas of low population density used for agriculture and as leisure spaces by the population of the megapolitan areas.[7] In many parts of Asia, the spatial juxtaposition of many of the larger city cores within heavily populated regions of intensive, mostly wet-rice agriculture based on a mixture of "skill-oriented" and "mechanical" technological inputs has created densities of population that are frequently much higher than in the suburban areas of the West.[8] This juxtaposition permits demographic densities similar to urban areas over extended zones of intensely cultivated rural areas located adjacent to urban cores. The considerable advances in transportation technology, particularly in relatively cheap intermediate transportation technology, such as two-stroke motorbikes, greatly facilitate the circulation of commodities, people, and capital in such regions, creating, in turn, large mega-urban regions.

Third, the Western paradigm of the urban transition, which draws its rationale from the historical experience of urbanization as it has occurred in Western Europe and North America in the nineteenth and twentieth centuries, is clearly not neatly transferable to the developing countries' urbanization process. The uneven incorporation of these Asian countries into a world economic system from the fifteenth century onward created divergent patterns of urbanization, which reflect the different interactions between Asian countries and the world system.[9] For example, the British, French and Dutch all developed the productivity of wet-rice agriculture in Southeast Asia.[10] In a similar manner, Japanese rule in Korea and Taiwan further accentuated the monocrop rice characteristics of parts of these countries as sources of supply for Japan's prewar empire. Geopolitical events determined that both these countries emerged into "fragile" independence with high rural densities and low levels of urbanization. On the contrary, British intervention in Malaysia created an urban system oriented to the production of export products on the west coast away from the heavily populated rice bowls of Kedah and Kelantan, limiting the possibilities of an emergent mega-urban region.

Because of these inadequacies in the conventional view, the concept of the "urban transition" needs to be positioned within a broader paradigm of the transition in the space-economy of countries. Such a paradigm would include (1) a heightened sensitivity to the historical elements of the urban and agrarian transition within specific countries; (2) an appreciation of the ecological, demographic and economic foundations of the urban and agrarian transition; (3) an investigation of the institutional components, particularly the role of the state in the development process; (4) a careful evaluation of the transactional components within given countries including transport, commodity, and population flows; and (5) a broad understanding of the structural shifts in the labor force reflecting economic change. Essentially, such an approach is an attempt to investigate the manner in which particular sets of conditions in one place interact with broader processual change. It is not so much concerned with the contrast between rural and urban as the space-economy changes but focuses instead on the interactions within the space economy as they affect the emergence of particular regions of economic activity. This view has important implications for policy making in the Asian context, for it poses a challenge to sectoral approaches to development planning.

Definitions and Parameters

Since this assertion is quite challenging to those who have vested interests in the persistence of the urban-rural paradigm, it is necessary to spell out in some detail the definitional components of this broader view of the "space-economy transition."

Figure 9.1 presents a model of the spatial configuration of a hypothetical Asian country, which I will label Asiatica Euphoria for the purposes of this exercise.[11]

In this example, five main regions of the spatial economy are identified as follows:

1. The major cities of the urban hierarchy, which are often dominated in the Asian context by one or two extremely large cities.

2. The peri-urban regions, which are those areas surrounding the cities within a daily commuting reach of the city core. In some parts of Asia, these regions can stretch for up to thirty kilometers away from the city core.

3. The regions labeled *desakota,* which are regions of an intense mixture of agricultural and non-agricultural activities that often stretch along corridors between large city cores.[12] These regions were previously characterized by dense populations engaged in agriculture, generally but not exclusively dominated by wet-rice.

4. Densely populated rural regions, which occur in many Asian countries, particularly those practicing wet-rice agriculture.

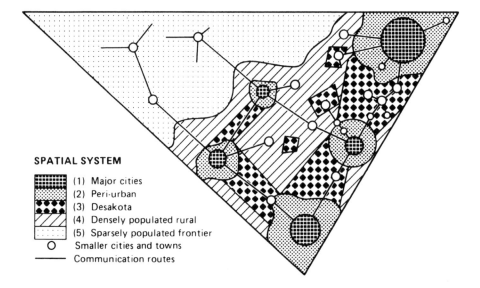

SPATIAL SYSTEM

(1) Major cities
(2) Peri-urban
(3) Desakota
(4) Densely populated rural
(5) Sparsely populated frontier
O   Smaller cities and towns
—   Communication routes

9.1 Spatial configuration of a hypothetical Asian country

5. Finally, the sparsely populated frontier regions found in many Asian countries that offer opportunities for land colonization schemes and various forms of agricultural development.

The model of the spatial economy is, of course, static and must change as the economy changes. The pace and characteristics of this settlement transition vary from country to country, reflecting the features of socioeconomic change at the macro level. The role that the growth of metropolitan cores and the *desakota* process play in this transformation is of major importance. The mega-urban regions that emerge often incorporate two large urban cores linked by effective transportation routes. These regions include the major cities, peri-urban zones, and an extensive zone of mixed rural-urban land use along such routes. Travel time between any two points in a region would probably be no more than three to four hours, but in most cases is considerably less. Mixed economic activities may also occur in villages in these zones, which are less accessible and where economic linkages are more reliant on social networks.

It should be stressed that this model of the transition of the space-economy is not intended to be universally applicable, but to fit the situation where one or more urban cores are located in densely settled peasant rural areas.[13] There may also be cases where the urban cores are located in lightly populated regions of plantation agriculture as in the case of Kuala Lumpur in Malaysia. The contrast between the two agroeconomic systems as they are reflected in socioeconomic systems, export trade, and class relations is not a new theme. It has been used by Baldwin for a theoretical exposition of patterns of development in newly settled regions, by Dowd to explain the differences in the settlement patterns of the American west and south, and by Morse to explain the different urban systems that evolved in the "hacienda" and "plantation" regions of Latin America.[14] These writers are not suggesting that a particular urban system results from a preexisting agroeconomic system, but rather that the existence of these agroeconomic systems provides the possibility for the emergence of certain urban systems and regions.

In the Asian context, the existence of high-density agricultural regions adjacent to large urban cores offers an opportunity for a particular form of mega-urban region to emerge. Their existence does not ensure the inevitability of the emergence of such regions. These will result from, for example, the policies of private and public sectors, the form of economic growth, and the position of the urban core relative to international connections. In the case of the Republic of Korea, with a precondition of high-density rice regions, the government adopted a strategy of concentrating on industrialization rather than agriculture, which led to slow growth in rural income and a release of surplus rural population into urban-based industrialization. Thus, South Korea was characterized by a metropolis-dominated urban hierarchy. By contrast, in a region of similar pre-existing rural densities such as Jogjakarta in Java, in a slow-growth situation there are only limited possibilities for drawing off surplus rural population to urban centers in other parts of the country, and the rural inhabitants engage in an intense mixture of non-agricultural and agricultural activity that permits survival but does not increase income.

There are at least three types of spatial economy transition occurring in Asia in regions that have the prerequisite of the historical evolution of high-density, mostly rice-growing agroeconomic niches.

First, there are those countries that have seen a decline in rural settlement, land use and agricultural population as the population has moved to urban centers. In such countries, agricultural land use may remain important as a reflection of government land or agricultural protection policies. This pattern has been associated with overall increases in income and productivity in which rural populations fall well behind those of urban areas. South Korea and Japan are examples of such a spatial economy transition. These countries will be labeled *desakota* Type I or *konjuka*, the Japanese term for landscapes that have a mixture of small farm plots, residences and industry. Such regions are characterized by rural landscapes in which most of the economically active work is in non-agricultural activities.[15]

Second, there are those regions in which, over varying periods of time, productivity gains in agriculture and industry, and secular shifts from agricultural to non-agricultural activities are focused particularly on the urban cores and adjacent regions. These changes are linked to rising household income, improved transportation linkages, and improved infrastructures. Examples occur in regions such as Nanjing-Shanghai-Hangzhou, the Central Plains of Thailand, the Taipei-Kaohsiung corridor, the Calcutta region and Jabotabek in Java. These may be identified as *desakota* Type 2, and are characterized by rapid economic growth compared to other regions of the country.

Third, there are those regions of high density in which economic growth is slow. Often such regions are located close to secondary urban centers that have slow economic growth, and are characterized by continuing high population growth, surplus labor and persistent low productivity in both agriculture and non-agriculture. Examples are the Jogjakarta region in Java, Kerala in South India, Bangladesh and the Sichuan Basin in the interior of China. These regions will be labeled *desakota* Type 3, and are characterized by slow growth of income and involuntary economic activity.[16]

The Emergence of the Extended Metropolitan Region in Asia

Figure 9.2 shows the location of the core regions in Asia as grouped into the three main *desakota* types. First are those countries that have experienced a rapid transformation of the spatial economy in terms of rural-to-urban shift in population, although agricultural land use may remain quite persistent. Japan and South Korea are the most prominent examples.[17]

Second, there are those regions of countries that have experienced a rapid change in their economic features in the past 30 years. An example is the Taipei-Kaohsiung corridor of Taiwan, which has experienced a declining proportion of agricultural employment from 56 to 20 percent between 1956 and 1980, and a concurrent growth of industrialization. Speare and his colleagues have estimated that the growth of small to medium-sized industries in rural areas slowed the growth rate of cities by 6 percent in the 1960s and 1970s.[18] At the same time, this region was characterized by a decline of staple crops as a proportion of the total agricultural value of production. Thus, over the past 30 years, although the production of rice has increased considerably, the share of rice as a proportion of gross agricultural receipts has dropped from 50 percent in 1950 to 34 percent in 1980. At the same time, other agricultural products have increased from 20 to 36 percent, and vegetables and fruit from 7 to 20 percent. More recently, there has been a rapid increase in fish farming (prawns), chicken rearing and other forms of capital-intensive agribusiness. This shift has led to a significant change in the pattern of female employment, with a decline from 52.5 percent (1965) in primary industry to 16 percent in 1980, and an increase in secondary industry from 18.2 to 43.7 percent.[19] Similar patterns are being exhibited in the Bangkok-Central Plains region of Thailand and the four major coastal zones of China. These regions,

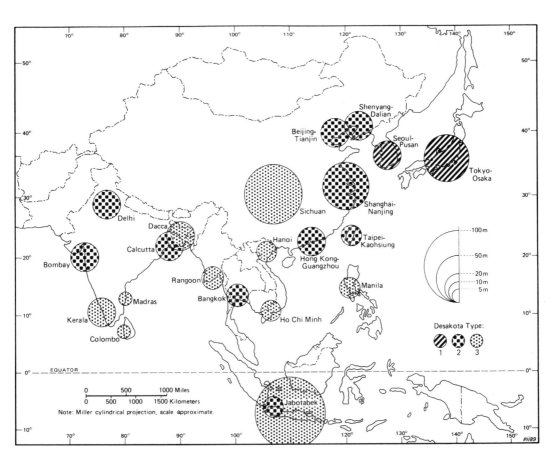

9.2 Growth of core areas in Asia

with only 12.5 percent of China's population, accounted for 46.4 percent of the value of industrial production and 13 percent of the value of agricultural output in 1986.

Third, there is a type of region that bears some spatial and economic resemblance to Type 2 but is characterized by changes that occur because of high population growth and slower economic growth. This situation results in the persistence of underemployment and self-employment in unpaid family work and enterprises. In such regions there may be a juxtaposition of elements of Type 1 and Type 2, producing a highly dualistic economic structure. Thus, technological inputs in agriculture may cause labor shedding and an increase in non-agricultural activities in the rural areas adjacent to urban cores. This phenomenon has been recorded in areas such as Kerala and Tamil Nadu. Although there is often some growth of small industry and other income opportunities, these regions are characterized by the persistence of low incomes, which reflect the slow structural transition in the allocation of labor. In some cases, regions continue to absorb population into agricultural areas (for instance, the Sichuan Basin) where non-agricultural employment has remained fairly static over the past forty years while the population has almost doubled in size.[20]

Conditions and Processes Underlying the Emergence of New Zones of Economic Interaction: *Desakota*

Given the diversity of these transitions, it may well be argued that the *desakota* have little in common with one another. However, certain common conditions and processes occur in these regions.

First, virtually all these regions are characterized by densely populated, small-holder cultivation agriculture, commonly wet-rice, which involves careful water management and agronomic practices.[21] Densities frequently approach 1,000 people per square kilometer of cultivated land. Historically, Oshima has argued, the pronounced seasonality and the intense labor of planting and harvesting have had two results: increasing population density, which has led to increasingly smaller farm plots, and uneven seasonal demands for labor inputs. During the off-season, "This dense population must look for off-farm employment since most farms are too small to generate enough income to live on … Monsoon rice-farming never became separated from nonagriculture as it was in the West where cropping came to be combined with animal husbandry in large capitalistic farms."[22] He goes on to argue that in the prewar centuries "monsoon agriculture kept large masses of workers tied down in rural areas, rendering the large labor supply inflexible."[23] In a pre-Green Revolution situation, the capacity of the population of rice-growing areas to increase and still produce enough rice to avoid famine even with very limited infrastructural investment is the basic explanation that Geertz provides for the growth of Java's population from 5 million to 25 million in 10 decades of slow economic growth.[24] This argument can be applied to many of the other Asian rice bowls in India, China, Japan, Korea and Southeast Asia. Bray reinforces this point with the following comment:

The organization of resources typical of a "skill-orientated" technology such as intensive rice farming dovetails very neatly with petty commodity production, which requires very little capital to set up a family enterprise and absorbs surplus labour without depriving the farm of workers at times of peak demand. It can be expanded, diversified or contracted according to market demands, but the combination with the rice farm guarantees the family subsistence. The products can be conveniently conveyed to national markets by merchants, who pay the villagers for their labour and often provide raw materials as well as information on the state of the market.[25]

Thus, it is possible to argue that the labor force of these rice-bowl areas was "culturally" prepared to commit its labor to various forms of "new" non-agricultural activity.

Second, in virtually all the rice-bowl areas there were large cities or clusters of cities such as Calcutta, Shanghai, Bangkok and Guangzhou that provided both opportunities for seasonal labor and important markets for rural rice and other products. The linkages with these cities were important for the surrounding rural areas for cultural and economic reasons.

Third, these regions were frequently characterized by a well-developed infrastructure of roads and canals that allowed an intense movement of commodities and people. Indeed, one is constantly reminded of the importance of water systems for these regions as the fundamental sustainers of the ecological system. Colonial impact, whether by Britain, Japan or Holland, did little to change these patterns. Indeed, by the provision of political stability and investment in infrastructure the colonial powers frequently enhanced the preconditions for growing populations.

Fourth, by the early 1950s, all of these regions were large, cheap labor reservoirs waiting to be tapped by state, international and private capital investment. The manner in which this labor was incorporated into non-agricultural activity varied markedly from country to country and region to region. Most successful were Japan, Taiwan and South Korea, where both industrialization and agricultural growth led the way in Asia. In these three countries, efforts were made to increase rural income through higher yield, guaranteed prices, diversification into non-rice crops, and increased opportunities for employment in rural industries. This effort was aided by physical infrastructure improvements such as rural roads, electrification, consolidation and irrigation. Increased mechanization released labor, particularly women, to work in industry. Institutional changes, particularly land reform and the introduction of higher yielding rice varieties, were crucial in this process. In addition, the state invested in major transportation linkages such as freeways and electrified railways, which pulled these regions closer to the urban cores. Of course, these processes did not prevent the movement of labor out of agriculture into non-agriculture and urban centers, which accelerated in Japan in the 1960s, in Korea in the 1970s, and in Taiwan in the 1980s. But political and institutional imperatives, particularly the need for food self-sufficiency, encouraged the persistence of rice farming and created *konjuka* landscapes.

In other countries, these processes moved more slowly, partly because the institutional changes of the "Three Tigers" could not be implemented. The Philippines is an excellent example of initial success and then slowdown because of bad government. In the late 1970s, however, other regions in Asia began to exhibit enough of the features responsible for the successes in Japan, Korea and Taiwan to achieve considerable growth. For example, the four regions of Hong Kong, Guangzhou Macao, Nanjing Shanghai Hangzhou, Beijing Tianjin-Tangshan and Shenyang-Dalian have exhibited all these features since 1978. Wang and Veeck have shown how remarkably these regions fit the model of *desakota*.[26] Other studies find the same processes occurring in the Central Plains of Thailand and even in the extended Calcutta Metropolitan Region, which has long had the reputation of being one of the main centers of world poverty.[27] Rice-bowl areas such as Kerala, Bangladesh, Jogjakarta and the Sichuan Basin, less favorably positioned from the viewpoint of state and private investment, exhibit a persistence of low income and continuing pressure of population on available resources.

Fifth, all the *desakota* regions were characterized by highly integrated "transactive" environments in terms of movement of people and commodities, for example. In many cases, the dense network of rural canals and waterways was central to this integration prior to the Second World War. The onset of technological developments in intermediate transportation since the 1950s has greatly accelerated this process.

Finally, it is important to acknowledge the role of the expansion of the global economy and the international division of labor, which create a situation where national governments responsible for gigantic, cheap labor pools have adopted different policies with respect to permitting or encouraging their countries' labor to be tapped for national and international industrial growth. In this respect, the location of *desakota* Type 1 and 2 regions adjacent to large cities and transportation points has been particularly important. From the viewpoint of many investors, investment in industry in these regions is cheaper for virtually all the factors of production, and they are able to avoid some of the diseconomies that exist in the large urban zones. Thus, these regions are important areas of subcontracting for a portion of the industrial production process.

To summarize, the regions designated as *desakota* have six main features.

1. They have been or are characterized by a large population engaged in small-holder cultivation of rice, which before the Second World War conducted considerable interaction through accessible transportation routes.

2. They are generally characterized by an increase in non-agricultural activities in areas that have previously been largely agricultural. These non-agricultural activities are very diverse, and include trading, transportation and industry. The increase in non-agricultural activity is characterized by a mixture of activities, often by members of the same household. Thus, one person may commute to the city to work as a clerk, another engage in farming, a third work in industry, and another find employment in retailing in the *desakota* zone. This mixture creates a situation in which the economic linkages within such a region may be as important as the dominance of the large cities in the megalopolis that draw the surrounding regions into their orbit.

3. The *desakota* zones are generally characterized by extreme fluidity and mobility of the population. The availability of relatively cheap transport such as two-stroke motorbikes, buses and trucks has facilitated relatively quick movement over longer distances than could be covered previously. Thus, these zones are characterized not only by commuting to the larger urban centers but also by intense movement of people and goods within the zone.

4. The *desakota* zones are characterized by an intense mixture of land use with agriculture, cottage industry, industrial estates, suburban developments and other uses existing side by side. Such a mix has both negative and positive effects. Agricultural products, particularly industrial crops, have a ready market, but the waste of industrial activity can pollute and destroy agricultural land. On the whole, these zones are much more intensely utilized than the American megalopolis, with regard to which Gottmann commented on the amount of woodland and recreational areas that exist. In the *desakota* zones of Asian countries, population pressures place greater demands on the available space.

5. Another feature of the *desakota* zones is the increased participation of women in nonagricultural labor. In part, this feature is associated with a demand for female labor in industry, domestic service and other activities, but it is also closely related to changing patterns of agricultural production in the *desakota* regions. Generally, agricultural production shows a shift from monocrop grain cultivation to increased diversity with production of livestock, vegetables and fruit, sometimes for national and interregional consumption.

6. Finally, *desakota* zones are to some extent "invisible" or "gray" zones from the viewpoint of the state authorities. Urban regulations may not apply in these "rural areas," and it is difficult for the state to enforce them despite the rapidly changing economic structure of the regions. This feature is particularly encouraging to the "informal sector" and small-scale operators who find it difficult to conform to labor or industrial legislation.

In essence, then, the central processers that shape these regions are the dynamic linkages between agriculture and non-agriculture, and investment seeking to utilize cheap labor and land within a distinctive agroecological setting. Ranis and Stewart have identified how expansion in agricultural output leads to an expansion in other activities and, conversely, how additional non-agricultural activity in the rural areas provides opportunities and incentives for raising agricultural productivity.[28]

In the *desakota* regions that show the greatest increase of both agricultural and nonagricultural income, there is a general rise in household income. Depending on the expenditure decisions of households (savings/expenditure ratios), there may be an increase in demand for local supplies, goods from urban centers and imports. Ranis and Stewart show significant variations in different regions. Thus, in Taiwan an increase in agricultural income in rural areas was associated with increased nonagricultural production-related employment and high increases in all linkages. In the Philippines, slower rates of agricultural production associated with a large population increase led to an increase in low-income non-agricultural employment and limited linkages with larger markets. The Philippine situation is typical of the "involuntary" and "distress" features of surplus labor markets first discussed by W. Arthur Lewis.[29]

Questions Concerning the *Desakota* Regions in Asia

The regions where the *desakota* processes are in full operation are clearly an important part of the "settlement transition" in Asia. For example, Zhou reported that the four key economic regions of China (Nanjing-Shanghai-Hangzhou, Hong Kong-Guangzhou-Macao, Beijing-Tianjin-Tangshan and Shenyang-Dalian) with approximately 12 percent of the nation's population in 1986-87 were responsible for 47 percent of its industrial output. These four key economic regions play a crucial role in the current phase of rapid economic growth in China. Similar arguments were presented by Liu and Tsai for Taiwan. Thus, there is a great deal of support for the assertion that these regions are highly significant foci for the development process. However, further data are needed to support the assertion, particularly with respect to the following questions:

In what manner are these new economic regions different from the "zones of urban influence" that are well established in the urban transition literature? In other words, if these zones are simply a greater areal extension of the "peri-urban" region of large cities that have been brought about by space-time collapse and transportation improvements, then what is different about them from the so-called peri-urban regions? In fact, the relationship between the urban cores and the adjacent regions is important to the sustainability of these regions, and therefore any study of these regions must investigate the urban core functions and the relationships with the surrounding regions.

Can economic data be collected to show processes operating that facilitate certain types of economic activities in these regions? For instance, are there diseconomies associated with large cities that facilitate the location of economic activities in such zones? Is the legislative environment in such zones more permissive (are taxes lower?) for certain types of activities? Are wage rates persistently lower? Are the social overhead costs lower in such regions? In other words, are there economic benefits that facilitate the growth of economic activities in these regions that may be a "growth generator" in the development process?

Are such regions likely to exhibit short-term persistence (up to 50 years), or are they simply a transitory phenomenon? Some evidence presented by Liu and Tsai suggests that in Taiwan the persistence of such a region, at least in the corridor between Taipei and Kaohsiung, is questionable. They show evidence that the population is concentrating in the northwest quadrant of Taiwan as the industrial and services characteristics of the economy change. This shift is associated with a decline in agricultural employment. Is there some point in the development process at which the agglomerative tendencies will take over? This type of question has important policy implications for countries such as China or India as their economies develop.

Issues of Policy Formation

Prevailing policy prescription for macrointervention in the spatial shift of population during development is broadly polarized between acceptance of big-city growth representing the "rational" development of economies of scale and agglomeration, and arguments in favor of the development of "small" and "intermediate" towns in the urban hierarchy, decentralization of industry, and frontier development.[30] Current developments raise the question of whether *desakota* regions represent a viable "middle" policy option and, if so, what kinds of policies need to be adopted. A range of "problems" result from the growth of urban cores and the *desakota* regions adjacent to them, including environmental degradation, waste removal and adequate delivery of social welfare. Before the issue of some form of "middle planning option" is tackled, it will be necessary for the governments of the region to deal with the fundamental issue of the usefulness of a rural-urban distinction. In reviewing the debate on "urban bias," Harriss and Moore explain this point as follows:

> There are two themes central and common to their ["urban bias" analysts] work. First, in attempting to explain national level patterns of economic resource allocation within a political economy framework, they use the concept of economic sectors, mainly the rural/agricultural versus urban/industrial categorization. Second, they suggest in varying degrees that the way in which sectoral conflicts influence the allocation of economic resources through state action has been the prime cause of slow rates of economic growth (and in Lipton's work, of growth biased against the poor) in developing countries since the Second World War.[31]

But what happens if the rural-urban dichotomy ceases to exist, as in the case of *desakota* zones? Then the whole policy debate on urban and rural allocation of resources becomes fuzzy and meaningless, unless one accepts Lipton's argument that "rural-urban is not a categorization of space alone. To see it like that is to underpin an incorrect, absolute distinction between geographical (residence, density), occupational, sectoral and class categorizations of households."[32]

All societies have working spatial definitions of urban and rural areas. These definitions are highly variable from country to country and are often changed. However, most definitions have some common elements such as size and political definition. For instance, in some countries all gazetted towns exceeding a population of ten thousand are regarded as urban; everything else is rural. In fact, it is more important to know two important economic pieces of information:

1. What is the contribution of agricultural and non-agricultural activities to the GDP of a given spatial unit (nation, province, and so on)?

2. What is the proportion of the working labor force employed in agricultural and non-agricultural work in a given spatial unit?

If this information were available over given time periods, it would be possible to develop a more precise definition of urban and rural areas.

One could conceive a rather simple matrix constructed at the level of small administrative units that would allow a fourfold spatial division of a country on a continuum from the most urban spatial unit to the most non-urban spatial unit (Figure 9.3).

Assuming some ideal statistical base, this type of analysis would enable the estimation of the contribution of the urban spatial units to the GDP, as compared to the non-urban spatial units. Temporal data, if available, would permit the assessment of the relative contribution of urban and non-urban areas to the GDP through time as well as the differences in the labor force over time. This kind of information would provide vital feedback to the government in assessing the spatial impact of its investment policies. Unfortunately, few developing societies possess data that can be analyzed in this way, relying instead on macrodata that conceal these significant differences between urban and non-urban areas.

There appear to be six priorities for many Asian countries if they are to develop pragmatic strategies that attempt to recognize the importance of the *desakota* regions. First, the government will have to make some significant decisions with respect to agricultural policy. All indications are that in most Asian countries, the "agricultural issue" is of central importance to *desakota* regions. The problem revolves around the need for a sufficient supply of foodstuffs and the "cultural" demand for agricultural activity in Asian countries.

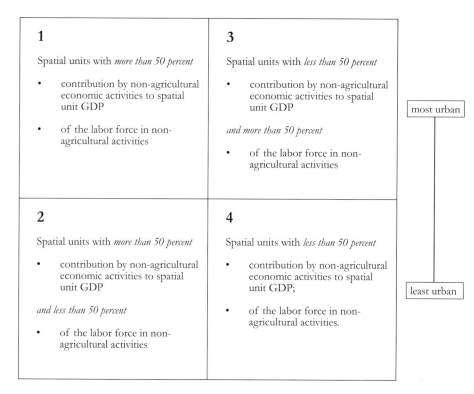

9.3 Spatial units and economic outputs

The crucial issue is how long rice growing, for example, will persist in *desakota* regions as economic growth proceeds. In the cases of Japan, Korea and Taiwan, it appears that policies will eventually reduce the role of rice in *desakota* areas. In other cases, labor is being released from rice growing as a result of technological changes over which governments apparently have little control.

Second, Asian governments will seriously need to consider in what manner the release of labor from agricultural labor pools is going to occur. Policies that slow down geographical relocation and foster *in situ* development should be given priority. Given the already high levels of development in these regions, they should not be expensive. Of course, the problems of the more "traditional" regions of *desakota*, such as Sichuan, are more intractable and should be tackled by more conventional development inputs that emphasize population control, delivery of basic needs and integrated rural development.

Third, Asian governments will have to recognize the reality of these zones of intense urban-rural interaction and direct much of their investment to these areas. This means making hard decisions against fostering small-town development and rural industrialization in less accessible areas without neglecting rural-integrated development schemes in such areas. Many governments should opt for policies of "modified regional growth pole" growth (emphasizing not just the urban pole but also the large mega-urban region of which it is part).

Fourth, Asian governments will need to monitor carefully the growth of economic activities in these zones for the obvious problems that will arise over conflict in incompatible land uses and environmental pollution, for example. This process will involve great care, for one of the major factors favoring the economic vitality of the *desakota* zones is the mixture of land uses.

Fifth, Asian governments will need to improve access in these zones of intense rural-urban interaction with improved roads and fast railway communication. In this respect, the building of the Shinkansen, the Seoul-Pusan Highway, and the Taipei-Kaohsiung Freeway have been crucial to the development of Japan, Korea and Taiwan, respectively. This costly investment reaps developmental rewards.

Finally, Asian governments should develop new spatial systems of data collection similar to those of the "living perimeters" of Taiwan, which will enable them to monitor effectively the impact of investment decisions on labor force composition and income, among others, within the *desakota* zones.

Of course, the timing of government strategies and fiscal ability to implement them are not easy to gauge. However, the demographic and economic reality of the growth of the *desakota* means that planning decisions relating to them cannot be postponed.

Conclusion

The historical evolution of the *desakota* regions has created a unique opportunity for Asian development. Whether this opportunity will be taken advantage of in all Asian countries remains to be seen, but certainly the challenge to urban versus rural growth, which seems so central to many Asian development strategies, can be resolved at least partially through the planned development of *desakota* regions.

Notes

1 Jean Gottmann, *Megalopolis: the Urbanized Northeastern Seaboard of the United States* (New York: Kraus, 1961) 257.

2 O. H. K. Spate and A. I. A. Learmonth, *India and Pakistan: A General and Regional Geography* (London: Methuen, 1967) 202.

3 Some of the ideas in this chapter were first put forward in an address to the International Conference on Asian Urbanization held at the University of Akron in April 1985. See Terry G. McGee, "*Urbanisasi* or *Kotadesasi?* Evolving Patterns of Urbanization in Asia," *Urbanization in Asia: Spatial Deimensions and Policy Issues,* eds. Frank J. Costa, Ashok K. Dutt, Laurence Ma and Allen G. Noble (Honolulu: University of Hawaii Press, 1989) 93-108.

4 United Nations, Centre for Human Settlements, *Global Report on Human Settlements* (Oxford: Oxford University Press, 1987).

5 Norton Ginsburg, "Extended Metropolitan Regions in Asia: A New Spatial Paradigm," *The Urban Transition: Reflections on the American and Asian Experiences* (Hong Kong: Chinese University Press, 1990) 21.

6 See Terry G. McGee, *Urbanisasi or Kotadesasi? The Emergence of New Regions of Economic Interaction in Asia,* Working Paper 87/8

(Honolulu: EWCEAPI, 1987). See also Norton Ginsburg, *The Urban Transition: Reflections on the American and Asian Experiences* (Hong Kong: Chinese University Press, 1990).

7 Jean Gottmann, *Megalopolis: the Urbanized Northeastern Seaboard of the United States* (New York: Twentieth Century Fund, 1961) 257.

8 This division between "skill-oriented" and "mechanical" technological inputs is used to buttress Bray's provocative arguments concerning the distinctive role of Asian wet-rice agriculture in the agrarian development processes in Asia. She argues persuasively that this agroeconomic system created very different conditions from the "Western model." This position is certainly central to some of the arguments of this chapter, but its acceptance does not rule out the application of the "mechanical" technological input (as reflected by capital replacing labor in these regions), as can be seen in the growth of agribusiness in the chicken industry in areas such as the Central Plains of Thailand. See Francesca Bray, *The Rice Economies: Technology and Development in Asian Societies* (Oxford: Basil Blackwell, 1986).

9   This argument is presented in much greater detail for Latin America in Richard M. Morse, "Trends and Patterns of Latin American Urbanization, 1750–1920," *Comparative Studies in Society and History* 16 (1974) 416-47; and Richard M. Morse, "The Development of Urban Systems in the Americas in the Nineteenth Century," *Journal of Interamerican Studies* 17, 1 (1975) 4-26.

10 See Christopher Baker, "Economic Reorganization and the Slump in South and Southeast Asia," *Comparative Studies in Social and Economic History* 23, 2 (1981) 325-49.

11 The diagram in Figure 9.1 was constructed by Mike Douglass of the Department of Urban and Regional Planning, University of Hawaii, and myself during the course of some extended evening discussions on the subject of the "urban transition." I am very grateful to him for his constant probing of my ill-formed ideas that formed the basis of earlier presentations of this model. See Mike Douglass, *Urbanization and National Urban Development Strategies in Asia, Indonesia, Korea, and Thailand*, Discussion Paper No. 8 (Honolulu: Department of Urban and Regional Planning, University of Hawaii, 1988).

12 The use of a coined Indonesian term taken from the two words *kota* (town) and *desa* (village) was adopted after discussions with Indonesian social scientists, because of my belief that there was a need to look for terms and concepts in the languages of developing countries that reflect the empirical reality of their societies. Reliance solely on the language and concepts of Western social science, which have dominated the analyses of non-Western societies, can lead to a form of "knowledge imperialism." In this text, I have used the term *desakota*, which can be used interchangeably with *kotadesa*.

13 The term "peasant" in this context applies not only to those farmers who own their land, but also to tenants operating small units of farmland.

14 Robert E. Baldwin, "Patterns of Development in Newly Settled Regions," *The Manchester School of Economic and Social Studies* 24 (1956) 161-79; and Douglas Dowd, "A Comparative Analysis of Economic Development in the American West and South," *Journal of Economic History* 16, 7 (1956) 558-74. See also Richard Morse, "Trends and Patterns"; and Morse, "Urban Systems in the Americas."

15 Harry T. Oshima, "The Transition From an Agricultural to an Industrial Economy in East Asia," *Economic Development and Cultural Change* 34, 4 (1986) 783-810.

16 Graeme Hugo, *Population Mobility in West Java, Indonesia* (PhD dissertation, Canberra: Australian National University, 1975); Patrick Guiness, *Harmony and Hierarchy in a Javanese Kampong* (Oxford: Oxford University Press, 1986); and Ali Ahmad, *Agricultural Stagnation and Population Pressure: The Case of Bangladesh* (New Delhi: Vikas Publishing House, 1984).

17 Yujiro Hayami, *A Century of Agricultural Growth in Japan* (Minneapolis: University of Minnesota Press, 1976); Otohiko Hasumi, "Rural Society in Postwar Japan, Part 1," *The Japan Foundation Newsletter* 12, 5 (1985) 1-10; Otohiko Hasumi, "Rural Society in Postwar Japan, Part 2," *The Japan Foundation Newsletter* 12, 6 (1985) 1-7; Norihiko Nakai, "Urbanization Promotion and Control in Metropolitan Japan," *Planning Perspectives* 3 (1988) 783-810; John Lewis, "Metropolitan Japan," *Planning Perspectives* 3 (1988) 783-810; and John Lewis, "The Real Security Issue: Rice," *Far Eastern Economic Review* (19 June 1981) 70-1.

18 Alden Speare, Paul Lie and Ching-lung Tsay, eds. *Urbanization and Development: the Rural-Urban Transition in Taiwan* (Boulder: Westview Press, 1988).

19 See Daniel Todd and Yi-Chung Hsueh, "Taiwan: Some Spatial Implications of Rapid Economic Growth," *Geoforum* 19, 2 (1988) 133-45; and Jack F. Williams, "Urban and Regional Planning in Taiwan: the Quest for Balanced Regional Development," *Tijdschrift voor Economische en Social Geografie* 79, 3 (1988) 175-87.

20 I am grateful to Rex Casinader and Wang Yaolin, PhD candidates in the Department of Geography at the University of British Columbia, for information on developments in South India and Sichuan.

21 An exception to this generalization appears to be the Beijing-Tianjin area, which is a region of intense mixture of crops. Since 1949, the southern part of the Shenyang-Dalian region has become an important area of rice production. The identification of "rice-growing" regions does not preclude the possibility of "mixed crop" systems developing similar population densities. For example, Polly Hill, *Dry Grain Farming Families: Hausaland (Nigeria) and Karnataka (India) Compared* (Cambridge: Cambridge University Press, 1982).

22 See Oshima, "The Transition from an Agricultural to an Industrial Economy," 784.

23 Ibid., 785.

24 Clifford Geertz, *Agricultural Involution: the Process of Ecological Change in Indonesia* (Berkeley: University of California Press, 1963).

25 Bray, *Rice Economies*, 135.

26 Wang Yaolin's PhD thesis research on the Shenyang-Dalian region is being carried out in the Department of Geography at the University of British Columbia.

27 See Mike Douglass, *Regional Integration on the Capitalist Periphery: the Central Plains of Thailand* (The Hague: Institute of Social Studies, 1984); and Mike Douglass, "Population Growth and Policies in Mega-cities: Calcutta," *Population Policy Paper No. 1* (New York: United Nations, 1986).

28 Gustav Ranis and Francis Stewart, "Rural Linkages in the Philippines and Thailand," *Macro-policies for Appropriate Technology in Developing Countries,* ed. Frances Stewart (Boulder: Westview Press, 1988) 140-91.

29 W. Arthur Lewis, "Economic Development with Unlimited Supplies of Labour," *The Economics of Underdevelopment*, ed. H. N. Agarwala and S. P. Singh (New York: Oxford University Press, 1963) 400-49. See also Geertz, *Agricultural Involution*; and Pierre Gourou, *L'Asie* (Paris: Libraire Hachette, 1953).

30 Yue-man Yeung, "Controlling Metropolitan Growth in Eastern Asia," *Geographical Review* 76, 2 (1986) 125-37.

31 John Hariss and Mick Moore, "Editors' Introduction to Special Issue on Development and the Rural-Urban Divide," *The Journal of Development Studies* 20, 3 (1984) 1-4.

32 Michael Lipton, "Urban Bias Revisited," *The Journal of Development Studies* 20, 3 (1984) 139-66, specifically 155.

Figure Credits

9.1   Original by Mike Douglass and the author.
9.2   Original by author.
9.3   Original by author.

THREE
PLANETARY URBANIZATION— OPENINGS

Is a planetary formation of complete urbanization being consolidated in the early twenty-first century? If so, what are its major experiential, social, spatial and environmental expressions, and what are its sociopolitical implications? What categories of analysis and methods of representation are needed to decipher such trends and transformations?

**Edward Soja &
J. Miguel Kanai
Neil Brenner &
Christian Schmid
Andy Merrifield
Neil Brenner
Christian Schmid
Kanishka Goonewardena**

10
THE URBANIZATION OF THE WORLD

Edward W. Soja and J. Miguel Kanai

Over the past 30 years, the world has been experiencing an unusually expansive and reconfigured form of urbanization that has defined a distinctively global urban age—one in which we can speak of both the urbanization of the entire globe and the globalization of urbanism as a way of life. This dynamic interrelationship between the urban and the global is the focus of this essay, which presents an overview of the urbanization of the world understood as the extension in the spatial reach of city-based societies, economies and cultures to every place on the planet. We see this extended form of contemporary urbanization not just as an adjunct to the globalization process, but also as its primary driving force, stimulating innovation, creativity and economic growth while at the same time intensifying social and economic inequalities and conflict filled political polarization. But as the world urbanizes, cities are being globalized. Not only is urbanization increasingly reaching everywhere, everywhere is increasingly reaching into the city, contributing to a major reconfiguration of the social and spatial structures of urbanism and creating the most economically and culturally heterogeneous cities the world has ever known.

The Urbanization of the World

There can be no doubt that more people are living in cities than ever before. Just how many is not easy to determine, because countries differ on the criteria used to define what is urban. It is now widely accepted, however, that 2006 marked a remarkable moment in the urbanization of the world. In its report, "The State of the World's Cities," the United Nations HABITAT office made a formal pronouncement that, for the first time, the majority of the world's population—nearly 3.3 billion—lived in urban agglomerations rather than in rural areas. This urban-rural tipping-point, however, is just one measure of a much more extensive, focused and accelerating urbanization process that has been spreading over the entire Earth's surface for at least the past 30 years.[1]

The urbanization of the world has brought with it new terms to describe what were conventionally called cities and metropolitan regions. The term "world city" emerged early in the 1960s to reflect the increasing global influences on urban life.[2] Influenced significantly by the work of Saskia Sassen in the early 1990s, the concept of the "global city" began to be widely used for the most influential financial command centers of the global economy. More recently, the world's largest agglomerations have taken on several additional descriptions.[3] The term we will use most often is the "global city region," defined as a new metropolitan form characterized by sprawling polycentric networks of urban centers clustered around one or more "historic" urban cores.[4] Particular emphasis is given here to "city regions" of more than one million inhabitants in their contiguous urbanized area; to "megacity regions," whose population exceeds 10 million; and to even larger emerging agglomerations that we tentatively call "megalopolitan city regions," which can be defined by their demographic and economic magnitudes as well as quasi-continental extents.

The global imprint of these regional agglomerations and their networked extensions is vividly illustrated in the satellite picture of the "world at night." Punctuating this view of the world are over 500 city-regions in the million-plus category. They occupy only a small portion of the Earth's surface, but they concentrate well over a billion residents and, almost surely, account for an even greater share of the world's built environment, economic wealth, cultural creativity and political power.[5] These million-plus city-regions form the peaks of the world map of population density and stand out as the primary power points of the urban global age.

Another vivid picture of the accelerating growth in the number of million-plus city-regions is presented in the series of maps on Figure 10.1 (next page). While there were only two cities—London and Beijing—that had more than 1 million inhabitants in the early nineteenth century, 100 years later that list had expanded to over a dozen cities and London was beginning to show the signs of megacity regional growth, which we now define as above the 10 million mark (indicated by a larger circle on the maps). In 1950, New York and Tokyo had actually surpassed that threshold, and joining London as thriving city-regions with a world orientation were Paris, Moscow, Shanghai Buenos Aires and Germany's Rhein-Ruhr area—all with populations of over 5 million. By the early 2010s, the number of million-plus metropolitan regions soared to 503, and the list of megacity regions expanded to 29. The urbanization of the world shows every sign of continuing at an accelerating rate.[6]

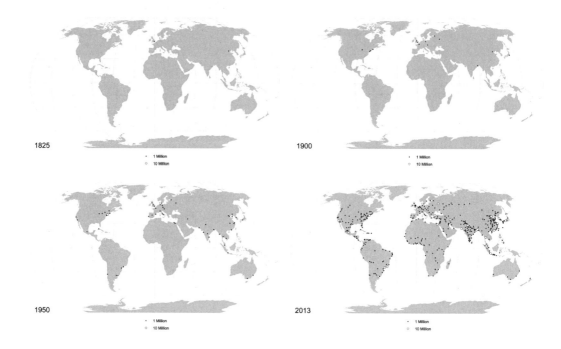

10.1 Accelerating the pace of change
City regions of 1 million people or more multiplied in the twentieth century. Today they accommodate a total of 1 billion people, reflecting their role as centers of global flows of people, capital, culture and information. While there were only a handful of city-regions of this scale up to the mid-twentieth century, the number soared to 450 by 2005.

Looking at the global distribution of the million-plus city regions on the 2013 map, both China (79) and India (53) have larger numbers than the United States (50). Regionally, Europe (60) has fewer million-plus city-regions than Latin America and the Caribbean (70) and almost the same number as the African continent (57). This distribution accentuates all the statistical evidence indicating an unusually rapid urbanization of the world's developing countries in the past half-century. In 1950, developing countries contained slightly less than 40 percent of the world's urban population and by 1970 they still accounted for less than 50 percent. This figure climbs dramatically after that, so that by 2005 only 30 percent of the world's urban dwellers are in "developed" countries, and almost four out of five urban dwellers in the year 2030 are expected to live in developing countries. Perhaps the most rapidly urbanizing continental region has been sub-Saharan Africa, which is expected to have a larger share of the world's urban population than Europe by 2030.[7]

The evolution of megacity regions also deserves attention. By the middle of the twentieth century, Greater New York City was the largest city-region in the world, with a population of over 10 million. But it was soon overtaken by Greater Tokyo, which became the first city-region to pass the 20 million mark at the time of Japan's high economic growth and the Tokyo Olympics in the mid-1960s. By 1985, there were still only nine megacity regions, but the list increased rapidly in the next two decades. Figure 10.2 lists the 29 agglomerations

	Rank	City-Region	Country	Population	Visual Comparison
1950					
	1	New York–Newark	United States of America	12,338,000	
	2	Tokyo	Japan	11,275,000	
	3	London	United Kingdom	8,361,000	
	4	Paris	France	5,424,000	
	5	Moscow	Russian Federation	5,356,000	
	6	Shanghai	China	5,333,000	
	7	Rhein–Ruhr North	Germany	5,295,000	
	8	Buenos Aires	Argentina	5,042,000	
	9	Chicago	United States of America	4,999,000	
	10	Kolkata (Calcutta)	India	4,446,000	
	11	Osaka–Kobe	Japan	4,147,000	
	12	Los Angeles	United States of America	4,046,000	
	13	Beijing	China	3,913,000	
	14	Milan	Italy	3,633,000	
	15	Berlin	Germany	3,337,000	
	16	Philadelphia	United States of America	3,128,000	
	17	Mumbai (Bombay)	India	2,981,000	
	18	Rio de Janeiro	Brazil	2,930,000	
	19	Saint Petersburg	Russian Federation	2,903,000	
	20	Mexico City	Mexico	2,883,000	
1985					
	1	Tokyo	Japan	30,304,000	
	2	New York–Newark	United States of America	15,827,000	
	3	Mexico City	Mexico	14,109,000	
	4	São Paulo	Brazil	13,395,000	
	5	Shanghai	China	12,395,000	
	6	Buenos Aires	Argentina	10,538,000	
	7	Osaka–Kobe	Japan	10,350,000	
	8	Mumbai (Bombay)	India	10,341,000	
	9	Los Angeles	United States of America	10,181,000	
	10	Kolkata (Calcutta)	India	9,946,000	
	11	Beijing	China	9,797,000	
	12	Seoul	Republic of Korea	9,549,000	
	13	Paris	France	9,105,000	
	14	Rio de Janeiro	Brazil	9,086,000	
	15	Moscow	Russian Federation	8,580,000	
	16	Cairo	Egypt	8,326,000	
	17	Tianjin	China	8,312,000	
	18	London	United Kingdom	7,667,000	
	19	Chicago	United States of America	7,285,000	
	20	Metro Manila	Philippines	6,888,000	
2005					
	1	Tokyo	Japan	34,700,000	
	2	Canton	China	26,400,000	
	3	Jakarta	Indonesia	26,000,000	
	3	Shanghai	China	26,000,000	
	5	Seoul	Republic of Korea	25,600,000	
	6	Delhi	India	23,700,000	
	7	Mexico City	Mexico	23,600,000	
	8	Karachi	Pakistan	22,300,000	
	9	Manila	Philippines	21,900,000	
	10	New York	United States of America	21,600,000	
	11	São Paulo	Brazil	21,400,000	
	12	Mumbai (Bombay)	India	21,200,000	
	13	Los Angeles	United States of America	17,100,000	
	14	Beijing	China	16,900,000	
	15	Osaka	Japan	16,800,000	
	16	Moscow	Russian Federation	16,300,000	
	17	Cairo	Egypt	16,000,000	
	17	Dacca	Bangladesh	16,000,000	
	19	Kolkata (Calcutta)	India	15,900,000	
	20	Buenos Aires	Argentina	14,500,000	
	21	Bangkok	Thailand	14,300,000	
	22	Tehran	Iran	13,800,000	
	23	Istanbul	Turkey	13,600,000	
	24	London	United Kingdom	13,300,000	
	25	Lagos	Nigeria	13,000,000	
	26	Rio de Janeiro	Brazil	12,800,000	
	27	Paris	France	10,600,000	

10.2 Measuring city size

The world's largest city-regions reveal the size and location of urbanization since 1950. Although advanced capitalist countries initially dominated, by 2005 15 of the 20 megacity regions were in the developing world with populations above 10 million in all 20.

over 10 million in 2013, along with the world's 20 largest cities in 1950 and 1985. Notable from this data is the shift in the world's urban center of gravity. In 1950, the 10 largest cities of the world included only three in what could be described then as developing countries (Shanghai, Buenos Aires and Calcutta). By 2013, the North Atlantic Basin could only claim New York among the 10 largest cities of the world. Only three more megacity regions (Los Angeles, London and Paris) were in North America and western Europe.

Emphasizing the regional dimension of the contemporary urbanization process helps to understand better both what has been happening to the size and geographical scope of urban agglomerations as well as to their internal configuration. Over the past 30 years, the modern metropolis has been experiencing a distinctively regional urbanization process, in which urbanism as a way of life, once confined to the historic central city, has been spreading outwards, creating urban densities and new "outer" and "edge" cities in what were formerly suburban fringes and greenfield or rural sites. In some areas, urbanization has expanded on even larger regional scales, creating giant urban galaxies with population sizes and degrees of polycentricity far beyond anything imagined only a few decades ago. Although the rate of population growth in some of the largest megacity regions has slowed somewhat in the face of official census data, when viewed from a broader spatial perspective the world's megacity regions have continued to expand in dramatic ways. An increasing share of the world's population is now being absorbed into expanding regional networks of cities, and in some cases city-regions are coalescing into even larger agglomerations in a process that can be called "extended regional urbanization."

Much can be learned about this extended form of regional urbanization by looking at recent developments in China, where at least three expansive megacity regions—in the Pearl River Delta and in the expanding hinterlands around Shanghai and Beijing—have been coalescing into a giant Chinese urban galaxy. Conservative estimates suggest that each of the megacity regions contains at least 40 million people, depending on how they are defined and bounded. Strong arguments can be made, however, that the actual populations are much higher. In less than one-third of a century, China has experienced what is almost certainly the largest scale of urbanization and the most rapid rural-to-urban transition in human history. In 1970, China could be described as a country of "limited urbanization," where less than 20 percent of the national population lived in cities. By the early twenty-first century, the urbanization rate of China had officially reached 40 percent—the world's average for developing countries—and it is expected to pass the 50 percent mark within the next decade.

This would represent a net addition of around half a billion people to the Chinese urban population. Yet even these figures probably underestimate the magnitude of Chinese urbanization, especially given the country's current GDP per capita and its unusually high industrialization rate.[8] The suspected undercounting can be attributed to several factors. There are recently urbanized areas that have not yet been reclassified from their rural designation, and there are many migrants from the countryside in cities who are still not counted as part of the urban population. Undercounting, however, is not just a problem of time-lags in the demographic measurement process; it also reflects China's policies restricting population mobility and emphasizing urbanization in the countryside. While the growth of smaller cities has been encouraged, increasing constraints were put on the concentration of the population in the largest cities in the coastal region. These interventions, however, did not stop the enormous demographic pull and economic synergism of the coastal urban cores, with the paradoxical result that the areas with the highest reported urbanization rates are also where the largest numbers of undercounted city residents are located.

Unauthorized and often unreported migrants are an increasing problem in the largest cities. In Shanghai alone, the so-called floating population of unregistered internal migrants is estimated to be between 3 and 4 million, adding almost 20 percent to the officially recognized population. As the economic stimulus of these large coastal agglomerations extends well into their regional hinterlands, many nearby "rural towns" have been industrializing rapidly and mushrooming in size.[9] The population of the formerly rural township of Dongguan, near Hong Kong and Shenzhen, for example, has reached more than 5 million. These newly industrialized (and urbanized) areas and populations, not always included in overall national urbanization statistics, are a vital part of the growth of polycentric, networked and increasingly interconnected megacity regions.

The emergence of expansive megacity regions more generally and of huge urban galaxies in particular are important hallmarks of the urban global age, extending the urbanization of the world well beyond officially designated urban areas. Despite their growing importance, however, these emerging megalopolitan city regions are not yet given much attention in the urban research community, nor among policymakers and data collectors around the world. Richard Florida, known for his work on creative cities, has recently pointed out that no major global institution compiles and reports systematic data for what are perhaps the most significant territorial units of today's global economy.[10] Assisted by satellite images, Florida has prepared a preliminary and selective mapping of what he calls the "New Megalopolises," megacity regions interconnected in vast amorphous fields. These are highly extended versions of older notions such as Patrick Geddes' "conurbation," Jean Gottmann's "megalopolis" and increasingly resemble the shape of Constantinos Doxiadis' *eperopolis*, literally "continental city" in Greek.

Using a slightly modified version of Florida's estimates of megalopolitan populations, three vast continental zones of macro-regional urbanization can be identified: in Northeast Asia, Western Europe and North America. The subregions comprising these three zones are listed on Figure 10.3 (next page). The super continental conurbation of Northeast Asia is the largest of the three, reaching over 300 million people based only on official statistics. Japan, a highly urbanized and regionally integrated country, contributes 115 million—

MEGACITY REGIONS	POPULATION (millions)

ASIA

Greater Sapporo	4.6
Greater Tokyo	54.7
Mid–Japan Osaka–Nagoya	36.1
Ky–Fuko–Shima Fukuoka, Hiroshima, Kitakyushu	20.0
Greater Seoul Seoul, Busan, Daegu, Taejon, Gwangju	43.8
Greater Taipei Taipei–Chungli, Kaohsiung–Tainan, Taichung	16.7
Greater Beijing Beijing, Tianjin, Tangshan	36.5
Shang–King Shanghai, Nanjing, Hangzhou	50.5
Hong–Zeng Shenzhen, Guangzhou, Hong Kong	40.0
Total	**302.9**

EUROPE

Greater Glasgow	3.8
Greater London London, Manchester, Liverpool, Leeds–Sheffield, Birmingham	49.1
Greater Dublin	3.5
Greater Madrid	5.8
Lis–Port Lisbon, Porto	9.7
Greater Paris	14.6
Euro–Lowlands Ruhr–Cologne, Amsterdam–Rotterdam, Brussels–Antwerp, Lille	50.0
Euro–Sunbelt Barcelona, Marseille, Valencia, Lyon	24.8
Euro–Heartland Stuttgart, Frankfurt, Mannheim	22.0
Urb–Italy Milan, Rome, Turin	46.9
Greater Prague	10.6
Euro–East Katowice, Budapest, Vienna	20.1
Total	**260.9**

NORTH AMERICA

Bos–Wash Boston, New York, Philadelphia, Washington	54.8
Tor–Buf–Chester Toronto, Buffalo, Rochester, Ottawa, Montreal	20.1
Chi–Pitts Pittsburgh, Cleveland, Detroit, Cincinnati, Chicago, Minneapolis	45.0
Chatlanta Atlanta, Charlotte, Raleigh	19.6
Gulf Coast Houston, New Orleans	9.3
So–Flo Miami, Tampa, Orlando, Jacksonville	13.7
Daustin Dallas, San Antonio, Austin	9.1
Bajalta California San Francisco, Los Angeles, San Diego, Tijuana, Las Vegas, Phoenix, Mexicali	42.0
Total	**213.6**

10.3 The rise of the massive city

Large-scale regional urbanization is a less well-known aspect of the contemporary urban world. City-regions have unprecedented, quasi-continental sizes with major agglomerations in Europe, East Asia and North America considered the main drivers of the global economy.

almost half of which is concentrated around Tokyo and the narrow Kanto Plain. The megacity regions in the coastal areas of China, the Korean peninsula and Taiwan are other areas of high economic and demographic dynamism.

The transnational megalopolitan population of Western Europe adds up to more than 260 million, with the largest cluster of 50 million in what Florida describes as the Euro-Lowlands, a densely urbanized region spreading across six countries and characterized by the absence of an overarching metropolitan center such as London or Paris. Connecting with the Euro-Lowlands to the northwest is an extended Greater London, and to the south lie the Euro-Heartland and Urb-Italy, to use Florida's names. This composite arc of development, concentrated around what some have called Europe's "Blue Banana," constitutes the continent's economic engine. In North America, where the megalopolitan population surpasses 200 million, the older Gottmann-identified megalopolises of Bos-Wash and Chi-Pitts have been extended to include the Golden Triangle of southern Ontario, and areas to the south and west in the United States. To this Atlantic-oriented zone must be added a growing Pacific Rim megalopolis stretching from Vancouver to Tijuana. At its core is the earlier California megalopolis of San-San (San Francisco-San Diego), now bulging outwards into Mexico and Nevada to form what some call Bajalta California.[11]

Several other megalopolitan zones can be seen taking shape around the world, adding new dimensions to the concept of extended urbanization. In Latin America, for example, Brazil's two leading city regions, São Paulo and Rio de Janeiro, have grown increasingly connected, both physically and functionally, while maintaining differentiated roles and cultural identities, as well as increasing decentralization, a socioeconomic polarization and territorial fragmentation.[12] A similar integration process is occurring in neighboring Argentina between the two leading metropolitan regions of Buenos Aires and Rosario, along a 300-kilometer corridor on the lower Paraná-Río de la Plata river basin.[13] Moreover, due to the development of a connecting infrastructure and increasing flows, these megacity regions can be extended further to include an incipient formation stretching across five countries, from Santiago de Chile to Belo Horizonte.

The South Asian subcontinent, certainly one of the largest zones of macroregional urbanization in the world, also deserves special consideration. Just looking at the megacity regions of the subcontinent, the list would include Delhi (23.7), Mumbai or Bombay (21.2 million), Kolkata or Calcutta (15.9), as well as Karachi in Pakistan (22.3) and Dhaka in Bangladesh (16). In addition, the city-regions of Bangalore (9.5) and Hyderabad (8.5) concentrating high-tech industries, India's automotive center of Chennai or Madras (9.5) in the south, the textile, chemical and pharmaceutical center of Ahmedabad (6.5) in the west, and Pakistan's second urban-industrial center of Lahore (9.3) are all on the way to becoming megacity regions.[14]

These 10 South Asian agglomerations add up to over 140 million already, and there are at least 45 more million-plus city regions in India alone. Urban centers are expected to further integrate into synergetic megalopolitan formations with the regional infrastructure now being developed, particularly the Golden Quadrangle mega-project, a network of express motorways linking India's largest megacity regions. While much research is dedicated to the challenging problems urbanization generates in the subcontinent, Anglo-American literature has so far not engaged with processes of large-scale megalopolitan growth in India to the extent that, for example, the now burgeoning literature on urban China has. Florida does not include the subcontinent in his maps of the New Megalopolises either. How best to identify the subregions of this zone of accelerating urbanization, and assess its economic potential in the global economy as well as for more socially inclusive and environmentally sustainable forms of urban development, will have to await further research.

The urbanization of the world can be extended still further, beyond the 500 million-plus city regions and the emerging megalopolitan city regions and urban galaxies. More than ever before, it can be said that the Earth's entire surface is urbanized to some degree, from the Siberian tundra to the Brazilian rainforest to the icecap of Antarctica, perhaps even to the world's oceans and the atmosphere we breathe. Of course, this does not mean there are dense agglomerations everywhere, but the major features of urbanism as a way of life— from the play of market forces and the effect of administrative regulations, to popular cultural practices and practical geopolitics—are becoming ubiquitous. To a degree not seen before, no one on Earth is outside the sphere of influence of urban industrial capitalism.

Globalization, Urbanization, Industrialization

The extended urbanization of the world opens up new ways of understanding the globalization of capital, labor and culture, and the forces that have led to the formation of a new mode of capitalist development—variously described as post-Fordist, flexible and information based. The spread of urbanism and the characteristics of urban industrial capitalism can be seen as the distinguishing feature of the current round of intensified globalization. Commercial capitalism was globalized centuries ago, creating mercantile world cities such as Amsterdam and London. Financial capital was diffused globally with the spread of colonialism and imperialism, centering financial power in such global command posts as London, Paris and New York. Over the past 30 years, global trade and financial flows have been expanding rapidly, but what is most new and different has been the globalization of productive or industrial capital—that is, investments in the production of goods, services and information, facilitated by the revolution in information and communications technology, and reorganized in what is now called the New Economy or flexible capitalism.[15]

Urbanization, industrialization and globalization have been intimately tied together at least since the Industrial Revolution. Few human activities gain as much from being located in dense urban agglomerations as industrial production or manufacturing. The clustering of producers and consumers in urban space gives rise to a variety of agglomeration economies, which can lead to greater productivity and technological innovation, thus creating a potential snowball effect that stimulates urban industrial expansion. This holds true not only for making pins and needles but also for the production and exchange of information, and the development of what are now being called the creative or cultural industries. As we have rediscovered in recent years, cities in themselves, as socially constructed human habitats, generate positive forces of creativity, innovation and economic development, as well as negative spillover effects that aggravate social inequality and environmental sustainability. Studying the powerful forces that emanate from agglomeration has become the springboard for some of the most exciting research findings in contemporary urban and regional studies.[16]

Globalization and the formation of a New Economy have not been leading to a post-industrial or posturban era, as many have claimed, but rather to a new and different round of urban industrialization that, in turn, is creating a new and different global geography of economic development. For most of the past 200 years, advanced forms of industrialization have been tightly confined geographically to the major urban centers of the advanced capitalist countries and, for much of the twentieth century, a few industrialized socialist countries. The familiar international division of labor consisting of First, Second and Third Worlds, often roughly reduced to a North-South divide, arose primarily from differences in the organizational form and level of urban industrial production and consumption.

This fairly stable geo-structural and territorial division of the world into industrialized and industrializing countries has been radically reconfigured over the past 30 years through the spread of urban industrialism into what can be called "new industrial spaces." Several generations of "Asian Tigers" have created a growing list of Newly Industrialized Countries or NICs, from the early group that included Hong Kong, Taiwan, South Korea and Singapore to the most recent explosion of urban industrial production in China and India, the two most populous countries on Earth. Ireland, once the classic case of an internal colony, became a Celtic Tiger, and at least until the global recession, one of the richest countries in Europe. Regardless of the variable fate of individual cases, the point is that the list of NICs continues to grow as a new global geography of industrialization emerges in conjunction with the urbanization of the world.

New industrial spaces have also been developing within nation states, as formerly non-industrialized areas experience rapid urban industrialization. The evolving regional geography of industrial development in China is one example, the regional power shift between the so-called Frostbelt or Rustbelt and the Sunbelt in the United States is another. At the scale of the metropolitan region, many new industrial complexes have emerged in what were once suburban or rural areas. The best-known example of this metropolitan expansion of urban industrialism is probably Silicon Valley, but similar "technopoles" and "silicon landscapes" have been developing in many other major city regions. The decentralization of industrial geographies within metropolitan regions has thus been accompanied to varying degrees by a simultaneous recentralization, thereby intensifying the trend towards greater polycentricity.

Globally extended and reconfigured urban industrialization has generated a set of paradoxical consequences with regards to the spread of a global culture. On the one hand, the world has been experiencing an increasing social, economic and cultural homogenization, with cities beginning to look what some commentators call a Coca-colonization or McDonaldization or simply an Americanization of the world. At the same time, new patterns of differentiation and geographically uneven development are emerging, as the general processes of urban globalization take particular forms in the world's major city regions. With their cultural hybridity, physical and social fragmentation, Latin American megacity regions exhibit multiple predicaments and new opportunities of particular interest in the age of urban globalization.[17]

However one explains the changes mentioned above, a strong argument can be made that the differences existing 30 years ago between what could then be described as First, Second and Third World cities and urbanization processes, while not entirely disappearing, have significantly decreased, as virtually all cities are experiencing some degree of globalization. This has led to the unexpected situation, in which we can learn just as much about the new urbanization processes from Mexico City, Johannesburg and Shanghai as we can from New York, London and Berlin.

The old International Division of Labour (IDL) has been significantly transformed by these simultaneous processes of global homogenization and differentiation. What was once conveniently characterized as North vs South, for example, has been broken into three continental zones focused on the three super-sized urban fields mentioned earlier. These three global core regions, North American, Western European and East Asian—along with their continental spheres of influence—define a new tripartite Global Division of Labour (GDL, as global replaces international) linked within and between each zone by inter-urban networks that transcend national borders and connect in an encompassing worldwide web. Increasingly, the geographical and functional organization of the global economy has come to hinge around a new power hierarchy of financial command centers, led by the three great "capitals of capital" London, New York and Tokyo, and buttressed by a growing number of ever more interconnected and synergetic global cities.[18]

Every one of the city regions articulates with the global cultural and political economy in different ways, creating a mixture of similarity and difference, along with a growing range of emergent hybridities and "fusions." Understanding how the general features of global urbanization combine with local particularities in the growing list of city-regions, megacity regions and emerging megalopolitan city regions will require rigorous and comprehensive comparative analysis. Such analyses must be especially cognizant of the multiple scales at which the urbanization process is expressed: global, supranational, national, subnational and regional, metropolitan, municipal, neighborhood and local.[19] Recognizing the need for rigorous comparative analyses of these multiscalar urban globalization processes, we will examine some of the major changes taking place within the world's cities and city regions.

An important starting point in looking at the changes that have taken place within urban regions over the past 30 years is what Mike Davis recently described as the mass production of slums.[20] The expansion of urban poverty has made "extended" slums and burgeoning informal economies a distinctive feature of both the urbanization of the world and the globalization of the urban. According to the United Nations, one out of three urban dwellers—more than one billion people—live in slums. Some have put the figure even higher. The global concentration of urban poverty is the other, darker side of the growing concentration of economic wealth and political power. Urban areas containing poorly housed and underemployed populations have been part of the industrial capitalist city from the very beginning, but never before have more people lived in urban slums than today. The largest slum populations are in the megacity regions in developing countries, in some cases accounting for more than three-quarters of all local inhabitants, but the expansion of transnational migrations has also created growing slums of what are now called the immigrant working poor in such global power centers as New York, Los Angeles and London.

A Planet of Slums

We live today in what Davis provocatively calls a "planet of slums." He attributes this explosion of urban poverty to an unquestioned embrace of market forces, the adoption of neoliberal forms of local, national and supranational governance, the attendant acceptance of debilitating structural adjustment programs imposed by the World Bank and the International Monetary Fund, reduced state responsibilities for social welfare, and the adoption of policies fostering liberalization, deregulation and decentralization of national economies. The globalization of the urban hinges around the massive expansion of slums, but it is only part of the story of urban restructuring.

Simultaneous with the growth of urban poverty has been an almost equally large expansion of the professional-managerial-executive and "creative" class, a largely neoliberal elite that is having a particularly influential effect on shaping the city-building process. This has led to the emergence of a new dualism in the world's major cities, quite different from the older division between industrial bourgeoisie and urban proletariat. The overseers-underclass dualism has grown in many parts of the developed world at the expense of what was, in the decades after the Second World War, a burgeoning middle class. Although it is difficult to quantify, the world's megacity regions may be nearing the point where nearly one-third of the population consists of wealthy residents of guarded and gated communities, super-rich suburbs and gentrified neighborhoods in the urban core, often starkly located next to the worst slums.

One must be careful, however, not to overemphasize or simplify this dualism. The re-stratification of urban social structures is much more complex, fragmented and multilayered. The fortunate fifth of the income distribution, for example, is probably more politically and culturally heterogeneous and unpredictable than ever before. Not only is there the traditional division between new and old wealth, the nouveau riche now symbolically attached to the neologism of yuppie, there are many variations that have developed within the upper income brackets over the past 30 years. Especially relevant to the city-building process, for example, is a growing polarity between those who "secede" from the city and urban responsibility by moving into insular gated communities and those who commit themselves much more to urban regeneration as gentrifiers and inner-city dwellers.

Specialized ethnic niches further complicate the restratification of class, creating growing disparities of wealth and social mobility among immigrant populations, as well as aggravating divisions between domestic and immigrant populations of the same ethnic group. One must also be careful not to assume a withering away of the old middle class due to the growing polarization between the rich and the poor. In many ways, a new globalized middle class is being reconstituted in the world's major city-regions, in between (and sometimes overlapping both) the upper 20 percent and the lower 40 percent of the income ladder. And it too is increasingly heterogeneous, fragmented and unpredictable in its politics.

What is perhaps most important to understand about the new urban division of labor, and also about its spatial expression, is that it is significantly different from what it was 30 years ago. There are some pervasive continuities with the past based on class, race and gender, but simply projecting past trends on to the present, without recognizing what is new and different, can lead to misunderstanding and oversimplification. Take, for example, one of the characteristic features of the new urban geography that has been emerging in many of the world's major city regions, the so called hollowing out of the historic central city core of its former domestic population. Should this be seen as a form of urban decay, signaling perhaps the declining significance of downtown nuclei in an age of the Internet and instant communications? Or is it just a product of continued suburbanization or the inevitable effect of market forces? What are the implications of decentralization and reduced inner city densities for public policy?

One interesting case is Osaka. Once reputed to be the densest city in Japan, central Osaka is now almost devoid of a resident population, but has experienced little of the urban decay seen in the West. Its large downtown is thriving as a center for commerce, office activities, entertainment and the creative industries. The inner ring around the center has become increasingly dense, and suburbanization not only sprawled outwards but also densified and agglomerated as part of the vast and polycentric Mid-Japan megacity region.

Greater Los Angeles provides another model of inner-city transformation. After the Watts Riots in 1965, as many as 1.5 million white and black, largely working class, residents of the inner ring surrounding downtown left the area, many settling further out in the Greater Los Angeles region. In the past four decades, however, nearly 5 million immigrants have moved into the same area. When combined with increasing suburban densities, this has transformed what was once the least densely populated major American metropolis into what is now the densest urbanized area in the United States, passing New York City's metropolitan region for the lead in 1990. At another extreme are American cities such as Detroit and St Louis, where the outflow of people and jobs has been far greater than the inflow of new migrants, reducing the total city population (but not that of the surrounding city region) to less than half its former size. Statistics showing inner-city population losses in other parts of the world, the special case of declining city populations in former East Germany and several other former-socialist countries, and some recent data indicating some population growth slowdowns or even decline in the central cities of Paris, Seoul and Manila, has led to a growing research and public policy interest on "shrinking cities," engaging with the implications of declining urban growth rates.[21]

It is difficult to make any generalizations about what has been happening to the older urban cores in the megacity regions of the world, for the variations are almost endless. This is one of the reasons that policy and planning for historic city centers has become so challenging and so competitive, generating whole new industries related to city-marketing and branding. Urban image-making relies on events such as international exhibitions, Olympic Games and architectural extravaganzas such as the Gehry-designed Guggenheim Museum in Bilbao. With decentralization and deregulation, every local government vies with the others to attract attention, investment and tourists. Although some lip service is often given to local problems of poverty and inequality, such competitive urban "wars" for investment, jobs, visitors and global image have, in many cities, diverted attention from social services and community welfare, thereby aggravating the increasing economic inequalities and social polarization that have been an integral part of the new urbanization processes.

In contrast to the varying fates of central cities, there is a fairly clear general trend affecting suburbia. In many developed-world city-regions, in conjunction with what Deyan Sudjic has called the rise of the "100-mile city," there has been a growing urbanization of suburbia, another of the paradoxical twists on urban globality.[22] As older inner-city areas have their former populations replaced by new immigrants, new urban growth is taking place in outer cities or edge cities, as once relatively homogeneous dormitory suburbs become cities in themselves. In many parts of former suburbia, there are now more jobs than bedrooms, increasing numbers of cultural and entertainment facilities, and growing problems of crime, drugs and traffic gridlock. In many cases, the old sociospatial dualism of urbanism and suburbanism as separate and distinct ways of life has begun to disappear, as the modern metropolis evolves into what might be called an exopolis, with the ex-signifying a growing external or outer city, as well as meaning an urban form quite different from anything known in the past.[23]

The polycentricity and complex urban networking of the megacity region reflects these changes, as city space becomes increasingly unbounded, reconfigured and rescaled. Everywhere cities are being reshaped by three interrelated forces: the globalization of capital, labor and culture; the formation of a "new economy" variably described as flexible, global and information-intensive; and the facilitating effects of a revolution in information and communications technology. Cities are no longer spatially defined by and confined to their old metropolitan hinterlands or commuting zones, as urban economies become geographically reconfigured into multiple scales that connect the local with the global in a nesting of larger and larger nodal regions and inter-urban networks.

In this concatenation of regional scales, the globalization of the urban begins to coincide with the urbanization of the globe. Sustaining this transformative process has been an extraordinary expansion of population movements and migrations, transnational, intranational and within the urban region itself. The nature, impact and public policy response to these mass movements of people, from global diasporas to local neighborhood gentrification, differ greatly from place to place, but nearly everywhere they are creating what can be described as crises of governance and planning. Exploring this growing crisis of governance and planning brings us to the concluding section.

Towards a New Urban Agenda

We live in a world where nearly one in six inhabitants is a slum dweller—and the numbers are growing. One outgrowth of the discussion about the simultaneous urbanization of the globe and the globalization of the urban, is the expectation that the problems associated with urban poverty and inequality are likely to shape local and global politics in the twenty-first century more than ever before and in ways that few have anticipated. As these and other urban problems intensify, programs dealing with them at a national scale have tended to decline nearly everywhere. This has shifted attention and hopes for the future to other scales of intervention, from the global and supranational to the regional and local.

As this rescaling of the urban action agenda progresses, it is becoming increasingly apparent that the existing governmental structures and institutions are not yet organized to deal with the new responsibilities and, in many cases, adamantly resist any changes in their authority and power. Resurgent nationalisms weaken the efforts of transnational organizations such as the United Nations or the European Union to deal with growing problems of urban poverty and social exclusion. Attempts to foster regional coordination at the sub-national and metropolitan scales are often met with localisms, as existing local governments turn instead to more entrepreneurial city-marketing strategies, competing for tourist and investment dollars.

Any attempt to create a new global action agenda for the urban age must begin with an awareness of the tensions that exist between established governmental structures and the need to find ways of strengthening more progressive forms of planning and policymaking at every geographical scale. Rather than bemoaning the difficulties of this task, however, we will identify some of the most positive developments that have been occurring in recent years with regards to the challenges and opportunities facing the city-building professions.

Urban and regional planning in the future will be increasingly shaped by new ideas about the generative effects of urban and regional economies. Prominent economists, drawing on the pioneering work of Jane Jacobs in *The Economy of Cities*, have been arguing that what can be called the stimulus of urban agglomeration is the primary cause of economic development in the world today. Dense and heterogeneous cities and city regions have become the driving forces of the global economy, generating enormous wealth as well as technological innovation and cultural creativity.

Planners and policymakers are accordingly giving increasing attention to promoting efficient regional economic integration, developing clustered forms of economic activity and enhancing conditions conducive to creativity and innovation. But at the same time, urban agglomerations can also function to intensify inequalities and social polarization, as well as contributing significantly to global environmental degradation. One major challenge for the future of the city-building professions is to find ways to take advantage of the economic power of city regions and the creative capacity of dense and heterogeneous urban populations, while at the same time controlling the accompanying negative spillover effects, from widening income inequalities and global warming to increased intercultural friction and conflict. Finding an appropriate structure of local and regional governance is crucial.

As the global reaches into the urban and urbanization spreads around the globe, new movements are emerging that are likely to affect local efforts to deal with urban poverty and inequality. Struggles over environmental issues and poverty become simultaneously local, urban, metropolitan, regional, national, supranational and global issues. They include the rise of what some call global civil society, global or cosmopolitan citizenship and identity, and the global justice movement.

At the supranational regional scale, perhaps the most important counter-trend to the entrepreneurial approach to planning has been occurring within the European Union, one of the most important seedbeds for a New Regionalism—or at least the revival of the older welfare-oriented urban and regional planning that had declined significantly with the rise of neoliberal state policies in the 1980s, and the unabated market-driven globalization that has occurred ever since.

There are examples of improved metropolitan governance worldwide. The case of London deserves particular attention. Reversing the trend towards fragmentary governance and lack of explicit territorial planning, the Greater London Authority has been reinstated and now Londoners can elect a citywide mayor who will be responsible for London's sustainable development as a global city within the South-East of England, the UK and Europe. In Mexico City, where residents have also recently regained the right to vote for a municipal mayor in the Federal District, there has also been an increased cooperation between the national government, the District and the surrounding State of Mexico where more than half of the city region's population lives. In South Africa, the region of Gauteng is the first in the world to be officially described as a global city-region. Increased cooperation between the Johannesburg, Tshwane (former Pretoria) and Ekurhuleni (former East Rand) metropolitan councils is leading to joint development programs and planning frameworks that will allow the city region to attain a competitive position in the global economy while reversing the fragmentary and racially exploitative patterns of apartheid urbanism.

Not all metropolitan reforms are state initiated. In the United States, many of the metropolitan initiatives of "growth with equity" have emerged from civil society, and particularly from coalitions of community-based and grassroots organizations that, through multiscalar organizing and coalition building, have been able to advance innovative and effective forms of community based regionalism.[24] New approaches to "building resilient regions" have been encouraged from another nongovernmental source, the John D. and Catherine T. MacArthur Foundation, which in 2007 announced the creation of a new research network aimed at expanding knowledge of "how regions shape the response to major national and demographic challenges."

In Latin America, a wave of local democracy has also swept the region, as urban social movements have been able to enter progressive electoral coalitions gaining control of city governments.[25] Latin American cities have been producing highly innovative urban planning strategies, ranging from the low-cost and socially inclusive rapid-transit systems of Curitiba and Bogotá to the community architecture projects of Caracas.[26] It is clear that the global urban agenda should not be understood as a single and centralized project, largely in the hands of elite institutions and empowered professionals.

There are many different ways to achieve greater social and spatial justice in combination with sustained and equitable urban development, but these efforts will require working at multiple scales of governance and in increasingly eclectic conditions. For the city-building professions more generally, and architects and designers in particular, this represents a special challenge. As Rem Koolhaas argues, "[this is] the first generation of architects that has had a direct experience of working in so many different urban systems at any one time."[27] As a result, they have the opportunity to shape realities that are attuned to both the larger imperatives of the urban global age and the localized and unique conditions of each individual city region. Especially important here is the need to reflect upon the ways form-making and site-specific physical interventions interact with the economic dynamism of urban agglomeration and its capacity to generate creativity, innovation and economic development. The interaction here must be made to work effectively in both directions.

159

Notes

1   It would have been noticed that the world became predominantly urban much earlier if, for example, a consistent definition of cities was adopted worldwide based on population densities, land uses, sources of income and cultural norms—rather than maintaining country-specific administrative demarcations that are often arbitrarily drawn.

2   See Peter Hall, *The World Cities* (London: Weidenfeld and Nicolson, 1966); and John Friedmann and Goetz Wolff, "World City Formation: An Agenda for Research and Action," *International Journal of Urban and Regional Research* 6 (1982) 309-44.

3   Peter J. Taylor and Robert E. Lang have listed 50 terms used to conceptualize new metropolitan forms and another 50 describing inter-metropolitan functional relations. See Peter J. Taylor and Robert E. Lang, "The Shock of the New: 100 Concepts Describing Recent Urban Change," *Environment and Planning A* 36,6 (2004) 951-8.

4   See Allen J. Scott, ed., *Global City Regions: Trends, Theory, Policy* (New York: Oxford University Press, 2001).

5   An interesting statistic is that almost 25 percent of the cities on this list are national capitals. Looked at in another way, nearly all but the smallest countries have their capital cities on the list, suggesting a general trend for capital cities to have grown especially rapidly over the past few decades. This can be explained in part by the concentration of institutional, political, police and military power and control, offering at least the impression of greater safety and stability.

6   According to an updated online listing of the "principal agglomerations of the world" compiled by Thomas Brinkhoff, there were 503 million-plus city regions and 29 megacities as of 2013. See Thomas Brinkhoff, *Major Agglomerations of the World*, http://www.citypopulation.de/world/Agglomerations.html (accessed July 1, 2013).

7   African urbanism raises many challenges to Western concepts of cities and urban development, an emerging and insightful literature is now emerging on how to think through this new urban majority. See Jennifer Robinson, *Ordinary Cities: Between Modernity and Development* (London: Routledge, 2006); Abdou Maliqalim Simone, *For the City Yet to Come: Changing African Life in Four Cities* (Durham: Duke University Press, 2004); and Susan Parnell and Edgar Pieterse "The 'Right to the City': Institutional Imperatives of a Developmental State," *International Journal of Urban and Regional Research* 34, 1 (2010) 146-62.

8   Aimin Chen, "Urbanization in China and the Case of Fujian Province," *Modern China* 32, 1 (2006) 99-130.

9   John Friedmann, *China's Urban Transition* (Minneapolis: University of Minnesota Press, 2005) 39.

10 Richard Florida, "The New Megalopolis; Our Focus on Cities is Wrong. Growth and Innovation Come From New Urban Corridors," *Newsweek* July 3, 2006, special edition. See also Richard Florida, Tim Gulden, and Charlotta Mellander, "The Rise of the Mega-Region," *Cambridge Journal of Regions, Economy and Society* 1, 3 (2008) 459-76.

11 Michael Dear and Gustavo Leclerc, eds., *Postborder City: Cultural Spaces of Bajalta California* (New York: Routledge, 2003).

12 Brian J. Godfrey, "Revisiting Rio de Janeiro and São Paulo," *Geographical Review*, 89, 1 (1999) 94-121.

13 D. Silberfaden, Latitude 33°41'S, Latitude 59°41'W, in the Argentine presentation at the tenth Architecture Biennale Venice.

14 Brinkhoff, *Major Agglomerations of the World*.

15 Edward Soja, *Postmetropolis: Critical Studies of Cities and Regions* (Oxford/Cambridge, MA: Blackwell Publishers, 2000).

16 See for instance Michael E. Porter, "The Competitive Advantage of the Inner City," *Harvard Business Review* 73, 3 (May–June 1995) 55-71; Michael E. Porter, "Location, Competition and Economic Development: Local Clusters in a Global Economy," *Economic Development Quarterly* 14, 1 (February 2000) 15-34; Michael Storper,

The Regional World: Territorial Development in a Global Economy (New York: Guilford Press, 1997); Michael Storper and Anthony J. Venables, "Buzz: Face-to-Face Contact and the Urban Economy," *Journal of Economic Geography* 4, 4 (2004) 351-70; Richard Florida, *The Rise of the Creative Class: and How It's Transforming Work, Leisure, Community and Everyday Life* (New York: Basic Books, 2002); and Edward Soja, "Writing the City Spatially," *City* 7, 3 (2003) 269-81.

17 See for instance George Yúdice, *The Expediency of Culture: Uses of Culture in the Global Era* (Durham: Duke University Press, 2003) and Nestor García Canclini, "Makeshift Globalization," *The Endless City*, eds. Richard Burdett and Deyan Sudjic (London: Phaidon, 2007) 186-91.

18 Saskia Sassen, ed., *Global Networks, Linked Cities* (New York: Routledge, 2002); and Peter J. Taylor, *World City Network: a Global Urban Analysis* (New York: Routledge, 2004).

19 Particularly useful in understanding these multiple scales of global urbanization is the hybrid (if awkward-sounding) notion of glocalization. This neologism focuses attention on the regions in between the macro and the micro, the global and the local, tying together these multiple scales and highlighting the spatial interplay of the general and the particular, endogenous and exogenous effects. See for example Erik Swyngedouw, "Neither Global nor Local: "Glocalization" and the Politics of Scale," *Spaces of Globalization: Reasserting the Power of the Local*, ed. Kevin R. Cox (New York: Guilford Press, 1997) 137-66.

20 Mike Davis, *Planet of Slums* (London/New York: Verso, 2006).

21 Philipp Oswalt, ed., *Shrinking Cities* (Ostfildern-Ruit: Hatje Cantz, 2005).

22 Deyan Sudjic, *The 100 Mile City* (London: A. Deutsch, 1992).

23 Soja, *Postmetropolis*.

24 Manuel Pastor, Jr., Peter Dreier, J. Eugene Grigsby III, and Marta López-Garza, *Regions that Work: How Cities and Suburbs Can Grow Together* (Minneapolis: University of Minnesota, 2000).

25 Daniel Chavez and Benjamin Goldfrank, eds., *The Left in the City: Participatory Local Governments in Latin America* (London: Latin America Bureau, 2004).

26 See Guy Battle, "Sustainable Cities," *The Endless City*, eds. Richard Burdett and Deyan Sudjic (London: Phaidon, 2007) 386-93; and Richard Burdett and Miguel Kanai, "City-building in an Age of Global Urban Transformation," *Cities: Architecture and Society* (Venice: Marsilio, 2006) 3-23.

27 Rem Koolhaas, "On Working Cities," *Cities: Architecture and Society* (Venice: Marsilio, 2006) 74.

Figure Credits

10.1 For 1825 and 1900: Tertius Chandler and Gerald Fox, *3000 Years of Urban Growth, Volume 413* (New York: Academic Press, 1974); for 1950: United Nations Population Division, *World Urbanization Prospects—The 2005 Revision*. http://www.un.org/esa/population/publications/WUP2005/2005WUP_DataTables11.pdf; and for 2013: Thomas Brinkhoff, *Major Agglomerations of the World*. http://www.citypopulation.de.

10.2 United Nations Population Division, *World Urbanization Prospects—The 2005 Revision*. http://www.un.org/esa/population/publications/WUP2005/2005WUP_DataTables11.pdf.

10.3 Authors' own calculations based on Richard Florida, "The new Megalopolis; Our Focus on Cities is Wrong. Growth and innovation Come From New Urban Corridors," *Newsweek* 3 July 2006, special edition.

11
PLANETARY URBANIZATION

Neil Brenner and Christian Schmid

During the last several decades, the field of urban studies has been animated by an extraordinary outpouring of new ideas regarding the role of cities, urbanism and urbanization processes in ongoing global transformations.[1] Yet, despite these advances, the field continues to be grounded upon a mapping of human settlement space that was more plausible in the late nineteenth and early twentieth centuries than it is today.

The early twentieth century was a period in which large-scale industrial city-regions and suburbanizing zones were being rapidly consolidated around the world in close conjunction with major demographic and socioeconomic shifts in the erstwhile "countryside." Consequently, across diverse national contexts and linguistic traditions, the field of twentieth century urban studies defined its theoretical categories and research object through a series of explicit or implied geographical contrasts. Even as debates raged regarding how best to define the specificity of urban life, the latter was universally demarcated in opposition to a purportedly "non-urban" zone, generally classified as "rural." As paradigms for theory and research evolved, labels changed for each term of this supposed urban-rural continuum, and so too did scholars' understandings of how best to conceptualize its basic elements and the nature of their articulation. For instance, the Anglo-American concept of the "suburb" and the French concept of *la banlieue* were introduced and popularized to demarcate further sociospatial differentiations that were occurring inside a rapidly urbanizing field.[2] Nonetheless, the bulk of twentieth-century urban studies rested on the assumption that cities—or, later, "conurbations," "city-regions," "urban regions," "metropolitan regions," and "global city-regions"—represented a particular *type* of territory that was qualitatively specific, and thus different from the putatively "non-urban" spaces that lay beyond their boundaries.

The demarcations separating urban, suburban and rural zones were recognized to shift historically, but the spaces themselves were assumed to remain discreet, distinct and universal. While paradigmatic disagreements have raged regarding the precise nature of the city and the urban, the entire field has long presupposed the existence of a relatively stable, putatively "non-urban" realm as a "constitutive outside" for its epistemological and empirical operations. In short, across divergent theoretical and political perspectives, from the Chicago School's interventions in the 1920s and the rise of the neo-marxist "new urban sociology" and "radical geography" in the 1970s, to the debates on world cities and global cities in the 1980s and 1990s, the major traditions of twentieth-century urban studies embraced shared, largely uninterrogated geographical assumptions that were rooted in the late nineteenth- and early twentieth-century geohistorical conditions in which this field of study was first established.

During the last 30 years, however, the form of urbanization has been radically reconfigured, a process that has seriously called into question the inherited cartographies that have long underpinned urban theory and research. Aside from the dramatic spatial and demographic expansion of major megacity regions, the last 30 years have also witnessed several far-reaching worldwide sociospatial transformations.[3] These include:

- *The creation of new scales of urbanization.* Extensively urbanized interdependencies are being consolidated within extremely large, rapidly expanding, polynucleated metropolitan regions around the world to create sprawling "urban galaxies" that stretch beyond any single metropolitan region and often traverse multiple national boundaries. Such mega-scaled urban constellations have been conceptualized in diverse ways, and the representation of their contours and boundaries remains a focus of considerable research and debate.[4] Their most prominent exemplars include, among others, the original Gottmannian megalopolis of "Bos–Wash" (Boston–Washington DC) and the "blue banana" encompassing the major urbanized regions in western Europe, but also emergent formations such as "San San" (San Francisco-San Diego) in California, the Pearl River Delta in south China, the Lagos littoral conurbation in West Africa, as well as several incipient mega-urban regions in Latin America and South Asia.

- *The blurring and rearticulation of urban territories.* Urbanization processes are being regionalized and reterritorialized. Increasingly, former "central functions," such as shopping facilities, company headquarters, research institutions, prestigious cultural venues, as well as spectacular architectural forms, dense settlement patterns and infrastructural arrangements, are being dispersed outwards from historic central city cores, into erstwhile suburbanized spaces, among expansive catchments of small- and medium-sized towns, and along major transportation corridors such as superhighways and rail lines.[5]

- *The disintegration of the "hinterland."* Around the world, the erstwhile "hinterlands" of major cities, metropolitan regions and urban-industrial corridors are being reconfigured as they are functionalized—whether as back office and warehousing locations, global sweatshops, agro-industrial land-use systems, recreational zones, energy generation grids, resource extraction areas, fuel depots, waste disposal areas or corridors of connectivity—to facilitate the continued expansion of industrial urbanization and its associated planetary urban networks.[6]

- *The end of the "wilderness."* In every region of the globe, erstwhile "wilderness" spaces are being transformed and degraded through the cumulative socioecological consequences of unfettered worldwide urbanization. In this way, the world's oceans, alpine regions, the equatorial rainforests, major deserts, the arctic and polar zones and even the earth's atmosphere itself, are increasingly interconnected with the rhythms of planetary urbanization at every geographical scale, from the local to the global.[7]

In our view, these geohistorical developments pose a fundamental challenge to the entire field of urban studies as we have inherited it from the twentieth century: its basic epistemological assumptions, categories of analysis, and object of investigation require a foundational reconceptualization in order to remain relevant to the massive transformations of worldwide sociospatial organization we are witnessing today. Under contemporary conditions, therefore, the urban can no longer be understood with reference to a particular "type" of settlement space, whether defined as a city, a city-region, a metropolis, a metropolitan region, a megalopolis, an edge city or otherwise. Consequently, despite its continued pervasiveness in scholarly and political discourse, the category of the "city" has today become obsolete as an analytical social science tool. Correspondingly, it is no longer plausible to characterize the differences between densely agglomerated zones and the less densely settled zones of a region, a national territory, a continent or the globe through the inherited urban/rural (or urban/non-urban) distinction. Today, the urban represents an increasingly worldwide condition in which political-economic relations are enmeshed.

This situation of *planetary urbanization* means, paradoxically, that even spaces that lie well beyond the traditional city cores and suburban peripheries—from transoceanic shipping lanes, transcontinental highway and railway networks, and worldwide communications infrastructures to alpine and coastal tourist enclaves, "nature" parks, offshore financial centers, agro-industrial catchment zones and erstwhile "natural" spaces such as the world's oceans, deserts, jungles, mountain ranges, tundra and atmosphere—have become integral parts of the worldwide urban fabric. While the process of agglomeration remains essential to the production of this new worldwide topography, political-economic spaces can no longer be treated as if they were composed of discrete, distinct and universal "types" of settlement.[8] In short, in an epoch in which the idea of the non-urban appears increasingly to be an ideological projection derived from a long dissolved, preindustrial geohistorical formation, our image of the urban likewise needs to be fundamentally reinvented.

Already four decades ago, Henri Lefebvre put forward the radical hypothesis of the complete urbanization of society, demanding a radical shift in analysis from urban form to the urbanization process. However, a systematic application of this fundamental thesis has yet to be undertaken.[9] Perhaps, in the early twenty-first century, the moment is now ripe for such an undertaking? Indeed, in our view, the epistemological foundations of urban studies must today be fundamentally transformed, and Lefebvre's formulation provides a highly salient starting point for such an effort. The epistemological shift towards the analysis of planetary urbanization requires new strategies of concrete research and comparative analysis that transcend the assumptions regarding the appropriate object and parameters for urban research that have long been entrenched and presupposed within the mainstream social sciences and planning/design disciplines. In close conjunction with such new research strategies, the investigation of planetary urbanization will require major theoretical and conceptual innovations. We need first of all new theoretical categories through which to investigate the relentless production and transformation of sociospatial organization across scales and territories. To this end, a new conceptual lexicon must be created for identifying the wide variety of urbanization processes that are currently reshaping the urban world and, relatedly, for deciphering the new emergent landscapes of sociospatial difference that have been crystallizing in recent decades. Last but not least, we require adventurous, experimental and boundary-exploding methodological strategies to facilitate the empirical investigation of these processes. Whether or not a distinct field of urban studies will persist amidst such theoretical, conceptual and methodological innovations is a question that remains to be explored in the years and decades ahead.

Notes

1 Saskia Sassen, "New Frontiers Facing Urban Sociology at the Millennium," *British Journal of Sociology* 51, 1 (2000) 143-59; and Ananya Roy, "The 21ˢᵗ Century Metropolis: New Geographies of Theory," *Regional Studies* 43, 6 (2009) 819-30.

2 Robert Fishman, *Bourgeois Utopias* (New York: Basic Books, 1989).

3 Edward Soja and Miguel Kanai, "The Urbanization of the World," this book, Ch. 10; Tony Champion and Graeme Hugo, eds., *New Forms of Urbanization* (London: Ashgate, 2005); and Allen J. Scott, ed., *Global City-Regions* (London: Oxford, 2001).

4 Peter Hall and Kathryn Pain, eds., *The Polycentric Metropolis* (London: Earthscan, 2006); Richard Florida, Tim Gulden and Charlotta Mellander, "The Rise of the Mega-region," *Cambridge Journal of Regions, Economy and Society* 1 (2008) 459-76.

5 Thomas Sieverts, *Cities Without Cities: An Interpretation of the Zwischenstadt* (London: Routledge, 2003); and Joel Garreau, *Edge City* (New York: Anchor, 1992).

6 Roger Diener, Jacques Herzog, Marcel Meili, Pierre de Meuron and Christian Schmid, *Switzerland—An Urban Portrait* (Zurich: Birkhauser, 2006). See also Christian Schmid, "A Typology of Urban Switzerland," this book, Ch. 26.

7 Roberto Luis Monte-Mór, "What is the Urban in the Contemporary World?," this book, Ch. 17; and Bill McKibben, *The End of Nature* (New York: Random House, 2006).

8 Edward Soja, *Postmetropolis* (Cambridge, Mass.: Blackwell, 2000); Allen J. Scott, *Metropolis* (Los Angeles: University of California Press, 1988).

9 Henri Lefebvre, *The Urban Revolution*, trans. Robert Bononno (Minneapolis, MN.: University of Minnesota Press, 2003).

12
THE URBAN QUESTION UNDER PLANETARY URBANIZATION

Andy Merrifield

> If we cannot produce a new theory, and I agree it is not easy, we can at least find
> new words … If we find new words we can hope to produce a framework of
> understanding. Without a framework, any means of instrumentality are futile.
>
> –Rem Koolhaas[1]

Perspective and Prospective

Near the beginning of the chapter "Perspective or prospective?" in *Le droit à la ville*, the Marxist urban studies godfather, Henri Lefebvre, alludes to the godfather of science fiction, Isaac Asimov. Barely a paragraph long, Lefebvre doesn't elaborate on this allusion. Yet even in its brevity Lefebvre's remark is intriguing. In this chapter, I try to develop what Lefebvre means, or at least what *I think* he might mean. Specifically, I want to use his comments to frame the theoretical and political dilemmas that confront progressives in our age of planetary urbanization. For here, Lefebvre is projecting the urban trajectory of his day—1967, the centenary of Marx's *Capital*—22,500 years into the future, into the sci-fi imaginary of Asimov's magisterial *Foundation* series, a drama dominated by the giant planet "Trantor," with 40 billion inhabitants; its entire land surface, 75 million square miles, is a single city, a thoroughly urbanized society of dazzling administrative and technological complexity, dominating a vast galaxy.

From outer space, at nighttime, says Asimov, Trantor looks like a "giant conglomeration of fireflies, caught in mid-motion and still forever."[2] "Trantor's deserts and its fertile areas were engulfed," he says, "and made into warrens of humanity, administrative jungles, computerized elaborations, vast storehouses of food and replacement parts. Its mountain ranges were beaten down; its chasms filled in. The city's endless corridors burrowed under the continental shelves and the oceans were turned into huge underground aqua-cultural cisterns."[3] Canopied under a ceiling of millions of steel domes, like a colossal iceberg, nine-tenths of Trantor's social life takes place underground in climate-controlled air and light, with programmed downpours. Nobody recognized day from night any longer, whether the sun shone or not, and after a while few cared. The countryside is but a fuzzy memory based on ancient hearsay; only the Imperial Palace and Trantor's University have real green space. Newcomers would tell you that the air seemed thicker in Trantor, the gravity much greater, its sheer immensity unnerving.

Asimov gives us a brilliant vision of urbanization taken to the max, a veritable utopia-cum-dystopia. In mentioning Asimov, Lefebvre already recognized in the late 1960s the seeds of Trantor in our urban midst. Through Asimov, he seems to call on us to open up our *perspective* on thinking about urban life, daring us to broaden it to the largest remit possible. He wants us to grasp the totality of capitalist urbanization—wholesale and full-scale—to live with that starling *immensity*, to make it our own. We might then be able to think more clearly about politics—about *prospective*, progressive politics under planetary urbanization.

By the time Lefebvre published *La révolution urbaine*, he had begun hinting at this new reality: not as a sci-fi reality, but as something that was already there, now: The complete urbanization of society," he says. He is being ironic, of course, but only slightly, because, he adds: "This hypothesis implies a definition: 'urban society' is a society that results from a process of complete urbanization. Today, it's virtual, tomorrow it will be real."[4]

The progression/periodization is evident: we should no longer talk of cities as such, said Lefebvre in *Le droit à la ville*; urban society is more appropriate. Yet in *La révolution urbaine* he began thinking that we should not even be talking of urban society but of *planetary urbanization*, of the complete urbanization of society, of something that's both here and about to come here soon. Trantor is here—not quite—but we can expect it any day now.

Fast-forward four decades: Asimov's extraterrestrial universe seems closer to home than ever, closer to Lefebvre's own terrestrial prognostications—planetary urbanization is creating a whole new spatial world (dis)order. As in 2006, the balance had tipped: the majority of the world's inhabitants, 3.3 billion people, now lived in urban agglomerations, not in rural areas. By 2030, this figure is set to be 4.9 billion, some 60 percent of the world's population. By then, an extra 590,000 square miles of the planet will have been urbanized, a land surface more than twice the size of Texas, incorporating an additional

1.47 billion urban dwellers. If the trend continues, by 2050, 75 percent of the planet earth will be urbanized.[5] In truth, these facts and figures aren't very interesting to the political urbanist. The real point is that urbanization is increasing its reach everywhere; the urban is shapeless, formless and apparently boundless, riven with new contradictions and tensions that make it hard to tell where borders reside and what's inside and what's outside.[6] An infinite array of concepts have been brandished to identify what this new city form might be: endless city, shrinking city, 100-mile city, global city, megacity, arrival city, indistinguishable city. What is interesting about these labels is that all try to follow Lefebvre's lead, all try to come to grips with the death of their object, or death of their subject—the city—knowing full well that something has happened, is happening, and that it is hard to get an analytical grip on it. The city was once whole and solid, steel and concrete, there and only there. Now, "it" is slippery, no longer an "it," not responding to the old laws of gravity. What is interesting, too, is that every label, no matter how diverse, how insightful, still struggles to retain the social scientific rigor of the term "city." Lefebvre was not so convinced. Urban society, he had announced in *Le droit à la ville*, "constitutes itself on the ruins of the city."[7] In *The Urban Revolution*, he reiterated this claim, more boldly and in increasing decibels: "the city exists only as a historical entity," "[it] no longer corresponds to a social object. Sociologically, the city is a pseudo-concept."[8] For that reason, let us stop using the term "city," he urges, let us change our terminology; let us name a new object that is not a physical object in the usual sense of the term; let us use instead the term "urban society," or "urban fabric;" let us try to identify a new theoretical and virtual object that is in the process of becoming. Urban fabric does not narrowly define the built environment of cities, but, says Lefebvre, indicates all manifestations of the dominance of the city over the countryside. Meanwhile, "urban society" serves a theoretical need and frames a political ambition. It is a hypothesis that is both a point of arrival for a bigger perspective on existing reality, and a point of departure for studying a new, emergent reality.

Blind Fields and Ways of Seeing

Urban society, Lefebvre says, outstrips our cognitive and sensory facilities; the mind boggles at the sensory overload that today's urban process places upon us. The problem, though, is compounded if we continue to think "city," perceive things through a "city" lens, through the notion of "objects," "categories" and "things," and through the traditional language and concepts of industrial growth. We need to change our perspective, rethink the urban, he says, in order to think prospectively.[9] Otherwise our epistemology will grope in a veritable "blind field." Urbanization is not a highly developed manifestation of industrialization, but—and this is the startling thing about Lefebvre's "urban revolution" thesis—industrialization has been a special sort of urbanization all along. Lefebvre flips the traditional Marxist notion of the historical development of the productive forces on its head; Marx thought industrialization had a sense, was its own finality, being the process as well as the product of the capitalist mode of production.

Marx and Engels never provided an explicit "urban mode of production," says Lefebvre, but if we look closely at their *oeuvre*, in a way they did: the city was itself a developmental force, the seat of modern industry, of the division of labor, of the reproduction of labor-power, of technological innovation; and the rise of the industrial city was not only vital for the expansion of productive forces, it was also politically crucial for an ascendant bourgeoisie asserting itself in the passage from feudalism to capitalism.[10] Marx did not know, and could never have known, that urbanization *harbors* the logic of industrialization. Marx had not seen that industrial production *implies* the urbanization of society; that mastering the potentialities of industry demands a specific understanding of the urban process. Beyond a certain level of growth, urbanization creates industrial production, *produces* industrialization, furnishes fertile conditions for the latter, converting industrial contradictions into contradictions of the city, eventually posing anew the urban question, converting it into the question of planetary urbanization.

The urban is now an ontological reality inside us, one that behooves a different *way of seeing*: it is a *metaphilosophical* problem of grappling with ourselves in a world that is increasingly urbanized. Another "way of seeing," another way of conceiving urbanization in our mind's eye, is to grasp it as a complex adaptive system, as a chaotic yet determined process.[11] As a concept, even a "virtual concept," the term "planetary urbanization" already connotes a shift in perspective, conjures up stirring imagery, maybe even rhetorical imagery that is seemingly extraterrestrial and futuristic. Already we are propelled into a realm in which our perceptual parameters are being stretched, broadened, opened out; somehow four-dimensionality seems dated. "Planetary" suggests something more alive and growing, something more vivid than the moribund "global" or "globalization." "Planetary" truly charts the final frontier, the telos of any earthly spatial fix, of an economic, political and cultural logic that has not been powered by globalization but is one of the key constituent ingredients of globalization, of the planetary expansion of the productive forces, of capitalism's penchant to annihilate space by time, and time by space.

The inner boundedness of the traditional city and of our traditional notion of the city form was prised open by the advent of the industrial city; by capitalist industrial production shedding its geographical and temporal fetters; by the development of new modes of transport; by the invention and reinvention of new technologies, products and infrastructure; by sucking people in when business cycles surged, only to spit them out when markets dipped. From once being absolute spaces, cities became relative spaces, spaces relative to one another in what would, in the second half of the twentieth century, become a global hierarchy, dictated by comparative economic advantage. This historical shift from the absolute to the relative preoccupied Lefebvre in his two great books from the 1970s: *The Urban Revolution* and *The Production of Space*.[12] He had taken these circumstances as somehow revolutionary, revolutionary in the Gramscian sense: as a passive revolution —pregnant with all things contrary, for sure, with progressive possibilities, yet counter-revolutionary, a kind of revolution from above, one in which, as Marx and Engels said in *The Communist Manifesto*, "the bourgeoisie had played a most revolutionary part."[13]

So when Lefebvre urges us to reframe the city as "the urban," he is urging us to abandon the standard frame, to reposition our vision and redescribe what we see as a Cubist artist might have seen it. This was akin to an Einsteinian revolution in the spatial and human sciences; akin to when Einstein began devising his general theory of relativity, problematizing the Newtonian conception of gravity, with its assumptions of absolute time and space. It was a new way of seeing our world, even if it all went beyond our immediate world, beyond our own capacity to see. Einstein's cosmology was itself the harbinger of quantum theory, for the probabilistic theories of "complementarity" and "uncertainty" pioneered in the 1920s and 1930s by Niels Bohr and Werner Heisenberg—even though Einstein had a hard time accepting that role. Moving away from the notion of a *city* toward *the urban* expressed a paradigm shift on a par with Einstein, a shift from the absolute to the relative, an affirmation of curved time and space, an acceptance that capitalist gravity does not only occur over absolute space, over a passive surface; space and time are themselves capitalist constructs, and the mass and velocity of commodities, of capital and money shifting around the market universe, create their own bending and warping of time and space, their own space-time dimensionality. The virtual reality of global financial markets plays havoc with isotropic planes of space and with linear conceptions of time, of present and future, confirming time's arrow, not only warping space but physically tearing it apart, too, creating a hidden speculative realm of financial quarks and neutrinos coursing forwards and backwards at the speed of light—at the touch of a trader's keyboard.

Concrete Abstractions and Abstract Expressionism

If a city is a complex adaptive system, the change in tack from "cities" (in the plural) toward "the urban" (in the singular) marks a simplifying movement, an analytical sidestep from the concrete to the abstract. The urban, we might say, is more precisely a *concrete abstraction*, the terrain of theoretical knowledge—or, in Lefebvre's lexicon, an "illuminating virtuality."[14] Thus, the urban represents a theoretical object and a "possible object," a *concrete abstraction* similar to how Marx posits the *world market* as the very basis of capitalism; to be sure, we could easily transpose "urban" for "world market" without losing any of Marx's clarity of meaning.

In *Capital, Volume III*, Marx said, "the immanent necessity of this mode of production is to produce the world market on an ever-enlarged scale."[15] In the *Grundrisse*, the sentiment is redoubled: "the tendency to create the world market is directly given in the concept of capital itself. Every limit appears as a barrier to be overcome."[16] In *Theories of Surplus Value—Part III,* he says it is "only foreign trade, the development of the market to a world market, which causes money to develop into world money and abstract labor into social labor. Abstract wealth, value, money, hence abstract labor, develop in the measure that concrete labor becomes a totality of different modes of labor embracing the world market."[17] In the sense that Marx describes things here, the world market is, like Lefebvre's "urban," an actual reality and a concept of reality. The world market and the urban are real enough, vital necessities for the reproduction of capitalism on an expanded scale; both are embodied in nameable people, in living agents and actual economic practices, in institutions and organizations; both are a vast web of exchange relations based around money and capital and culture. Yet, at the same time, both should be conceived as fluid processes circulating around the globe; both flow as non-observable phenomena, too.

Another way in which we might frame "the urban" is actually the way Spinoza conceived substance in Part I of *Ethics*. Substance, for Spinoza, is the very essence of nature and reality, its bedrock content, indivisible in itself and only perceivable and conceivable through its manifold and manifold *attributes*. Each attribute, says Spinoza, "expresses the reality or being of the substance."[18] Substance is, of course, Spinoza's pantheistic theory of God, his notion that God is immanent in all reality, including ourselves; but maybe the form of this notion holds, too, for the immanent nature of the urban, for its complex ontological tissuing, for the fabric that now clothes our daily lives. What is being affirmed here is the urban as a single, indivisible substance whose attributes—the built environment, transport infrastructure, population densities, topographical features, social mixes, political governance—are all the formal *expressions* of what pervades it ontologically. These attributes, in short, are how the urban looks and how it can be seen and known.

Like the giant drip canvases of Jackson Pollock, and the fractals his art is meant to represent, there is chaos to these attributes yet underlying order to its substance, to *the* substance, to the underlying urban structure. If Cubist art captured the relativizing tendencies and contortions of an emergent urban space, the spontaneous flowing skeins and explosive nebulae of Pollock's late Abstract Expressionism offer pictorial representations of the formless form of planetary urbanization. It is often said of Pollock's mural-size drip paintings, especially those completed between 1947 and 1950, that they give the impression of infinite expandability, an experiential feeling of expansion and enlargement, a volatile dynamism that seems to want to break free of its own borders.[19] As Pollock himself was wont to claim, "here there's no center, no beginning, no middle or end"; entering necessitates a daring leap onto a moving train, not knowing quite where it is headed, only having a vague sense of where it has been. "Unframed space" is how Pollock's widow, artist Lee Krasner, described these paintings; boundless kinetic energy, chaotic and dense processes of high complexity containing an almost hidden scaling order—just like contemporary urbanization.[20]

Pollock's skeins and swirls, spirals and drips are often so intense, so dense, that they engulf the whole canvas; there is no space left, little daylight between buildings and roads, no more developable canvas surface. The imagery is electrodynamic, hydraulic and energetic, and somehow quintessentially urban. What is equally significant here is how this perspective evokes what Clement Greenberg called "the crisis of the easel picture," the crisis of the classic framing—maybe the classic framing of the city.[21] Greenberg's intent was to affirm the de-centered, polyphonic picture, one that did away with an upright viewpoint and dispensed with any beginning, middle and end. Greenberg invoked a principal ingredient: "fatal ambiguity."[22]

Chaos and repetition cohere in free-flowing composition, mimicking the flows of capital unleashed in the deregulated world market. Flows of investment that produce space, that seemingly have the same vital, spontaneous energy of a Pollock loop, power the "secondary circuit" of capital into real estate, a circuit of investment that formerly ran parallel to the "primary circuit" of capital, to industrial production, but which now, Lefebvre says, has grown to be relatively more important in the overall global economy.[23] The secondary circuit flows as fixed and usually immovable capital, such as office blocks and transport infrastructure, roads and warehouses, marinas and apartment complexes, a whole built investment for production and consumption, all of which has its value imprisoned in space and cannot be devalued without immanent destruction.[24]

The secondary circuit was once a "buffer" against crisis, says Lefebvre; now we know that it is the mainstay of a global and increasingly planetary urban economy, one of the principal sources of capital investment, and hence over the past 15 to 20 years the medium and product of a worldwide real estate boom.[25] But the secondary circuit is a source of new instabilities and problems, too, particularly when it gets lubricated by financial (fictitious) capital and underwritten by the state. In the early 1970s, Lefebvre said this secondary circuit got caught up in the "consensual" politics of state neomanagerialist bureaucrats negotiating with a new species of entrepreneurial private-sector neoliberals. In the 1980s, the neoliberal paradigm foisted themes of growth, productivity and competitivity upon the dominant political-economic ideology, running roughshod over concerns for equality, democracy and social justice. Transnational monopoly capital began to gobble everything up everywhere in order to increase value-added and accumulate capital. Capital danced to the same frantic beat that Marx sketched in his *Manifesto*. The explosion of urban growth has consequently been a process of uneven development, of homogeneity and fragmentation. Rural places and suburban spaces have become integral moments of neoindustrial production and financial speculation, becoming absorbed and being reconfigured into new world-regional zones of exploitation, into megalopolitan regional systems, a phenomenon that also swallowed up old-style city-forms, as urbanization shed its skin and corroded its shell.

Never before—even more than in Lefebvre's day—has the urban process been so bound up with finance capital and with the caprices of the world's financial markets. The global urbanization boom, with its seemingly insatiable flows into the secondary circuit of capital, has depended on the creation of new mechanisms to wheel and deal fictitious capital and credit money, on new deregulated devices for legalized looting and finagling, for asset stripping and absorbing surplus capital into the built environment. David Harvey neatly labels all this "accumulation by dispossession," upgrading and updating Marx's theory of "primitive accumulation," mobilizing it in a twenty-first-century neoliberal context.[26] Accumulation by dispossession signals other fresh terrains for speculation and market expansion: asset-stripping through mergers and acquisitions, raiding of pension funds, biopiracy, privatization of hitherto common assets such as water and other public utilities, and the general pillaging of hitherto publicly owned property. Baron Haussmann once tore into central Paris, into its old neighborhoods and poor populations, dispatching the latter to the periphery while speculating on the center; the built urban form simultaneously became a property machine and a means to divide and rule; today, neo-Haussmannization, in a similar process that integrates financial, corporate and state interests, tears into the globe, sequesters land through forcible slum clearance and eminent domain, valorizing it while banishing former residents to the global hinterlands of postindustrial malaise.

Separation and Encounters: "The Urban Consolidates"

Such universalizing tendencies based on market relations create unification and integration, positive, dynamic energy and the creative power of attraction and incorporation; yet, as in all particle physics, there is also negative energy repulsion, minus charges, generating a dialectical force field in which centers oppose peripheries. The demarcation is no longer a definitive split between strict opposites; nor is it any simple urban-rural, North-South divide. Rather separation, Lefebvre would have it, is *immanent* within the accumulation of capital itself, *immanent* within its secondary circuit of capital. "In this case," he says, "the frontier line doesn't pass between the city and the country, *but is within the interior of the phenomenon of the urban*, between a dominated periphery and a dominating center."[27]

Separation and segregation are social realities that Lefebvre hates. They are the enemy of urbanization, he says, "the enemy of assemblies and encounters," profoundly anti-urban impulses, enemies of what his own potted definition of "the urban" is: centrality in space, assembly in space, encounters in space, a dense and differential social space.[28] Separation "breaks the unifying power of urban form."[29] But the dialectical form of the urban is, of course, that it is formless, formless because urbanization tends to break any limits that try to circumscribe its own form. It is like trying to know, with certainty, both the movement and position of a subatomic particle, both its wave and particle characteristic— the paradox between process and product, between movement and outcome, between urbanization and the urban. However, at the same time, there is, strangely, a form of sorts to the urban— even if that form is empty in itself: it is always relative form, floating form, contingent and uncertain form, only becoming real, only beginning to define itself ontologically when the urban is filled by a certain notion of proximity, by people and activity, by events coming together in this proximity, creating concentration and simultaneity, as well as density and intensity.

This is doubtlessly why the idea of "urban fabric" or "urban tissue" is such powerful imagery, so suggestive a terminology. With it, we can begin—or should be able to begin—to grasp the urban as organic tissue, as fine-grained texturing, as a mosaic and fractal form that has some delicate content, some feel to it, something we can touch and manipulate in our own conceptual hands, think feelingly, as it were. We know when it is there—and when it is not. The urban creates nothing, is nothing, serves no purpose and has no reality *outside* of a human reality—outside of exchange, outside of union, outside of human proximity, human concentration and human encounter. "The signs of the urban," Lefebvre says, "are signs of assembly: the things that promote assembly (the street and its surface, stone, asphalt, sidewalks) and the requirements for assembly (seats, lights)."[30] The urban is, he says:

> pure form: a place of encounter, assembly, simultaneity. This form has no specific content, but is a center of attraction and life. It is an abstraction, but unlike a metaphysical entity, the urban is a concrete abstraction, associated with practice. Living creatures, the products of industry, technology and wealth, works of culture, ways of living, situations, the modulations and ruptures of the everyday—the urban accumulates all content. But it is more than and different from accumulation. Its content (things, objects, people, situations) are mutually exclusive because they are diverse, but inclusive because they are brought together and imply their mutual presence. The urban is both form and receptacle, void and plenitude, superobject and nonobject, superconconsciousness and the totality of consciousness.[31]

Few, perhaps, have so beautifully defined something so indefinable.

The urban is nothing in itself, nothing outside dynamic social relations, a coming together of people. As long as human beings can come together, as long as separation can be resisted, there is always a possibility of *encounters* between people. We must offset separation, Lefebvre insists, separation between people and things; we must overcome the obstacles that promote opacity of relationships, that restrict separated particularities coursing around in prefabricated space. In *The Urban Revolution,* Lefebvre uses another beautiful turn of phrase: *l'urbain rassemble* (the urban consolidates).[32] The urban brings everything together, and transforms everything in that coming together: capital and goods, people and information, activity and conflict, confrontation and cooperation. The urban concentrates things, intensifies, creates simultaneity and difference, creates difference where no awareness of difference existed; ditto, what was once distinct and isolated becomes conscious of its own universality in that particularity. The urban consolidates: it is both particle and wave, flow and thing; its own random uncertainty principle that prevails in everyday life. Yet if we follow Lefebvre's own premise about urban society, about urban reality, the more urbanization continues to carpet over the whole world, the more encounters are likely to take place, and the more a *politics of the encounter* will punctuate and define our urban landscape of the future.

The urban is not the passive surface over which people encounter other people: the sheer proximity of people to other people, the sheer simultaneity of activities, of events and chance meetings *is the very definition of the urban itself*. In encountering one another, people produce space, urban space; they become urban people, Lefebvre says, "polyvalent, polysensorial, capable of complex and transparent relationships with the 'world.'"[33] Density intensifies the capacity for encounters, and encounters intensify the capacity of that density. This is a shifting conjoining of people, a kind of kaleidoscope in floating space, a spatial kaleidoscope, one that has little to do with absolute location. It is an understanding, too, that problematizes the right to the city: right to *what* city?[34] If urbanization is planetary, if the urban—and urban society—is everywhere, does this mean the right to the metropolitan region, the whole urban agglomeration? Does it still make sense to talk about the right to the city, as if this is something monocentric and clear-cut? The city is dead, classical humanism is dead, Lefebvre announces, gleefully, provokingly; but the urban persists, he says, grows and grows, as does the yearning for another sort of humanism, and for another sort of urban praxis.

So if the urban process is open-ended and if urbanization is global and boundless, any transformative politics presumably need to be likewise. If one loses the right to the city, then one gains a capacity to forge a politics based upon the encounter—a more freefloating, dynamic and relational militancy, to be sure, yet one perhaps more apt for our age of formless metropolitanization, one more attuned to a political landscape in which new social media can and have become subversive weaponry. In any politics of the encounter, the urban is a *place*, a site for action, not an actor itself; to see the urban as an actor is to fetishize the urban, is to fetishize space. As an "it," the urban does nothing in itself; its role is that of a dynamic sociospatial sphere in which the *betweenness* of people is ever so much more intense, ever so much more immediate and palpable, ever more likely to erupt should that social proximity and diversity, that concentration and simultaneity, elicit human bonding or human breakdown. Almost always will meaningful encounters comprise the construction of use values as opposed to the appropriation of exchange values; and almost always will meaningful encounters unfurl on streets that now internalize the world, streets that we can rename *world market streets*, urban streets that express a fragile planetary ecology as well as a rapacious global economy.

We have witnessed the politics of the encounter on the streets of Tunis, Cairo, Athens and Madrid—and in Manhattan, with Occupy Wall Street protests. In all these instances, encounters unfold in the heart of "the city," yet the stakes of organization and protest are not about the city *per se*; rather, they are something about *democracy*, in conditions of capitalist crisis, something more vast and simple than the city as we once knew it, ensembles of bodies, hastened together by digital media such as Facebook and Twitter. The Occupy Wall Street movement began in September 2011, when a handful of dogged activists ventured to the center of America's financial universe, justifiably griping about growing income inequality and the stranglehold of big money and corporations over US democracy. The turnout was small and its impact initially disappointing. But within a month, amazingly, a social movement was taking hold, and gathering strength and numbers; the protest suddenly captured popular imagination—not only of ordinary Americans but of disaffected people worldwide.

Encamped in Lower Manhattan's Zuccotti Park, thousands of demonstrators began organizing themselves without organizations or leaders. An online global "conversation," mobilizing favorable public opinion, soon grew as offline street protests. Inspired by "Arab Spring" uprisings, it took place across the planet: not only in New York but in Los Angeles, Madrid, Rome, Stockholm, Lisbon, London, Sarajevo, Hong Kong, Berlin, Athens and Sydney (the list is in no way exhaustive). In the process, demonstrators everywhere have revealed themselves and shown to the world that masses of young and old people share the same sense of frustration and rage. Along the way, *indignados* have discovered their own numbers: "We-are-the-99-percent!" Participants have simultaneously acted and reacted, been both affected and affecting; joy and celebration, tenderness and abandon, online and offline activism, all have found structuring, all somehow find definition.

Centrality and Citizenship: Here Comes Everybody?

Toward the end of his life, Lefebvre suggested that "the right to the city," as a proverbial "cry and demand," "implies nothing less than a new revolutionary conception of citizenship."[35] Typically, Lefebvre never tells us what he means by "revolutionary citizenship." Yet we might infer today that revolutionary citizenship has to imply something other than the right to the city, which is too inward-looking in its political expressiveness. Citizenship must be conceived as something *urban*, as something territorial, yet one in which this territoriality is narrower and broader than both "city" and "nationality"; a citizen of the block and neighborhood becomes a citizen of the world, a universal citizen rooted in place, encountering fellow citizens across the corridor and at the other end of the planet. Urbanization makes this sense of belonging possible, makes it both broader and narrower, even as it sometimes rips up the foundation of one's own dwelling space.

This kind of citizenship is one in which *perception* replaces passport and *horizon* becomes almost as important as habitat. This perception is simultaneously in place and in space, offline somewhere local, and online somewhere planetary, somewhere virtual. If we want to call this perception a newly formulated cognitive map in our heads, we can.[36] What is important in this mapping is that it maps the totality, that it works when people see these two realms coming together, when perception (as a structure of feeling) and horizon (as a way of seeing) conjoin, somehow meet one another, *encounter* one another, suddenly give rise to a singular political awareness, to a potential political citizenship.

The politics of the encounter are not about the right to the city. In the right to the city, politics hold that there is still something solid to reclaim, to have a right over, like the

Communards reclaiming central Paris when there was a clear-cut center. The politics of the encounter hinge upon another conception of *centrality* which is not necessarily about being at the center of things; it does not imply some absolute center, geographically located in absolute space, but is a locus of actions that attract and repel, that structure and organize a social space, that define the urban. Centrality is not the way Lefebvre once defined it in *Le droit à la ville*, as an absolute center of a city that needs taking back; urban politics cannot invoke that model anymore.[37] Instead, centrality is something that is the cell form of the urban, it is atomic structuring, its *sine qua non*.

Centrality is crucial to any politics of encounter because it is through the encounter that centrality unfolds; this, in turn, flips back dialectically because centrality then makes more encounters possible. Centrality calls out for content, for people and acts, for situations and practical relationships. It implies a simultaneity, a simultaneity of everything that comes together in a social act at a point, around that *node*, and at a certain time. Centrality is movable, always relative, never fixed, always in a state of constant mobilization and negotiation; sometimes it de-centers itself. Invariably, it requires something more open, more *horizontal*. Here the encounter expresses an encounter between people that has become an encounter between *citizens*, people who no longer ask for their rights, for the rights of man, for the right to the city, for human rights: these citizens meeting one another make no rights claims, posit no empty signifiers.[38] They don't even speak—not in the conventional sense of the term; they just do, just act, affirm themselves as a group, as a collectivity, as a "general assembly," wanting to take back that which has been dispossessed. They don't plead with or ask any interlocutor for anything abstract, for they have little expectation of any rights, and don't want any rights granted. If they say anything, citizens of the encounter, citizens of the occupation, speak a language that the group has only just collectively invented.

Occupations like encounters in Zuccotti Park and at London's St. Paul's Cathedral aren't hippie things, aren't like 1968; it would be a mistake to draw too many historical parallels, other than that both movements drummed drums and sang joyous songs. Forget 1968: today's urban occupational politics are something radically new and different, something fresher, more futuristic, electric rather than acoustic. The greatest difference forty-odd years on are the *social media*: they change everything; all bets are now off, and, indeed, all bets are very much now on. Social media change the *tactics*, the *tempo* and the *terrain* of any activism —the three Ts. True, the protagonists are also young and usually educated, sometimes super-educated; almost everywhere, a disproportionate percentage of protestors hail from privileged groups from the highest rungs of society. And yet, for these privileged, college-educated kids, an upending economy shows no signs of letting them benefit from any rosy capitalistic future. Today's young activists form a loose coterie of "youth-interrupted," the careerless, prospectless, assetless generation—the NINJA (no income, no job and no assets) generation, as Gordon Gekko called them in Oliver Stone's film *Wall Street 2: Money Never Sleeps*.[39]

Yet they're wising up fast, knowing that they can no longer have any expectations, that the reality of the *now* merits no expectations. What they have voiced is a broadly anti-capitalist agenda, a systemic indignation. And participants gel because of affinity, because of a common identification, because they share and want to express common notions, about themselves and about their world. Meanwhile, the gelling takes hold quasi-anarchically as organization spreads out like a tentacle. Social media are central to helping all this come into play, come into being, into becoming; to helping transform a virtual presence into a physical presence, and vice versa. Citizens in the encounter comprise disparate groups of people who have an uncanny knack of engineering "smart spontaneity," of creating encounters in the heat of the moment and in the heat of the movement. Like bourgeois production they arrange just-in-time rendezvous. Twitter and Facebook, mobile phones and SMS messaging, Blackberry BBM texting, have all collapsed space and diminished the time of organizing.

Social media enable groups to often punch above their weight, to mobilize the few while having the significant impact of the many. At the same time, anonymous minorities soon discover that they are not so anonymous and alone as they once thought, that others who are like them are out there, too, are everywhere, and that they are actually an emergent majority, one in the making, one making itself; if not a "Here Comes Everybody," then certainly a "Here Comes Every*buddy*."[40] The pun is James Joyce's, from *Finnegans Wake*, seemingly giving the nod to Facebook addicts everywhere, to the millions upon millions who now cohere as a sort of "mega-underground."[41] What is significant about this "mega-underground" is that its virtual reality has revealed itself in actual material reality, on the ground somewhere, in the formation of face-to-face groups, in the formation of crowds of occupiers, stepping out of the shadows. A disconnected group is now getting connected, a mega-underground casting off its invisibility to embody itself in physical space.

The tactics of this movement, as well as the tempo of its dynamics, of its ebbing and flowing and crowd coalescence, of its just-in-time activism, create a new terrain of struggle, different from the streets of Paris in the 1960s, different from the campus revolts, different from the barricade-building of old. Just as it is silly to think that revolutions are realized online, it is almost as silly to underplay how strong-tie and weak-link politics nourish each other. In a sense, together, they create a new time and space of protest; the temporal aspect is perhaps obvious, the spatial perhaps not. Indeed, this new space is a space neither rooted in place nor circulating in space, but rather one inseparable combination of the two, an insuperable unity that we might describe as urban: an abstraction becoming concrete, the concrete becoming abstract.

But squares like Tahrir in Cairo or Zuccotti Park in Manhattan are urban public spaces not for reason of their pure concrete physicality, but because they are meeting places between virtual and physical worlds, between online and offline conversations, between online and offline encounters. That is why they are public: because they enable public discourses, public conversations to talk and meet each other, quite literally. They are public not because they are simply there, in the open, in a city center, but because these spaces are made public by people encountering one another, there. The efficacy of these spaces for any global movement is defined by what is going on both inside and outside these spaces, by the here and the there, by what is taking place in them and how this taking place is greeted outside them, by the rest of the world, how it inspires the rest of the world, how it communicates with the rest of the world, how it becomes the rest of the world. The relationship can only ever be reciprocal, the inside and the outside, the here and the there, the absence and the presence.

The occupation dramatizes the necessarily expansive nature of revolt against planetary capitalism, drawing the outside within itself while enlarging its own sphere of activity, propelling it onto the outside. From this standpoint, the question of geography is now tantamount to the question of teleportation, of being here and there at once, or almost at once, of absences as much as presences, of particles and waves expressing their specific, dynamic complementarity. As such, the stake of protest is not strictly the city nor even the urban; yet perhaps, just perhaps, there is something about contemporary planetary urban society that enables these protests to be made, that permits and engenders such a definition of protest, a definition in which people collectively can now express themselves publicly, encounter one another, and talk to one another, as citizens in front of the whole wide world.

This is perhaps how Henri Lefebvre might have conceived his notion of revolutionary citizenship were he still with us today. At least this is how he *should* have conceived it. And if we can take leave where his *La pensée Marxiste et la ville* left off, the complete urbanization of the world will continue to mean job cuts, deindustrialization, layoffs, downsizing and unemployment—the whole bit of contemporary work (and postwork) relations we recognize in our midst, the contextual reality for continued mega-underground occupational activism.[42] Therein lie the threats and the promise of urban protest. Because as long as there is a *mob* constituency out there, making itself, encountering one another in public, there are reasons to be cheerful and relatively optimistic. As long as the enemy of encounter— segregation and separation—can be offset, the politics of the encounter will continue to be part and parcel of the process of planetary urbanization.

Perhaps the politics of the encounter really boil down to mobs of people encountering other mobs of people. In *Foundation*, Asimov presents "mob analysis" as the watchword for *psychohistory*, the brainchild of mathematician Hari Seldon, who formulates psychohistory to predict the future in statistical fashion.[43] Rulers of Trantor became very interested in Seldon because they felt he could help make the future theirs; Seldon soon became one of the most important men in the galaxy and assumed the role of First Minister under Emperor Cleon I's rule. For the scientist Asimov (he had a PhD in chemistry), the concept of psychohistory was modeled on the kinetic theory of gases. Molecules making up gases move about in absolutely random fashion, in any direction, in three dimensions and at a wide range of speeds. Nobody can predict the behavior of a single molecule. Yet, as a mass of molecules, as gases, you can somehow describe what the motions would be on average, and from there work out the gas laws with an enormous degree of predictability.

Asimov applied this notion to human beings. (In Asimov's *Foundation* books, there is no alien presence, no non-human life, save human-made robots: his vision of the universe is all the more interesting because it is all too human.) All of us have free will, all of us as individuals exhibit behavior and act in ways that defy predictability. Still, for vast numbers of people, for diverse societies, for "mobs" of people, Asimov's Seldon suggests that some sort of predictability is possible, as for gases. Thus psychohistory is "mob analysis," predicting mob behavior as intruding, intervening in historical contingency. The politics of mobs, then, are like the kinetic theory of gases, and the idea has considerable salience because it suggests something about the prospect of group encounters intervening in the historical-geographical logic of urbanization, intervening in a world without work or cities. Although here, perhaps, it is not so much psychohistory as *psychogeography* that is more akin to mob analysis, implying any act of centralizing human behavior, any human agglomeration, is likely to create at a certain time and in a certain space a gathering of people that resembles a gathering of gases, a certain coming together of movement and stasis, of particle and wave. This encounter will possess its own kinetic energy; sometimes negative energy, like indiscriminate rioting (British cities witnessed this not so long ago), but also positive energy, its own Brownian motion, perhaps generating an energy that is enough to alter the course of history (and geography).

Should such an encounter really take hold, really gel, the social configuration would be a kind of political superstring theory realizing itself, a transformative conjoining around a collective *boson*. Like particle physicists today, we know, theoretically and mathematically from our radical hypotheses that this collective reality exists, even if we have never yet witnessed it empirically. We are 99 percent sure that the figures stack up, that those in the boson will be the 99 percent. If that ever happens—when it happens—we will see before our eyes a beautiful *collideorscape* (the portmanteau is also Joyce's, from *Finnegans Wake*), a "collision and escape," a kaleidoscope of sorts, a passage into another political reality.[44]

What might this *collideorscape* resemble? Once again, the imagery, the pictorial representation of resistance, the sight of a politics of the encounter unfolding in our mind's eye, might come from abstract expressionism, from Jackson Pollock, from his 1950s canvas entitled *Number 32*, which currently hangs in Düsseldorf's Kunstsammlung Nordrhein-Westfalen museum. Pollock's patterning depicts the very act of *fusion*, of people becoming what Sartre called a *le groupe en fusion* (fused group).[45] Only two colors make up Pollock's masterpiece *Number 32*: a light tan-colored canvas brown over which are splattered skeins of jet-black swirls. One is struck by the energy that radiates from this composition; if you verge too close, it sucks you into its spiraling vortex. Energy enters via thin whirls and curves, thin threads of spontaneous black. Yet there are points of convergence, snowflakes and dendrites, where the black paint thickens and is nodal, highly charged. Modest inputs spiraling inwards seem, at these points of fusion, about to release enormous outputs, energy that pushes outwards, a diffusion unleashing a quantity-quality reaction, a critical mass of power. They kindle radical eruptions, not random explosions, volcanic happenings rather than unannounced anarchy, because here there's underlying regularity, some inner structuring order. For in this imagery we not only glimpse radical fractals, attributes of Spinozian urban substance, but also the physicists' concept of *wormhole* coming to life, illusive shortcuts, tiny trails toward liberation.[46]

Wormholes create new regions of planetary urban space, blaze new spatial territories, a new political space-time dimension that secretly links, makes a bridge, or subterranean tunnel, between social movements everywhere. Wormholes complete the encounter, transmit *messenger particles* that unite all struggles across the planet. Charged particles, as I've said, transmit negative, repulsive energy, frequently telling other particles to "move apart"; yet every particle also has an opposite charge, has powers of attraction that say "come together." In our contemporary, ever-expanding urban universe, little loops of energy generate incredible force; they literally make the world go around, light it up with electricity. It is time for political struggles to really energize this new planetary charge, and to convert it into unprecedented cosmic singularity—into a new *concrete* expressionism.

Notes

1   Rem Koolhaas, "In Search of Authenticity," *The Endless City*, eds. Richard Burdett and Deyan Sudjic (London: Phaidon, 2007) 320.
2   Isacc Asimov, *Foundation* (London: Voyager Paperback, 1955) 11.
3   Isaac Asimov, *Foundation's Edge* (London: Granada Publishing, 1983) 62.
4   Henri Lefebvre, *La révolution urbaine* (Paris: Gallimard, 1970) 7.
5   Richard Burdett and Deyan Sudjic, eds., *The Endless City* (London: Phaidon, 2007).
6   Louis Wirth, in his classic essay "Urbanism as a Way of Life," still gives one of the best takes on matters: "The degree to which the contemporary world may be said to be 'urban,'" Wirth says, "is not fully or actually measured by the proportion of the total population living in cities. The influences which cities exert upon social life are greater than the ratio of the urban population would indicate, for the city is not only in ever larger degrees the dwelling-place and the workshop of the modern man, but it is the initiating and controlling center of economic, political, and cultural life that has drawn the most remote parts of the world into its orbit and woven diverse areas, peoples, and activities into a cosmos." See Louis Wirth, "Urbanism as a Way of Life," *The American Journal of Sociology* XLIV (1938), 2.
7   Henri Lefebvre, *Le droit à la ville* (Paris: Anthropos, 1968) 83.
8   Henri Lefebvre, *The Urban Revolution*, trans. Robert Bononno (Minneapolis: University of Minnesota Press, 2003) 57.
9   Ibid., chapter 2.
10 Henri Lefebvre, *La pensée Marxiste et la ville* (Paris: Casterman, 1972).
11 As John Berger says in his groundbreaking text on art criticism, *Ways of Seeing*: "It is seeing which establishes our place in the surrounding world; we explain that world with words, but words can never undo the fact that we are surrounded by the world. The relation between what we see and what we know is never settled. Each evening we see the sun set. We know that the earth is turning away from it. Yet the knowledge, the explanation, never quite fits the sight." See John Berger, *Ways of Seeing* (Harmondsworth: Penguin, 1972), 7.
12 Lefebvre also devotes considerable attention to the passage from the feudal (commercial) city to the capitalist (industrial) city in another 1970s book: *La pensée Marxiste et la ville*. See Henri Lefebvre, *La pensée Marxiste et la ville*, chapter 2, 39-41 and 45-69. The argument is interestingly bedded down in Karl Marx and Friedrich Engels, *The German Ideology* (New York: International Publishers, 1970 [1846]).
13 Karl Marx and Friedrich Engels, *The Communist Manifesto* (New York: Penguin, 2011 [1848]) 67.
14 Lefebvre, *The Urban Revolution*, 17.
15 Karl Marx, *Capital, Volume III* (New York: International Publishers, 1967 [1894]) 333.
16 Karl Marx, *Grundrisse der Kritik der politischen Ökonomie* (Harmonsworth: Penguin, 1973[1857]) 408.
17 Karl Marx, *Theories of Surplus Value—Part III* (Moscow: Progress Publishers, 1975 [1862]) 253.
18 Benedictus de Spinoza, *Ethics* (London: Everyman Edition, 1993 [1677]) 9.
19 Claude Cernuschi and Andrzej Herczynski, "Cutting Pollock Down to Size: the Boundaries of the Poured Technique," *Pollock Matters*, eds. Ellen G. Landau and Claude Cernuschi (Boston: McMullen Museum of Art, Boston College, 2007).
20 Ibid.
21 Clement Greenberg, "The Crisis of the Easel Painting," *Art and Culture* (Boston: Beacon Press, 1961).
22 Ibid., 155.
23 Lefebvre, *The Urban Revolution*, 159.
24 David Harvey, *Limits to Capital* (Oxford: Blackwell, 1982).
25 Lefebvre *The Urban Revolution*, 159.
26 David Harvey, *The New Imperialism* (New York: Oxford University Press, 2003).

27 Lefebvre, *The Urban Revolution,* 152, emphasis added.

28 Ibid.

29 Ibid., 124.

30 Ibid., 118.

31 Ibid., 118-9.

32 Ibid., 174.

33 Lefebvre, *Le droit à la ville,* 110.

34 Andy Merrifield, "The Right to the City and Beyond: Notes on a Lefebvrian Reconceptualization," this book, Ch. 31; and Andy Merrifield, *The Politics of the Encounter: Urban Theory and Protest Under Planetary Urbanization* (Athens: University of Georgia Press, 2013).

35 Henri Lefebvre, "Dissolving City, Planetary Metamorphosis," this book, Ch. 34; and Henri Lefebvre et al. (eds.), *Du Contrat de Citoyenneté* (Paris: Syllepse, 1985).

36 Fredric Jameson, "Postmodernism, or the Cultural Logic of Late Capitalism," *New Left Review* 146 (July–August 1984) 53-92.

37 Lefebvre, *Le droit à la ville.*

38 The other tricky thing about "rights" these days is how they underwrite a great deal of conservative policy about personal responsibility and individual freedom. Be it Tea Party or Tory Party, the Right on both sides of the Atlantic now defiantly champions rights, embraces their claims, peddles the right of (wealth) citizens to challenge public service providers, to contest, opt out and attack any state action that is not in some way geared toward bolstering private enterprise. Even Lefebvre's sacred urban right figures in the mainstream's arsenal, re-appropriated and defanged in, for instance, the UN-Habitat's 2010 Charter and the World Bank's manifesto for addressing the ills of the global poverty trap. Meanwhile the right to this and that has been proclaimed so frequently by radicals, from so many different walks of life, that the concept is not pretty much a political banality (Merrifield, "The Right to the City and Beyond," this book, Ch. 31).

39 *Wall Street 2: Money Never Sleeps* (Oliver Stone, 2010).

40 Andy Merrifield, "Crowd Politics, or, 'Here Comes Everybuddy,'" *New Left Review* 71 (September–October, 2011).

41 Bill Wasik, "Crowd Control," *Wired Magazine* (January 2012).

42 Lefebvre, *La pensée Marxiste et la ville,* chapter 2.

43 Asimov, *Foundation.*

44 James Joyce, *Finnegans Wake* (New York: Penguin, 1976 [1939]) 143.

45 Jean Paul Sartre, *Critique of Dialectical Reason—Volume I* (London: Verso, 1976).

46 Brian Greene, *The Elegant Universe* (New York: Vintage, 2000) 264-5.

13
THESES
ON URBANIZATION

Neil Brenner

In the early 1970s, a young Marxist sociologist named Manuel Castells, then living in exile in Paris, began his soon-to-be classic intervention on *The Urban Question* by declaring his "astonishment" that debates on "urban problems" were becoming "an essential element in the policies of governments, in the concerns of the mass media and, consequently, in the everyday life of a large section of the population."[1] For Castells, this astonishment was born of his orthodox Marxist assumption that the concern with urban questions was ideological. The real motor of social change, he believed, lay elsewhere, in working-class action and anti-imperialist mobilization. On this basis, Castells proceeded to deconstruct what he viewed as the prevalent "urban ideology" under postwar managerial capitalism: his theory took seriously the social construction of the urban phenomenon in academic and political discourse, but ultimately derived such representations from purportedly more foundational processes associated with capitalism and the state's role in the reproduction of labor power.

Four decades after Castells' classic intervention, it is easy to confront early twenty-first-century discourse on urban questions with a similar sense of astonishment—not because it masks the operations of capitalism but because it has become one of the dominant metanarratives through which our current planetary situation is interpreted, both in academic circles and in the public sphere. Today, advanced interdisciplinary education in urban social science, planning and design is flourishing in major universities, and urban questions are being confronted energetically by historians, literary critics and other humanities-based scholars. Physical and computational scientists and ecologists are likewise contributing to urban studies through their explorations of new satellite-based data sources, georeferencing analytics and GIS technologies, which are offering more differentiated perspectives on the geographies of urbanization than have ever before been possible.[2] Classic texts such as Jane Jacobs' *The Death and Life of Great American Cities* and Mike Davis' *City of Quartz* continue to animate discussions of contemporary urbanism, and more recent, popular books on cities, such as Edward Glaeser's *Triumph of the City*, Jeb Brugmann's *Welcome to the Urban Revolution*, and Richard Florida's *Who's Your City?*, along with documentary films such as Gary Hustwit's *Urbanized* and Michael Glawogger's *Megacities*, are widely discussed in the public sphere.[3] The 2010 World Expo in Shanghai was focused on the theme of *A Better City, A Better Life*, and major museums, expos and biennales from New York City and Venice to Christchurch and Hong Kong are devoting extensive attention to questions of urban culture, design and development.[4] The UN Habitat Programme has famously declared the advent of an "urban age" due to the world's rapidly increasing urban population.[5] This city-centric vision of the current geohistorical moment has been further popularized through a series of Urban Age conferences in some of the world's major cities, which have been organized and funded through a joint initiative of the London School of Economics and the Deutsche Bank.[6] Even debates on climate change and the future of the biosphere are being directly connected to questions about urbanization. The planetary built environment—in effect, the sociomaterial infrastructure of urbanization—is now recognized to be contributing directly to far-reaching transformations of the atmosphere, biotic habitats, land-use surfaces and oceanic conditions that have long-term implications for the metabolism of both human and non-human life forms.[7]

These intellectual and cultural reorientations are synchronous with a number of large-scale spatial transformations, institutional reorientations and social mobilizations that have intensified the significance and scale of urban conditions. First, the geographies of urbanization, which have long been understood with reference to the densely concentrated populations and built environments of cities, are assuming new, increasingly large-scale morphologies that perforate, crosscut and ultimately explode the erstwhile urban/rural divide (Figure 13.1). As Edward Soja and Miguel Kanai explain:

> … urbanism as a way of life, once confined to the historical central city, has been spreading outwards, creating urban densities and new 'outer' and 'edge' cities in what were formerly suburban fringes and green field or rural sites. In some areas, urbanization has expanded on even larger regional scales, creating giant urban galaxies with population sizes and degrees of polycentricity far beyond anything imagined only a few decades ago. … [I]n some cases city regions are coalescing into even larger agglomerations in a process that can be called "extended regional urbanization."[8]

13.1 As this iconic satellite image of nighttime lights illustrates, the geographies of urbanization have exploded the boundaries of city, metropolis, region, and territory: they have assumed a planetary scale.

Second, across each of the major world economic regions, spatially selective policy initiatives have been mobilized by national, state and provincial governments to create new matrices of transnational capital investment and urban development across vast zones of their territories.[9] While these state strategies sometimes target traditional metropolitan cores, they are also articulating vast grids of accumulation and spatial regulation that cascade along intercontinental transportation corridors, large-scale infrastructural, telecommunications and energy networks, free trade zones, transnational growth triangles and international border regions. This extended landscape of urbanization is now a forcefield of crisscrossing state regulatory strategies designed to territorialize long-term, large-scale investments in the built environment and to channel flows of raw materials, energy, commodities, labor and capital across transnational space (Figure 13.2, next page).

Third, within this tumult of worldwide sociospatial and regulatory reorganization, new vectors of urban social struggle are crystallizing. Michael Hardt and Antonio Negri have recently suggested that the contemporary metropolis has become a locus of sociopolitical mobilization analogous to role of the factory during the industrial epoch. For them, the metropolis has become the "space of the common" and thus the territorial basis for collective action under conditions of globalizing capitalism, neoliberalizing states and reconstituted Empire.[10] In many urban regions around the world, the notion of the right to the city, developed in the late 1960s by Henri Lefebvre, has now become a rallying cry for social movements, coalitions and reformers, both mainstream and radical, as well as for diverse global NGOs, UNESCO and the World Urban Forum.[11] The urban is thus no longer only a site or arena of contentious politics, but has become one of its primary stakes. Reorganizing urban conditions is increasingly seen as a means to transform the broader political-economic structures and spatial formations of early twenty-first-century world capitalism as a whole (Figure 13.3, page 185).

13.2 New transnational geographies of state intervention into the urban process are emerging, as illustrated in Felipe Correa's map of the project portfolio for the Initiative for the Integration of Regional Infrastructure in South America (IIRSA).

These trends are multifaceted, volatile and contradictory, and their cumulative significance is certainly a matter for ongoing interpretation and intensive debate. At minimum, however, they appear to signify that urban spaces have become essential to planetary political-economic, social and cultural life, and socioenvironmental conditions. Across diverse terrains of social research, policy intervention and public discourse, the configuration of urban(izing) built environments and urban institutional configurations is now thought to have major consequences for the futures of capitalism, politics and indeed for the planetary ecosystem as a whole. For those who have long been concerned with urban questions, whether in theory, research or practice, these are obviously exciting developments. But they are also accompanied by new challenges and dangers—not the least of which is the proliferation of deep confusion regarding the specificity of the urban itself, both as a category of analysis for social theory and research, and as a category of practice in politics and everyday life.[12]

• • •

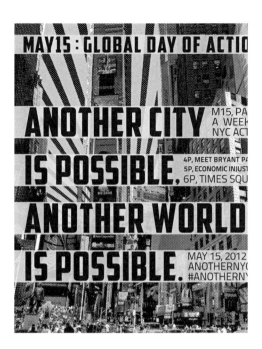

13.3   Another city, another world, 2011. Poster by Ange Tran, *Not an Alternative*

Writing in the late 1930s, Chicago School urban sociologist Louis Wirth famously delineated the analytical contours of urbanism with reference to a classic triad of sociological properties—large population size, high population density and high levels of demographic heterogeneity.[13] For Wirth, the spatial coexistence of these properties within urban areas distinguished such zones from all other settlement types, and justified the deployment of specific research strategies, the tools of a distinct field of urban sociology, to investigate them. By contrast, in the early twenty-first century, the urban appears to have become a quintessential floating signifier: devoid of any clear definitional parameters, morphological coherence or cartographic fixity, it is used to reference a seemingly boundless range of contemporary sociospatial conditions, processes, transformations, trajectories and potentials. Ash Amin and Nigel Thrift describe this state of affairs as follows:

> The city is everywhere and in everything. If the urbanized world now is a chain of metropolitan areas connected by places/corridors of communication (airports and airways, stations and railways, parking lots and motorways, teleports and information highways), then what is not urban? Is it the town, the village, the countryside? Maybe, but only to a limited degree. The footprints of the city are all over these places, in the form of city commuters, tourists, teleworking, the media, and the urbanization of lifestyles. The traditional divide between the city and the countryside has been perforated.[14]

The emergent process of extended urbanization is producing a variegated urban fabric which, rather than being simply concentrated within nodal points or confined within bounded regions, is now woven unevenly and yet ever more densely across vast stretches of the entire world. Such a formation cannot be grasped adequately through traditional concepts of cityness, metropolitanism or urban/rural binarisms, which presuppose the coherent, areal separation of distinct settlement types. Nor can it be understood effectively on the basis of more recent concepts of global(izing) cities, since most variants of the latter likewise presuppose the territorial boundedness of urban units, albeit now understood to be relationally networked with other cities via transnational webs of capital, labor and transportation/communication infrastructures.[15] Paradoxically, therefore, at the very moment in which the urban appears to have acquired an unprecedented strategic significance for an extraordinarily broad array of institutions, organizations, researchers, actors and activists, its definitional contours have become unmanageably slippery. The apparent ubiquity of the contemporary urban condition makes it now seem impossible to pin down.

Under these conditions, the field of urban theory, as inherited from Wirth, Castells and other major twentieth-century urbanists, is in a state of disarray. If the urban can no longer be understood as a particular kind of place—that is, as a discrete, distinctive and relatively bounded type of settlement in which specific kinds of social relations obtain—then what could possibly justify the existence of an intellectual field devoted to its investigation?

• • •

At present, the world of academic urban studies is host to a variety of "morbid symptoms" that appear to signify the latest among a long succession of epistemological crises that have periodically ricocheted through the field since its origins nearly a century ago.[16] Among the most specialized, empirically oriented researchers, the formidable tasks of data collection, methodological refinement and concrete investigation continue to take precedence over the challenges of grappling with the field's decaying epistemological foundations. Disciplinary and subdisciplinary specialization thus produces what Henri Lefebvre once termed a "blind field" in which concrete investigations of time-honored themes continue to accumulate, even as the "urban phenomenon, taken as a whole" is hidden from view.[17] Meanwhile, among those urbanists who are reflexively concerned to confront such questions, there is growing confusion regarding the analytic foundations and *raison d'être* of the field as a whole. Even a cursory examination of recent works of urban theory reveals that foundational disagreements prevail regarding nearly every imaginable issue—from the conceptualization of *what* urbanists are (or should be) trying to study to the justification for *why* they are (or should be) doing so and the elaboration of *how* best to pursue their agendas.[18] This situation has engendered a kind of "academic Babel" in which, even amidst productive conceptual innovations, the fragmentation of urban realities in everyday political-economic and cultural practice is being replicated relatively uncritically within the discursive terrain of urban theory.[19]

A particularly problematic tendency, in this context, is the contextualist turn that has become fashionable among many urbanists who have been influenced by Latourian actor-network theory and associated, neo-Deleuzian concepts of assemblage. Especially in their ontologically inflected variants, such approaches reject abstract or macrostructural forms of argumentation in favor of place-based narratives and thick descriptions, which are claimed to offer a more direct means of accessing the microsocial contours of a rapidly changing urban landscape.[20] Such positions may partially circumvent some of the structuralist blind-spots of earlier meta-theoretical positions, and some also succeed in opening up fruitful new horizons for inquiry into urban processes, particularly in relation to the role of nonhuman agents in the structuration of places. Unfortunately, however, most work on urban assemblages does not begin to confront, much less resolve, the foundational epistemological conundrums outlined above.[21] Here, too, the concept of the urban is attached to an extraordinarily diffuse array of referents, connotations and conditions, all too frequently derived from everyday categories of practice, which are then unreflexively converted into analytical commitments. The field's theoretical indeterminacy is thus further entrenched, while the *context of context*—the broader geopolitical and geoeconomic dimensions of contemporary urbanization processes and associated forms of worldwide capitalist restructuring, dispossession and uneven spatial development—is analytically "black-boxed."[22]

Is there any future for urban theory in a world in which urbanization has been generalized? Should urbanists simply affirm the apparent amorphousness of their chosen terrain of investigation and resign themselves to the task of tracking the social life and spatial form of generically defined places? Or should urban studies today be pursued using the aspatial framework controversially proposed by Peter Saunders in the 1980s, which emphasized constitutive social processes (in particular, collective consumption) rather than their materializations in spatial forms?[23] Or, more radically still, is it perhaps time to speak of *the field formerly known as urban studies*, consigning work in this realm of inquiry to a phase of capitalist modernity whose sociospatial preconditions have now been superseded? In a provocative recent reflection, the eminent urban sociologist Herbert Gans suggests as much, proposing to replace the inherited *problematique* of urban studies with that of a "sociology of settlements" based upon reinvented typologies of human spatial organization and a less rigid understanding of inter-place boundaries.[24] Unlike Saunders, Gans insists that the field under discussion must retain a spatial component, but he opts to abandon the cartography of urban settlement space that has long underpinned urban sociology, including his own pioneering investigations since the 1960s.

It is tempting to follow Gans' lead, and thus to confront emergent landscapes of urbanization with a more or less blank conceptual slate, devoid of the unwieldy epistemological baggage associated with the last century of debates on cities, metropolitan forms and urban questions. But doing so would entail reintroducing a version of Castells' earlier rejection of urban discourse as pure ideology. Such a position would be poorly equipped to explain the continued, powerful resonance of the urban across diverse realms of theory and research, as well as its widespread invocation as a site, target or project in so many arenas of institutional reorganization, political-economic strategy and popular struggle. Surely, the intensified engagement with urban conditions and potentialities, as broadly sketched above, is indicative of systemic sociospatial transformations under way across the contemporary world, and of the ongoing effort to construct what Frederic Jameson once called a *cognitive map* through which to secure cartographic orientation under conditions of deep phenomenological dislocation.[25]

Whatever its ideological dimensions, and they are considerable, the notion of the urban cannot be reduced to a category of practice; it remains a critical conceptual tool in any attempt to theorize the ongoing creative destruction of political-economic space under early twenty-first century capitalism.[26] As Lefebvre recognized, this process of creative destruction (in his terms, "implosion-explosion") is not confined to any specific place, territory or scale; it engenders a "problematic," a syndrome of emergent conditions, processes, transformations, projects and struggles, that is connected to the uneven generalization of urbanization on a planetary scale.[27] A case must be made, therefore, for the continuation of urban theory, albeit in a critically reinvented form that recognizes the relentlessly dynamic, creatively destructive character of "the urban phenomenon" under capitalism, and on this basis aspires to decipher newly emergent patterns of planetary urbanization. In Ananya Roy's appropriately combative formulation, this is surely an ideal moment in which "to blast open new theoretical geographies" for a rejuvenated approach to critical urban studies.[28]

• • •

Without intending to short-circuit the process of restless, open-ended theoretical experimentation that such an endeavor will require, the remainder of this essay presents a series of theses intended to provoke debate regarding the contemporary planetary urban condition, the state of our intellectual inheritance in the academic fields devoted to its investigation, and the prospects for developing new conceptual strategies for deciphering emergent urban realities and potentialities across places, territories and scales. Several of these theses are connected to the vast academic literature on urban studies that has been under development for nearly a century. Other theses confront an analytical terrain to which little urban research corresponds, or which has previously been approached via routes that generally fall outside the rubric of urban studies, at least in the sense in which that field has traditionally been understood.

While these theses advance an argument for continued attention to urban questions, they propose a reconstituted vision of the "site" of such questions. As Andrea Kahn has productively emphasized, the demarcation of urban sites always entails complex epistemological, political and cartographic maneuvers; urban sites are "multiscalar, heteroglot settings for interactions and intersections" rather than discreet, pregiven or self-contained spatial artifacts.[29] More abstractly, however, the theoretical orientation developed here suggests that the urban character of *any* site, from the scale of the neighborhood to that of the entire world, can only be defined in substantive terms, with reference to the historically specific sociospatial processes that produce it. As conceived here, therefore, the urban is a "concrete abstraction" in which the contradictory sociospatial relations of capitalism (commodification, capital circulation, capital accumulation and associated forms of political regulation/contestation) are at once territorialized (embedded within concrete contexts and thus fragmented) and generalized (extended across place, territory and scale and thus universalized).[30] As such, the concept of the urban has the potential to illuminate the creatively destructive *patterning* of modern sociospatial landscapes, not only within cities, metropolitan regions and other zones traditionally considered to be impacted by urbanism, but across the space of the world as a whole.[31]

In methodology, if not also in substance, these propositions take inspiration from Henri Lefebvre's call for a metaphilosophy of urbanization—an exploratory approach that "provides an orientation …, opens pathways and reveals a horizon" rather than making pronouncements regarding an actualized condition or a completed process.[32] Insofar as inherited cognitive maps of the urban condition have proven increasingly inadequate, if not obsolete, the tentative, experimental quality of this method appears highly salient. A new cognitive map is urgently needed, but its core elements have yet to cohere in an intelligible form. Accordingly, many of the propositions outlined below are no more than speculative outlines for avenues of conceptualization and investigation that have yet to be pursued. Their potential to inform future mappings of the planetary urban condition remains to be explored and elaborated. Figure 13.4 (next page) offers a schematic summary of some of the distinctions presented in the text.

1. *The urban is a theoretical construct.* The urban is not a pregiven site, space or object—its demarcation as a zone of thought, representation, imagination or action can only occur through a process of theoretical abstraction.[33] Such abstractions condition "how we 'carve up' our object of study and what properties we take particular objects to have."[34] As such, they have a massively structuring impact on concrete investigations of all aspects of the built environment and sociospatial restructuring. In this sense, questions of conceptualization lie at the heart of all forms of urban research, even the most empirical, contextually embedded and detail-oriented. They are not mere background conditions or framing devices, but constitute the very interpretive fabric through which urbanists weave together metanarratives, normative-political orientations, analyses of empirical data and strategies of intervention.

2. *The site and object of urban research are essentially contested.* Since the formal institutionalization of urban sociology in the early twentieth century, the conceptual demarcation of the urban has been a matter of intense debate and disagreement across the social sciences.

Since that time, the trajectory of urban research has not only involved an accumulation of concrete investigations in and of urban(izing) spaces, but the continual theoretical rearticulation of their specificity as such, both socially and spatially. During the last century, many of the great leaps forward in the field of urban studies have occurred through the elaboration of new theoretical "cuts" into the nature of the urban question.[35]

3. *Major strands of urban studies fail to demarcate their site and object in reflexively theoretical terms.* In much of twentieth-century urban studies, cities and urban spaces have been taken for granted as empirically coherent, transparent sites of research. Consequently, the urban character of urban research has been conceived simply with reference to the circumstance that its focal point is located within a place labeled a "city." However, such mainstream, empiricist positions cannot account for their own historical and geographical conditions of possibility: they necessarily presuppose determinate theoretical assumptions regarding the specificity of the city and/or the urban that powerfully shape the trajectory of concrete research, generally in unexamined ways. Critical reflexivity in urban studies may only be accomplished if such assumptions are made explicit, subjected to systematic analysis and revised continually in relation to evolving research questions, normative-political orientations and practical concerns.[36]

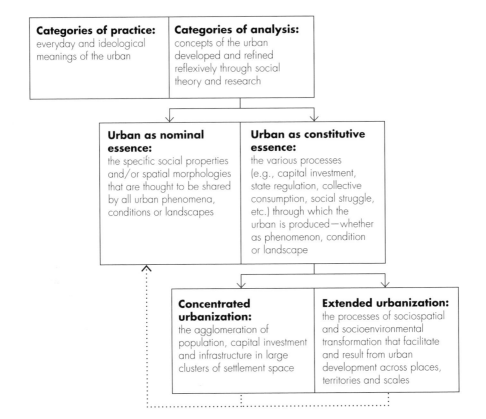

Categories of practice: everyday and ideological meanings of the urban

Categories of analysis: concepts of the urban developed and refined reflexively through social theory and research

Urban as nominal essence: the specific social properties and/or spatial morphologies that are thought to be shared by all urban phenomena, conditions or landscapes

Urban as constitutive essence: the various processes (e.g., capital investment, state regulation, collective consumption, social struggle, etc.) through which the urban is produced—whether as phenomenon, condition or landscape

Concentrated urbanization: the agglomeration of population, capital investment and infrastructure in large clusters of settlement space

Extended urbanization: the processes of sociospatial and socioenvironmental transformation that facilitate and result from urban development across places, territories and scales

13.4 Some useful distinctions for a theory of planetary urbanization.

4. *Urban studies has traditionally demarcated the urban in contrast to putatively non-urban spaces.*
    Since its origins, the field of urban studies has conceived the urban as a specific type
    of settlement space, one that is thought to be different, in some qualitative way, from
    the putatively non-urban spaces that surround it—from the suburb, the town and
    the village to the rural, the countryside and the wilderness.[37] Chicago School urban
    sociologists, mainstream land economists, central place theorists, urban demographers,
    neo-marxian geographers and global city theorists may disagree on the basis of this
    specificity, but all engage in the shared analytical maneuver of delineating urban
    distinctiveness through an explicit or implied contrast to sociospatial conditions
    located "elsewhere."[38] In effect, the terrain of the non-urban, this perpetually present
    "elsewhere," has long served as a *constitutive outside* that stabilizes the very intelligibility
    of the field of urban studies. The non-urban appears simultaneously as the ontological
    Other of the urban, its radical opposite, and as its epistemological condition of
    possibility, the basis on which it can be recognized as such (Figure 13.5).[39]

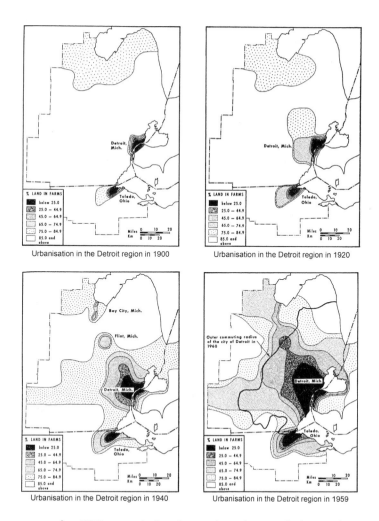

Urbanisation in the Detroit region in 1900

Urbanisation in the Detroit region in 1920

Urbanisation in the Detroit region in 1940

Urbanisation in the Detroit region in 1959

13.5 In this time-series representation from 1973, geographer Brian Berry used a simple empirical indicator to demarcate the changing urban/rural interface—percentage of land allocated to agricultural functions.

5.   *The concern with settlement typologies (nominal essences) must be superseded by the analysis of sociospatial processes (constitutive essences).* The development of typologies of settlement space, urban and otherwise, requires the delineation of a nominal essence through which the distinctiveness of particular sociospatial forms or conditions is to be understood. This methodological aspiration has long preoccupied major strands of twentieth century urban theory, and it persists within several important contemporary urban research traditions. However, it is time for urbanists to abandon the search for a nominal essence that might distinguish the urban as a type of settlement (whether conceived as a city, a city-region, a megacity, a metropolis, a megalopolis or otherwise) and the closely associated conception of other spaces (suburban, rural, wilderness or otherwise) as being non-urban due to their supposed separation from urban conditions, trends and effects. Instead, in order to grasp the production and relentless transformation of spatial differentiation, urban theory must prioritize the investigation of constitutive essences—the *processes* through which the variegated landscapes of modern capitalism are produced.[40]

6.   *A new lexicon of sociospatial differentiation is needed.* The geographies of capitalism are as intensely variegated as ever: contemporary urbanization processes hardly signify the transcendence of uneven spatial development and territorial inequality at any geographical scale. However, a new lexicon of sociospatial differentiation is needed in order to grasp emergent patterns and pathways of planetary urban reorganization. Today, spatial difference no longer assumes the form of an urban/rural divide, but is being articulated through an explosion of developmental patterns and potentials *within* a thickening, if unevenly woven, fabric of worldwide urbanization.[41] Consequently, inherited vocabularies of settlement space, both vernacular and social-scientific, may offer no more than a working epistemological starting point for such an endeavor. They can only be rendered critically effective within a framework that emphasizes the perpetual *churning* of sociospatial formations under capitalism rather than presupposing their stabilization within built environments, jurisdictional envelopes or ecological landscapes. Such an approach has been pioneered with impressive systematicity by a team of scholars, architects and designers at the ETH-Studio Basel, leading to the development of the "urban portrait" of Switzerland (Figure 13.6).[42]

Crucially, the zones depicted on the map are conceived not as enclosed territorial arenas or as embodiments of distinct settlement types, but rather as indicators of contradictory yet interconnected processes of sociospatial restructuring under conditions of ongoing industrial, labor, politico-regulatory and environmental reorganization. They demarcate the geographical inheritance of earlier rounds of urban restructuring, as well as the territorial framework in which future urban pathways and potentials are to be produced.

7. *Urban effects persist within an intensely variegated sociospatial landscape.* This endeavor must also attend systematically to the ongoing production and reconstitution of urban ideologies, including those that propagate visions of the city as a discreet, distinct and territorially bounded unit, whether in opposition to the rural or nature, as a self-contained system, as an ideal type or as a strategic target for intervention.[43] While the critical deconstruction of such urban effects has long been central to the project of critical urban theory, this task has acquired renewed urgency under conditions of planetary urbanization, in which the gulf between everyday cognitive maps and worldwide landscapes of creative destruction appears to be widening.[44] What practices and strategies produce the persistent experiential effect of urban social discreteness, territorial boundedness or structured coherence? How do the latter vary across places and territories? How have such practices and strategies, and their effects, been transformed during the course of world capitalist development, and under contemporary conditions?

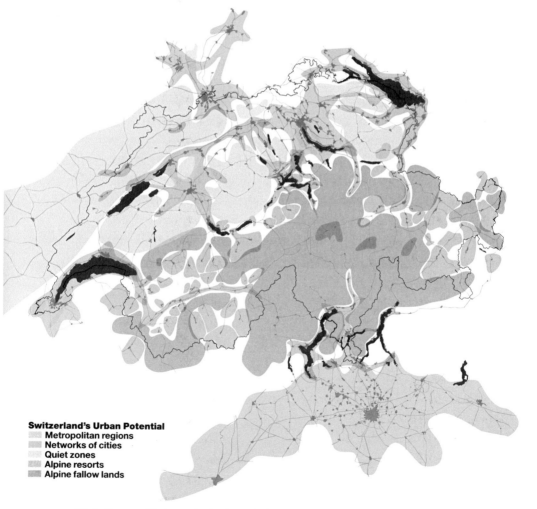

Switzerland's Urban Potential
Metropolitan regions
Networks of cities
Quiet zones
Alpine resorts
Alpine fallow lands

13.6 This map of the Swiss urban landscape by the ETH Studio Basel replaces the traditional urban/rural binarism with a fivefold classification of metropolitan regions, city networks, quiet zones, alpine resorts and alpine fallow lands (See also the discussion of this map by Christian Schmid, "A Typology of Urban Switzerland," this book, Ch. 26).

8.	*The concept of urbanization requires systematic reinvention.* Because of its attunement to the *problematique* of constitutive essences, the concept of urbanization is a crucial tool for investigating the planetary urban process. To serve this purpose, however, the concept must be reclaimed from the city-centric, methodologically territorialist and predominantly demographic traditions that have to date monopolized its deployment. Traditional approaches equate urbanization with the growth of particular types of settlement (cities, urban areas, metropolises), which are conceived as territorially discrete, bounded and self-contained units embedded within a broader non-urban or rural landscape. Additionally, such approaches usually privilege purely demographic criteria, such as population thresholds and/or density gradients, as the basis on which to classify urban development patterns and pathways. Urbanization is thus reduced to a process in which, within each national territory, the populations of densely settled places ("cities") are said to expand in relative and absolute terms. This is the model that has been used by the United Nations since it began producing data on world urban population levels in the early 1970s, and it underpins contemporary declarations by prominent urbanists and academics that an "urban age" is now under way because more than half the world's population purportedly lives within cities.[45]

While such understandings capture meaningful dimensions of demographic change within an evolving global settlement system, they are limited both empirically (the criteria for urban settlement types vary massively across national contexts) and theoretically (they lack a coherent, reflexive and historically dynamic conceptualization of urban specificity). By contrast, several previously marginalized or subterranean traditions of twentieth-century urban theory may offer useful conceptual elements and cartographic orientations for a revitalized theory of urbanization.[46] The possibility that the geographies of urbanization transcend city, metropolis and region was only occasionally considered by postwar urban theorists, but under contemporary planetary conditions it has an extraordinarily powerful intellectual resonance.

9.	*Urbanization contains two dialectically intertwined moments—concentration and extension.*[47] Urban theory has long conceived urbanization primarily in terms of agglomeration—the dense concentration of population, infrastructure and investment at certain locations on a broader, less densely settled territorial plane. While the scale and morphology of such concentrations is recognized to shift dramatically over time, it is above all with reference to this basic sociospatial tendency that urbanization has generally been defined (Figures 13.7 and 13.8).

Considerably less attention has been devoted to the ways in which the process of agglomeration has been premised upon, and in turn contributes to, wide-ranging transformations of sociospatial organization and ecological/environmental conditions across the rest of the world. Though largely ignored or relegated to the analytic background by urban theorists, such transformations—materialized in densely tangled

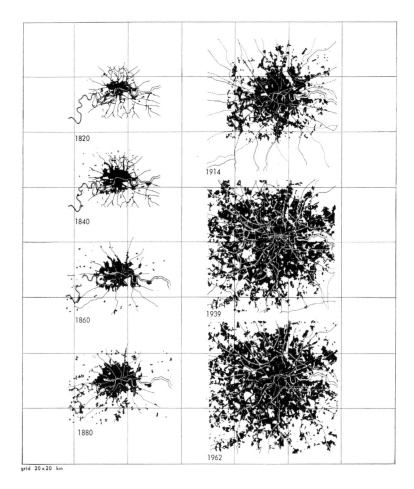

13.7 During the evolution of modern capitalism, the scale of concentrated urbanization has expanded considerably—as illustrated in this map of London's long-term spatial evolution.

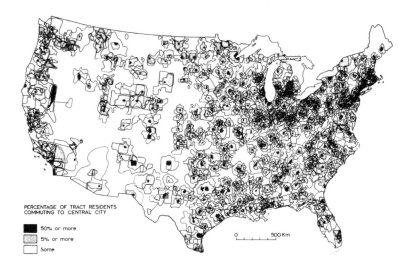

13.8 The process of concentrated urbanization encompasses flows of workers within and around large-scale agglomerations, as illustrated here in Brian Berry's famous visualization of commuting sheds in the postwar USA.

circuits of labor, commodities, cultural forms, energy, raw materials and nutrients—simultaneously radiate outwards from the immediate zone of agglomeration and implode back into it as the urbanization process unfolds. Within this extended, increasingly worldwide field of urban development, agglomerations form, expand, shrink and morph continuously, but always via dense webs of relations to other places, territories and scales, including to realms that are traditionally classified as being outside the urban condition. The latter include, for example, small and medium-sized towns and villages in peripheralized regions and agro-industrial zones, intercontinental transportation corridors, transoceanic shipping lanes, large-scale energy circuits and communications infrastructures, underground landscapes of resource extraction, satellite orbits and even the biosphere itself. As conceived here, therefore, urbanization involves both concentration and extension: these moments are dialectically intertwined insofar as they simultaneously presuppose and counteract one another.

This proposition suggests, on the one hand, that the conditions and trajectories of agglomerations (cities, city-regions and the like) must be connected analytically to larger-scale processes of territorial reorganization, circulation (of labor, commodities, raw materials, nutrients and energy) and resource extraction that ultimately encompass the space of the entire world (Figures 13.9 and 13.10). At the same time, this perspective suggests that important socioenvironmental transformations in zones that are not generally linked to urban conditions—from circuits of agribusiness and extractive landscapes for oil, natural gas and coal to transoceanic infrastructural networks, underground pipelines and satellite orbits—have in fact been ever more tightly intertwined with the developmental rhythms of urban agglomerations. Consequently, whatever their administrative demarcation, sociospatial morphology,

13.9 The development of urban agglomerations hinges upon increasingly dense, worldwide transportation infrastructures: they are an essential expression of extended urbanization.

population density or positionality within the global capitalist system, such spaces must be considered integral components of an extended, worldwide urban fabric (Figure 13.11, next page).

This dialectic of implosion (concentration, agglomeration) and explosion (extension of the urban fabric, intensification of interspatial connectivity across places, territories and scales) is an essential analytical, empirical and political horizon for any critical theory of urbanization in the early twenty-first century.

• • •

We thus return to the classic question posed by Castells in *The Urban Question* four decades ago: "Are there specific urban units?"[48] Under conditions in which urbanization is being generalized on a planetary scale, this question must be reformulated as: "Is there an urban *process?*"

Much like the nation-form, as analyzed by radical critics of nationalism, the urban-form under capitalism is an ideological effect of historically and geographically specific practices that create the structural appearance of territorial distinctiveness, coherence and boundedness within a broader, worldwide maelstrom of rapid sociospatial transformation.[49] Insofar as the field of urban studies has long presupposed the "unit-like" character of the urban, or sought to explain it with reference to a putative nominal essence that inheres within the organization of settlement space, the urban effect has been naturalized rather viewed as a puzzle requiring theorization and analysis. To the degree that urbanists perpetuate this naturalization through their choices of categories of analysis, the field

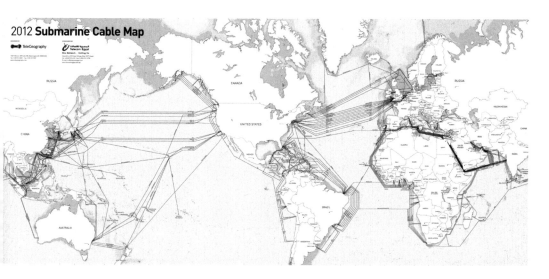

13.10 The vast territories of the world's oceans have become strategic terrains of extended urbanization through undersea cable infrastructures (shown here), as well as through shipping lanes and undersea resource extraction systems.

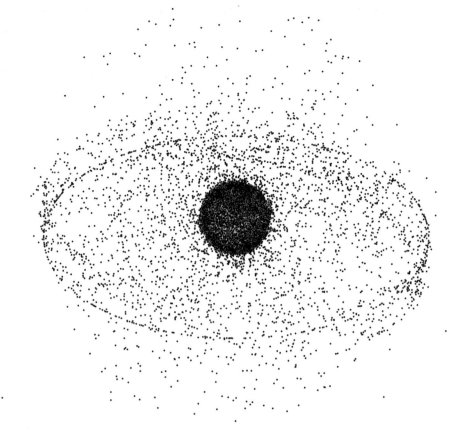

13.11 The field of extended urbanization is pushed upwards into the earth's atmosphere through a thickening web of orbiting satellites and space junk.

remains bound within an epistemological straightjacket analogous to that which constrained nationalism studies prior to the process-oriented interventions of scholars such as Nicos Poulantzas, Benedict Anderson and Etienne Balibar, among others, over three decades ago. The task of deciphering the interplay between urbanization and patterns of uneven spatial development remains as urgent as ever, but territorialist notions of the city, the urban and the metropolis are today increasingly blunt conceptual tools for that purpose.

These considerations suggest several possible future horizons for urban theory and research, including the following:

- *The creative destruction of urban landscapes.* Capitalist forms of urbanization have long entailed processes of creative destruction in which socially produced infrastructures for capital circulation, state regulation and sociopolitical struggle, as well as socio-environmental landscapes, are subjected to systemic crisis tendencies and are radically reorganized. Urban agglomerations are merely one among many strategic sociospatial sites in which such processes of creative destruction have unfolded during the geohistory of capitalist development. What is the specificity of contemporary forms of creative destruction across place, territory and scale, and how are they transforming inherited global/urban geographies, socio-environmental landscapes and patterns of uneven spatial development? What are the competing political projects, neoliberal and otherwise, that aspire to shape and rechannel them?

- *Geographies of urbanization.* How has the relation between concentrated and extended urbanization evolved during the history of capitalism? Since the first industrial revolution of the nineteenth century, the big agglomerations and metropolitan centers have long been among the primary arenas of capitalist creative destruction— they have served as the "front lines" of strategies to produce, circulate and absorb surpluses of capital and labor, and thus to facilitate the dynamics of world-scale capital accumulation.[50] To what degree has the extended landscape of urbanization, with its increasingly planetary infrastructures of capital circulation, nutrient and energy flow, and resource extraction, today become a strategically essential, if not primary, terrain of capitalist creative destruction? In the age of the Anthropocene, in which the logics of capitalist industrialization have indelibly transformed the systems of planetary life, are there new crisis-tendencies and socioecological barriers— including food supply disruptions, resource depletion, water scarcity, new forms of environmental vulnerability and the manifold, place-specific expressions of global climate change—that are destabilizing the developmental rhythms of extended urbanization? What are the implications of such processes for the future forms and pathways of concentrated urbanization and, more generally, for the organization of human built environments?

- *Political horizons.* Current debates on the right to the city have productively drawn attention to the politics of space and the struggle for the local commons within the world's giant cities, the densely agglomerated zones associated with the process of concentrated urbanization. However, the foregoing analysis suggests that such struggles must be linked to a broader politics of the global commons that is also being fought out elsewhere, by peasants, small landholders, farm workers, indigenous populations and their advocates, across the variegated landscapes of extended urbanization. Here, too, the dynamics of accumulation by dispossession and enclosure have had creatively destructive effects upon everyday life, social reproduction and socioenvironmental conditions, and these are being politicized by a range of social movements across places, territories and scales. Increasingly, such transformations and contestations of the extended built environment of capital circulation resonate with, and occur in parallel to, those that have long been percolating within and around urban agglomerations.[51] The approach proposed here opens up a perspective for critical urban theory in which connections are made, both analytically and strategically, among the various forms of dispossession that are being produced and contested across the planetary sociospatial landscape.

Once the "unit-like" character of the urban is understood as a structural product of social practices and political strategies, and no longer as their presupposition, it is possible to position the investigation of urbanization, the creative destruction of political-economic space under capitalism, at the analytical epicenter of urban theory. It is the uneven extension of this process of capitalist creative destruction onto the scale of the entire planet, rather than the formation of a worldwide network of global cities or a single, world-encompassing megalopolis, that underpins the contemporary *problematique* of planetary urbanization.

Notes

1 Manuel Castells, *The Urban Question: A Marxist Approach* (Cambridge: MIT Press: 1977 [1972]) 1.

2 David Potere and Annemarie Schneider, "A Critical Look at Representations of Urban Areas in Global Maps," *GeoJournal* 69 (2007) 55-80; Shlomo Angel, *Making Room for a Planet of Cities* (Cambridge: Lincoln Institute of Land Policy, 2011); and Paolo Gamba and Martin Herold, eds., *Global Mapping of Human Settlement* (New York: Taylor & Francis, 2009).

3 Jane Jacobs, *The Death and Life of Great American Cities* (New York: Modern Library, 1965); Mike Davis, *City of Quartz* (New York: Vintage, 1991); Edward Glaeser, *Triumph of the City* (New York: Tantor, 2011); Jeb Brugmann, *Welcome to the Urban Revolution* (New York: Bloomsbury, 2010); Richard Florida, *Who's Your City?* (New York: Basic, 2008); Gary Hustwit, dir., *Urbanized* (Plexifilm, 2011); and Michael Glawogger, dir., *Megacities* (Fama Film AG, Lotus Film, 1998). For a strong critique of Glaeser, Brugmann and Florida, among others, see Brendan Gleeson, "The Urban Age: Paradox and Prospect," *Urban Studies* 49, 5 (2012) 931-43.

4 David J. Madden, "City Becoming World: Nancy, Lefebvre and the Global-Urban Imagination" this book, Ch. 30; Gavin Kroeber, *Experience Economies: Event in the Cultural Economies of Capital* (MDesS Thesis, Cambridge: Graduate School of Design, Harvard University, 2012); Jorinde Seijdel and Pascal Gielen, eds., "The Art Biennial as a Global Phenomenon: Strategies in Neoliberal Times," *Cahier on Art and the Public Domain* 16 (2009).

5 United Nations Centre for Human Settlements, *An Urbanizing World: Global Report on Human Settlements* (Oxford: Oxford University Press for the United Nations Centre for Human Settlements (HABITAT), 1996). For historical contextualization and detailed critique of this proposition, see Neil Brenner and Christian Schmid, "The 'Urban Age' in Question," this book, Ch. 21.

6 Ricky Burdett and Deyan Sudjic, eds., *The Endless City: The Urban Age Project by the London School of Economics and Deutsche Bank's Alfred Herrhausen Society* (London: Phaidon, 2006).

7 Nathan Sayre, "Climate Change, Scale, and Devaluation: The Challenge of Our Built Environment," *Washington and Lee Journal of Energy, Climate and Environment* 1, 1 (2010) 92-105; and Timothy Luke, "At the End of Nature: Cyborgs, 'Humachines' and Environments in Postmodernity," *Environment and Planning A* 29, 8 (1997) 1367-80.

8 Edward W. Soja and J. Miguel Kanai, "The Urbanization of the World," this book, Ch. 10, page 146.

9 Neil Brenner, *New State Spaces: Urban Governance and the Rescaling of Statehood* (New York: Oxford University Press, 2004); Felipe Correa, "A Projective Space for the South American Hinterland: Resource-Extraction Urbanism," *Harvard Design Magazine* 34 (2011) 174-85; Bae-Gyoon Park, Asato Saito, and Richard Child Hill, eds., *Locating Neoliberalism in East Asia: Neoliberalizing Spaces in Developmental States* (Oxford: Blackwell, 2011); Aihwa Ong, "Graduated Sovereignty in South-East Asia," *Theory, Culture and Society* 17, 4 (2000) 55-75.

10 Michael Hardt and Antonio Negri, *Commonwealth* (Cambridge: Harvard University Press, 2009) 250.

11 Margit Mayer, "The 'Right to the City' in Urban Social Movements," *Cities for People, Not for Profit: Critical Urban Theory and the Right to*

the City, eds. Neil Brenner, Margit Mayer and Peter Marcuse (New York: Routledge, 2011) 63-85; David Harvey, *Rebel Cities: From the Right to the City to the Urban Revolution* (London: Verso, 2012); Andy Merrifield, "The Politics of the Encounter and the Urbanization of the World," *CITY* 16, 2 (2012) 265-79; Christian Schmid, "Henri Lefebvre, The Right to the City and the New Metropolitan Mainstream," *Cities for People, not for Profit: Critical Urban Theory and the Right to the City*, eds. Neil Brenner, Margit Mayer and Peter Marcuse (New York: Routledge, 2012) 42-62.

12 The distinction between categories of analysis and categories of practice is productively developed in Rogers Brubaker and Frederick Cooper, "Beyond Identity," *Theory & Society* 29 (2000) 1-47. For a powerful meditation on its applications to urban questions, see David Wachsmuth, "City as Ideology," this book, Ch. 23.

13 Louis Wirth, "Urbanism as a Way of Life," *Classic Essays on the Culture of Cities*, eds. Richard Sennett and Engelwood Cliffs (New York: Appleton-Century-Crofts, 1969 [1937]) 143-64.

14 Ash Amin and Nigel Thrift, *Cities: Reimagining the Urban* (London: Polity, 2002) 1.

15 Neil Brenner and Christian Schmid, "Planetary Urbanization," this book, Ch. 11. In their book *Cities*, Amin and Thrift develop a productive version of this critique, albeit one that is oriented towards a very different methodological pathway than that forged here.

16 On earlier crises, see Manuel Castells, "Is There an Urban Sociology?" *Urban Sociology: Critical Essays*, ed. Chris G. Pickvance (London: Tavistock, 1976) 33-59; and Janet Abu-Lughod, *The City is Dead Long Live the City*, Monograph No. 12 (Berkeley: IURD Monograph Series, Institute of Urban and Regional Development, University of California Berkeley, 1969). On contemporary challenges see, among other works: Christian Schmid, "Patterns and Pathways of Global Urbanization: Towards a Comparative Analysis," this book, Ch. 14; Ananya Roy and Aihwa Ong, eds., *Worlding Cities: Asian Experiments and the Art of Being Global* (Oxford: Wiley-Blackwell, 2011); Ananya Roy, "The 21st Century Metropolis: New Geographies of Theory," *Regional Studies* 43, 6 (2009) 819-30; and Sharon Zukin, "Is There an Urban Sociology? Questions on a Field and a Vision," *Sociologica* 3 (2011) 1-18.

17 The concept of a blind field is borrowed from Henri Lefebvre's ferocious polemic against overspecialization in mainstream urban studies, a situation that in his view contributes to a fragmentation of its basic object of analysis and to a masking of the worldwide totality formed by capitalist urbanization. See Henri Lefebvre, *The Urban Revolution*, trans. Robert Bononno (Minneapolis: University of Minnesota Press, 2003 [1970]) 29, 53.

18 For useful overviews and critical assessments of this state of affairs, see Edward Soja, *Postmetropolis* (Oxford: Blackwell, 2000); and Roy, "The 21st Century Metropolis: New Geographies of Theory" Another useful resource on such debates is the journal *CITY: Analysis of Urban Trends, Culture, Theory, Policy, Action*, which devotes extensive attention to discussions of theoretical/epistemological foundations and their political ramifications.

19 On the concept of "academic Babel" see Lefebvre, *The Urban Revolution*, 54.

201

20 Key texts in this line of research include Ignacio Farías and Thomas Bender, eds., *Urban Assemblages: How Actor-Network Theory Changes Urban Research* (New York: Routledge, 2010); Bruno Latour and Emilie Hermant, *Paris: Invisible City*, trans. Liz Carey-Libbrecht. http://www.bruno-latour.fr/livres/viii_paris-city-gb.pdf, 2006 [1998]; Colin McFarlane, "Assemblage and Critical Urbanism," *CITY* 15, 2 (2011) 204-24; and Colin McFarlane, "The City as Assemblage: Dwelling and Urban Space," *Environment and Planning D: Society and Space* 29 (2011) 649-71.

21 An important exception to this generalization is the work of Ignacio Farías, "Introduction: Decentering the Object of Urban Studies," *Urban Assemblages: How Actor-Network Theory Changes Urban Research*, eds. Ignacio Farías and Thomas Bender (New York: Routledge, 2010) 1-24, who explicitly confronts such issues and proposes a radical, if controversial, rethinking of the urban question. A more cautious assessment of the potential of such approaches in urban research is presented in Thomas Bender, "Reassembling the City: Networks and Urban Imaginaries," *Urban Assemblages: How Actor-Network Theory Changes Urban Research*, eds. Ignacio Farías and Thomas Bender (New York: Routledge, 2010) 303-23.

22 On the notion of a context of context, see Neil Brenner, Jamie Peck and Nik Theodore, "Variegated Neoliberalization: Geographies, Pathways, Modalities," *Global Networks* 10, 2 (2010) 182-222. A version of this line of critique is developed in Neil Brenner, David J. Madden and David Wachsmuth, "Assemblage Urbanism and the Challenges of Critical Urban Theory," *CITY* 15, 2 (2010) 225-40; as well as David Wachsmuth, David J. Madden and Neil Brenner, "Between Abstraction and Complexity: Meta-Theoretical Observations on the Assemblage Debate," *CITY* 15, 6 (2011) 740-50.

23 Peter Saunders, *Social Theory and the Urban Question*, second edition (London: Routledge, 1986 [1981]).

24 Herbert Gans, "Some Problems of and Futures for Urban Sociology: Toward a Sociology of Settlements," *City & Community* 8, 3 (2009) 211-19.

25 Frederic Jameson, "Cognitive Mapping," *Marxism and the Interpretation of Culture*, eds. Cary Nelson and Lawrence Grossberg (Chicago: University of Illinois Press, 1988) 347-57. Jameson's neo-Althusserian concept builds upon yet supersedes the strictly phenomenological notion introduced by urban designer Kevin Lynch in his classic text, *The Image of the City* (Cambridge: MIT Press, 1960).

26 On the creative destruction of urban space, see David Harvey, *The Urban Experience* (Baltimore: Johns Hopkins University Press, 1989).

27 Lefebvre, *The Urban Revolution*.

28 Roy, "The 21st Century Metropolis," 820. The notion of an "urban phenomenon" is from Lefebvre, *The Urban Revolution*.

29 Andrea Kahn, "Defining Urban Sites," *Site Matters: Design Concepts, Histories, and Strategies*, eds. Carol Burns and Andrea Kahn (New York: Routledge, 2005) 287.

30 Łukasz Stanek, *Henri Lefebvre on Space: Architecture, Urban Research and the Production of Theory* (Minneapolis: University of Minnesota Press, 2011) 151-6; Christian Schmid, *Stadt, Raum und Gesellschaft: Henri Lefebvre und die Theorie der Produktion des Raumes* (Stuttgart: Franz Steiner Verlag, 2005); Neil Brenner, "Between Fixity and Motion: Accumulation, Territorial Organization and the Historical Geography of Spatial Scales," *Environment and Planning D: Society and Space* 16, 4 (1998) 459-81.

31 The notions of the global, the planetary and the world are likewise philosophically and politically contested, and require further unpacking. See, among other works, Stuart Elden, "The Space of the World," *New Geographies* 4 (2011) 26-31; Hashim Sarkis, "The World According to Architecture: Beyond Cosmopolis," *New Geographies* 4 (2011) 104-8; and Madden, "City Becoming World," this book, Ch. 30. See also the various texts assembled in Henri Lefebvre, *State, Space, World: Selected Essays*, eds. Neil Brenner and Stuart Elden, trans. Gerald Moore, Neil Brenner and Stuart Elden

(Minneapolis: University of Minnesota Press, 2009). For present purposes, it must suffice simply to note that the "world," as used here, refers to a planet-encompassing zone of action, imagination and potentiality that is dialectically co-produced with the urban: it is not simply "filled in" through the global extension of urbanization, but is actively constituted and perpetually reorganized in and through urban sociospatial relations. This point is lucidly developed by Madden, "City Becoming World," this book, Ch. 30.

32 Lefebvre, *The Urban Revolution*, 66.

33 Castells, *The Urban Question*; Abu-Lughod, *The City is Dead—Long Live the City*; and Don Martindale, "Prefatory Remarks: The Theory of the City in Max Weber," *The City* (New York: Free Press, 1958) 9-64.

34 Andrew Sayer, "Defining the Urban," *GeoJournal* 9, 3 (1984) 281. See also Andrew Sayer, "Abstraction: A Realist Interpretation," *Radical Philosophy* 28 (1981) 6-15.

35 Saunders, *Social Theory and the Urban Question*; Mark Gottdiener, *Social Production of Urban Space*, second edition (Austin: University of Texas Press, 1985); and Andy Merrifield, *Metromarxism* (New York: Routledge, 2002).

36 Castells, "Is There an Urban Sociology?"

37 Wirth, "Urbanism as a Way of Life"; and Gans, "Some problems of and Futures for Urban Sociology."

38 Debates on the urban question as a scale question represent a partial exception to this generalization, since they entail analytically contrasting the urban to supra-urban scales (a vertical comparative vector) rather than to extra-urban territories (a horizontal comparative vector). See among other works, Neil Brenner, "Restructuring, Rescaling and the Urban Question," *Critical Planning* 16, Summer (2009) 60-79.

39 The urban/non-urban binarism is productively exploded in William Cronon's classic book on the simultaneous development of Chicago and the Great West, *Nature's Metropolis: Chicago and the Great West* (New York: Norton, 1991). The same set of issues is powerfully explored in Alan Berger's brilliant study of waste landscapes and horizontal urbanization in deindustrializing North America. See Alan Berger, *Drosscape: Wasting Land in Urban America* (Princeton: Princeton Architectural Press, 2006). One of the first attempts explicitly to treat the non-urban as a zone of theoretical significance to the project of urban theory is the recent issue of *MONU (Magazine on Urbanism)* 16, titled "Non-Urbanism" (2012).

40 The distinction between nominal and constitutive essences is derived from Sayer, "Defining the Urban." On process-based theorizing, see the following: David Harvey, *The Limits to Capital* (Chicago: University of Chicago Press, 1982); and Bertell Ollman, *Dialectical Investigations* (London: Routledge, 1993). The process-based methodology proposed here has long underpinned historical-geographical materialist approaches to sociospatial theory, but with a few major exceptions, its full ramifications for the theoretical foundations of urban research have yet to be fully elaborated. Important exceptions include the chapters included in Nik Heynen, Maria Kaika and Erik Swyngedouw, eds., *In the Nature of Cities: Urban Political Ecology and the Politics of Urban Metabolism* (New York: Routledge, 2006). Particularly when it is shed of its latent "methodological cityism," the concept of urban "metabolism" is an extremely fruitful analytical tool for advancing such a methodology. See Hillary Angelo and David Wachsmuth, "Urbanizing Urban Political Ecology: A Critique of Methodological Cityism," this book, Ch. 24; and David Wachsmuth, "Three Ecologies: Urban Metabolism and the Society-Nature Opposition," *Sociological Quarterly* 53, 4 (2012) 506-23.

41 This is the core thesis of Roger Diener, Jacques Herzog, Marcel Meili, Pierre de Meuron and Christian Schmid, eds., *Switzerland—An Urban Portrait, Volume 1-4* (Basel: Birkhäuser, 2006). For excerpts and selections, see several of the contributions to this book by Christian Schmid, including chapters 4, 6, 14 and 26.

42 Ibid.

43 See Wachsmuth, "City as Ideology," this book, Ch. 23.

44 A similar concern with the gulf between experience and the totality produced by capital animates Jameson's classic theorization of cognitive mapping. See Jameson, "Cognitive Mapping," 347-57.

45 This argument is assessed and criticized in Brenner and Schmid, "The 'Urban Age' in Question," this book, Ch. 21.

46 See, among other works, John Friedmann and John Miller, "The Urban Field," *Journal of the American Planning Association* 31, 4 (1965) 312-20; Jean Gottmann, *Megalopolis* (Cambridge: MIT Press, 1961); Constantinos Doxiadis and J.G. Papaioannou, *Ecumenopolis: The Inevitable City of the Future* (New York: W.W. Norton, 1974); and above all, Lefebvre, *The Urban Revolution*.

47 This thesis and, in particular, the distinction between concentrated and extended urbanization, is derived from ongoing collaborative work with Christian Schmid; I am grateful for his permission to present it here in this highly abbreviated form. The concept of extended urbanization was initially proposed by Monte-Mór in a pioneering investigation of the Brazilian Amazon. See his contributions to this book, "Extended Urbanization and Settlement Patterns in Brazil: An Environmental Approach," Ch. 8, and "What is the Urban in the Contemporary World?" this book, Ch. 17. See also Roberto Luís Monte-Mór, *Modernities in the Jungle: Extended Urbanization in the Brazilian Amazon* (Ph.D. Thesis, Los Angeles: Department of Urban Planning, University of California Los Angeles, 2004).

48 Castells, *The Urban Question*, 101.

49 Manu Goswami, "Rethinking the Modular Nation Form: Toward a Sociohistorical Conception of Nationalism," *Comparative Studies in Society and History* 44, 4 (2002) 770-99. This claim is developed productively in relation to urban ideology by Wachsmuth, "City as Ideology," this book, Ch. 23; a closely analogous account is implicit within David Harvey's concept of structured coherence in Harvey, *The Urban Experience*.

50 Harvey, *The Urban Experience*.

51 An argument along these lines is suggested in the literature on the "new enclosures," especially Massimo De Angelis, *The Beginning of History: Value Struggles and Global Capital* (London: Pluto, 2007). For wide-ranging analyses of emergent forms of contestation over the global commons (including issues related to the appropriation of land, water, air and food), see Nik Heynen, James McCarthy, Scott Prudham and Paul Robbins, eds., *Neoliberal Environments* (New York: Routledge, 2007); Fred Magdoff and Brian Tokar, eds., *Agriculture and Food in Crisis: Conflict, Resistance, and Renewal* (New York: Monthly Review Press, 2011); and Richard Peet, Paul Robbins and Michael J. Watts, eds., *Global Political Ecology* (New York: Routledge, 2011).

Figure Credits

13.1 National Aeronautics and Space Administration (NASA). http://visibleearth.nasa.gov/view.php?id=55167.

13.2 Used with permission from Ange Tran, *Not an Alternative*.

13.3 Used with permission from Felipe Correa, Harvard GSD.

13.4 Original by the author.

13.5 Brian Berry, *The Human Consequences of Urbanization: Divergent Paths in the Urban Experience of the Twentieth Century* (New York: St. Martin's Press, 1973) 39-42.

13.6 Roger Diener, Jacques Herzog, Marcel Meili, Pierre de Meuron, and Christian Schmid, *Switzerland—An Urban Portrait, Volume 1* (Basel: Birkhäuser, 2006) 209.

13.7 Constantinos Doxiadis, *Ekistics: An Introduction to the Science of Human Settlements* (Oxford: Oxford University Press, 1968) 200. By permission of Oxford University Press.

13.8 Brian Berry, *Geographic Perspectives on Urban Systems* (Englewood Cliffs: Prentice Hall, 1970) 44-5.

13.9 Nikos Katsikis, Urban Theory Lab, Harvard-GSD. Compilation of road, rail and marine transportation networks. Road and rail networks are based on the Vector Map Level 0 (VMap0) data set released by the National Imagery and Mapping Agency (NIMA) in 1997. Marine routes are based on the global commercial activity (shipping) data set compiled by The National Center for Ecological Analysis and Synthesis (NCEAS). http://www.nceas.ucsb.edu/globalmarine.

13.10 www.telegeography.com

13.11 http://earthobservatory.nasa.gov/IOTD/view.php?id=40173, accessed on June 29, 2012.

14
PATTERNS AND PATHWAYS OF GLOBAL URBANIZATION: TOWARDS COMPARATIVE ANALYSIS

Christian Schmid

The past two decades have seen a fundamental change in the speed, scale and scope of urbanization. Transcending all forms of physical, political and social borders, urbanization has become a global phenomenon. At the same time, differences both between and within cities have become more pronounced. Despite the global sprawl of urban areas, the individual development of cities reveals considerable specificity and path dependency. This has led to the evolution of a wide range of different urban forms and constellations.

We are now faced with an urban universe that is constantly bringing forth new developments. The challenge is to improve our understanding of contemporary urbanization processes and to decipher their implications and effects. New concepts and terms are needed to designate these new urban forms and processes. Despite intense efforts, the concepts developed so far are not sufficient for comprehensively describing and explaining these new urban developments. Little is yet understood regarding the form, extent and implications of these urbanization processes and their variations across places. What is still lacking is a comparative approach enabling the detection and explanation of the differences that are today developing. The challenge is thus further to develop a comparative approach that can apprehend the general tendencies of urbanization, while at the same time illuminating the specificities of each urban area.

Tracing Global Urbanization

Urban development has radically changed in recent years. All over the world, new patterns of urbanization are evolving, "creating the most economically, socially, and culturally heterogeneous cities the world has ever known."[1] Existing urban forms are dissolving and polymorphous urban regions are taking shape. Extremely heterogeneous in structure, they include old city centers as well as formerly peripheral areas.

At the same time, extremely rapid urbanization has led to the emergence of completely new urban forms in the megacities of the global South. Informal modes of urbanization, which were long regarded as temporary aberrations, are increasingly becoming core elements of urban expansion that can no longer be ignored. It is instead to be expected that informal forms of urbanism will become a permanent feature of urban development.

Contemporary urbanization is closely linked with globalization. In an increasingly networked world, industrialization on a global scale has experienced massive acceleration and expansion. This has a dual effect on urbanization: on the one hand, the new global economy has led to strong economic growth in cities, attracting a large number of migrants. Some cities have become centers of decision-making and innovation, and are developing into strategic nodes of the globalized economy.[2] Other cities, predominantly located in emerging economies, are attracting the growing global manufacturing industry. On the other hand, industrialization and rationalization of agriculture works as a push factor and causes additional migration from rural areas to the cities. The increasingly complex mechanisms of urban growth are further aggravated through continuing population growth in many parts of the world. Accelerated urbanization leads to considerable concentration processes in already densely populated urban areas, as well as to dramatic patterns of sprawl manifested in the massive expansion of urban areas into the countryside.[3] In this way, globalization leads to an intensification of urbanization, while urbanization simultaneously acts as a major driving force of globalization.

The unprecedented dimension and speed of urbanization has dramatic consequences. Today, there are around 500 city-regions with populations exceeding one million, around 20 megacity regions with over 10 million residents, and some extended urban areas, such as Tokyo and the Pearl River Delta, with more than 40 million inhabitants (see Figues 10.1, 10.2, and 10.3 on pages 144, 145, and 148).[4] These regions form large, networked and strongly urbanized spaces, which are structured quite heterogeneously. They may include various agglomerations, metropolitan regions and networks of cities, as well as large green spaces and sparsely settled zones.[5] Other far-reaching sociospatial transformations include the blurring and rearticulation of urban territories, the disintegration of the "hinterland" and the end of the "wilderness."[6]

Case Studies and Urban Models

Until recently, urban research remained largely dominated by analyses of individual cities. Accordingly, the understanding of urban development is to a large extent still determined by ideal-typical models. As early as the 1920s, the Chicago School of urban sociology used the example of Chicago as the basis for its famous concentric ring model of urban development.[7] In the 1990s, the Los Angeles School emerged as an antithetical model shaped largely by the discipline of urban geography. It declared Los Angeles, with its massive urban sprawl and polycentricity, to be a paradigmatic example of urban development at the end of the twentieth century.[8] In architecture too, the emphasis was on learning from individual cities; well-known examples included *Learning from Las Vegas* and *Delirious New York*.[9] These examples show that, until the end of the twentieth century, the focus was mainly on developments in the West, especially in North America. This dominance of Western models has been increasingly questioned in recent times.[10] Currently, there is a constant flow of new research and investigations of cities across the world. However, the overwhelming majority of these case studies continue to be case-based monographs, leading again to the promotion of particular cities, such as Mexico City, Shanghai, Dubai or Lagos as spectacular new examples of urban development. While such specific cases can be helpful for identifying typical new developments, they offer little insight into broader processes of global urbanization or their differentiated regional and local patterns. Instead, there is a danger of generalization based on spectacular individual cases, or a reductionist view of highly complex, varied and differentiated processes, resulting in simplified models of contemporary urban conditions and forms.

New Processes of Urbanization

Another important strand of urban research involves the analysis of processes and trends. This strand focuses less on the individual city than on the process of urbanization itself. This approach has gained prominence since the 1980s, when fundamental changes in urbanization became visible and the focus shifted to entirely new trends and processes, heralding a new phase of urban research. Many new concepts and terms have been developed in recent years to designate various newly emerging urban phenomena.[11] First, the emergence of global cities and world cities as strategic hubs of the global economy was investigated and their implications for urban development processes were explored across various places.[12] Second, processes of restructuring and reinvestment in mainly low- and middle-income urban areas were analyzed, with particular attention to processes of gentrification and urban regeneration.[13] Third, entirely new developments were observed in the former urban peripheries of metropolitan regions, where a wide variety of new urban configurations emerged and were referred to as, among other names, "edge cities," "exopolis," and "*Zwischenstadt*" ("in-between cities").[14] Fourth, during the past decade, new patterns of restructuring and uneven spatial development have been detected in the global North and South. In particular, there has been a massive growth of cities in the global

South and a trend towards megacity formation, accompanied by the consolidation of multiple forms of informal settlements.[15] Finally, especially in the deindustrializing zones of the older capitalist world, the phenomenon of shrinking cities has attracted considerable attention.[16]

The many anthologies on these issues have led to important insights and have productively illuminated various aspects of global urbanization. Many of these studies make use of a comparative perspective. Nevertheless, they usually consist in compilations of interesting but distinct case studies by different authors. Accordingly, the examples presented are not genuinely comparable, and are rarely, if ever, subjected to systematic comparison. Furthermore, they often remain focused on a single topic or theme, thus occluding the need for a more comprehensive overview of contemporary worldwide urbanization patterns and pathways.

On Comparative Urban Studies

Demands for more systematic approaches to comparative research in urban studies have been increasingly put forward, and there is an ever growing number of studies of specific aspects of global urbanization.[17] Examples include the *Multiplicity* project, the studies conducted by Peter J. Taylor and the *Globalization and World Cities* (GaWC) research network, the International Network for Urban Research and Action (INURA) volume on contested metropolises, and a recent comparative study of European megacity regions by Peter Hall and Kathy Pain.[18] Additionally, some important overviews of diverse aspects of global urbanization have recently been published, including the catalogue of the 2006 Venice Biennale, the book *The Endless City*, part of the LSE's Urban Age project, and the study of the geography of globalization by Jacques Lévy and his team.[19]

None of these examples, however, is a comparative study in the strict sense. Efforts to carry out a comprehensive, systematic comparison of urban development under globalizing capitalism are still in their early stages. One of the first systematic studies in this field is Janet Abu-Lughod's detailed comparison of the historical development of the three US metropolises, New York, Los Angeles, and Chicago.[20] But major theoretical and methodical difficulties have arisen here too, and the result is less a full comparative analysis than a temporally parallel interpretation of urban development within the three cities.[21] In his comparison of four African cities, AbdouMaliq Simone offers a further important perspective for comparative urban research, and Jennifer Robinson has advanced the remarkable proposal to analyze all cities as "ordinary," thus countering the persistent exoticization of Non-Western cities in mainstream urban discourse.[22] Further examples for efforts to advance comparative urban studies include the work of Julie-Anne Boudreau and her colleagues, that of Fulong Wu and Nicholas Phelps, as well as that of Harris.[23]

As all these examples show, the comparative analysis of cities and urban areas is facing many difficulties. The complex processes involved in the restructuring of cities and urban regions require a new understanding of contemporary urbanization. In particular, what is needed is a dynamic approach to urban studies that not only detects and describes the emergence of new urban forms, but also focuses on the mechanisms of urbanization processes and explains how general tendencies take shape in specific places. I now illustrate some of my own experiences in this field.

Capitales Fatales

The first comparative study I was involved in was an analysis of contemporary urban politics and the unfolding of new urbanization processes in Zurich and Frankfurt.[24] This study was based on the theories on world cities and global cities that had just been introduced into German-speaking debate at that time. The two cities were analyzed by two separate teams in a parallel fashion, with the same basic concepts and analytical tools. It could be seen that both cities were undergoing very similar processes: both were old industrial cities that were experiencing massive economic restructuring, thus becoming global financial centers, and manifesting trends comparable to those of large global cities like New York or London. This is why we called them "*capitales fatales.*" By focusing on the parallel trends of urban development in the two cities, it was possible to understand how globalization was produced, and to identify the decisive elements of the transformations that were reshaping globalizing cities—on the one hand, the restructuring and gentrification of inner city areas, and on the other, the emergence of new centralities, corporate headquarters and advanced business services in the urban peripheries, producing urban patterns that were similar to those observed in North America around the same time. These developments also led to the emergence of a regional scale of urbanization and opened up the question of new regional politics. At the same time, the effects of local politics and the strong influence of urban social movements were observed in both cities, thus indicating the strong articulation of global and local processes, a phenomenon that was conceptualized at the time through the term "glocalization."[25]

The New Metropolitan Mainstream

Another example of this comparative approach is the ongoing project of the International Network for Urban Research and Action (INURA) on the "new metropolitan mainstream." This term has been coined to describe a broad range of phenomena that have recently emerged in cities around the world.[26] Initially, this new metropolitan mainstream is articulated as a norm that defines what is to be regarded as "urban" or "metropolitan," while also presenting certain standards, models and templates for urban planning and design that have been circulated among municipal governments and city councils around the world. For example, the promotion of "soft" location factors, of "quality of life" for elites, and of a prestigious blend of cultural amenities and services for luxury consumption is today an increasingly standard policy goal for attracting capital investment and highly qualified workers. Accordingly, many contemporary cities all over the globe have been equipped with skyscrapers, flagship projects, and "star" architecture. This "standard metropolitan architecture" is becoming an important new fuel for global urbanization patterns. In this context, a remarkable shift in models for the "urban future" has taken place. Today, "new" metropolises such as Dubai, Shanghai and Singapore are much more likely to be seen as models for the future of urban development than the "old" Western metropolises such as Paris or New York.[27]

As an effect of these policies, processes of gentrification and of the commodification of the urban are spreading on a global scale, deep into the cities of the South, into the former urban peripheries, and even into smaller cities. These trends also entail a significant rescaling of urban development. Processes of gentrification and displacement are no longer limited to individual neighborhoods; rather, entire intra-urban areas and even large parts of metropolitan regions are upgraded and transformed into zones of reproduction for metropolitan elites. A massive increase in land and real estate prices, and the accompanying housing crisis, have already seriously restricted access to these areas for less privileged sections of the population. In order to learn more about these processes, INURA embarked upon a collective mapping project that has traced the various elements of the new metropolitan mainstream in more than thirty cities, bringing together scientists, professionals and practitioners. Initial results were presented at an exhibition in conjunction with the 20th INURA conference held in Zurich in 2010.[28]

Switzerland—An Urban Portrait

A different approach and methodological design was applied in the project of ETH Studio Basel, *Switzerland—An Urban Portrait*.[29] The aim of this research was not primarily to compare individual cities, but to analyze the urbanization of the territory and, more generally, the urban condition of contemporary Switzerland. The theoretical and methodological framework developed in this project has enabled us to detect different forms of urbanization and various types of urban potential. The theoretical starting point was Henri Lefebvre's famous hypothesis of the complete urbanization of society, already put forward in 1970.[30] This hypothesis involves a decisive change in analytical perspective, from the classical distinction between urban and rural areas, which has been dominant in urban theory for so long, towards an approach to the differences that are emerging across a worldwide urbanizing landscape.[31] This study put forth three elementary criteria for determining and analyzing today's urban phenomena: networks, borders, and differences.[32] On the basis of these criteria, it was possible to describe the entire territory in urban terms and to develop a typology of urbanized areas in Switzerland: metropolitan regions, networks of cities, quiet zones, Alpine resorts and Alpine fallow lands.[33]

With this analysis, it is also possible to compare individual cities, such as the metropolitan region of Zurich and the Région Lémanique, around Lake Geneva, with the two main centers Geneva and Lausanne (Figure 14.1 and 14.2, next page). These two regions contain quite diverse features and patterns. If mapped appropriately, this diversity becomes visible. The project constructed different layers (including built-up areas, transport systems, commuter zones, etc.), which were superimposed to produce an approximate outline of the regions. If these patterns are compared, it is clear that they are very different, and that these differences have considerable effects on daily life. Zurich is thus characterized by urban sprawl and reveals a strong regional dimension and a complex polycentric structure. In contrast, the Région Lémanique is clearly divided into two catchment areas around the two centers of Lausanne and Geneva. The region of Geneva has a very unusual urban form: on the one hand there is a compact monocentric city, and on the other there is an amorphous urban area stretching into France, separated from the city of Geneva by the national border and a greenbelt. Nevertheless, this urbanized area is completely dependent on and oriented towards the city of Geneva in everyday life; it forms a reservoir for cheap labor and offers affordable land for houses and villas. Thus, the map reveals a hidden reality, with which everyone is familiar but which was generally ignored in political debates.

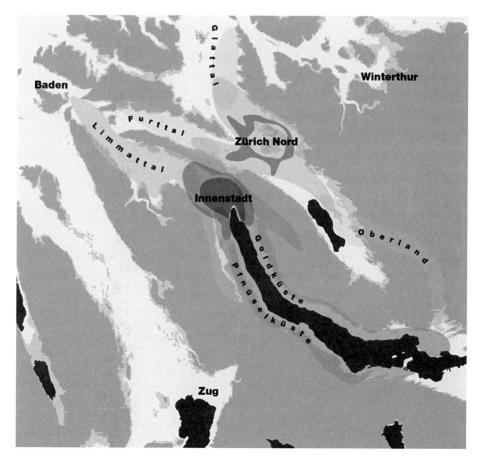

14.1 Region Zürich: urban configurations

Geneva has thus developed two sides: the splendid, well-known international city oriented towards the lake, and the neglected backside beyond the border, hardly connected with the city—"*l'autre Genève*" ("the other Geneva").

This analysis of urbanization patterns presents a snapshot of the current situation. However, it is equally crucial to understand why and how these patterns developed. Such an endeavor requires a historical analysis of the dynamics of urbanization processes.

A Historical Territorial Approach

Within the framework of an interdisciplinary research project involving architects, geographers and historians, which also included a comparative analysis of Zurich and Geneva, we developed such a historical analysis of urbanization and territorial regulation.[34] The project was based on the regulation approach, which was theoretically extended to include a territorial dimension. At the heart of this framework is the concept of the "territorial relation" (*rapport territorial*), which defines the specific field of regulation of the territory.[35]

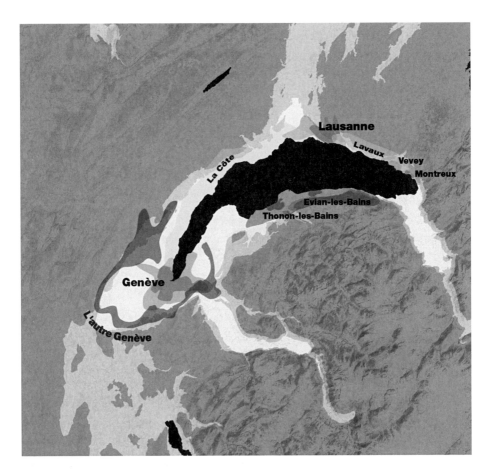

14.2 Région Lémanique: urban configurations

The main instrument applied in this research project was periodization, which was used to compare individual models of urbanization and to identify the specificity of their trajectories. Periodization has long been developed and applied in the social sciences and has also figured crucially in debates on Fordism, its crisis and its "post-Fordist" aftermath.[36] However, in the context of comparative approaches to urban development, the challenge consists in analyzing local trajectories, which are articulated with supralocal cycles but nevertheless show a certain degree of independence. Furthermore, this periodization should be able to illuminate processes of urbanization, which in turn requires that various phases of the production of space be distinguished analytically. While these are linked to more general social processes, they follow a logic of their own and accordingly display a different kind of dynamic.

The details of this analysis cannot be elaborated here, but one result of the research was particularly striking: it turned out that conditions at the beginning of the urbanization process in the early nineteenth century had a decisive impact on the further development of both cities. At that time, Zurich was a relatively small city of about 10,000 inhabitants, which had a certain political power, but was economically not very important. However, it was located in the geographical center of the most industrialized region of Switzerland and thus soon became the functional center of this industrialized region and the largest city in Switzerland. Even today, Zurich is oriented intensively towards this region and also forms an important center of the global economy. By contrast, Geneva developed differently. At the beginning of the nineteenth century, it was by far the largest city in Switzerland with about 25,000 inhabitants. It formed a Protestant city-state with almost no territory. Outside the city walls was the "enemy": a predominantly Catholic and rural population. Thus, Geneva represented in many respects the opposite model to Zurich—and both cities today still articulate these fundamental differences.

This example clearly shows how the historical pathway of urban development is engraved into the territory, and how entrenched legacies of urbanization survive, influencing contemporary patterns of urban development. This insight suggests the need for a twofold analysis—first, an account of (contemporary) patterns of urbanization; and second, an investigation of the (historical) pathways of urbanization that produced those patterns.

Three Dimensions of Urbanization

According to Henri Lefebvre's theory of the production of space, the urbanization process can be analyzed in three dimensions—first, the production of material elements and structures; second, the processes of regulation and representation; and third, socialization and learning processes.[37]

Material structures. First, urban space is perceived space. As such, it is a space of material interaction that is opened up by all kinds of networks and information flows. Interaction processes are inscribed upon the urban space; they form shapes and patterns, from the earliest dirt trails to modern-day fiber-optic networks. This aspect of the material production of space has already been clearly conceptualized by David Harvey as the production of the built environment.[38] Harvey also identified the main contradiction of this production process, in particular, the contradiction between fixity and motion. For, in order to allow for large-scale movements in space, it is necessary to produce a fixed and immobile infrastructure (such as high-speed rail networks, airports and the like).[39] In economic terms, this requires massive, long-term investments that have great influence on later patterns of spatial development. Once decisions on such infrastructures are taken, they establish the material bases of nodes and networks, and thus also define centralities and peripheries at all spatial scales. A huge effort is needed to change these structures, and they therefore survive for a very long time. These material structures are deeply embedded in the city, and they have massive effects on everyday life, for they define the lines along which the urban fabric takes shape and evolves historically.

Regulation and representation. Second, the city can be analyzed as a conceived space, or as a representation of space. The everyday understanding of what a city is depends upon the social definition of urban space. If we ask somebody in Paris and someone else in Los Angeles to define the city, quite different answers will emerge. And these answers are strongly influenced by the dominant concepts of space, and thus by the image of the city, the blueprint or the map, and also by the plan that attempts to define and pin down the characteristics of urban space. All these various definitions are specific representations of space. They describe discursive demarcations of the content of urban space and entail corresponding strategies of inclusion and exclusion. Definitions of the city thus become a complex force field in which diverse strategies and interests converge and clash. These assume the form of explicit and implicit procedures and rules that regulate the process of urbanization in particular ways. Representations of space are thus related to power and define how space is used and reproduced. They not only determine how we discuss, but how we act.

Socialization and learning processes. Third, the city is always a lived space as well—a place of residents, who use it and appropriate it in their everyday practices. Urban space can be identified as the place of difference: its specific quality comes from the simultaneous presence of quite distinct worlds and concepts of value, of ethnic, cultural and social groups, and of activities, functions and knowledge. Urban space establishes the possibility of bringing all these diverse elements together and making them productive. At the same time, however, there is also a tendency for the elements to cut themselves off and become separate. How these differences are experienced in actual daily life is crucial. The qualities of urban space are embedded in our history and in our everyday experiences, and are a result of socialization processes that are always contextualized in concrete places. Thus, processes of socialization and learning play a decisive role in determining the shape of everyday life in a city.

Models of Urbanization

These three basic dimensions can be applied to the analysis of the contemporary urban process. While urbanization lays the groundwork for the generation of urban situations, these are only created through the interplay of multiple actions. Urbanization is always a physical process shaped by specific local conditions, structures and constellations. Therefore, the process of global urbanization does not necessarily homogenize the entirety of urban space. Quite the contrary, differences within urban space are arguably increasing under contemporary conditions.[40]

Accordingly, in different places, various models of urbanization have evolved. Individual urbanization models are determined, beneath other factors, by a wide range of historical experiences, traditions and value systems. They are transmitted as commonly accepted collective processes of socialization and learning, with the built environment playing an important role as the material basis of everyday experience. While many conditions of urbanization are organized at a national or even global scale, fundamental differences in urbanization patterns persist within individual countries. The examples of New York, Los Angeles and Chicago, of Toronto, Montreal and Vancouver, of Milan, Rome and Naples, and even of Zurich, Geneva and Basel provide sufficient evidence to support this thesis.

In order to understand such differences, we must often look back over a long period, for the models of urbanization are deeply inscribed in the history of a territory, just as, conversely, history constantly inscribes itself anew as a territory evolves; during this process, earlier strata are not obliterated, but rather tend to be overwritten, as in a palimpsest. As a result, a great variety of models of urbanization are developing. It is crucial to understand their origins, their pathways of development, and their possible impacts, in order to detect and explore the specific urban potentials they might contain.

How can models of urbanization be analyzed? The problem we face today is that cities no longer constitute delimited units; they are highly dynamic, multifaceted and complex. A twofold approach is required in order to grasp these factors. On the one hand, a "horizontal," synchronic analysis is needed which starts from the current situation of the territory, determines the expansion of and interaction between urban regions, and reveals variations in the process of urbanization. On the other hand, urban development has to be understood and conceived as a historical process of production and ongoing transformation. This requires a "vertical," diachronic analysis. Only through a combination of both perspectives can the specificity of an urban region be identified and understood.

Patterns of Urbanization

Horizontal analysis examines the structure of the city and urban situations as they are at a given moment. While increasingly exact data and detailed methods are available for analyzing the structure of a city, experience has shown that, in most cases, such approaches to mapping spatial phenomena and distributions only create the appearance of precision. Urbanization is a complex process that is constantly changing shape. Therefore, no single representation can provide more than a mere snapshot. Furthermore, urban reality comprises quite diverse attributes that are superimposed in layers. Accordingly, many different lines of demarcation can be drawn, depending on the observer's perspective and heuristic interest.

The nighttime lights map (Figure 13.1, page 183) is one of the most popular images that are currently used to illustrate patterns of global urbanization. In fact, this image does not grasp urbanization directly, but displays rather a form of pollution, namely light pollution. It serves here as a metaphor to show how urbanized areas are seen from the outside. It has indeed been used as a putatively "scientific" indicator for the delimitation of urban mega-regions, and it was also one of the main components used to construct the "urban extents," or built-up urban areas, in one of the major contemporary approaches to geospatial visualization (Figure 14.3).[41] Whatever their deficiencies, both maps do clearly reveal some of the tremendous differences in urbanization patterns around the globe. These patterns and differences must now be analyzed more closely, and both their historical production processes and contemporary implications revealed.

Such an analysis must also address the question of scale: urban realities exist on different scales; the various urban networks differ in spatial extent; and many are also superimposed upon one another and interconnected. At the top end of the scale are vast megalopolises or "urban galaxies," whose expansion is continental.[42] At the next level are urban mega-regions or conurbations, which represent large, extensively urbanized and networked spaces.[43] Examples include Greater Tokyo, but also the Swiss Plateau. These urban mega-regions can again be structured quite heterogeneously within themselves, and may include various agglomerations, metropolitan regions, or networks of cities, but also large green spaces and sparsely settled zones.[44] Individual regions may again be structured quite heterogeneously within themselves—their structure may be monocentric, bipolar, or polycentric—and may be composed of various urban configurations. It is important to look at the interference of the different scales and to move up, down and across in and through the analysis.[45]

Pathways of Urbanization

On the basis of the horizontal analysis, a vertical or historical analysis should follow. It descends into the past to identify the defining moments of urban culture that have inscribed themselves into the terrain and collective memory. Subsequently, the analysis must ascend in order to attempt to reconstruct the decisive lines of development and to draft a timeline that demarcates the dominant constellations of power and the most important fields of conflict. In particular, it is crucial to identify the constants and the discontinuities in the process of urban development.

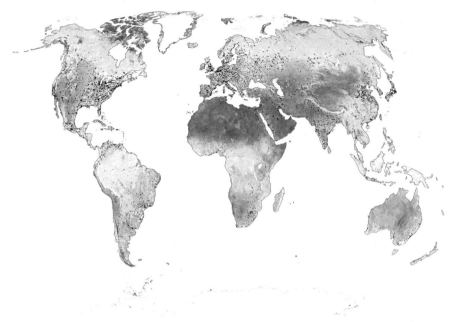

14.3 Global urbanization: urban extents.

This analysis does not simply aim to reconstruct the history of a city, but is intended to detect the ways in which history remains present in the contemporary situation and influences future developments. The aim is to understand the path-dependency of urbanization processes. As Lefebvre pointed out, no social space disappears completely, because it forms the starting point for subsequent development. Every social space therefore survives in one form or another. It will leave traces that may be visible or hidden monuments, urban structures, or even specific symbols survive, albeit often in seclusion, but they remain effective. It is important to conduct an exact analysis of these historic aspects.

The Urban as Open Horizon

The examples presented above show very different ways of comparing urban development, but they also reveal certain basic qualities of contemporary urbanization. Urbanization necessarily implies the materialization of global tendencies in local contexts. The forms and consequences of this materialization hinge upon the specificities of each place. Consequently, urbanization is not a homogenizing, globally predetermined process, but path-dependent and differentiating, one that entails new creations and inventions as global tendencies intermesh with local conditions. Urbanization can thus be understood as a constant struggle for new solutions and a relentless search for new spatial forms. The result is often unpredictable and full of surprises. We should therefore not only examine urban forms, but must embed them within broader urbanization processes and their uneven rhythms. A certain form identified and analyzed today might be completely transformed or may even have disappeared in a few years' time.

Under these conditions, comparative urban analysis is more essential than ever: it can help us develop a better understanding of the local conditions in which global processes materialize, and in so doing, it can help us explore and realize the possibilities and potentials that might be available for future patterns and pathways of urbanization.

Notes

1   Edward Soja and J. Miguel Kanai, "The Urbanization of the World," this book, Ch. 10.

2   Saskia Sassen, *The Global City: New York, London, Tokyo* (Princeton: Princeton University Press, 1991); and Allen J. Scott, ed., *Global City-Regions: Trends, Theory, Policy* (Oxford: Oxford University Press, 2000).

3   Shlomo Angel, Stephen Shappard and Daniel Civco, *The Dynamics of Global Urban Expansion* (Washington: Department of Transport and Urban Development and the World Bank, 2005); and Robert Lang, *Edgeless Cities: Exploring the Elusive Metropolis* (Washington DC: Brookings Institutions Press, 2003).

4   Richard Florida, Tim Gulden and Charlotta Mellander, "The Rise of the Mega-Region," *Cambridge Journal of Regions, Economy and Society* 1, 3 (2008) 459-76.

5   Roger Diener, Jacques Herzog, Marcel Meili, Pierre de Meuron and Christian Schmid, *Switzerland—An Urban Portrait* (Basel: Birkhäuser, 2006).

6   Neil Brenner and Christian Schmid, "Planetary Urbanization," this book, Ch. 11.

7   Robert Park and Ernest Burgess, *The City* (Chicago: The University of Chicago Press, 1925).

8   Allen J. Scott and Edward Soja, eds., *The City: Los Angeles and Urban Theory at the End of the Twentieth Century* (Berkeley and Los Angeles: University of California Press, 1996).

9   Robert Venturi, Denise Scott Brown and Steven Izenour, *Learning from Las Vegas: The Forgotten Symbolism of Architectural Form* (Cambridge: MIT Press, 1972); and Rem Koolhaas, *Delirious New York: A Retroactive Manifesto for Manhattan* (Oxford: Oxford University Press, 1978).

10 Mike Davis, *Planet of Slums* (London: Verso, 2006); and Ananya Roy, "The 21st Century Metropolis: New Geographies of Theory," *Regional Studies* 42, 1 (2008) 1-12.

11 Peter Taylor and Robert Lang, "The Shock of the New: 100 Concepts Describing Recent Urban Change," *Environment and Planning A* 36, 6 (2004) 951-8.

12 John Friedmann, "The World City Hypothesis," *Development and Change* 17, 1 (1986) 69-84; Sassen, *The Global City*; and Neil Brenner and Roger Keil, eds., *The Global Cities Reader* (New York: Routledge, 2006).

13 Neil Brenner and Nik Theodore, eds., *Spaces of Neoliberalism: Urban Restructuring in Western Europe and North America* (Oxford and Boston: Blackwell, 2002); Neil Smith, "New Globalism, New Urbanism: Gentrification as Global Strategy," *Spaces of Neoliberalism: Urban Restructuring in North America and Western Europe*, eds. Neil Brenner and Nik Theodore (London: Blackwell, 2002) 80-103; Frank Moulaert, Arantxa Rodriguez and Erik Swyngedouw, *The Globalized City—Economic Restructuring and Social Polarization in European Cities* (Oxford: University Press Oxford, 2003); and Libby Porter and Kate Shaw, eds., *Whose Urban Renaissance? An International Comparison of Urban Regeneration Strategies* (London: Routledge, 2009).

14 Joel Garreau, *Edge City: Life on the New Frontier.* (New York: Doubleday, 1991); Edward Soja, "Inside Exopolis: Scenes From Orange County," *Variations on a Theme Park*, ed. Michael Sorkin (New York: The Noonday Press, 1992) 94-122; and Thomas Sieverts, *Cities Without Cities: An Interpretation of the Zwischenstadt* (London: Spon Press, 2003).

15 Josef Gugler, ed., *Cities In the Developing World: Issues, Theory and Policy* (Oxford: Oxford University Press, 1997); Peter Marcuse and Ronald van Kempen, eds., *Globalizing Cities: A New Spatial Order?* (Malden and Mass: Blackwell, 2000); Davis, *Planet of Slums*; Robert Neuwirth, *Shadow Cities: A Billion Squatters, a New Urban World* (New York: Routledge, 2005); Ananya Roy and Nezar AlSayyad, eds., *Urban Informality: Transnational Perspectives from Latin America, the Middle East, and South Asia* (New York: Lexington Books, 2004); and Alfred Brillembourg, Kristin Feireiss and Hubert Klumpner, *Informal City: Caracas Case* (Munich: Prestel Verlag, 2005).

16 Philipp Oswalt and Tim Rieniets, eds., *Atlas of Shrinking Cities* (Ostfildern-Ruit: Hatje Cantz, 2006).

17 Jan Nijman, "Introduction: Comparative Urbanism," *Urban Geography* 28, 1 (2007) 1-6; Kevin Ward, "Towards a Comparative (Re)Turn in Urban Studies? Some Reflections," *Urban Geography* 29, 5 (2008) 405-10; Colin McFarlane, "The Comparative City: Knowledge, Learning, Urbanism," *International Journal of Urban and Regional Research* 34, 4 (2010) 725-42; and Jennifer Robinson, "Cities in a World of Cities: The Comparative Gesture," *International Journal of Urban and Regional Research* 35, 1 (2011) 1-23.

18 Stefano Boeri and Multiplicity, "USE: Uncertain States of Europe," *Mutations*, eds. Rem Koolhaas, Sanford Kwinter, Stefano Boeri, and Nadia Tazi (Bordeaux: ACTAR / arc en rêve, 2000) 338-483; Peter Taylor, *World City Network: A Global Urban Analysis* (London and New York: Routledge, 2004); INURA and Raffaele Palosicia, eds., *The Contested Metropolis: Six Cities at the Beginning of the 21ˢᵗ Century* (Berlin: Birkhäuser, 2004); and Peter Hall and Kathy Pain, *The Polycentric Metropolis: Learning From Mega-City Regions in Europe* (London: Earthscan, 2006).

19 Ricky Burdett and Sarah Ichioka, *10ᵗʰ International Architecture Exhibition: Cities, Architecture, and Society, Volume 1* (Verona: Marsilio, 2006); Ricky Burdett and Deyan Sudjic, eds., *The Endless City: The Urban Age Project* (London: Phaidon Press, 2007); and Jacques Lévy, ed., *L'invention Du Monde: Une Géographie De La Mondialisation* (Paris: Sciences Po Press, 2008).

20 Janet Abu-Lughod, *New York, Chicago, Los Angeles: America's Global Cities* (Minneapolis: University of Minnesota Press, 2009).

21 Neil Brenner, "World City Theory, Globalization and the Comparative-Historical Method: Reflections on Janet Abu-Lughod's Interpretation of Contemporary Urban Restructuring," *Urban Affairs Review* 36, 6 (2001) 124-47.

22 AbdouMaliq Simone, *For the City yet to Come: Changing African Life in Four Cities* (Durham NC: Duke University Press, 2004); and Jennifer Robinson, *Ordinary Cities: Between Modernity and Development* (London and New York: Routledge, 2006).

23 Julie-Anne Boudreau, Pierre Hamel, Bernard Jouve and Roger Keil, "New State Spaces in Canada: Metropolitanisation in Montreal and Toronto Compared," *Urban Geography* 28, 1 (2007) 30-53; Fulong Wu and Nicholas Phelps, "From Suburbia to Post-Suburbia in China? Aspects of the Transformation of the Beijing and Shanghai Global City Regions," *Built Environment* 34, 4 (2008) 464-81; and Andrew Harris, "From London to Mumbai and Back Again: Gentrification and Public Policy in Comparative Perspective," *Urban Studies* 45, 12 (2008) 2407-28.

24 Hansruedi Hitz, Roger Keil, Ute Lehrer, Klaus Ronneberger, Christian Schmid and Richard Wolff, *Capitales Fatales: Urbanisierung und Politik in den Finanzmetropolen Frankfurt und Zürich* (Zurich: Rotpunkt, 1995).

25 Erik Swyngedouw, "Neither Global nor Local: Glocalization and

the Politics of Scale," *Spaces of Globalization*, ed. Kevin Cox (New York and London: Guilford, 1997) 137-66.

26 Christian Schmid, "Henri Lefebvre, the Right to the City and the New Metropolitan Mainstream," *Cities for People, not for Profit: Critical Urban Theory and the Right to the City*, eds. Neil Brenner, Peter Marcuse and Margit Mayer (London and New York: Routledge, 2011) 42-62.

27 Roy, "The 21st Century Metropolis: New Geographies of Theory."

28 See International Network for Urban Research and Action (INURA) at www.inura.org. A publication of the results is in preparation.

29 Diener, Herzog, Meili, de Meuron and Schmid, *Switzerland—An Urban Portrait*.

30 Henri Lefebvre, *The Urban Revolution*, trans. Robert Bononno (Minneapolis: University of Minnesota Press, 2003).

31 See Georg Simmel, "The Metropolis and Mental Life," *Georg Simmel on Individuality and Social Forms*, ed. Donald Levine (Chicago and London: The University of Chicago Press, 1971) 324-39; and Louis Wirth, "Urbanism as a Way of Life," *American Journal of Sociology* 44, 1 (1938) 1-24.

32 See also Christian Schmid, "Networks, Borders, Differences," this book, Ch. 4; Schmid, "The Urbanization of Switzerland," this book, Ch. 18; and Schmid, "A Typology of Urban Switzerland," this book, Ch. 26.

33 See Christian Schmid, "A Typology of Urban Switzerland," this book, Ch. 26.

34 See Daniel Marco, Christian Schmid, Christa Hirschi, David Hiler and Jan Capol, *La ville: villes de crise ou crise des villes. Rapport scientifique final pour le 'Fonds national suisse de la recherche scientifique* (Institut d'Architecture de l'Université de Genève: Geneva, 1997).

35 Christian Schmid, "Urbane Region und Territorialverhältnis: Zur Regulation des Urbanisierungsprozesses," *Unternehmen Globus—Facetten Nachfordistischer Regulation*, eds. Michael Bruch and Hans-Peter Krebs (Münster: Westfälisches Dampfboot, 1996) 224-53.

36 Alain Lipietz, *La société en sablier: le partage du travail contre la déchirure sociale* (Paris: La Découverte, 1996).

37 Henri Lefebvre, *The Production of Space*, trans. Donald Nicholson Smith (Oxford: Blackwell Press, 1991); and Christian Schmid, "Henri Lefebvre's Theory of the Production of Space: Towards a Three-Dimensional Dialectic," *Space, Difference, Everyday Life: Reading Henri Lefebvre*, eds. Kanishka Goonewardena, Stefan Kipfer, Richard Milgrom and Christian Schmid (London: Routledge, 2008) 27-45.

38 David Harvey, *The Urbanization of Capital* (Oxford: Blackwell, 1985).

39 Neil Brenner, "Between Fixity and Motion: Accumulation, Territorial Organization and the Historical Geography of Spatial Scales," *Environmental and Planning D: Society and Space* 16, 4 (1998) 459-81.

40 Jacques Herzog and Pierre de Meuron, "The Particular and the Generic," *The Endless City*, eds. Ricky Burdett and Deyan Sudjic (New York: Phaidon Press Inc., 2007) 324-27.

41 Florida, Gulden and Mellander "The Rise of the Mega-Region"; See Deborah Balk, Francesca Pozzi, Gregory Yetman, Uwe Deichmann and Andy Nelsonc, "The Distribution of People and the Dimension of Place: Methodologies to Improve the Global Estimation of Urban Extents," CIESIN-Columbia University, the World Bank and the University of Leeds (2004). ftp://ftp.ecn.purdue.edu/jshan/proceedings/URBAN_URS05/balk-etal.pdf.

42 Jean Gottman, *Megalopolis* (New York: The Twentieth Century Fund, 1961); and Soja and Kanai, "The Urbanization of the World," this book, Ch. 10.

43 Florida, Gulden and Mellander, "The Rise of the Mega-Region."

44 Diener, Herzog, Meili, de Meuron and Schmid, *Switzerland—An Urban Portrait*.

45 Neil Brenner, "Rescaling the Urban Question," *Globalization of Urbanity*, eds. Josep Acebillo, Jacques Lévy and Christian Schmid

(Mendrisio: Accademia di architettura—Università della Svizzera italiana / Barcelona: ACTAR, 2012) 78-93.

Figure Credits

14.1 Roger Diener, Jacques Herzog, Marcel Meili, Pierre de Meuron, and Christian Schmid, *Switzerland—An Urban Portrait, Volume 3* (Basel: Birkhäuser, 2006) 633.

14.2 Same as above, 533.

14.3 Global Rural-Urban Mapping Project, Alpha Data, Columbia University (New York, 2005).

15
THE COUNTRY AND THE CITY IN THE URBAN REVOLUTION

Kanishka Goonewardena

1

Urban theory today is in some turmoil, much like the urbanized world with which this increasingly fragmented yet worldwide discourse is concerned. No one school of thought dominates urban studies today, unlike during the Fordist-era hegemony of the Chicago School or the subsequent influence of Marxian urban political economy following path-breaking works by David Harvey and Manuel Castells in the early 1970s.[1] A much more diverse discursive field becomes readily visible today to any reader of the leading academic journals on urban issues. Even among those perspectives that are generally considered critical or Left, there seems to be more of a cacophony and than a polyphony: "assemblage urbanism," "subaltern urbanism," "global urbanism," "global suburbanism," "planetary urbanism," "the right to the city" and other current theoretical tendencies betray no common core or cause.

2

While the novel qualities of these brands of inquiry are surely to be welcomed, it would also be useful to historicize this scattering of thought trajectories on the urban terrain. How could one make sense of the appearance of such a disparate range of urban theories in the present conjuncture? The widespread perception that we have just entered "an urban age," commonly understood as a world in which there are suddenly more people living in cities than in rural areas, certainly explains at least some of the current surge of interest in cities.[2] Beyond such general interest, however, what are the salient features of contemporary urban thought? In this evidently disorganized and wide-ranging field, one tendency of the "subaltern" and "postcolonial" wings of the "global urbanism" school is particularly striking: here, quite a few critical strands of new inquiry into especially Southern cities now appear as so many therapeutic attempts to deal with Mike Davis's acute but foreboding assessment of our urban world as a "planet of slums."[3] And they often involve in reaction a celebration of this or that chosen aspect of urban life: creativity, ingenuity, informality or some other salutary attribute of the subaltern multitudes. An adaptation of a famous phrase from Antonio Gramsci suggests itself: pessimism of the habitat, optimism of the inhabitant! Yet this opposition between objective and subjective aspects of the urban—between the grim structuralist space of the slum and the Deleuzean vitalism of the subaltern voice—conceals as much as it reveals. The dramatic tension enacted there between an inhuman condition and an irrepressible human spirit is often gripping and moving; but it is also a means of misrecognizing and misrepresenting struggles between groups of human beings and the nature of their spatial mediations. Unresolved in much contemporary urban theory with regard to these spatially mediated social struggles is the very meaning of the urban, as Neil Brenner and Christian Schmid have firmly underlined in their recent contributions to the literature on "planetary urbanization."[4] If "the urban question" can no longer be addressed in the once dominant terms of the "human settlement" (late Chicago School) or the "excrescence of capital" (early urban political economy), then how should it be approached so that the role of urbanization in the uneven development of capitalism *and* in emancipatory political possibilities within and against it comes into focus?[5]

3

A fundamental difficulty attends this question about urbanization—a process that, as Davis puts it, "must be conceptualized as [a] structural transformation along, and intensified interaction between, every point of an urban-rural continuum."[6] The problem has to do with the inconvenient opposition between the "global," "complete" or "planetary" reach of the urban phenomenon and the anti-totalizing hangover from postmodernist toasts to difference, which still seems to urge many critical urbanists among others to keep away from ostensibly oppressive "metanarratives," such as capitalism and, it has to be said, urbanization. Yet at the same time, given the vast temporal, territorial and existential distances that beg to be bridged in any apprehension of the urban as a *world-historical* phenomenon, critical urban theory is also compelled to consider all concrete particulars in terms of what Marx and Engels called "universal intercourse" (*allseitiger Verkehr*) in the *Communist Manifesto*, and in so doing adopt some conception of totality.[7] It would be better of course if the concept of totality so adopted were dialectical and open-ended, unlike what postmodernism typically imagines it to be. The philosophical challenge here would be to avoid privileging either identity or difference, but to think through their concrete mediations—so that we may act on them, for the sake of another, possible world. Urban theory therefore stands to benefit in particular from the reappropriation of ideas from two prolific writers in the Western Marxist tradition, Henri Lefebvre and Raymond Williams, both of whom are noted both for their original contributions towards an open-dialectical concept of totality and their path-breaking explications of the role of urbanization in that totality. Their offerings to a concept of urbanization by way of totality and space would be rendered all the more poignant, moreover, if complemented with punctual references to Marx's classic reflections on the transition to capitalism.

4

Lefebvre's work has become familiar of late in urban studies and several other academic disciplines dealing with "space"; Williams, partly because of his professional identification as a literary critic, remains relatively unknown to or undervalued by many students of urban theory. Within the Anglo-American literature on Western Marxism, moreover, both writers have occupied unjustly subordinate positions in comparison to some other luminaries in this tradition, such as Lukács and Sartre, Althusser and Gramsci, or those associated with the Frankfurt School.[8] And rarely have the pioneering works of Lefebvre and Williams been studied in juxtaposition, in spite of an impressive range of common and intersecting interests on culture, everyday life, language, space and of course ("long," "urban," "socialist") revolution inspired by Marx.[9] Yet the most basic questions concerning worldwide urbanization now call for a joint reexamination of their remarkable works— especially on the dialectical mediations of space and social struggle as they pertain to the fundamental relations between city, country and capitalism, which in turn would bring us to the intersections of urbanization, imperialism and colonization.

5

Two texts in particular suggest that they be read together, even if their authors themselves do not seem to have been much aware of each other's endeavors: *The Urban Revolution* (1970) by Lefebvre and *The Country and the City* (1973) by Williams. Now, the sense that the very air of the city is liberating (*die Stadtluft macht frei*) goes back to the Middle Ages, as recalled by Max Weber with reference to the hopes of serfs escaping from feudal lords. Yet, "if the history of the city is a history of freedom," writes Guy Debord, "it is also a history of tyranny" involving forms of sociospatial domination applied to "not only the countryside but the cities themselves." For Debord, then, "the city has served as the historical battleground for the struggle for freedom without yet having been able to win it."[10] A quite similar dialectic of alienation and emancipation animates both *The Urban Revolution* and *The Country and the City*, wherein the development of capitalism and the struggle for socialism are studied—in the most original and sustained ways—as sociospatial processes.

The significance of Lefebvre and Williams to radical urban studies and critical theory is most efficiently assessed by way of their key contributions to Marxist thought. In Lefebvre's case, this lies above all in the new conception of *totality* he proposes, as a complement to the base-superstructure model with which Marxism has traditionally understood social-historical reality as a whole.[11] Lefebvre's theory of totality in fact presents in compendium the totality of his *oeuvre*, drawing within a single perspective the three major themes to which he devoted multiple volumes in the postwar era: everyday life, space and the state. Here "the urban" figures as a crucial *level* of social totality, whose spatial dimension includes several scales, extending from the local to the global. In Lefebvre's formulation, this urban level exists in a mediated relationship with two other levels of social reality that have their own spatial scales: the level of "everyday life" consisting of our quotidian routines and aspirations and the level of "the global" consisting of the state and capital.[12] It is within this three-tiered theory of totality, which stresses the pivotal location of the urban as the dominant mediation between the everyday and the global, that Lefebvre's concept of "the urban *revolution*" makes most sense—as (capitalist) historical *process* as well as (socialist) political *project*.

7

As an intervention in Marxism and social theory more generally, the primary significance of *The Urban Revolution* lies in its audacious (hypo)thesis: namely, that *urbanization* has surpassed industrialization, modernization and other such processes identified by variously specialized scientists of society as the ever more decisive means by which the development and survival of capitalism is assured. The key term here is not the "city" understood as a type of human settlement; nor is the vital variable the proportion of the population living in such settlements called "cities." What is of essence is rather the process of urban*ization* itself— the dialectic of sociospatial implosion and explosion that has produced, in short, an *urban society*. If a visual image were needed, it would be that of an *urban fabric* spreading itself over the earth's surface, gathering all kinds of places and people into its far-flung and firm embrace. The making of such a fully urbanized world at the planetary scale—which clearly includes evolving relations between city and country, shaped by the global forces of capital and the state—is the first meaning of "the urban revolution." Its second meaning insists, with many radical political activists throughout history, that "another world is possible," referring to the revolutionary struggle for a sociospatial order released from the logics of capital and state that produced and still dominate the actually existing world—a *possible* and *different* world.

8

Key aspects of Lefebvre's concept of urbanization in *The Urban Revolution* recall some classic ruminations on city and country by Marx and Engels. In *The German Ideology* (1845), "the antagonism between town and country" appears as both expression and vehicle of the "transition from barbarism to civilization." Here the spatial division of town and country is dialectically linked to the social division of labor and the consequent "division of the population into two great classes," all of which can "only exist within the framework of private property." For Marx and Engels, therefore, "the abolition of the antagonism between town and country" becomes "one of the first conditions of communal life"—i.e., communism.[13] A few years later, a famous—or infamous, given its apparent metropolitan and Eurocentric bias—passage in *The Communist Manifesto* (1848) illustrates how:

> ... [t]he bourgeoisie has subjected the country to the rule of the towns. It has created enormous cities, has greatly increased the urban population as compared with the rural, and has thus rescued a considerable part of the population from the idiocy of rural life. Just as it has made the country dependent on the towns, so it has made barbarian and semi-barbarian countries dependent on the civilized ones, nations of peasants on nations of bourgeois, the East on the West.[14]

9

While *The German Ideology* already registers the passage from "barbarism to civilization" as a spatial as much as a social process via the city-country relation, the more historical-geographical perspective of the *Manifesto* develops this insight further by adding an essential scalar dimension to it. Now the basic spatial form of capitalism leaps across several scales, from the more close-to-home, country-city horizon through the borders among unequal nations to a worldwide East-West divide—suggesting a deeper logic of center-periphery that territorializes capitalism as a mode of *colonization*. The seeds of a theory of uneven and combined development are very much present here, as is the immediate recognition that communism must produce its own space, in anti-colonial opposition to the bourgeoisie that creates "a world after its own image" as "the constantly expanding market for its products chases [it] over the whole surface of the earth."[15] Hence, the ninth of the ten-point political program briskly laid out in the *Manifesto*, advocating the "gradual abolition of the distinctions between town and country."[16]

10

A substantive conception of capitalism as a mode of colonization develops relatively late in Lefebvre's *oeuvre*, although his four volumes devoted to everyday life do on occasion employ the term colonization in a metaphorical way, to think through the increasing subjection of the everyday level of our social reality to the dictates of a "bureaucratic society of controlled consumption."[17] A substantive conceptual innovation occurs as he moves on from his studies of the urban level of totality begun in the 1960s to the global level in the 1970s, wherein the role of the state in the production of space and the survival of capitalism is specifically examined. Lefebvre's view of the global level primarily in terms of the state (*neo-dirigisme*) and capital (*neoliberalism*) falls in line with Fernand Braudel's considered opinion professed upon the completion of his legendary historical work *Capitalism and Civilization* (1955–1979): "Capitalism only triumphs when it becomes identified with the state, when it is the state."[18] Particularly in his four-volume study *De l'État* (1976–1978), Lefebvre now advances such concepts as "becoming worldwide" (*mondialisation*), "state mode of production" (*le mode de production étatique*) and "state-space" (*l'espace étatique*) to pursue a fully territorialized theorization of the geopolitical-economy of late capitalism. Here emerges a definition of colonization that is most pertinent to studies of "planetary urbanization," which was clearly influenced by Lefebvre's proximity to the living conditions and everyday struggles of postcolonial immigrants, students and assorted subalterns in the peripheral spaces of Paris: "Wherever a dominated space is generated and mastered by a dominant space—where there is periphery and center—there is colonization."[19]

11

No one has studied the country-city dialectic with the power and passion of Raymond Williams, who was once described as "the most authoritative, consistent and original socialist thinker in the English-speaking world" by a former editor of *New Left Review*.[20] Terry Eagleton, his former student at Cambridge University and the leading British Marxist critic today, writes of a "strange, profound, unclassifiable work" that Williams "had more trouble getting finished than probably any other, since its themes touched him to the quick": *The Country and the City*.[21] Yet it seems that these themes have not adequately been understood, not just in urban theory, but also in cultural studies, due in part to the sheer depth of interpretation one encounters in this inimitable book, which combines a classical style of "close reading of texts" reminiscent of Williams's one-time teacher F. R. Leavis and his own potent brand of "cultural materialism." So it is best to hear in Williams's own words what it is about, which is often not what one reads in literary-critical reviews of this book that tend to miss its "underlying social, economic and historical analysis":

> My central case in *The Country and the City* was that these two apparently opposite and separate projections—country and city—were in fact indissolubly linked, within the general and crisis-ridden development of a capitalist economy which had itself produced this division in its modern forms.[22]

12

That "strange, profound, unclassifiable" quality of *The Country and the City*—a thoroughly autobiographical work—may be demystified somewhat with reference to the exemplary intellectual and political career of its author. Like many of Lefebvre's writings, Williams's oeuvre could usefully be understood in terms of a lasting engagement with the base-superstructure conception of totality in Marxism—a subject of intense scrutiny from his first book to the last. With many other critics, he was dissatisfied with the reductive implications and applications of this conception, which allowed no genuine role for culture in history. At the same time, however, he had no patience for notions of culture that did not contain a historical and materialist understanding of social relations. Both of these convictions, pursued through a series of vigorous engagements with Marx, Engels and especially the great Italian philologist and communist Sebastiano Timpanaro, yielded for Williams and others an enormously productive framework for thinking *culture as politics* that is much closer to Gramsci's communism than postmodern cultural studies: "cultural materialism."[23] Its fruits are abundantly evident in *The Country and the City*, where Williams extracts from two of the most loaded words in the English language a stunning historical-cultural geography of the development of capitalism in England. That it is a story of barbarism beneath civilization is perhaps predictable; not so is the skill and erudition with which Williams reveals, in a relentless deconstruction of the categories of country and city, and the related ideologies of progress and the pastoral, the bitter realities of class struggle in space, at home and abroad. One looks in vain for a better proof of Walter Benjamin's thesis: "There is no document of civilization which is not at the same time a document of barbarism."[24]

13

The pronounced Gramscian aspect of Williams's work is hardly accidental. For he was an intellectual—traditional as well as organic—in the sense Gramsci understood these terms: a Cambridge don who was also a lifelong partisan and artisan of Left politics outside of the lecture hall. After a stint in adult education after the Second World War, he was a key figure in the making of the British "New Left" in the 1950s who helped found *New Left Review* in 1960; the main drafter of the *May Day Manifesto* in 1968; a founder of the Socialist Society in 1982; and "in many less formal ways Williams was sponsor, contributor and guide to a host of radical educational, cultural and political ventures, across more than three decades, which sought to go beyond the narrow and elitist assumptions of the Labour establishment."[25] Directly relevant to the perspective of *The Country and the City* was Williams's involvement in the radical politics of the 1960s, especially the anti-war movement and the Vietnam Solidarity Campaign, which sharpened his interest in imperialism and forms resistance to it—both rural and urban, in the metropolis and the colony. Not inconsequently, an anti-colonial standpoint becomes unmistakable in the political orientation of *The Country and the City*, even in its treatment of that most iconic concentration of social and symbolic power in the English landscape: as Robin Blackburn aptly notes, Williams unearths in no uncertain terms "the process of capitalist despoliation at home and colonial slavery abroad behind the culture of the English "country house" and the conventions of a pastoral mode that conjured them away."[26]

Such an anti-colonial perspective in a study of the landscape and literature of England is not to be taken for granted—especially from a Western writer, Left or not. It is to Williams's credit that he is refreshingly and consistently keen to highlight the global implications and lessons of the foundational English experience of country and city in the transition to capitalism, which lies at the root of imperialism and colonization in the modern world. For "much of the real history of city and country, within England itself, is from an early date a history of the extension of a dominant model of capitalist development to include other regions of the world."[27] Not only does this "extension" mean that "the country-houses which were the apex of a local system of exploitation that had many connections to these distant lands"—in other words, that "the country-houses of late George Eliot, of Henri James and of their etiolated successors are ... country-houses of capital rather than of land."[28] It also directs our attention to some radical sociospatial changes that took place in the colonies themselves, as relations between them and the "old queen of the waves" shifted from a predominantly mercantile mode of metropolitan profiteering backed up military means to one premised on what Marx called "so-called primitive accumulation."[29] Williams refers in this regard to "the slave trade from Africa," "the new rural economy of the tropical plantations" and other forms of colonial dispossession recorded in the novels of R. K. Narayan, Mulk Raj Anand, James Ngugi, Elechi Amadi, Chinua Achebe and Wilson Harris—urging English men and women to read *these* authors in order to "get a different and necessary perspective" on their own country that they will not find in Rudyard Kipling, E. M. Forster or George Orwell.[30] For "what happened in England has since been happening ever more widely, in new and dependent relationships between all the industrialized nations and all the other 'undeveloped' but economically important lands."[31] As to what this history of unequal relations means with respect to the two keywords of his study, Williams is clear: "one of the last models of "city and country" is the system we now know as imperialism."[32]

15

A considerable overlap exists between *The Country and the City* and the "So–Called Primitive Accumulation" section concluding the first volume of Marx's *Capital*. Both recount in varied detail how "capital comes dripping from head to toe, from every pore, with blood and dirt;" and how "this history, the history of ... expropriation, is written in the annals of mankind in letters of blood and fire."[33] Both acknowledge also the never-ending nature of this "process of divorcing the producer from the means of production," especially with reference to colonization.[34] According to Marx:

> The capitalist relation presupposes a complete separation between the workers and the ownership of the conditions for the realization of their labour. As soon as capitalist production stands on its feet, it not only maintains this separation, but reproduces it on a constantly extending scale.[35]

So why is it labeled "so-called"? One plausible interpretation would suggest that this process of expropriation and separation, although it *"appears* as "primitive" [*ursprünglich*] because it forms the *pre*-history of capital," belongs in reality just as much to the *history* of capitalism, including the present.[36] A closer reading of Marx's text with reference to the classical political-economic doctrine he is critiquing here suggests however a better explanation—with some implications for our understanding of capitalism in terms of country and city.

16

The excessive frequency with which Marx used words like "blood," "fire," "terror," "violence," "plunder," "conquest," "robbery," "murder," "fraud," "force," *"coup d'état"* and so on to describe "so-called primitive accumulation" signals what he was most determined to prove—namely, that "the methods of primitive accumulation are anything but idyllic."[37] The reigning opinion of classical political economy was just the reverse, as Harvey demonstrates in a lucid paraphrasing of Adam Smith's influential opinion on this matter:

There were some people that were hard working and some people who were not. Some people who could be bothered, and some people who could not be bothered. And the result of that was, bit by bit, those who were hard working, and could be bothered, accumulated some wealth. And eventually, those who could not be bothered, could not accumulate wealth, in the end, in order to survive, preferred, actually, to give up their labor power as a commodity, in return for a living wage.[38]

On Smith's view, then, there really exists no such thing as "originary accumulation" in the Marxist sense of a bloody and brutal *transition* to capitalism—i.e., a *qualitative* change in social and property relations with attendant spatial transformations. What he calmly called "previous accumulation" in *The Wealth of Nations* is rendered simply as the natural consequence of an inherent human tendency found in all people, lazy as well as laborious, to "truck, barter and exchange."[39] The difference between Smith and Marx here, signified by the phrase "so-called," leads to different interpretations of capitalism. Smith's account essentially entails a mercantilist view that explains capitalism in terms of a seemingly peaceful prior accumulation of wealth in the age-old marketplace rather than a radical change in social and property relations. By contrast, Marx's narrative dwells on the dispossession of the peasantry as the extra-economic precondition for establishing a fundamentally new set of social and property relations that simultaneously invents the "free and rightless" [*vogelfrei*] laborer and turns wealth into *capital*. The serene seat of the former (exchange, money) is the city; the crime scene of the latter (production, capital) lies in the countryside.[40]

The transition from feudalism to capitalism was the subject of a groundbreaking debate extended over several rounds of influential publications from the 1950s until the late 1980s that (re)asserted, on balance, the agrarian origins of the capitalist mode of production in the English countryside, in opposition to interpretations of the same history grounded on allegedly neo-Smithian notions.[41] This debate became a magnetic artifact of Left intellectual culture around the world and found remarkable resonance especially in agrarian studies, as could be seen by its ongoing treatment as a focal point in the *Journal of Peasant Studies*. A truly international array of critical writers, including many from the South, engaged in this exchange. Here was a crowd that approached the high standard set by Ananya Roy in her recent call for "new geographies of theory" in the field of urban studies—a most salutary plea to terminate the Eurocentric hegemony of urban theory by admitting more conceptual reflections on the urban by scholars and activists based in the South.[42] It is ironic, then, that while agrarian studies achieved a level of geographical diversity and critical insight that Roy would appreciate by pursuing the transition debate with such infectious enthusiasm, her own field of urban studies remained largely oblivious to it—in spite of its obvious focus on the relations between city, country and capital. This is of course not entirely surprising, given the disciplined provincialism fostered by our academic division of labor, and the self-serving tendency to valorize one's own guarded object of study at the expense of others. Yet the conspicuous non-consumption of the transition debate in the field of urban studies counts as a missed opportunity for urbanists to have engaged substantively with forms of "primitive accumulation," past and present, which provide an indispensible reference point for any approach that sees urbanization as social and political struggle.

18

"All I know is, I had a cow and Parliament took it."[43] Such was the thought of a "poor man" in England at the mercy of an Enclosure Act of Parliament—as imagined and penned by the versatile English writer Arthur Young (1741–1820) who, upon disillusionment with the social consequences of the enclosures that he himself once prosecuted as Secretary of the Board of Agriculture, also wrote: "I had rather that all the commons of England were sunk in the sea, than that the poor should in future be treated on enclosing as they have been hitherto."[44] That sentiment, not what he did in office, would be much appreciated today by poor men and women in rural India, at least those farmers among them still managing to stay alive. Over a quarter of a million farmers have committed suicide there since 1995, when the National Crime Records Bureau started reporting such data, four years into the age of neoliberalism in India. The renowned journalist Palagummi Sainath, author of a biting survey of rural poverty in India, *Everyone Loves a Good Draught*, and Rural Affairs Editor for *The Hindu*, says that this number of 270,940 amounts, for the census decade of 2001–2011, to an annual average of 16,743 suicides: 46 farmers a day; one farmer every half-hour.[45] And he offers to sum up in five words the Indian agrarian crisis underlying these figures recording "the largest wave of suicides in history" ("the drive toward corporate farming"), and the method, in five words ("predatory commercialization of the countryside"), and the result, in five words ("the biggest displacement in our history").[46] Five more words are hardly needed—ongoing and so-called primitive accumulation—except to note that what happens in the farm has a lot to do with what happens in the town.

19

In demographic scale and volumes of "blood and dirt," what Marx witnessed in Victorian England pales in comparison to the present transition to capitalism in India. It is therefore a logical place to look for the most courageous struggles against and perspicuous critiques of contemporary capitalist development, such as the "Maoist" movement of tribal peoples of central India and the scholarship of intellectuals like Aijaz Ahmad, Amiya Bagchi, Jan Bremen, Jayati Ghosh, Utsa Patnaik, Prabhat Patnaik and others who happen to be conspicuously missing from metropolitan publications on subaltern and postcolonial studies.[47] Utsa Patnaik, India's top agricultural economist and a world authority on the agrarian question, has been particularly active in bringing to the public domain the bitter truth of neoliberal capitalism: *absolute immiserization*. Below in Figure 15.1 is a table published by Prabhat Patnaik in *The Hindu*, which puts the growth of absolute poverty in India during the post-1991 neoliberal years ("India Shining") into historical perspective[48]:

> The concept of absolute poverty, first proposed by Marx, has for long been widely discredited—by many Marxists too, barring a few exceptions such as Immanuel Wallerstein—with reference to the rise of living standards in the OECD zone, as evidenced by a once fattening middle class sprawled in suburban houses equipped with creature comforts far beyond even the wildest dreams of Engels in Manchester.[49] But on the global evidence marshaled by Utsa Patnaik, absolute immiserization hits one like a blast from not the past, but the future.[50]

20

The essence of Utsa Patnaik's argument about absolute immiserization consists in noting that the question of "capitalism and the production of poverty" cannot be addressed in a Eurocentric way, as it generally has been, but only in a global perspective. Only within such a framework can a true picture of historical capitalism emerge; and only then can proper account be taken of the means by which Europe dealt with its vagabond problem and forgot about absolute immiserization. In the case of England, Williams notes: "We can see in the Industrial novels of the mid-nineteenth century how the idea of emigration to the colonies was seized as a solution to the poverty and overcrowding of cities."[51] Seized, indeed it was. Patnaik has some numbers: Britain had a population of 12 million in 1821 and between 1821 and 1915, 16 million Britons emigrated, meaning that "on average half of the entire annual increment to its population left Britain every year for a century."[52] And a rhetorical

Year	Urban Poverty Rate	Rural Poverty Rate
1973 / 1974	60	56
1983 / 1984	58.5	56
1993 / 1994	57	58.5
2004 / 2005	64	69.5
2009 / 2010	73	76

15.1 Poverty rates in India, 1973–2010

question: what would it have entailed for India to export its unemployment problem on a similar scale from independence until today? Colonies would have had to be found to emigrate nearly half a billion Indians. But the actually dispossessed Indians, Chinese and other victims of what Harvey calls "accumulation by dispossession" have nowhere to go.[53] At the same time, metropolitan cities are also no longer able to do now what they did about it then. Not emigration but mass incarceration of the racialized urban underclass in the US—as illuminated by radical geographer Ruth Wilson Gilmore—is symptomatic of new solutions to old problems in the metropolis, where the urban experiences of diasporas from former colonies cannot properly be described as *post*colonial.[54] The beast of absolute immiserization is slouching towards a center struggling to hold.

21

The rural landscape sketched by Sainath and "the planet of slums" surveyed by Davis are, to say the least, related. The concept of urbanization proposed by Lefebvre and the relation between country and city studied by Williams both suggest that the world of Davis and the world of Sainath are in fact one world. But the prevailing academic division of labor has not effectively illuminated the dialectical unity of that world. As we know only too well, that world has for long been split into two overly self-referential worlds—one urban, one rural. As a result, both have been understood one-sidedly. Yet "the urban revolution" as Lefebvre conceived it and the kind of socialism intimated by Williams demand that they be united—in political practice as much as critical theory. But what are the prospects of the *International Journal of Urban and Regional Research* forming a radical united front with the *Journal of Peasant Studies?* Not very good, I am afraid, given the historical evidence. Yet the need highlighted by Neil Brenner to link forthwith the politics of "the right to the city" to the "politics of the global commons that is also being fought elsewhere, by peasants, small landholders, farmworkers, indigenous populations and their advocates" suggests precisely such a united political front, the theoretical anchor of which must surely be a concept of "production of space" not limited to *either* the city *or* the country, but mindful of their dialectical relations in the uneven development of capitalism.[55] Here Lefebvre and Williams, by ushering us out of our traditional specializations and their settled categories, offer vital resources for a radical politics of the dispossessed of the world and also a measure of the challenges lurking in such a planetary and revolutionary project. While much work remains to be done about it, of course, one thing is now certain concerning the Urban Question and the Agrarian Question: be delighted we surely must, if ever the twain should meet!

For Ben Kohl (1954–2013)—activist, scholar, friend.

Notes

1   Manuel Castells, *The Urban Question: A Marxist Approach* (Cambridge: MIT Press, 1977 [1972]); and David Harvey, *Social Justice and the City* (Baltimore: Johns Hopkins University Press, 1973).

2   Neil Brenner and Christian Schmid, "The 'Urban Age' in Question," this book, Ch. 21.

3   Mike Davis, "Planet of Slums," *New Left Review* 26 (2004) 5-34.

4   Neil Brenner and Christian Schmid, "Planetary Urbanization," this book, Ch. 11.

5   The phrase is from Neil Smith, "Preface" to Henri Lefebvre, *The Urban Revolution*, trans. Robert Bononno (Minneapolis: University of Minnesota Press, 2003 [1970]), xvii.

6   Davis, "Planet of Slums," 7. It is interesting to note that the authority invoked by Davis in this apt definition of urbanization is a book on the plight of the peasants: Gregory Guldin, *What's a Peasant to Do? Village Becoming Town in Southern China* (Boulder: Westview Press, 2001).

7   On the concept of totality often invoked by Lefebvre and Williams, see Martin Jay, *Marxism and Totality: The Adventures of a Concept from Lukács to Habermas* (Berkeley: University of California Press, 1984), as well as Fredric Jameson's contributions to this topic discussed in Kanishka Goonewardena, "The Urban Sensorium: Space, Ideology and the Aestheticization of Politics," *Antipode* 37, 1 (2005) 46-71.

8   Perry Anderson, *Considerations on Western Marxism* (London: Verso, 1976). For an account of Lefebvre's oeuvre as a Marxist, see Kanishka Goonewardena, "Henri Lefebvre," *The Wiley-Blackwell Companion to Major Social Theorists, Volume 2*, ed. George Ritzer and Jeffrey Stepnisky (Chichester: Wiley-Blackwell, 2011), 44-64. On Williams, see Terry Eagleton, ed., *Raymond Williams: Critical Perspectives* (London: Polity, 1989); Robin Blackburn, "Introduction," *Resources of Hope: Culture, Democracy, Socialism* (London: Verso, 1989) ix-xxiii; and Raymond Williams, *Politics and Letters: Interviews with "New Left Review"* (London: Verso, 1979).

9   For an excellent exception, see Andrew Shmuely, "Totality, Hegemony, Difference: Henri Lefebvre and Raymond Williams," *Space, Difference, Everyday Life: Reading Henri Lefebvre*, eds. Kanishka Goonewardena, Stefan Kipfer, Richard Milgrom and Christian Schmid (New York: Routledge, 2008) 212-30.

10   Guy Debord, *The Society of the Spectacle*, trans. Ken Knabb (San Francisco: The Bureau of Public Secrets, 2002 [1976]) 176. http://www.bopsecrets.org/SI/debord/7.htm (accessed July 10, 2013).

11   See Jay, *Marxism and Totality*.

12   On the distinction between level and scale, see Lefebvre, *The Urban Revolution*, 77-102; Stefan Kipfer, "Why the Urban Question Still Matters: Reflections on Rescaling and the Promise of the Urban," *Leviathan Undone? Towards a Political Economy of Scale*, eds. Roger Keil and Rianne Mohan (Vancouver: UBC Press, 2009) 67-83; Kanishka Goonewardena, "Marxism and Everyday Life: On Henri Lefebvre, Guy Debord and Some Others," *Space, Difference, Everyday Life: Reading Henri Lefebvre*, eds. Kanishka Goonewardena, Stefan Kipfer, Richard Milgrom, and Christian Schmid (New York: Routledge, 2008) 117-33.

13   Karl Marx and Friedrich Engels, *The German Ideology* (1932 [1845/46]). www.marxists.org (accessed on July 10, 2013).

14   Karl Marx and Friedrich Engels, *Manifesto of the Communist Party* (1848). www.marxists.org (accessed on July 10, 2013).

15   Ibid.

16   Ibid.

17   Henri Lefebvre, *Everyday Life in the Modern World*, trans. Sacha Rabonovitch (New Brunswick: Transaction Books, 1984 [1971]).

18   Fernand Braudel, *Afterthoughts on Material Civilization and Capitalism*, trans. Patricia M. Ranum (Baltimore: Johns Hopkins University Press, 1977) 64.

19   Henri Lefebvre, *De l'État*, tome IV (Paris: Union générale d'éditions, 1978) 173-174. For a more detailed examination of the development of the concept of colonization in Lefebvre's work, see Stefan Kipfer and Kanishka Goonewardena, "Urban Marxism and the Post-colonial Question: Henri Lefebvre and "Colonization," *Historical Materialism* 21, 2 (2013) 1-41. A superb account of Paris in the late 1960s, including the anti-colonial dimensions of May 1968, is available from one of the most acute readers of Lefebvre: Kristin Ross, *May '68 and Its Afterlives* (Chicago: University of Chicago Press, 2002).

20   Blackburn, "Introduction," ix.

21   Eagleton, *Raymond Williams*, 5.

22   Raymond Williams, *Resources of Hope: Culture, Democracy, Socialism*, ed. Robin Gable (London: Verso, 1989) 227.

23   Raymond Williams, *Marxism and Literature* (Oxford: Oxford University Press, 1977); and Raymond Williams, *Problems in Materialism and Culture* (London: Verso, 1980). See also Perry Anderson, "On Sebastiano Timpanaro," *London Review of Books* (May 10, 2001) 8-12.

24   Walter Benjamin, "Theses on the Philosophy of History," *Illuminations*, ed. Hannah Arendt, trans. Harry Zohn (New York: Schocken, 1968) 256.

25   Blackburn, "Introduction," xi; emphases added.

26   Ibid., xv.

27   Raymond Williams, *The Country and the City* (Oxford: Oxford University Press, 1973) 279.

28   Ibid., 280, 282.

29   Karl Marx, *Capital: A Critique of Political Economy, Volume 1*, trans. Ben Fowkes (London: Penguin [New Left Review], 1976 [1867]) 870, 873-940.

30   Williams, *The Country and the City*, 282, 285.

31   Ibid., 279; emphasis added.

32   Ibid.

33   Marx, *Capital*, 926, 875.

34   Ibid., 875.

35   Ibid., 874.

36   Ibid., 875; emphases added. The German phrase Marx used for "so-called primitive accumulation" was *sogennante ursprüngliche Akkumulation*, which can be more literally and accurately rendered as "so-called *originary* accumulation." "Primitive" suggests connotations not present in the German text.

37   Ibid., 874.

38   David Harvey, *Reading Marx's* Capital, *Volume 1*, recorded video lecture 12: *Capital* chapters 26–33 (minute range: 20–22). www.davidharvey.org (accessed July 10, 2013).

39   Adam Smith quoted in Marx, *Capital*, 873. For a thorough account of the social and philosophical background of Adam Smith and classical political economy that is mindful of the agrarian origins

of capitalism, see David McNally, *Political Economy and the Rise of Capitalism: A Reinterpretation* (Berkeley: University of California Press, 1988).

40 Marx, *Capital,* 896.

41 The key contributions to this debate include: Rodney Hilton, ed., *The Transition from Feudalism to Capitalism* (London: Verso, 1976); Robert Brenner, "Agrarian Class Structure and Economic Development in Pre-Industrial Europe," *Past and Present* (1976) 30-74; Robert Brenner "The Origins of Capitalist Development: A Critique of Neo-Smithian Marxism," *New Left Review* I/104 (1977) 25-92; T. H. Ashton and C. H. E. Philpin, eds. *The Brenner Debate: Agrarian Class Structure and Economic Development in Pre-Industrial Europe* (Cambridge: Cambridge University Press, 1985). For a fine recent review of this literature with new reflections in contemporary imperialism, see Ellen Meiksins Wood, *The Origin of Capitalism: A Longer View* (London: Verso, 2002).

42 Ananya Roy, "The 21ˢᵗ Century Metropolis: New Geographies of Theory," *Regional Studies* 43, 6 (2009) 819-30.

43 Arthur Young quoted in Williams, *The Country and the City*, 99.

44 Ibid., 66-67. Williams also traces here the instructive career of Young.

45 Palagummi Sainath, "Farmer's Suicide Rates Soar Above the Rest," *The Hindu* (18 March 2012). www.thehindu.com (accessed July 10, 2011). Sainath notes here and elsewhere how suicide rates are fraudulently under-reported by some states, referring to the most authoritative study of farmers' suicides in India: K. Nagaraj, *Farmers' Suicides in India: Magnitude, Trends and Spatial Patterns* (Chennai: Madras Institute of Development Studies, 2008).

46 Palagummi Sainath, "Neoliberal Terrorism in India: The Largest Wave of Suicides in History," *Counterpunch*, February 12, 2009. www.counterpunch.org (accessed July 10, 2013).

47 For two iconic and contrasting critiques of postcolonial studies, see Aijaz Ahmad, *In Theory: Classes, Nations, Literatures* (London: Verso, 1992); and Gayatri Chakravorty Spivak, *A Critique of Postcolonial Reason: Toward a History of the Vanishing Present* (Cambridge: Harvard University Press, 1999).

48 *The Hindu*, "Poverty has Increased," May 20, 2013. www.thehindu.com (accessed July 10, 2013). The poverty rate is defined by the Planning Commission of India: in urban areas as the percentage of the population with access to less than 2,100 calories a day; and in rural areas as the proportion below 2,400 calories a day.

49 Immanuel Wallerstein, *Historical Capitalism*, Third Edition (London: Verso, 2011).

50 For a condensed version of her argument and evidence, see Utsa Patnaik, *Capitalism and the Production of Poverty*, T. G. Narayan Memorial Lecture 2012, Asian College of Journalism, Chennai, India. www.thehindu.com/multimedia/archive/00893/T_G__Narayanan_Memo_893967a.pdf (accessed July 10, 2013). The research upon which she defends the absolute immiserization thesis is global and collaborative: see for, example, Utsa Patnaik and Sam Moyo, *The Agrarian Question in the Neoliberal Era: Primitive Accumulation and the Peasantry* (Cape Town: Pambazuka Press, 2011); Utsa Patnaik, *The Republic of Hunger and Other Essays* (London: Merlin, 2008); and Utsa Patnaik, *The Agrarian Question and the Development of Capitalism in India* (Oxford: Oxford University Press, 1986).

51 Williams, *The Country and the City*, 281.

52 Utsa Patnaik, *The Agrarian Question and the Development of Capitalism in India*, 6-7.

53 David Harvey, *The New Imperialism* (Oxford: Oxford University Press, 2005).

54 Ruth Wilson Gilmore, *Golden Gulag: Prisons, Surplus, Crisis and Opposition in Globalizing California* (Berkeley: University of California Press, 2007).

55 Neil Brenner, "Theses on Urbanization," this book, Ch. 13, page 199.

Figure Credits

15.1 Prabhat Patnaik, "Poverty has Increased," *The Hindu* (Delhi) May 20, 2013.

FOUR
HISTORICAL
GEOGRAPHIES OF
URBANIZATION

If urbanization includes yet transcends the process of city building, how can the historical geographies of these intertwined processes be conceptualized in relation to ongoing transformations of place, landscape, territory and environment at various spatial scales?

Álvaro Sevilla-Buitrago
Roberto Luis Monte-Mór
Christian Schmid
Edward Soja
Stefan Kipfer

16
URBS IN RURE: HISTORICAL ENCLOSURE AND THE EXTENDED URBANIZATION OF THE COUNTRYSIDE

Álvaro Sevilla-Buitrago

[T]his whole kingdom, as well the people as the land, and even the sea, in every part of it, are employed to furnish something, and I may add, the best of everything, to supply the City of London with provisions.

–Daniel Defoe[1]

Enclosure is one process that unifies proletarians throughout capital's history.

–Midnight Notes[2]

In the spatio-temporal schema opening *La révolution urbaine* Henri Lefebvre incorporates a crucial landmark in the formation of the urban society. Towards the sixteenth and seventeenth centuries, he says, "an event of great importance occurred": not only was the city beginning to play so central a role that "the whole [sociospatial formation] seemed to shift"—the traditional contrast between the city and the country was also dissolving as the latter became "no more than ... the town's 'environment,' its horizon, its limit."[3] This chapter uses English parliamentary enclosure as a paradigmatic illustration of the process Lefebvre describes and, more broadly, as a lens to interpret a particular feature of capitalist urbanization: its drive to extend its operational landscapes to large-scale spatial formations beyond conventional zones of urban agglomeration. Most of the recent literature on historical enclosure has focused on the local singularities of the process and its impact on rural social structures. Yet, an investigation of the spatialities of enclosure reveals its substantive role in the wider production of new territorial formations across different scales at the dawn of capitalism. Such an analysis should be taken as an opportunity not only to link the historiographical account and current studies of ongoing enclosure across the world, but also as a fundamental step towards developing a genealogical approach to contemporary trends of urbanization on a planetary scale.[4]

Read from the specific perspective of urbanization theory, English enclosure provides a telling insight into the nature of capitalist territorialization as a dialectical combination of moments of urban concentration and extension. In using these notions, I follow this book's reassessment of Lefebvre's analysis of the "implosion-explosion" of urban territories as the main feature of capitalist spatiality.[5] *Concentrated urbanization* designates the process of agglomeration of population, economic activity, governmental apparatuses, cultural hegemonies and metabolic consumption of energy and raw materials in amalgamated densifications of the urban fabric. Concomitantly, *extended urbanization* refers to the construction of operational networks beyond the immediate zones of agglomeration through the mobilization and circulation of subsidiary aspects of the foregoing elements— labor power, commodities, resources and nutrients, political and cultural forms. These networks generate discrete condensations of the urban fabric across different places, territories and scales that in turn underpin, reinforce and alter the patterns of concentration in the system's cores. The capitalist mode of territorialization incorporates and unevenly distributes both concentration and extension as dialectically intertwined moments that continuously reshape inherited sociospatial formations. Although I will suggest some preliminary ruminations about the historical contours of this dialectic, the present chapter focuses, more modestly, on providing a first step towards understanding the historical role of extended urbanization in the production of the operational landscapes of capitalism.

Drawing on Marx's approach to original accumulation at the dawn of capitalism, I characterize the waves of parliamentary enclosures that unfolded in England between the seventeenth and nineteenth centuries as an exercise of original or *ex-novo* extended urbanization—an initial stage in the subsumption of non-urban realms under specifically capitalist modes of uneven spatial development, involving new divisions of labor, distributional systems for raw materials and commodities, political and cultural formations and so forth. Along with the economic, technical and infrastructural changes in this period, these waves of enclosure provided an opportunity to rescale the social fabric of rural enclaves, restructuring the linkages between city and countryside along a range of different dimensions. Non-urban, non-capitalist territories were increasingly subordinated to the operational landscapes of national and international trade networks, which in turn expanded across the globe as new resources circulated through the system. Such transformations undermined the relative autonomy of preexisting, comparatively self-contained lifeworlds in the countryside.[6] Previous rural social structures that combined use-value oriented everyday routines and a relatively bounded, discrete sphere of market-oriented practices were superseded by an intensifying, potentially totalizing form of capitalist territorial organization. This transformation was achieved through a profound, spatially-driven alteration of property relations, spatial divisions of labor and forms of social reproduction that in turn hinged upon the concerted, systematic intervention of the state. The process of original extended urbanization thus reveals the violent, yet legally mediated operations of dispossession that constitute the new urban territories of capitalism.

The bulk of this chapter is dedicated to the study of English parliamentary enclosure as a way to delve into broader questions regarding the nature and historical geographies of worldwide capitalist urbanization. Throughout this discussion, in investigating the extended landscapes of early capitalist urbanization, I also devote particular attention to the dialectic between *original* (*ex-novo*) and *ongoing* enclosure processes, which are conceived as two interdependent yet analytically specific moments linking past and present logics of spatial creative destruction, both within and outside of urban agglomerations. I argue that any investigation of the interplay between concentrated and extended urbanization also requires careful attention to both the *ex-novo* and ongoing dimensions of enclosure processes under capitalism.

Defining Original Extended Urbanization

In part eight of *Capital,* Marx identifies English parliamentary enclosure as one of the fundamental steps of "so-called primitive accumulation" (*ursprüngliche Akkumulation*—better translated as *original* accumulation) between the seventeenth and nineteenth centuries, a move that laid the basis for the creation of the capital relation through the "[divorce of] the worker from the ownership of the conditions of his own labor."[7] The notion of original accumulation has received significant attention and reconsideration in recent attempts to understand current dynamics of neoliberalization around the world.[8] Many of these approaches aim to correct and expand Marx's hypothesis so that original accumulation appears not only as a temporally distinct episode in the prehistory of capitalism, but also as a still ongoing logic of accumulation by dispossession which, especially since the 1970s, has underpinned the restructuring of global capitalism.

The fact is, however, that Marx himself had loosened his otherwise crude identification of original accumulation with English enclosure when he suggested that:

> In the history of primitive accumulation, all revolutions are epoch-making that act as levers for the capitalist class in the course of its formation; but this is true above all for those moments when great masses of men are suddenly and forcibly torn from their means of subsistence, and hurled onto the labour-market as free, unprotected and rightless proletarians. The expropriation of the agricultural producer, of the peasant, from the soil is the basis of the whole process. *The history of this expropriation assumes different aspects in different countries, and runs through its various phases in different orders of succession, and at different historical*

epochs. Only in England, which we therefore take as our example, has it the classic form.[9]

Indeed, this historical and geographical extension echoes a previous formulation in Marx's manuscript *Pre-Capitalist Economic Formations*, where he investigated not only the separation of labor from land—including both free petty landownership and access to communal land—but also, and more broadly, the disappearance of the precapitalist community's relative independence and the eclipse of the lifeworld attached to it as important preconditions for the emergence of capitalism. What later appears in *Capital* as a neat extrication of the nexus between property, the division of labor and social reproduction is here tinged with a quasi-ontological flavor. Before the process of capitalist dispossession, Marx says, "[t]he individual is related to himself as a proprietor ... Where this *prerequisite* derives from the community, the others are his co-owners, who are so many incarnations of the common property"; even in more developed social formations "[t]he common property which formerly absorbed everything and embraced them all ... subsists as a special *ager publicus*," public fields that provide the basis for the survival of communal bonds. The purpose of labor under these conditions "is not the *creation of value* [but] the maintenance of the owner and his family as well as of the communal body as a whole."[10] In other words, the social reproduction of the community is basically oriented towards the preservation of the regimes of relative self-subsistence and self-government upon which communal autonomy is based. Enclosure entails the destruction of these regimes and is therefore embedded in the broader Marxian ontology of alienation.[11]

The central constituent of original accumulation, then, consists not only of the deprivation of the means of production, but more broadly, it involves the wide-ranging processes in which the independence of pre- or non-capitalist social formations is disarticulated through the erosion of their capacity to appropriate their life realms, to organize the social division of labor and to control the material bases of social existence.[12] In this sense, original accumulation undermines the autonomy of precapitalist communities as their institutions are dismantled and their members are rendered more and more dependent on the wage relation and the markets to subsist. As Michael Perelman demonstrates, this aspect was not a by-product of other social and economic transformations, but an explicit goal of the ascendant ruling class at the dawn of capitalism—capital used original accumulation as "a weapon to decompose society's natural desire to protect itself from [market] rule."[13]

This extension of the conceptual field of dispossession from the *means of production* to the broader *means of independence* in the sphere of social reproduction resonates productively with the recent debate about enclosure and the ongoing character of original accumulation. David Harvey has recently provided a vibrant account of how contemporary capitalism has overcome current economic and financial crisis tendencies by opening new arenas of accumulation by dispossession across the planet, including in the core zones of the global North that underwent industrialization at least a century ago, if not earlier.[14] Echoing

Marx's focus on the different facets of original accumulation, Harvey identifies four elements—privatization, financialization, crisis-management and state redistribution—as key moments within contemporary processes of accumulation by dispossession, suggesting that privatization stands among the others as its "cutting edge."[15] Despite their fundamental contributions to illuminating current forms of neoliberalization, most contemporary discussions of dispossession and enclosure have focused on the *material* dimensions of privatization processes—comprising a wide range of realities from the plundering of natural resources and the global commons to the commodification of the genetic commons—while overlooking the less obvious but equally important issue of the *means of autonomy* beyond the strictly economic sphere. The latter include, among other aspects, knowledge and skills for social organization, collective institutions and imaginaries, everyday spatialities and affective bonds underpinning community cohesion, and so forth. As I argue below, the case of English parliamentary enclosure provides an extremely powerful, far-reaching example of the historical articulation between processes of dispossession and original accumulation at a wide range of different levels, from the purely economic to the political and cultural dimensions.

Most crucially for the concerns of this book, the enclosure acts pursued this goal by deploying *a new spatial rationality* that mobilized territory as an instrument for the production of social order while radically reworking previous scalar configurations of the relation between city, countryside and the wider international trade networks to which both were increasingly connected.[16] Drawing a parallel with the expanded notion of *ursprüngliche Akkumulation* suggested above, this process can be described as one of *original extended urbanization*—an inaugural stage in a newly emergent regime of capitalist urbanization. The onset of original extended urbanization entailed the condensation of urban patterns of sociospatial structuration in the countryside. These extended urban formations reshaped preexisting rural lifeworlds, eroding their relative autonomy in the social division of labor and the sphere of social reproduction as they were rescaled into broader economic, social and political networks defined by a logic of capital accumulation. The vectors of urban society penetrated the countryside through this consolidation and extension of a specifically capitalist spatial division of labor, imposing new codes and practices on territories that, to a great extent, had previously given themselves their own rules and forms of social organization, either on a feudal basis or through subsequent articulations of communal and private institutions.[17] In turn, this process imploded back on cities themselves, as they were subsequently redefined by their reinforced role as mediators in the expanding operational landscapes of the capitalist world-system.

As is the case with original accumulation, the process of original extended urbanization should not be interpreted as an isolated point in the history of capitalism, but must be understood as a constant, ongoing dynamic in which non-urban realms have been relentlessly incorporated and rewoven into these operational landscapes. But what differentiates the dynamic of territorial subsumption—the inaugural or initial phase that characterizes *original* extended urbanization—from subsequent, more general trends of urbanization under modern capitalism?

In confronting this question, it is productive to consider the ways in which the dialectic between original and ongoing accumulation by dispossession has been explored in contemporary debates on primitive accumulation. Such discussions illuminate the historical and ongoing subsumption of labor to capital in a way that generates useful insights for our own explorations of the subordination of the country to urban formations under capitalism. As indicated, the English historical case does not exhaust the narrative of original accumulation in *Capital*. Early on, in *Value, Price and Profit*, Marx had warned that, once established, the "[s]eparation between [l]abor and the [i]nstruments of [l]abor" had to be "reproduce[d] upon a constantly increasing scale."[18] Rather than being a purely historical account, as some authors have indicated, the Marxian analysis of original accumulation "allow[s] us to read the past as something that survives in the present" and "prevents us from seeing the historical time of the capitalist mode of production as merely linear and progressive."[19]

We can, therefore, think of processes of *ursprüngliche Akkumulation* as being constituted by two analytically distinct, geographically uneven but historically coterminous moments, whose dialectic allows capitalism to consolidate and reproduce itself in time and space. Drawing on Massimo de Angelis' terminology, we can identify:

1. An *ex-novo* moment of original accumulation, characterized by the taming of precapitalist social spaces and pools of labor. This entails the advancement of the *extensive* frontier of capitalism with a spatial focus on areal, absolute territorial expansion (*exo-colonization*).

2. An *ongoing* moment of accumulation by dispossession, characterized by the continuous reworking and creative destruction of already capitalist realms of social life, as the subsumption of labor is deepened and new aspects of sociality are commodified and recommodified. This entails a deepening of the *intensive* frontier of capitalism with a focus on the continual reconfiguration of the inner structure of social space (*endo-colonization*).[20]

Under present conditions, *both* moments of original accumulation are clearly operative. This discussion has important implications for the analysis of extended urbanization, which likewise contains *ex-novo* and ongoing developmental moments. Thus understood, (a) original extended urbanization designates the *ex-novo* production of territorial heteronomy— the dismantling of traditional city-hinterland balances and relatively self-contained rural lifeworlds and divisions of labor through an intensified connection and subsumption of the countryside by which it increasingly becomes a mere functional appendix of the broader urban networks that command sociospatial organization under capitalism. Concomitantly,

(b) ongoing extended urbanization refers to subsequent waves of sociospatial restructuring that reproduce and deepen the conditions of territorial heteronomy in subaltern areas that are already inside the system, constantly reshaping the geographies of core/periphery relations associated with agglomerations and their dispersed operational landscapes. The difference among these moments resides not only in their relative historical-geographical context, but in their aims and in the conditions and means of their development.

The *ex-novo* subsumption of erstwhile non-capitalist realms is achieved through the direct extra-economic intervention of the state. Merely economic forms of coercion are too slow or unable to transform many aspects of their organization, especially in regards to local forms of social reproduction; it is these new political measures and institutional strategies, not the markets, that push the process forward by enforcing novel, capitalist modes of production and social reproduction. In so doing, the politics of original accumulation tendentially replace a form of dispossession that was based upon individual acts of violent expropriation—the dispersed violence of feudal and piecemeal enclosure—with an emergent juridical modality of coercion based upon the state-enforced universality of socially and territorially standardized legal codes.[21]

In a similar manner, the penetration of urban logics and markets into non-urban territories is preceded by the implementation of a broader political economy mediated through historically and geographically specific state spatial practices to uproot inherited systems of land use permitting the collective appropriation of social resources. The new urban order emerges from the interstices of a foreign territory, beating its path against a set of practices and institutions that produce friction and hinder its advance. Robert Dodgshon has explored this phenomenon with reference to the *inertial* character of societal organization, which he considers to be rooted in the properties of historical systems of spatial organization.[22] Everyday cultures, customs, institutions and the like are spatially reified, he suggests, so that a great part of social resistance against change is actually rooted in the entrenchment or rigidity of extant spatial practices and their routines of social appropriation. Insofar as these spatialities provide the conditions for the persistence of the old order, social change can only occur through their destabilization, erosion or removal. These observations may help illuminate the intensified role of state action in the penetration and disarticulation of non-urban, non-capitalist territories during the *ex-novo* moment of original extended urbanization. For it is precisely through the mobilization of new governmental techniques that the "inertia" of inherited, precapitalist sociospatial arrangements was subjected to the transformative pressures associated with capitalist forms of territorialization.

Subsequent rounds of sociospatial restructuring of the peripheries of the urban system can be understood as successive waves of *ongoing* extended urbanization, as capitalism reworks the sociospatial fabric of already incorporated territories to achieve the conditions for new rounds of accumulation. The operational landscape of extended urbanization, therefore, is not forged once and for all with the destruction of postfeudal social spaces, but is likewise continually creatively destroyed, at once deterritorialized and reterritorialized, during the course of world capitalist development, to support the diverse political-economic processes associated with successive forms of capitalist agglomeration and centralization. The role of the state shifts here, as does the form of violence involved in this process of restructuring. On the one hand, state coercion is not only formally dissolved into the "neutrality" of law, but also naturalized in the social relations fostered by new regulatory frameworks.[23] Paraphrasing Marx, we can say that "the silent compulsion of economic relations" deepens the conditions of submission of peripheral areas to the urban system; enshrined in law, the quotidian violence of spatial divisions of labor and heteronomous social reproduction develops additional, discrete restructurings of sociospatial practices on an everyday basis.[24] On the other hand, the concealed character of coercion disappears when direct extra-economic force is mobilized to unleash new assaults upon the remaining, non-commodified forms of social existence, crushing resistance to the newly emergent processes of creative destruction and dispossession.[25] Figure 16.1 summarizes the key elements of this argument.

Crucially, as is the case with the dialectic of original and ongoing accumulation by dispossession, the dual process of *ex-novo* and ongoing extended urbanization is not specific

	Accumulation by Dispossession	**Original Extended Urbanization**
Ex-novo moment	Initial subsumption of labor to capital Expropriation of the people's means of autonomy State foundation of labor markets Extensive frontiers of accumulation	Inaugural subsumption of the countryside within urban operational landscapes Enclosure/dismantling of self-contained sociospatial assemblages State constitution of capitalist spatial divisions of labor Exo-colonization/focus on areal, absolute territorial expansion
Ongoing moment	Intensified subsumption of labor to capital State restructuring of labor markets Transformation (increasing commodification) of the conditions for the reproduction of the working class Intensive frontiers of accumulation	Deepened subsumption of the countryside in urban operational landscapes State reterritorialization of capitalist spatial divisions of labor Expanded enclosure of non-commodified sociospatial reproduction in already-capitalist territories Endo-colonization/focus on reorganizing the inner structure of social space

16.1 The dialectic between the *ex-novo* and ongoing moments of extended urbanization in relation to accumulation by dispossession

to any particular historical stage of capitalism, but should be regarded as constitutive of the system's global evolution. *Ex-novo* extended urbanization constitutes a precise moment in the reterritorialization of particular places or regions, but at the same time, it continuously reappears across diverse areas of the globe as capital shifts in space through successive waves of territorial and scalar restructuring, incorporating new enclaves to its basic sociospatial rationalities.[26] In turn, peripheral territories that are already integrated within urbanized operational landscapes undergo successive rounds of ongoing extended urbanization, as core agglomerations mediate new waves of spatial creative destruction as they confront new accumulation crises. This complex, nonlinear character of urbanization should therefore be regarded as a central aspect of the capitalist mode of territorialization.

Open-field System, Common Right and Parliamentary Enclosure

Enclosure was the process by which open field land subject to communal crop regulation and common right obligations was transformed into land held in severalty, that is, private individual ownership free from any communal bond and usually with physical boundaries separating one person's land from the rest.[27] The process of regulated enclosure—as opposed to uncontrolled encroachment—had been practiced since the thirteenth century, especially to consolidate land holdings, which in the ancient Saxon patterns preserved in the open-field system were usually divided and scattered throughout the parish into narrow strips. However, pre-parliamentary, piecemeal enclosure had had a limited scope—usually only a part of the parish was enclosed, preserving common land and common rights. Even if these piecemeal enclosures sought economic improvement and private profit, for the most part they remained subject to what Edward Thompson called a local moral economy, where individual interests were balanced with custom and communal necessity.[28] Since pre-parliamentary enclosure was locally decided and negotiated, the communal ties—and the possibility of reprisals and social disorder—limited the extent of interventions.

Starting in the beginning of the seventeenth century, enclosure acts constituted a new step in which Parliament centralized the process and provided a common framework and procedure for the development of local interventions in cases where other forms of enclosure were particularly difficult to implement. Initially each parish had to develop its own bill (Figure 16.2). From the end of the seventeenth century, the number of enclosure acts rapidly increased, and during the eighteenth century—when the pace and scope of enclosure accelerated—this mechanism superseded traditional modes of piecemeal enclosure by agreement between private owners. The peak of activity concentrated between 1755 and the mid-1830s, fostering the passing of the Inclosure Consolidation Act of 1801 and the General Inclosure Act of 1836, subsequently followed by another General Act in 1845. These general acts reinforced the tendency to legal normalization and homogenization of a national regulatory framework by setting more detailed general conditions for all interventions and obviating the need for individual laws in each parish. Throughout the entire period, enclosure acts were widely used for their systematic potential

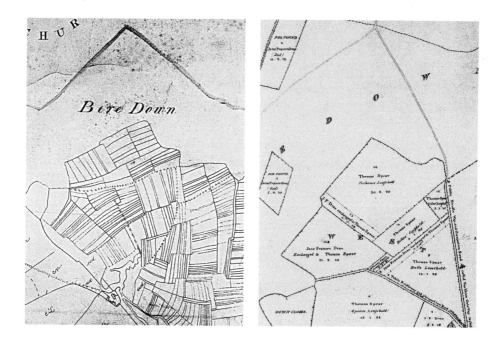

16.2 The Bere Regis enclosure, Dorset, 1846. The extracts illustrate the situation before and after parliamentary enclosure on Bere Down: the pre-enclosure cadaster showing the subdivision of the open field (left) and the award map (right).

to reterritorialize those regions that presented more resistance to change, areas where the open-field system was widespread, with the greatest proportion of common land or with deeply entrenched communal practices (Figure 16.3, next page). Unlike earlier patterns of enclosure, which were piecemeal and partial, the newly imposed acts affected the entire parish, including common land, wastes and so forth.[29]

In order to understand the impact of enclosure, it may be useful to briefly describe how the open-field system worked and its relation to common right. Superimposed upon the complex medieval patterns of property was a regime of social land use, a field system, which both predated and partially survived feudal arrangements of ownership. The open-field system included three elements, each with its own rules for the regulation of common right.[30] In the first place, there were the arable fields, with their characteristic pattern of long, narrow strips and a crop regime that was agreed upon collectively. Each farmer held rights over one or several strips of land scattered over the parish, usually arranged so that every owner received plots with varying soil quality.[31] After harvesting, these fields were used as common pastureland for up to eight months, hence the name of *commonable land* by which they were known. The rest of the land was *common land* and, in turn, divided into two types: common meadows, distributed annually in a similar way to the arable fields among local landowners and tenants for use as pastureland or individual crops, and also subject to collective usufruct after harvesting; and different forms of common pastures and waste land, permanently available for common usage under a specific regulatory framework. The open-field system was dominant in the richest and most densely populated regions—the

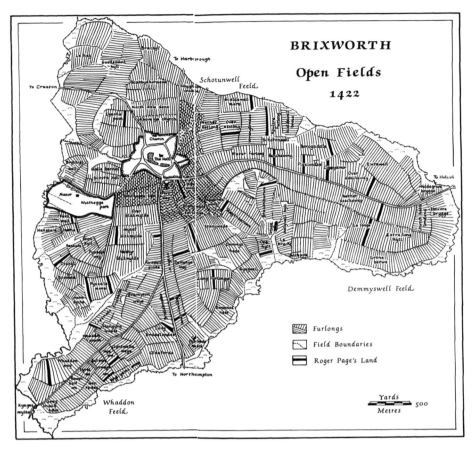

16.3 The open field of Brixworth, Northamptonshire, in 1422, as reconstructed by David Hall
Note how the yardland of one person is evenly scattered throughout the fields of the village.

Midlands, parts of Southern England and, with its own particular features, East Anglia—
and constituted 53 percent of the total surface area of England around 1600 (Figure 16.4).[32]

In 1914, when the formal process of enclosure was abandoned, only 4.6% of the land
operated under the open-field system. The impact of such radical transformation can be
fully understood only in connection to the extinction of individual and collective autonomy
it involved in relation to common right as well as the communal self-management of
productive cycles within the parish. Common and commonable lands were a fundamental
resource for a great part of the population that lacked any property but enjoyed common
rights, including rights of pasturage, hunting, fishing, gleaning, the gathering of fuel and
others. Common right provided an informal source of income that became a key element
of household economies in the poor's attempt to resist exclusive dependence on wage
labor and the extension of markets. To name but a few examples, gleaning could provide
enough grain to prepare bread during a whole year, the equivalent to an adult male's two-
month salary; fuel could be collected for the whole winter, the equivalent to a six-week
salary; if a family was lucky enough to buy a cow, the earnings derived from it could rise

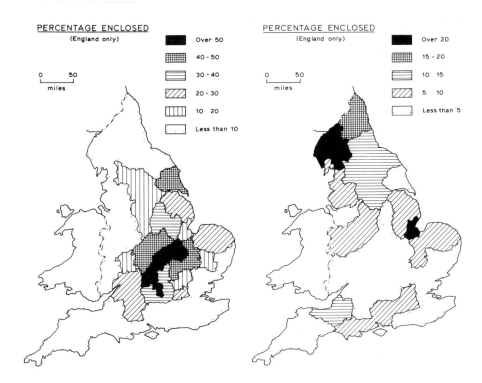

16.4 The enclosure of open field (left) and of common and waste land (right) as a percentage of county area (England only), c. 1750–1870

to a male's annual wage.[33] These informal resources provided the basis for small farmers and the poor to resist the advance of a new social division of labor and its associated pattern of commodified social reproduction. The members of the ruling classes and their ideological representatives—not only the landed gentry but also new industrialists, merchant-manufacturers and political economists—were indeed all too conscious of how extant territorialities and spatial practices attached to common land were hindering the emergence of the new capitalist order.[34] Commons were a "nest and conservatory of sloth," a "hindrance to Industry, … Nurseries of Idleness and Insolence" that made "[d]ay labour … disgusting" and impeded the creation of the reserve army of surplus labor demanded by the new economy.[35] Enclosure would deprive the poor of that "sort of independence" produced by the commons, securing "that subordination of the lower ranks of society which in the present times is so much wanted"; thus "labourers [will] work every day in the year, and have their children … put out to labour *early*."[36] More importantly for our reading of parliamentary enclosure through the lens of urbanization theory, the benefits of such territorial transformation would not only be felt in the countryside, but also in the emerging hybrid landscapes of production across the nation at large:

> [I]f by converting the little farmers into a body of men who must work for others more labour is produced, it is an advantage which the nation should wish for … the produce being greater when their joint labours are employed on one farm,

there will be a surplus for manufacturers, and by this means manufactures, one of the mines of this nation, will increase, in proportion to the quantity of corn produced.[37]

Parliamentary Enclosure as Original Extended Urbanization

The process of dispossession, then, was not a form of unintended collateral damage associated with agrarian "improvement" under nascent capitalism, but represented a key element within an emergent territorial strategy that was replacing traditional bonds and balances between the country and the city at a range of different levels. This strategy contributed to the construction of a rescaled urban operational landscape designed to fulfill new national and potentially global aspirations (Figure 16.5). England, many contemporary observers suggested, had to supersede the Dutch in the overseas trade and become the new hegemon in the developing capitalist world-system.[38] All national resources—not only agriculture, but also manufacture, mining, the timber industry and, more generally, *labor*—thus had to be mobilized in that endeavor. To this end, a variety of state mercantilist policies were enacted from the end of the seventeenth century forwards, including the protection of the national market and progressive relaxation of regional and local market regulation, state borrowing to support the development of modern financial markets, legal incentives to facilitate private infrastructural investment, naval aggression and colonial expansion and so forth.[39] Enclosure acts were seen as an essential element within that project insofar as they helped consolidate one of its essential conditions of possibility: the reconfiguration of the land-workforce nexus according to newly emerging demands from rescaled markets and systems of production.

The enclosure acts provided a more systematic, homogeneous and centralized means to transform property relations by dismantling locally variegated regimes of ownership

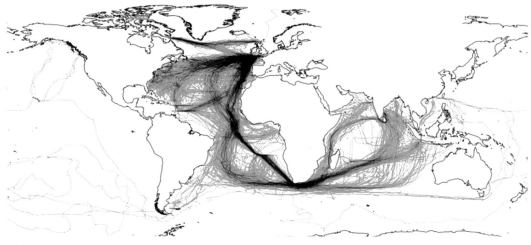

16.5 British trade routes as shown by ship logs, c. 1750–1800

and common right-based access to land, and hence for imposing conditions of wage dependence.[40] The augmented commodification of labor and land generated by these shifts can be interpreted as an essential expression of original extended urbanization at that time. It facilitated the penetration of new activities and schemes of production into the countryside, disseminated by increasingly mobile merchant-manufacturers escaping the constraints of traditionally regulated production and trade in guild towns, and weaving more tightly interlinked networks between major mercantile cities and their operational landscapes.[41] In this way, the division of labor and land use systems were released from the control of the parish and incorporated into expanding markets, processes that in turn subjected farming to a "yoke of improvement" that was increasingly dictated by the conditions of international exchange rationales rather than those of relatively self-contained regional markets. The whole countryside thus became a key zone of engagement for the coming industrial explosion, providing an important reserve of dispossessed labor power to work in the expanding system of rural domestic manufacture and later to migrate to the growing industrial cities (Figure 16.6). A new rural/urban landscape of production was emerging that would transform the role of mercantile hubs and foster the booming development of new industrial agglomerations.

But economic change was only one aspect of the *ex-novo* moment of extended urbanization. Other dimensions of territorial transformation must also be considered that permit a more precise understanding of its multilayered character. While the following discussion is hardly exhaustive, it is intended simply to underscore some of the political, cultural and physical dimensions of enclosure acts and their consequences for the reshaping of the urban fabric during this period.

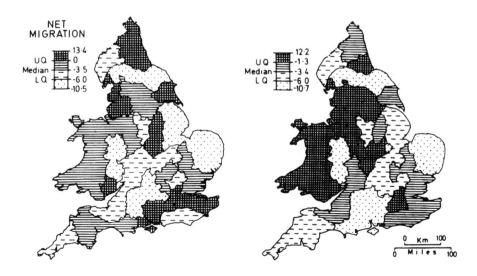

16.6 Net migration in England and Wales by counties between 1781–1800 (left) and 1801–30 (right). The average decadal rate of change per 1,000 is shown in four quartile groups. The regions with higher rates of enclosure in Figure 16.5 usually present net outmigration.

The eclipse of rural autonomy discussed above was manifested in the *political* erosion of local institutions in the wake of parliamentary acts. Prior to enclosure, the open-field system was regulated on a local basis, through agencies and bodies that were closely linked to the daily life in the parish, a scalar scheme that partially allowed the survival of local moral economies and forced the commoners to engage in constant, intra-local negotiations in order to reach the agreements required for land cultivation.[42] The whole community was directly or indirectly involved in this collective self-management: "The hamlet was the unit of cultivation, not the farm. The farmer did not farm as he chose, but according to the method prescribed for him, by common agreement guided by custom."[43] Ingrained in everydayness and customary routine, this arrangement layered the social fabric of the parish with a network of reciprocal bonds and duties that reinforced community cohesion—even if, for some members, this system was experienced as a collective burden on private initiative. Feudal enclosure had partially disarticulated previous Saxon schemes of commonality, but the process usually reproduced the central role of local institutions. Later forms of pre-parliamentary enclosure occurred largely through locally negotiated, piecemeal agreements, and as such, they were balanced and limited by tradition, communal necessity and the fear of social disorder. Crucially, these long entrenched vectors of rural autonomy and (sometimes compulsory) commonality were abruptly removed by the enclosure acts, which transferred negotiations to parliamentary control, thereby rendering useless the manorial courts and parish structures, and effectively destroying the nexus of local communal institutions. London became a hub of political control as the new national regulatory framework was consolidated.

Original extended urbanization was also articulated through at least one other transformed relation between land and political power. During the heyday of parliamentary enclosure, from the end of the seventeenth century and into the nineteenth century, land was still "the most permanent form of asset and the principal fount of influence and power."[44] Yet, although landowners still held political power, the countryside's traditional role as a reserve for the old landed peerage was increasingly undermined. Urban commercial and financial elites bought rural estates to attain a social standing that granted them political representation. While such trends were by no means new, they had been largely restricted prior to parliamentary enclosure due to the extraordinary diversity of rural ownership patterns and regimes of possession, which inhibited most urban investors from venturing into the strange territories characteristic of medieval and postmedieval social dispersion. Enclosure acts simplified the incursion of these urban "foreign" agents into the countryside through various forms of legal and managerial homogenization, which imposed and extended a single model of exclusive dominion across the erstwhile countryside. Such a model was, in effect, perfectly attuned with the expansion of a calculative logic in an era of booming economic exchange and incipient industrial development.[45]

It should also be considered how *cultural* and *symbolic* spatializations associated with enclosure urbanized the countryside. The enclosure acts paved the way for the material reconfiguration of landscape for aesthetic purposes. The expansion of the networks of gentry tourism throughout Europe produced a new symbolic economy that had a direct influence on the image and imagination of national territories. Highly idealized representations of foreign pastoral settings ricocheted across England as now-mature gentlemen established their country estates, creating gardens that evoked the travel memories of their youth. Embodied in the new visual regimes of picturesque scenery, a redefined rural landscape became the object of conspicuous consumption and class distinction.[46] The growing size and formal ambition of such gardens and landscapes required integrally consolidated land holdings in which the designers could deploy their schemes, and of course, the process of enclosure provided precisely that opportunity.[47] Contrary to the official discourse of agrarian "improvement," many enclosures were not only aimed at economic development, but also at the creation of such pleasure gardens, especially for urban landowners seeking a place to stay away from the city. Significantly, the booming picturesque aesthetic of the eighteenth century—with its serpentines and gently curved, Hogarthian "lines of beauty and grace"—was actually contemporaneous and interconnected with a massive deployment of geometric, increasingly homogenized landscapes of production.[48] Both forms of landscape were indeed related to the nascent planned reterritorialization associated with parliamentary enclosure.[49] Trapped in its own spatial phantasmagoria, the gentry mobilized the garden both as a symbol of social respectability and as a buffer concealing the more forbidding landscapes of straight walls and fences that actually underpinned the rise to economic power of that class (Figure 16.7). In fact, the fake, "more-natural-than-Nature" rurality imposed on the picturesque garden was indeed all-too-urban—it embodied a new aesthetic imagination popularized on the latest fashion of landscape painting and pastoral poetry, which by the eighteenth century were the result of an urban reimagination

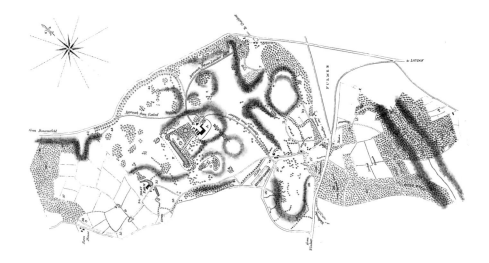

16.7 Humphry Repton's design for the pleasure garden of Bulstrode (Buckinghamshire). The garden around the house acts as a "natural," loosely outlined buffer that conceals the "ugliness" of the surrounding enclosed, geometrically distributed land in the fringes of the estate. Only the drive planned by Repton goes into these landscapes of production as a device both to control labor and to add diversity to the aesthetic experience of the landowner.

of the countryside.[50] Taken together, these diverse representational shifts and landscape transformations composed a further transformation of the erstwhile countryside in the realm of cultural formations and visual identity.

The enclosure acts also paved the way for the growing operationalization of the countryside in relation to other major transformations that were soon to occur in the big cities of England, especially through the expansion of transportation and communications infrastructures. Once the erstwhile non-capitalist peripheries had been included in capitalist systems of land use organization, they could be more closely incorporated into a network of distribution that assured their functionality for the city and, by implication, for emergent systems of industrial production and circulation across the national territory and beyond. The project of creating and extending road, turnpike, canal and later railroad networks at this progressively larger scale engendered major design challenges that were confronted above all through the establishment of a kind of spatial and legal *tabulae rasae* intended to overcome property rights issues and physical obstacles (Figure 16.8).

Thanks to their comprehensive potential to include all the land—both common and arable—within a parish in a single system of property allocation, the enclosure acts provided exactly such a framework. Indeed, as they were implemented across various territorial scales, they routinely incorporated considerations on the projected layout of new, large-scale transportation and communications infrastructures; it was not uncommon for such issues to be mentioned explicitly as one of the major aims of the intervention. The generalization in the use of enclosure acts from the end of the seventeenth century and their intensification towards the last third of the eighteenth century and the beginning of the nineteenth century occurred in parallel to the approval of statutory authority acts for infrastructural development, which granted for-profit corporations and private investors the right to fix the price and enforce the sale of land, to claim labor from inhabitants along the path of the infrastructure and to levy fees on users.[51]

Crucially, enclosure acts were also eventually used to manage and promote the expansion of the cities themselves. Landowners increasingly came to use them as legal weapons for consolidating their holdings and appropriating urban commons in the city fringes of booming agglomerations in order to develop new residential or industrial enclaves.[52] The same technique that had been introduced to promote extended urbanization in the countryside was now imploding back into the cities. In their reinvented role as mediators within the operational landscapes of an expanding capitalist world-system, the spatial cores of mercantile and later industrial agglomeration were now also subject to intense transformative pressures. In effect, parliamentary enclosure was now being mobilized to facilitate new rounds of *concentrated* urbanization. Its potential to deploy capitalist spatializations across different territories and scales was now more explicit than ever before (Figure 16.9, page 254).

Conclusions

By the beginning of the nineteenth century, enclosure was becoming a sort of universal *territorial equivalent* for the development of the variegated, multifarious forms of capitalist urbanization: a spatial fulcrum or pivot through which different types of territories could be transformed and managed using a similar rationale across different scales. At this time, enclosure was reaching its peak importance as a political-legal mechanism for urbanizing the English countryside while also being used increasingly to orchestrate and accelerate the land use transformations associated with concentrated forms of urbanization in the emerging industrial agglomerations of Britain. At the same time, it was also morphing into a global device of territorial transformation as Britain expanded its imperialist project across the

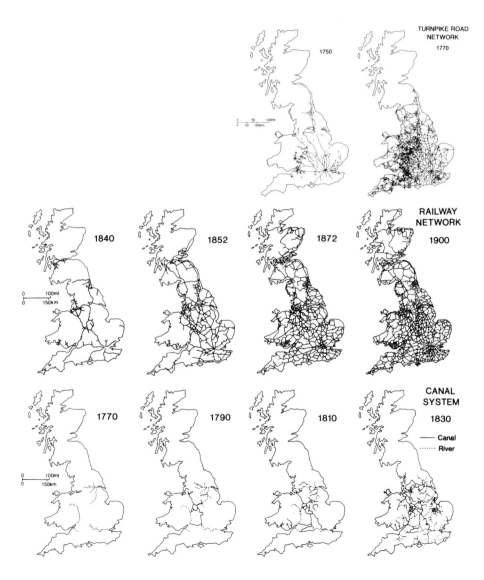

16.8 The successive development and thickening of several infrastructural networks in the eighteenth and nineteenth centuries.

world.[53] The spatial strategy of enclosure was exported to the colonies as a moment of land dispossession, as an instrument to submit foreign populations to new spatial divisions of labor, and as a way to reconfigure extant territorial formations. In effect, as capitalist urbanization was assuming a worldwide horizon, enclosure and dispossession were likewise increasingly being globalized as basic elements of the capitalist mode of territorialization.

In this chapter, I have interpreted parliamentary enclosure as an instance of original or *ex-novo* extended urbanization, a key moment in the consolidation of a new formation of city/countryside relations and associated territorial, social and economic ramifications at the dawn of English capitalism. But to what extent can this analysis inform an investigation of subsequent rounds of original and ongoing extended urbanization during later stages of capitalist development and, in particular, today?

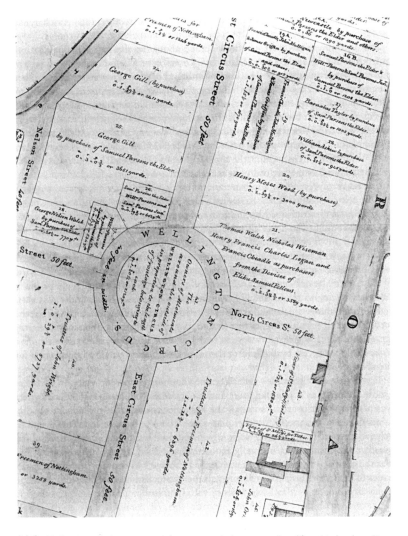

16.9 Enclosure applied in a situation of concentrated urbanization. Detail from Notthingham Common Fields enclosure map (1846), showing properties laid out as a fully formed urban tissue.

Enclosure, conceived as a form of spatially driven dispossession, should be regarded as a constitutive moment in the study of the historical geographies of capitalist urbanization, not only in England but globally. Enclosure operates through an interrelated set of nested layers of sociospatial transformation. Each of them hinges upon dispossession, and connects to the others in forms that are specific to particular places and moments of capitalist evolution. Yet, the overall compound results in a generalized reconfiguration of territorial hierarchies and formations that consolidates and expands the urban system at different scales. The constitutive moments of enclosure are:

- *Transformation of property and land rights regimes*. Privatization is a key moment of enclosure and capitalist reterritorialization, but dispossession is often related, more generally, to the dismantling of communal regimes of social reproduction. As is the case with other forms of capitalist spatialization, calculation, abstraction and homogenization usually play an important role in this process.

- *Redistribution of resources*. Regimes of access to resources (crops, minerals, water, and other raw materials and sources of energy) are reconfigured, usually as a result of the transformation of property systems. The mobilization of resources as a means to secure autonomy and render other agents or groups dependent remains a fundamental drive under capitalist forms of territoriality, but the latter entail more historically specific strategies for appropriating and instrumentalizing such resources, and thus for relentlessly expanding, thickening and rescaling the urban fabric as a whole.[54]

- *Restructuring spatial divisions of labor and modes of social reproduction*. The previous moves, which entail the monopolization of land and resources, are used by ruling class elites to impose new economic relations upon the subaltern classes. Both labor and processes of social reproduction are gradually subsumed under commodity forms, thereby securing the further expansion of the system. These processes are developed through spatially uneven reconfigurations of extant divisions of labor that involve new functional landscapes of production and social reproduction.

- *State intervention*. As an instrument in the production of national and international economic space, enclosure is a fundamental moment of the state mediation of urbanization processes, which hinges upon intensive forms of intervention to unlock strongly resistant, spatially entrenched articulations of land, resources and labor. Even if private or corporate actors are usually the final beneficiaries of enclosure, the state remains a key agent in conducting the process, providing the adequate legal framework, legitimizing the violence involved in dispossession, and designing the resulting territories as efficient landscapes for accumulation.

- *Political heteronomization*. The dismantling of communal bonds after enclosure is accompanied by the gradual erosion and disappearance of communal bodies of government at the local scale. State intervention undermines local autonomy, normalizes political formations and produces the peripheries of the urban fabric as subaltern sites.

- *Urban fabric.* Enclosure provides the material and legal bases for the development and tightening of the urban fabric across the territories incorporated into the system. Given the specific role of these extended areas of urbanization within the broader operational landscape, the urban fabric is usually condensed in the form of sites of production and extraction and in infrastructures of transportation and communication. However, the materialization of the urban fabric in peripheral areas can adopt other, less obvious forms, as their apparently natural and rural qualities are mobilized in specifically urbanizing regimes of production, management and symbolic representation.

Through the interaction between these vectors of sociospatial change, enclosure reshapes existing territorial formations. It provides the conditions for the incorporation of non-urban, non-capitalist spaces into the operational landscapes of urbanization, eroding their previous relative autonomy at a range of different levels and transforming them into functional, subaltern territories within wider spatial divisions of labor and exchange networks. Additionally, enclosure reworks the links and hierarchies within the system and, eventually implodes back into agglomerations themselves as another moment of concentrated urbanization. In this expanded scope, enclosure operates as part of a wider spatial rationale, a universal territorial equivalent between different trends of spatialization, producing new relations between city, countryside and the broader international networks to which the former are increasingly connected.

This multilayered framework of analysis appears as potentially transferable to subsequent scenarios of *ex-novo* and ongoing urbanization within the geohistory of capitalism and, particularly, to current processes of neoliberalized, planetary urbanization. In any case, these considerations should be taken as merely tentative steps that require further development both in their historical specificity and in broader evolutionary terms, especially in relation to contemporary experiences. An effort to periodize and develop comparative studies of the larger historical-geographical configurations of enclosure under capitalism seems crucial in order to develop the preliminary approach presented here. Can we, for instance, think of specifically imperialist, Fordist-Keynesian or post-Keynesian/neoliberal formations of enclosure? What are the particular features of such formations in their articulation to successive stages of capitalist urbanization (both concentrated and extended) and associated strategies of state regulation? How are new moments of *ex-novo* and ongoing extended urbanization intertwined throughout these phases? How do they rework and creatively destroy inherited territorial configurations and the extant urban fabric?

As I have suggested, English parliamentary enclosure did not exhaust the dynamics of *ex-novo* extended urbanization. Even though it may be considered classic or paradigmatic, this case represents merely one example of a larger trajectory of capitalist territorial subsumption. New rounds of *ex-novo* and ongoing extended urbanization are unleashed around the world as capital strives to colonize any non-capitalist spaces contained on the planet and to deepen the subaltern condition of already incorporated sites of exploitation. The whole system of territorialization, indeed, is constantly revolutionized as it gets rewoven within successive phases of capitalist development. The fact that this evolutionary pattern has seemingly intensified over recent decades under conditions of worldwide neoliberalization provides a further intellectual and political rationale for an interest in its historical evolution. Yet, it would be premature to take the aspects and moments identified in this chapter as elements in a universal, stabilized account of the dynamics of original extended urbanization. They should be understood instead as provisional explorations pointing towards a particular framework of analysis that may be adapted to other cases. The degree to which this initial analytical framework requires adjustment and updating to study contemporary phenomena is, after all, an indication of how capitalism continually transforms its strategy and its mode of territorialization in order to survive and expand. The patterns and vectors of dispossession, territorial subsumption and uneven spatial development remain, nevertheless, present at the core of its evolution and ongoing expansion.

Notes

1   Daniel Defoe, *Tour Through the Eastern Counties of England* (New York: Cassell, 1888 [1722]) 27.

2   Midnight Notes, "Introduction to The New Enclosures," *Midnight Notes* 10 (1990) 1-9, 1.

3   Henri Lefebvre, *The Urban Revolution*, trans. Robert Bononno (Minneapolis: University of Minnesota Press, 2003 [1970]) 11. For a discussion of the strengths and weaknesses of Lefebvre's historical schema, see Stuart Elden, *Understanding Henri Lefebvre: Theory and the Possible* (London: Continuum, 2004) 130-2; and Andy Merrifield, *Henri Lefebvre: a Critical Introduction* (New York: Routledge, 2006) 87-9.

4   Neil Brenner, "Theses on Urbanization," this book, Ch. 13.

5   For a more detailed conceptualization of the dialectic between concentrated and extended urbanization see Brenner, "Theses on Urbanization," this book, Ch. 13, as well as, Neil Brenner & Christian Schmid, "The 'Urban Age' in Question," this book, Ch. 21; and Roberto Luís Monte-Mór, "What is the Urban in the Contemporary World," this book, Ch. 17. For a description of the spatiality of contemporary capitalism as a dialectic of implosion-explosion of urban formations, see also Lefebvre, *The Urban Revolution*, 14-15; and Neil Brenner, "The Urban Question as a Scale Question: Reflections on Henri Lefebvre, Urban Theory, and the Politics of Scale," *International Journal of Regional and Urban Research* 24 (2000) 369-370.

6   I am not suggesting that these rural formations were idyllic, autonomous islands detached from precapitalist and proto-capitalist networks. They were, no doubt, embedded in regional divisions of labor and, depending on their location, partially articulated to national markets. See Mark Overton, *Agricultural Revolution in England: the Transformation of the Agrarian Economy, 1500–1850* (Cambridge: Cambridge University Press, 1996); and J. A. Yelling, "Agriculture 1500–1730," *An Historical Geography of England and Wales*, eds. Robert A. Dodgshon and Robin A. Butlin, Second Edition (London: Academic Press, 1990). Yet a great part of the local everyday life in such zones remained disconnected

from the emerging trends of production and trade restructuring in the cities and was largely based on self-contained modes of social reproduction. This is precisely the sense of the new interpretation of the city-country relation provided by Hal Draper in his translation of the famous passage in *The Communist Manifesto* in which Marx and Engels refer to the '*Idiotie des Landlebens*' as the *isolation* (not "idiocy") of rural life. See Hal Draper, *The Adventures of the Communist Manifesto* (Alameda: Center for Socialist History, 2004) 220.

7   Karl Marx, *Capital, Volume 1* (London: Penguin, 1976) 874. On the translation of the concept "*ursprüngliche Akkumulation*" into English, see Werner Bonefeld, "Primitive Accumulation and Capitalist Accumulation: Notes on Social Constitution and Expropriation," *Science & Society* 75 (2011) 386; and Michael Perelman, *The Invention of Capitalism: Classical Political Economy and the Secret History of Primitive Accumulation* (Durham: Duke University Press, 2000) 25-26. Marx identified the deprivation of the producer from the means of production as the main form of original accumulation, but he also distinguished other concomitant "chief moments" in the process—colonialism, the exploitation and murder of indigenous peoples, slavery, and the technology of public debt. See Marx, *Capital, Volume 1*, 915; and Rohit Negi and Marc Auerbach, "The Contemporary Significance of Primitive Accumulation," *Human Geography* 2 (2009) 89.

8   See Tony C. Brown, "The Time of Globalization: Rethinking Primitive Accumulation," *Rethinking Marxism: a Journal of Economics, Culture & Society* 21 (2009) 571-84; Massimo De Angelis, "Separating the Doing from the Deed: Capital and the Continuous Character of Enclosures," *Historical Materialism* 12 (2004) 57-87; Jim Glassman, "Primitive Accumulation, Accumulation by Dispossession, Accumulation by 'Extra-Economic' Means," *Progress in Human Geography* 30 (2006) 608-25; David Harvey, *The New Imperialism* (Oxford: Oxford University Press, 2003); David Harvey, "Neo-liberalism as Creative Destruction," *Geographiska Annaler, Series B* 88 (2006) 145-58; David Harvey, "The Future

of the Commons," *Radical History Review* 109 (2011) 101-7; Alex Jeffrey, Colin McFarlane, and Alex Vasudevan, "Rethinking Enclosure: Space, Subjectivity, and the Commons," *Antipode* 44 (2012) 1247-67; Midnight Notes, "Introduction to The New Enclosures"; Michael Perelman, "Primitive Accumulation from Feudalism to Neoliberalism," *Capitalism Nature Society* 18 (2007) 44-61; and Alex Vasudevan, Colin McFarlane and Alex Jeffrey, "Spaces of Enclosure," *Geoforum* 39 (2008) 1641-46.

9 Marx, *Capital, Volume 1*, 876, emphasis added.

10 Karl Marx, *Pre-Capitalist Economic Formations,* trans. Jack Cohen (London: Lawrence & Wishart, 1964) 67.

11 As Jim Glassman and Sandro Mezzzadra have suggested, this aspect links original accumulation to subsequent stages of capitalism, providing a basis for understanding enclosure and dispossession as more than merely historical phenomena. See Jim Glasman, "Primitive Accumulation," 615; and Sandro Mezzadra, "The Topicality of Prehistory: a New Reading of Marx's Analysis of 'So-called Primitive Accumulation,'" *Rethinking Marxism: a Journal of Economic, Culture & Society* 23 (2011) 307.

12 Bonefeld, "Primitive Accumulation and Capitalist Accumulation," 397; Glassman, "Primitive Accumulation," 610; and Midnight Notes, "Introduction to The New Enclosures," 3.

13 Perelman, *The Invention of Capitalism;*" Perelman, "Primitive Accumulation;" and Bonefeld, "Primitive Accumulation and Capitalist Accumulation," 384.

14 Harvey, *The New Imperialism*, 157. See also Perelman, "Primitive Accumulation," 620; and Rohit Negi and Marc Auerbach, "Primitive Accumulation, Capitalism and Development," *Human Geography* 2 (2009) 101.

15 Harvey, "Neo-liberalism as Creative Destruction," 153-5.

16 Álvaro Sevilla-Buitrago, "Territory and the Governmentalisation of Social Reproduction: Parliamentary Enclosure and Spatial Rationalities in the Transition From Feudalism to Capitalism," *Journal of Historic Geography* 38 (2012) 209-19.

17 J. M. Neeson, *Commoners: Common Right, Enclosure and Social Change in England, 1700–1820* (Cambridge: Cambridge University Press, 1993).

18 Karl Marx, *Value, Price, and Profit* (Chicago: C. H. Kerr, 1913) 74.

19 Silvia Federici, *Caliban and the Witch: Women, the Body, and Primitive Accumulation* (New York: Autonomedia, 2004) 12; and Mezzadra, "The Topicality of Prehistory," 305. Likewise, Werner Bonefeld has suggested that original accumulation must be seen not only as a historical precondition of capitalism, but also as an outcome and necessary element of its expansion throughout its *longue durée* development. See Bonefeld, "Primitive Accumulation and Capitalist Accumulation," 380.

20 De Angelis, "Separating the Doing and the Deed," 66. For the dialectic of extensive accumulation (based on the creation of the wage relation) and intensive accumulation (based on the transformation of the conditions of existence of wage labor), see Michel Aglietta, *A Theory of Capitalist Regulation: the US Experience,* trans. David Fernbach (London: Verso, 2000) 71-2. Jim Glassman uses the metaphor of an *"extensive* (geographical) and an *intensive* (social) frontier" of primitive accumulation to show its enormous sociospatial range of activities. See Glassman, "Primitive Accumulation," 622. The similar notions of exo- and endo-colonization are suggested in Jason Read's interpretation of primitive accumulation as a key moment in the capitalist production of subjectivity. See Jason Read, *The Micro-Politics of Capital: Marx and the Prehistory of the Present* (Albany: State University of New York Press, 2003) 27.

21 Marx, *Capital, Volume 1*, 885, 899-900; and Read, *The Micro-Politics of Capital*, 28.

22 Robert Dodgshon, *Society in Time and Space: a Geographical Perspective on Change* (Cambridge: Cambridge University Press, 1998).

23 Read, *The Micro-Politics of Capital*, 28.

24 Marx, *Capital, Volume 1*, 899.

25 Ibid.; and Harvey, "Neo-liberalism as Creative Destruction," 153.

26 Rosa Luxemburg, *The Accumulation of Capital,* trans. Agnes

Schwarzchild (London: Routledge, 2003); Neil Smith, *Uneven Development: Nature, Capital, and the Production of Space*, Third Edition (London: Verso, 2010); Neil Brenner, "A Thousand Leaves: Notes on the Geographies of Uneven Spatial Development," *Leviathan Undone? Towards a Political Economy of Scale*, eds. Roger Keil and Rianne Mahon (Vancouver: University of British Columbia Press, 2009) 27-49; and Neil Brenner, "Restructuring, Rescaling, and the Urban Question," *Critical Planning* 16 (2009) 60-79.

27 Michael Turner, *Enclosures in Britain, 1750–1830* (London: Macmillan, 1984) 11. For bibliographies of studies on historical enclosure stretching back to the 1860s see Jerome Blum, "English Parliamentary Enclosure," *Journal of Modern History* 53 (1981) 477-504; Gregory Clark and Anthony Clark, "Common Rights to Land in England, 1475–1839," *Journal of Economic History* 61 (2001) 1009-36; and G. E. Mingay, "Introduction," E. C. K. Gonner, *Common Land and Inclosure* (London: MacMillan, 1966) xxxiii-liii.

28 Edward P. Thompson, "The Moral Economy of the English Crowd in the Eighteenth Century," *Past and Present* 50 (1971) 76-136.

29 Turner, *Enclosures in Britain*.

30 Alan R. H. Baker and Robin A. Butlin, eds., *Studies of Field Systems in the British Isles* (Cambridge: Cambridge University Press, 1973); John Chapman, "Field Systems and Enclosure," *International Encyclopedia of Human Geography, Volume IV*, eds. Rob Kitchin and Nigel Thrift (Amsterdam: Elsevier, 2009) 112-118; Joan Thirsk, "The Common Fields," *Past and Present* 29 (1964) 3-25; and Jan Z. Titow, "Medieval England and the Open-Field System," *Past and Present* 32 (1965) 86-102.

31 Carl Johan Dahlman, *The Open Field System: a Property Right Analysis of an Economic Institution* (Cambridge: Cambridge University Press, 1980); and Stephen J. Rippon, Ralph M. Fyfe and Anthony G. Brown, "Beyond Villages and Open Fields: the Origins and Development of a Historic Landscape Characterised by Dispersed Settlement in South-west England," *Medieval Archeology* 50 (2006) 31-70.

32 George C. Homans, "The Explanation of English Regional Differences," *Past and Present* 42 (1969) 18-34; and J. R. Wordie, "The Chronology of English Enclosure, 1500–1914," *The Economic History Review* 36 (1983) 483-505.

33 John Lawrence Hammond and Barbara Hammond, *The Village Labourer* (London: Longman, Green & Co, 1912) 107; Jane Humphries, "Enclosures, Common Rights, and Women: the Proletarianization of Families in the Late Eighteenth and Nineteenth Centuries," *Journal of Economic History* 50 (1990) 17-42; Neeson, *Commoners*, 158-84; and Leigh Shaw-Taylor, "Parliamentary Enclosure and the Emergence of an English Agricultural Proletariat," *Journal of Economic History* 61 (2001) 640-62.

34 Maurice Dobb, *Studies in the Development of Capitalism* (London: Routledge and Kegan Paul, 1963); and Perelman, *The Invention of Capitalism.*

35 Charles Vancouver, *General View of the Agriculture of Hampshire* (London: R. Phillips, 1810) 496; John Bellers, *An Essay Towards the Improvement of the Physick: With an Essay for Implying the Able Poor* (London: J. Sowle, 1714) 40; and John Billingsley, *General View of the Agriculture in the County of Somerset* (London: W. Smith, 1794) 37.

36 J. Bishton, *General View of the Agriculture in the County of Salop* (Brentford: P. Nodbury, 1794) 24-5.

37 John Arbuthnot, *An Inquiry into the Connection between the Present Price of Provisions and the Size of Farms* (London: T. Cadell, 1773) 128-9.

38 See Giovanni Arrighi, *The Long Twentieth Century: Money, Power, and the Origins of our Times* (London: Verso, 1994).

39 Daniel Bogart and Gary Richardson, "Property Rights and Parliament in Industrializing Britain," *Journal of Law and Economics* 54 (2011) 241-74; David Ormrod, *The Rise of Commercial Empires: England and the Netherlands in the Age of Mercantilism, 1650–1770* (Cambridge: Cambridge University Press, 2003); and Thompson, "The Moral Economy of the English Crowd in the Eighteenth Century."

40 Humphries, "Enclosures, Common Rights, and Women"; and Edward P. Thompson, *Customs in Common: Studies in Traditional*

41 Dobb, *Studies in the Development of Capitalism*; and Karl Polanyi, *The Great Transformation: the Political and Economic Origins of our Time* (Boston: Beacon Press, 2001).

42 Dahlman, *The Open Field System*; and Neeson, *Commoners*.

43 Gilbert Slater, "The Inclosure of Common Fields Considered Geographically," *Geographical Journal* 29 (1907) 36.

44 G. E. Mingay, *The Gentry: the Rise and Fall of a Ruling Class* (London: Longman, 1976) 17.

45 Jeremy Crampton and Stuart Elden have underscored how the increasing interrelation of calculative logics and political thinking during the seventeenth century opens the path to a transformed politics of space. This idea is further developed in Stuart Elden's study of Foucault's analysis of modern governmentalities. See Jeremy Crampton and Stuart Elden, "Space, Politics, Calculation: an Introduction," *Social & Cultural Geography* 7 (2006) 681-5; and Stuart Elden, "Governmentality, Calculation, Territory," *Environment and Planning D: Society and Space* 25 (2007) 562-80. For an interpretation of parliamentary enclosure as an emerging spatial rationality and its deployment of calculation as a moment of spatial homogenization, see Sevilla-Buitrago, "Territory and the Governmentalisation of Social Reproduction."

46 John Dixon Hunt, *Gardens and the Picturesque: Studies in the History of Landscape Architecture* (Cambridge, Mass: MIT Press, 1992); and John Dixon Hunt and Peter Willis, eds., *The Genius of the Place: The English Landscape Garden, 1620–1820* (Cambridge, Mass: MIT Press, 1988).

47 Ann C. Bermingham, *Landscape and Ideology: the English Rustic Tradition, 1740–1860* (Berkeley: University of California Press, 1986).

48 William Hogarth, *The Analysis of Beauty* (London: W. Strahan, 1772) 52-3.

49 Raymond Williams, *The Country and the City* (Oxford: Oxford University Press, 1973) 120-6.

50 John Barrell, *The Dark Side of Landscape: the Rural Poor in English Painting, 1730–1840* (Cambridge: Cambridge University Press, 1980).

51 Bogart and Richardson, "Property Rights and Parliament in Industrializing Britain."

52 H. R. French, "Urban Common Rights, Enclosure and the Market: Clitheroe Town Moors, 1746–1802," *The Agricultural History Review* 51 (2003) 40-68; and Roger J. P. Kain, John Chapman, and Richard R. Oliver, *The Enclosure Maps of England and Wales, 1595–1918* (Cambridge, Cambridge University Press, 2004) 7.

53 This point is concisely summarized by Edward P. Thompson: "[t]he same era that bore witness to the expropriation of the English peasant from his common lands saw the Bengal peasant made a parasite in his own country … the dispossession of the commoners of England … [was] the [template] for the Settlement of Bengal" (Thompson, *Customs in Common*, 170, 173-4). The point is also borne out in the historiography of British colonialism in various contexts. See also Joseph Michael Powell, *The Public Lands of Australian Felix* (Melbourne: Oxford University Press, 1970); and Sumit Guha, *Environment and Ethnicity in India, 1200–1991* (Cambridge: Cambridge University Press, 1992).

54 Claude Raffestin, *Pour une géographie du pouvoir* (Paris: Librairies techniques, 1980); and Robert David Sack, *Human Territoriality: Its Theory and History* (Cambridge: Cambridge University Press, 1986).

Historical Geography and Economic History (Folkestone: Archon, 1980) 59-61.

16.5 James Cheshire, English Shipping Routes 1750-1800, online at http://spatial.ly/wp-content/uploads/2013/06/info_history_shipping_sml.jpg.

16.6 Richard Lawton, "Population and Society, 1730-1914," *An Historical Geography of England and Wales*, eds. Robert A. Dodgshon and Robin A. Butlin, second edition (London: Academic Press, 1990) 297-8.

16.7 Humphry Repton, *Observations on the Theory and Practice of Landscape Gardening* (London: T. Bensley, 1805) 66.

16.8 Nigel Thrift, "Transport and Communication," *An Historical Geography of England and Wales*, eds. Robert A. Dodgshon and Robin A. Butlin, second edition (London: Academic Press, 1990) 457-463.

16.9 Kain, Chapman and Oliver, *The Enclosure Maps of England and Wales 1595-1918*, 8.

Figure Credits

16.1 Original by author.

16.2 Roger J. P. Kain, John Chapman, and Richard R. Oliver, *The Enclosure Maps of England and Wales, 1595–1918* (Cambridge, Cambridge University Press, 2004) 42, 44.

16.3 David Hall, *The Open Fields of Northamptonshire* (Northampton: Northamptonshire Record Society, 1995) 10-11.

16.4 Michael Edward Turner, *English Parliamentary Enclosure: Its*

17
WHAT IS THE URBAN IN THE CONTEMPORARY WORLD?

Roberto Luís Monte-Mór

The relationship between the city and the countryside is situated historically and theoretically at the center of human societies. The city's domain over the countryside, as the result of the division between intellectual and manual labor and through the market's command over productive activities, has marked human societies since ancient times, and particularly in the modern capitalist industrial societies to which we belong. However, the adjectives *urban* and *rural*, referring to the city and the countryside, only recently gained autonomy in the sense of referring to a range of cultural, socioeconomic and spatial relations between forms and processes deriving from them respectively, however without allowing the dichotomous clarity that characterized them until the last century. On the contrary, the borders between urban and rural space are increasingly diffuse and difficult to identify. This may occur because these adjectives currently lack their original substantive reference, to the extent that city and countryside are both no longer pure concepts that are easy to identify or demarcate. What are the cities of Belo Horizonte, São Paulo, Rio de Janeiro, Bela Vista de Minas, or any other large, medium-sized, or even small cities in contemporary Brazil or in the world? Where do they begin, and where do they end? On the other hand, what is the countryside today? Does it consist of remote villages or the outskirts of cities, the so-called rural area? Is it large ranches, agribusinesses, or settlements of the Landless movement, in the Northeast, the savannah (*cerrado*), or the Amazon? At any rate, the definition of the limits and nature of both the city and rural versus urban areas is increasingly diffuse and difficult.

Cities in Brazil are defined legally by the city limits of municipal centers and districts (or townships), and thus what are considered urbanized territories and populations include the city limits of towns serving as the seats of municipal districts or townships. However, urbanized areas encompass broad areas neighboring on cities whose integrated urban space extends over adjacent and distant territories, in an expansion process that began in the nineteenth century and was accelerated irreversibly in the twentieth century.

In addition, the cities, or the political and sociocultural space formed on the basis of them, became the center of organization for society and the economy. On the international scale, a handful of cities organize and command major interest blocs and reorder global economic space.[1] On the local, regional and national scales the cities define forms of organization and the location of both economic activities and population; they also provide the reference points for social identities and define modes of community constitution. Indeed, central concepts in contemporary life derive from the city's spatial form and social organization. The Greek notion of *polis* comes from the concept of politics; the Latin *civis* and *civitas* give us citizen, citizenship, city and civilization, implying the existence of cities. Peoples which did not produce cities, such as the semi-nomads of Americas, were considered uncivilized, as opposed to the Mayan, Aztec and Inca "civilizations," even though ethnohistorical, anthropological and archeological approaches now question such classifications and the very concept of city.[2]

Latin also gives us the term *urban*, with a double connotation: *urbanum* (plow) came from the sense of settlement, the physical form of the space demarcated by the furrow of the plow pulled by the sacred oxen, marking the territory for Roman production and life; thence came the terms *urbe* and *urbs*, the latter referring to Rome, the Imperial city and center of the world, which disappeared until the resurgence of large cities in the modern era. The term *urban* was retrieved in the sixteenth century to refer to the Imperial city, especially the city that was headquarters to the British Empire under construction, where the word *city* relates to the financial center London as opposed to the countryside in the Victorian Age.[3]

City and countryside, opposite and complementary sociospatial elements, thus constitute the centrality and periphery of power in sociospatial organization. The city, according to the prevailing view of political economy, results from the deepening sociospatial division of labor and the opening to other communities and regularized processes of exchange. It also implies sedentary life, sociospatial hierarchy, and a power structure sustained by the extraction of a regular surplus from collective production, in addition to regular flows of goods and people between communities. The city thus presupposes the emergence of a dominant class that extracts and controls this collective surplus through ideological processes accompanied by the use of force.

According to Paul Singer, the city is the mode of sociospatial organization that allows the ruling class to maximize the regular extraction of surplus production from the countryside and to transform it into a food base for its own sustenance and that of the army that guarantees its regular extraction.[4] This therefore establishes what Henri Lefebvre referred to as the *political city*, that is, the city that maintains its domain over the countryside (with the resulting extraction of surplus production) based on political control.[5] In this context, the countryside is the space for production and the city is the space for control of the surplus, the locus of political and ideological power, which extracts from the countryside the conditions for the reproduction of the ruling class and its direct military and civil servants. According to the heterodox hypothesis presented by Jane Jacobs and rejected for decades, the city has always been more productive than the countryside, which in fact guaranteed its domain, while it often produced the rural space *a posteriori*.[6] This precedence of the city over the countryside has been reclaimed in the legendary city of Jericho, among others.[7]

However, Lefebvre proposes that one envision a continuum stretching from the political city to the mercantile city and the industrial city up through what he terms the "critical zone" (the *urban*). The first passage within this continuum is marked by the entry of the marketplace inside the walls of the cities controlled by the monasteries or castles. Encouraged by the fair (which can be regional and even international), the elites gradually allowed the entry of the bourgeoisie into the sphere of power, soon shifting the centrality of the palaces and monasteries to the market square, consolidating this economy which has its privileged space in the cities.

Thus, the *mercantile city*, the central place where regional surpluses were voluntarily brought and marketed, resulted from the entry of the bourgeoisie into the city (and eventually taking it over). The merchant burghers gave the political city a new meaning and force, transforming it into a mercantile center. The countryside-city relationship thus underwent its first major shift, and the extraction of surplus production was no longer made possible only by political/ideological and military coercion, but also resulted from a voluntary shift from the countryside towards the city as the articulating location for market exchange. The shift from the countryside to the city was thus marked by the economy: the countryside's production was only realized on the market square, thus modifying and expanding the city's domination over the countryside. Note also the synergy of urban life in the mercantile city, the central place for innovation and for the provision of goods and services for production in the countryside, and also the privileged space for community life where the division of labor was being deepened through the specializations and complementarities that developed there.

The Industrial City, the City-Countryside Relationship and the Emergence of the *Urban*

The second transformation associated with the shift from the city to the urban was marked by the entry of industry into the city, a long process in Western history.[8] In fact, urbanization as we understand it today began with the industrial city. Until the emergence of factory-based industry and its concentration in European cities, the urbanization process was limited to a handful of cities where power and/or the market were concentrated. There were few human agglomerations that could now be called cities during the period preceding the industrial revolution. The proportion of the total population living in cities was no more than 20 percent in nearly all of the countries, and the city was a fundamental precondition for the development of industry, concentrating in just a few cities, as in Brazil until recently, the consumer population, workers, and general conditions of production for the installation of factories. These general conditions of production, whether existing or to be created, include: the state's provision of the legal apparatus that guarantees relations of private ownership and the free circulation of commodities (including land and the labor force), transportation and communications services, and provision of the basic infrastructure and services for industrial and financial capital, as well as for the reproduction of the labor force.[9]

The industrial city, was thus marked by the entry of production into the center of power, bringing with it the working class, the proletariat. The city began to not only control and market the production of the countryside, but also to transform and add value to it in unprecedented ways and degrees. The countryside, until then predominantly isolated and self-sufficient, began to depend on urban-industrial production for basic foodstuffs and consumer goods. According to Lefebvre, this shift meant the total subordination of the countryside to the city.[10]

In the industrial city there was also a radical transformation. Industry imposed its production-centered logic on the city. Meanwhile the city's space, previously organized as the privileged locus for the economic surplus, political power, and cultural *fiesta*, while being legitimized and ruled as (collective) use value, became increasingly privatized and subordinated to exchange value. According to Lefebvre, the city itself also became an industrial product, constructed according to the same economic laws ruling the production process. The privileged space for the reproduction of society was thus subordinated to the logic and needs of industry, combining the necessary conditions of production, including the collective reproduction of the labor force, synthesized in housing. Castells defined the specificity of urban space within the capitalist economic system as the privileged locus for the reproduction of the labor force, made possible by the concentration of the means of collective consumption.[11]

The urbanized space, in this context, thus began to operate as a function of the demands placed on the state both to serve industrial production and especially to support the various needs associated with the collective reproduction of the labor force. The large industrial cities, which then extended beyond their peripheries, aimed mainly to accommodate factories and their suppliers and workers, generating in turn wide urbanized areas around them, namely the metropolitan areas.

However, the city, as the locus for the triad of collective surplus, political power, and cultural *fiesta* did not disappear, since it synthesized the society that generated it. Lefebvre describes metaphorically what happened to it: the industrial city underwent a dual process of *implosion* and *explosion*.[12] Implosion took place through the centrality of surplus/power/ *fiesta*, concentrating and reactivating the symbols of the citadel that were being threatened by the industrial logic. Explosion occurred, meanwhile, on the surrounding space by extending the urban fabric in this new sociospatial form/process according to the demands of industrial production and collective reproduction, bearing with it the conditions of production that had previously been restricted to the cities, over the immediate countryside, and eventually also reaching into the more remote regional spaces. The urban fabric thus synthesizes the process in which the urban phenomenon is extended over the countryside and virtually over the regional and national space as a whole.

Contemporary Urbanization: Its Extended Nature and Other Implications

In short, what is urban in the contemporary world, this fabric that is born in the cities and extends beyond them, over the countryside and regions? Urban, from this perspective, is a synthesis of the old city-countryside dichotomy, a third element in the city-countryside dialectic. It is the material and sociospatial manifestation of contemporary urban- industrial society, now extended virtually throughout the entire territory. Lefebvre uses the expression *urban society* to denote the dialectical synthesis of the city-countryside dichotomy, which is now overcome in the contemporary stage of capitalism, to which he refers as "the bureaucratic society of controlled consumption."[13] As he argues, the urban, or contemporary urban-industrial space, extends virtually throughout the territory via the *urban fabric*:

> The urban fabric proliferates, spreads, and corrodes the remains of agrarian life. These words, "the urban fabric," do not strictly designate the built-up domain of cities, but the set of manifestations of the city's predominance over the countryside. From this view, a second home, a highway, a supermarket in the middle of the countryside, are all part of the urban fabric.[14]

However, the industrial city, which earlier overflowed onto surrounding areas, now gives rise to a new form of urbanization which simultaneously extends the city's own sociopolitical/ spatial praxis and urban-industrial space (which Lefebvre called *urban praxis*) to social space as a whole. To the extent that the urban fabric extends through territory, it takes with it the seeds of the *polis*, of the *civitas*, of the urban praxis that was previously specific and limited to the city's internal space. The political struggle for control of the collective means of reproduction that characterized the 1970s, and the urban social movements that emerged during that period showed that citizenship claims were closely tied to cities and urban areas. However, the 1980s showed that these movements had extended beyond such limits, now stretching across the entire social space. Social movements lost the adjective "urban" to the extent that they came to encompass rural and traditional populations, such as indigenous peoples, rubber tappers, and landless workers, among others.

Thus, the urban question had become the spatial question itself, and urbanization came to constitute a metaphor for the production of contemporary social space as a whole, potentially covering the entire national territory in urban-industrial forms. On the other hand, the politicization proper to urban space, which had now been extended to regional space, reinforces popular concerns over the quality of daily life, the environment, and the expanded reproduction of life. The industrial became subjected, at least virtually, to the limits of the urban and the demands of reproduction. In this context, as Lefebvre recognized, the repoliticization of urban life becomes a repoliticization of social space as a whole: "… the issue of space, which subsumes the problems of the urban sphere (the city and its extensions) and daily life (controlled consumption) replaced the issue of industrialization."[15]

I have used the term *extended urbanization* to describe the spatio-temporal materialization of the processes of production and reproduction resulting from the confrontation between the industrial and the urban, along with the sociopolitical and cultural issues intrinsic to the *polis* and the *civitas* that have now been extended beyond urban agglomerations to social space as a whole.[16] This term is intended to reclaim central aspects of the urban phenomenon, combining the sociospatial dimension and the political element implicit within *urban praxis*. This reality, urban society, virtually imposes itself in Brazil today, constituting a new condition for understanding contemporary social space.

The Extended Urbanization of Contemporary Brazil

Given the above, one can already speak of a virtually urban society in Brazil. Brazilian urbanization intensified in the latter half of the twentieth century, when industrial capitalism gained traction in the country and dynamized the economy based on the consolidation of the large industrial cities, particularly São Paulo, the national hub. The transformation of an agro-export economy into an economy centered on import substitution for the domestic market redefined the *industrial city* as a pole for growth and selective transformations in Brazilian territory and society.

The *industrial city* emerged in Brazil from two main watersheds, which were not necessarily mutually exclusive: the first, the transformation of the political city, the traditional headquarters for state bureaucracy and the space for controlling the rural oligarchies linked to the agro-export economy, into a *mercantile city*, marked by the presence of export capital and/or the concentration of commerce and central support services for rural productive activities in a center for industrial production; the second, the creation and/or capture of small cities as spaces for mono-industrial production by large industries. Only these industrial cities, whether large or small (mono-industrial), combined the conditions required by industrial capitalism, where the state regulated the relations between capital and labor, made infrastructure investments, guaranteed the means for collective consumption, in a word, created the general conditions of production for industry. These conditions of production were limited to what Milton Santos called the "urban archipelago," highlighting the fragmented and disarticulated nature of Brazilian urban society.[17] In this context, the industrial city was the central component in the capitalist dynamic, linking to outside commercial cities and urban centers which channeled production to their area of influence and control. Only these cities additionally concentrated the possibilities for access to the facilities of modern life, citizenship and urbanity.

The urban fabric in Brazil had its origin in the territorial policy (both concentrating and integrative) practiced by the military governments following the centralization and expansionism of the Vargas period and the interiorization (i.e., inland shift) of development during the Kubitschek Administration. The dyad "Energy and Transportation" was expanded to investments in infrastructure, communications, and industrial and financial services, among others. International capital coming to Brazil joined the construction industry, the subsidized large landholdings, and agribusiness as part of the agreements among the domestic and regional economic elites to support (inter) national militarism. The state apparatus, labor and social security legislation, communications networks, urban and social services (for production and consumption) extended through the urban fabric virtually throughout the country, from the dynamic centers to the frontiers of natural resources.

Beginning in the 1970s, urbanization extended virtually throughout the Brazilian territory, integrating the various regional spaces into the urban-industrial centrality emanating from São Paulo, developing into the network of regional metropolises, medium-sized cities, and urban centers affected by large-scale industrial projects and finally reaching the small cities in the various regions, particularly where the modernization process gained a more intense, extended dynamic. "There is no longer an agrarian issue; the issue is now urban on a national scale," proclaimed economist/sociologist Francisco de Oliveira at the meeting of the Brazilian Society for the Advancement of Science in 1978, in a paper that came to be known as the "roadmap for Brazilian urbanization."[18]

Extended urbanization encompasses this urbanization process that occurred beyond the cities and urbanized areas, bearing with it the urban-industrial conditions for production and reproduction, as well as the urban praxis and the sense of modernity and citizenship. In the last 30 years, extended urbanization has impacted practically the entire country, reaching from the metropolitan regions and linking to the industrial centers, the sources of raw materials, following the transportation, energy, and communications infrastructures, creating and extending the conditions of production and the means for collective consumption necessary for the forms of Fordist industrial production that were implanted in the country beginning with the "Brazilian miracle." In the late twentieth century, the urban made its presence felt throughout the national territory, particularly on the Amazon and Central-West frontiers, where the production of space already occurred through an urban-industrial base emanating from the metropolitan centers and their spin-offs in the agrarian areas linked to the country's agro-industrial base.

In this broader sense, one can speak of an extended urbanization imposing itself on Brazilian space far beyond the cities, integrating rural and regional spaces with urban-industrial space through the expansion of the material base required by the contemporary society and economy and the relations of production which are (or should be) reproduced by the production of space itself. Within this context there is a multiplication of (urban) frontiers, both internally and on the fringes of agglomerations, as well as in regional and rural spaces incorporated into the prevailing urban-industrial logic. Extended urbanization thus moves along various transportation corridors and communications and services networks in "new" regions like the Amazon and the Central-West, but also in "old" regions like the Northeast, in residual spaces of more developed regions, and in the "islands of rural life" in the hinterlands of Minas Gerais or São Paulo. All over Brazil, the urban-industrial logic imposes itself on contemporary social space, defining what is urban in our present-day life.

Notes

1 John Friedmann, *Life Space and Economic Space: Essays in Third World Planning* (Oxford: Transaction Books, 1988); and Saskia Sassen, *The Global City* (Princeton: Princeton University Press, 1991).

2 Roberto Luís Monte-Mór, *Modernities in the Jungle: Extended Urbanization in the Brazilian Amazonia* (PhD dissertation, Los Angeles: University of California, 2004).

3 Instituto Antônio Houaiss de Lexicografia, *Dicionário Houaiss da Língua Portuguesa* (Rio de Janeiro: Objetiva, 2001); and Lexicon Publications, *The New Lexicon Webster's Dictionary of the English Language* (New York: Lexicon Publications, 1987); Raymond Williams, *The Country and the City* (New York: Oxford University Press, 1973); and Raymond Williams, *Keywords: A Vocabulary of Culture and Society* (London: Fontana Paperbacks, 1983).

4 Paul Israel Singer, *Economia Política da Urbanização; Ensaios* (São Paulo: Editora Brasiliense, 1973).

5 Henri Lefebvre, "The Right to the City," *Writings on Cities* (Cambridge: Blackwell, 1996 [1968]) 63-184; and Henri Lefebvre, *The Urban Revolution*, trans. Robert Bononno (Minneapolis: University of Minnesota Press, 2003 [1970]).

6 Jane Jacobs, *The Economy of Cities* (New York: Random House, 1969).

7 Edward Soja, *Postmetropolis: Critical Studies of Cities and Regions* (Cambridge: Blackwell, 2000).

8 Kingsley Davis, "Urbanization of the Human Population," *Scientific American: Cities*, ed. Kingsley Davis (1965) 3-24.

9 Christian Topalov, *Capital et propriété foncière: introduction à l'étude des politiques foncières urbaines* (Paris: Centre de sociologie urbaine, 1973); and Jean Lojkine, *Le Marxisme, l'état et la question urbaine* (Paris: Presses universitaires de France, 1977).

10 Henri Lefebvre, "From City to Urban Society," this book, Ch. 2, page 43.

11 Manuel Castells, *The Urban Question: A Marxist Approach* (Cambridge: MIT Press, 1977 [1972]).

12 Lefebvre, *The Urban Revolution*.

13 Ibid.; and Henri Lefebvre, *Everyday Life in the Modern World*, trans. Sacha Rabonovitch (New Brunswick: Transaction Books, 1984 [1971]).

14 Lefebvre, *The Urban Revolution*, 17.

15 Henri Lefebvre, *The Production of Space*, trans. Donald Nicholson (Cambridge: Blackwell, 1991) 89.

16 See Roberto Luís Monte-Mór, "Extended Urbanization and Settlement Patterns: An Environmental Approach," this book, Ch. 8; Roberto Luís Monte-Mór, "Urban and Regional Planning: Impact on Health and the Environment," *International Perspectives on Environment, Development, and Health: Toward a Sustainable World*, eds. Gurinder S. Shahi, Barry S. Levy, Al Binger, Tord Kjellström and Robert Lawrence (New York: Springer, 1997) 554-66; and Roberto Luís Monte-Mór, "Outras Fronteiras: Novas Espacialidades na Urbanização Brasileira," *Urbanização Brasileira: Redescobertas*, ed. Leonardo Barci Castriota (Belo Horizonte: Editora C/Arte, 2003) 260-71.

17 Milton Santos, *Técnica, Espaço, Tempo: Globalização e Meio Técnico-Científico Informacional* (São Paulo: Editora Hucitec, 1994).

18 Francisco Oliveira, "Acumulação Monopolista, Contradições Urbanas, e a Nova Qualidade do Conflito de Classes," *Contradições urbanas e movimentos sociais*, second edition, ed. José Álvaro Moisés (Rio de Janeiro: Paz e Terra, 1977) 65-76.

18
THE URBANIZATION OF SWITZERLAND

Christian Schmid

One central observation constitutes the point of departure in analyzing current forms of urbanization in Switzerland: its cities are still comparatively small. Switzerland is marked by an urban structure based on small cities and by highly decentralized urbanization. Even the largest agglomerations barely exceed a million inhabitants. This type of urbanization reflects two related basic conditions: the distinctively Helvetian autonomy of communes and a long history of decentralized industrialization.

If we examine the current picture of settlements in Switzerland, there is only one territorial unit evident as a structuring influence: the commune (Figure 18.1). National and cantonal borders recede far into the background by comparison. Helvetian federalism has led to the entire country being covered with a fine-meshed, cellular territorial structure. All of the just under 3,000 communes in Switzerland, ranging from small hamlets with a few dozen inhabitants to urban communes with several hundred thousand residents, have essentially the same rights and possess astonishingly far-reaching authority, particularly in the area of planning.[1]

The second basic condition is decentralized industrialization. In Switzerland, as in many other areas of Western Europe, industrialization started at the countryside and not in the cities. On the one hand, manpower and water power as energy sources were available there; on the other, the power elites of the cities had long prevented industrialization within the

18.1 Communal borders and settlements in Switzerland

city walls. Even as late as the end of the ancient regime, cities were still very small and their distribution on the territory showed a distribution on the territory showed a fine-meshed pattern. In 1798, only Geneva—with about 25,000 residents—achieved any significant size. All the other cities had fewer than 15,000 inhabitants.[2]

This fact in itself is neither astonishing nor unique. Comparable circumstances prevailed in many regions at the time. What is unusual, however, is that this decentralized structure survived the industrial revolution and the founding of the nation-state, and still characterized Switzerland at the end of the twentieth century.

Decentralized Urbanization

Population growth aptly illustrates the course of the urbanization process over the last 150 years. Several different historical patterns of urbanization can be observed that correspond with astonishing clarity to the phases of industrial development. The following reconstruction and analysis of the process of urbanization in Switzerland uses the periodization that was developed as part of the regulation approach.[3]

Liberal Development Model

Early industrialization in Switzerland led to the formation of three core industrial regions: northeastern Switzerland with its textile industry, which later evolved into the machine industry and the banking center of Zurich; northwestern Switzerland, where the textile industry evolved by way of the dye industry into the chemical and later pharmaceutical industries; and the Jura mountain range in southwestern Switzerland, with its clock and watch industry (Figure 18.2).

This basic decentralized urban structure was transformed only marginally through the Industrial Revolution. Around the middle of the nineteenth century, an expansive process of urbanization affected Switzerland as well as other countries. City limits—the walls and fortifications—were demolished, and cities expanded into the open country. Zurich, Basel and Winterthur developed into substantial industrial centers. In many regions, however, industrial growth followed the basic decentralized pattern of early industrialization: in the Jura and eastern Switzerland, as well as in Valais and central Switzerland, the industrialized zones that developed were comprised of small towns. The first tourist centers arose in sections of the Alps that were easily accessible. At the same time, there was a mass exodus from broad sections of rural Switzerland, particularly from the central Alps and a broad band in the Swiss Plateau, which included nearly all of the rural regions in the cantons of Aargau and Lucerne. The phase between 1850 and 1890 revealed a typical decentralized pattern of urbanization. A few larger industrial cities emerged in this industrial landscape, but they were quite small in comparison to those in most other parts of Europe.

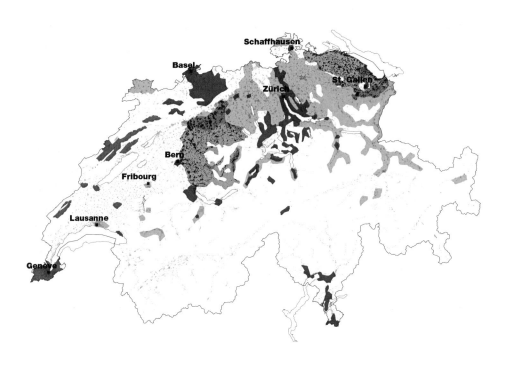

⬜ Cotton
▦ Linen
⬛ Silk
⬛ Watch making
▪ Cities with more than 5,000 inhabitants around 1798

18.2 Industrialization and urbanization at the end of the eighteenth century

Between 1890 and 1930, during the Taylorist phase of development, the decentralized form of urbanization was accentuated. This phase was characterized by the transition to a model of intensive, technologically oriented industrialization. In Switzerland, the leading role of the textile industry gradually gave way to the machine and watch industries, and also the chemical industry. Nevertheless, industrial growth during this phase continued to be decentralized. In eastern Switzerland and along the south base of the Jura mountain range, industrialized urban belts emerged, which consolidated into a continuous belt from St. Gallen to Biel. This pattern of sprawling urbanization also characterized the northern Jura, Valais, and central Switzerland.

Only a few towns developed into big cities. In such cases, population growth increasingly affected the suburbs as well; cities grew by incorporating neighboring communes, but they were still much smaller than those outside Switzerland. Only four cities—Zurich, Basel, Geneva and Bern—had more than a 100,000 residents in 1930. In several alpine regions there was a rise in tourism, particularly in Klosters-Davos, in the Engadine Valley, in the southern Valais and in central Switzerland. Emigration was now confined to smaller areas in the Alps and the few industrialized regions of the Swiss Plateau. The only significant emigration was from the valleys on the south side of the Alps. The overall picture is thus a uniform, decentralized pattern of urbanization. On the eve of the Second World War, nearly all of Switzerland was industrialized, without any pronounced peripheries, but also without any genuinely large cities.

Fordist Development Model

After the Second World War, Switzerland, like all Western industrialized nations, adopted a Fordist development model. It formed the basis for the enduring economic miracle of the postwar period. The typical Fordist model was essentially based on combining standardized mass production with mass consumption, the development of the welfare state, and increased state intervention in economic development (Keynesianism). Switzerland developed a special variety of Fordism that differed from the classical model in several respects. Helvetian Fordism was based only to a limited extent on mass production. Swiss industry increasingly specialized instead in labor-intensive, high-quality and technologically advanced consumer and capital goods that were produced by small to medium-sized companies with a large number of qualified skilled workers. This led to extensive industrial growth in which most companies expanded at their existing location.

Thus Switzerland's basic decentralized industrial structure was largely retained even in the Fordist development phase, and the belt-like urbanization in eastern Switzerland and along the southern base of the Jura Mountains saw further growth. At the same time, however, there was a process of spatial concentration: Switzerland's five largest cities—Zurich, Basel,

Geneva, Bern and Lausanne—evolved into urban centers and specialized sites for the service sector. By the mid 1960s, the population in most of the large cities had peaked and growth shifted increasingly to suburban belts. Notably, however, communes were no longer incorporated; true to their federalist orientation, they resisted such efforts with all their power. This resulted in a process of suburbanization that formed agglomerations of typical concentric patterns.

The overall picture now revealed a surprising feature that was overlooked in debates at the time: two distinct development trends—extensive, decentralized industrial growth and the formation of urban centers—overlapped, bringing about sprawling concentrations of population. In greater Zurich in particular, but also in greater Basel, on Lake Geneva and in the area around Bern, the growth zones were spread out. Conversely, there were large, contiguous areas of out-migration—in the central Alps, on the one hand, and in the three rural zones of the Swiss Plateau and the lower alpine region (eastern Switzerland, around Napf Mountain, and between Fribourg and Lausanne). Today, these areas are the country's "quiet zones."[4] Despite these concentration trends, the basic territorial structure in Switzerland as a whole remained essentially the same for more than a century. As late as 1970, the country was still an industrial nation that retained a decidedly decentralized urban structure (Figure 18.3).

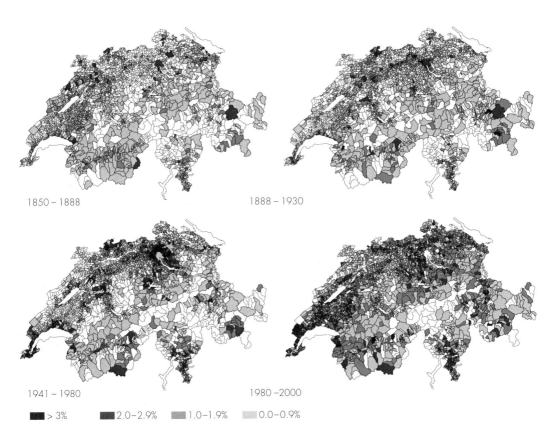

1850 – 1888

1888 – 1930

1941 – 1980

1980 – 2000

■ > 3%   ■ 2.0–2.9%   ■ 1.0–1.9%   0.0–0.9%

18.3 Average annual population increase

A Completely Urbanized Switzerland

In the early 1970s, this decentralized pattern of development began to undergo a fundamental transformation. Previously, most urban regions had spread concentrically around a core city, but since the 1970s, urbanization has seen the rise of increasingly complex, polycentric patterns and even new forms of peripheral urbanization.

In the 1970s, the Fordist model fell into crisis in nearly all industrial nations of the West, and in the course of the 1980s, a new postfordist or liberal-productivist model crystallized.[5] The latter may be characterized by the goals of flexibilization, deregulation and globalization. In contrast to the rigid, highly regulated Fordist model, it is distinguished by a notable fluidity of production processes, labor markets, financial organization, and consumption patterns as well as a proportionately high degree of socioeconomic and cultural heterogenization and fragmentation.

Switzerland was hit particularly hard by these changes. With the onset of the economic crisis and the beginnings of globalization, the limitations of the Helvetian development model were thrown into sharp relief in the early 1970s, and a radical restructuring of the industrial landscape resulted. One by one, nearly all industrial sectors experienced a deep crisis, first the textile industry in eastern Switzerland, then the watch industry in the Jura. The decline of the metal and machine industries followed in the 1980s and 1990s. No other Western industrial nation experienced such a drastic economic downturn, and few showed weaker economic growth in the 1980s and 1990s.

In this new, liberal-productivist development phase, the various sectors of the economy followed different strategies. Whereas small and medium-sized industrial companies, even despite drastic restructuring measures, had only limited success in retaining their international competitiveness, several leading industrial companies significantly improved their national and international position by pursuing a strategy of multinationalization. They shifted a large percentage of their production abroad, where costs were lower, retaining in Switzerland primarily the skilled and critical functions of the company (management, marketing, research and development). The banking industry expanded as well, and thanks to the specific advantages of its Swiss location (neutrality, labor peace, business-friendly economic policies, banking secrecy, social and political stability, hard currency), it profited more than most from the upswing in the global financial system.

This economic restructuring resulted in a fundamental transformation of the Helvetian economy, which ultimately led to a new development model. On the one hand, fewer skilled industrial jobs were cut or sent abroad; on the other, the significance of crucial economic activities and the number of highly skilled jobs increased. In Switzerland a "headquarters economy" was established that specialized in organizing trans-national production processes and controlling the circulation of global capital.

As a consequence of this development, the specialized regional production complexes of the headquarters economy began to converge in specific metropolitan regions: the global financial system in Zurich, specialized financial services in Geneva, and the chemical and pharmaceutical industries in Basel. By contrast, the other industrial sectors, including high-tech sectors, continued to be decentralized.[6]

An analysis of contemporary patterns of gross value added and labor productivity shows a clear polarization in the main economic sectors of Switzerland. On the one hand, there are the financial services and the chemical/pharmaceutical industries, which in 1998 generated more than 200,000 Swiss francs per job, and which since 1980 have shown an increase in labor productivity of more than 25%. On the other hand, agriculture, forestry and tourism achieved just over 40,000 Swiss francs of value added per job, and labor productivity has actually decreased during the past two decades. The other economic branches are grouped in a narrow middle field with a value added of about 100,000 Swiss francs and only a slight increase in labor productivity of around 15%.[7]

The uneven spatial distribution of these branches has led to a regional concentration of dynamic, innovative and high value-added economic activities, a process that has accelerated since the mid-1990s. The losers in this process are not just the peripheral regions but increasingly the small and medium-sized centers.[8] As a consequence, regional incomes are drifting further apart. In 1999, per capita incomes in the cantons that were entirely or partially within commuter belts of metropolitan regions (Zurich, Zug, Schwyz, Glarus, Schaffhausen, Basel-Town/Basel-Country and Geneva) ranged between 50,000 and 80,000 Swiss francs. Not only was this above average, but it reflected disproportionately high growth during the last two decades. By contrast, per capita income in most of the other cantons was around 40,000 francs, which represented moderate growth. At the bottom of the rankings, in terms of both per capita income and growth, were the cantons of Valais, Jura, and Obwalden.[9]

New Urban Landscapes

This fundamental economic restructuring went hand in hand with an equally drastic transformation in the process of urbanization. The pattern of urbanization discussed previously, with its consolidating, decentralized industrial belts and its concentrically growing agglomerations, began to break down. A highly complex and differentiated pattern of urbanization arose in its place and produced fundamentally new urban landscapes.

Networked, polycentric urban regions formed not only in the vicinity of the metropolitan centers, but also around small and medium-sized cities. While many inner cities experienced a new economic and cultural upswing, with abandoned industrial and infrastructural areas becoming desirable locations for the headquarter economy and high income urban professionals, there was a coincident development in which centrality was dispersed. In suburban belts and in undefined urban intermediary zones, new, diffuse centers formed, with extensive infrastructure, shopping centers, entertainment sites, and in some cases highly skilled jobs. These regions are dominated by a new form of urban mobility that is directed eccentrically and tangentially. Meanwhile, nearly all everyday activities are governed by it. On the edges of the large agglomerations, a variety of urbanization forms can also be observed that are not adequately described by the concept of "peri-urbanization." Detached houses, consumer facilities, industrial plants, and small businesses are settling around villages and towns, creating a dense network of restless movement between communes.

Maps of population development do not illustrate these complex relationships accurately, because they merely depict the sum of these diverse trends. Nevertheless, it is striking that the strongest growth in population is found primarily along the edges of major agglomerations. In a general sense, the process of urbanization is increasingly losing its contours; it is undirected, sprawling and covers the whole territory. The complete urbanization of Switzerland has become reality.[10]

Notes

1   See Roger Diener, Jacques Herzog, Marcel Meili, Pierre de Meuron and Christian Schmid, *Switzerland—An Urban Portrait, Volume 2: Borders, Communes—A Brief History of the Territory* (Basel: Birkhäuser, 2006).

2   François Walter, *La Suisse urbaine, 1750–1950* (Geneva: Éditions Zoé, 1994) 52.

3   For the following section, see Alain Lipietz, "New Tendencies in the International Division of Labor: Regimes of Accumulation and Modes of Regulation," *Production, Work, Territory: The Geographical Anatomy of Industrial Capitalism*, eds. Allen J. Scott and Michael Storper (London: Allen & Unwin, 1986) 16-40; and Alain Lipietz, *La société en sablier: le partage du travail contre la déchirure sociale* (Paris: La Découverte, 1996); as well as Hansruedi Hitz, Christian Schmid, and Richard Wolff, "Boom, Konflikt und Krise: Zürichs Entwicklung zur Weltmetropole," *Capitales Fatales: Urbanisierung und Politik in den Finanzmetropolen Frankfurt und Zurich*, ed. Hansruedi Hitz, Roger Keil, Ute Lehrer, Klaus Ronneberger, Christian Schmid and Richard Wolff (Zurich: Rotpunktverlag, 1995) 208-82; Christian Schmid, "A New Paradigm of Urban Development for Zurich," *The Contested Metropolis: Six Cities at the Beginning of the 21st Century*, eds. INURA and Raffaele Paloscia (Basel: Birkhäuser, 2004) 237-46.

4   On the "quiet zones," see Christian Schmid, "A Typology of Urban Switzerland," this book, Ch. 26.

5   Lipietz, *La société en sablier*.

6   See Patrick Dümmler, Christof Abegg, Christian Kruse, Alain Thierstein, Institut für Raum und Landschaftsentwicklung (IRL) ETH Zurich, *Standorte der innovativen Schweiz: Räumliche Veränderungsprozesse von High-Tech und Finanzdienstleistungen* (Neuchâtel: Bundesamt für Statistik, 2004).

7   Neue Regionalpolitik (NRP), *Schlussbericht der Expertenkommission zur Überprüfung und Neukonzeption der Regionalpolitik* (Zurich: 2003) 34.

8   See Martin Schuler, Manfred Perlik and Natascha Pasche, *Nichtstädtisch, rural oder peripher – Wo steht der ländliche Raum heute? Analyse der Siedlungs und Wirtschaftsentwicklung in der Schweiz* (Bern: Bundesamt für Raumentwicklung, 2004) 10.

9   NRP, *Überprüfung und Neukonzeption der Regionalpolitik*, 26.

10 See Christian Schmid, "Traveling Warrior and Complete Urbanization in Switzerland," this book, Ch. 6.

Figure Credits

18.1   Roger Diener, Jacques Herzog, Marcel Meili, Pierre de Meuron, and Christian Schmid, *Switzerland—An Urban Portrait, Volume 3* (Basel: Birkhäuser, 2006) 177.

18.2   Same as above, 179. Sources: Beatrix Mesmer ed. *Geschichte der Schweiz – und der Schweizer*, volume 2 (Basel: Helbing & Lichtenhahn, 1982) 111; and Walter, *La Suisse urbaine*, 52.

18.3   Same as above, 180. Source: Swiss Federal Statistical Office, Federal Population Census, 1850-2000, Neuchâtel.

19
REGIONAL URBANIZATION AND THE END OF THE METROPOLIS ERA

Edward W. Soja

A fundamental and far-reaching change in the very nature of the urbanization process has been taking place over the past 30 years. Efforts to capture its essential features have generated a substantial literature on urban restructuring and many defining terms such as postmodern, postindustrial, postfordist, neoliberal, informational, flexible, and global.[1] My objective here is to present a convincing argument that what has been happening to cities all over the world in the past three decades is best described as a shift from a distinctively metropolitan mode of urban development to an essentially regional urbanization process. Regional urbanization is still in its early stages of development but has advanced far enough in some metropolitan regions for its defining features to be analyzed and understood—and for urban scholars to begin to recognize that the era of the modern metropolis may be ending.

Metropolitan Urbanization

The metropolitan mode of urban development has been so dominant for so long a time, that it is assumed by many to be the only form of contemporary urban growth and change. This often idealized and universalized view of the modern metropolis as the highest stage of the urbanization process has injected an encompassing dualism into urban studies, reflecting perhaps the most characteristic feature of metropolitan urbanization, the division of the metropolis into separate and essentially different urban and suburban worlds or ways of life. The urban world, the city, is densely filled with heterogeneous cultures, thick layers of social interaction, abundant sources of creativity and entertainment, as well as crime, drugs, intrigue, corruption and vice. Suburbia or suburbanism as a way of life is, in contrast, starkly homogeneous in almost every way: in how families are organized and function, in where one sleeps and where one works and shops and seeks recreation, in the repetitious rhythms and routines of everyday life.

For most of the past century, this dualism has been consolidated and extended through an urbanization process driven mainly by expansive and often sprawling suburban growth, arising in large part from a selective decentralization of economic, political and cultural power from the once much more dominant city centers. This prevailing dynamic of metropolitan urbanization has spawned a fulsome critical urban literature filled both with wellsprings of nostalgia for some real or imagined earlier form of urban agglomeration as well as waves of antipathy and revulsion for the tedious monotony and cultural backwardness of classical suburbia. So great has been the hammerlock that the urban-suburban dualism has maintained on how we think about the city, that even where its essential features have begun to disappear the changes often remain unnoticed or else re-absorbed into the same old divisions and binary discourses.

This disconnection reminds me of what was happening in the interwar years with the rise of the influential Chicago School of Urban Ecology. Even as the metropolitan urbanization process was advancing all around them, the Chicago scholars persisted in theorizing the sociospatial conditions that characterized the still prevailing nineteenth-century industrial capitalist city: compact, densely centralized, growing almost organically from the residential and industrial agglomeration in the teeming center, neatly organized in urban rings and wedges surrounded by a vaguely defined "commuting zone," all part of what was summarily called "the city." With urban scholarship fixated on continuities with the past, indeed projecting them as idealized models for the future, the new urbanization processes transforming the fundamental nature of urban life were largely overlooked. Decades later, some would recognize the possibility of a new "metropolitan" urban form taking shape," but the idealized Chicago School models of nineteenth-century urbanization continued to dominate urban theory well into the twentieth century. Relics of concentric zonation and axial sectors were searched for and could almost always be found in the modern metropolis, but these comforting geohistorical continuities helped very little in understanding the then contemporary urban condition.

It can be argued that a remarkably similar situation exists today in urban studies broadly defined. Theory and practice, empirical analysis and critical thinking, continue to revolve around an urbanization process that is in the midst of a profound reconfiguration. Many continue to assume that there is but one mode of urbanization, one model of urban-suburban form and function, which may go through periods of perturbation and restructuring but remains essentially constant in its fundamental structures and dynamics.

Almost all contemporary urban scholars dismiss the Chicago School models (often, I would argue, for the wrong reasons), yet remain fixed on a singular, universal and constant model of the metropolis as divided clearly into city and suburb. What I am arguing here is first, that metropolitan urbanization must be recognized as a distinct phase in the development of the industrial capitalist city, growing out of an earlier phase of more highly centralized industrial urbanism, and second, that this metropolitan phase is currently being superseded by a new phase of multiscalar regional urbanization.

Regional Urbanization and the Great Density Convergence

So what then is this multiscalar process of regional urbanization and how does it differ from earlier phases in the development of the industrial capitalist city? The best place to start is with what can be called the great density convergence, a still ongoing change in the sociospatial organization of the modern metropolis. A simplified diagram illustrates this definitive trend. In Figure 19.1, the vertical axis measures population density, the horizontal axis indicates distance from the city center.

The early capitalist city had a steep density gradient falling precipitously from the center to what was clearly the countryside, as described by the line A-B in the diagram. As Engels observed in Manchester and the Chicago School codified iconically for the American city, industrialization tended to be concentrically agglomerated around the urban core. The majority of factories as well as the great mass of the urban proletariat and its associated

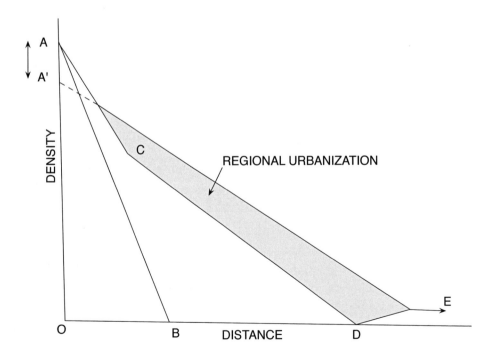

19.1 Density chart

labor reservoir of unemployed, often immigrant and/or minority residents, were densely concentrated in rings of relative residential quality around the magnetic, centripetal city center. Outside what was clearly the city was a shadow area where the new industrial bourgeoisie (the third new population group defining urban industrial capitalism and its unprecedented surge in urban growth) competed with the landed gentry for manor houses, villas, and local socioeconomic status, while maintaining commuter access to their wealth-generating factories in the city center. Unplanned as such, the earliest industrial capitalist cities, when physical features and preexisting urban forms did not interfere, tended toward a fairly regular spatial morphology, especially with regard to the geographical segregation of social status based on class or income.

Metropolitan urbanization as it began to develop in the last decades of the nineteenth century jumbled up, but rarely erased, many of the earlier regularities and reordered them around the urban-suburban dualism. This led in most cases to a small reduction of population density in the city center, as some activities and households once densely clustered in the urban core began to move out to the periphery. Accompanying these early decentralizing trends, however, were other forces such as the formation of expansive corporate monopolies and later Fordist and Keynesian policies that led to new clusters of corporate headquarters and government bureaucracies in growing central business districts and civic centers. This often skyscrapered refilling of the downtown core typically required removal of at least some of the concentrated urban poor from the best central sites, a process that was rationalized in public policy as a search for urban renewal. Struggles over centrality involving different segments of capital, labor, and the state each striving for different land uses was a characteristic feature of metropolitan urbanization.

The defining feature of metropolitan growth, however, was found not so much in the center but in the urban periphery, as expanding numbers of white- and later blue-collar workers moved out to create what was to become largely middle-class suburbia. While there remained a steep density gradient around the center, a breakpoint developed between high urban and lower suburban densities (ACD). There was also a second and mobile boundary (at D) defining the outer edge of constantly expanding suburban growth. Factories and jobs were no longer as centralized as they were before but the poorest residents tended to remain densely concentrated in the "inner city" (the term "outer city" was rarely if ever used) as selective suburbanization siphoned off the relatively wealthier middle classes. Constellations of autonomous suburban municipalities grew around the city and would together, in many modern metropolises, contain a population greater than that of the urban core. As cogently noted by neo-Marxist urban scholars in the 1970s, the postwar metropolis was inherently unstable and prone to social unrest revolving around the increasing impoverishment and joblessness of the urban core, standing in stark contrast to the comfortable, expanding and increasingly working class suburbs.[2]

The recovery from war and the Great Depression in the US and elsewhere was driven as much as anything else by the economic stimulus of mass suburbanization. Automobile-centered suburban life hungrily expanded consumer demand and pressured governments to invest enormous amounts of public funds to sustain the increasingly expensive and expansive infrastructure of sprawling automobile-dependent metropolitan urbanization. Library loads of literature accumulated describing these two contrasting and tensely interconnected worlds of the modern metropolis. The urban cores of modern metropolises around the world exploded in the 1960s, however, marking the beginning of the end of the metropolis era. Never again would metropolitan urbanization be precisely what it was for the first two-thirds of the twentieth century.

Returning to the diagram and the great density convergence, the new urbanization processes unleashed by the urban crises of the 1960s initiated a pronounced morphological change. In most of the world's major metropolises, there was some degree of "hollowing out" of the central city, a reduction in density caused primarily by the outmigration of domestic populations. In some cases, this was more than compensated for by transnational immigration so that central densities were either maintained or, in some cases, increased significantly. This is shown in the diagram by the two direction arrows for line AA^I, as the net effect on central city density varies enormously. What is not shown in the density figures, however, is another defining feature of regional urbanization, arising from an extraordinary change in the demographic and cultural composition of the inner and outer city populations.

Reconstituting the Inner and Outer Cities

Prior to 1970, the poor were increasingly concentrated in the inner city, even in the metropolises of the Third World where the center was often dominated historically and geographically by the wealthy elite. This concentration, however, was largely domestic in the sense of being comprised of national citizens rather than foreign migrants (although foreign migration had already begun in parts of the industrialized world before 1970). The new concentration of what some now call the immigrant working poor (to contrast with the welfare dependant domestic underclass) is the outgrowth of a profound globalization of the urban population, creating the most culturally and economically heterogeneous cities the world has ever known. This cultural and economic heterogeneity of the urban poor, emerging amidst a spreading homogenization of built environments, visual landscapes, and popular tastes and fashions, is one of the hallmarks of regional urbanization and has been the trigger for many related developments, including the rise of a new cultural politics, the reconstitution of urban identities and increasing social and political polarization revolving primarily around conflicts between domestic and immigrant populations.

It is almost impossible to generalize about what has been happening to central cities in the regional urbanization process as the emerging conditions vary enormously. Detroit lost

600,000 people and has never quite recovered despite expensive efforts at "renaissance." Osaka lost almost all its inner-city residents, most moving into the densifying Kansai region (Osaka-Kobe-Kyoto), but its commercial and business-oriented inner city is thriving and vibrantly alive. In Los Angeles, more than a million white and black residents left the inner city over the past 30 years, but at least five million migrants from nearly every country on earth poured in, increasing central densities to Manhattan levels. In the neighborhood where I grew up in the Central Bronx, earlier tenements and later high rise residential towers have been replaced by tiny row houses with patches of grass in front, lowering densities substantially and suggesting something akin to the suburbanization of the city.

This variability and instability in the rapidly changing urban cores of the regional metropolis has deeply affected urban planning and policy making, focusing attention on the problems of the "old downtown." This has sparked the growth of such "regenerative" strategies as city marketing, city branding, and the search for a cultural or architectural fix following the now well-known model of the Frank Gehry-designed Guggenheim Museum in Bilbao or the dozens of repetitive projects by other "starchitects." In most cases, this drew attention and investment away from issues of social welfare and poverty alleviation that drove earlier efforts at urban renewal, as socially conscious planners were transformed into competitive entrepreneurs and city salespersons. With such complexity and variability in outcomes, it becomes almost impossible to generalize about the future of any given inner city.

It is much easier to identify a general trend affecting the suburban rings. With some exceptions, suburbia is becoming increasingly dense and demographically as well as economically differentiated. Conventional sprawl continues but is ebbing significantly, not because so-called smart and sustainable growth is spreading but due to another characteristic feature of regional urbanization, the increasing urbanization of suburbia. Almost everywhere, suburbia and suburban ways of life are changing, becoming more dense and heterogeneous, more like what the urban used to be. New terms have proliferated to describe these changes: edge cities, outer cities, exopolis, peripheral urbanization, postsuburbia, technoburbs, metroburbia.[3] In Figure 19.1 above, the line A^{1}E indicates the flattening out and extension of the density gradient and points to the increasing erosion of the formerly relatively clear boundary between the urban and the suburban, a marked homogenization of the urban landscape from center to periphery. Where this process is most pronounced, the longstanding urban-suburban dualism of metropolitan urbanization has almost disappeared, as the age of mass suburbanization shifts to one of mass regional urbanization, a filling in so to speak of the entire metropolitan area.

Density convergence plays a key role in the emergence of a distinctive new urban form, the expansive, polynucleated, densely networked, information-intensive, and increasingly globalized *city region*. The concept of city region is often seen as just a minor twist in the terms used to describe urban globalization, from the earlier "world city" to the more recent "global city."[4] I am arguing here, however, that the city region is not just an expression of globalization but represents a more fundamental change in the urbanization process, arising from the regionalization of the modern metropolis and involving a shift from the typically monocentric dualism of dense city and sprawling low-density suburbanization to a polycentric network of urban agglomerations where relatively high densities are found throughout the urbanized region.

Causes and Consequences of Regional Urbanization

Three major forces have been driving the regional urbanization process and shaping the formation of city regions: the globalization of capital, labor, and culture; economic restructuring and the formation of a new economy; and the facilitative effects of the revolution in information and communications technologies. Transnational migration flows in particular have refilled many metropolitan cores, contributing to the flattening out of metropolitan density gradients, especially through the urbanization of suburbia. A complex mix of deindustrialization and reindustrialization as well as decentralization and recentralization have worked to reorganize the social and spatial structure of almost every modern metropolis, creating the foundations for the emergence of a more flexible, globalized, and neoliberal mode of urban industrial capitalism, a "new economy."

Density convergence can also be linked to the increasing cultural and economic heterogeneity of the regional metropolis and the associated social and political polarization arising not only from traditional class and racial divisions, but increasingly from growing clashes between domestic and immigrant populations. Perhaps the most disturbing and challenging feature of regional urbanization has been its intensification of economic inequalities and social polarization. The new economy has characteristically squeezed the once voluminous middle classes of the modern metropolis, with a small spurt of yuppies and the super-rich rising from the economic pressures while a much larger flow moves downward into poverty or near poverty. The income gap between the richest 5 percent and poorest 40 percent in the US is now greater than it ever has been, and while the stronger welfare states of Western Europe have ameliorated the intensification of income inequality they all are facing major political problems arising from clashes between domestic and immigrant populations and cultures, in the urban core as well as former suburbs, as in the *banlieues* of Paris.

Increasing regional densities, growing cultural heterogeneity, and rising economic inequalities also play a part in the spread of what Mike Davis called "security-obsessed urbanism," an urban condition charged with paranoid fear of the seemingly chaotic and incomprehensible character of today's inner as well as outer cities.[5] This obsession with security and protection has encouraged domestic outmigration from the city centers in many different ways, ranging from racially induced white flight to the so-called secession of the rich, the movement of the relatively well off to guarded and gated communities and "privatopias" hoping to insulate themselves from the invasive dangers of the inner city. Surveillance cameras and high-tech alarm and security systems are now almost everywhere.[6] Public spaces are eroding as privatization spreads across the urban landscape and the regional metropolis is embedded with a "carceral" archipelago of fortressed new enclosures.

There are many other negative manifestations of regional urbanization and the growing density convergence. Longstanding problems related to the jobs-housing-transit imbalance, the degree to which the distribution of jobs, affordable housing, and available mass transit facilities do not match, are being aggravated further by urban restructuring. Homelessness expands in various ways in the inner city, ranging from the abject poverty of those hopelessly stranded in the streets to the relative deprivation of vital workers (police, firefighters, teachers) unable to find affordable accommodation near where they work. In rapidly urbanizing suburbia, booming new cities often grow well in advance of job creation, forcing large portions of the local workforce to commute more than two hours each way to work. In some cases, this leads to rising rates of divorce, child and spouse abuse, suicide, home foreclosures, impacted schools, bankrupt public services, conditions once associated with inner city slums but now arising in what some call postsuburbia.[7]

The characteristic features associated with regional urbanization are also contributing to increasing environmental degradation at multiple scales from the local to the transnational and global. From more positive geo-economical perspectives, the city is increasingly being seen as a generative source of economic development, technological innovation and cultural creativity; but the city and the regional city in particular is also the generator of major negative spillover effects, from increasing economic inequalities and social polarizations to worsening air and water pollution, climate change, and global warming.[8] The environmental justice debate at the global scale is not only about whether and how much climate change might be caused by human actions. It must also address the likelihood that resurgent urbanization and especially the regional urbanization process that is reconfiguring the modern metropolis are the *primary* cause of accelerated environmental degradation all over the planet and must be recognized as such in any attempt to deal with the accompanying problems. This becomes more starkly evident when regional urbanization is viewed in its multiscalar manifestations.

Extended Regional Urbanization

That the line A¹E in Figure 19.1 above does not quite touch the base is indicative of the unconstrained character of regional urbanization. The modern metropolis, in a significant sense, has become "unbound." Just as the clear internal border between city and suburb has begun to disappear, the external boundary of the city region is becoming less confining, opening up the urban hinterland to ever larger regional scales. More than ever before, the urbanization process is global in its reach and impact. Its sociospatial effects do not just decline with distance from the center to some outer boundary, they become virtually asymptotic, never and nowhere completely absent. This multiscalar spread of regional urbanization is almost impossible to understand if one maintains a conventional metropolitan perspective.

The city region is the anchor and archetype of this multiscalar regional urbanization. Its growing importance and recognition is exemplified in a recent decision by the United Nations to collect data on the size of city populations not by metropolitan region but by city region. A related change in defining the size of cities was adopted some time ago by the US Census Bureau. Data are now collected on the size and population density of what are called urbanized areas, defined by the relatively contiguous area of densities greater than 1,000 per square mile. The urbanized area of New York, for example, covers 23 counties and has the largest total population. In 1990, however, the Los Angeles urbanized area, whether defined as two counties (Los Angeles and Orange) or five (with parts of San Bernardino, Riverside, and Ventura added), surpassed New York as the densest in the US, a stunning turnaround as Los Angeles was probably the least dense major metropolis 30 years earlier.

The comparison between Los Angeles and New York is reflected in the difference between the lines A^1E and ACD in the density decay diagram. New York more closely resembles the metropolitan urban model (ACD), while Los Angeles presents an advanced form of regional urbanization, with dense outer cities and an intermixture of the urban and suburban, more comparable to the polycentric regional cities that have emerged around Washington DC, the San Francisco Bay Area, and, for that matter, around European cities such as London and Paris, and in the Randstad in the Netherlands, arguably the first city region to be defined as such.

According to UN data, there are now close to 500 city regions of more than one million inhabitants in the world. They contain at least a third of the entire world's population and, according to some estimates, nearly two-thirds of the world's wealth and an even larger share of its innovative capacity. This pronounced concentration in the world's city regions is another major expression of regional urbanization, even more so than the now often repeated UN statistic that the majority of the 6 to 7 billion people on earth now live in cities. But regional urbanization does not stop at the boundary of the city region. Edging higher in scale is the megacity region, with a population of at least 10 million but now growing, in some cases, to over 50 million. Even larger "megalopolitan" city regions coalescing together many city regions of various sizes, are creating the largest regional conurbations the world has ever known.[9] The Pearl River Delta in South China has more than 60 million inhabitants; the Yangtze Delta-Greater Shanghai region now surpasses 80 million; and if one added together the two adjacent megacity regions on Honshu (Tokyo-Yokohama, Osaka-Kobe-Kyoto), the total population would be over 100 million.[10]

Regional urbanization extends still further to vast subcontinental urban "galaxies" of more than 250 million inhabitants, the largest being in Eastern Asia, Western Europe, and Atlantic and Pacific North America. Today, it can be argued that every square inch of the world is urbanized to some degree, with the influences and effects of regional urbanization, the latest phase in the development of urban industrial capitalism, extending into the Amazon rainforest, the Siberian tundra and even the shrinking Antarctic icecap. What all this suggests is that the accelerated globalization process of the past 30 years has been carrying with it, and may be primarily defined by, the qualities and conditions associated with a regionalized version of the industrial capitalist city. Globalization and the new urbanization processes are intricately intertwined and interdependent in ways we are only beginning to understand.

The New Regionalism: Some Concluding Remarks

The growing recognition and importance of regional urbanization arises not only from its role in the reconfiguration of the metropolitan mode of urban development and its integral association with the globalization of capital, labor and culture, but also from other significant developments in the ways we think about the world around us. Two developments in particular help to clarify the meaning and significance of regional urbanization, the unprecedented diffusion of critical spatial thinking that some now call the *spatial turn* and the related rise of innovative applications of a spatial perspective that has come to be known as the New Regionalism.[11] They provide a useful way of concluding this essay and opening up new possibilities for further discussion.

The concept of regional urbanization is to a significant degree a product of the pronounced and transdisciplinary spatial turn, the diffusion of spatial thinking to almost every academic discipline and subject area. This unprecedented spread of thinking critically about the spatiality of human life is much more than a passing fad. It represents a sea change in Western intellectual thought, an ontological and epistemological correction of a distorted world view that arose in the second half of the nineteenth century as an exaggerated and space-blinkered form of social historicism, a privileging of time and historical thinking that would persist in powerful ways up to the present.[12] Today, we are beginning to see a rebalancing of social, historical and spatial perspectives. Space is now being seen by more and more scholars in much the same way we have previously viewed time, as dynamic, problematic, developmental, ideologically charged, and filled with action, dialectics, process and social causality, rather than fixed, dead background, container, stage, extrasocial environment.

However one views the spatial turn, there can be little doubt that more scholars than ever before are adopting some form of a spatial perspective, even if only in the use of spatial metaphors. This has reinforced the development and widened the understanding of many concepts that relate to the spatiality of human life, including networks, territory, scale, agglomeration, and regions. It has also focused attention on what can be called critical studies of cities and regions. It is from this eclectic interpretive focus and framework that the concept of regional urbanization emerges most directly. Spurring these developments further has been a radical reconceptualization of regions and regionalism built primarily on new ideas and discoveries about the extraordinary generative effects of cities and cohesive city regional economies.

As presented most assertively by Michael Storper in *The Regional World*, this New Regionalism interprets regions not simply as receptacles or reflections of social and economic processes but as fundamental units of social life comparable to markets, states, and families. Cohesive regional economies, and especially those built around the network of agglomerations that define the city region, are also being seen today as the source of powerful yet rarely studied and still poorly understood generative forces. Some geographical economists now claim that these generative forces emanating from the global hierarchy of megacity regions are the *primary* (most important among many) causes of contemporary economic development, technological innovation, and cultural and artistic creativity.[13] The positive effects of agglomeration are now entering the economics textbooks as "Jane Jacobs externalities," honoring the work many economists recognize as the earliest to identify this generative spark of urban life.[14] Emerging more slowly has been the related recognition that the generative force of urban agglomeration can also generate diseconomies, increasing social inequality and polarization, expansive environmental degradation, and other negative effects.

These regionally defined agglomeration effects, positive and negative, represent perhaps the most path-breaking and potentially transformative discovery arising from the cumulative literature on urban restructuring, globalization and the new economy. Until very recently, there was almost nothing written about the stimulus of urban agglomeration, or "synekism," as I have called it.[15] Today, it is becoming the central theme for a growing literature that extends well beyond the fields of urban and regional studies as they have been formerly defined. Carried forward by the transdisciplinary spatial turn, regional perspectives and such related concepts as the city region and regional urbanization are likely to become increasingly important and widespread over the next several decades.

Notes

1   Edward W. Soja, *Postmetropolis: Critical Studies of Cities and Regions* (Oxford: Blackwell Publishers, 2000); and Konstantina Soureli and Elise Youn, "Urban Restructuring and the Crisis: A Symposium with Neil Brenner, John Friedmann, Margit Mayer, Allen J. Scott and Edward W. Soja," *Critical Planning* 16 (2009) 34-60.

2   Harvey, *Social Justice and the City* (Baltimore: Johns Hopkins University Press, 1973); and Manuel Castells, *The Urban Question: A Marxist Approach* (Cambridge: MIT Press, 1977).

3   Joel Garreau, *Edge City: Life on the New Frontier* (New York: Doubleday, 1991); Rob Kling, Spencer C. Olin and Mark Poster, eds., *Postsuburban California: The Transformation of Orange County Since World War II* (Berkeley: University of California Press, 1991); Soja, *Postmetropolis*; and Paul L. Knox, *Metroburbia, USA* (New Brunswick: Rutgers University Press, 2008).

4   John Friedmann, "The World City Hypothesis," *Development and Change* 17, 1 (1986) 69-83; and Saskia Sassen, *The Global City: New York, London, Tokyo* (Princeton: Princeton University Press, 2001) 1991.

5   Mike Davis, *City of Quartz: Excavating the Future in Los Angeles* (New York: Verso, 1990).

6   Evan Mackenzie, *Privatopia: Homeowner Associations and the Rise of Residential Private Government* (New Haven: Yale University Press, 1994).

7   Soja, *Postmetropolis*, 260-2.

8   Edward L. Glaeser, "The New Economics of Urban and Regional Growth," *Oxford Handbook of Economic Geography*, eds. Gordon L. Clark, Meric S. Gerler, and Maryann P. Feldman (New York: Oxford Univeristy Press, 2000) 83-98.

9   Richard Florida, "The New Megalopolis: Our Focus on Cities is Wrong," *Newsweek* July 3, 2006, special edition.

10 Edward W. Soja and J. Miguel Kanai, "The Urbanization of the World," this book, Ch. 10.

11 Barney Warf and Santa Arias, eds., *The Spatial Turn: Interdisciplinary Perspectives* (New York: Routledge, 2009); Edward W. Soja, "Take Space Personally," *The Spatial Turn: Interdisciplinary Perspectives*, eds. Barney Warf and Santa Arias (New York: Routledge, 2008); Michael Storper, *The Regional World: Territorial Development in a Global Economy* (New York: Guilford Press, 1997); Edward W. Soja, "The New Regionalism: A Conversation with Edward W. Soja," interviewer Renia Ehrenfurt, *Critical Planning* 9 (2002) 5-12; and Edward W. Soja, "Regional Planning and Development Theories," *The International Encyclopedia of Human Geography* (Amsterdam, Elsevier, 2009) 259-70.

12 Edward W. Soja, *Postmodern Geographies: the Reassertion of Space in Critical Social Theory* (Oxford: Blackwell Publishers, 1989); and Michel Foucault, "Of Other Spaces," *Diacritics* 16 (1986) 22-7.

13 John F. McDonald, *Fundamentals of Urban Economics* (New York: Prentice-Hall, 1997).

14 Jane Jacobs, *The Economy of Cities* (New York: Random House, 1969).

15 Soja, *Postmetropolis*.

Figure Credits

19.1   Original by author.

20
WORLDWIDE URBANIZATION AND NEOCOLONIAL FRACTURES: INSIGHTS FROM THE LITERARY WORLD

Stefan Kipfer

When hypothesizing about the complete urbanization of society in *The Urban Revolution*, Henri Lefebvre insisted that this process was worldwide but virtual—incomplete and uneven.[1] Among other things, this was so because urbanization remained shot through with territorial relations between dominant and dominated social spaces. Lefebvre proposed that these relations between "centers" and "peripheries" can be compared across scalar divides, and that they also refract, in part, the very historical realities (of "city" and "countryside") that urbanization helps supersede. The not-only metaphorical language he used to describe center-periphery relations ("colonization") cautions us to be mindful of how neocolonial realities, past and present, still weigh on the urban world. Two generations after the publication of Lefebvre's book, this point is still relevant, even though the Three Worlds of the postwar period have been reconfigured and the center of gravity of worldwide urbanization has long shifted away from Euro-America. A comparative analysis of the boundary-destroying dynamics of global urbanization must take into account the reterritorializing neocolonial and neoimperial forces that fracture urban landscapes.

Undertaking such a comparative project is daunting—and vastly exceeds the scope of this chapter. For present purposes, I underscore the importance of such a historical-materialist project by using the literary world as an entry point. We know from Marxist and postcolonial debates that literary texts represent acute mediations between everyday life and the totality of imperial, patriarchal capitalism. These debates approximate Lefebvre's view that urban research should also further a critique of everyday life. My example will be *Texaco*, the thematically most "urban" novel by Patrick Chamoiseau, the Martinique-born writer and promoter of creole literature in the French Antilles.[2] Published in 1992, *Texaco* is a landmark in Caribbean and French literature and has been acclaimed far beyond the Creole-French world, including by Derek Walcott, Junot Díaz and Austin Clarke.[3] *Texaco* places "slum" clearance in postwar Fort-de-France, Martinique in a historical context that reaches back to the last years of slavery prior to 1848. In the novel, the legacies of colonial slavery continue to fracture urbanizing Martinique and clash with Chamoiseau's conception of creole urbanism as a tension-ridden but hopefully deterritorializing force. The novel about the hometown of Frantz Fanon thus points to the continued relevance of the latter's countercolonial—not postcolonial—critique for urban analysis.[4]

Texaco opens a window into the historical transformations that usher in the urban revolution in Martinique. In *Texaco*, the urban makes an appearance as a form of centrality/difference built upon territorialized social relations. As such, it refracts "city" and "countryside" and embodies both hope and repulsion. Yet the territorial relations in urbanizing Martinique, still a French *département*, rearticulate a history of town and country that is formally, not indirectly, colonial, as in Lefebvre's main reference point of postwar French urbanism. *Texaco* thus reminds us that concepts developed in one context must be translated carefully to analyze another.[5] We have argued elsewhere that great caution is warranted when "globalizing" Lefebvrian insights.[6] Lefebvre's urban hypothesis, and his commitment to a multipolar world of knowledge creation, provide us with vital resources for deciphering the urban field and its possibilities not only in Europe. Yet to actualize these resources requires us to move beyond Lefebvre, for whom the starkness of the urban revolution emanates from the transformation of the historic "city" and "countryside" in Western Europe. The novel *Texaco* shows how creole urbanism refracts the contradictions of worldwide urbanization through the racially stratified social mixing characteristic of Antillean plantation economies. It thus underscores that the character of the urban in Martinique is, in comparative terms, coeval: contemporaneous and connected to worldwide (including French) urbanization processes, but also inflected with the histories of city and country in the Caribbean.

Worldwide Urbanization and Revolution

In 1970, Lefebvre argued that society was in the process of being urbanized completely. He made this argument about the world as a whole, not only about national urban systems, within which much urban analysis was contained at that time. Linking the production of space to the production of the world, Lefebvre's claim thus remains vital for any contemporary discussion of worldwide urbanization.[7]

Lefebvre meant his claim as a hypothesis about a virtual reality, not a *fait accompli*. Urbanization thus cannot be grasped adequately in objectivist terms, with disciplinary methods of analysis that are obsessed with pinning down the empirical content and extent of actually existing urbanization in a falsely concrete fashion. Understanding urbanization, for Lefebvre, requires a method of transduction that links reality with possibility.[8]

For Lefebvre, worldwide urbanization represents a multifaceted field-in-formation-and-mutation. Urbanization is not reducible to the physical extension and increasing demographic weight of existing settlements that happen to be described as "urban."[9] Lefebvre's focus was on a multiplicity of processes—the expansion of the built environment, the relative weight of land rent in accumulation, and the industrialization of agriculture, among others. These processes all help disarticulate the integrity of seemingly self-evident spatial forms (such as "city" and "countryside") that appear to contain social relations and to demarcate them from "nature." In contrast, Lefebvre holds that generalized, worldwide urbanization is now the main medium through which social relations relate to nature. Agricultural questions remain crucial, but should be investigated in relation to urbanization.[10] Indeed, Lefebvre's hypothesis forces us to ask if, where and how agriculture retains its autonomous rural character, and whether it continues to be built upon qualitatively distinct social relations.[11]

Of particular interest to Lefebvre was the phenomenon of centrality. For him, the capitalist version of urbanization necessarily involves the production of centrality/difference as a fleeting spatial form with a key role in condensing and reshaping spatial peripheries. For him, the revolutionary quality of modern capitalist urbanization lies in its tendency to undermine existing articulations of spatial and sociopolitical centrality, and to create new such articulations by bringing together differences that serve as productive forces (for capital and the state) and resources (for oppositional social forces). As Brenner and Schmid have pointed out, this dialectical implosion/explosion of "the city" can be grasped, in part, as a shifting interplay of spatial concentration and spatial extension at various scales.[12]

A crucial aspect of Lefebvre's analysis of urbanization as a decomposition and recomposition of centralities is political. The most far-reaching aspect of Lefebvre's hypothesis is the insight that relationships of domination between center and periphery cannot be subsumed under the categories that defined the terms of revolutionary theory when he wrote *The Urban Revolution* in 1970 (for instance, "city," "country," "industry," "agriculture"). For Lefebvre, territorial relations of domination are to be understood *within* the urban field. They help shape the distinct ways in which the form of centrality brings together differences. Revolutionary theory can thus no longer be conceptualized in classical terms, whether as (1) an extension of urban-industrial-proletarian struggle, (2) an encirclement of cities by peasant movements, or (3) a united front linking "city" and "countryside" as if these were fixed, pregiven entities.

Lefebvre's discussion of riots, uprisings and urban guerrillas late in *The Urban Revolution* underscores his concern that the implosion/explosion of the "city" could recreate the conditions for new revolutionary mobilizations from multiple peripheries, old and new, in pursuit of new forms of social and spatial centrality. Lefebvre's text thus expressed and theorized the emergent global constellation of social movements that was "1968" in a provocatively new, specifically urban way.[13] Theoretically, Lefebvre's doubled understanding of the urban revolution—as both a process of transformation and a revolutionary possibility—is articulated most powerfully through his language of "levels." For him, the urban as spatial form represented an intermediate level of analysis in a tension-fraught field, caught between the routines and aspirations of everyday life and the "big" or "global" institutions of capitalist modernity, notably the state.

The ultimate importance of urban research for Lefebvre, thus flows directly from the role of urbanization as the main medium through which our everyday lives are connected to totality, the broader social order of capitalism and its relations to nature. Without such an emphasis on the urban as level, Lefebvre believed, urban research will continue to be no more than a hyphenated subfield within the academic division of labor, one that remains subservient to "high" theory, is subject to periodic identity crises, and, still worse, can be readily instrumentalized by statist forms of urbanism and modern planning apparatuses. Also, without reference to the urban as level, and its associated mediations to both everyday life and the broader social order, urban politics is reduced to a merely local, municipal or city-regional concern in Left oppositional strategies.

On Uneven Urbanization

Lefebvre's urban work, including his hypothesis of global urbanization, offers challenges for comparative urban research. For Lefebvre, global urbanization cannot be confined to the study of urban regions and their inter-relationships. It is a multiscalar affair that includes but cuts across local, regional, national and continental territorial configurations.[14] Claims to the urban, fleeting or temporarily fixed articulations of centrality and difference, can also vary in their scalar reach. Lefebvre's multiscalar vision also holds for the question of "colonization." Originally a metaphor to sharpen his critique of everyday life, the term colonization ended up denoting, in Lefebvre's work, territorial relations of domination between central and peripheral spaces at various scales, both in former colonies and in imperial heartlands. Lefebvre's insight is that colonial or neocolonial relations of domination are increasingly mediated by the urban field. They are not confined to the historic divides between "city" and "countryside." To put it differently, the form of centrality/difference that is the urban is itself shot through with territorial forms of domination, some of which may be tied to imperial colonialism.[15]

Methodologically, two implications follow for the comparative investigation of urbanization.[16] First, Lefebvre's hypothesis regarding the boundary-defying character of urbanization implies a form of relational comparison that supersedes methodological nationalism and territorialism, permitting sociospatial relations within the urban field to be compared without being neatly confined to the typical units of comparative analysis (nation, continent, First, Second or Third World).[17] Second, Lefebvre's language of colonization invites us to pay attention to how colonial history has shaped center-periphery relations in today's urbanizing world. Taking up this invitation can lead to studies of racialized territorial relations that are articulated to colonialism either indirectly ("colonization" in postcolonial contexts, such as contemporary London or Paris) or directly (persisting colonial or neocolonial occupation in Palestine, indigenous North America, and France's overseas territories).[18]

We need to take Lefebvre's suggestions as just that, as gestures towards more sustained, worldwide comparative analyses. For the force of his argument lies in the contrast he develops between the boundary-defying yet fractured geography of modern urbanization and the city-countryside divide characteristic of precapitalist Europe, where urban life stood in a relationship of "internal exteriority" to feudalism.[19] Lefebvre uses this contrast to demarcate a line of transformation from the "political city" and the "commercial city" to the "industrial city" and, finally, to the contours of a worldwide urban reality under twentieth-century neocapitalism. In this neocapitalist context, Lefebvre became cognizant of the boundary-dissolving tendency of capitalist urbanization to both implode and explode the centralities of the historic city.[20] A key meaning of the urban revolution, in his framework, thus lies in process by which city and countryside are superseded as object-like markers of qualitatively distinct practices in European history. At the same time, he recognized, claims to "urban" and "rural" life can persist in ideological, symbolic and imagined forms *within* an emergent, amorphous urban field.[21]

Lefebvre's work as a whole does not lend itself to the linear-progressivist "urbanism" that underlies various Eurocentrisms.[22] His rural sociological work was deeply sensitive to the historical variability of city-country relationships in Europe itself and gestured towards a global comparative approach to agricultural questions.[23] Lefebvre thus did not treat urbanization as an evolutionary transition from rural life. Nonetheless, his urban work gives us little sense of how global urbanization varies in relation to a much wider range of historical trajectories beyond Europe. In turn, it does not explore how Europe was itself formed in relation to other histories (including histories of "city" and "countryside") via colonial imperialism. For such an understanding, we must extend and recast substantively Lefebvre's own basic procedure to link histories of space and urbanization to transformations in modes of production. We need to focus on the comparatively distinct ways in which city-countryside relations emerged in *different* precapitalist, tributary social formations before being reshaped in *distinct ways* in articulation with merchant and industrial capitalism and the associated forces of colonialism and imperialism.[24]

Western Europe is not of course the only region in which the urban revolution has transformed histories shaped by stark interplays of city and countryside. North African urbanization, for example, is impossible to understand without reference to the historical relationships between dynastic military and commercial urbanism, settled agriculture and tribal-nomadic networks, as already sketched by the famous fourteenth-century historian Ibn Khaldoun.[25] But such qualitative and social urban-rural contrasts did not inform precapitalist geographies everywhere. As we know from contemporary students of *desakota* urbanization in Southeast Asia, and as Wing-Shing Tang has likewise reminded us with respect to Chinese urban history, physical boundaries between settlement forms can hide urban-rural social continua organized by imperial administrations. Very different from the city-countryside divide of West European feudalism, such continua are essential reference points for understanding the most dynamic, currently ongoing urban revolutions as well as the twin processes of agricultural restructuring and depeasantization that sustain them.[26]

Lefebvre's brief historical sketch of global urbanization in *The Urban Revolution* also obscures the degree to which city-country relationships are being revolutionized according to qualitatively distinct temporalities. While Lefebvre elsewhere insisted on the articulation of multiple rhythms, both cyclical and linear, in different parts of urban Europe, his work does not paint a global comparative picture of such temporal multiplicity.[27] But we know that, in colonial contexts based on territorial systems of labor control (which tried to separate "urban" production from "rural" reproduction, as in British-dominated extractive economies in Africa) or based on the reinstitution of semi-feudal agriculture (in parts of Latin America and South Asia), city-country divides were materially *(re-)instituted* during the history of modern capitalism rather than being subverted and transposed in the manner Lefebvre described for southern France, for example.[28]

Crucially for the present discussion, Caribbean plantation economies also organized novel divisions of labor between city (colonial town) and countryside (plantation). After the eradication of indigenous populations, slave-based economies helped develop a geopolitically and socially distinct regional pattern of development. Tightly integrated into French, English, Spanish and Dutch imperial economies, these quintessentially modern, albeit not fully capitalist, economies of mass production imposed new forms of city-countryside relation. Fully integrated economically, colonial towns and plantations related to each other through a distinct mix of physical proximity (given the small size of the islands) and starkly racialized forms of residential and legal segregation (after the historical consolidation of "racial" codes of labor control).[29] In the twentieth century, these common patterns animated successive anticolonial arguments for regional self-determination as well as claims to regionally specific crosscultural, creole or African-Caribbean cultural forms.[30] Notwithstanding comparative differences among Caribbean plantation economies, they help us interpret urbanism in Martinique, an "old" French colony claimed in 1635 and defined by black slavery (as codified by the *Code Noir*) from 1685 until 1848.[31]

In current debates, two avenues seem to be on offer to address the limitations in Lefebvre's comparative field of vision on the urban revolution. As already mentioned, students of planetary urbanization have built upon Lefebvre's work to map the extended dimensions of urbanization, and on this basis, to question thing-like conceptions of the city as bounded settlement.[32] At the same time, authors who draw upon a range of influences, including strands of postcolonialism, have started to deconstruct the Euro-American biases in urban theory. In welcome challenges to such Euro-American traditions of "Metromarxism," including the work of Lefebvre, the postcolonial critique has productively recentered the geography of urban theory and has begun to infuse research on the global North with sensibilities and analytic insights derived from studies of the metropoles of the urban South.[33] Both approaches cut across inherited divides of comparative research, albeit in distinctive ways and for different reasons.

To understand the meaning of urban revolutions in North and South, I propose paying greater attention to the ways in which the unevenness of the urban revolution is articulated in different spatio-temporal contexts under modern imperial capitalism. This approach, which presupposes Lefebvre's conceptualization of the urban as level, requires that we analyze the world-historical forces that have sustained and naturalized key spatial distinctions (for instance, between colonial and imperial; and between first, second and third, as well as between urban and rural worlds) in previous rounds of comparative urban analysis. Embedded or reinvented in built environments, state forms and everyday practices, these forces continue to shape urban trajectories, despite the fact that global urbanization is cutting across inherited comparative geographies in novel ways. To account for such continuity-in-discontinuity, this chapter contributes to the project of reconstructing radical urban theory by reestablishing contacts between marxist and countercolonial currents. In this case, the reconstruction draws on selective insights from research on colonial, Third-World and dependent cities in the 1970s and 1980s which, it is important to remember, helped form the intellectual agendas of English-speaking radical geography.[34]

Literature: An Entry Point into Global and Comparative Urbanization

One entry point to the "big" questions of comparative and global urban research is literature. Literature—writing deemed especially valuable by bourgeois society—can be said to "mediate" totality in ways that bring out the contradiction between potentiality and actuality, fantasy and historical reality.[35] Lefebvre himself suggested that literature expresses social life, emanating from as well as surpassing in fantasy the realities of a given context.[36] From this point of view, criticism should be seen as an attempt to revisit the content and form of literary texts in order to bring to life, and bring closer to our lives, the lived realities that are refracted in literature. As urban analysis, criticism should highlight the contradictions between reality and fantasy which literature includes in acute but not always intentional ways.

Translating Lefebvre's literary insight into this discussion, the promise of literature lies in its capacity to illuminate aspects of totality through representations of everyday life. Focusing on the spatial forms articulated in literary texts may thus present us with insights into the relationship between large-scale historical forces and everyday routines and aspirations.[37]

Lefebvre's work is exemplary here: his exposition of the notion of the festival in Rabelais later allowed him to trace the transposition of festivality from the early modern countryside to France's urban revolutionary moments in 1871 and 1968. His work on Rabelais thus anticipated his foundational claim that the urban revolution does not simply erase rural and urban life but recomposes city and countryside, both symbolically and ideologically.

The methods of comparative literature provide an opening for analyses of city and countryside across the North/South divide. This is true whether we insist on the idea of Third World literature or claim that we live in one world, albeit one in which colonial-imperial histories continue unevenly to shape contemporary experience.[38] For instance, the social realist treatment of metropolitan life and its broader articulations could be compared in the work of Emile Zola, Mulk Raj Anand and Ousmane Sembène, provided such a comparison is carefully embedded in historical and geographical contexts. More generally, as Neil Lazarus has argued in a discussion relating the ideas of Raymond Williams, Marshall Berman, David Harvey, Lao She and Rohinton Mistry, literary treatments of land, environment, city and countryside can illuminate the historical geographies of urban-rural relationships and the shock-experience of modernity in both colonial and postcolonial metropoles.[39]

Lazarus' point is important not only for literary theory but also for comparative urban research. His argument demonstrates that literary themes are comparable across contexts because they are neither culturally relative nor purely universal in a homogenizing sense.[40] Lazarus' claims also jive with Harry Harootunian's approach to the "coeval" character of modernity. Drawing on Walter Benjamin and Tosaka Jun, as well as Henri Lefebvre, Harootunian's work on everyday life in interwar Japan suggests that modernity is not a product of diffusion from Europe (as claimed by modernization theorists), nor is it incommensurate with the experiences and conditions of the European form of modernity (as suggested in key strands of area studies and postcolonial theory). Instead, as a regime of the new incorporating fragments of the past, the modern everyday represents a "minimal unity" of the capitalist world, even as it is inflected with comparative specificity across places and territories.[41] We may thus hypothesize, with both Lefebvre and Lazarus, that the urban can be found simultaneously in multiple, interlinked contexts, literary and otherwise. Yet, as Harootunian's framework suggests, this regime of centrality/difference continually rearticulates specific historical-geographical contents, not least divergent histories of city and country.

Creolizing the Urban Revolution

Born and raised in Martinique in 1953 but living in France for extended periods, Patrick Chamoiseau has been writing since the early 1970s. His work encompasses plays, novels, screenplays, autobiographical accounts, childrens' tales, literary manifestos, political essays and columns. He attributes great autobiographical significance to his urban childhood in Fort-de-France, the capital of Martinique.[42] Indeed, Chamoiseau's work responds in many ways to the urban revolution in Martinique. After the Second World War and the transformation of Martinique into a *département* of France in 1946, this revolution appeared at first in the unmistakenly statist forms of French Fordism. As he reports in *Écrire en pays dominé*:

> As the 1946 law started having wider effects, the country changed at great speed: concrete construction becomes king, glass windows, lamps, red lights, first television sets, automobile ecstasy, triumphant social housing blocks, sanitary plumbing, social assistance, family allowance payments, airplanes, roads and highways, schools, ready-to-wear clothing, stores, hotels, supermarkets, advertising … [43]

Key works by Chamoiseau, including *Solibo Magnifique, Chronicle des sept misères* and *Texaco,* illustrate the mortal danger that urbanization-modernization posed for key island institutions—local markets, the Creole language, storytelling and self-built urbanism. The urban tapestry being draped over Martinique, he believed, threatened to "sterilize" island life and to "invalidate" anti-colonial claims.[44]

However, from these works and others, we also learn that the urban revolution in Martinique assumed a more directly neocolonial character than its mainland French counterpart to which it remained tied. Driven by the postwar crisis of the sugar economy and profoundly dependent on metropolitan capitalism for tourism, commodity exports and transfer payments, Fordist urbanization in Martinique had an artificial quality. Given the limited capacity of Martinique's towns to absorb labor surpluses, informal settlements expanded and migration to France magnified. In turn, it became evident that departmental status represented a form of neocolonial domination. Instead of emancipation and equality within the confines of the French state, this arrangement intensified cultural assimilation even as it also reproduced a pigmentocratic, "shadist" class structure, in which divisions between the old slaveholding families, French administrators, a mulatto middle class and the working class (descended from slaves and plantation laborers) have been overdetermined by fine-grained, racialized distinctions between shades of skin color.

Chamoiseau responded to urbanization in multiple ways—including revolt, nostalgia and ambiguous accommodation. His entry to the literary scene as a rebel theater director and screenwriter in the 1970s was deeply shaped by local student activism for independence in the 1960s and the banana workers' strike in 1974.[45] These followed the 1959 revolt in which, during three days of rioting against racist humiliation and rising food prices, inhabitants claimed the center of Fort-de-France.[46] To Chamoiseau's generation, this political conjuncture highlighted the contradictions of political assimilation in Martinique and the tensions in older intellectuals like Aimé Césaire. A larger-than-life father figure, Césaire inspired younger radicals with his manfestos for a revolutionary countercolonialism even as he helped implement Martinique's departmental status as a life-long mayor of Fort-de-France and a member of France's National Assembly. Chamoiseau later interpreted the revolts of 1959 as Martinique's modest, inconclusive contribution to worldwide anticolonialism.[47] At the time, his theatrical work added to the charged historical context and helped politicize the relationship between formal French, the language of the administrators and the assimilated middle class, and Creole, the popular classes' oral language, long prohibited in school and often derided by elites and expatriates.

The struggle over language in the 1970s helped prepare the ground for the creole movement of the 1980s, represented by authors like Raphaël Confiant, Jean Bernabé and Maryse Condé, as well as by Chamoiseau himself. Epitomized by Bernabé, Confiant, and Chamoiseau's 1988 manifesto *Eloge de la créolité*, this movement embarked on a quest for a specifically Antillean, indeed Caribbean, cultural identity—creole.[48] Bernabé, Confiant and Chamoiseau refused to mimic the protocols of established French literature and also rejected the alternative Césaire had helped develop in the 1930s and 1940s—the search for the African roots of Caribbean culture (*négritude*). While their critiques seemed to echo Fanon's earlier claim about the double impasse in Caribbean cultural politics (the "great white error" of assimilation and the "great black mirage" of *négritude*), they did not follow Fanon, who asserted the primacy of politics in national culture and placed his Caribbean engagements in a context of tri-continental revolution.[49] Instead, they privileged poetic knowledge over anticolonial militancy in their search for an "internal" form of cultural subjectivity that was neither African nor European, but specifically Caribbean. They thus recast political sovereignty in the region as a *ramification* of their artistic project to revamp—to creolize—modern literature.[50]

In their quest to affirm the cultural specificity of creole as identity, language and form of literary expression, Bernabé, Chamoiseau and Confiant vacillated between a situated, sometimes romantic opposition to France's falsely universal cultural imperialism, and open-ended proclamations for cultural mixing and epistemic complexification.[51] On the one hand, the authors treated creole as a state of being, *créolité*—an authentic source of self not rooted in "racial" hierarchy but permeated by a sense of cultural, linguistic, customary, religious and "racial" diversity that is deemed profound, essential and sedimented, and may thus be expressed in ecological metaphors ("magma," "mangrove").[52] On the other hand, they also discussed creole as a form of becoming—*créolisation* as a process by which the world as a whole undergoes cultural diversification, akin to the transformation of New York City's migrant neighbourhoods. In this aspect, the authors were closer to their predecessor, critic and collaborator Edouard Glissant's *Discours Antillais*, which was published in 1981.[53] Literary analysts have suggested that this mix of a romantic-essentializing posture and a postmodern-cosmopolitan sensibility, which displaces the countercolonialisms of both Césaire and Fanon, signaled a partial accommodation to neocolonial realities. It enabled others to appropriate arguments by the creole movement in order to promote a color-blind, folkloristic Martinique. For the organizers of the elite cultural project *Tous Créoles*, for example, everyone, including the ruling families descended from white slaveholders (*békés*), can lay equal claim to creole culture.[54] In this generic view of creolization, the differences that come together in urbanizing Martinique are left in their alienated state. Their complicity with racialized capitalism is not problematized.

Texaco

Chamoiseau's *Texaco* embodies many of the tensions within the creole movement on an explicitly urban terrain. Named after a shantytown bearing the name of the oil company on whose ground it developed, *Texaco* zeroes in on the struggles of shantytown dwellers against the "slum" clearance schemes in Fort-de-France. This literary critique of urban renewal does not take the form of a social realist counternarrative in the tradition of anticolonial liberation novels. Instead, *Texaco* deploys the techniques of creole writing, which attempt to "conquer" the French language with oral Creole.[55] Blurring genres and languages, it infuses literary French with Creole vocabulary, figures of speech and oral rhythms. It also combines oral testimony with written historical documents and the narrator's commentary. The story of *Texaco* is told through multiple voices—the oral account of Marie-Sophie Laborieux, the Texaco inhabitant and activist; the memories of her late father, Esternome Laborieux, which are embedded in Marie-Sophie's own narrative; the commentaries by Christ, the town-planner; and the interventions by the storyteller Chamoiseau. This collage-like form allows Chamoiseau to infuse the relationship between Texaco residents and the authorities housed in "solid" Fort-de-France with memories of slavery, colonial violence and resistance.[56] This technique also makes clear that urban Martinique has long been a confluence of multiple rhythms and temporalities, all of which are refracted pervasively through language.[57] Conquered by the struggles chronicled in the text, formal-French Fort-de-France "integrates some of the soul of Texaco," the informal-Creole shantytown which, as the Creole pronunciation makes clear, embodies Marie-Sophie's voice (*teks-a-ko* = text-future-body).[58]

In *Texaco*, the urban holds the key to grasping the sociospatial transformation of Martinique. The book retraces the transfiguration of the peculiar divide between city and countryside that shaped Martinique's plantation economy and the spatial imaginaries that emerged from it.[59] During slavery, the colonial garrison and port towns (Saint Pierre, Fort-de-France) and the plantations (*habitations*) were both components of a single, integrated, always already modern colonial economy. Yet they were demarcated from each other in racialized terms in order to facilitate supervision and labor control. As we learn from the trials of the character Esternome in the novel, "racial" demarcation made even freed blacks, who were nominally allowed to leave the plantation, subject to constant suspicion in the towns, which were dominated by a pigmentocratic hierarchy of French administrators, white slaveholders (*béké*), and assimilated mulatto inhabitants. The hostile character of colonial urban life pushed the plantation slaves' emancipatory aspirations away from the towns and towards subsistence agriculture and the mountains, the refuge of *maroons* (fugitive slaves).

The slaves' capacity to resort to subsistence agriculture or escape, also to British islands, helped accelerate the implementation of abolition in 1848 and constituted a source of resistance against labor control in the postemancipation plantation economy.[60] In the following decades, however, the appeal of rural smallholding was undercut by debt bondage, the proletarianization of plantation agriculture, and migration to the sugar factories. Finally, the crisis of the sugar economy in late colonial and early departmental Martinique furthered the decomposition of the colonial divide between town and plantation and the growth of informal habitats such as Texaco. Through the multiple voices he mobilizes, Chamoiseau brilliantly shows how rural imaginaries of revolt and emancipation exhausted themselves and were embeddded within an integrated urban field. As demonstrated in the 1959 revolt, earlier quests for autonomy and land–such as the struggles between slaves in their plantation huts (*case-nègres*) and plantation owners in their houses (*grand-cases*)—got recast in the spatial, social and multisensory struggle between the fragile, ramshackle and self-built shantytowns, including Texaco, and the solid, planned and orderly Fort-de France (*l'En-ville*).[61] In this struggle, shantytown dwellers strike compromises with reform-oriented forces, including Aimé Césaire, who later described his mayoral role as a mission to "get people out of their shanties."[62] In the novel, Césaire appears as a paternalist figure ("papa Césaire") and as a force of hope, a black mayor in a white and mulatto City Hall who achieves a veritable "Césaire effect," limiting forceful and arbitrary evictions.[63]

In *Texaco*, the urban expresses profound contradictions—between the promise of freedom and persistent racial hierarchy, between cosmopolitan openness and economic parasitism. On the one hand, *Texaco* illustrates Chamoiseau's conviction that, after the exhaustion of revolt during slavery and following emancipation, new political possibilities are most likely to emerge in and through urban space.[64] Urban Martinique is defined by "nodes of connection" that refract differences: they facilitate creative interactions among a diversity of inhabitants and thus allow "creolization [to] unfold." More open to the world than homogenized plantation life, urbanizing Martinique promises an escape from the stifling control of the slaveholders.[65] The Creole term for town (*l'En-ville*) makes clear that the city is not a thing (a physical form or bounded territory) but a *claim*, an existential project to move into and occupy space, however fleetingly.[66] Chamoiseau sees the promise of diverse urban Martinique in the deterritorializing, chaotic life-force that permeates it, an errant "*drive*" that holds traces of marooning slave resistance and invades the rationalism of the orderly Fort-de France proper. Alluding to Deleuze and Guattari's notion of rhizome, he deploys the plant metaphor "mangrove" to show how in Texaco, the multiple, complexly combined (creolized) and not-just human energies in Martinique's history permeate urban life symbolically, swamp-like and in horizontal, lateral fashion.[67] Here, informal urbanism is valorized. Shanty entrepreneurs and survival artists (*"djobeurs"*), who cobble together a subsistence and invade Fort-de-France in search of marginal deals and petty jobs, play a heroic role akin to that of the fugitive slaves (*maroons*) and the plantation workers in earlier periods of struggle.[68]

On the other hand, *Texaco* shows how mangrove urbanism is continuously fractured by patriarchal neocolonialism. Indeed, the most critical dimensions of *Texaco* lie in its depiction of *situated, concrete* resistance—the struggles of black, Creole-speaking shanty dwellers to resist demolition, fight assimilation and appropriate Fort-de-France as a whole for dignity and political recognition.[69] Here, informal survival tactics, including self-help, are only one way to "conquer *l'En-ville*."[70] In Texaco, shanty dwellers must deal with slumlordism, petty exploitation, permanent insecurity and gendered violence, including rape and physical assault. As is common in shantytown politics, they do so under female leadership, in this case that of the fierce, resourceful Marie-Sophie Laborieux.[71] They intervene collectively in "vertical" power relations. They work with allies such as Mayor Aimé Césaire and communist lawyers at City Hall to rehabilitate and solidify shanties. And with direct action, they confront the forms of domination—whether of law, bulldozer, baton or formal French—that sustain the rule of departmental administrators, *békés,* and the mulatto petty bourgeoisie. To actualize the possibilities of creole urbanism, political strategies must tackle the relations of force that subtend the state and govern the landscape. It is through such strategies that Marie-Sophie and her neighbors succeed in forcing the *béké* landowner to give up his claims to Texaco and retreat to his caste-like residential enclave.[72]

Conclusion: On the Coeval Character of the Urban

Texaco holds a number of lessons for students of worldwide urbanism. First, it shows how material networks of generalized urbanization on a worldwide scale have complicated established understandings of urban geographies, while also remaining intimately bound up with stark territorial relations of domination, some of which rearticulate earlier historical geographies and spatial oppositions. Still an overseas *département*, Martinique is today covered by the urban tapestry produced by French tourism and circuits of mass consumption. And yet, it remains shaped by the deeply racialized relations between centers of decision-making and the spaces inhabited by slave descendents. These relations recompose, in the contemporary neoliberal context, the particular, entrenched divides between the urban and rural spaces of Martinique's history as a plantation economy since the seventeenth century. The implication is clear: the boundary-defying dynamics of worldwide urbanization must be investigated in ways that reveal their role in mediating distinct historical geographies of state, capital, patriarchy and empire.

Second, *Texaco* underlines the importance of spatial imaginaries of city and country in the global urbanization process. The book chronicles urbanization as being mediated through twin processes of agricultural transformation and metropolitan expansion, inextricably tied to each other via intense processes of economic restructuring, migration and political struggle. In so doing, *Texaco* also represents the shifting symbolic terrains of political engagement. It demonstrates how the anti-urbanism that so strongly characterized struggles against slavery and colonialism reached a decisive impasse in the postwar period, during departmentalization. Yet *Texaco* also powerfully underlines the crucial importance of land struggles in (neo)colonial contexts, as Gillian Hart and Fernando Coronil have both pointed out with reference to other global regions.[73] In the novel *Texaco*, the memory of anticolonial conflict, both on the plantation and in the hills, continues to shape contemporary struggles over land, recognition and political power, but now within the urbanizing fields of departmentalized Martinique. Of course, in other contexts, land questions will be politically articulated differently in relation to urbanization. Research on worldwide urbanization must therefore proceed in a manner that is intensely attentive to the situated meaning and ongoing contestation of claims to city and countryside within the broader historical geographies of capitalist development.[74]

Third, *Texaco* provides a basis for understanding the experience of urbanism in a comparative yet global perspective. Following Harootunian, the urban(izing) world may be viewed as having a coeval character, much like that of modernity as a whole, that regime of the new that embodies fragments of the past in enduringly distinct ways. The urban thus represents a form (of centrality/difference) that is infused with qualitatively distinct historical-geographical content, and as such, it is neither a result of European diffusionism nor a function of purely relative cultural traits. As Chamoiseau's *Texaco* shows, urban Martinique is contemporaneous with and closely connected to French urbanism, and yet, the symbolic meanings of urbanity and rurality in the island's urban transformation are strongly shaped by the neocolonial dynamics that transformed the uneven geographies of its modern plantation economy. In Chamoiseau's Martinique, then, the urban is legible as a form of centrality/difference in a wider urbanization process, even as it is fraught with place-specific contradictions. In *Texaco*, tensions between real-existing differences and desires for a different urban life permeate creole urbanism itself. They express themselves as a clash between the cosmopolitan tendency towards cultural mixing and the persistently deep sociospatial divides of "racial" capitalism.

Fourth, *Texaco* speaks to the importance of "informality" as a key theme in what Ananya Roy has described as the new geographies of urban theory that are emerging in the early twenty-first century.[75] The novel treats informality as a complex modality of everyday life rather than as a simple imprint of structural forces, or, worse, as a pathology.[76] More specifically, *Texaco* demonstrates the politically contradictory character of informal urbanism. Life in Texaco embodies the profound tensions between courage and despair, agency and vulnerability, collective mobilization and individual ruthlessness. The novel valorizes the heroic efforts of survival artists and their capacity to destabilize formal Fort-de-France by invading it with fleeting, individualized, ambiguous, subsistence-driven occupations. Yet the book also clearly underscores the neocolonial character of informality and narrates the ways in which shantytown dwellers translate the unforgiving tensions in their daily life into explicitly political forms of action—organized, collective and generalizing—that intervene in the extended state of departmentalized Martinique. In effect, then, *Texaco* cautions against one-sided treatments of urban informality, whether celebratory or pessimistic.[77] It forces us to investigate how and under what conditions informal urbanisms may constitute sources for political mobilization—critical, radical or conservative—in a neoimperial, capitalist world.

Finally, *Texaco* paradoxically demonstrates the continued relevance of countercolonial critique for urban analysis. As an exponent of the creole literary movement, Chamoiseau mobilizes organic, flow-like metaphors against neocolonial urban renewal. These metaphors resonate with Deleuze and Guattari's rhizomatic vitalism. Indirectly, therefore, *Texaco* provides a suggestive reference point for evaluating some of the neo-Deleuzian currents that have recently asserted themselves in comparative urban research. Chamoiseau insists on the subversive character of informal urbanism, which he likens to a mangrove-like force—multirooted and complexly entangled. But in *Texaco* itself, the creolizing dynamics of informal urbanism cannot escape the compartmentalized confines of departmentalized Martinique. In this sense, importantly, they do not exhaust Chamoiseau's own complex narrative. For purposes of comparative research, Chamoiseau's account underscores the double limitations of hybridizing ontologies and their horizontal, deterritorializing desires: they cannot, in themselves, grasp the structured, patterned historical geographies (such as neocolonialism) they cut across; and they offer few clues about how to transform actually existing diversities, creolized or otherwise, with forms of political action that can challenge the multilayered, also vertical relations of domination and exploitation in which they are embedded.[78] Chamoiseau himself underlined the weight of neocolonialism in a recent comment on the riots and general strikes against inflation and unemployment that hit Guadeloupe and Martinique, as well as Guyane and La Réunion, in 2009. The tenacious neocolonial power structures that the movements faced in these struggles still overshadow and deform everyday life in the urbanized French Antilles.[79]

Notes

1 Henri Lefebvre, *The Urban Revolution*, trans. Robert Bonnono (Minneapolis: University of Minnesota Press, 2003).

2 Patrick Chamoiseau, *Texaco* (Paris: Gallimard, 1992).

3 Wendy Knepper, *Patrick Chamoiseau: A Critical Introduction* (Jackson: University Press of Mississippi, 2011) 25-6.

4 I have developed this argument at length in other contexts in collaboration with Kanishka Goonewardena. See Stefan Kipfer, "The Times and Spaces of (De-)colonization: Fanon's Counter-Colonialism, Then and Now," *Living Fanon*, ed. Nigel Gibson (New York: Palgrave, 2011) 93-104; Kanishka Goonewardena and Stefan Kipfer, "Creole City: Culture, Capital, and Class in Toronto," *The Contested Metropolis: Six Cities at the Beginning of the 21th Century*, ed. International Network of Urban Research and Action (Berlin: Birkhäuser, 2004) 225-30.

5 On the uses of Gramsci's notion of "translation" for such global-comparative purposes, see Stefan Kipfer and Gillian Hart, "Translating Gramsci in the Current Conjuncture," *Gramsci: Nature, Space, Politics*, eds. Mike Ekers, Gillian Hart, Stefan Kipfer and Alex Loftus (London: Blackwell, 2013) 323-43.

6 Stefan Kipfer, Christian Schmid, Kanishka Goonewardena and Richard Milgrom, eds., "Globalizing Lefebvre?" *Space, Difference, and Everyday Life: Reading Henri Lefebvre* (New York: Routledge, 2008) 285-305.

7 Lefebvre, *Urban Revolution*.

8 Ibid., 5.

9 Neil Brenner, "Theses on Urbanization," this book, Ch. 13; Neil Brenner and Christian Schmid, "The 'Urban Age' in Question," this book, Ch. 21.

10 See Kanishka Goonewardena, "The Country and the City in the Urban Revolution," this book, Ch. 15.

11 This question, which Lefebvre asked in his rural sociological work in the 1940s, set the tone for his urban investigations ("Problèmes de sociologie rurale," *Du rural à l'urbain* (Paris: Anthropos, 1970) 38-40). As ongoing debates about the state of world agriculture indicate, the question is more crucial than ever. Provided one eschews both peasant essentialist and linear-teleological perspectives on agriculture, one can see that imperial capitalism poses deep epistemological problems not only for urban studies but also for rural sociology and peasant studies. Two generations of uneven agricultural restructuring have forced researchers to differentiate agricultural from peasant and land questions and problematize the label "rural" one often attaches to all three. See Farshad A. Araghi, "Global Depeasantization, 1945-1990," *Sociological Quarterly* 36, 2 (1995) 358; and Henry Bernstein, "Once Were/Still are Peasants? Farming in a Globalising 'South,'" *New Political Economy* 11, 3 (2006) 403.

12 Neil Brenner and Christian Schmid, "The 'Urban Age' in Question," this book, Ch. 21.

13 See Samir Amin, Giovanni Arrighi, Andre Gunder Frank and Immanuel Wallerstein, *Transforming the Revolution: Social Movements and the World System* (New York: Monthly Review Press, 1990).

14 Stefan Kipfer, "Why the Urban Question Still Matters: Reflections on Rescaling and the Promise of the Urban," *Towards a Political Economy of Scale*, eds. Roger Keil and Rianne Mahon (Vancouver: University of British Columbia Press, 2009) 67-83.

15 Given the deep limitations of Lefebvre's work on colonialism and racism, we can only make this point with the help of his countercolonial contemporaries, notably Frantz Fanon. See Stefan Kipfer and Kanishka Goonewardena, "Urban Marxism and the Post-colonial Question: Henri Lefebvre and 'Colonization,'" *Historical Materialism* 21, 2 (2013) 1-41.

16 Stefan Kipfer, "Comparative Perspectives on 'Colonization' and Urbanization," Contribution to "Writing the lines of connection: Unveiling the strange language of urbanization," Nasra Abdi, Nathalie Boucher, Mariana Cavalcanti, Stefan Kipfer, Edgar Pieterse and Vyjayanthi Rao. *International Journal of Urban and Regional Research* 32, 4 (2008) 989-1027.

17 Gillian Hart, *Disabling Globalization* (Berkeley: University of California Press, 2002).

18 See our interpretation of public housing redevelopment in Paris and Toronto, which we see as a form of "colonization," that is, as a way of reorganizing territorial relations that also recomposes colonial racism (Stefan Kipfer and Kanishka Goonewardena, "Henri Lefebvre and 'Colonization': From Reinterpretation to Research," *Urban Research and Architecture: Beyond Henri Lefebvre*, eds. Ákos Moravánszky, Christian Schmid and Lukasz Stanek (forthcoming).

19 John Merrington, "Town and Country in the Transition to Capitalism" *New Left Review* 93 (1975) 71-92.

20 Lefebvre, *The Urban Revolution*, 9-16, 32-44.

21 See also David Wachsmuth, "City as Ideology," this book, Ch. 23. Of course, Lefebvre was not the only one to make this point. On Raymond Williams, see Goonewardena, "The Country and the City in the Urban Revolution," this book, Ch. 15.

22 See, for example, R. J. Holton, *Cities, Capitalism, Civilization* (London: Allen & Unwin, 1986).

23 Lefebvre, "Perspectives de la sociologie rurale," 63-78.

24 Aidan Southall, *The City in Time and Space* (Cambridge: Cambridge University Press, 1998); and Anthony King, *Urbanism, Colonialism, and the World Economy* (London: Routledge, 1990).

25 Ibn Khaldun, *The Muqaddimah: An Introduction to History*, trans. Franz Rosenthal (Princeton: Princeton University Press, 2005); Janet Abu-Lughod, *Rabat: Urban Apartheid in Morocco* (Princeton: Princeton University Press, 1980) 9-51.

26 T. G. McGee, "The Emergence of Desakota Regions in Asia: Expanding a Hypothesis," *The Extended Metropolis: Settlement Transition in Asia*, eds. Norton Ginsburg, Bruce Koppel and T. G. McGee (Honolulu: University of Hawaii Press) 3–26; and Wing-Shing Tang, "Where Lefebvre Meets the East Nowadays: Urbanisation in Hong-Kong," *Urban Research and Architecture: Beyond Henri Lefebvre*, eds. Ákos Moravánszky, Christian Schmid and Lukasz Stanek (forthcoming). See also John Friedmann, *China's Urban Transition* (Minneapolis: University of Minnesota Press, 2005). On the question of the autonomy of urban life in precolonial India and Africa, see Romila Thapar, *The Penguin History of Early India* (Delhi: Oxford, 2003); and Catherine Coquery-Vidrovitch, *Histoire des villes d'Afrique noire des origines à la colonisation* (Paris: Albin Michel, 1993).

27 Henri Lefebvre, *Elément de rythmanalyse: introduction à la connaissance des rythmes* (Paris: Syllepse, 1992).

28 Bill Freund, *The African City* (New York: Cambridge University Press, 2007) 65-141; and King, *Urbanism, Colonialism, and the World Economy*, 52.

29 C. L. R. James, "From Toussaint L'Ouverture to Fidel Castro," *The Black Jacobins*, second edition (New York: Vintage, 1989) 391-2; and King, *Urbanism, Colonialism, and the World Economy*, 31.

30 Famous arguments for regional self-determination include those by C. L. R. James, "From Toussaint L'Ouverture to Fidel Castro; Daniel Guérin, *Les Antilles Décolonisées* (Paris: Présence Africaine, 1956); and Frantz Fanon, "Blood Flows in the Antilles under French Domination," *Toward the African Revolution*, trans. Haakon Chevalier (New York: Grove, 1988) 167-9. Among the many crucial voices on crosscultural, diasporic or creole Caribbean culture, one can find Fernando Ortíz, Alejandro Carpentier, Derek Walcott and Kamau Braithwaite (as well as those discussed further below).

31 Dale W. Tomich, *Through the Prism of Slavery: Labour, Capital and the World Economy* (Lanham: Rowman and Littlefield, 2004) 120-36.

32 Neil Brenner, "Theses on Urbanization," this book, Ch. 13; and Neil Brenner and Christian Schmid, "The 'Urban Age' in Question," this book, Ch. 21. See also Roger Diener, Jacques Herzog, Marcel Meili, Pierre de Meuron, Christian Schmid, *Switzerland—An Urban Portrait*,

Volumes 1–4 (Basel: Birkhäuser, 2006); and Neil Brenner and Nikos Katsikis, "Is the Mediterranean Urban?" this book, Ch. 27.

33 Jennifer Robinson, *Ordinary Cities: Between Modernity and Development* (New York: Routledge, 2006); Ananya Roy, "The 21st-Century Metropolis: New Geographies of Theory," *Regional Studies* 43, 6 (2009) 819-30; and AbdouMaliq Simone, *City Life from Jakarta to Dakar: Movements at the Crossroads* (New York: Routledge, 2010).

34 Diane E. Davis, "Cities in Global Context: A Brief Intellectual History," *International Journal of Urban and Regional Research* 29, 1 (2005) 92-109. Of course, the conception of Marxist and countercolonial traditions advanced here goes much beyond the macropolitical economic research program that dominated work on colonial and Third World cities in the 1970s and 1980s.

35 On the specificity of literary texts, see Terry Eagleton, *Literary Theory: An Introduction* (Minneapolis: University of Minnesota Press, 2008) 9. On literature as mediation, see Fredric Jameson, *The Political Unconscious: Narrative as a Socially Symbolic Act* (Ithaca: Cornell University Press, 1981).

36 Henri Lefebvre, *Rabelais* (Paris: Les Editeurs Français Réunis, 1955) 19, 29.

37 As Kanishka Goonewardena has pointed out, following both Jameson and Lefebvre, mediation and totality as method may yield a form of "cognitive mapping" different from cartographic visualization. See "The Urban Sensorium: Space, Ideology and the Aestheticization of Politics," *Antipode* (2005) 46-71.

38 For this contrast, see the classic exchange between Fredric Jameson ("Third-World Literature in the Era of Multinational Capitalism," *Social Text* 15 (1986), 65-88) and Ajaz Ahmad (*Theory: Classes, Nations, Literatures* (London: Verso, 1992) 122-35). For a discussion, see Neil Lazarus, *The Postcolonial Unconscious* (Cambridge: Cambridge Universty Press, 2011) 89-113.

39 Lazarus, *The Postcolonial Unconscious*, 56-69.

40 Lazarus asserts a mode of criticism that eschews the one-sidedly deterritorializing orientation in postcolonial criticism (and its tendency to read the world of literature for signs of cultural flux and themes such as migrancy, hybridity, liminality, transnationality). He suggests that doing justice to urban and rural questions requires a sensitivity to themes that resonate in countercolonial, materialist-feminist and marxist registers—including mode of production, class, land, imperialism, state, patriarchy, national liberation, social revolution. He joins Priyamvada Gopal and Peter Hallward, among others, when he argues that the problem with postcolonialism does not lie in its debt to literary criticism, but in its penchant for deterritorializing literary themes. This penchant risks deflecting our attention from the territorial transformations wrought by imperial-capitalist urbanization—see also Peter Hallward, *Absolutely Postcolonial* (New York: Manchester University Press, 2001); and Priyamvada Gopal, *Literary Radicalism in India: Gender, Nation and the Transition to Independence* (London: Routledge, 2005). I am adapting these arguments to suggest that Chamoiseau's *Texaco* reveals much more about neocolonial urbanism than one would expect if one were only to emphasize the neo-Deleuzian, rhizomatic allusions in the text.

41 Harry Harootunian, *History's Disquiet: Modernity, Cultural Practice, and the Question of Everyday Life* (New York: Columbia University Press, 2000) 18, 61-2.

42 Knepper, *Patrick Chamoiseau*, 21.

43 Patrick Chamoiseau, *Ecrire en pays dominé* (Paris: Gallimard, 1997) 69-70.

44 Ibid., 224, 74.

45 Knepper, *Patrick Chamoiseau*, 10-17, 32-58.

46 See also Fanon, "Blood."

47 Patrick Chamoiseau, *La Biblique des derniers gestes* (Paris: Gallimard, 2002).

48 Jean Bernabé, Patrick Chamoiseau, and Raphaël Confiant, *Eloge de la Créolité* (Paris: Gallimard, Presses Universitaires Créoles, 1989).

49 Frantz Fanon, "West Indians and Africans," *Toward the African Revolution,* trans. Haakon Chevalier (New York: Grove, 1988) 27.

50 Bernabé, Chamoiseau and Confiant, *Eloge de la Créolité,* 37-8, 39,
66, 57-9.

51 The ambiguities of the creole movement are widely noted—see Knepper, *Patrick Chamoiseau,* 25-30, 98-9; and Margaret Majumdar, *Postcoloniality: The French Dimension* (New York: Berghan, 2007) 151-5. Christine Chivallon points out that the ambiguities in the use of créolité and creolisation reveal multiple, even contradictory meanings. See "Créolisation universelle ou singulière? Perspectives depuis le Nouveau Monde," *L'Homme* (2013) 207-8. As we have argued in another context (Toronto), invoking creolization is not always a critical act, not least because an affirmation of cultural mixing does not necessarily undermine racialized reification (Goonewardena and Kipfer, "Creole City: Culture, Capital, and Class in Toronto").

52 Bernabé, Chamoiseau and Confiant, *Eloge de la Créolité,* 13, 20, 26-8.

53 Edouard Glissant, *Le discours Antillais* (Paris: Gallimard, 1997); Bernabé, Chamoiseau and Confiant, *Eloge de la Créolité,* 51, 30-31. This take on creolization can have liberal undertones, as two books Chamoiseau coauthored with Glissant indicate. They leveled a critique at the mixophobic racism of the Sarkozy government (and its talk of "national identity") while also applauding the Barack Obama presidency as a hopeful step in the creolization of the world. See Patrick Chamoiseau and Édouard Glissant, *Quand les murs tombent: L'identité nationale hors-la-loi?* (Paris: Galaade Editions, 2007); and Patrick CHamoiseau and Édouard Glissant, *L'intraitable beauté du monde: Adresse à Barack Obama* (Paris: Galaade Editions, 2009).

54 Christiane Chivallon, *L'esclavage: du souvenir a la mémoire* (Paris: Karthala, 2012) 514-23; and Richard Price and Sally Price, "Shadowboxing in the Mangrove," *Cultural Anthropology* 12, 1 (1997) 3-36. Confiant took a hint from Césaire when he argued that *créolité* needed to be wrested from the white ruling class. See Raphaël Confiant, *Aimé Césaire: une traversée paradoxale du siècle* (Paris: Ecrire, 2006) 273. Yet, "conciliatory" notions of *créolité* and *créolisation* (Chivallon) as indeterminate maelstrom of complexity and cultural diversity are easy to find in creolist texts (Bernabé, Chamoiseau and Confiant, *Eloge de la Créolité,* 26-9, 51-5; Confiant, *Aimé* Césaire, 277; and Chamoiseau, *Ecrire en pays dominé,* 281-317).

55 Barnabé, Chamoiseau and Confiant, *Eloge de la Créolité,* 46-7.

56 On *Texaco*'s form, see Christine Chivallon and Dorothy Blair, "Images of Creole Diversity: A Reading of Patrick Chamoiseau's *Texaco*," *Cultural Geographies* 4, 3 (1997) 318-36; and Knepper, *Patrick Chamoiseau,* 112-29. I will emphasize the tensions between the postmodern aspects of creole literature and neocolonial historical forces, both of which impose their presence in *Texaco*.

57 Chamoiseau, *Texaco*, 370-3.

58 Ibid., 487; and Knepper, *Patrick Chamoiseau,* 128.

59 On spatial imaginaries in the history of African American politics, see George Lipsitz, *How Racism Takes Place* (Philadelphia: Temple University Press, 2011) 51.

60 On the role of subsistence provision, see Tomich, *Through the Prism of Slavery*, 153, 170-91. On the role of fugitives, see Robin Blackburn, *The Overthrow of Colonial Slavery 1776-1848* (London: Verso, 2011) 496-8.

61 Chamoiseau, *Texaco*, 218-22, 360, 401. The spatial dimensions of Chamoiseau's novels reveal a profound interest in the morphology and built environment of Martinique, as his illustrated works indicate (Lorna Milne, *Patrick Chamoiseau: Espaces d'une écriture antillaise* (Amsterdam and New York: Rodopi, 2006).

62 Césaire, cited in Patrice Louis, *Conversation avec Aimé Césaire* (Paris: Arléa, 2004) 51.

63 Chamoiseau, *Texaco*, 322, 454-5.

64 Chamoiseau, *Ecrire en pays dominé,* 182; and Samia Kassab-Charfi, *Patrick Chamoiseau* (Paris: Institut Français, 2012) 77.

65 Ibid., 196; Chamoiseau, *Texaco*, 89; and Chamoiseau, *Ecrire en pays dominé,* 183.

66 Chamoiseau, *Texaco*, 492.

67 Chamoiseau, *Ecrire en pays dominé,* 187, 279-80, 294.

68 Chamoiseau, *Texaco*, 304-5.

69 Ashley Dawson, "Squatters, Space and Belonging in the Underde-

veloped World," *Social Text* 22, 4 (2004) 30.

70 Chamoiseau, *Texaco*, 320.

71 As Maryse Condé has pointed out, female characters do not typically play such a central and strong role in the works by Bernabé, Chamoiseau and Confiant (cited in Price and Price, "Shadowboxing in the Mangrove," 19-20).

72 Ibid., 465-66.

73 Hart, *Disabling Globalization*; and Fernando Coronil, "Towards a Critique of Globalocentrism: Speculations on Capitalism's Nature," *Public Culture* 12, 2 (2000) 351-74.

74 Stefan Kipfer, "City, Country, Hegemony: Gramsci's Spatial Historicism," *Gramsci: Nature, Space, Politics*, eds. Mike Ekers, Gillian Hart, Stefan Kipfer, and Alex Loftus (London: Blackwell, 2013) 83-103. Symbolic urbanization can have different ramifications depending on the context. Christian Schmid's research on the complete urbanization of Switzerland had critical-polemical purchase given nationalist conceptions of the country as a non-metropolitan, rural-alpine place governed by an infinite number of small, autonomous municipalities (Diener, Herzog, Meili, de Meuron, and Schmid, *Switzerland—An Urban Portrait*; and see also Christian Schmid, "The Urbanization of Switzerland," this book, Ch. 18). Mapping extended urbanization may help problematize imbrications of anti-urbanism, nationalism and state where these are dense and often regressive (Britain, Canada, the USA). However, urbanizing political language is politically ambiguous, even in these contexts, as Schmid and Brenner have themselves indicated in a critique of "urban age" discourses and their technocratic or neoliberal interpretations of world-wide urbanization ("The 'Urban Age' in Question," this book, Ch.21). Indeed, where claims to the non-urban embody subaltern and progressive, even radical forms of resistance (Naxalite India, Zapatista Chiapas, the Brazil of the MST, and parts of indigenous North America, for example), a symbolic urbanization of politics can be positively problematic.

75 Roy, 'The 21st-Century Metropolis."

76 Simone, *City Life from Jakarta to Dakar*.

77 Compare Mike Davis—*Planet of Slums* (London: Verso, 2006)—with Richard Pithouse's critique, "A Politics of the Poor: Shack Dweller's Struggles in Durban," *Journal of Asian and African Studies* 43, 1 (2008) 63-94.

78 This point requires further discussion, of course. Beyond a full engagement with debates on assemblage urbanism and its applications (see various issues of the journal *City* in 2011), it requires a deeper comparison of Deleuzian, Bergsonian and Spinozian themes with Marxian and countercolonial traditions. For Lefebvre's musings on Deleuze, see *Le temps des méprises* (Paris: Stock, 1975) 172-3, 209-10; and Attilio Belli, "Differential Space and Hospitality: Starting from a Nietzschean Lefebvre," *Crios* 4 (2012) 41-51. For sharp notes on Marx and Deleuze, see Isabelle Garo, "Deleuze, Marx and Revolution," *Critical Companion to Contemporary Marxism*, eds. Jacques Bidet and Stathis Kouvelakis (Leiden: Brill, 2008) 605-24; and Jean-Jacques Lecercle, "Deleuze, Guattari, and Marxism," *Historical Materialism* 13, 3 (2005) 35-55.

79 Patrick Chamoiseau, "Nous avons intériorisé l'infériorité," *Le Monde Hors Série* (Jan-Feb 2010) 26-7.

**FIVE
URBAN STUDIES
AND URBAN
IDEOLOGIES**

What are the limitations and blind-spots of inherited and contemporary approaches to the urban question in relation to emergent worldwide urbanization patterns? What is the role of ideological (mis)representations of the city and the urban in historical and contemporary strategies to shape sociospatial and environmental transformations?

**Neil Brenner &
Christian Schmid
Brendan Gleeson
David Wachsmuth
Hillary Angelo &
David Wachsmuth
Andy Merrifield**

21
THE "URBAN AGE" IN QUESTION

Neil Brenner and Christian Schmid

Foreboding declarations about contemporary urban trends pervade early twenty-first-century academic, political and journalistic discourse. Among the most widely recited is the claim that we now live in an "urban age" because, for the first time in human history, more than half the world's population today purportedly lives within cities. Across otherwise diverse discursive, ideological and locational contexts, the urban age thesis has become a form of doxic common sense around which questions regarding the contemporary global urban condition are framed.

While thinkers as diverse as H.G. Wells, Patrick Geddes and Oswald Spengler had predicted the worldwide explosion of urbanization since the turn of the twentieth century, eminent demographer Kingsley Davis appears to have been the first scholar to predict, on strictly empirical grounds, the advent of an urban transition on a world scale.[1] Although urban historian Adna Weber (1899) had pioneered the statistical investigation of city population growth in diverse national contexts at the turn of the twentieth century, it was only in the 1940s that the size of the world's entire urban population became a topic of sustained research and debate among demographers, sociologists and historians.[2] Louis Wirth opened his classic 1937 text on urbanism by speculating on this question, and Kingsley Davis devoted a major portion of his career over the next several decades to its systematic empirical exploration.[3] Davis himself generally adopted a rigorously scientific tone, but his data, methods and analyses were quickly appropriated to frame speculations regarding the global urban predicament. In a typical example, in the inaugural issue of *Urban Affairs Quarterly,* architect and UN housing analyst Ernest Weissman built upon Davis' demographic data to anticipate a *fin de siècle* world-scale urban transition.[4] Adopting an apocalyptic tone that would be soon become *de rigueur* in such projections, Weissman argued that over 60 percent of the world's population would be urban as of 2000; that the resultant "urban crisis in the world" would require a "rate of construction ... over 40 times that of the past"; and that this situation would in turn "harbor dangers for human progress no less frightening than atomic warfare."[5]

UN research teams had been systematically tracking global population levels since 1951, and began to produce worldwide urban population estimates as of 1968.[6] It was only as of the mid-1980s, however, that UN analysts began to anticipate a world-scale urban transition in their regular reports on human settlement trends. An issue of a UNESCO magazine from 1984 on "The Urban Explosion" articulated an early version of this claim:

> The universalization of urbanism is a new fact. Before the year 2000, for the first time in the history of humanity, the world will have more town dwellers than country dwellers ... This demographic and urban evolution is taking place in the context of an economic crisis and the imbalance in population distribution will be accompanied by an increasing gap in the distribution of wealth.[7]

During the following decade, this prediction was repeated within the UN's regular reports on *World Urbanization Prospects*, and by the mid-1990s it had become the framing observation around which the UN Centre for Human Settlements (UN-Habitat) opened its second *Global Report on Human Settlements*.[8] During the early 2000s, a series of UN studies declared the dawn of this "urban age" to be imminent, and in 2007 two major UN agencies framed their yearly reports around the following dramatic assertions:

> In 2008 the world reaches an invisible but momentous milestone. For the first time in history, more than half its human population, 3.3 billion people, will be living in urban areas.[9]

> Sometimes it takes just one human being to tip the scales and change the course of history. In the year 2007, that human being will either move to a city or be born in one. Demographers watching urban trends will mark it as the moment in which the world entered a new millennium, a period in which, for the first time in history, the majority of the world's people will live in cities.[10]

Since the mid-2000s, the thesis of an urban age has also gained considerable international prominence and resonance through the work of The Urban Age Project, a multisited conference series and research initiative organized through the Cities Programme at the London School of Economics (LSE) and funded through a major grant from the

Deutsche Bank's Alfred Herrhausen Society. The LSE-Deutsche Bank project has to date produced two graphically striking and widely distributed volumes, *The Endless City* and *Living in the Endless City*, both of which are framed with direct reference to the UN agency demographers' assertions.[11] Although the LSE-Deutsche Bank volumes contain a range of substantive arguments and place-specific narratives regarding the contemporary global urban condition, the overarching thesis of an urban age is its central framing device. As the volumes' editors explain:

> Given that more than half the world's population is now living in cities—a number that is likely to reach 75 percent by 2050, while it was only 10 percent in 1900— … urban questions have become truly global ones, with significant consequences for the future of our planet.[12]

The urban age thesis is also prominently represented on the cover images of both LSE-Deutsche Bank volumes through a series of numbers, percentages and symbols that highlight the 50 percent global urban population threshold that is claimed to have recently been crossed (Figure 21.1). These pictorial illustrations of the urban age thesis serve as powerful, accessible branding devices through which the LSE-Deutsche Bank project represents its perspective on global urban research and practice.

But the urban age thesis is not only the province of UN demographers and the LSE-Deutsche Bank research team. Since the late 1990s, it has been embraced with increasing frequency in international urban scholarship and policy research, often by influential thinkers and practitioners, as a convenient metanarrative for framing a wide variety of investigations within or about cities. Thus, in the early 2000s, Rem Koolhaas' Harvard

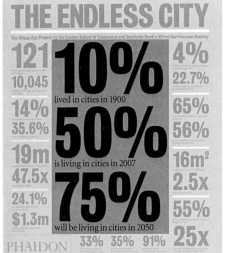
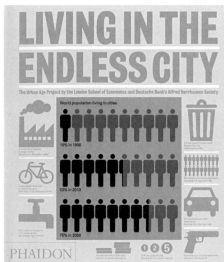

21.1 The urban age as a branding device

research team opened its *Mutations* report with a page-sized, large-font rendition of the UN's urban age thesis (Figure 21.2).

Similarly, Manuel Castells introduces a volume on urban inequality and community action in the developing world by suggesting that:

> Our blue planet is fast becoming a predominantly urban world. Probably around the time you are reading this book, we will be crossing the threshold of 50 percent of the world's population living in urban areas, up from 37 percent in 1970 … The forces behind this process of accelerated urbanization appear to be irreversible.[13]

The claim is dutifully repeated by the editors of a 2008 special issue of the respected journal *Science*: "cities are now home to more than half the world's 6.6 billion humans. By 2030, nearly 5 billion people will live in cities."[14] The trope is also repeated by researchers working for the consulting firm McKinsey & Company in a recent report on the economic role of cities: "the world is in the throes of a sweeping population shift from the countryside to the city … for the first time in history, more than half of the world's population is now living in towns and cities."[15] Even the fiercely critical urbanist Mike Davis opens *Planet of Slums* with his own formulation of the UN's declaration:

> Sometime in the next year or two, a woman will give birth in the Lagos slum of Ajegunle, a young man will flee his village in west Java for the bright lights of Jakarta, or a farmer will move his impoverished family into one of Lima's innumerable *pueblos jovenes*. The exact event is unimportant and it will pass entirely unnoticed. Nonetheless it will constitute a watershed in human history,

At the outset of the twentieth century, 10% of the population lived in cities

In 2000, around 50% of the world population lives in cities

In 2025, the number of city-dwellers could reach 5 billion individuals (two thirds of them in poor countries)

Source: Global Urban Observatory

21.2 The urban age as framing metanarrative

comparable to the Neolithic or Industrial revolutions. For the first time the urban population of the earth will outnumber the rural.[16]

As the above quotations indicate, the urban age thesis is today repeated with monotonous regularity across diverse discursive, institutional and political terrains, including by some of the most influential urban intellectuals of our time.[17] Indeed, countless additional examples of this seemingly omnipresent discursive trope could be enumerated from international organizations (including the UN, the World Bank and the World Health Organization), research reports by governmental and non-governmental agencies, international scholarly journals, magazine and newspaper articles, as well as from planning, design and consultancy documents, conference dossiers and public presentations by politicians, developers, architects and urbanists around the world. The urban age appears, in short, to have become a *de rigueur* framing device or reference point for nearly anyone concerned to justify the importance of cities as sites of research, policy intervention, planning/design practice, investment or community activism. Much like the notion of modernization in the 1960s and that of globalization in the 1980s and 1990s, the thesis of an urban age appears to have become such an all-pervasive metanarrative that early twenty-first-century readers and audiences can only nod in recognition as they are confronted with yet another incantation of its basic elements.

This chapter argues that, despite its long history in urban demography and its increasingly widespread influence in contemporary scholarly and policy discourse, the urban age thesis is a flawed basis on which to conceptualize contemporary world urbanization patterns: it is empirically untenable (a statistical artifact) and theoretically incoherent (a chaotic conception). This critique is framed against the background of postwar attempts to measure the world's urban population, whose main methodological and theoretical conundrums remain fundamentally unresolved in early twenty-first-century urban age discourse. The chapter concludes by outlining a series of methodological perspectives for an alternative understanding of the contemporary global urban condition.

Background: The Postwar Debate on Urban Population Thresholds

Since the 1950s, when systematic research on the world's urban population was first attempted, analysts wrestled with a fundamental empirical and theoretical problem: how to determine the appropriate spatial boundaries of the areas whose populations were to be measured? Given the relentless dynamics of sociospatial restructuring that have continually reworked the boundaries, scale and morphology of urbanization since the nineteenth century, it would seem futile to impose statistical or analytical fixity upon any settlement space, urban or otherwise, for even the most basic demographic calculation. Yet is not precisely such a fixity required in order to measure the size of a population at any scale? Since the earliest attempts to measure the world's urban population, this thorny issue has been confronted through diverse methodological strategies, but it has never been adequately resolved. Demographic approaches attempt to solve this fundamentally spatial problem—where to draw the boundaries of an urban(izing) territory?—by converting it into a numerical one: how many inhabitants are required, within a *predefined* jurisdictional unit, to justify its classification as "urban"? Thus emerged the debate on urban population thresholds (UPTs), which began in the 1930s and persists up to the present.[18]

Kingsley Davis was one of the earliest contributors to such debates. In one of his most influential confrontations with this challenge, derived from his pioneering efforts to construct a World Urban Resources Index with his colleagues at Columbia University, he initially worked with a rather loose, contextually embedded notion of "cities" as having substantially larger populations than smaller "towns" and surrounding areas during a given historical period.[19] While Davis suggested that the relevant UPT would vary historically, he ventured a definition of "genuine urbanization" as a situation in which "a substantial portion of the population lived in towns and cities."[20] This notion was formalized as: "$U = P_c / P_t$" (U = urbanization; P_c = population of cities; and P_t = total population); the key insight was that urbanization rates could fluctuate "independently of the absolute number of people living in cities" because they were contingent upon absolute (national) population size.[21] On this basis, reflecting on the period of capitalist modernization that ensued following the first industrial revolution, Davis introduced what is probably one of his better-known analytical maneuvers: he proposed a primary definition of cities as places containing a population of 100,000 or more, and a secondary one based on a smaller population threshold of 20,000. Following from this, in an adventurous foray into what was then a largely uncharted statistical terrain, he and his colleagues produced some of the first estimations of world urban population since 1800, as well as some forecasts regarding future trends. A half century prior to the urban age declarations of UN-Habitat and the LSE-Deutsche Bank team, Davis confidently proclaimed that "the human species is moving rapidly in the direction of an almost exclusively urban existence."[22] A decade later, he was even more specific in his prediction: "At the 1950-1960 rate the term 'urbanized world' will be applicable well before the end of the century."[23]

But why a UPT of 100,000 and not a smaller or larger one? Davis offered no theoretical justification for his choice: he simply demonstrated what such a criterion, as well as his secondary one of 20,000, would entail in empirical terms for the urban measurements in question, both at a world scale and among the major world regions.[24] From the late 1950s and throughout the 1960s, along with his colleagues at Columbia's Bureau of Applied Social Research and Berkeley's Institute of International Studies, Davis intensified his efforts to fine-tune and deploy this scheme in the interest of creating a data set whose basic units were suitable for cross-national comparisons. Despite several important technical and empirical modifications to the original formula, the specificity of such units was bracketed, or treated merely in passing. Their definition was understood primarily as a methodological challenge—as a "problem of comparability" resulting from the lack of standardized cross-national data and "the technical problems presented by this deficiency."[25]

And yet, even as Davis' statistical calculations appeared to reify the urban condition based on a relatively arbitrary UPT, he occasionally articulated a more nuanced understanding of the historical-geographical transformations that were unfolding around him. He thus concluded one of his early studies by insisting that "one must guard against assuming that cities will retain their present form."[26] In a speculative but prescient passage that pointed beyond the confines of a purely demographic approach, Davis succinctly outlined the dramatic processes of metropolitan expansion and dispersion that were already profoundly altering inherited urban and regional configurations during the early postwar period in which he was writing. In so doing, he considered the possibility that "rurality" might disappear entirely in conjunction with the consolidation of a totally "new kind of urban existence":

> At the periphery, it may well be that the metropolis and the countryside, as the one expands and the other shrinks, will merge together, until the boundaries of one sprawling conurbation will touch those of another, with no intervening pure countryside at all.[27]

In subsequent writings, Davis reiterated this acknowledgment with reference to intensifying "suburbanization and fringe development" in the "advanced societies," which he considered to cause "the entire process of urbanization [to] become ambiguous."[28] However, Davis left to others the task of reconciling such insights and predictions with his own, far more influential statistical estimations, the coherence of which hinged upon a tightly circumscribed, if not static, understanding of human settlement space.

The spatial essence of Davis' conceptualization was succinctly captured in a map produced by the UN's Division of Economic and Social Affairs, typical of several such maps produced by prominent urban social scientists during this time.[29] Embedded within a text that repeatedly underscored the limitations of extant UN urban data in light of comparability problems as well as ongoing dynamics of sociospatial and demographic restructuring, the map nonetheless represented the state of knowledge on world urbanization by adopting a uniform UPT of 20,000 for all national data sets. Continental and sub-continental land masses were coded according to national urbanization levels as recorded in 1960 (Figure 21.3).

From a contemporary point of view, three key aspects of this representation of world urbanization are particularly striking. First, the map contains no attempt to represent urban or rural areas, or even major cities. While the UN researchers considered the urban/rural divide to be a quantitative fact, demonstrable through hard demographic data, they appeared to consider the task of demarcating its precise spatial boundaries to be irrelevant, whether within or among states or continents. Consequently, the bulk of the world map is empty—the only lines of demarcation are national borders, subcontinental divisions and continental land masses. Second, the map articulates a vision of urbanization in which national territories and, through an aggregation technique, continents and subcontinents, are viewed as the natural scales of urbanization. In this manner, the UN researchers spatialized Davis' conceptualization of urbanization rates as a proportional measurement (city population growth as a proportion of national population growth). Within this framework, the geographical locations and spatial boundaries of cities and metropolitan regions were inconsequential; what mattered were their differential population sizes relative to those of larger units (national territories, subcontinents, continents). Third, although the map represents urbanization levels as an encompassing property of large-scale territories, its authors recognized that the "urban" phenomena contained within the latter were, in practice, quite heterogeneous, even in purely demographic terms. Differences among cities whose populations exceeded the specified UPT of 20,000 were not captured in the map; nor were similarities among such putatively urban locations and those settlements that, due to their lower population levels, were classified as non-urban or rural. In this way, the quest to code entire territories according to aggregate urbanization levels entailed a rather dramatic statistical and cartographic simplification of *de facto* patterns of internal sociospatial differentiation. However, for the UN-DESA research team, this homogenizing representation of national, subcontinental or continental territories was considered appropriate given the need to grasp differential urbanization patterns on a *world* scale. While contemporary urban age metanarratives are grounded upon updated data, we argue below that they have reproduced in nearly identical form the underlying conceptual orientations, geographical imaginaries and representational strategies associated with this methodologically territorialist model of world urbanization from the 1960s.

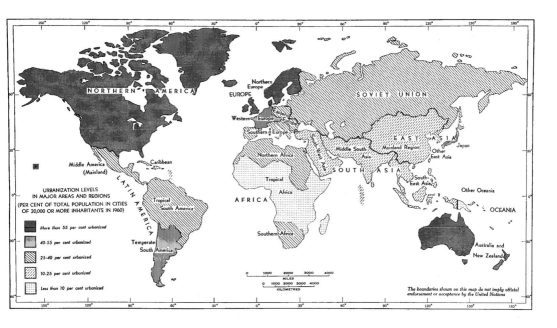

21.3 The UN applies Kingsley Davis' territorialist approach to world urbanization in 1969.

The Theoretical Imperative: Postwar Critiques of Urban Demography

In contrast to Kingsley Davis's empirical and methodological confrontation with the problem of defining the urban (population) unit, Louis Wirth had insisted on its fundamentally theoretical character nearly two decades earlier.[30] Even at that time, population-based definitions of cities had achieved such prominence among urban historians, sociologists and demographers that Wirth was motivated to open his major theoretical statement on urbanism with a frontal attack on them. In broad empirical terms, Wirth recognized the practical need for such definitions, but on a theoretical level he considered them ahistorical and indeterminate. Whether the relevant UPT was set at 2,500, 4,000, 8,000, 10,000, 25,000 or 100,000, Wirth maintained a purely population-based definition of the urban condition was "obviously arbitrary," since "no definition of urbanism can hope to be satisfying if numbers are the sole criterion."[31] Insofar as UPT definitions always relied upon the boundaries of extant local and regional administrative units, they had to be viewed as artifacts of juridical convention rather than as indicators of sociologically meaningful circumstances.

Moreover, Wirth argued, given the constant flow of people across such boundaries, population-based definitions of urban areas provided no more than a rough, and often highly misleading, indication of urbanity. Ostensibly "non-urban" settlement units located on the fringes of metropolitan centers often had more in common with the latter areas than with larger towns situated in more isolated regions. He thus curtly dismissed the demographers' apparent assumption that "urban attributes abruptly ceased to be manifested beyond an arbitrary boundary line."[32] In a formulation that is strikingly reminiscent of Marx and Engels' characterization of the capitalist world economy in *The Communist Manifesto*, Wirth insisted that the twentieth-century urban condition had to be understood with reference to thickening webs of connectivity among dispersed, differentiated, expanding and unstable constellations of metropolitan social organization, and increasingly, to an emergent worldwide horizon towards which urbanization processes were radiating:

> The degree to which the contemporary world may be said to be "urban" is not fully or accurately measured by the proportion of the total population living in cities. The influences which cities exert upon the social life of man [*sic*] are greater than the ratio of the urban population would indicate, for the city is ... the initiating and controlling center of economic, political, and cultural life that has drawn the most remote parts of the world into its orbit and woven diverse areas, peoples, and activities into a cosmos.[33]

However, despite Wirth's recognition of the spatially expansive, boundary-superseding dimensions of urbanization, his theory of urbanism was almost completely insulated from such insights, and from the largely uncharted analytical and empirical terrain they opened up.[34] His theory was instead premised on the assumption that social life continued to be—indeed, necessarily *is*—organized into coherently bounded spatial envelopes ("human settlements") that could be neatly typologized, and whose demographic properties (including his classic triad of size, density and heterogeneity) engendered distinctive forms of social behavior within those boundaries. In other words, even if UPTs could not be relied upon to classify the spatial unit in question, Wirth continued to presuppose that this unit would naturally be characterized by certain sociospatial properties—discreteness, coherence and boundedness. It is this element of Wirth's theory that has been canonized in twentieth century urban sociology, but we shall see that his critique of urban demography—and, more generally, his insistence on the fundamentally theoretical character of the urban question—are far more relevant to contemporary discourse on the world urban condition.

The Marxian interventions of the young Manuel Castells in the 1970s resonate in unexpected ways with Wirth's earlier critique of urban demography.[35] Although he dismissively characterized Wirth's theory of urbanism as a culturalist account of intra-national spatial diffusion, Castells opened *The Urban Question* with a ferocious critique of urban demography that was essentially identical to that which the Chicago School sociologist had presented four decades previously. Surveying at some length the various UPTs that had been embraced by previous urban scholars, as well as by the United States Census Bureau and the European Conference of Statistics, Castells bluntly rejected them as expressions of a "statistical empiricism."[36] Like Wirth, Castells doubted the reliability of "criteria of administrative practice" for analytical purposes, since they could not adequately capture "the acceleration of the rhythm of urbanization throughout the world."[37] Despite his otherwise sharp disagreements with Wirth, Castells likewise insisted that the only viable delimitation of the urban unit would have to occur on theoretical grounds.[38] Because of the "almost complete lack of correspondence between [juridical and] political frontiers and the specificity of their social content," as well as the constantly changing form and scale of urbanization processes under modern capitalism, Castells unwittingly concurred with Wirth that purely empirical and territorial definitions of the urban—including those associated with UPTs—would remain doomed to arbitrariness, inconsistency and nearly immediate obsolescence.[39] While the influence of the young Castells' proposed theoretical solution to this problem has long since waned, his emphasis on the intrinsically theoretical character of the urban is, like that of his erstwhile sociological antagonist Wirth, a highly salient analytical reference point for contemporary urban studies, especially in relation to the urban age thesis.

The sharply critical epithets launched by Wirth in the 1930s and redeployed by Castells in the 1970s against the use of UPTs in the study of urbanization—*arbitrary, empiricist, ahistorical*—apply with striking accuracy to contemporary versions of the urban age thesis. Accordingly, in what follows, we subject early twenty-first-century urban age discourse to a contemporary critique. This critique is intended to apply to the broad constellation of urban age references, discourses, metanarratives and projects that were surveyed at the outset of this article. However, because the UN's collection of urban data continues to be treated by "end-users ... as if it is absolute truth" and remains the authoritative bibliographical reference for contemporary proclamations of an urban age, it is given specific attention here.[40]

Urban Age as Statistical Artifact

Before returning to the theoretical critiques of urban demography developed by Wirth and Castells, some major empirical problems with the urban age thesis require attention. Foremost among these is the continued lack of agreement on what needs to be measured, and at what spatial scale, in analyses of world urbanization. Across national contexts, including in the UN's data sets, there is no standardized definition of the urban unit on which basis population size, density or other proposed indicators of urbanization levels are to be measured. In effect, the same problems of data compatibility and boundary demarcation that vexed Kingsley Davis and his colleagues in the 1950s and 1960s remain completely unresolved in the urban data sets that have been assembled regularly by the UN Population Division from the early 1970s up through the most recent revision of *World Urbanization Prospects* in 2011.[41]

The problem has been discussed extensively among UN demographers and statisticians since the 1950s, leading the organization to issue and regularly update general guidelines regarding the appropriate means to delineate localities.[42] Nonetheless, UN researchers have recurrently concluded that national statistical offices are best positioned to determine how the "urban/rural boundary" should be demarcated. The UN's continued reliance on such "state-istics" for its supposedly global urban analyses is unsurprising since, as Peter J. Taylor notes, "large-scale data collection on human activities has its origins in state needs and continues to be dominated by states."[43] To the degree that the UN has proposed a technical resolution to this conundrum, its recommendations resonate closely with those introduced by Kingsley Davis in the mature phase of his work on the topic in the late 1960s at Berkeley—namely, the combination of population size indicators with subsidiary ones pertaining to density, labor market structure and infrastructural outlays.[44] But even if implemented consistently, such strategies would still hinge on data resolved at the scale of (subnational) state administrative units, albeit now recombined in an effort to account for *de facto* patterns of agglomeration and land use within adjacent juridical units. In practice, however, even these modest proposals for enhancing cross-national data compatibility have proven impossible to implement due to the persistence of nationally specific census practices and the UN's continued reliance on such state-centric data for its analysis of urbanization. Consequently, as Champion concludes, "the bottom line is that the world's major source of published international comparative statistics on urban population—the United Nations—is still using essentially the same 'spectacles' as it adopted half a century ago."[45]

Those weathered "spectacles" have generated an extremely blurry vision of the global urban condition. In particular, the wildly divergent criteria of urbanity used by national census bureaus—whether administrative, population-based or otherwise—have profoundly skewed the UN's estimations of world urban population. Evidence of these problems is readily available in the UN's own data tables and analytical reports, and they have also been examined extensively by critical demographers.[46] As of the 2001 revision of *World Urbanization Prospects*, 109 UN member countries (38 percent) used administrative criteria as the sole or primary basis for their urban definitions.[47] This meant that some municipalities or localities were declared to be urban regardless of population size or other indicators, while others, often large and densely settled, were excluded by administrative fiat. This also meant that significant population clusters located on the peri-urban fringes of large metropolitan settlements, but positioned outside the city's official administrative borders, were often classified as "non-urban." In the same data sample, population size was used as the sole or primary criterion for 98 national urban classifications (34 percent)—but UPTs varied quite widely across national contexts, from as little as 100 in Uganda, 200 in Iceland and Sweden, or 400 in Albania, up to 2,000 in Angola and Cuba, 5,000 in Botswana and Zambia, and 10,000 in Benin and Italy.[48]

These problems have been further intensified insofar as many countries frequently change their official urban classifications, whether with reference to individual city boundaries or more general settlement typologies. Such definitional recalibrations may produce dramatic fluctuations in national and—in highly populous countries such as China, India, Brazil or Nigeria—*world* urban population levels due entirely to classificatory modifications. An equally serious problem relates to the timing of census data collection, which varies considerably across national states. Consequently, the population data used in the UN's urban analyses are often derived from divergent years. No less than 38 percent of the data used in the UN's 2001 *Urbanization Prospects* were more than eight years old (this figure was 56 percent for African countries); 43 percent of the global urban data were between three and eight years old.[49] The use of such varied indicators and classificatory schemata has generated some counterintuitive statistical outcomes. In a detailed overview, Satterthwaite lists several typical examples:

> Mexico can be said to be 74 or 67 percent urban in 2000, depending on whether urban centres are all settlements with 2500 or more inhabitants or all settlements with 15,000 or more inhabitants. China's level of urbanization in 1999 could have been 24%, 31% or 73% depending on which of three official definitions of urban populations was used … [I]n 1996, 18 percent of Egypt's population lived in settlements with between 10,000 and 20,000 inhabitants and that had many urban characteristics including significant non-agricultural economies and occupational structures. These were not classified as urban types—although they would have been in most other nations. If they were considered urban, this would mean that Egypt was much more urbanized, causing major changes to urban growth rates.[50]

The case of India adds an additional layer to the confusion: its national census bureau neglects to classify a huge number of small and medium-sized towns with populations exceeding 5,000 as urban; if it were to do so, the country's urban population would instantly exceed the fabled 50 percent threshold.[51] Many additional examples could be enumerated, but the basic problem is evident: "[T]he units in which city populations are expressed can vary across all of the relevant dimensions: across countries, within countries and over time for a given city."[52] Consequently, "the scale of the world's urban population is strongly influenced by the urban criteria used within the largest population nations."[53]

Given these systemic problems of data comparability within the UN's "state-istics," is there any salvageable *empirical* content to the notion of an urban age? Clearly, populations are growing and changing around the world; their distribution across the sociospatial landscape is constantly being reshuffled; and so too is the territorial morphology and demographic composition of politico-administrative units across the world interstate system. Thus, even if its precise contours and timing may be difficult to measure, might a world urban transition nonetheless be unfolding, signaling some qualitative shift in the "way of life" experienced by most people on the planet? Or, is the UN's famous prediction that a 50 percent global urban threshold has been crossed merely an artifact of inadequate "state-istical" procedures that assimilate fundamentally heterogeneous conditions under a crudely simplistic classificatory scheme?

From a strictly empirical point of view, there are two main strategies for confronting these questions. The first involves recognizing the limits of extant UN data collection techniques, abandoning the notion of a rigid 50 percent global UPT, and postulating a broad *trajectory* of rural-to-urban sociospatial reorganization across all or most states in the world system, thus yielding aggregate evidence of an ongoing world-scale transition. Satterthwaite suggests such a resolution as follows:

> [T]he world's level of urbanization is best understood not as a precise figure (50 percent in 2008) but as being between 45 and 55 percent, depending on the criteria used to define urban areas. It might be that the much-discussed transition to more than half the world's population living in urban areas actually took place some years ago, with its recognition delayed by various governments deliberately understating their urban populations by classifying most small urban centres as rural.[54]

In this approach, the notion of a worldwide rural-to-urban transition is preserved intact, but its precise timing and sociospatial expressions are considered to be more fluid than in official UN analyses—it is, in effect, understood as a long-term, world-scale secular trend rather than as a conjunctural transformation. However, just as in UN documentation, the urban/rural distinction and the notion of a discrete urban "unit" are perpetuated. The main modification here is a greater level of reflexivity and flexibility in interpreting the heterogeneous forms of data that are subsumed under the urban age postulate.

A second, potentially more radical strategy involves abandoning the UN's approach to data collection, with its dependence on state-centric sources, and elaborating new, spatially disaggregating approaches based on remote sensing techniques.[55] Such satellite-based data sources on urbanization have been under development since the early 1990s, and are now being mobilized with increasing technical sophistication in several US and European labs, research institutes and universities, including Columbia University's Earth Institute, the Oak Ridge National Lab and the European Environmental Agency. Major initiatives along these lines include, among others, the generation of nighttime lights satellite data by the National Oceanic and Atmospheric Administration (NOAA) and other government agencies, the development of new forms of georeferenced population data (the Global Rural-Urban-Mapping Project [GRUMP], the Gridded Population of the World [GPW], and the Landscan Global Population Database), and the elaboration of georeferenced data sets on global land cover (for instance, CORINE Land Cover and MODIS Urban Land Cover). The major attraction of such approaches is that they permit the investigation of changing patterns of agglomeration, population distribution, land cover and land use that are no longer completely reliant on national census data. The new array of mapping possibilities that flow from such techniques are productively complicating the representation of planetary urbanization processes.[56]

Whether recent developments in remote sensing might facilitate theoretically innovative interpretations of the global urban condition is a question that requires more sustained exploration elsewhere.[57] Here our concern is less to evaluate the empirical viability of the aforementioned two strategies, than to suggest that both must be subjected to the same standard of theoretical reflexivity upon which Wirth and Castells had so forcefully insisted in their critical assessments of mainstream twentieth-century urban demography. From this point of view, the limitations of the contemporary urban age thesis cannot be effectively transcended by means of empirical maneuvers alone, be it through creative reinterpretations of the UN's census-based data or through the construction of georeferenced mappings of key indicators such as population density, land cover or nighttime light patterns. Like both Wirth and Castells, we contend that an intractable theoretical problem is hidden "behind false evidence" within any purely data-based approach to urban research—namely, the *qualitative* significance of the label "urban" as an analytical basis for demarcating and interpreting sociospatial transformations.[58] In the absence of theoretical reflexivity regarding this fundamental question, even the most sophisticated forms of urban data, georeferenced or otherwise, represent no more than inchoate heaps of information—in effect, early twenty-first-century forms of the "statistical empiricism," which Castells had so ferociously decried four decades ago.[59]

Urban Age as Chaotic Conception

If the empirical edifice of the urban age thesis is unstable, its theoretical foundations are obsolescent, having been eroded through the dramatic forward-motion and geographical reorganization of the urbanization process that the thesis purports to be documenting. The basic problem is the *de facto* sociospatial fluidity and relentless dynamism of the urban phenomenon under modern capitalism: its endemic tendency to explode inherited morphologies of urbanism at all spatial scales; to create new, rescaled formations of urbanized territorial organization; and, as Wirth presciently recognized, to promote the "urbanization of the world" by intensifying sociospatial independencies across places, territories and scales.[60] The resultant, unevenly woven urban fabric is today assuming extremely complex, polycentric forms that no longer remotely approximate the concentric rings and linear density gradients associated with the relatively bounded industrial city of the nineteenth century, the metropolitan forms of urban development that were consolidated during the opening decades of the twentieth century or, for that matter, the tendentially decentralizing, nationalized urban systems that crystallized across the global North under Fordist-Keynesian capitalism.[61] As Soja and Kanai explain:

> ... urbanism as a way of life, once confined to the historical central city, has been spreading outwards, creating urban densities and new "outer" and "edge" cities in what were formerly suburban fringes and green field or rural sites. In some areas, urbanization has expanded on even larger regional scales, creating giant urban galaxies with population sizes and degrees of polycentricity far beyond anything imagined only a few decades ago ... [I]n some cases city regions are coalescing into even larger agglomerations in a process that can be called "extended regional urbanization."[62]

Merrifield characterizes the transformation in closely analogous terms:

> The urbanization of the world is a kind of exteriorization of the inside as well as interiorization of the outside: the urban *unfolds* into the countryside just as the countryside *folds* back into the city ... Yet the fault lines between these two worlds aren't defined by any simple urban-rural divide, nor by anything North-South; instead, centers and peripheries are *immanent* within the accumulation of capital itself ... Absorbed and obliterated by vaster units, rural places have become an integral part of post-industrial production and financial speculation, swallowed up by an "urban fabric" continually extending its borders, ceaselessly corroding the residue of agrarian life, gobbling up everything and everywhere in order to increase surplus value and accumulate capital.[63]

Kingsley Davis explicitly recognized these powerful tendencies towards expanded urbanization and "shrinking rurality" already in the 1950s, but he continued to conceptualize the "city" (or, eventually, the metropolitan region) as the basic unit within which the demographic dynamics of urbanization were contained, both analytically and geographically.[64] Concomitantly, like most postwar social scientists, Davis persisted in labeling the inchoate realm located "outside" or "beyond" the expanding city using the traditional notion of the rural, even though he clearly recognized that its coherence and discreteness were being steadily compromised through metropolitanization, suburbanization, megalopolis formation and various forms of industrial, residential and infrastructural decentralization. Remarkably, contemporary declarations of an urban age replicate this methodological opposition by embracing the identical conceptual framework and geographical imaginary that Davis had relied upon—in particular, the core assumption that global settlement space can and must be divided neatly into urban or rural containers. On this basis, the thesis posits an ineluctable shift of population, in both relative and absolute terms, to the urban side of this dualism.

While urban age discourse is usually put forward as a set of empirical claims regarding demographic and social trends, the latter are premised upon an underlying theoretical and cartographic framework whose core assumptions, once excavated and scrutinized, are deeply problematic. Figure 21.4 presents a stylized overview of the key elements

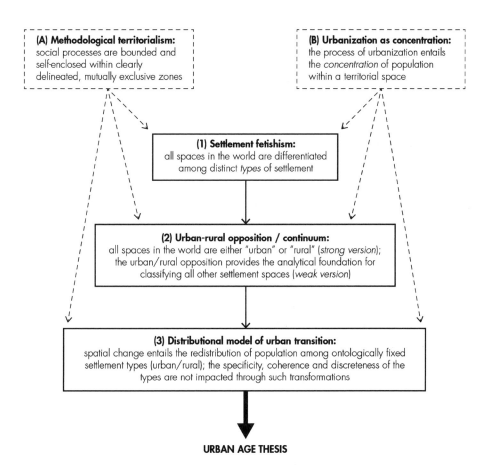

21.4 Conceptual architecture of the urban age thesis (note: dashed lines and arrows indicate a contributing influence; bold lines and arrows indicate a core theoretical assumption)

within this framework and their links to broader methodological tendencies in nineteenth and twentieth-century urban social science. Urban age discourse is articulated in diverse methodological forms and ideological guises, but the elements presented in this figure can be viewed as its theoretical foundation.

First (A), the theory is methodologically territorialist insofar as, like many entrenched traditions of twentieth-century social science, it assumes the territorial boundedness, coherence and discreteness of the spatial units in which social relations unfold.[65] Methodologically territorialist approaches presuppose rather than examine or explain the historical construction and reconstitution of territorial boundaries at any spatial scale; they ignore the historical specificity and political instrumentalities of territory as a form of sociospatial organization; and they often bracket the role of non-territorial sociospatial processes such as place-making, networking and rescaling that likewise figure crucially in the structuration of political-economic relations.[66] Second (B), urban age theory conceptualizes urbanization primarily or exclusively with reference to the concentration of population within cities or urban settlements. While this conceptualization is fairly standard within most major twentieth-century traditions of urban studies, it can be argued that such understandings bracket the ways in which the formation of cities and urban zones is premised upon and in turn triggers a range of large-scale, long-term sociospatial transformations beyond the agglomeration itself, across less densely settled places, territories and scales.[67] The aforementioned intellectual influences have impacted diverse strands of twentieth-century social science and urban studies, but in the contemporary notion of an urban age they have converged to form a particularly obfuscatory vision of the global urban condition.

As Figure 21.4 indicates, the intellectual core of the urban age thesis is (1) the methodologically territorialist assumption that the world is divided into discrete types of settlement, the classification of which facilitates understanding of major demographic and socioeconomic trends. On this basis, (2) the urban/rural opposition is presented as the analytical foundation for such classifications, an assumption that in turn hinges upon the largely uninterrogated claim (B) that certain unique social conditions obtain within cities or agglomerations that do not exist elsewhere. In most urban age discourse, this opposition is understood in zero-sum terms: all of settlement space must be classified as either urban or rural; the extension of the former thus entails the shrinkage of the latter. Although this conceptualization is most commonly traced to Wirth's influential theory of urbanism, his analysis was in fact, as noted above, reflexively attuned to the role of urbanization in intensifying interspatial interdependencies and reorganizing territorial organization across the world.[68] Occasionally, urban age arguments are grounded upon weaker versions of this assumption, with the urban/rural opposition used to demarcate a continuum of settlement types rather than being presented as an either/or ontological choice.[69] But even within this more differentiated approach, the urban/rural opposition serves as an epistemological anchor for the exercise of classifying purportedly distinct types of settlement space. Whether presented as a dualism or as a continuum, this model engenders (3) a distributional notion of urban transition in which sociospatial change is said to occur through the reapportionment of populations from rural to urban settlement types. The possibility that these entrenched envelopes of settlement space might themselves be deconstructed or transformed through the process of sociospatial restructuring is thereby excluded from consideration by definitional fiat.

Some version of this constellation of assumptions is presupposed in all contemporary versions of the urban age thesis, but they are on display in a particularly pure form in Figure 21.5, which is drawn from the most recent edition of the United Nations publication *World Urbanization Prospects*.[70] These visualizations of the UN's most recent set of urban data embody, paradigmatically, the theoretical and cartographic framework associated with the notion of an urban age. The bottom portion of Figure 21.5 represents the evolution of

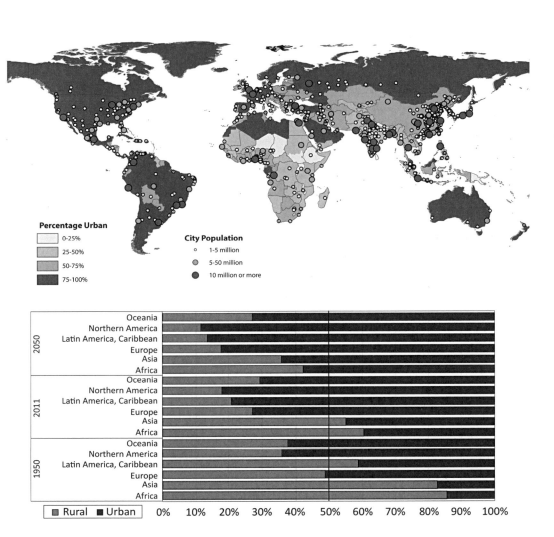

21.5 The ontological division of settlement space among urban and rural zones in recent UN data and images

global population geography through the application of a binary urban/rural classification to each global region in 1950, 2011 and 2050, respectively. In this understanding, the distribution of global population may shift, like the sands in an hourglass, but the containers in which populations are located remain ontologically fixed. The urban/rural opposition is thus conceived as a constant, unchanging feature of global settlement space, one that applies universally across social formations and time-periods. The top portion of Figure 21.5 spatializes this set of assumptions in the form of a world map depicting urbanization levels in all national territories. Despite its updated data and its slightly modified visualization technique, this map is analytically identical to that produced by UN researchers in 1969 (see Figure 21.3 page 317).[71] As in the 1960s, urbanization is still represented as a property of national territories, which are once again graphically coded according to their respective percentage levels of urban (non-rural) population. While the top portion of Figure 21.5 also depicts the locations and population levels of some of the world's largest cities, its main purpose is to classify national territories using the dualistic urban/rural cartography outlined above.[72]

In the 1950s, the urban/rural dualism offered a conceptual reference point for empirically oriented UN demographers concerned to understand observed differentials in infant mortality and fertility rates among populations in different settlement types.[73] Today, however, this dualism, and the broader concept of an urban age to which it has been attached, have come to serve a broader academic and sociocultural purpose. The sense that cities are changing and growing with unprecedented speed and intensity; that more of the world's habitable territory is becoming "urban"; that the erstwhile countryside is being eroded or degraded; and that these tendencies represent something of a milestone in global human development—these sweeping generalizations, however simplistic, appear to offer a workable "cognitive map" for navigating a rapidly restructuring worldwide sociospatial landscape defined by turbulence, uncertainty and rampant crisis tendencies, at once social, spatial and environmental.[74] Consequently, the popularity of the urban age thesis, whether in scholarly, political and corporate discourse or in everyday life, would appear to be connected to the ways in which, however crudely, it gestures towards naming and beginning to interpret what are indeed widely experienced as profound, even epochal, transformations of urban sociospatial organization around the world.

Our claim, however, is that this cognitive map obfuscates much more than it reveals regarding contemporary urbanization processes. Particularly in light of the wide-ranging and disruptive sociospatial transformations outlined by Soja and Kanai and Merrifield in the passages quoted above, the theoretical cartography associated with the notion of an urban age functions as a chaotic conception, in the precise technical sense defined by Sayer: "[it] divides the indivisible and/or lumps together the unrelated and the inessential, thereby 'carving up' the object of study with little or no regard for its structure and form."[75]

First, the urban age thesis *divides the indivisible* insofar as it treats urban and rural zones as fundamentally distinct, thereby ignoring the pervasive imprint of urbanization processes on settlement spaces that, whether based on criteria of population size, administrative classification or otherwise, are officially categorized as rural. The invocation of an analytical or ontological divide among these purportedly distinct types of spaces prevents exploration of their structuration by some of the same political-economic processes, including capital accumulation, state regulation, the privatization of common resources (including land), financialization, migration and socioenvironmental degradation/transformation. Once such an analysis is undertaken, the use of the designation "rural" becomes highly problematic, at least as a category of social scientific analysis.[76] Increasingly, the urbanization process has become a global condition rather than simply a "way of life" that is confined to certain types of settlement space as opposed to others.[77] This emergent planetary formation of urbanization is deeply uneven and variegated, and emergent patterns and pathways of sociospatial differentiation within and across this worldwide urban fabric surely require sustained investigation at various geographic scales.[78] However, because of its reliance on a long outdated urban/rural dualism, the notion of an urban age is a crude instrument for this purpose.

Second, the urban age thesis *lumps together the unrelated and the inessential* due to its inadequate specification of what specific phenomena are meant to be contained within each term of the urban/rural dualism. As used within urban age discourse, both of these categories are generalized to the point of meaninglessness; each refers to extremely heterogeneous conditions within and among national territories. For the most part, the notion of the rural used within urban age discourse is simply a "black box": it refers to the residual zones of settlement that are purportedly "not urban," but this is done without specifying what features these spaces might share across contexts, whether in terms of population size, density or composition, land use, labor markets, or any other indicators. More problematically still, in contrast to this pervasive black-boxing of the rural, the notion of the urban used within urban age discourse is radically *over*specified. The concept of the urban associated with the urban age thesis is used to refer to so many divergent conditions of population, infrastructure and administrative organization that it loses any semblance of analytical coherence. While the notion of an urban age is generally meant to imply a worldwide shift towards an encompassing, worldwide urban condition, its evidentiary base encompasses a vast spectrum of settlement conditions, ranging from small and medium-sized towns to regional centers, metropolitan cores, large city-regions and sprawling megacities with populations exceeding 10 million.[79] Yet there "is little in common between small market towns in areas with stagnant economies in (say) Argentina, China and India and Buenos Aires, Shanghai and Delhi."[80] Given the sweeping heterogeneity of settlement configurations and transformative processes that are subsumed under the notion of an urban age, it is highly questionable whether any meaningful theoretical content can be ascribed to it.

We thus return to the theoretically reflexive orientation towards the urban question emphasized by both Wirth and Castells many decades ago. As both authors insisted, without reflexive theoretical specification, the concept of the urban will remain an empty abstraction devoid of substantive analytical content and thus a blunt tool for deciphering or illuminating the nature of the conditions, processes and transformations to which it is applied. Unless the proponents of the urban age thesis can explicate what specific phenomena—sociospatial, demographic, administrative, or otherwise—unify the ostensibly unrelated or inessentially connected zones of settlement that obtain with its sweepingly vague categorization of settlement space, then this crucial methodological condition has not been met; the term will remain no more than an empty abstraction.

Conclusion: Towards an Investigation of Planetary Urbanization

Even when they are grounded upon chaotic conceptions, hegemonic understandings of major social processes may have wide-ranging impacts, for they mediate expert and popular discourse, representation, imagination and practice in relation to matters of considerable consequence for the organization of political-economic relations. Accordingly, as Wachsmuth argues, the ideological dimension of urbanization requires sustained analysis and deconstruction by critical urban theorists, especially under conditions in which entrenched formations of sociospatial organization are radically reorganized to produce new landscapes of urbanization whose contours remain blurry, volatile and confusing, and are therefore particularly subject to fetishized forms of narration, representation and visualization.[81]

It would be extremely valuable, therefore, to track the ways in which the notion of an urban age has been disseminated and naturalized among powerful actors and institutions across the world urban system, and has, by consequence, influenced any number of policies related to the global urban condition.[82] For instance, Satterthwaite suggests that the skewed data associated with the urban age thesis have had particularly problematic ramifications in policy debates related to urban poverty, public health and greenhouse emissions in the global South.[83] One could also readily envision a range of related policy areas, including labor markets, housing, education, transportation, infrastructure development and energy provision, in which the theoretical precepts associated with this thesis (and, indeed, any other model that rigidly delineates a rigid urban/rural divide) have engendered distorted, confused and misleading understandings of the multiscalar forces shaping contemporary urbanization patterns around the world.[84]

A more wide-ranging analysis of the practical effectivities of the urban age thesis would be of considerable interest and import at every conceivable spatial scale, not least for those committed to promoting more socially just and ecologically viable forms of urbanization in both North and South. For the moment, however, such an endeavor has only just begun to be pursued in relation to specific places and policy regimes in which the urban age thesis has garnered explicit attention among policy makers, for instance due to the intense local publicity generated through the LSE-Deutsche Bank's traveling conference initiatives in southern megacities.[85]

Can an alternative cognitive map of emergent urbanizing formations be constructed, one that supersedes the manifold limitations and blind-spots associated with urban age discourse and other contemporary ideologies of urbanization? The urgency of this task is blunted by the entrenched empiricism that dominates so much of contemporary urban social science and policy discourse, leading researchers to emphasize concrete investigations and associated visualizations rather than interrogating the underlying conceptual assumptions and cartographic frameworks around which they are organized. This problem has been long recognized by radical spatial theorists, but it continues to impede theoretical innovation in early twenty-first-century urban studies due to the persistence of stubbornly entrenched spatial ideologies that treat the urban as a pregiven, self-evident formation to be investigated or manipulated. However, as Ananya Roy has argued in a powerful critique of the hegemony of Euro-American urban theories: "It is time to blast open theoretical geographies, to produce a new set of concepts in the crucible of a new repertoire of cities."[86] In a similar vein, Jennifer Robinson has recently called for a "rich and fragmented array of ongoing conversations across the world of cities" that will serve to unsettle parochially defined theoretical certainties.[87] We strongly support these calls to supersede inherited urban epistemologies, but wish to connnect them, in particular, to a new conceptualization of urbanization processes both within and beyond those settlement spaces that are demarcated as "cities."

While it is not possible here to elaborate our alternative approach to such an endeavor in detail, we conclude by outlining a series of epistemological guidelines that follow from the preceding critique of the urban age thesis. Our own current work on planetary urbanization is grounded upon these precepts, but we believe they could productively inform a variety of heterodox engagements with the urban question under early twenty-first century conditions.

- *The urban and urbanization are theoretical categories.* The urban is not a pregiven, self-evident reality, condition or form—its specificity can only be delineated in theoretical terms, through an interpretation of its core properties, expressions or dynamics. It is essential, therefore, that twenty-first-century debates on urban questions reflexively embrace the need for conceptual abstractions related to the changing form and geography of urbanization processes. Without this recursive work of theory, the field of urban studies will be poorly equipped to decipher the nature and implications of the complex, multiscalar transformations they aspire to understand. Urban age discourse represents a particularly egregious expression of the latter tendency and its associated intellectual and cartographic hazards.

- *The urban is not a universal form but a historical process.* In contrast to inherited concepts of the urban as a definitionally fixed unit or static form, its meanings and expressions must be understood to evolve historically in relation to broader patterns and pathways of global capitalist development. Thus conceived, urbanization is a process of continual sociospatial transformation, a relentless "churning" of settlement types and morphologies that encompasses entire territories and not just isolated "points" or "zones" within them. As Lefebvre insisted, the study of urban forms must be superseded by the investigation of urbanization *processes* at all spatial scales.[88]

- *The sociospatial dimensions of urbanization are polymorphic, variable and dynamic.* Much of twentieth-century urban studies embraced a methodologically territorialist cartography in which the urban was treated as a distinct, relatively bounded settlement type, assumed to be separate from purported non-urban zones located beyond or outside it. Urban age discourse represents only the most recent, influential exemplar of this long entrenched methodological tendency. Such territorialist and settlement-based understandings of cityness had a basis in the morphologies of industrial and metropolitan urbanization during the nineteenth and twentieth centuries, but even then they represented only partial, one-sided depictions of a polymorphic, variable and relentlessly dynamic landscape of urbanization. However, given the accelerated differentiation of urban landscapes across the world since the 1980s, it is clear that settlement-based understandings of the urban condition have now become obsolete. The urban cannot be plausibly understood as a bounded, enclosed site of social relations that is to be contrasted to non-urban zones or conditions. It is time, therefore, to explode our inherited assumptions regarding the morphologies, territorializations and sociospatial dynamics of the urban condition.

- *Urbanization involves both concentration and extension.* Once urbanization is seen as a process that transforms diverse zones of the world, another entrenched methodological tendency must be superseded—namely, the exclusive or primary focus of urban scholars on agglomerations, the densely settled zones (cities, metropolitan regions, megacity regions, and so forth) in which population, economic activities and infrastructural systems are clustered. In this model, which underpins not only the urban age thesis but much of twentieth-century urban theory, the non-urban realm is interpreted simply as an empty field, as an indeterminate outside that serves to demarcate the urban condition from its purportedly exurban or rural "other." However, throughout the history of modern capitalism, this terrain has been neither empty nor disconnected from the process of agglomeration; it has actually evolved dynamically through a complex, constantly thickening web of economic, social and ecological connections to the heartlands of urban concentration across every zone of the world economy. Though largely ignored or relegated to the analytic background by urban theorists, such transformations—materialized in densely tangled circuits of labor, commodities, cultural forms, energy, raw materials and nutrients—

simultaneously radiate outwards from the immediate zone of agglomeration and implode back into it as the urbanization process unfolds. Within this extended, increasingly worldwide field of urban development and infrastructural equipment, agglomerations form, expand, shrink and morph continuously, but always via dense webs of relations to other places, whose historical patterns and developmental pathways are in turn mediated ever more directly through their modes of connection/ disconnection to the hegemonic zones of urban concentration. These observations suggest a methodological starting point for a radically reinvented approach to (capitalist) urbanization: the development of the concept of *extended urbanization* to complement and reposition the emphasis on agglomeration processes that has long underpinned urban research.[89] Such a concept, we believe, has major implications for periodizations of urbanization since the emergence of industrial capitalism, and it also has considerable potential to guide research on the early twenty-first century urban condition.

- *Urbanization has become a planetary phenomenon.* Today, urbanization is a process that affects the entire world and not just isolated parts of it. The urban represents an increasingly worldwide, if unevenly woven, fabric in which the sociocultural and political-economic relations of capitalism are enmeshed. This situation of planetary urbanization means that even sociospatial arrangements and infrastructural networks that lie well beyond traditional city cores, metropolitan regions, urban peripheries and peri-urban zones have become integral parts of a worldwide urban condition.[90] Concomitantly, the urban-rural opposition that has long underpinned the epistemology of urban concepts has been profoundly destabilized, at once in social science, planning practice and in everyday life. There is, in short, no longer any *outside* to the urban world; the non-urban has been largely internalized within an uneven yet planetary process of urbanization. Under these conditions, the urban-rural binarism is an increasingly obfuscatory basis for deciphering the morphologies, contours and dynamics of sociospatial restructuring under early twenty-first century capitalism.

- *Urbanization produces constantly new differentiations.* Urbanization is a process of constant transformation and leads continuously to the production of new urban configurations and constellations. Zones of urbanization, and the urban condition more generally, should not be treated as homogeneous—neither in the contemporary era nor during earlier historical periods. Rather, urbanization processes produce a wide range of sociospatial conditions across the world that require contextually specific analysis and theorization. As discussed above, the urban age thesis encloses each side of the urban/rural divide within an analytical black box. It focuses on the distribution of population among the two boxes rather than exploring their substantive contents, conditions of emergence or developmental pathways. As such, each term within the dualism is no more than an empty abstraction since neither is adequately attuned to the massive patterns of differentiation and variegation that characterize urbanization processes. Consequently, and rather urgently, these black boxes must now be opened, and their contents explored. Today's planetary urban universe reveals a wide variety of differentiated and polarized situations, conditions and contestations that require contextually specific yet theoretically reflexive investigation.

• *A new vocabulary of urbanization is needed.* Inherited analytical vocabularies and cartographic methods do not adequately capture the changing nature of urbanization processes, and their intensely variegated expressions, across the contemporary world. Emergent patterns and pathways of planetary urbanization therefore require the development of new analytical approaches, methods and concepts, including experimental and speculative ones, as well as new visualizations of evolving sociospatial and sociometabolic conditions. In short, a new lexicon of urbanization processes and forms of territorial differentiation is required in order to grasp the unstable, rapidly changing geographies of early twenty-first-century capitalism.[91]

The analytic maneuvers proposed here are no doubt contentious, and they surely require further, more detailed elaboration elsewhere. While many readers may object to the admittedly radical methodological consequences we have derived from our critique of urban age discourse, we hope that our proposals will help stimulate a wider debate regarding how best to conceptualize the contemporary global urban condition. From our point of view, such a debate is long overdue not only among urbanists, but among all scholars, practitioners and activists concerned to understand, and thereby to reshape, the sociospatial fabric of our shared planetary existence.

Notes

1   David Madden, "City Becoming World: Nancy, Lefebvre, and the Global-Urban Imagination," this book, Ch. 30; and Kingsley Davis, "The World Demographic Transition," *American Journal of Sociology* 60, 5 (1955) 429-37.

2   Adna F. Weber, *The Growth of Cities in the Nineteenth Century: a Study in Statistics"* (New York: Macmillan, 1899); and Kingsley Davis, *World Urbanization: 1950–1970, Volume II: Analysis of Trends, Relationships and Development,* Population Series No. 9 (Berkeley: Institute of International Studies, University of California, 1972).

3   Louis Wirth, "Urbanism as a Way of Life," *Classic Essays on the Culture of Cities,* ed. Richard Sennett (Engelwood Cliffs: Prentice Hall, 1969 [1937]) 144; Kingsley Davis, "The World Demographic Transition," *Annals of the American Academy of Political and Social Science* 237, 1 (1945) 1-11; Davis, "The World Demographic Transition"; Kingsley Davis, *The World's Metropolitan Areas* (Berkeley and Los Angeles: International Urban Research, Institute for International Studies, University of California Press, 1959); Kingsley Davis, "The Urbanization of the Human Population," *Scientific American* 213, 3 (1965) 40-53; Kingsley Davis, *World Urbanization: 1950–1970, Volume I: Basic Data for Cities, Countries, and Regions,* Population Monograph Series No. 4 (Berkeley: Institute of International Studies, University of California, 1969); and Davis, *World Urbanization: 1950–1970, Volume II.*

4   Ernest Weissman, "The Urban Crisis in the World," *Urban Affairs Quarterly* 1 (1965) 65-82.

5   Ibid., 66, 69, *passim.*

6   Davis, *World Urbanization: 1950–1970, Volume II,* 5.

7   Edouardo Glissant, "The Urban Explosion," *The UNESCO Courier* 38 (1984) 24, 25.

8   United Nations Human Settlement Programme (UN-Habitat), *An Urbanizing World: Global Report on Human Settlements, 1996* (Oxford: Oxford University Press for UN-Habitat, 1996) xxi.

9   United Nations Population Fund (UNFPA), *State of World Population 2007: Unleashing the Potential of Urban Growth* (New York: United Nations Population Fund, 2007) xxi; http://www.unfpa.org/swp/2007/english/introduction.html (accessed 14 June 2012).

10 United Nations Human Settlement Programme (UN-Habitat), *The State of the World's Cities Report 2006/2007—30 years of Shaping the Habitat Agenda* (London: Earthscan for UN-Habitat, 2007).

11 Ricky Burdett and Deyan Sudjic, eds., *The Endless City* (London: Phaidon, 2006); and Ricky Burdett and Deyan Sudjic eds., *Living in the Endless City* (London: Phaidon, 2010).

12 Ricky Burdett and Phillip Rode, "The Urban Age Project," *The Endless City,* eds. Ricky Burdett and Deyan Sudjic (London: Phaidon, 2006) 8.

13 Manuel Castells, "Preface," *Livable Cities? Urban Struggles for Livelihood and Sustainability,* ed. Peter Evans (Berkeley: University of California Press, 2002) ix.

14 Caroline Ash, Barbara R. Jasny, Leslie Roberts, Richard Stone, and Andrew M. Sugden, "Reimagining Cities," *Science* 319, 5864 (2008) 739.

15 McKinsey Global Institute, *Urban World: Mapping the Economic Power of Cities* (London: McKinsey & Company, 2011) 3.

16 Mike Davis, *Planet of Slums* (London: Verso, 2006) 1.

17 Brendan Gleeson, "Critical Commentary. The Urban Age: Paradox and Prospect," *Urban Studies* 49, 5 (2012) 931-43.

18 Leo F. Schnore, "Urbanization and Economic Development: the Demographic Contribution," *American Journal of Economics and Sociology* 23, 1 (1964) 37-48; David E. Bloom, David Canning, Günther Fink, Tarun Khanna, and Patrick Salyer, "Urban Settlement: Data, Measures, Trends," *Urbanization and Development: Multidisciplinary Perspectives*, eds. Jo Beall, Basudeb Guha-Khasnobis and Ravi Kanbur (Oxford: Oxford University Press, 2010); and Mark Montgomery, "The Demography of the Urban Transition: What We Know and Don't Know," *The New Global Frontier*, eds. George Martine, Gordon McGranahan, Mark Montgomery and Rogelio Fernandez-Castilla (London: Earthscan, 2010).

19 K. Davis, "The Origins and Growth of Urbanization in the World"; Kingsley Davis and Hilda Hertz Golden, "Urbanization and the Development of Pre-industrial Areas," *Economic Development and Cultural Change* 3, 1 (1954) 6-26.

20 Davis, "The Origins and Growth of Urbanization in the World," 433.

21 Davis and Hertz Golden, "Urbanization and the Development of Pre-industrial Areas," 7.

22 Davis, "The Origins and Growth of Urbanization in the World," 434.

23 Davis, "The Urbanization of the Human Population," 52; see also Davis, *World Urbanization 1950–1970, Volume II*, 121.

24 Davis, "The Origins and Growth of Urbanization in the World," 434, *passim*.

25 Jack P. Gibbs and Leo F. Schnore, "Metropolitan Growth: an International Study," *American Journal of Sociology* 66, 2 (1960) 160; and Davis, *The World's Metropolitan Areas*, 1-2.

26 Davis, "The Origins and Growth of Urbanization in the World," 437.

27 Ibid.

28 Davis, "The Urbanization of the Human Population," 44.

29 See Homer Hoyt, "World Urbanization," *According to Hoyt: 50 Years of Homer Hoyt* (Washington: Homer Hoyt, 1966 [1962]) 329; Brian J. L. Berry, "City Size Distributions and Economic Development," *Economic Development and Cultural Change* 9, 4 (1961) 580 and Figure 1 in Berry's text, which built extensively on Kingsley Davis' data and methods. See also United Nations Department of Economic and Social Affairs (UN-DESA), *Growth of the World's Urban and Rural Population, 1920–2000*, Population Studies, 44 (New York: United Nations, 1969).

30 Wirth, "Urbanism as a Way of Life."

31 Ibid., 145.

32 Ibid., 146.

33 Karl Marx and Friedrich Engels, "The Communist Manifesto," *Karl Marx: Selected Writings*, second edition, ed. David McLellan (London: Oxford University Press, 2000 [1848]) 248-9; and Wirth, "Urbanism as a Way of Life," 143-4.

34 Neil Brenner, "Louis Wirth's Radiant Urbanism: a Contribution to the Investigation of World Urbanization," Working Paper (Cambridge: Urban Theory Lab, Harvard University, 2013).

35 Manuel Castells, *The Urban Question: a Marxist Approach* (Cambridge: MIT Press, 1977 [1972]).

36 Ibid., 10.

37 Ibid., 11, 15.

38 Ibid., 101-12.

39 Ibid., 235.

40 Barney Cohen, "Urban Growth in Developing Countries," *World Development* 32, 1 (2004) 25. The UN has regularly updated its data and, to a lesser extent, its methods of data collection in various ways since the late 1960s (for an overview see Tony Champion, "Lest We Re-invent the Wheel: Lessons From Previous Experience," *New Forms of Urbanization*, eds. Tony Champion and Graeme Hugo [London: Ashgate, 2004]). The most recent collection of UN urban data is available in the 2011 revision of its series, *World Urbanization Prospects* (United Nations Department of Economic and Social Affairs, Population Divison (UN-DESA-PD), *World Urbanization Propects, the 2011 Version* [New York: United Nations, 2012]); an online version of the report provides the raw data files as well as a variety of maps and graphs based on the latter (http://esa.un.org/unup/). While this discussion subjects several key aspects of the UN's approach to severe criticism, it should be acknowledged that the organization's long-term commitment to the collection of worldwide urban data has contributed a valuable starting point for analyses of planetary urbanization patterns. Despite the problems discussed below, the most recent version of *World Urbanization Prospects* includes useful data on city-size distributions and city population levels in some of the world's largest metropolitan regions since the 1970s. The challenge, we argue, is to devise new methods of data collection and analysis that more effectively illuminate the long-term trajectory of sociospatial restructuring under capitalism. Confronting this challenge entails a significant labor of *(re)conceptualization* in relation to the fundamental nature of urbanization itself. See Neil Brenner and Christian Schmid, "Planetary Urbanization," this book, Ch. 11; Neil Brenner, "Theses on Urbanization," this book, Ch. 13; Christian Schmid, "Patterns and Pathways of Global Urbanization: Towards Comparative Analysis," this book, Ch. 14; Christian Schmid, "Networks, Borders, Differences," this book, Ch. 4; Roger Diener, Jacques Herzog, Marcel Meili, Pierre de Meuron, and Christian Schmid, *Switzerland—An Urban Portrait* (Zurich: Birkhäuser, 2006); and Henri Lefebvre, *The Urban Revolution*, trans. Robert Bononno (Minneapolis, University of Minnesota, 2003 [1970]). To the degree that influential authors and organizations appropriate the UN's data and analyses uncritically, as if they offered an unmediated window into "raw facts" of the global urban condition, the need for this labor of reconceptualization is obscured.

41 United Nations Department of Economic and Social Affairs (UN-DESA-PD), *World Urbanization Prospects, the 2011 Version*.

42 For a detailed overview, see Champion, "Lest We Re-invent the Wheel."

43 Peter J. Taylor, *A Brief Guide to Quantitative Data Collection at GaWC, 1997-2001* (Loughborough: Globalization and World Cities Research Network: Loughborough University, 2002) 1. http://www.lboro.ac.uk/gawc/guide.html (accessed 30 May 2012).

44 In the late 1960s, researchers from the UN Population Division appear to have directly appropriated the new measurement techniques that were being developed in Davis' research lab during this time. In a terse footnote to the book-length culmination of his decades-long investigation, Davis (*World Urbanization 1950–1970 Volume II*, 6, footnote 6) indicates as much, suggesting that UN statisticians had adopted his Berkeley research team's methodological innovations without proper attribution after several visits by high-ranking UN officials to his lab.

45 Champion, "Lest We Re-invent the Wheel," 41.

46 Philippe Bocquier, "World Urbanization Prospects: An Alternative to the UN Model of Projection Compatible with Urban Transition Theory," *Document de Travail DIAL* (Paris: Unité de Recherche CIPRÉ, 2004); Champion, "Lest We Re-Invent the Wheel"; Cohen, "Urban Growth in Developing Countries"; David Satterthwaite, "The Transition to a Predominantly Urban World and its Underpinnings," *Human Settlements* (London: International Institute for Environment and Development / IIED, 2007); David Satterthwaite, "Urban Myths and the Mis-use of Data the Underpin Them," *Urbanization and Development*, eds. Jo Beall, Basudeb Guha-Khasnobis and Ravi Kanbur (Oxford: Oxford University Press, 2010); Montgomery, "The Demography of Urban Transition"; and Tony Champion and Graeme Hugo, eds., *New Forms of Urbanization* (London: Ashgate, 2004).

47 United Nations Department of Economic and Social Affairs

Population Division, *World Urbanization Prospects, the 2001 Revision* (New York: United Nations, 2002).

48 Bloom, Canning, Fink, Khanna, and Salyer, "Urban Settlement," 22-3; Martin Brockerhoff, "An Urbanizing World," *Population Bulletin* 55, 3 (2000) 6; Cohen, "Urban Growth in Developing Countries," 26; and Hirotsugu Uchida and Andrew Nelson, "Agglomeration Index: Towards a New Measure of Urban Concentration," *Urbanization and Development*, eds. Jo Beall, Basudeb Guha-Khasnobis, and Ravi Kanbur (Oxford: Oxford University Press, 2010) 41. The remaining 28 percent of countries used economic criteria, other criteria, or failed to list their basis for classification (see Bloom, Canning, Fink, Khanna, and Salyer, "Urban Settlement," 23; and Champion, "Lest We Re-invent the Wheel," 34-35).

49 Cohen, "Urban Growth in Developing Countries," 27.

50 Satterthwaite, "Urban Myths," 84, 85.

51 Ibid., 84.

52 Mark Montgomery and Deborah Balk, "The Urban Transition in Developing Countries," *Global Urbanization*, eds. Eugenie Birch and Susan Wachter (Philadelphia: University of Pennsylvania Press, 2011) 93.

53 Satterthwaite, "Urban Myths and the Mis-use of Data that Underpin Them," 85.

54 Ibid., 85.

55 David Potere and Annemarie Schneider, "A Critical Look at Representation of Urban Areas in Global Maps," *Geojournal* 69 (2007) 55-80; David Potere, Annemarie Schneider, Schlomo Angel, and Danial Civco, "Mapping Urban Areas on a Global Scale: Which of the Eight Maps Now Available is More Accurate?" *International Journal of Remote Sensing* 30, 24 (2009) 6531-58; and Montgomery and Balk, "The Urban Transition in Developing Countries."

56 Shlomo Angel, "Making Room for a Planet of Cities," *PolicyFocus Report* (Cambridge: Lincoln Institute of Land Policy, 2011); and Potere and Schneider, "A Critical Look at Representation of Urban Areas in Global Maps."

57 Neil Brenner and Nikolaos Katsikis, *Is the World Urban? Towards a Critique of Geospatial Ideology* (Moscow: Strelka Press, 2014).

58 Castells, *The Urban Question*, 234.

59 Ibid., 10.

60 Wirth, "Urbanism as a Way of Life," 143-4.

61 Lefebvre, *The Urban Revolution*; Edward W. Soja and J. Miguel Kanai, "The Urbanization of the World," this book, Ch. 10; Edward Soja, "Regional Urbanization and the End of the Metropolis Era," this book, Ch. 19; Andy Merrifield, "The Right to the City and Beyond," this book, Ch. 31; Neil Brenner and Christian Schmid, "Planetary Urbanization," this book, Ch. 11; Christian Schmid, "Patterns and Pathways of Global Urbanization: Towards Comparative Analysis," this book, Ch. 14; Christian Schmid, "Networks, Borders, Differences," this book, Ch. 4 ; Neil Brenner, "Theses on Urbanization," this book, Ch. 13; and Peter Hall and Kathy Pain, *The Polycentric Metropolis* (London: Earthscan, 2006).

62 Edward W. Soja and J. Miguel Kanai, "The Urbanization of the World," this book, Ch. 10, page 146.

63 Merrifield, "The Right to the City and Beyond," this book, Ch. 31, pages 524, 525.

64 Davis, "The Origins and Growth of Urbanization in the World," 437.

65 Peter Taylor, "The State as Container: Territoriality in the Modern World-System 1994," *Progress in Human Geography* 18, 2 (1994) 151-62; and Neil Brenner, *New State Spaces* (New York: Oxford University Press, 2004).

66 Stuart Elden, "Land, Terrain, Territory," *Progress in Human Geography* 34 (2010) 799-817; Bob Jessop, Neil Brenner, and Martin Jones, "Theorizing Socio-Spatial Relations," *Environment and Planning D: Society and Space* 26, 3 (2008) 389-401.

67 Herbert Gans, "Some Problems of and Futures for Urban Sociology," *City and Community* 8, 3 (2009) 211-9; Edward Soja, *Postmetropolis* (Cambridge: Blackwell, 2000); Neil Brenner and Christian Schmid, *Towards a Theory of Extended Urbanization*, (Urban Theory Lab, Harvard GSD and ETH Zurich, 2012); Soja, "Regional Urbanization and the End of the Metropolis Era," this book, Ch. 19; Alan Berger, *Drosscape* (New York: Princeton Architectural Press, 2006); and Brenner, "Theses on Urbanization," this book, Ch. 13.

68 Wirth, "Urbanism as a Way of Life."

69 See, United Nations Department of Economic and Social Affairs (UN-DESA), "Growth of the World's Urban and Rural Population, 1920-2000," 66.

70 United Nations Departemtn of Economic and Social Affaris (UN-DESA-PD), *World Urbanization Prospects, the 2011 Revision.*

71 United Nations Department of Economic and Social Affairs (UN-DESA), "Growth of the World's Urban and Rural Population, 1920–2000."

72 Formally identical recent visualizations of the UN's urban population data include a time-series approach produced by UNICEF (http://www.unicef.org/sowc2012/urbanmap/) and a color-coded mapping by a journalist from *The Guardian* (http://image.guardian.co.uk/sys-files/Guardian/documents/2007/06/27/URBAN_WORLD_2806.pdf). See also Urban Theory Lab-GSD, "Envisioning an Urban Planet—Materials," this book, Ch. 28.

73 Tony Champion and Graeme Hugo, "Introduction," *New Forms of Urbanization*, eds. Tony Champion and Graeme Hugo (London: Ashgate, 2004) 5.

74 Fredric Jameson, "Cognitive Mapping," *Marxism and the Interpretation of Culture*, eds. Lawrence Grossberg and Cary Nelson (Chicago: University of Illinois Press, 1988).

75 Soja and Kanai, "The Urbanization of the World," this book, Ch. 10; Merrifield, "The Right to the City and Beyond," this book, Ch. 31; and Andrew Sayer, *Method in Social Science*, second edition (New York: Routledge, 1992) 138.

76 Keith Halfacree, "Rethinking Rurality," *New Forms of Urbanization*, eds. Tony Champion and Graeme Hugo (London: Ashgate, 2004).

77 Lefebvre, *The Urban Revolution*; Merrifield, "The Right to the City and Beyond," this book, Ch. 31; and Soja, "Regional Urbanization and the End of the Metropolis Era," this book, Ch. 19.

78 Schmid, "Patterns and Pathways of Global Urbanization," this book, Ch. 14; and Schmid, "Networks, Borders, Differences," this book, Ch. 4.

79 Montgomery, "The Demography of Urban Transition."

80 Satterthwaite, "Urban Myths," 96.

81 David Wachsmuth, "City as Ideology," this book, Ch. 23; see also Kanishka Goonewardena, "The Urban Sensorium: Space, Ideology, and the Aestheticization of Politics," *Antipode* 37, 1 (2005) 46-71.

82 For a brilliant example of how to track this process of interspatial policy transfer and mutation across scales and territories in the context of contemporary neoliberalization tendencies, see Nik Theodore and Jamie Peck, "Framing Neoliberal Urbanism: Translating 'Common Sense' Urban Policy Across the OECD Zone," *European Urban and Regional Studies* 19, 1 (2012) 20-4; and Jamie Peck and Nik Theodore, "Recombinant Workfare, Across the Americas: Transnationalizing 'Fast' Social Policy," *Geoforum* 41, 2 (2010) 195-208.

83 Satterthwaite, "Urban Myths," 95-96.

84 Terry McGee, "Managing the Rural-Urban Transformation in East Asia in the 21st Century," *Sustainability Science* 3, 1 (2008) 155-67. See also McGee, "The Emergence of *Desakota* Regions in Asia," this book, Ch. 9.

85 Nikhil Anand and Anne Rademacher, "Housing in the Urban Age," *Antipode* 43, 5 (2011) 1748-72.

86 Ananya Roy, "The 21st Century Metropolis: New Geographies of Theory," *Regional Studies* 43, 6 (2009) 820.

87 Jennifer Robinson, "Cities in a World of Cities: The Comparative Gesture," *International Journal of Urban and Regional Research* 53, 1 (2011) 19.

88 Henri Lefebvre, *The Urban Revolution*.

89 The term "extended urbanization" was introduced by Roberto Luis Monte-Mór in his studies of the urbanization of the Amazon in the mid-1990s: see Monte-Mór, "Extended Urbanization and

Settlement Patterns" and "What is the Urban in the Contemporary World?," this book, Chs. 8 and 17. The concept has also been recently deployed by Edward Soja. See "Regional Urbanization and the End of the Metropolis Era," this book, Ch. 19. While we draw upon these authors' vocabulary, our conceptualization is specific to the theoretical framework developed here and elsewhere for investigating the *problematique* of planetary urbanization. For a more detailed account, see Brenner and Schmid, *Towards a Theory of Extended Urbanization*.

90 We have begun to explore this proposition through a series of investigations of several "extreme territories" of urbanization—the Amazon, the Arctic, the Himalayas, the Gobi desert, the Pacific Ocean, the Sahara desert, Siberia and the atmosphere—in the Urban Theory Lab-GSD. This work—which combines spatialized political economy, critical cartography and geocomparative analysis—is intended at once to illuminate ongoing transformations in these remote zones of the world economy *and* to forge new theoretical categories for the study of urbanization.

91 Several projects to develop such a vocabulary are under way, building upon the concepts, methods and cartographic strategies developed in an earlier investigation of the urban fabric of Switzerland produced by ETH Studio Basel (see Christian Schmid, "A Typology of Urban Switzerland," this book, Ch. 26). More recently, the research project on "Patterns and Pathways of Planetary Urbanization," organized through the ETH Future Cities Laboratory Singapore, is comparing urbanization processes in nine large urban areas (Tokyo, Hong Kong / Shenzhen, Singapore, Kolkata, Istanbul, Lagos, Paris, Mexico City and Los Angeles). By exploring the wide variety of contemporary urbanization processes, this project is intended to destabilize inherited concepts of the urban and productively to expand our urban imagination. See also Schmid, "Patterns and Pathways of Global Urbanization," this book, Ch. 14.

Figure Credits

21.1 Ricky Burdett and Deyan Sudjic, eds., *The Endless City* (London: Phaidon, 2006) cover image; and Ricky Burdett and Deyan Sudjic, eds., *Living in the Endless City* (London: Phaidon, 2010) cover image.

21.2 Rem Koolhaas, *Mutations: Harvard Project on the City* (Barcelona: Actar, 2000) 1-2.

21.3 United Nations Department of Economic and Social Affairs (UN-DESA), *Growth of the World's Urban and Rural Population, 1920–2000*, Population Studies, 44 (New York: United Nations, 1969) map 1.

21.4 Original by authors

21.5 Redrawn from United Nations Department of Economic and Social Affairs, Population Division (UN-DESA-PD), *World Urbanization Prospects, the 2011 Revision* (New York: United Nations, 2012) http://esa.un.org/unpd/wup/Analytical-Figures/Fig_2.htm and http://esa.un.org/unpd/wup/Maps/maps_urban_2011.htm (accessed 14 June 2012).

22
WHAT ROLE FOR SOCIAL SCIENCE IN THE "URBAN AGE"?

Brendan Gleeson

Introduction: The Superannuation of Social Science?

In October 2010, the influential physicists Luis Bettencourt and Geoffrey West published an article in the leading scientific journal, *Nature*, which presented "a unified theory of urban living." The theory's exposition needed less than two pages of the journal, but the problem and its solution were epic in scale: "To combat the multiple threats facing humanity, a "grand unified theory of sustainability" with cities and urbanization at its core must be developed."[1] The authors identified the need for "an integrated, quantitative, predictive, science-based understanding of the dynamics, growth and organization of cities."[2] An empirical survey of urbanization trends revealed that "surprisingly, size is the major determinant of most characteristics of a city; history, geography and design have secondary roles."[3]

The "unified theory" is textbook positivism. The influence of time and space, the fundaments of human social organisation, are found to be "surprisingly" uninfluential variables in a theory of urbanism. It is the physical quantum of population that explains the quintessentially social phenomenon of urbanization. Bettencourt and West believe that all can be explained through the idea—indeed, *the law*—of "superlinear scaling," meaning that as city populations grow, their dynamism (measured variously) increases disproportionately but uniformly. The superlinear multiplier is 1.15—that is, for every

100 percent of population growth, there is an increase of 115 percent in socioeconomic "goods" and "bads":

> On average, as city size increases, per capita socio-economic quantities such as wages, GDP, number of patents produced and number of educational and research institutions all increase by approximately 15% more than the expected linear growth. There is, however, a dark side: negative metrics including crime, traffic congestion and incidence of certain diseases all increase following the same 15% rule. The good, the bad and the ugly come as an integrated, predictable, package.[4]

In a postpositivist era, it might be expected that the bold assertion of naturalism on a leading human question—"urban living" no less—would draw critical comment from social scientists.[5] Strangely, there is little evidence that it did. Joel Kotkin was critical in *The New York Times*, but the mainstreams of urban scholarship seem to have ignored the "unified theory."[6] Although obviously outside the realm of urban studies, *Nature* is a leading, widely discussed scientific outlet. The article's propositions have been further expounded by West in a number of public and broadly reported fora.[7] They have also been broadcast by the influential US economist Paul Romer in international work promoting his econocratic model of urbanism, "charter cities."[8]

In December 2010, *The New York Times* reported excitedly that "A Physicist Solves the City," and interviewed West at length. West enthused, "I've always wanted to find the rules that govern everything ... I had this hunch that ... every city was also shaped by a set of hidden laws."[9] The urban neophyte told the *Times* that "he didn't want to be constrained by the old methods of social science."[10] He asserted that "urban theory" was a "field without principles," much like "physics before Kepler pioneered the laws of planetary motion in the 17th century." The physicist rejected the inscrutable annals of social science; he "wanted to begin with a blank page, to study cities as if they had never been studied before. He was tired of urban theory—he wanted to invent urban science."[11] Fatigued by theory, the intrepid West "set out to solve the City."[12]

The interest of quantitative science grew. In July 2011, sensing a Eureka moment, Marcus du Sautoy, Simonyi Professor for the Public Understanding of Science at Oxford University, conveyed the "superlinear" finding with enthusiasm in an article in the UK newspaper *The Daily Mail*. His TV series "The Code," broadcast on BBC2 around this time, had shown "how numbers can explain everything around us."[13] The golden nugget was the "magic number of 1.15," its luster confirming "the beauty of mathematics."[14] A major efficiency dividend for human knowledge glowered in the discovery. Social explanation, and its tedious contingencies, seemed destined for superannuation, given that "[m]athematics is the code that controls not only our world and everything in it, but even us, a jumble of millions of individuals."[15]

A snowball, it seemed, had started to run down a widening hill of interest. In June 2012, *The Economist* lent its authoritative voice to the chorus of approval for the new urban physics. A piece entitled "The Laws of the City" proclaimed that "a deluge of data makes cities laboratories for those seeking to run them better."[16] An indication of the possibilities for wider policy "take up" emerged a few months later when two respected Australian social scientists enthusiastically cited *The Economist*'s piece, and in particular, the superlinear "finding," in an opinion editorial in the influential *Australian Financial Review*.[17]

With all this in mind, it is remarkable to think that the *Nature* paper and its noisy dispersions have not aroused attention, not to say amazement, amongst urban scholars. This episode seems emblematic, more generally, of a contemporary decline in the influence and reach of urban social science, by which I mean the cross-disciplinary field of scholarship that deploys the epistemologies and methodologies of the social sciences to study human urbanization. This may be a relative, not absolute, weakening of social scientific presence in an era witnessing a rapidly growing interest in urbanization. In many respects, urban studies in Anglophone countries seems vibrant enough, if measured by the amount and velocity of publishing and the steadily expanding number of dedicated journals.[18] However, the field of urban studies may not be engaging directly enough with a rapidly growing conversation about cities within the physical sciences, which is grounded upon suppositions that are patently hostile to the main postulates of social science. The first premise eschewed by the new urban revolutionaries is that cities are social, not natural, artifacts.

Yet this intellectual starting point is problematic, to say the least, given the irrefutably *social* ontology of urbanization. Four decades ago, Harvey stated the point succinctly:

> Urbanism may be regarded as a particular form or patterning of the social process. This process unfolds in a spatially structured environment created by man. The city can therefore be regarded as a tangible built environment—*an environment which is a social product*.[19]

His definition was as much intervention as prescription in an era dominated by positivistic geography and urban "science" that was frequently hostile to any social ontology of spatial arrangements.[20]

The "new urban conversation" has welcomed the fact that humanity is now preponderantly an urban species, *homo urbanis*. For the past seven or more years, the United Nations has strongly broadcast the message of a new urban ascendancy.[21] The major transnational institutions have meanwhile accorded greater significance to cities and their challenges.[22] Added to this, a parade of new popular literature noisily honks the arrival of the "urban age." These offerings include books such as *The Triumph of the City* by Harvard economist Edward Glaeser, and *Welcome to the Urban Revolution* by the Canadian urban "practitioner and thinker" Jeb Brugmann.[23] *Arrival City* by British-Canadian journalist Doug Saunders, exalts the rise of *homo urbanis* and the cities where the newest urban migrants gather.[24] *Aerotropolis* is meanwhile ordained as *The Way We'll Live Next* by management scholars John Kasarda and Greg Lindsay.[25] This popular urban literature is almost exclusively North American, and emanates mostly from journalists, consultants and media savvy academics in business schools and economics departments.[26]

This new "urbanology" is a tide of interest and ambition flowing into broad readerships and constituencies that heretofore showed little concern for urban issues.[27] The books have been generally reviewed favorably in key print media outlets that normally evince little interest in formal urban scholarship, including *The New York Review of Books*, *The New York Times*, *Publisher's Weekly*, and, in the UK, *The Independent*, *The Economist*, *The Evening Standard*, *The Financial Times* and *The Guardian*. Saunders' *Arrival City* was released by nine national publishers around the globe and was judged "a remarkable achievement" by Britain's former Prime Minister, Gordon Brown. In Australia, the commentator Elizabeth Farrelly excitedly reported in *The Sydney Morning Herald* the enthusiasm of former Prime Minister Paul Keating and former Opposition leader Malcom Turnbull for Glaeser's book.[28] In broadening the appeal of urban issues, the new literature has furthered the work of popular urbanists, such as Richard Florida, and the evangelistic fervour of applied design movements, including the "new urbanism."[29]

Urbanology is also a tide flowing into the urban studies field from "non-traditional" quarters. Unlike the recent contributions of physical scientists, some of the new popular literature is not linked in any meaningful way to the mainstreams of scholarship. Its significance and implications are surely ambiguous but should not be discounted. Several questions are raised by such discussions. To what extent do the new popular urbanists acknowledge or draw upon the tradition of social scientific (and lately environmental scientific) scholarship that has investigated and debated the human experience of urbanization? To what extent, and in what ways, will the newer entrants into urban research be willing to adopt and deploy the methods and orientations of urban science?

A large issue, which has considerable bearing on these questions, is the potential for the new urban commentary to resuscitate some of the intellectual failings that were debated and contested in the social sciences over the past half century—especially those of positivism and its kindred guises, naturalism and determinism. It is notable that the new urbanology displays a strong predilection for a law-bound view of urbanization.[30] The urbanologists' premises and projections lean commonly on abstractions about the overarching nature and power of the urban process. For example, Brugmann's chapter subtitles signal this faith in a knowable, if secreted, urban process: "The Hidden Logic of Global Urban Growth," "The Inevitable Democracy of the City," "The Irrepressible Economics of Urban Association."[31] Glaeser offers the natural metaphor of the ant nest to explain human urbanization: "Humans are an intensely social species that excels, like ants or gibbons, in producing things together. Just as ant colonies do things that are far beyond the abilities of isolated insects, cities achieve much more than isolated humans."[32] If so, this would compound the positivistic influence of the physical science that has lately taken an interest in the question of urbanization. Indeed, the scientists cited above consider this conundrum *solved*.

The new urban conversation, in its various forms, seems as yet to have aroused little awareness and debate in urban scholarship. An exception is the set of reviews of Brugmann's book, together with his response, in a recent issue of *Dialogues in Human Geography*.[33] Brugmann's academic interlocutors pointed, *inter alia*, to the absence of theoretical framing in his book, and by consequence a failure to present an account of how social power shapes urbanization.[34] The implication is that his work has developed in isolation from social science. This could not be said of Glaeser's work, which proceeds from economic scholarship that is distinctly neoclassical.

This chapter considers these shifts from the perspective of critical social science, especially in the form presented in Andrew Sayer's recent work.[35] This perspective is avowedly anti-positivistic and opposes those forms of social science that rely heavily upon naturalistic or deterministic approaches. Sayer reinstates the importance of a confident, outwardly aware social science that seeks engagement with issues fundamental to human flourishing. Urbanization is clearly such an issue in the present age. This is confirmed by the recent rapid growth in attention to cities in policy and popular fora. And yet, as with another great issue of the age, global warming, there is evidence—partial but suggestive— that social science is being sidelined from a rapidly growing field of human concern. In climate change debate and policy, the sociologists Beck and Shove report a similar diminution of social explanation.[36] Shove observes that "policy proceeds on the basis of a characteristically thin account of the social world."[37] The contention is that thought and practice are irredeemably weakened by the breach between human imperative and social science. This chapter essays the apparent opening of such a cleavage in the urban field. The objectives are, first, to propose an explanation for this; second, to consider its consequences for explanation and human response; and lastly, to explore prospects for a new social scientific engagement of that most compelling human issue, the urban ascendancy.

The discussion proceeds in three parts. The first considers the apparent dimming of social scientific influence on urban debate. After this, analysis is made of the regressive possibilities that may thrive in the contemporary breach between social and urban explanation. The chapter's last offering is a sketched prospectus for a resocialization of urban debate and practice. This will necessitate, amongst other things, resolution of how the insights and methods of the natural sciences are to be reconciled to a revivified social urbanism. It will also mean, pace Sayer, commitment to conversation with the ever wider human publics that claim an interest in urbanization.[38]

The Dimming of Urban Social Science?

Urban attention has risen recently in policy and popular fora, expressing recognition of a newly urban human age. At the same time, however, social scientific influence seems to have waned within this burgeoning interest. The reasons for the apparent waning of social scientific explanation in urban thought and practice are probably too varied and complex for one exposition. Importantly, this is not to overstate an incipient, if progressive, problem. There remains a large social scientific enterprise dedicated to the explanation of urbanization. Within urban studies, critical social theory retains vibrancy.[39] What is at issue is the dwindling *relative* standing and influence of social science in debates that have been invigorated and enlarged by new institutional, political and popular recognition of the significance of urbanization to human prospects.

What are the ideological, institutional and scientific developments that have variously outflanked, ignored, or undermined (sometimes from within) the claims of social science in urban understanding, debate and practice? By way of explanation I point not so much to changes in the object of inquiry, urbanization—important as that is—as to the currents of knowledge, formal and otherwise, that have sought to explain it. The emphasis here is the reformations of urban knowledge in recent decades, and the intellectual, institutional and political economic forces that have driven these new directions. The changing courses of urbanization are not neglected, but the emphasis is on new epistemological imperatives over ontological changes. To be sure, the increasing empirical and policy manifestation of new urban conditions has generated shifts in scholarship, debate and practice.[40] The starkest example is the environmental crisis and the intellectual and institutional responses this has generated.[41] Equally there have been profound alterations to the governance, cultural make-up, and economic geography of urbanization, manifesting variously at different spatial and political economic scales, especially and with increasing force at the global level. In the sociocultural register, for example, Beck insists upon cosmopolitanism as a defining reality of the contemporary urban age.[42]

With ontological change in mind, what have been the major structural influences on urban scholarship and debate? To elaborate, what political-economic and institutional changes have reframed the nature of urban inquiry, ostensibly to the disadvantage of social science? Arguably in the past three decades or so, the terms, possibilities and priorities of urban scholarship and debate have been recast by five shifts:

1. The rise of neoliberalism and its pervasive, if variegated, institutional influence, especially the increasing preference for aspatial social explanation and, allied to this, the gradual, sometimes sudden, suppression of spatial social sciences;

2. New formations and reformations of knowledge and epistemological suppositions within the social sciences themselves, including the "long night" of postmodernism

during the 1990s during which the terms and ambition of social explanation were radically challenged;

3. A heightening of aesthetic interest in urbanization and urban knowledge and practice, partly reflecting the influence of postmodernism and the neoliberal urbanisms that strengthened in the wake of ongoing structural economic reform and economic integration at national and global levels[43];

4. Burgeoning institutional and cross-sectoral interest in urbanization, especially from the new urbanology, reflecting the increasingly accepted postulate of an "urban age" marked by the global demographic preponderance of urban living and the simultaneous ascendancy of cities as technological, political and cultural pivots of the global economy; and

5. Recent interest in urban explanation from the physical sciences, including through the (re)deployment of naturalistic epistemologies and methods, and reflecting also the long rise of environmental and resource issues and responses in cities and in urban thought and practice.

The intention here is to focus on the last two dynamics, as they have the strongest contemporary influence and, arguably, are the least debated influences in urban studies. The first three influences are briefly related.

The long rise to near hegemony of neoliberalism, especially in the West, has been a weakening force on critical social science.[44] Although in essence a class project, neoliberalism has been closely associated with, indeed legitimized by, a number of intellectual movements that have considerably influenced the format of the social sciences—notably, neoclassical economics, public choice theory, hyperliberalism and some variants of postmodernism.[45] Although contested and resisted, the disciplinary and institutional changes effected included a withering of commitment to spatial and urban subfields, such as urban economics, urban history, economic history, and urban sociology. The discipline of economics gained new ascendancy in scholarship, public policy and popular culture. Its spatial traditions and insights were largely evacuated by the neo-classical turn. Barnes now describes neo-classicism as "*the* school of economics … ubiquitous, hegemonic and mainstream."[46] The more recent attempt to foster a "New Economic Geography" has not aroused a general reemergence of spatial ontology. Interestingly, it is instead the new urbanology of writers such as Glaeser that appears to be making stronger headway in reestablishing urban and spatial dynamics as legitimate concerns for economics.

Postmodernism and poststructuralism were for a brief time—largely in the 1990s—decisive and unsettling forces in the social sciences and humanities, especially in the Anglophone world. Woodard and Jones report that "today the hullabaloo over postmodernism has waned, but it manages to live on in some contexts."[47] It was corrosive to critical social science: suspicious of "normativity," preferring to unsettle rather than explain, and sceptical about the possibility of judgement.[48] The general effect, as Sayer explains it, was to undermine the capacity of social science to engage with human themes, especially in popular and policy settings.[49] This seemed to confirm the charge of reaction leveled at postmodernism by critics such as Harvey and Eagleton, who emphasized its tendency, both explicit and unintended, to varnish political neoliberalism.[50]

It is, however, surely also true that postmodernism and poststructuralism helped to further root out the residuum of earlier positivism in the social sciences. Sayer finds that many of the "inhibitions" of contemporary social science have a "poststructuralist provenance," but he also acknowledges the powerful reflexive energies of the critiques that opposed modernist science, including the work inspired by Foucault.[51] Textual and discursive analysis did much to expose hidden assumptions and to disrupt reductionism, as much as it may have also engendered a drift to relativism and ethical restraint.

And yet, as Beauregard observes, in textual analysis "politics is a topic for discussion and not a field of action."[52] Sayer finds that postmodernism and poststructuralism continued the project of "de-naturalization" (albeit in a variety of ways) and opposition to intellectual dogmatism. Ultimately, however, "while reflexivity might certainly be regarded as an intellectual virtue, it amounts to a highly limited notion of critique."[53] The fundamental problem is the "directionless character of [such] de-naturalizing critique."[54]

Postmodernism did evince a strong interest in the "urban." Woodard and Jones define postmodernism as "an important *architectural, aesthetic* and intellectual movement."[55] Dear argued for a "postmodern urbanism" that was strongly preoccupied with aesthetic and design themes—many of which were genuinely novel and disruptive of oppressive or limiting traditionalism.[56] In this sense, however, the "postmodern turn" impelled an aestheticization of urban thought that was not to the advantage of social scientific urbanism. Davison and Fincher explain postmodernism as a "destabilizing" force in urban studies that unsettled notions of the public good and progress that had long guided urban commentary, especially in the applied field of planning.[57]

This historiographical sketch arrives at the early years of the present millennium. The general picture is of a social science somewhat exhausted and depleted by: the various and complex workings of political neoliberalism; ideologically driven change to disciplinary priorities; and the entropic, if brief, reign of postmodernism. Our analysis now turns to the final two dynamics of change listed earlier, which mark a new widening of the breach between social science and urban thought.

The New Urban Enthusiasm and its Discontents

The shifts explained above were corrosive to urban social science, and emerged as much from within its borders as without. At least for a time, many urban scholars shared Dear's enthusiasm for a "postmodern urbanism" before it reached the "dead end" foreseen by Sui.[58] The new urban analyses proceeding from popular urbanology and the physical sciences are less corrosive and more in open antipathy to social scientific urbanism. They are distinctive not identical oppositions, but with a strong area of overlap in their positivistic assumptions and preferences. The physical scientific urbanism is rather undiluted in this respect. Urbanology, by contrast, harbours positivism as a tendency, sometimes leavened with recognition of the role of social processes in shaping the course of urbanization. Taken together, however, as popular and policy conversation tends to do, the two influences prosecute a generally determinist view of urban change.

In a separate review, I have explained at some length the positivism that partly if clearly characterizes the new urbanology.[59] It runs as Arendt would have it, like a "red thread" through voluminous urban commentary. The strand of positivism most strongly apparent in the literature is that of naturalism, which asserts a unity of method between the natural and social sciences, to the exclusion of social determination.[60] The urbanologists' premises and projections frequently lean on naturalized abstractions about the overarching "power" of the urban process. A totalizing, law-bound view of urbanization is never far from the surface of discussion. Brugmann, for example, seeks "the hidden logic of global urban growth."[61] He is taken to task for this by both Nicholls and Purcell, who think that his search for hidden laws neglects the obvious fact of social power.[62]

The new urbanology leans heavily towards naturalized ontology, stressing unity not contradiction; connection, not disconnection; certainty not contingency. Brugmann's chapter subtitles signal this faith in a knowable, if secreted, urban process: "The Hidden Logic of Global Urban Growth," "The Inevitable Democracy of the City," "The Irrepressible Economics of Urban Association." He offers a unifying construct "the City," that conveys

> ... the merging of cities throughout the world into a single, converging system that is reordering the most basic dynamics of global ecology, politics, markets, and social life.[63]

The tendency to naturalism, and its determinations, is in tension with the explicit social concerns of the urbanologists. Brugmann, Saunders and Glaeser have generally progressive values, each embracing social and ecological sustainability in different ways. The "challenge" of global urban poverty is a central theme—though Glaeser also states that "there's a lot to like about urban poverty."[64] Their frameworks nonetheless bear many determining assumptions—for example, Glaeser's "near perfect correlations between urbanization and prosperity."[65] They are not, however, unyieldingly deterministic. Thus Glaeser acknowledges that whilst "the city has triumphed …, sometimes city roads are paved to hell."[66] Testimony to naturalism arises in the urbanologists' enthusiasm for physical density as a determining force (for good) in human relations. Glaeser opens his book with the claim that "cities are expanding enormously because urban density provides the clearest path from poverty to prosperity."[67] Further, he asserts that "human creativity is strong, especially when reinforced by urban density."[68]

Potentially then, in urban thought and debate, the "crypto-positivism" of urbanology has the potential to reinforce the neopositivism of the physical sciences. The two conversations seem yet to meet and partner, but the dance cards are surely marked. In urban social science, this possibility and its broader prospects remain unrecognized. Concern arises not merely from antithesis to social science, but also the wider implications of positivist (re)ascendancy for human thought and response in an urban age. From the 1970s, there emerged a broad consensus in the Western social sciences that the long dominance of positivism had eroded human knowledge and too often licensed, actively or otherwise, institutional oppression and political reaction.[69] It was judged necessary for a while to speak of "postpositivist social science" as both a marker of the new intellectual consensus and a watchword against regression. The never-quite-defeated claims of determinism and naturalism are constantly enjoined and adjudicated in the mainstreams of social sciences through mechanisms such as peer review and scholarly critique.

The new urban positivism, at least in prospect, may conceivably reinforce the neoliberal urbanism that has plagued human urban life in recent decades.[70] The sympathies of urbanology certainly lie with market capitalism. Most of its contributors are consultant/advisors and their works tend to highlight and favor urban entrepreneurship. For example, the impressively credentialed Kasarda is Professor of Strategy and Entrepreneurship in the Kenan-Flagler Business School at the University of North Carolina at Chapel Hill, and director of the Frank Hawkins Kenan Institute of Private Enterprise. Glaeser, the Harvard economist, works—with originality to be sure—within a strongly neoclassical economic framework.

By contrast, the emergent urban physics seems more inclined to the idea of structural change, at least in terms of urban administration. It ultimately seeks a simpler, predictable world that is best managed by experts. Bettencourt and West make the point:

> The difference between "policy as usual" and policy led by a new quantitative understanding of cities may well be the choice between creating a "planet of slums" or finally achieving a sustainable, creative, prosperous, urbanized world expressing the best of the human spirit.[71]

In *A World at Risk*, Ulrich Beck points to the ever heightening prospects for authoritarianism as a means for resolving intractable socioecological problems.[72] Already, he argues, "it is experts who are governing where politicians are nominally in charge."[73] Innocently or not, the expertise of urban physics stands ready to assist the cause of sound management.

Conclusion: Prospectus for Urban Social Science

Tobler's "First Law of Geography" was a memorable epithet for positivism: "Everything is related to everything else, but near things are more related than distant things."[74] "Pythonesque," perhaps, but this outlook is now being recalled into service in the sweeping legal proclamations of urban physics and urbanology. "Cities are the absence of physical space between people and companies," states Glaeser.[75] Proximity and scale are the all determining quanta. West boasts, "I don't know anything about this city or even where it is or its history, but I can tell you all about it. And the reason I can do that is because every city is really the same."[76]

The regression in human knowledge and prospect threatened by positivism has been well essayed in critical social science.[77] While the eternal salience of anti-positivism may not be in doubt, Sayer finds contemporary critical social science at low ebb.[78] He believes it has sunk to a "minimalism," marked by a residualized commitment to anti-naturalism and criticism (reduction of illusion), but lacking the animus for *critique* that exposes not only false beliefs, but their genesis and ideological function. In urban studies, even the first defence of anti-naturalism seems to have been breached and is now in danger of being overrun by the neopositivistic accounts reviewed above. Added to this, the authority and confidence of critical knowledge seems to have been weakened by the progressive and long-term influence of positivism and postmodernism, both of which in contrasting ways problematized a socially determined view of human progress.[79] At the same time, evidence of human regress mounts inexorably.[80] The shadow of a timid, relativized social science flickers weakly behind major human debates on both climate change and urbanization.

How, then, to restore to confidence and influence critical social scientific urbanism? Two agendas seem integral to a new social scientific prospectus in urban studies:

- First, to renew the cause of anti-naturalism, but without neglecting the need to respond to natural imperatives; and

- Second, to restore confidence in values and judgement in science, and thereby to strengthen its presence and influence in key human debates.

The first agenda is axiomatic to social scientific renewal. To oppose naturalism is not to deny nature, the substrate and first materiality of human society. Urbanization is an increasingly important part of this natural substrate—as Beauregard put it recently, "to engage 'the urban' is to engage the materiality of human existence."[81]

A globe imperiled by ecological risk demands a new willingness in social science to recognize and absorb the claims of environmentalism, and more challengingly, the constructs and testimony of natural science. In this sense, naturalism—the view of nature as an all-determining force—must be counterposed to naturalistic social science, which accepts the fact of determination, arising from the human encounter with ecology. For Roy Bhaskar, the point of critical social science is to seek emancipation from unwanted determinations, including surely what appear to be natural ordinations (for example, resource scarcity).[82] Of course, as Sayer points out, the identification of unwanted and unloved determinations is never easy; it is a social task that goes to the core of human political expression and action.[83] It also beckons, as no other imperative does quite so compellingly, encounter and collaboration between the natural and social sciences to identify and prioritize the surest steps to human flourishing. And some dependencies, such as human solidarity, are to be preserved not upturned on the road to emancipation.

Critical social science by definition rejects a unity of method with physical science (positivism), but it must still rely upon the latter's evidentiary and conceptual base to comprehend human ecology. The engagement between the social sciences and modern ecology is now long standing. In 1998, Davison and Fincher found that environmentalism was a leading edge of urban social inquiry in Australia. Luke has likewise stated the case for "contemporary urbanism as public ecology."[84] Now, in a maturing encounter, and given further impetus by the speed and scale of global ecological default, there are serious attempts at construct transfer from the natural to social sciences. The principal example is that of "resilience," which has recently become especially manifest in urban scholarship and policy discussion.[85] In an age of perturbation and risk, the idea and its scientific connotations are undeniably compelling.

The new social scientific enthusiasm for resilience flags the danger of commonsensical application—embodied, for instance, in the transposition of a scientific concept across disciplinary understandings through the medium of conventional wisdom. As Simmie and Martin observe with considerable understatement, "there are issues about abducting a model from one disciplinary field … to another."[86] Has the rapid take-up of the resilience marker in urban environmental advocacy short-circuited the critical adjudicative processes that normally filter the movement of concepts across scientific fields? Evans finds a trail leading back to naturalism, citing the wider potential of resilience thinking to "depoliticize urban transition … by constraining governance within a technocratic mode that remains inured to the tropes of scientific legitimacy."[87] Critical social science is central to human ecology and thus to wider debate on the human prospect. In its quest for ecological insight and influence it must, however, avoid the pitfalls and snares of naturalism, especially the lure of methodological unity. This is to be sure a difficult work-in-progress.

Finally, how to replenish the springs of judgement in urban social science? This is a necessary step towards a new assertiveness for critical urban studies in a wider debate on contemporary cities and urbanism. In this respect, the bravura of the new urban commentaries is to be admired. The broadcast journalism of urbanology has boldly asserted its values, eclectic as they may be, including preferences for entrepreneurialism, environmental sustainability, relentless innovation, human density and facilitative governance. It has undeniably rendered service in the field of human debate, instating the importance of urbanization as a core human concern. The new urban physics has similarly disported confidence and predisposition, including for science, empirical authority, managerial response and technical solution. Both contributions, arguably, are also freighted with illusion and ideological service, intended or otherwise—to naturalism and its reactionary possibilities; to econocratic thought and its regressive, limiting consequences; and to conventional wisdom that is innately hostile to science. Critical social science would judge these illusions harmful to human prospect. Brenner provides the manifesto for the critical alternative to conventional urban wisdom:

> Critical urban theory is … grounded on an antagonistic relationship not only to inherited urban knowledges, but more generally, to existing urban formations. It insists that another, more democratic, socially just, and sustainable form of urbanization is possible, even if such possibilities are being suppressed through dominant institutional arrangements, practices and ideologies. In short, critical urban theory involves the critique of ideology … and the critique of power, inequality, injustice, and exploitation, at once within and among cities.[88]

All this underlines the need for social science to renew its prosecution of explanatory critique. For Sayer "critique in this strong sense … seeks to identify cases where false beliefs have a self-confirming character by helping to maintain circumstances ('real appearances') that support those beliefs and also are likely to be favorable to dominant groups."[89] The short form is that critique opposes power that seeks to dominate and constrain human flourishing. As Sayer insists, it necessitates an *explicit* vision of what flourishing is, meaning an inclusive species-wide prospect for human realization and well being.[90] In the theater of public debate, it is not enough for critique to shout out objections to the bad. It must take the stage and present its vision of human good or suffer, as it recently has, invisibility and irrelevance.

Therein lays, perhaps, the central challenge for social science: to offer the conceptual—that is, *theoretical*—means for human urban aspiration. Beauregard recently admonished social science for paying too much attention to the urban object and too little to its theorization.[91] His admonition seems borne out by contemporary urban debates, scholarly and popular, which are littered with new markers and labels—the many tags of urban classification, much of it fluttering free from the mainstreams of social theory. Instead, new cities are discovered and made to walk on thin conceptual legs. These rickety constructions of contemporaneity step over the deeper historical currents of social science.

Commentaries proclaim their visions of desirable urbanism in modish language: the entrepreneurial city; the smart city; the creative city; the knowledge city.[92] The common wrapping is a bright universalism that masks the agonies of a failing world. None of these can surely withstand the test of critique: all bear the illusions and desires of structures that have generated a world marked by urban misery for many and grave ecological danger for all.[93] Arraigned against them are the fragmented ideals of social scientific urbanism: the cosmopolitan city; the just city; the green city; the rebellious city—*disjecta membra* of progressive urban thought that float outside the popular consciousness.[94] They are powerful, estimable pages of a new urban testimony. How to bind them in an imaginary that refuses the doom of a darkening human ecology, in the quest for a unifying, but *not unitary*, ideal that declines the fatalism of a "postpolitical age" and solicits new prospects for *homo urbanis?*

Intentionally or otherwise, the illusions of the new urban commentaries clear the way for what Jane Jacobs, at the end of her long life, feared was the "Dark Age Ahead."[95] Jacobs saw such rising "hubris" as one sees clouds before a disastrous storm. But all this is mere criticism—enough of portent, an end to declamation. What does critical social science hold to be the "good city"? To restate Glaeser, *which city* should triumph in the human imagination?

Notes

1 Luis Bettencourt and Geoffrey West, "A Unified Theory of Urban Living," *Nature* 467 (2010) 912.

2 Ibid.

3 Ibid.

4 Ibid., 913.

5 Trevor Barnes, "Positivism," *The Dictionary of Human Geography*, eds. Derek Gregory, Ron Johnston, Geraldine Pratt, Michael Watts and Sarah Whatmore, Fifth edition (Chichester: Wiley-Blackwell, 2009) 557-9.

6 Jonah Lehrer, "A Physicist Solves the City," *The New York Times* 17 December 2010. http://www.nytimes.com/2010/12/19/magazine/19Urban_West-t.html?pagewanted=all&_r=0 (accessed 8 November 2012).

7 See Geoffrey West, "The Surprising Math of Cities and Corporations," *TEDGlobal* (2011). http://www.ted.com/talks/geoffrey_west_the_surprising_math_of_cities_and_corporations.htm (accessed 9 August 2011).

8 See http://chartercities.org/blog/160/geoffrey-west-on-scaling-phenomena-in-cities (accessed 13 March 2012).

9 Lehrer, "A Physicist Solves the City," MM46.

10 Ibid.

11 Ibid.

12 Ibid.

13 Marcus Du Sautoy, "Physicist Discovers that the Reason We All Live in Cities is…1.15," *Daily Mail Online* 30 July 2011. http://www.dailymail.co.uk/news/article-2020527/Physicist-Geoffrey-West-discovers-reason-live-cities-1-15.html (accessed 20 March 2012).

14 Ibid.

15 Ibid.

16 "The Laws of the City: A Deluge of Data Makes Cities Laboratories for Those Seeking to Run Them Better," *The Economist* 23 June 2012.

17 Glenn Withers and Andrew MacIntyre, "Smart Growth Doesn't Rest on Laurels," *The Australian Financial Review* 6 August 2012, 26.

18 Holding aside the argument that these may be doubtful measures of disciplinary health.

19 David Harvey, *Social Justice and the City* (London: Edward Arnold, 1973) 196, emphasis added.

20 Barnes, "Positivism."

21 David Whitehouse, "Half of Humanity Set to Go Urban," *BBC News* 19 May 2005. http://news.bbc.co.uk/2/hi/science/nature/4561183.stm (accessed 13 March 2012).

22 OECD, *Cities and Climate Change* (Paris: OECD Publishing, 2010); World Bank, *Cities and Climate Change: an Urgent Agenda* (Washington: World Bank, 2010); UN-Habitat, *Global Report on Human Settlements, 2011*, Abridged Edition (London: Earthscan, 2011); and UNICEF, *Children in an Urban World* (New York: UNICEF, 2012).

23 Edward Glaeser, *The Triumph of the City: How Our Greatest Invention Makes Us Richer, Smarter, Greener, Healthier, and Happier* (Harmondsworth: Penguin, 2011); and Jeb Brugmann, *Welcome to the Urban Revolution: How Cities are Changing the World* (New York: Bloomsbury Press, 2009).

24 Doug Saunders, *Arrival City: How the Last Great Migration is Changing Our World* (Sydney: Allen & Unwin, 2010).

25 John Kasarda and Greg Lindsay, *Aerotropolis: The Way We'll Live Next* (New York: Farrar, Straus and Giroux, 2011).

26 A recent geographical exception is the new book by British writer Peter D. Smith, *City: A Guidebook for the Armchair Traveller* (London:

Bloomsbury Press, 2012).

27 Brendan Gleeson, "The Urban Age: Paradox and Prospect," *Urban Studies* 49, 5 (2012) 1-13.

28 Elizabeth Farrelly, "Be Happy, Be More Interesting, Be Dense," *The Sydney Morning Herald* 20 October 2011. http://www.smh.com.au/opinion/society-and-culture/be-happy-be-more-interesting-be-dense-20111019-1m809.html (accessed 2 October 2012).

29 Richard Florida may be counted amongst the new urbanologists—witness his recent popular work, *The Great Reset: How the Postcrash Economy Will Change the Way We Live and Work* (New York: Harper, 2011).

30 Gleeson, "The Urban Age."

31 Brugmann, *Welcome to the Urban Revolution*.

32 Glaeser, *The Triumph of the City*, 247.

33 *Dialogues in Human Geography* 1, 2 (2011).

34 See, for example, Walter Nicholls, "Review of *Welcome to the Urban Revolution*" *Dialogues in Human Geography* 1, 2 (2011) 265-8; and Mark Purcell, "Review of *Welcome to the Urban Revolution,*" *Dialogues in Human Geography* 1, 2 (2011) 263-5.

35 Andrew R. Sayer, *Why Things Matter to People: Social Science, Values and Ethical Life* (Cambridge: Cambridge University Press, 2011).

36 Ulrich Beck, "Climate for Change, or How to Create a Green Modernity?" *Theory, Culture & Society* 27, 2–3 (2010) 254-66; and Elizabeth Shove, "Social Theory and Climate Change: Questions Often, Sometimes and Not Yet Asked," *Theory, Culture & Society* 27, 2–3 (2010) 277-88.

37 Shove, "Social Theory and Climate Change," 247.

38 Sayer, *Why Things Matter to People*.

39 Neil Brenner, "What is Critical Urban Theory?" *CITY 13*, 2–3 (2009) 298-307.

40 Ibid.

41 Timothy W. Luke, "'Global Cities' vs. 'global cities': Rethinking Contemporary Urbanism as Public Ecology," *Studies in Political Economy* 70 (2003) 11-33.

42 Ulrich Beck, *World at Risk* (Cambridge: Polity, 2009).

43 See Michael J. Dear, *The Postmodern Urban Condition* (Oxford: Blackwell, 2000); and Mike Hodson and Simon Marvin, *World Cities and Climate Change* (Milton Keynes: Open University Press, 2010).

44 Andrew W. Sayer, "Who's Afraid of Critical Social Science?" *Current Sociology* 57, 6 (2009) 767-86.

45 As explained by David Harvey, *A Brief History of Neoliberalism* (New York: Oxford University Press, 2005).

46 Trevor Barnes, "Neo-classical Economics," *The Dictionary of Human Geography*, eds. Derek Gregory, Ron Johnston, Geraldine Pratt, Michael Watts and Sarah Whatmore, Fifth Edition (Chichester: Wiley-Blackwell, 2009) 495.

47 Keith Woodard and John Paul Jones, "Postmodernism," *The Dictionary of Human Geography*, eds. Derek Gregory, Ron Johnston, Geraldine Pratt, Michael Watts and Sarah Whatmore, Fifth Edition (Chichester: Wiley-Blackwell, 2009) 568.

48 Terry Eagleton, *The Illusions of Postmodernism* (Oxford: Wiley-Blackwell, 1996).

49 Sayer, "Who's Afraid of Critical Social Science?"; and Sayer, *Why Things Matter to People*.

50 David Harvey, *The Condition of Postmodernity* (Oxford: Wiley-Blackwell, 1989); and Eagleton, *The Illusions of Postmodernism*.

51 Sayer, *Why Things Matter to People*, 240.

52 Robert A. Beauregard, "What Theorists Do," *Urban Geography* 33, 4 (2012) 485.

53 Sayer, *Why Things Matter to People*, 241.

54 Ibid., 225.

55 Woodard and Jones, "Postmodernism," 566, emphasis added.

56 See also Nan Ellin, *Postmodern Urbanism* (New York: Princeton Architectural Press, 1999).

57 Graeme Davison and Ruth Fincher, "Urban Studies in Australia: A Road Map and Ways Ahead," *Urban Policy and Research* 16, 3 (1998) 183-97.

58 Dear, *The Postmodern Urban Condition*; and Daniel Z. Sui, "Postmodern Urbanism Disrobed: or Why Postmodern Urbanism is a Dead End for Urban Geography," *Urban Geography* 20, 5 (1999) 403-11.

59 Gleeson, "The Urban Age."

60 Roy Bhaskar, *The Possibility of Naturalism: a Philosophical Critique of the Contemporary Human Sciences* (London: Routledge, 1998); and Barnes, "Positivism."

61 Brugmann, *Welcome to the Urban Revolution*.

62 Nicholls, "Review of *Welcome to the Urban Revolution*"; and Purcell, "Review of *Welcome to the Urban Revolution*."

63 Brugmann, *Welcome to the Urban Revolution*, 24.

64 Glaeser, *The Triumph of the City*, 9.

65 Ibid., 7.

66 Ibid., 6.

67 Ibid., 1.

68 Ibid., 67.

69 Bhaskar, *The Possibility of Naturalism*.

70 Mike Davis, *Planet of Slums* (London: Verso, 2006); and Hodson and Marvin, *World Cities and Climate Change*.

71 Bettencourt and West, "A Unified Theory of Urban Living," 913.

72 Beck, *World at Risk*.

73 Ibid., 110.

74 Waldo Tobler cited by Barnes, "Positivism," 559.

75 Glaeser, *The Triumph of the City*, 6.

76 Lehrer, "A Physicist Solves the City," MM46.

77 Derek Gregory, *Ideology, Science and Human Geography* (London: Hutchinson, 1978).

78 Sayer, "Who's Afraid of Critical Social Science?"

79 Ibid.; and Sayer, *Why Things Matter to People*.

80 Beck, *World at Risk*; and Davis, *Planet of Slums*.

81 Beauregard, "What Theorists Do," 485.

82 Bhaskar, *The Possibility of Naturalism*.

83 Sayer, *Why Things Matter to People*.

84 Roger Keil, "Urbanism," *The Dictionary of Human Geography*, eds. Derek Gregory, Ron Johnston, Geraldine Pratt, Michael Watts and Sarah Whatmore, Fifth Edition (Chichester: Wiley-Blackwell, 2009) 792.

85 J. P. Evans, "Resilience, Ecology and Adaptation in the Experimental City," *Transactions of the Institute of British Geographers* 36, 2 (2011) 223-37.

86 James Simmie and Ron Martin, "The Economic Resilience of Regions: Towards an Evolutionary Approach," *Cambridge Journal of Regions, Economy and Society* 3 (2010) 42.

87 Evans, "Resilience, Ecology and Adaptation in the Experimental City," 233.

88 Neil Brenner, "What is Critical Urban Theory?," *CITY 13*, 2-3 (2009) 198.

89 Sayer, "Who's Afraid of Critical Social Science?" 770.

90 Ibid; Sayer, *Why Things Matter to People*.

91 Beauregard, "What Theorists Do."

92 A recent Urban Age conference in London explored the "Electric City" and the cause of urban technological innovation (see: http://ec2012.lsecities.net/). Esteemed sociologist and speaker Richard Sennett sounded a note of doubt, cautioning that "no one likes a city that's too smart" (Richard Sennett, "No One Likes a City that's Too Smart," *The Guardian UK* 4 December 2012).

93 UNICEF, *Children in an Urban World*; and Beck, *World at Risk*.

94 Leonie Sandercock, *Towards Cosmopolis: Planning for Multicultural Cities* (London: John Wiley, 1998); Susan Fainstein, *The Just City* (Ithaca: Cornell University Press, 2011); Nicholas Low, Brendan Gleeson, Ray Green and Darko Radovic, *The Green City: Sustainable Homes, Sustainable Suburbs* (London: Routledge, 2004); and David Harvey, *Rebel Cities* (London: Verso, 2012).

95 Jacobs thundered against "ideologies that promise prefabricated answers for all circumstances" in *Dark Age Ahead* (New York: Random House, 2004) 115. She had "neoconservative ideologues" in mind (Ibid., 114).

23
CITY AS IDEOLOGY
David Wachsmuth

Introduction

Could the concept of the city now be ideological? Henri Lefebvre suggested as much in *The Urban Revolution*:

> The concept of the city no longer corresponds to a social object. Sociologically it is a pseudoconcept. However, the city has a historical existence that is impossible to ignore…. An image or representation of the city can perpetuate itself, survive its conditions…. In other words, the "real" sociological "object" is an image and above all an ideology![1]

A common assessment of *The Urban Revolution* is that its claims of an emerging urban society were at best premature. And this may be so. But there is a broader methodological point lurking in the particular usage Lefebvre makes of the word "city" (usually *ville* but occasionally *cité*). He uses the term to refer only to a historical phenomenon (e.g., the mercantile city and the industrial city) or to a present-day representation (the image or concept of the city), and implies that *these are one and the same object*. Yesterday's sociological truths may become today's ideologies.

It is in this spirit rather than self-contradiction that we can interpret Lefebvre's discussion of the city as a sociological "pseudoconcept" only two years after speaking of the "right to the city:" the *analysis* of urban society requires new conceptual tools even as the *experience* of urban society remains tethered to some extent to the traditional, historical idea of the city.[2] This observation offers a strategy for resolving a central dilemma of contemporary urban and spatial theory: how to reconcile the explosion of the city form with the tenacity of the city concept?

In this chapter, I answer this question by way of a theoretical reexamination of the traditional concept of the city—and its legacy in the context of urbanization processes that exceed it. By the "traditional city," I refer to the analytical tradition handed down through Western social science via the Chicago School of urban sociology, in particular, which could be summarized via three tropes: the city-countryside opposition, the city as a self-contained system, and the city as an ideal type. They are the common epistemological core of Park, Burgess, McKenzie, Wirth and Redfield's approach to the city, despite the different substantive features of the city these different scholars emphasized, such as Park's ecological succession or Wirth's size/density/diversity triad.[3] Together, these three tropes define the city as an analytical form, and they have historically comprised something like the collective unconscious of Anglo-American urban studies.

The argument proceeds as follows: 1) I argue that, in the North Atlantic at least, we should neither dismiss the concept of the city as outdated nor try to resuscitate it as an category of analysis, but rather treat it as a category of practice: a *representation* of urbanization processes that exceed it. 2) Furthermore, I argue that the city-as-a-representation is not neutral or innocent, but rather is *ideological*, in the sense that its partiality helps obscure and reproduce relations of power and domination that critical spatial theory seeks to expose and confront. 3) I substantiate these claims by examining the three tropes of the traditional city not as analytical features, but as ideological projects.

New Urban Forms, New Urban Concepts

Recent decades have witnessed a bewildering proliferation of new urban morphologies and processes, and an equally bewildering proliferation of new concepts to capture them. Simply witness Taylor and Lang's non-exhaustive list of 100 such concepts.[4] Only a few have become major research concerns in urban studies (e.g., "world city network") while most have remained niche ideas (e.g., "slurbs" or "archipelago economy"), but it is hard to look at this list without seeing in it a sort of meta-argument for qualitative change—in other words, an "urban revolution."[5]

Taylor and Lang themselves offer two possible responses to the eruption of new urban concepts: "One is to celebrate the variety: the world, especially the urban world, is inherently 'messy'.…. The other is to suspect that there is more than a little incoherent thinking abroad in contemporary urban studies."[6] A third—and in my view more persuasive—approach would be to accept *both* of these responses but then move on to *historicize* the relationship between the concepts and the material processes being conceptualized. The urban world might be "inherently 'messy'" and there may be "incoherent thinking" as Taylor and Lang suggest, but these things have always been true. If the forms of urban spatial change afoot in the contemporary era are particularly amenable to messiness and incoherent conceptualization, an explanation for this fact should lie not just in the forms themselves, but in the *interaction* between them and the concepts traditionally used to describe them.

The impulse more often has been to assume that new material arrangements will cast off their old discursive trappings (and presumably secrete new ones). Jürgen Habermas, for example, observes that "our concept of the city is connected to a form of life," and then suggests, "that form of life has changed so much that the concept that grew out of it can no longer keep pace," and so "the question arises whether the very *concept* of the city has not been superseded."[7] The impression we are left with is that the concept of the city is withering away, deprived of the material form that gave it birth.

And yet … the old idea of the city persists. Taylor and Lang claim that the terms describing new urban spaces suggest a negation of the idea of the traditional city, an argument seconded by Merrifield.[8] But nearly a third of Taylor and Lang's terms are simply "____ city," with some descriptor filling in the blank. In other words, it seems that the only thing that has been forgotten in this explosion of new critical urban research is the stubborn tenacity of the city concept itself. The problem is that, while the traditional concept of the city is no longer a convincing one, the obvious remedies are equally unconvincing. On the one hand would be an attempt to recuperate the term "city" (perhaps with a novel prefix to make it term 101 on Taylor and Lang's list) as an adequate analytical concept corresponding to some pattern of contemporary urbanization—but which pattern? Amin and Thrift, for example, claim that "the possibility of recognizing cities as spatial formations gives us a legitimate object of analysis," but proceed to offer an account of these formations whose very heterogeneity seems to contradict the claim.[9] On the other hand would be a preemptory dismissal of the city-concept altogether, as Merrifield suggests[10]—but the idea has proven tenacious, and we should account for that rather than simply wish it away.

To avoid the false necessity implied by these poles, we instead could move perpendicularly to both of them if we approached the city not as a category of *analysis,* but as a category of *practice*: a concept *arising* out of a given social practice rather than adequately *grasping* it. After all, a concept that has undeniable ongoing purchase in everyday life may nevertheless be a "chaotic" one for the purposes of theory-building and empirical research.[11] This distinction makes explicit the non-identity of (and potential radical difference between) "categories of everyday social experience, developed and deployed by ordinary social actors" and "the experience-distant categories used by social analysts."[12] Inspired by this distinction, I want to reinterpret the city-concept as a category of practice, and in particular as *ideology*.

The Urbanization of Ideology

The term "ideology" has nearly as many meanings in social theory as there are authors who have written about it,[13] and any reading of it must be selective. Here I draw on the "negative"[14] or "critical"[15] tradition, according to which ideology expresses the way that the forms of appearance of social reality under capitalism are systematically distorted to the benefit of some and the detriment of others. While critical conceptions of ideology often draw on a realist philosophy which posits an experience-independent "objective" reality which science can hope to access[16]—they do not require a radical distinction between "Science" and "Ideology" which maintains that the former can somehow escape the latter completely.[17] It is sufficient simply to posit that: 1) different theoretical and practical understandings have varying degrees of adequacy to the phenomenon they attempt to understand, with adequacy here being defined as distinguishing *necessary* properties from *contingent* ones[18]; and 2) some (more ideological) forms of understanding, which claim to understand the reality of things, actually do not manage to penetrate much beyond those things' forms of appearance. As Andrew Sayer lucidly argues, "it does not follow from the fact that all knowledge is fallible, that it is all *equally* fallible."[19]

Drawing on the critical usage of ideology, my argument is that, in the context of the contemporary North Atlantic, "the city" is a form of appearance corresponding only partially and problematically to urban reality. Or, rather, real*ities* in the plural: critical geographical scholarship shows that they are multiple, complex and contradictory. But the concept of the city obscures this multiplicity, at the very same time that it is a product of it. The city is an *ideological representation* of urbanization processes rather than a *moment* in them.

The premise for this claim is that the experience of urban space is necessarily partial, and that representations are the corollary to any complex social process that we cannot immediately experience in its totality. Representation is a cognitive shorthand, a way of rendering *conceivable* aspects of social reality that exceed our ability to *perceive* them. As Goonewardena explains, en route to a theorization of the "urban sensorium" to which I will return shortly:

> Now, if society were actually transparent, that is, if the totality of the structure of social relations were directly accessible to everyday human consciousness—then there would be no pressing need for an ideological representation of it. But it is clearly not so.[20]

Representations are not optional. Goonewardena makes this observation with respect to capitalism itself, but more modest social ensembles also elude our direct perception. What about urbanization? Surely so, particularly if we define the term expansively as Lefebvre would have us do, as a multiscalar process of the production and reproduction of the built environment, linking global structures of capital and the state with practices of everyday life[21]—a process that historically characterized the space of the city but has since shattered that space and become generalized. How can planetary urbanization be comprehended *except* through representation?[22]

Here it is worth emphasizing the difference between the city-urbanization relationship I have in mind and the standard understanding of this relationship in urban and spatial theory. Risking some oversimplification, the standard understanding of the city-urbanization relationship—both in mainstream and more critical traditions—is one of moment and process. "Process" because urbanization has been understood as a transformation over space and time: of population,[23] of urbanism as a way of life and its corresponding form of settlement space,[24] of relations of accumulation[25] and social reproduction,[26] or of some combination of these. "Moment" because, in the standard understanding, cities are the still frames which the urbanization process comprises: stop the process at any point in time, and the discrete spaces you observe are the extent of urbanization. Within this metatheoretical consensus, there have been disputes about whether the city or urbanization is the proper object of analysis, but no real disagreement about the basic relationship between the terms.[27]

In contrast to this standard understanding, I am here following Andrew Sayer's suggestion to treat the city as a "thought object" rather than a "real object," or, in the sociological language I have been using, as a "category of practice" rather than a "category of analysis."[28] This theoretical maneuver shifts the explanatory task away from condensing complex urbanization processes into the objective city-moments that comprise them, and toward charting how these processes are experienced and interpreted by social actors in everyday life and thus formed into practical representations. While urbanization might now be a planetary process, it is not lived or experienced as one.

This implies that any tenable concept of the city will look less like a scientific abstraction and more like a cognitive map.[29] After all, depicting the spontaneous representations that arise directly out of everyday urban spatial practice was precisely the goal of Kevin Lynch's justly celebrated exercises in cognitive mapping. But I have in mind something closer to Jameson's cognitive map of postmodern totality, which, as Goonewardena reminds us, was meant explicitly to despatialize an operation that for Lynch was always self-evidently spatial.[30] Totality, Jameson argued, could "obviously" not be represented spatially, so the exercise in mapping it might be able to "transcend" the spatiality of the map. And the same could be said about urbanization and the everyday experience of it: *there is no reason to think that it can be adequately mapped.* As insightful as Lynch's cognitive maps are, we risk a kind of design-fetishism if we imagine that the experience of urban space can be adequately reduced to a cartographic representation. If we redirected Jameson's impulse to despatialize the cognitive map back toward Lynch's original object of analysis, then, what would we find? What would a non-cartographic representation of urban spatial practice look like?

Perhaps it would look like the traditional idea of the city. "The city" is a concept that mediates our everyday experience of urbanization processes that are too complex for us to directly perceive. It is only tenable as a phenomenal category, not an analytical one. It would be meaningless and formalistic to suggest that there is one mass representation of people's relationship to the urbanization processes they experience. But in the context of the contemporary North Atlantic at least—the historical-geographical ensemble that has inherited both the intellectual tradition of the traditional city and the urban forms that inspired it—we must look for reasons that something like the traditional city remains a plausible representation of urbanization processes that have exceeded it. Moreover, we must investigate to what extent "the city" faithfully represents these processes and to what extent it distorts them as ideology. The concern is not that our everyday representations of the city might be "wrong" in analytic terms (because who would expect the categories of practice used by social actors to be the same as the categories of analysis developed by social scientists?), but rather that—as social imaginaries in Castoriadis' sense—they help structure and legitimate a social order founded on exploitation.[31]

Once we treat the city as a category of practice, the claim that the traditional Western concept of the city is an ideological one is not so far fetched. After all, we have known that partial, everyday representations of urban space are likely to be structured in particular ways at least since Simmel's "The Metropolis and Mental Life," which effectively describes an ideological environment (the "blasé attitude" and the feeling of social distance) arising out of certain patterns of urbanization (generalized relations of money-exchange and an enormous density of social interaction).[32] This question is what Goonewardena has theorized in the contemporary moment as the "urban sensorium."[33] His lynchpin is the contention that the gap between the global structures of capitalism and our consciousness of them in everyday life (ideology *par excellence*) is paralleled by a similar gap between the structures of urban space and our consciousness of them in the phenomenal experience of the city. Goonewardena thus suggests that the contemporary urban sensory environment (the "sensorium") systematically obscures not only the structure of urban space, but thereby the basic workings of capitalism itself.

Put momentarily in Althusserian terms,[34] if the city is a representation of people's imaginary relationship to real processes of urbanization, then what types of urban subjects does capitalist urbanization interpellate—and what ideas of the urban? For it is not only the case, as Goonewardena argues, that our experience of urban space selectively structures our understanding (i.e., representations) of capitalism, but the reverse is also true: our experience of capitalism selectively structures our understanding (i.e., representations) of urban space. Manuel Castells developed this latter claim via what he called simply *the* "urban ideology"[35]—the belief that the city, along with its generalization within an "urban society," is the causal force for social transformations that in fact are driven by class antagonism. Such analyses, he argued, falsely suggest the viability of a common front of all urban citizens against common urban problems. Raymond Williams had a similar critique of the misidentification of capitalism as urbanization, calling it the "the last protecting illusion in the crisis of our own time."[36]

In effect, Castells and Williams build on previous debates about the proper research object for urban studies while more directly raising the political implications of these debates.[37] Scholastic debates about what a city is and what urban studies should be, they imply, are an expression of a constitutive ambiguity in the role of urbanization within capitalist society—the very topic that Lefebvre attempted to historicize.[38] But while Castells and Williams identify a similar problematic, each stops somewhat short of explaining it. If urbanized capitalism persistently appears simply as urbanism, we should be able to explain why this is so as part of a theory of urbanized capitalism itself. Here, Lefebvre offers some suggestive aphorisms, but nothing really approaching a theory.

We can find such a theory in David Harvey's work. Harvey analyzes the urban process and its ideological forms of appearance integrally, identifying the production of fetishized understandings of sociospatial relations within the city.[39] But he does not ask *whether the city itself could be considered a fetish*, and this is the additional step I am taking. The most fruitful way to understand the traditional concept of the city and its persistence in the North Atlantic in the face of a qualitatively transforming urban landscape is as a phenomenological category—a practical understanding of urban space—which distorts what it represents. The concept of the city is not "obsolete," and we do not need to "reinvent" it for contemporary urban conditions. The concept of the city is ideological.

Accordingly, I now return to the three tropes of the traditional city—the city-country opposition, the city as a self-contained system, and the city as an ideal type—and briefly indicate how it might have come to be that they have progressively faded as adequate *analytical descriptions* of urbanization processes in the Global North, yet remained plausible *ideological representations* of these processes. As indicated above, I have singled out these three tropes as the dominant *formal* delineations of the city common to Western social science and particularly the Chicago School of urban sociology, in spite of the large variety of *content* the city-concept has been called upon to grapple with. I critically reconstruct these three features of the city-concept as ideological dimensions of contemporary urbanization, by commenting in each case on 1) the historical development of the trope as a feature of capitalist urbanization and as a social-scientific concept via the Chicago School; 2) the phenomenal experience of urbanization in relation to the trope; and 3) state and capitalist projects that have shored up the trope and thus the traditional concept of the city. What follows is intended not to break new empirical ground, but rather to reprise a familiar periodization of the urban process in a different context, and in so doing to shed light on an important contemporary instance of the social production and experience of space: the city as ideology.[40]

City and Country: Beyond the Spatial Division of Labor

The first trope, both historically and logically, is the opposition of city and country, the *sine qua non* of the traditional concept of the city. It is only once city and non-city came to be seen as separate social orders, that an identifiable urban social science came into existence, delineating its object of analysis in contrast to a non-urban outside: the countryside, the wilderness, the traditional village, etc. And it is precisely this opposition between city and countryside whose apparent obsolescence has been central to new approaches to understanding urban space. Yet the opposition remains central to urban experience, and to strategies of uneven development encouraging and leveraging this experience. In other words, the city-country opposition upon which the traditional concept of the city rests is not obsolete but ideological.

The separation of city and country under nineteenth-century Western European industrialization is a familiar story that needs no detailed rehearsing here: from the enclosure of the commons and the dispossession of peasants from the land, to the concentration of the workforce in the rapidly growing metropolises alongside manufacturing fixed capital.[41] This historical development of the spatial division of labor between industry and agriculture also corresponded to other city-country distinctions within the socially produced landscapes of capitalism: spatial mappings of social understandings.

One of these is the assumption that urban and rural are spatial containers for society and nature respectively.[42] Nature, external to the city, provides the raw materials to be transformed, within the city, into society, and provides a periodic escape from the pressures of society via its leisure spaces. The industrial revolution's concentration of manufacturing and population in Western European cities (and the corresponding deindustrialization and depopulation of the countryside) made this a plausible idea, and prompted a range of social responses by the end of the nineteenth century, from urban-oriented social reform movements to planning and design interventions, such as Howard's garden cities and a landscape architecture oriented towards providing green sanctuaries from busy urban life—typified by Olmsted and Vaux's Central Park.[43]

The other important guise of the city-country opposition is a morally inflected distinction between urban and rural ways of life. From the Chicago School, we owe this distinction to Louis Wirth and Robert Redfield, but the best historical analysis of it belongs to Raymond Williams.[44] Here, the city is the site of progress and the future, but also depravity, impersonality, and imbalance. The country, meanwhile, is the site of tradition and the past, but also morality, togetherness, and harmony. This understanding existed, as Williams notes, in some form or another for hundreds of years, but became a widespread experience and hence basis for social mobilization during the industrial revolution, directly motivating many of the radicals and utopian socialists of the nineteenth century.[45]

These three mappings of the city-country opposition (division of labor, society and nature, and way of life) are analytically distinguishable, but in practice tend to overlap and blur. The mainstream of Western urban studies via the Chicago School relied simultaneously on all three mappings as the basis for a teleological analysis of capitalist urban social transformation, which took a stable or self-evident division between city and country for granted. The separation of the city from the non-city thereby also became the separation of the city from history—an ideological timelessness that gave the Chicago School research program its clarity, but ultimately also led it to run aground when this assumption became manifestly insupportable.[46]

By contrast, the neo-Marxist renaissance in geography and urban theory historicized the city-country opposition, but assumed that it had been "overcome." Castells, Harvey, Lefebvre and Smith all carry this assumption, generally by reading city and country narrowly (as Marx himself did) as the spatial division of labor and capital between industry and agriculture. This mapping has indeed become decisively attenuated throughout the Global North and in many parts of the Global South, starting with the industrialization of agriculture: as Michael Perelman points out in reference to the twentieth-century US, many of the workers who left the farm and migrated to the city remained part of the agricultural production process, producing agricultural machinery and inputs such as tractors and chemical fertilizers to be metabolized by an increasingly small farming workforce.[47] More recently, the suburbanization of industry has accomplished a similar result in the opposite direction.

It would be a mistake, however, to simply close the file because city and country no longer correspond to the spatial division of labor in advanced capitalist economies. All three of the dominant historical mappings of city and country remain, to varying degrees, plausible representations of everyday life in advanced capitalist urban society, even if the precise referents have changed. And these representations are actively encouraged and produced through strategies of accumulation and state power.

In contemporary American public discourse, for example, small towns and the suburbs have readily occupied the position of the "country" in moral inflections of the city-country opposition (e.g., "Wall Street" versus "Main Street"). And not by accident: this is precisely how the suburbs were conceived of and marketed—as an escape from the evils of the city, and as a return to traditional small-town values.[48] Meanwhile gentrification projects, in the United States and throughout the world, have been consistently and successfully marketed as opportunities for cutting-edge, "progressive" urban living.[49] In both cases, the ongoing subjective salience of urban/non-urban distinctions has been actively encouraged as a strategy of accumulation, alongside equally consequential state representations of space, such as funding formulas for national and regional investment schemes, and censuses and geospatial data collection and operationalization.

Similarly, for all that agriculture has long been as industrialized as automobile manufacturing, cities still tend to be experienced as gray and the countryside as green. In the United States in particular, suburbanization has substantively undermined any objective coherence to the society-nature mapping of city and country, but in such a way that suburban living continues to be widely construed as non-urban and closer to nature. Michael Bell reports similar findings in his ethnography of a small English village, where the city-countryside opposition remains central to social identity and to practical interpretations of class.[50] And there is money to be made selling this "out-in-nature" experiential frame to city dwellers: across the North Atlantic, expanded circuits of tourism allow easy access to sustainability-oriented "eco-tourism" schemes or to amenity-heavy premium nature retreats.[51] Similar processes are at work in "sustainable city" projects, which have become important components of entrepreneurial urban governance strategies—what While et al. have called the "greening of the growth machine."[52] These projects trade on narratives of the *return* of nature to the city, and thus rely on a representation of urban environments as non-natural *except* where they incorporate superficially green elements, such as city parks or suburban lawns.[53] Only the gray city can be greened.

These representational dimensions of the separation of city and country have not waned alongside the political-economic blurring of the spatial division of labor. After decades of suburbanization and revolutions in mobility and communication technologies, the city-country opposition is incoherent as a category of analysis but coherent as a category of practice. And is this disjuncture simply a coincidence, a value-free curiosity? Of course not: the systematic production of the desire to flee the gray, decrepit city for the green, suburban countryside and then the desire to return to the edgy, modern, greening city have been central to uneven development on the regional scale for the last 50 years.[54] The space between city and country as a category of practice and a category of analysis is the space of ideology.

City as a System: The Urban Lifecycle and the Commuting Zone

The second trope of the traditional city is the city as a self-contained system. This trope has informed generations of scholarship on cities as urban worlds with their own endogenous logic, internally integrated but externally differentiated from surrounding hinterlands and other cities-as-systems. In fact, it did so long before cities in the Global North reasonably approximated such systems, during the Fordist-Keynesian era of metropolitan urbanization and city-suburban integration. Unlike the city-country opposition, the trope of the city as a self-contained system existed in theory before it existed in practice. And while the trope persists to some extent in urban studies, like the city-country opposition it has mostly been relegated to the theoretical dustbin, even as it continues to inform everyday representations of the urban and strategies of accumulation.

Prior to the industrial revolution, social commentators in the West generally understood the city not as its own independent social world but rather as expressive of general social relations writ large. The separation of city and countryside challenged this understanding, however, and gave Western social science the trope of the city as a distinctive, self-contained social system, most influentially via the pioneering work of the Chicago School of sociology. Robert Park used the metaphor of a "mechanism" to describe the system-properties of the city, while Ernest Burgess proposed to understand the city as an organism.[55] Alongside his famous concentric-circle model of Chicago, Burgess described an urban system within which people and their social ties circulate, integrate, and disintegrate in an unceasing metabolic process. The organicist idea is a dynamic one, but it is remarkably autarchic. Burgess' urban organism endlessly reproduces itself with barely any reference to the outside world: the urban metabolism has no fuel. In actual fact, the apparent development of cities as integrated social worlds was predicated on massive, continuing inflows of capital, resources and people from outside, a state of affairs captured in subsequent iterations of the urban metabolism concept.[56]

A preoccupation of the Chicago School's investigation of the urban organism was a search for its laws: the rules of the city-system. This preoccupation was in fact widespread throughout geography and urban studies in the twentieth century, including within the neo-Marxist revival; Castells' search for the functional specificity of the urban demonstrates this clearly.[57] And while such universalistic urban scholarship is now less common than it once was (although see the mathematical laws of urbanism from Bettencourt et al. for a prominent counter-example[58]), the city-as-system trope persists latently in urban studies via methodological localism—the analytical privileging of the local scale as a means of decoding its internal structure.[59] However, since the 1980s, critical approaches within urban and spatial theory have largely dispensed with the idea of cities as self-contained systems, just as they have dispensed with the opposition between the city and the countryside. Research on the relationship between globalization and urbanization, urban rescaling and networked urbanism has shown the contemporary North Atlantic urban world to be a multiplex, hybrid one, whose component city-systems are always partial and perforated.[60] But there is an intuitive phenomenal logic to the city as a self-contained system, both in temporal and spatial terms, which raises the possibility that the trope persists ideologically even as it has faded analytically.

In temporal terms, the cyclical and uneven patterns of urban change suggest an analogy between the urban ecosystem and the "natural world," where ecosystems and their components are seen to experience a lifecycle. The physical environment of cities evolves, ages, and decays, and the social environment seems to as well. New infrastructural growths emerge where a break in the urban canopy lets sunlight (or capital) shine through, and every so often a fire sweeps away old growth and sets the stage for new. Such ecological metaphors make it easier to see the city as a self-contained system. The see-saw pattern of uneven development at the urban scale appears as the local logic of a system in motion, when it substantively implies the opposite—the systematic penetration and remaking of urban spaces by regional, national and global capital.[61] This is ideology in the classic sense: a form of appearance which makes it more difficult to understand the underlying exploitative reality. The apparent inevitability of the urban lifecycle has long justified and facilitated urban accumulation by dispossession.[62]

In spatial terms, an important source of the plausibility of the city-as-a-system trope is the daily spatial practice most typical of large, motorized urban agglomerations in the Global North: commuting. Burgess' original formulation of the urban-ecosystem idea emphasized the importance of *non-routine* movement of people within the city, but routine movement—commuting—has proved far more influential in efforts to characterize, and in fact to create, the unity of an urban area.[63] Functional definitions of urban space—rooted abstractly in economic interconnection between places, and concretely in commuting ties—originated in the United States around the beginning of the twentieth century as a means of defining an integrated urban economic space when many such spaces had expanded beyond municipal or county borders.[64] The commuting zone has subsequently been widely adopted by statistics-gathering agencies worldwide as the accepted way to measure and compare urban areas in regional, national, and international contexts, and considerable effort has been exerted to establish the consistency of different definitions.

But there was an important historical transition from efforts to *identify* cities-as-systems to efforts to *create* them—the imperative to remake and integrate urban areas around the urban lifecycle and the daily commute. This imperative is readily identifiable in modernist urbanism—as Aksoy and Robins argue, "the modern city, like the modern nation, was imagined as a space that should be unitary, coherent and ordered"[65]—but did not become a decisive force in the production of space until the period of Fordist-Keynesian national industrial development after the Second World War. Throughout Western Europe, functional integration within and between urban regions was a central component of spatial Keynesianism, with local administrations serving as the policy vehicles for wide-ranging national programs of infrastructure investment, welfare state development, and metropolitan institution building. In the United States, suburbanization played a macroeconomic role similar to the welfare state in Western Europe, mobilizing effective demand into new economies of scale, and here the key vector for functional urban integration was highway construction typified by Robert Moses on the regional scale and the Eisenhower interstate highway system on the national scale.[66] Within urban areas, the task was to render central business districts maximally accessible to daily commuters from the new suburbs. Since existing large cities already had dense downtowns, often predating automobiles entirely, this was not easy, and required large-scale, violent demolition of neighbourhoods for new transportation infrastructure.[67] But by the end of the 1960s, American urban regions had generally been refashioned into integrated commuting regions.

However, even after the period of major highway construction ended, the Fordist-Keynesian era continued to see state policy deliberately and repeatedly employed to ensure that the urban lifecycle continue to churn. Students of urban planning in the United States will be familiar with federal- and state-government planners' use of the neighbourhood-lifecycle theory to justify destructive policies of "planned shrinkage" in deindustrializing metropolises.[68] These technocratic and capital-led efforts to remake cities as integrated systems did not happen without opposition. Community resistance to mega projects, urban renewal, and planned shrinkage was often fierce and sometimes successful. Still, these transformations of urban space were squarely at the center of a postwar (sub)urban ideology of universal automobility that was broadly shared.[69]

Since the 1970s, meanwhile, state and capitalist investments in the production of urban space in the Global North have increasingly abandoned the "modern infrastructural ideal" of integrated cities in favor of what Graham and Marvin have called "splintering urbanism"—neoliberalized, customized infrastructure networks that privilege competitiveness over equity.[70] But, while the city as an self-contained system thus might appear to be as dead in practice as it is in theory, splintering urbanism may have had the contradictory effect of decreasing the objective coherence of urban areas while potentially increasing their subjective coherence. To use the example of commuting patterns in the United States: the suburb-to-central-city commute for which metropolitan highway networks were constructed has shrivelled next to intra-suburban commuting. More strikingly, the proportion of commuters who commute outside their metropolitan area has been growing at almost three times the rate of commuting overall since 1980, and now stands at eight percent of the total.[71] This may seem a small figure, but metropolitan areas are specifically designed to aggregate commuting patterns, and they are constantly redefined to account for such developments. Despite statisticians' best efforts, the commuting zone—the state representation of the city as an integrated system—is slowly unraveling.

But what has happened to the subjective experience of commuting? For one, the daily labor migration has become a daily reproductive migration. That is, the trip from home to work and back has become a smaller and smaller share of the daily commute, and "is now festooned with associated and integrated trips … dropping things off in the morning and picking them up on the way home."[72] Whereas in the early twentieth century the spatial practice of an urban working-class American would have been clustered relatively tightly around the home and the workplace, now that spatial practice is increasingly diffuse—a pattern observable (although to a lesser degree) throughout the automobile-centered urban world. In other words, even as the commuting zone in aggregate is splintering, each individual commuter's everyday experience has come to resemble an aggregated commuting zone. The metropolitan area as the sum of one million point-A-to-point-B commutes is giving way to one million personal metropolitan areas. As the objective basis for considering the city a system unified by automobility declines, the subjective basis for experiencing it as such may have increased—and with it the plausibility of "common urban front" ideologies which minimize racial and class divisions and present the city as a space of equality even in the face of the systematic dismantling of the provisioning of this equality.

City as an Ideal Type: Urban Competitiveness

The third and final trope of the traditional concept of the city is the idea that cities are fundamentally comparable to one another—that "the city" in general is an ideal type, of which individual cities are discrete instances. Put pithily: every city is a city. In combination with the previous two tropes, the city as an ideal type provides the dominant formal framework for the study of urban space in the twentieth century: cities are externally differentiated from the countryside, internally integrated as self-contained systems, and related to each other as instances of the same type. More so than the previous two tropes, assumed ideal-typical urban comparability remains strongly present in urban studies, although arguably there have been multiple "universes" of urban comparison that until recently have only infrequently overlapped—most notably the Global North and the Global South.[73] In recent decades, this trope has metastasized into a key axis of globalized entrepreneurial urban governance.

The paradigmatic ideal-typical conception of the city, as with the previous two tropes, belongs to the Chicago School. Chicago ethnographer Robert Redfield uses the Weberian language explicitly to contrast the type of "folk society" with that of "urban society," while Louis Wirth's tripartite definition of the city as large, dense and diverse similarly constructs an ideal type in contrast to a rural settlement.[74] In both cases, and in ideal-typical urban scholarship more generally, the concept of the city is not meant to capture all the diversity of social conditions existing in any given urban area, but rather to analytically accentuate certain key features. And, while the specific features vary from analysis to analysis (Amin and Thrift provide a good overview of the diversity of content captured by the term "city"[75]), what is consistent is the assumption that there is some inherent condition of comparability underlying the city. Here we can note that, as problematic as Redfield's folk-urban typology is, it had at least the virtue of explicitly identifying its condition of comparability: modernization. More often the underlying comparability of cities has simply been assumed rather than argued: the City floats outside history, while an endless variety of specific cities enters and exits the world stage.

Although the trope of the city-country opposition emerged both in practice and in theory under industrialization in the nineteenth century, the city was conceptualized as an integrated system before it was made so under postwar Fordism-Keynesianism. Likewise, although *scholars* have long compared cities, in *practical* terms the city as an ideal type belongs squarely to the neoliberal era, under the guise of *urban competitiveness*.[76] Urban competitiveness is a keyword describing entrepreneurial urban governance oriented toward attracting globally mobile capital investment as a means of economic survival.[77] Not all urban entrepreneurs are targeting the same "spaces of competition"—global cities such as New York and

London are generally understood to be competing within a different global space from export processing zones in Manilla or Shenzen, for example. But across the world, there has been a striking generalization of the need to compete and the potential limitlessness of the global urban competitive playing field.

Competitiveness (or its lack) is often portrayed in the media and mainstream scholarly accounts as a natural, almost ontological property of cities in the contemporary globalizing economy, and thus has become an urbanized instance of Margaret Thatcher's famous pronouncement that "there is no alternative" to neoliberal capitalism. In the global political-economic landscape, competition between cities is widely viewed as inevitable. But such competition is better understood not as a property of city-ness, but rather as a structural effect of coalitions of local elites mobilizing to defend and promote their geographically fixed interests, as in analyses of urban growth machines and territorial alliances.[78] Such elite coalitions seek to muster as broad a base of support as possible for their favored policies, and one prominent means of doing so is the fostering of ideologies of local community—a local, united "us" to compete against a non-local "them."[79] Of course not all feelings of local community are ideological, and, as Harvey notes, capitalist attempts to foster local community as an accumulation strategy are an uncertain business that can backfire through the inadvertent encouraging of local communities of resistance.[80] Still, the systematic efforts of boosters, entrepreneurial urban governance agents, and growth-oriented local media are aimed at producing a depoliticized representation of a unitary city competing in a world of similarly unitary cities—precisely the trope of the city as an ideal type, but in practical, ideological form.[81]

The implications of this political and discursive framework for comparing cities are clearly illustrated by a recent policy statement from the Greater London Authority:

> London ... needs to compare itself with other cities for the purpose of identifying best practice for policy. ... It is our view that having a common standard is more important that having the right standard since in some senses if there is a common standard which represents city-regions in a reasonably consistent way then that itself is the "right" standard.[82]

Translation: comparison is necessary, never mind what is being compared. Taylor and Lang's list of 100 concepts to describe recent urban change should make it clear that this trope has increasingly little analytical purchase on the contemporary urban world.[83] Many of the terms they identify describe new inter-urban systems that, when taken together, suggest heterogeneity and variegation to be the emerging urban norm. So it is striking that the last 30 years have seen the emergence and consolidation of an urban governance paradigm rooted in the broad and necessary comparability of bounded cities on a global scale.

A recent innovation in urban policy which has been key in facilitating this comparison is urban benchmarking.[84] Actors ranging from international think tanks to popular media to municipal chambers of commerce now routinely publish "competitiveness reports" and lists of "best places to live" which are widely reported on in local media. Local elites deploy the same discourse in attempting to build support for favored policy interventions, again working through (and often with the overt support of) local media and appealing to national media coverage to make the case.[85] The result is a nexus of media, public opinion and portable urban policy oriented around the competitive threat from other cities, and a discursive uniformity of intuitive urban comparability.

The general phenomenon of local elites or politicians attempting to muster broad local support for an economic development agenda favorable to a narrow range of interests is certainly not unique to the neoliberal era, as Logan and Molotch's historical analysis of the growth machine in the United States demonstrates.[86] But the ubiquitous assumption that competitiveness is a (or even *the*) key problem of urban governance is of recent origin. No doubt there are other factors one could focus on to help explain the ongoing intuitiveness of the city as an inherently comparative unit even despite political economic restructuring making such an understanding increasingly implausible in analytical terms. But urban competitiveness illustrates straightforwardly a confluence of elite interests and everyday understandings, which is characteristic of all three of the tropes of the traditional city I have been discussing.

Conclusion: Who Benefits from the City as Ideology?

This essay is an attempt to deal with the specter of the city that hangs over critical urban and spatial theory, and it is one part séance and one part exorcism. The preceding discussion is tentative, but it should suffice to illustrate the following dilemma. In recent decades, qualitatively new patterns of urbanization have transformed inherited sociospatial landscapes and thereby called into question the coherence of the city as the basic unit of urban analysis. But these patterns have not necessarily had the same impact on everyday consciousness of urbanization—the "cognitive maps" of these new urban spaces may still resemble the traditional city. So on the one hand, we have complex patterns of urban growth that have exceeded the traditional idea of the city, while on the other, we have the ongoing salience of the city-concept to everyday urban spatial practice. The former suggests the futility for critical spatial theory of continuing to bend the concept of the city to fit these new forms of urbanization—what I have elsewhere called "methodological cityism"[87]—while the latter suggests the importance of not simply abandoning the concept altogether. What I have outlined here is a third way: to treat the city as a category of practice, as a representation of people's relationship to urbanization processes, rather than an as a category of analysis adequate to describe these processes themselves. But in a specific sense: we should systematically interrogate the city not simply as a neutral representation, but as ideology—as a structured misrecognition that critical urban theory and practice must confront and seek to change alongside the sociomaterial forms that produce it. Such a project implies treating the "right to the city" with some caution, since as an emancipatory urban imaginary, it is only one potential orientation within the wider field of "the city" as a normative concept, a concept always already laden with power relations.[88]

After all, the adequacy of the three tropes of the traditional city I have discussed is not the same for all social actors. Just as the idea that "hard work pays off" is ideological but adequate to capitalists, the traditional concept of the city is ideological but adequate to urban elites—the problem in both cases is that these ideologies are *not* adequate to most people. Suburbanization and gentrification as accumulation strategies, sold on the myths of city and country; metropolitan integration, sold on the myths of automobility and the urban lifecycle; urban competitiveness, sold on the myths of an urban us versus them. Radical geography and urban theory must uncover and resist both the policies and the myths. At least many or most workers know that they are being exploited in the labor market; at a minimum we need to strive for the same understanding about the city.

The challenge is that these ideological tropes do not endure simply because elite actors want them to; they continue to correspond to a common experience of urban society, and thereby influence scholarly as well as everyday understandings of urbanization in the Global North. The geographical specificity of the traditional city-concept is significant in its own right: the three tropes of the traditional city all have North Atlantic provenance, and their problematic dissemination around the world as mobile capital, mobile policy, and mobile theory are all of a piece. The project of generating "new geographies of theory" thus also must entail a critique of the old geographies that have persisted too long.[89]

Notes

1   Henri Lefebvre, *The Urban Revolution*, trans. Robert Bononno (Minneapolis: University of Minnesota Press, 2003 [1970]) 57; translation amended.

2   Henri Lefebvre, "The Right to the City," *Writings on Cities* (Cambridge: Blackwell, 1996 [1968]) 63-184.

3   Robert Park, "Succession, an Ecological Concept," *American Sociological Review* 1, 2 (1936) 171–9; and Louis Wirth, "Urbanism as a Way of Life," *Classic Essays on the Culture of Cities*, ed. Richard Sennett (New York: Appleton-Century-Crofts, 1969 [1937]) 143-64.

4   Peter J. Taylor and Robert E. Lang, "The Shock of the New: 100 Concepts Describing Recent Urban Change," *Environment and Planning A* 36 (2004) 951–8.

5   Lefebvre, *The Urban Revolution*.

6   Taylor and Lang, "The Shock of the New," 955.

7   Jürgen Habermas, "Modern and Postmodern Architecture," *The New Conservatism*, ed. Jürgen Habermas and trans. Sherry Nicholsen (Cambridge: MIT Press, 1989) 17.

8   Andy Merrifield, "The Urban Question under Planetary Urbanization," this book, Ch. 12.

9   In this context, it is striking to note that powerful and long-overdue challenges to the hegemony of Anglo-American urban theory have tended (implicitly or explicitly) to confirm the city as a lowest common denominator for urban theory, even as they expose the parochialisms with which it has traditionally been treated for example, Jennifer Robinson, "Cities in a World of Cities: The Comparative Gesture," *International Journal of Urban and Regional Research* 35, 1 (2011) 1–23. Also see Ash Amin and Nigel Thrift, *Cities: Reimagining the Urban* (London: Polity, 2002) 2.

10   Merrifield, "The Urban Question Under Planetary Urbanization," this book, Ch. 12.

11   Andrew Sayer, *Method in Social Science*, Second Edition (London: Routledge, 1992).

12   Rogers Brubaker and Frederick Cooper, "Beyond 'Identity'," *Theory and Society* 29, 1 (2002) 4.

13   Terry Eagleton, *Ideology: An Introduction* (New York: Verso, 1991).

14   Jorge Larrain, *Marxism and Ideology* (London: Macmillan, 1983).

15   Trevor Purvis and Alan Hunt, "Discourse, Ideology, Discourse, Ideology, Discourse, Ideology," *The British Journal of Sociology* 44, 3 (1993) 473-99.

16   Sayer, *Method in Social Science*.

17   Louis Althusser, "Ideology and Ideological State Apparatuses," *Lenin and Philosophy and Other Essays*, trans. Ben Brewster (New York: Monthly Review Press, 2001) 127-86.

18   Andrew Sayer, "Abstraction: a Realist Interpretation," *Radical Philosophy* 28, Summer, (1981) 6-15.

19   Ibid., 7; emphasis in original.

20   Kanishka Goonewardena, "The Urban Sensorium: Space, Ideology and the Aestheticization of Politics," *Antipode* 37, 1 (2005) 52.

21   Lefebvre, *The Urban Revolution*.

22   Neil Brenner, "Theses on Urbanization," this book, Ch. 13.

23 Kingsley Davis, "The World Demographic Transition," *Annals of the American Academy of Political and Social Science* 237, 1 (1945) 1–11; UN-HABITAT, *State of the World's Cities 2008/2009* (London: Earthscan, 2008); and Neil Brenner and Christian Schmid, "The 'Urban Age' in Question," this book, Ch. 21.

24 Wirth, "Urbanism as a Way of Life."

25 David Harvey, *The Urban Experience* (Baltimore: Johns Hopkins University Press, 1989).

26 Manuel Castells, *The Urban Question: A Marxist Approach* (Cambridge: MIT Press, 1977).

27 David Harvey, "Cities or Urbanization?" this book, Ch. 3.

28 Andrew Sayer, "Defining the Urban," *GeoJournal* 9, 3 (1984) 279-85.

29 Kevin Lynch, *The Image of the City* (Cambridge: MIT Press, 1960); and Katie M. Mazer and Katharine N. Rankin, "The Social Space of Gentrification," *Environment and Planning D: Society and Space* 29 (2011) 822-39.

30 Fredric Jameson, (1991) *Postmodernism, or, The Cultural Logic of Late Capitalism* (Durham: Duke University Press, 1991); and Goonewardena, "The Urban Sensorium," 56-7.

31 Cornelius Castoriadis, *The Imaginary Institution of Society* (Cambridge: MIT Press, 1987).

32 Georg Simmel, "The Metropolis and Mental Life," *On Individuality and Social Forms*, ed. Georg Simmel (Chicago: University of Chicago Press, 1971) 324-39.

33 Goonewardena, "The Urban Sensorium."

34 Althusser defined ideology as "a 'representation' of the imaginary relationship of individuals to their real conditions of existence." See Althusser, "Ideology and Ideological State Apparatuses," 162.

35 Castells, *The Urban Question.*

36 Raymond Williams, *The Country and the City* (Oxford: Oxford University Press, 1973) 96.

37 Francisco Benet, "Sociology Uncertain: the Ideology of the Rural-Urban Continuum," *Comparative Studies in Society and History* 6, 1 (1963) 1-23; Manuel Castells, "Is There an Urban Sociology?" *Urban Sociology: Critical Essays*, ed. Chris G. Pickvance (London: Methuen & Co, 1976) 33-59; Ernest Manheim, "Theoretical Prospects of Urban Sociology in an Urbanized World," *American Journal of Sociology* 66, 3 (1960) 226-9; and Louis Wirth, "Rural-Urban Differences," *Classic Essays on the Culture of Cities*, ed. Richard Sennett (New York: Appleton-Century-Crofts, 1969) 165-9.

38 Lefebvre, *The Urban Revolution.*

39 Harvey, *The Urban Experience*, chapter 8.

40 Ibid., chapter 1.

41 See Michael Perelman, *The Invention of Capitalism* (Durham: Duke University Press, 2000); and Karl Polanyi, *The Great Transformation* (Boston: Beacon Press, 1944).

42 David Wachsmuth, "Three Ecologies: Urban Metabolism and the Society-Nature Opposition," *Sociological Quarterly* 53, 4 (2012) 506-23.

43 Ebenezer Howard, *Garden Cities of To-Morrow* (Cambridge: MIT Press, 1965); and Anne Whiston Spirn, (1995) "Constructing Nature: The Legacy of Frederick Law Olmsted," *Uncommon Ground*, ed. William Cronon (New York: W.W. Norton, 1995) 91-113.

44 Wirth, "Urbanism as a Way of Life;" Robert Redfield, "The Folk Society," *The American Journal of Sociology* 52, 4 (1947) 293-308; and Williams, *The Country and the City.*

45 Craig Calhoun, *The Question of Class Struggle: Social Foundations of Popular Radicalism During the Industrial Revolution* (Chicago: University of Chicago Press, 1982).

46 Benet, "Sociology Uncertain."

47 Michael Perelman, "Mechanization and the Division of Labor in Agriculture," *American Journal of Agricultural Economics* 55, 3 (1973) 523-6.

48 Robert Fishman, *Bourgeois Utopias: the Rise and Fall of Suburbia* (New York: Basic Books, 1987).

49 Neil Smith, *The New Urban Frontier* (New York: Routledge, 1966).

50 Michael Bell, *Childerley: Nature and Morality in a Country Village* (Chicago: University of Chicago Press, 1995).

51 Ben Brewster and Michael Bell, "The Environmental Goffman: Toward an Environmental Sociology of Everyday Life," *Society and Natural Resources* 23, 1 (2009) 45-57; and David B. Weaver and Laura J. Lawton, "Twenty Years On: The State of Contemporary Ecotourism Research," *Tourism Management* 28 (2007) 1168-79.

52 Aiden While, Andrew E. G. Jonas and David Gibbs, "The Environment and the Entrepreneurial City," *International Journal of Urban and Regional Research* 28, 3 (2004) 549-69.

53 Roger Keil and John Graham, "Reasserting Nature: Constructing Urban Environments after Fordism," *Remaking Reality*, eds. Bruce Braun and Noel Castree (New York: Routledge, 1998) 100-25.

54 Smith, *The New Urban Frontier.*

55 Robert Park, "The City: Suggestions for the Investigation of Human Behavior in the City Environment," *The American Journal of Sociology* 20, 5 (1915) 577-612; and Ernest Burgess, "The Growth of the City," *The City*, eds. Robert Park and Ernest Burgess (Chicago: University of Chicago Press, 1925) 47-62.

56 Abel Wolman, "The Metabolism of Cities," *Scientific American* 213, 3 (1965) 178-93; see Wachsmuth, "Three Ecologies" for a historical overview.

57 Castells, *The Urban Question*; and Neil Brenner, "The Urban Question as a Scale Question," *International Journal of Urban and Regional Research* 24, 2 (2000) 361-78.

58 Luís Bettencourt, José Lobo, Dirk Helbing, Christian Kühnert and Geoffrey B. West, "Growth, Innovation, Scaling, and the Pace of Life in Cities," *Proceedings of the National Academy of Sciences* 104, 17 (2007) 7301-06.

59 Neil Brenner, "Is There a Politics of 'Urban' Development?" *The City in American Political Development*, ed. Richardson Dilworth (New York Routledge, 2009) 121-40.

60 John Friedman and Geotz Wolff, "World City Formation: An Agenda for Research and Action," *International Journal of Urban and Regional Research* 6, 2 (1982) 309-44; Saskia Sassen, *The Global City: New York, London, Tokyo.* (Princeton: Princeton University Press, 1991); Brenner, "The Urban Question as a Scale Question"; Neil Brenner, *New State Spaces: Urban Governance and the Rescaling of Statehood* (Oxford: Oxford University Press, 2004); Erik Swyngedouw and Nikolas Heynen, "Urban Political Ecology, Justice and the Politics of Scale," *Antipode* 35, 5 (2003) 898-918; and Stephen Graham and Simon Marvin, *Splintering Urbanism* (New York: Routledge, 2001).

61 Neil Smith, *Urban Development: Nature, Capital, and the Production of Space, Third Edition.* (Athens: University of Georgia Press, 2008).

62 John T. Metzger, "Planned Abandonment: The Neighborhood Life-Cycle Theory and National Urban Policy," *Housing Policy Debate* 11, 1 (2000) 7-40.

63 Burgess, "The Growth of the City."

64 Henry S. Shryock, Jr. "The Natural History of Standard Metropolitan Areas," *The American Journal of Sociology* 63, 2 (1957) 163-170.

65 Asu Aksoy and Kevin Robins, "Modernism and the Millennium," *City* 2, 8 (1997) 26.

66 Richard Florida and Marshall Feldman, (1988) "Housing in US Fordism," *International Journal of Urban and Regional Research* 12, 2 (1988) 187-210.

67 Marshall Berman, *All That Is Solid Melts into Air* (London: Penguin, 1988).

68 Metzger, "Planned Abandonment."

69 Mimi Sheller and John Urry, "The City and the Car," *International Journal of Urban and Regional Research* 24, 4 (2000) 737-57.

70 Graham and Marvin, *Splintering Urbanism.*

71 Alan E. Pisarski, *Commuting in America III: The Third National Report on Commuting Patterns and Trends* (Washington: Transportation Research Board, 2006) 52-3.

72 Ibid., 151.

73 Robinson, "Cities in a World of Cities."

74 Redfield, "The Folk Society"; and Wirth, "Urbanism as a Way of Life."

75 Amin and Thrift, *Cities.*

76 Colin McFarlane, "The Comparative City: Knowledge, Learning,

Urbanism," *International Journal of Urban and Regional Research* 34, 4 (2010) 725-42.

77 David Harvey, "From Managerialism to Entrepreneurialism: The Transformation in Urban Governance in Late Capitalism," *Geografiska Annaler, Series B* 71, 1 (1989) 3-17; and Neil Brenner and David Wachsmuth, "Territorial Competitiveness: Lineages, Practices, Ideologies," *Planning Ideas That Matter: Livability, Territoriality, Governance and Reflective Practice,* ed. Bishwapriya Sanyal, Lawrence J. Vale, and Christina D. Rosan (Cambridge: MIT Press, 2012) 179-204.

78 John R. Logan and Harvey Molotch, *Urban Fortunes: the Political Economy of Place* (Berkeley: University of California Press, 1987); and David Harvey *The Limits to Capital* (New York: Verso, 2006).

79 Kevin R. Cox, "Ideology and the Growth Coalition," *The Urban Growth Machine,* eds. Andrew E. G. Jonas and David Wilson (Albany: SUNY Press, 1999) 21-36; and Castells, *The Urban Question.*

80 Harvey, *The Urban Experience,* 236.

81 Mark Boyle, "Growth Machines and Propaganda Projects," *The Urban Growth Machine,* eds. Andrew E. G. Jonas and David Wilson (Albany: SUNY Press, 1999) 55-70; Harvey, "From Managerialism to Entrepreneurialism;" and Logan and Molotch, *Urban Fortunes,* 70-3.

82 Alan Freeman and Paul Cheshire, "Defining and Measuring Metropolitan Regions: A Rationale," paper presented to OECD conference, Paris, (2006) 2. www.oecd.org/dataoecd/50/29/37788230.pdf

83 Taylor and Lang, "The Shock of the New."

84 Francis J. Greene, Paul Tracey and Marc Cowling, "Recasting the City into City-Regions," *Growth and Change* 38, 1 (2007) 1-22.

85 Eugene J. McCann, "'Best Places': Interurban Competition, Quality of Life and Popular Media Discourse," *Urban Studies* 41, 10 (2004) 1909-29.

86 Logan and Molotch, *Urban Fortunes.*

87 Hilary Angelo and David Wachsmuth, "Urbanizing Urban Political Ecology: A Critique of Methodological Cityism," this book, Ch. 24.

88 Bob Catterall, "Editorial," *City* 15, 3-4 (2011) 285-8.

89 Ananya Roy, "The 21st-Century Metropolis: New Geographies of Theory," *Regional Studies* 43, 6 (2009) 819-30.

24
URBANIZING URBAN POLITICAL ECOLOGY: A CRITIQUE OF METHODOLOGICAL CITYISM

Hillary Angelo and David Wachsmuth

Introduction: The Green City in an Urban World

At the dawn of what is being heralded as the "urban millennium," the city has found a new "wish image."[1] Urban areas expand relentlessly and fears of global warming and environmental catastrophe loom ever greater, and the "green" or "sustainable city" is taking a leading role in planning and policy discourse.[2] From radical critique to technocratic reform, these two ideas have tripped along hand in hand: if more than half of the world is now urban, hopes for its future must rest on the shoulders of the green, sustainable city.[3]

In one sense, the idea of the green city is nothing new: nature has long been prescribed as a cure for the city's social ills. Social reformers and utopians in late nineteenth-century Europe and early twentieth-century United States advocated for and engineered escape routes from dense, dirty urban slums, which included weekends in the countryside, summer camps for children, and large public parks. In another sense, though, the contemporary green city marks a significant change. An increasingly urban world seems to make escape-the-city solutions untenable—where to escape to?—and so it is not surprising that public policy and elite discourse across the world has increasingly turned instead to reimagining the city itself along greener, more sustainable lines.[4]

In this context, urban political ecology (UPE) seemingly could not be more relevant, with its urbanized analysis of resource flows and environmental struggles. And while UPE has done an exemplary job of investigating environmental questions in cities, it has been curiously quiet on the very feature of the contemporary urban world that should make it so relevant: the dimensions of urbanization processes that exceed the confines of the traditional city. These dimensions are now considerable indeed, as recent scholarship on "planetary urbanization," "worlding cities" and the "urban age" all attest—even if there is as yet no consensus on the precise character and scope of these new dimensions.[5]

What is the role of urban political ecology in these debates on an increasingly urban planet? If we take the pervasiveness of urban sustainability discourses in contemporary elite policy circuits and the popular imagination to imply a corresponding pervasiveness of socionature within planetary urban processes, then urban political ecology has the potential to be more than just the study of nature in the city. It could contribute to a new theory of urbanization that simultaneously foregrounds nature as it deemphasizes cities *per se*. Indeed, as we discuss below, this was one of the goals of UPE's founding theorists, and a goal that is still attainable.

In this chapter, we tell the story of UPE in the context of planetary urbanization—its premises, its promise, and where it got off track—and argue that these earlier ambitions need to be more substantively integrated into current research in the field. We recount the history of UPE as a project both of introducing political ecology to the city and of reinterpreting urbanization along constitutively socionatural lines; we develop a Lefebvrian critique of UPE's *methodological cityism* in its failure to live up to the second of these aspirations; and we suggest how the field could reorient itself to being a *political ecology of urbanization* rather than a *political ecology of cities*.

The History: How Political Ecology Came to the City

Why did it take political ecology so long to come to the city? If we look at Blaikie and Brookfield's classic definition of the field, after all, its urban dimension seems perfectly obvious in retrospect.

> The phrase "political ecology" combines the concerns of ecology and a broadly defined political economy. Together this encompasses the constantly shifting dialectic between society and land-based resources, and also within classes and groups within society itself.[6]

Society, land use, class: it is not a stretch to see these as urban questions. And the contributions to "human ecology"—one of the two fields that are generally understood to have spawned political ecology—of the Chicago School urban sociologists are hardly insignificant. So it is perhaps because political ecology from its inception was understood by its practitioners to be above all concerned with the politics of environmental degradation and environmental rehabilitation that it was a presumptively non-urban field.[7] The city, as the very antithesis of "environment" in the popular and scholarly imaginations, might feature political struggles over land use and resources, but it is a site where nature was understood to be already subjugated to society—where no rehabilitation was possible because there was no "environment" left to be rehabilitated.[8] In the present era of urban environmental crisis, what an unconvincing story this now appears. But how else to explain this urban myopia?

One way or the other, political ecology developed in happy indifference to the urban world, and by the 1990s had become a robust research program focused mainly on the politics of land use in non-urban (and non-Western) spaces. Not that it had not undergone its own internal transformations, the most significant being a broadly poststructuralist reassessment of Blaikie and Brookfield's "dialectic between society and land-based resources." Scholars such as Arturo Escobar, Richard Peet and Michael Watts drew on concepts such as hybridity and social construction to challenge above all the stable category of "nature" that had underlain mainstream political ecology from the beginning.[9] For Escobar, the result of this exercise was to redefine political ecology such that it no longer relied on the concept, but instead helped account for its ongoing social construction: "Political ecology can be defined as the study of the manifold articulations of history and biology and the cultural mediations through which such articulations are necessarily established."[10] The result of this and other allied interventions was an approach that had much in common with actor-network theory, as Latour himself explored.[11]

It was in the midst of this poststructuralist reassessment of political ecology that Erik Swyngedouw made his initial call for an *urban* political ecology.[12] There were two sides to his argument: first, an attempt to reconcile the society/nature and material/discursive binaries at work in political ecology through a novel approach to hybridity he termed "socionature"; and second, a proposal to extend the reach of political ecology into urban studies, in particular through the medium of water. Both were achieved through a retheorization of urbanization as "a political-ecological process with water as the entry point; water that embodies, simultaneously and inseparably, bio-chemical and physical properties, cultural and symbolic meanings, and socio-economic characteristics."[13] This argument dovetailed with David Harvey's influential contention that "there is nothing *unnatural* about New York City," to produce a surge of new critical research into the production of urban socionatures, much of which was organized under the banner of urban political ecology.[14]

So, from the beginning, urban political ecology had two related goals: to bring the methodology of political ecology into urban settings to which it had hitherto not been applied, and to retheorize urbanization itself as a process of socionatural and not just social transformation. Roger Keil, another of the field's founders, further extended the ambition of this latter goal by suggesting that UPE was particularly well suited to meet the theoretical and empirical challenges posed by what Lefebvre called "urban society."[15] In a 2003 review of the field's burgeoning literature, he argued that "to speak now about UPE as central to urban studies in general may be interpreted as responding to Lefebvre's challenge to create an urban science for an urban world."[16]

The urban intervention in political ecology was long overdue. For all political ecology's 1990s success at analyzing society and nature integrally, by training its analytical lens almost exclusively on the countryside or wilderness it unreflexively reproduced one of the most enduring facets of the society/nature opposition: its spatial mapping onto town and country, respectively.[17] It is no coincidence, then, that Swyngedouw's first elaboration of the need for an urban political ecology was simultaneously his major contribution to rethinking the society-nature opposition in general, through the portmanteau of "socionature."[18] The city was the great, uncharted frontier for analyzing the co-production of the social and the natural.

And this frontier had remained uncharted not only in political ecology. As an intervention in critical urban studies, Swyngedouw's early work on socionature and the elaborations that followed within UPE accomplished two simultaneous "denaturings." They demolished what remained of the Chicago School vision of cities as social worlds *analogous* to nature (obeying naturalized laws of development) and its blindness to the material ways in which nature, even in its most obvious green forms, was implicated in the production of these urban social worlds. Instead of seeing cities as social rather than natural, or urban injustice and inequality as natural rather than social, UPE made cities visible as *political* worlds, the politics of which are constitutively socionatural.

UPE helped bring to critical urban studies a new vision of the traditionally understood city: as a product of a global "metabolic socio-environmental process that stretches from the immediate environment to the remotest corners of the globe."[19] It provided a lens through which to analyze both cities and things in cities as historical, material socionatural assemblages, and the transformation of nature in urban environments as bound up in broader processes of uneven development. Following Swyngedouw's 1996 programmatic statements, texts such as Matthew Gandy's *Concrete and Clay*, Maria Kaika's *City of Flows*, and the essays compiled in the edited volume *In the Nature of Cities* each helped crystallize the socionatural city.[20]

In tandem with the greater ontological clarity afforded by this image, conceptions of urban socionatures also helped open up new avenues for urban theory and politics. As urban social movements increasingly framed their battles in ecological terms—most notably through the language of environmental justice—and spectres of environmental disaster haunted the urban imaginary, UPE provided a language through which radical urban theory and politics could forge alliances with these movements.[21] Connecting society and nature under the heading "urbanization" not only clarified urbanists' understanding of the production of urban built environments, but, crucially, also enabled the critical reframing of urban environmental problems in broader economic, social, and historical context. The political payoff of UPE's analytic focus on the production of nature has thus been the insistence that, to address problems of nature in cities such as environmental injustice and pollution, interventions must be made at the level of the social order, contrary to planners and theorists of the 1850s—and the present moment!—who argued that it was the "nature of the city and not that of society that needed to change."[22] UPE's framework, particularly in its Marxist strands, at once provided (1) shields against liberal, anti-urban ideologies that continue to rely on false dualisms such as town/country, urban/rural, and nature/culture as prescriptions for social problems—by preserving certain kinds of nature and providing access to it, or cleaning up dark, disorderly cities with planning interventions of the garden city legacy; (2) arrows to penetrate and expose deep, structural economic and social injustices; and (3) language for cross-issue alliance building among social and environmental activists.[23]

Following early programmatic statements, there has been a slow but steady uptake of research under the UPE rubric. Most subsequent work has filled in the analytical frame initially provided with empirical case studies describing the production of urban socionatures or injustices of urban environmental conditions with increasing sophistication. One branch of recent literature in the family describes the processes of production of specific socionatural forms, often in relationship to the city as a whole.[24] Another investigates the political economies of particular "natural" resources, taking up questions of management, distribution and access, by focusing on negative externalities, environmental justice, and sustainability.[25] Work on neoliberal natures has begun to describe specific forms and patterns under different urban political economic regimes, while a few outliers include applications of UPE's framework to related theoretical issues, settings—in particular suburbia and exurbs—and conceptions of politics.[26]

Methodological Cityism

Yet as we find the terrain of socionature and urban environmental injustice increasingly well mapped, it is hard not to notice that UPE's success has been rather one-sided. Recall from above that the UPE theorization of urbanization had two major ambitions. First, its socionatural moment: an explicit attempt to rethink urbanization as "a social process of transforming and reconfiguring nature."[27] Second, a Lefebvrian moment: as Keil puts it, "the realization that what we call 'the urban' is a complex, multiscale and multidimensional process where the general and specific aspects of the human condition meet," and thus that the object of analysis in the study of contemporary urbanization must be "urban society" rather than the city *per se*.[28] It is the first, socionatural moment that has been best elaborated theoretically and substantiated empirically: UPE has succeeded in bringing political ecology to the city. The Lefebvrian moment in its theorization of the urban, meanwhile, remains an ambition as yet unfulfilled.

But should we be surprised by this outcome? For all the early UPE texts' rhetorical appeals to a Lefebvrian conception of urbanization, the implications of such an understanding for the study of urban socionatures were rarely if ever substantively articulated, either theoretically or through the selection of empirical research sites. Beyond its banner statements, UPE did not systematically elaborate a distinctive concept of—or research program for—urbanization as a set of processes that are not reducible to the city. Suggestively, Swyngedouw himself uses the terms "urbanization" and "city" interchangeably, as if the former is simply the spread of the latter. In his initial formulation of the idea of urban political ecology, he refers to the project on one page as "the political ecology of the city" and on the next as "the political ecology of the urbanization process."[29] More recently he has asserted, "Modern urbanization or the city can be articulated as a process of geographically arranged socio-environmental metabolisms."[30] Which is it: urbanization or the city? One is a process, the other a site which is one (but not the only) outcome of that process. Surely they are not the same thing.

Moreover, it is precisely the relationship between them—the city as a specific although variegated socionatural form and urbanization as a global socionatural process—which Lefebvre calls on us to reevaluate, and which UPE seemed so well positioned to do. The early theorization of urban political ecology by Swyngedouw, echoed by Keil, was not only an attempt to insert nature into the production of cities, but also an attempt to assert the centrality of urbanization to broader socionatural processes that political ecologists studied.[31] Yet not only has political ecology itself continued to stubbornly exclude the city from its analysis, but the bulk of empirical research in urban political ecology has been tethered exclusively to the city, in both its site selection and analytical framework. The global socionatural dimensions of urbanization that span city and countryside, and whose insufficient investigation was apparently one of the main motivations behind the research program in the first place, have, in practice, remained largely unexplored.

Thus we find actually existing UPE guilty of *methodological cityism*. The city is its near-exclusive analytical lens for studying contemporary processes of urban social transformation that are not limited to the city. Here we build upon previous discussions of methodological nationalism and methodological localism, while departing from the scalar analytic which motivates this scholarship.[32] Methodological localism, for instance, refers to a privileging, isolation and perhaps naturalization of the local scale in situations where supralocal scales are also significant. By contrast, within urban political ecology in particular and urban studies in general, methodological *cityism* would refer to an analytical privileging, isolation and perhaps naturalization of the city in studies of urban processes where the non-city may also be significant.

Methodological cityism is rampant in UPE, where, in contrast to the more speculative pronouncements in self-consciously understood theoretical texts, the dominant implicit concept of urbanization in the literature to date is the city as an outcome of diverse socionatural processes. This theoretical and methodological frame then self-evidently offers up the city as its empirical research site. Though UPE understands the uneven *production* of urban environments—spatially, socionaturally, politically—as a global process, the uneven "urban environments" that are *produced* continue to be understood as discrete, bounded *cities*, both in the strands of research that describe the production of urban socionatures and in those that focus on environmental injustice. To use the excellent edited volume *In the Nature of Cities* as an example, the overwhelming majority of its case studies are analyses of the social production of nature within cities.[33] Only one piece, David Pellow's connection of high-tech consumerism in Western cities to the environmental devastation that accompanies computer recycling operations in the Global South, systematically takes up Keil's call to investigate urbanization as a "complex, multiscale and multidimensional process," by examining the different forms the urbanization process takes, or what effects it has, in different locations and at different scales.[34]

While there is certainly nothing problematic *per se* about urban research being conducted in cities, when such research takes as its *methodological* premise the city as a site as opposed to urbanization as a process, the result is the failed Lefebvrian promise we have documented. Methodological cityism does not in this case entail an *a priori* or ontological denial of the non-city aspects of urban processes, but it has resulted in the absence of substantive engagement with them, and it has naturalized the city as the sole analytical terrain of urban analysis. Much as methodological nationalism incorporates an understanding of global political-economic processes into what remains a nation-state-centric analytic, methodological cityism here peaceably coexists with a sophisticated theoretical understanding of region-, nation- or planet-spanning urbanization processes.[35] And indeed, UPE's analyses of cities as products of global socionatural processes are unparalleled, as the march of empirical cases in its second generation (described above) demonstrates. With titles such as "An Urban Political Ecology of _____," bridges, sewer systems, and other city assemblages become illustrations of the relationship between the social and the natural, of transformation, circulation, distribution, and metabolism. But outside the city—silence.

Alternately, when UPE authors examine urban environmental injustice—not the *production* of parks and sewer systems, but who has access to them, who is left out, and who suffers— they have similarly, overwhelmingly, restricted themselves to the city.[36] Some research is banging at the walls of this unnecessary box—Paul Robbins's work on lawns moves fluently between city, suburb and beyond, as does Keil's more recent work on global suburbanisms and exurban spaces.[37] But still: is strip mining in the Appalachian mountains any less a case of urban environmental injustice than polluted rivers from sewage treatment plants in the Bronx? If it is, why? And if it's not, why doesn't UPE study it?

An urban political ecology that moved beyond methodological cityism could answer such questions—and is in fact very well-poised to do so—by investigating urbanization processes in their totality. William Cronon's *Nature's Metropolis*, a study of the co-production of town and country in Chicago and its hinterland, is one example of this kind of investigation, albeit one that is less attentive to the questions of power and politics that motivate UPE.[38] Another similarly insightful contribution, and more politically attuned, is Henderson's study of the settling of California.[39] And in fact, Cronon was an early inspiration to UPE. Swyngedouw approvingly cites Cronon, as does Kaika in *City of Flows*.[40] But the contrast on this point between *Nature's Metropolis* and *City of Flows* is instructive. Kaika contextualizes her study of Athens' sewer system in a framework of urbanization in which "the world" is defined as "a historical geographical process of perpetual metabolism in which 'social' and 'natural' processes combine in a historical geographical 'production process of socionature.'"[41] Her own analysis stretches well beyond Athens' municipal boundaries, but Kaika pulls her Lefebvrian punch by citing Cronon as an example—alongside Gandy in New York, Davis in LA, and Harvey in New York City—of an effort to account for the socionatural production of a *city*. His work is invoked *not*, as it might be, to highlight how Athens' aqueducts can't be understood outside their broader regional context, but to show us that "*cities* are dense networks of interwoven sociospatial processes," and to help us imagine a thing such as *London* as socionatural.[42] She is correct, of course, and yes, we must focus on the distinct forms of particular socionatures. But here again we are retelling Harvey's story: that there is nothing unnatural about New York. Or Chicago, or Athens, or Los Angeles, or London, *ad infinitum*.

The question left unanswered is not "in what way are these cities natural?," but "in what way are they urban?" If the socionatural processes that produced Cronon's Chicago—the city—equally actively produced the Great West as an agricultural region of which Chicago was a hub, then what makes Chicago more distinctly urban than its superficially greener neighbor? Chicago's stockyards are urban, but aren't equally its hogs and grain—and these at their moments of production, long before their physical arrival downtown? Though Lefebvre's provocative rethinking of urbanization as a process that encompasses town and country, city and wilderness, is approvingly cited by Swyngedouw and his co-authors, it is rarely elaborated through UPE's socionatural lens, theoretically or empirically. Instead, as Keil notes, "most research [in UPE] while recognizing the globalized societal relationships with nature that constitute urban life today, and the complex governance processes that regulate them, has looked at individual or comparative case studies, not at the networked matrix itself on which urban-nature relations are made and unmade."[43]

To be sure, sometimes a city lens is methodologically appropriate. For example, research on urban social movements and community activism—an important focus of the environmental justice wing of UPE—is often rightly contained within a single city (or entails a comparison among multiple discrete cities) to the extent that these movements are place-bound. And even when process-focused urban research is the more suitable methodological choice, it can be challenging to undertake, not least on logistical grounds, since it may involve physically disparate sites with ambiguous geographical boundaries.

Methodologically, cityist studies have at least the virtue of research design simplicity, but that simplicity is not always (or often) compatible with their objects of inquiry.

In tandem with UPE's methodological cityism comes the fact that it and political ecology persist as two solitudes. Indeed, the degree to which political ecology, including its most critical wing, has almost completely ignored its urban counterpart is astonishing. Two recent magisterial surveys of critical political ecology and a special issue of *Human Organization* devote between them not one word to UPE as a research program and no more than a few words to urbanization as a problematic relevant to the broader discipline.[44] This is not necessarily a problem for political ecologists, few of whom presumably hold to a Lefebvrian analysis of urbanization as the emerging dominant mode of global social change. But for urban political ecologists, many of whom presumably *do* hold to such an analysis, the disciplinary divide is problematic indeed. We argue—and suspect Swyngedouw and his colleagues would agree—that strip mining is no less an "urban" political ecological problem than urban agriculture. What about political ecology's "amenity migrants," those city expatriates who increase rural or exurban property values in their search for spiritual renewal and authentic culture?[45] Are they any less urban?

The disciplinary divide is drawn between what we might call the political ecology of cities and the political ecology of the countryside, and the methodological focus of the former helps widen the divide. It is time, we suggest, for UPE to return to its Lefebvrian roots and take up again its motivating *urban* themes, by challenging us to move beyond the city to develop a political ecology of urbanization.

A Political Ecology of Urbanization

A fruitful place to begin such a project is to return to Lefebvre's contention that "the city no longer corresponds to a real social object," and that the proper object of analysis for urban studies would soon have to become a worldwide urban society exploding out of the historical space of the city.[46] After the metropolitanization of medieval European cities in the eighteenth and nineteenth centuries sharpened the qualitative differences between town and country, Lefebvre argued, postwar decentralization undermined these differences, rendering the town-country opposition an insufficient basis for understanding urban change.[47] Urbanization processes would thus have to be traced far beyond the physical boundaries of cities, and increasingly analyzed as global or planetary phenomena, while cities themselves would need to be analyzed as phenomenological or even ideological phenomena.[48] As Harvey has argued and as Brenner has recently affirmed, a long legacy of city-focused urban studies has thus failed to do justice to the complexity of contemporary urban reality.[49] The urban is a process, not a site:

> Urbanization must then be understood not in terms of some socio-organizational
> entity called "the city" (the theoretical object that so many geographers,

demographers and sociologists erroneously presume) but as the production of specific and quite heterogeneous spatio-temporal forms embedded within different kinds of social action.[50]

In the contemporary context, the processual dimensions of planetary urbanization take (at a minimum) two broad forms. First, "urbanism as a way of life" is no longer coterminous with the city as a form of settlement space (if indeed it ever was).[51] Economic globalization, the information and communications technology revolution, and related sociocultural transformations have scrambled inherited spatial divisions of labor and of consumption in ways that make a mockery of the city-countryside division. Second, urban systems are being rearticulated at a range of scales, from the enormous megaregions emerging within both the Global North and South to networks of migration and policy that connect North and South and indeed blur the lines separating them.[52] And though these new urban geographies are constituted at ever-larger—even planetary—scales, they are constitutively uneven, connecting some spaces as they disconnect others. The result is that the city, as a signifier of or way of experiencing complex urbanization processes, stands in an increasingly problematic relationship to these processes, and is not necessarily a methodologically sound frame for studying them.[53] An urban studies that is (city) site-focused rather than (urban) process-focused thus risks ignoring much of what is distinctive about the contemporary urban world.

To say that UPE's current research program does not systematically address these dimensions of urbanization is not to say that they have gone unnoticed. Gestures in the direction of a process-oriented urban studies have been visible at least since the original publication of *The Urban Revolution* in 1970, both in and outside of the bounds of self-consciously urban research.[54] Sociospatial transformations of the past half-century have troubled a range of modernist binaries, and cyborgs, artificial natures, and information and communication technologies have prompted new analytical tools for exploring the relationship between society and nature as well as interconnectivity between places.[55] New geographies of global production and international finance in the 1980s and 1990s highlighted a changing relationship between an increasingly urbanized world and cities as territorial objects.[56] The possibilities of new electronically mediated environments prompted parallel questions in cultural studies and the humanities about non-linear narratives and spaces, and contemporary social theory continues to grapple with the relationship between changing city forms and forms of citizenship, community, and governance.[57] Among political scientists, Timothy Luke, in his work on "global" cities—with emphasis on the word "global" as scope and process, rather than "Global" cities as particular places where such forces "burrow"—explicitly defines urbanization in processual terms and discusses its effects on natural resources and social inequality outside the limits of a particular city.[58] Most recently in urban studies, two of the most vibrant approaches to thinking across the crumbling boundaries of the formally bounded city have been the study of networked infrastructure and "assemblage" urbanism.[59] While otherwise springing from different intellectual sources, both chart urban processes that incorporate nature and extend beyond the boundaries of the traditional city.

A wide range of research has, from a variety of disciplinary perspectives, demonstrated that the relationship between cities as sites and global urban processes is an increasingly complex one. Topics as diverse as finance, epistemology, governance, material infrastructure, and vulnerability have pulled the focus from place to process, begged a wider view from city to world, and produced research that treads the connections and ruptures between "cities" as particular places and the networks, systems, people and problems that increasingly connect them. Layered together, such work begins to bring a densely connected but unevenly differentiated urban fabric into focus; cities as research objects fade into the background, giving way to the multiple processes, materials and networks that constitute them. But such efforts are the exception rather than the rule. More to the point for UPE, they generally proceed without directly taking up questions about the nature of urbanization itself, and when they do, for the most part they eschew the language of urban political ecology. For example, in a symposium in *Capitalism Nature Socialism*, Heynen, Robbins, Perkins and Swyngedouw themselves turn to concepts such as neoliberalization and privatization—rather than "urbanization"—to describe what we might think of as "urban" transformations of the governance, enclosure, and valuation of nature in a range of city and non-city sites.[60]

Regardless of the reasons, and in spite of the programmatic statements of UPE's founders, actually existing UPE is mainly a research program into the politics of nature within cities. But if scholars of broader questions of urbanization are content to answer them without drawing on UPE's insights, and UPE's practitioners are content to focus on the city to the exclusion of the broader questions, what is the problem? The problem is a lost opportunity: UPE could—should, even—be at the forefront of current scholarship that deals with exactly these questions of the relationship between the city as an artifact and processes of urban transformation. But in fact it has been marginal. And this, we argue, is the practical consequence of a methodological cityist research program in which the city has remained the privileged lens for studying contemporary processes of urban transformation that are not limited to the city.

There are at least two avenues along which a refocused UPE could fulfill its Lefebvrian promise and contribute to a planetary, ecological, political understanding of contemporary urbanization. The first would be to investigate processes of socionatural transformation that systematically differentiate, within specific regions or at larger scales, city from non-city—in other words, to show how urbanization produces, materially or representationally, spaces understood as urban or rural, or materials understood as natural or social. Such studies could dislodge the city from its current role as the container for research that calls itself urban political ecology and reposition it as a research object to be explained, alongside its non-city counterparts such as the "countryside," "wilderness," and "nature."

This research could make explicit the link between how contemporary understandings of "nature" take specific shape in particular urban contexts and their role in subsequent urban transformation, and could in principle be conducted at a diverse range of scales, from the body to the regional. Extended to social theory, such an understanding of the interaction between urban processes and experiential selectivities of particular environments could also elucidate important aspects of social and political life.[61] Other studies might involve confronting the morphological differences between sites, for example, reassessing rural and wilderness areas—the traditional sites of political ecology—in order to consider how socionatural processes spanning city and countryside differentiate the two at the same time as they connect them.

The second avenue along which UPE could follow urbanization out of the city would be to more rigorously interrogate its global uneven development, tracing features of the urban world across the planet and integrating those that rarely if ever appear in cities. In effect, urban political ecology could apply the insights of commodity chain analysis, simultaneously de-fetishizing economy and territory, to distinctive aspects of urban society.[62] David Pellow does this by showing the global ecological dimensions to the Western consumption of high-tech devices, and thereby implicitly elaborates an urban metabolism that neither relegates nature to an asocial role nor reifies the city as the privileged domain of agency and politics for urban environmental questions.[63] Similar strategies could be pursued to connect urbanisms outside the Anglo-American world to the global socionatural processes of which they are part.[64]

Conclusion

Encouragingly, recent research—much of it by young scholars—has begun prodding UPE in this direction by selecting research sites that venture beyond the boundaries of the traditional city while still using "urban" tools for analysis. Darling has reflexively studied the production of "rural" nature as analogous to "urban" phenomena, while Perkins' study of a Minnesota watershed area implies the same by using UPE literature for what is not explicitly identified as an "urban" site.[65] Two recent articles have likewise challenged methodological cityism in UPE: Parés et al. counterposing "suburban" and urban natures, and Kitchen using Sieverts' concept of the *Zwischenstadt* to help reconcile his implicit understanding of UPE's account of the "urban forest" (forests located in cities) with South Wales' apparently non-urban geography.[66] This direction is encouraging. But alongside the selection of non-city research sites that implicitly challenge inherited assumptions in urban studies, we continue to require methodologically adventurous, explicit theoretical challenges to these assumptions. Thus we have written this chapter as a provocation. As much of the world's collective gaze is turning towards an apparently green and urban horizon, we challenge urban political ecology to return to its Lefebvrian roots: to help us understand the present and, critically, to participate in imagining the urban future.

Notes

1   Walter Benjamin, "Paris, the Capital of the Nineteenth Century," *The Arcades Project*, ed. Rolf Tiedemann, trans. Howard Eiland and Kevin McLaughlin (Cambridge: Belknap Press of Harvard University Press, 1999).

2   UN-HABITAT, *State of the World's Cities 2010/2011: Bridging the Urban Divide* (London: Earthscan, 2011); UN-HABITAT, *State of the World's Cities 2006/2007: 30 Years of Shaping the Habitat Agenda* (London: Earthscan, 2006); and UNFPA, *State of the World Population 2007: Unleashing the Potential of Urban Growth* (New York: United Nations Fund, 2007).

3   See David Harvey, "The Right to the City," *New Left Review* 53 (2008) 23-40; Luís M. A. Bettencourt, José Lobo, Dirk Helbing, Chrstian Kühnert and Geoffrey B. West, "Growth, Innovation, Scaling, and the Pace of Life in Cities," *Proceedings of the National Academy of Sciences* 104, 17 (2007) 7301-06; and Edward L. Glaeser, *Triumph of the City: How Our Greatest Invention Makes Us Richer, Smarter, Greener, Healthier, and Happier* (New York: Penguin, 2011).

4   Roger Keil and John Graham, "Reasserting Nature: Constructing Urban Environments After Fordism," *Remaking Nature: Nature at the Millennium*, eds. Bruce Braun and Noel Castree (New York and London: Routledge, 1998).

5   On planetary urbanization, see the other contributions to this book. On worlding cities, see AbdouMaliq Simone, "On the Worlding of African Cities," *African Studies Review* 44, 2 (2001) 15-41; Ananya Roy, "The 21ˢᵗ-Century Metropolis: New Geographies of Theory," *Regional Studies* 43, 6 (2009) 819-830; and Ananya Roy and Aihwa Ong, eds., *Worlding Cities: Asian Experiments and the Art of Being Global* (Malden: Blackwell, 2011). On the "urban age," see UN-HABITAT, *State of the World's Cities 2006/2007*; and Richard Burdett and Deyan Sudjic, eds., *The Endless City: The Urban Age Project by the London School of Economics and Deutsche Bank's Alfred Herrhausen Society* (London: Phaidon, 2007).

6   Piers Blaikie and Harold Brookfield, *Land Degradation and Society* (London: Methuen, 1987) 17.

7   Susan Paulson, Lisa L. Gezon and Michael Watts, "Locating the Political in Political Ecology: An Introduction," *Human Organization* 62, 3 (2003) 205-17.

8   Ludwig Trepl, "City and Ecology," *Capitalism, Nature, Socialism* 7, 2 (1996) 85-94.

9   Arturo Escobar, "After Nature: Steps to an Antiessentialist Political Ecology," *Current Anthropology* 40, 1 (1999) 1-30; and Richard Peet and Michael Watts eds., *Liberation Ecologies: Environment, Development, Social Movements* (New York and London: Routledge, 2000).

10 Escobar, "After Nature," 4.

11 Bruno Latour, *Politics of Nature: How to Bring the Sciences into Democracy* (Cambridge: Harvard University Press, 2004).

12 Erik Swyngedouw, "The City as Hybrid: On Nature, Society and Cyborg Urbanization," *Capitalism, Nature, Socialism* 7, 2 (1996) 65-80.

13 Ibid., 76.

14 David Harvey, *Justice, Nature and the Geography of Difference* (Malden: Blackwell, 1996) 186, emphasis in original.

15 Henri Lefebvre, *The Urban Revolution*, trans. Robert Bononno (Minneapolis: University of Minnesota, 2003 [1970]).

16 Roger Keil, "Progress Report: Urban Political Ecology," *Urban Geography* 24, 8 (2003) 728-9.

17 David Wachsmuth, "Three Ecologies: Urban Metabolism and the Society-Nature Opposition," *The Sociological Quarterly* 53, 4 (2012) 506-23.

18 Swyngedouw, "The City as Hybrid."

19 Nik Heynen, Maria Kaika and Erik Swyngedouw, "Urban Political Ecology: Politicizing the Production of Urban Natures," *In the Nature of Cities: Urban Political Ecology and the Politics of Urban Metabolism*, eds. Nik Heynen, Maria Kaika, and Erik Swyngedouw (New York and London: Routledge, 2006) 5.

20 Matthew Gandy, *Concrete and Clay* (Cambridge: MIT Press, 2003); Maria Kaika *City of Flows* (New York and London: Routledge,
    2005); and Nik Heynen, Maria Kaika, and Erik Swyngedouw, eds., *In the Nature of Cities: Urban Political Ecology and the Politics of Urban Metabolism* (New York and London: Routledge, 2006).

21 Mike Davis, *Ecology of Fear: Los Angeles and the Imagination of Disaster* (New York: Vintage, 1999).

22 Kaika, *City of Flows*, 17.

23 Nik Heynen, "Green Urban Political Ecologies: Toward a Better Understanding of Inner-city Environmental Change," *Environment and Planning A* 38 (2006) 499-516.

24 Susannah Bunce and Gene Desfor, "Introduction to Political Ecologies of Urban Waterfront Transformations," *Cities* 24, 4 (2007) 251-8; Gene Desfor and Lucian Vesalon, "Urban Expansion and Industrial Nature: a Political Ecology of Toronto's Port Industrial District," *International Journal of Urban and Regional Research* 32, 3 (2008) 586-603; Jason Cooke and Robert Lewis, "The Nature of Circulation: The Urban Political Ecology of Chicago's Michigan Avenue Bridge, 1909–1930," *Urban Geography* 31, 3 (2010) 348-68.

25 Karen Bickerstaff, Harriet Bulkeley and Joe Painter, "Justice, Nature, and the City," *International Journal of Urban and Regional Research* 33, 3 (2009) 591-600; Elena Domene and David Sauri, "Urbanization and Class-produced Natures: Vegetable Gardens in the Barcelona Metropolitan Region," *Geoforum* 38, 2 (2007) 287-98; and Alex Aylett, "Conflict, Collaboration and Climate Change: Participatory Democracy and Urban Environmental Struggles in Durban, South Africa," *International Journal of Urban and Regional Research* 34, 3 (2010) 478-95.

26 Nik Heynen, James McCarthy, Scott Prudham and Paul Robbins, eds., *Neoliberal Environments: False Promises and Unnatural Consequences* (New York and London: Routledge, 2007); Erik Swyngedouw and Nik Heynen, "Urban Political Ecology, Justice and the Politics of Scale," *Antipode* 35, 5 (2003) 898-918; Roderick P. Neumann, "Political Ecology: Theorizing Scale," *Progress in Human Geography* 33, 3 (2009) 398-406; Laura Taylor, "No Boundaries: Exurbia and the Study of Contemporary Urban Dispersion," *Geojournal* 76, 4 (2011) 323-39; Erik Swyngedouw, "The Antinomies of the Postpolitical City: in Search of a Democratic Politics of Environmental Production," *International Journal of Urban and Regional Research* 33, 3 (2009) 601-20.

27 Erik Swyngedouw, "Metabolic Urbanization: the Making of Cyborg Cities," *In the Nature of Cities: Urban Political Ecology and the Politics of Urban Metabolism*, eds. Nik Heynen, Maria Kaika and Erik Swyngedouw (New York and London: Routledge, 2006) 35.

28 Keil, "Progress Report," 725; and see also Heynen, Kaika and Swyngedouw, "Urban Political Ecology," 5.

29 Swyngedouw, "The City as Hybrid," 74-5.

30 Ibid., 35.

31 Keil, "Progress Report."

32 John Agnew, "The Territorial Trap: the Geographical Assumptions of International Relations Theory," *Review of International Political Economy* 1, 1(1994) 53-80; Andreas Wimmer and Nina Glick Schiller, "Methodological Nationalism and Beyond: Nation-state Building, Migration and the Social Sciences," *Global Networks* 2 (2002) 301-34; and Neil Brenner, "Is there a Politics of "Urban" Development? Reflections on the US Case," *The City in American Political Development*, ed. Richardson Dilworth (New York: Routledge, 2009).

33 Heynen, Kaika and Swyngedouw, *In the Nature of Cities*.

34 David N. Pellow, "Transnational Alliances and Global Politics: New Geographies of Urban Environmental Justice Struggles," *In the Nature of Cities: Urban Political Ecology and the Politics of Urban Metabolism*, eds. Nik Heynen, Maria Kaika and Erik Swyngedouw (New York and London: Routledge, 2006).

35 Wimmer and Glick Schiller, "Methodological Nationalism and Beyond."

36 Gandy, *Concrete and Clay*; and Julie Sze, *Noxious New York: The Racial Politics of Urban Health and Environmental Justice* (Cambridge: MIT Press, 2006).

37   Paul Robbins, *Lawn People: How Grasses, Weeds, and Chemicals Make Us Who We Are* (Philadelphia: Temple University Press, 2007); and Roger Keil and Douglas Young, "Fringe Explosions: Risk and Vulnerability in Canada's New In-between Urban Landscape," *Canadian Geographer/Le Géographe canadien* 53, 4 (2009) 488-99.

38   William Cronon, *Nature's Metropolis: Chicago and the Great West* (New York: W. W. Norton & Co, 1991).

39   George L. Henderson, *California and the Fictions of Capital* (Philadelphia: Temple University Press, 1999).

40   Swyngedouw, "The City as Hybrid"; and Kaika, *City of Flows*.

41   Ibid., 22.

42   Ibid., 22, emphasis added.

43   Roger Keil, "Transnational Urban Political Ecology: Health and Infrastructure in the Unbounded City," *The New Blackwell Companion to the City*, eds. Gary Bridge and Sophie Watson (Oxford: Blackwell, 2011) 716.

44   Paul Robbins, *Political Ecology: A Critical Introduction* (Oxford: Blackwell, 2004); Timothy Forsyth, *Critical Political Ecology: The Politics of Environmental Science* (New York: Routledge, 2003); and Susan Paulson, Lisa L. Gezon and Michael Watts, "Locating the Political in Political Ecology (special issue)," *Human Organization* 62, 3 (2003).

45   Laurence A. G. Moss, ed., *The Amenity Migrants: Seeking and Sustaining Mountains and Their Cultures* (Wallingford: CABI, 2006).

46   Lefebvre, *The Urban Revolution*, 57.

47   Stefan Kipfer, Parastou Saberi and Thorben Wieditz, "Henri Lefebvre: Debates and Controversies," *Progress in Human Geography* (2012) 5. http://phg.sagepub.com/content/early/2012/05/29/0309132512446718

48   Brenner, "Theses on Urbanization," this book, Ch. 13; and Wachsmuth, "City as Ideology," this book, Ch. 23.

49   David Harvey, "Cities or Urbanization," this book, Ch. 3; and Brenner, "Theses on Urbanization," this book, Ch. 13.

50   Harvey, "Cities or Urbanization," this book, Ch. 3, page 62.

51   Louis Wirth, "Urbanism as a Way of Life," *American Journal of Sociology* 44, 1 (1938) 1-24.

52   Manuel Castells, *The Rise of the Network Society: the Information Age, Volume 1*, Second Edition (Malden: Blackwell, 2000); Catherine L. Ross, ed., *Megaregions: Planning for Global Competitiveness* (Washington: Island Press, 2009); John Harrison and Michael Hoyler, eds., *Megaregions: Globalization's New Urban Form?* (Cheltenham: Edward Elgar, forthcoming); and Eugene McCann and Kevin Ward, eds., *Mobile Urbanism: Cities and Policymaking in the Global Age* (Minneapolis: University of Minnesota, 2011).

53   Andrew Sayer, "Defining the Urban," *Geojournal* 9, 3 (1984) 279-85; and Wachsmuth, "City as Ideology," this book, Ch. 23.

54   See Clovis Ultramari and Rodrigo José Firmino, "Urban Beings or City Dwellers? The Complimentary Concepts of 'Urban' and 'City,'" *City & Time* 4, 30 (2010). http://www.ceci-br.org/novo/revista/viewarticle.php?id=143.

55   Manuel Castells, *The Information City: Information Technology, Economic Restructuring, and Urban-Regional Process* (Oxford: Basil Blackwell, 1989); Castells *The Rise of the Network Society*; and Donna Haraway, "A Cyborg Manifesto: Science, Technology, and Socialist-Feminism in the Late Twentieth Century," *Simians, Cyborgs, and Women: The Reinvention of Nature* (New York: Routledge, 1991).

56   John Friedmann and Goetz Wolff, "World City Formation: An Agenda for Research and Action," *International Journal of Urban and Regional Research* 6 (1982) 309-344; and Saskia Sassen, *The Global City: New York, London, Tokyo*, Second Edition (Princeton: Princeton University Press, 2001).

57   Italo Calvino, *Invisible Cities*, trans. William Weaver (New York: Harcourt, 1974); Paul Auster, *City of Glass* (New York: Penguin, 1987); Richard Skeates, "The Infinite City," *City* 2, 8 (1997) 6-20; Michael Crang, "Urban Morphology and the Shaping of the Transmissable City," *City* 4, 3 (2000) 303-15; Patsy Healey, "On Creating the 'City' as a Collective Resource," *Urban Studies* 39, 10

(2002) 1777-92; and Martin Coward, "Between Us in the City: Materiality, Subjectivity, and Community in the Era of Global Urbanization," *Environment and Planning D: Society and Space*, 3 (2012) 468-81.

58   Timothy Luke, "Global Cities vs. 'global cities': Rethinking Contemporary Urbanism as Public Ecology," *Studies in Political Economy* 70 (2003) 16.

59   Stephen Graham and Simon Marvin, *Splintering Urbanism: Networked Infrastructures, Technological Mobilities and the Urban Condition* (New York: Routledge, 2001; Ignacio Farías and Thomas Bender, eds., *Urban Assemblages: How Actor-Network Theory Changes Urban Research* (London and New York: Routledge, 2010); Neil Brenner, David J. Madden and David Wachsmuth, "Assemblage Urbanism and the Challenges of Critical Urban Theory," *City* 15, 2 (2011) 225-40; and Colin McFarlane, "Assemblage and Critical Urbanism," *City* 15, 2 (2011) 204-24.

60   Nik Heynen and Paul Robbins, eds., "The Neoliberalization of Nature: Governance, Privatization, Enclosure, and Valuation (symposium)," *Capitalism Nature Socialism* 16, 1 (2005).

61   Hillary Angelo, "Bird in Hand: How Experience Makes Nature," *Theory and Science* 42, 4 (2013) 351-68; and Michael Bell, *Childerley: Nature and Morality in a Country Village* (Chicago: University of Chicago Press, 1995).

62   Jennifer Bair and Marion Werner, "Commodity Chains and the Uneven Geographies of Global Capitalism: a Disarticulation Perspective," *Environment and Planning A* 43, 5 (2011) 988-97.

63   Pellow, "Transnational Alliances and Global Politics."

64   Robinson, "Global and World Cities"; AbdouMaliq Simone, "People as Infrastructure: Interesting Fragments in Johannesburg," *Public Culture* 16, 3 (2004) 407-29; and Colin McFarlane, "Sanitation in Mumbai's Informal Settlements: State, 'Slum,' and Infrastructure," *Environment and Planning A* 40, 1 (2008) 88-107.

65   Eliza Darling, "The City in the Country: Wilderness Gentrification and the Rent Gap," *Environment and Planning A* 37, 6 (2005) 1015-32; and Harold A. Perkins, "Manifestations of Contradiction: Lakes within the Production/Consumption Dialectic," *Antipode* 38, 1 (2006) 128-49.

66   Marc Parés, Hug March, and David Saurí, "Atlantic Gardens in Mediterranean Climates: Understanding the Production of Suburban Natures in Barcelona," *International Journal of Urban and Regional Research* 37, 1 (2012) 328-47; Lawrence Kitchen, "Are Trees Always 'Good?' Urban Political Ecology and Environmental Justice in the Valleys of South Wales," *International Journal of Urban and Regional Research* (2012). http://dx.doi.org/10.1111/j.1468-2427.2012.01138.x; and Thomas Sieverts, *Cities Without Cities: an Interpretation of the Zwischenstadt* (New York and London: Routledge, 2003).

25
WHITHER URBAN STUDIES?

Andy Merrifield

In talking about urban studies I can only talk from and for the perspective I know best: the critical urban tradition that developed out of Marxism in the 1970s, as pioneered by the likes of Henri Lefebvre, David Harvey and Manuel Castells. I tried to document and contribute toward this tradition in my book *Metromarxism,* where I claimed some of the best urban studies has been done by certain Marxists, and some the best Marxism has been done by certain urban theorists.[1]

If we look back at the debates that raged in the 1970s, one of the biggest was about the nature of the urban. Just what is the urban anyway? What is a city? Why should it command such interest for critical scholars? The obvious rejoinder is that the city plays a special role under capitalism—indeed was important in the birth of capitalism itself. The city assumes a twin role: an engine for capital accumulation, on the one hand, and a site for social/class struggle, on the other. It is crucial for the expansion of capitalism and for overthrowing capitalism. It is a theoretical object of curiosity because it is a political subject of necessity.

All of which bodes the question what is this "it"? In *The Urban Question*, Castells wondered what could we possibly mean by "city," and what is this concept "urban"? Why urban sociology and not simply sociology? Why urban geography and not simply geography? Of course, Castells was trying to figure out the *specificity* of the city, for both theory and politics, and it's a question we might still want to ponder.[2]

If anything, the question takes on renewed significance today because our world assumes a very different urban form than it did in the 1970s. Since 2006, the majority of the world's population is, we're told, urbanized, with some 3.3 billion dwellers living in urban agglomerations of some guise or another; and, if trends continue, this is set to increase exponentially. By 2030, 60 percent of planet earth will be urban; by 2050, 75 percent.

• • •

Yet beyond mere curiosity, what do these figures imply? Are they significant? Is urban studies a numbers-game anyway? In 1938, the American sociologist Louis Wirth expressed a skepticism about "measuring" the degree to which the contemporary world is "urban" from the proportion of the total population living in cities. The influence cities exert upon social life, he said, is greater than any statistical population ratio might infer. The urban isn't a physical entity delimited in space but its very own *cosmos*, Wirth said, its very own "way of life."[3]

Never anyone terribly interested in numbers, Henri Lefebvre always said that a fuller understanding of our urban age could only be reached through conceptualization of the whole, through conceptualization of what he termed "planetary urbanization." In 1970, Lefebvre posited "the complete urbanization society."[4] In his day, he said it was virtual but one day it might become real. Lefebvre is the last of a pretty extinct species: a philosopher of the city—or, better, a "metaphilosopher" of the city. I use this notion of "philosopher" in the ancient Greek tradition; not as somebody who is detached, solitary and contemplative, dealing with rarified abstractions, but as somebody who is completely engaged in politics and questions of democracy. Indeed, the very bedrock for ancient Greek philosophy were questions that linked the polis to democracy. The city, philosophy and politics were synonymous. (The philosopher Hippodamus of Miletus was the first city planner, initially proposing a grid pattern and a zoning scheme, as well as a central *agora* open square, that place of gathering and assembly so dear to democracy; and we know how Plato, in *The Republic*, said much about how cities relate to democracy—or, as in Plato's case, to too much democracy.)

The point here is that philosophy, the city, and political engagement went together. Within the field of urban geography, particularly in UK urban geography, there are certain things that today militate against this noble philosophical tradition. One is the dominance of the positivist-empiricist tradition. Why so? The reason may be obvious in our age of "experts" and "technocrats," in this era some describe as "postpolitical": positivism has always tried to rid itself of politics behind the shield of quantification and "objectivity." In that sense, positivism/empiricism is a convenient methodology for technocrats trying to find consensus without conflict. After all, their opinions are neutral and expert; their knowledge isn't value-laden, right? Yours, if it's critical and theoretically partisan, is warped, ideological.

The second reason for the prioritization of empirical data—which ties in neatly with the first reason—is that it can raise money for the corporate university, can more easily capture grant money, more easily produce a "knowledge commodity," a knowledge that may be calculated and evaluated in an institution's competitive yearnings and chart-topping desires. Very little money, if any, is doled out to work on theory, therefore theory/philosophy is unimportant because it is financially unimportant. To be sure, it is extremely difficult to evaluate and judge its "impact" on any spreadsheet.

You no longer think about a problem: you spend your time thinking about filling in a grant proposal about a problem. This creates a certain superficiality to the idea of doing "research": research constitutes amassing data; it rarely means thinking deeply about a problem, certainly not formulating concepts about this problem, and then engaging in a politics around that problem. This isn't helpful in the development of deeper, critical understandings of the urban problematic. Arguably, it creates a discipline that is at heart anti-intellectual. And anti-intellectualism doesn't "impact" well in the long run.

On the other flank, neither does sloppy theorizing, or theorizing divorced from political and social engagement. Consequently, there are dangers of "pure" theorizing, too, especially the sociologicalization of certain forms of continental philosophy, and here we might indict those who try to "adopt" or "instrumentalize" in some kind of disembodied abstract way the usual suspects, thinkers like Badiou, Rancière, Zizek, Deleuze & Guattari, and even Lefebvre. "Thoughts without content are empty," said Kant in *Critique of Pure Reason*; although he also said "thoughts without concepts are blind." And so we hobble along, between analytical emptiness and conceptual blindness …

• • •

Still, a reloaded urban studies doesn't mean middle-ground: it suggests a thorough reframing of the urban question, of dealing adequately with the *ontological* question, that of being in the world, of being in an urban world. Within this conceptualization, we need to dispense with all the old chestnuts between North and South, between developed and underdeveloped worlds, between urban and rural, between urban and regional, between city and suburb, and so forth. (Just as we need to dispense with the old distinctions between public and private, state and economy, politics and technocracy.) From this standpoint, frontier lines don't pass between any North-South or urban-rural divide but reside *"within the phenomenon of the urban itself,"* as Lefebvre says in *The Urban Revolution.*[5] Hence the need to conceptualize and politicize how the globe is no longer demarcated through definitive splits between strict opposites: all demarcations and frontier lines are *immanent* within urban society, between dominated peripheries and dominating centers that exist all over the planet.

The notion of immanence is writ large in Marx's as well as Spinoza's thought, and is instructive for our own urban problematic. Immanence is everywhere is Marx's vocabulary.

Marx said that *value* is immanent to capitalism, so is the *world market*, which is the very basis of capitalism, of what it is and what is emergent in its very Being; we could easily transpose "urban" for "world market" without losing any clarity of Marx's meaning. As for Spinoza, he called the immanent force of nature and reality *substance*. Substance is the bedrock content to human reality, perceivable and conceivable only through its manifold *attributes*. Substance is, of course, Spinoza's pantheist theory of God, his notion that God is immanent in all reality, including ourselves; but maybe the form of this notion holds, too, for the immanent nature of the urban, for its complex ontological tissuing, for the fabric that now clothes our daily lives.

What is being affirmed here is the urban as a single substance whose attributes—the built environment, transport infrastructure, population densities, topographical features, social mixes, political governance—are all the formal *expressions* of what pervades it ontologically. We might even say that the "city" is an attribute of the urban. These attributes are how the urban looks and how it can be seen and known. What we might also say, following this, is that the urban isn't out there, necessarily observable and measurable, but that it is immanent in our lives, an ontology not an epistemology: *it isn't a transitive attribute of our society but the immanent substance of our society.*

Within this conceptualization, it's possible to conceive planetary urbanization as the progressive production of undergrowth as well as overgrowth. In other words, the urban isn't simply bricks and mortar, high-rise buildings and autoroutes: it manifests itself as a process that produces skyscrapers as well as unpaved streets, highways as well as back roads, by-waters and marginal zones that feel the wrath of the world market—its absence as well as its presence. This process involves dispossession of land, sequestering of the commons, and eminent domain. The urban now signifies a new form of "dependency," justifying cultural, technological and economic obsolescence in rural economies. In the 1970s, the peasant sociologist Andrew Pearce spoke of the expansion of an "Urban-Industrial-Complex" into the world's rural areas, which sanctioned agricultural production through an urban reward system.[6] Today, we'd have to rename that complex an "Urban-Financial-Complex," with a reward system that penalizes and disciplines agricultural production, doing so planetarily, doing so from multiple centers of urban corporate power.

• • •

We should stop using the term city, Lefebvre says, and adopt instead the terminology "urban society." Urban society, he was fond of saying, "is built upon the ruins of the city."[8] The city is a pseudo-concept, a historical concept, not an analytical reality. In pushing for the notion of urban society, Lefebvre is asking us to open the floodgates, to quit bounding something, to give up on solidity and the security of an absolute and embrace something relative and open, something *becoming*. We should leave behind the *form* of the city and embrace the apparent *formlessness* of urban society.

I say "apparent" because we might remember there's nothing formless as such about Lefebvre's conception of space; he was keen to emphasize that space is global, fragmented and hierarchical in one fell swoop. It is a mosaic of stunning complexity, punctuated and textured by centers and peripheries, yet a mosaic in which the "commodity-form" gives this patterning its underlying definition. If we wanted to delve into the cell-like molecular structure of this urban substance, of this urban space, we could perhaps see it as an immense accumulation of commodities, bounded by the "commodity-form," even while its "value-form" is boundless. The commodity-form *vis-à-vis* the value-form is a key distinction Marx makes at the beginning of *Capital.* It was one way, after all, in which he could talk about how things have particularity and generality *at the same time*, have intrinsic form yet are also extrinsically formless. I would like to see the urban pictured in the same analytical light, as something with structure and form, as something as functionally chaotic—Lefebvre's "rational delirium"—yet as fractally ordered as a series of subatomic particles.[8]

We have to be imaginative about how we might conceive this reality. We could see it the way an atomic physicist might see it but really we are talking about something very vast—a terrestrial planetary universe. The commodity-form of space would represent the place-bound, fixed built-form, the built landscape of what Sartre in *Critique of Dialectical Reason* called the "practico-inert."[9] Meanwhile, the value-form would constitute a diffusive web of social relations, networked and stretched beyond place. If we wanted to push it further, the interaction between this value- and commodity-form is a bit like the way Roquentin, the protagonist from Sartre's *Nausea*, interacts with the world the inanimate objects, and the nausea that that engenders for living, conscious beings: how this inanimate, fixed world conditions and provides the passive frame for our active lives, and how we must somehow render it dynamic. Now our nausea is political and collective.[10]

So within this conception, just *what is* the specificity of the urban, if indeed there is any specificity? There is and there isn't specificity, since it's a specificity of complementarity, an understanding that sees the urban as a complex circuit card, as a networked tissue, as a mosaic, stitched together with pieces of delicate fabric. Outside of human woof and weft, the urban creates nothing, is nothing. The urban serves no purpose and has no reality outside of human reality, outside of exchange and union, outside of human proximity and concentration, outside of human encounter and intensity. Nodes of intensity that resonate, that connect with other nodes of intensity, that fuse together and create energy and electricity, incandescent light.

• • •

Why posit "urban society"? What's Lefebvre up to here, what's his point? Perhaps it isn't just an analytical trope he's employing so much as a political strategy. Again, Spinoza can come to our aid. When he wrote *Ethics* and affirmed substance as the bedrock of life and nature, he coined three different kinds of knowledge. The first was the sort that occurred at the level of everyday life, with its chaos and disorder, a level totally legitimate and real for life yet an *inadequate* idea for fully understanding that life; the second kind of knowledge sees a bigger pattern of human *relationships* behind that chaos, understanding the interconnectivity of human life, the *common notions* that keep it together, intact, more or less. With a third kind of knowledge that understanding is pushed even further, to an intuitive reason of human experience, and here I am thinking that this might better describe urban life, our future becoming, the substance to our lives, and the basis for improved and sustained common notions.

The major reason Spinoza developed this third kind of knowledge was that he saw something more fruitful at stake, something open to human beings: a society that affirms its dependence and interdependence of all, as a tissue of collective belonging. Similarly, Henri Lefebvre thinks there is something more humanly fruitful and politically worthwhile in affirming his own third kind of knowledge: urban society. The capacity for extended and deepening common notions is thereby augmented, provided separations and segregations can be warded off, kept at bay. By reaching out to understand the common ingredients that bond us we can then reach inward to understand ourselves as both a people and individuals. Such is the promise of a "third kind" of urban knowledge. That seems to be Lefebvre's point; and even if it isn't, we should make this point for him.

Lefebvre might have called this knowledge a "right to the city," but he also saw it as a new kind of *citizenship*, of revolutionary citizenship, based upon encounters between people, encounters that *reveal themselves though the negation of distance and though the reaching out to distance*. Citizenship is the point of convergence of both, a dialectic that is both a *perception* and a *horizon*, a structure of feeling as well as a new way of seeing ourselves and our planet. It is a citizenship conceived as something *urban*, as something territorial yet one in which territoriality is narrower and broader than both "city" and "nationality"; a citizen of the block, of the neighborhood, becomes a citizen of the world, a universal citizen rooted in place, encountering fellow citizens across the corridor and at the other end of the planet. Urbanization makes this sense of belonging possible, negating distance between everybody, piling people on top of one another, next to one another. Meanwhile, social media helps people reach out to distance, extend the distance of their lives, the horizons of their ways of seeing, of seeing themselves and other people.

A new kind of citizenship might emerge out of this, an urban citizenship of workers without salaried work, of students without careers (the NINJA generation: "No Income, No Job and No Assets"), of poor and middle-class people without homes, of retirees without pensions—a Here Comes Everybody (HCE) of people sharing a single planetary domain, one great big shit pot together. In *La pensée Marxiste et la ville* (1972), Lefebvre expressed a simple formula: the more cities upsize and the more urban society emerges, the more steady salaried work will downsize. Urban society will somehow be a "postwork" society in the sense that Marx hinted at in the *Grundrisse*, when we all eventually get "suspended" from the "immediate form of production," giving rise to a latent political constituency whose only real terrain left for struggle won't be the workplace but the urban itself.[11]

We're back with the ancient Greeks—or maybe with the-not-so-ancient-Greeks—for whom politics was (is) always experienced and enacted in the urban *agora*; to that extent nothing much has changed under planetary urbanization, excepting that the *agora* has now gotten bigger and vaster—a virtual and physical world combined into one. (The citizens of Athens didn't work 2,500 years ago; they were the aristocratic rulers who presided over the common folk—the slaves and strangers. Today, similarly, a new Greek citizenry emerges without work; not because they're aristocrats but because of economic crisis and Eurozone austerity measures.) Today's agora is a new kind of "common field" (Sartre) in which the passivity of the world of corporate things, of the built financial landscape, of the spectacular "practico-inert," is rendered active and affective, because it is filled with ordinary people who, united by common notions, *create* a function rather than *respond* to one (like a hoard of shoppers).

There are those of course who fear this *agora*, who want to close it down physically, seal it off virtually, censor cyberspace—the *agoraphobics*. But there are others who know that nowadays it isn't workers of the world who unite, who have a world to win, as Marx and Engels announced in the *Manifesto*; it's more that people have a whole world to occupy, to occupy as their own backyards.[12] There is a ruling class in this process of planetary urbanization, this class process of neo-Haussmannization; they are global and now put the infamous Baron's spadework to shame. But, in the wake of Occupy, they're nonetheless nervous. Neo-Haussmannization tears into the entire planetary urban fabric, and fronts the progressive production of core and periphery, of centers of power and wealth and of spaces of dispossession and marginalization; and this everywhere, with little concern for either city or countryside.

Critical urban theory and philosophy must comprehend and create a new terrain for political interventions—for militant, revolutionary politics—in a process that is itself revolutionary. Indeed, as Lefebvre says, "the urban" is revolutionary, and, as such, the revolution will be urban. That in a single line summarizes the gist of *The Urban Revolution*.[13] It's a project that still lives on, in both directions. And a lot of conceptual and political steady work remains to be done, in the right direction.

Notes

1 Andy Merrifield, *Metromarxism: A Marxist Tale of the City* (New York: Routledge, 2002).

2 Manuel Castells, *The Urban Question: A Marxist Approach* (London: E. Arnold, 1977).

3 Louis Wirth, "Urbanism as a Way of Life," *Classic Essays on the Culture of Cities*, ed. Richard Sennett (Engelwood Cliffs: Prentice Hall, 1969 [1937]) 143-64.

4 Henri Lefebvre, *The Urban Revolution*, trans. Robert Bononno (Minneapolis: University of Minnesota Press, 2003 [1970]).

5 Lefebvre, *The Urban Revolution*.

6 Andrew Pearce, "Metropolis and Peasant: The Expansion of the Urban-Industrial Complex" *Peasants and Peasant Societies,* ed. Teodor Shanin, Second Edition (London: Blackwell, 1987) 76.

7 Henri Lefebvre, "The right to the city," *Writings on Cities* (Cambridge: Blackwell, 1996 [1968]), 126.

8 Lefebvre, *The Urban Revolution*, 118.

9 Jean Paul Sartre, *Critique of Dialectical Reason, Volume I* (London: Verso, 1976).

10 Jean Paul Sartre, *Nausea* (Norfolk: New Directions, 1949).

11 Henri Lefebvre, *La pensée Marxiste et la ville* (Paris: Casterman, 1972); and Karl Marx, *Grundrisse der Kritik der politischen Ökonomie* (Harmondsworth: Penguin, 1973 [1857]).

12 Karl Marx and Friedrich Engels, *The Communist Manifesto* (New York: Penguin, 2011 [1848]).

13 Lefebvre, *The Urban Revolution*.

SIX
VISUALIZATIONS—
IDEOLOGIES AND
EXPERIMENTS

How to develop appropriately differentiated spatial representations of historical and contemporary urbanization processes? What taxonomies are most effective for mapping a world of generalized urbanization, massive uneven spatial development and continued territorial differentiation? What are the limits and possibilities of inherited mapping strategies and new geospatial data sources for developing a critical cartography of planetary urbanization?

**Christian Schmid
Neil Brenner &
Nikos Katsikis
Urban Theory Lab-GSD**

26
A TYPOLOGY OF URBAN SWITZERLAND

Christian Schmid

Switzerland is today a completely urbanized country with new urban landscapes that can no longer be apprehended with the classic understanding of the city. There are still a lot of cows on the Swiss meadows, but we have to recognize them as urban cows, even if they are still widely viewed as symbols of bygone, rural ways of life. Indeed, many contemporary images and spatial representations continue to reproduce the stereotypical vision of Switzerland as a basically rural country. Such representations have a strong influence not only on the specialized discourses of planning and urbanism, but also in the public sphere: they inform political debates, popular understandings and even imaginations of the future. Against such backward oriented representations, new approaches must be developed to illuminate the diverse patterns and pathways of urbanization that are reshaping this country. With the project *Switzerland—An Urban Portrait,* ETH Studio Basel has produced a novel, alternative spatial representation of urban Switzerland.[1] On the basis of a newly developed analytical framework derived from Henri Lefebvre's theory of the production of space, this project pursued a thorough analysis and mapping of urban Switzerland, resulting in the development of an urban typology that, for the first time, shows how the entire territory of Switzerland has been urbanized.[2]

Historical analysis shows that the traditional image of Switzerland as a "rural" country has not corresponded to reality for the past 150 years.[3] Since the industrial revolution, Switzerland has been almost entirely industrialized. The historical urbanization process of the nineteenth and twentieth centuries did, however, have a decidedly decentralized character, since commune-based federalism largely prevented urban concentrations or, where it couldn't suppress them, at least took care to hide them. This all but prevented the development of an urban self-image for Switzerland. Even today, large sections of the country are dominated by a pronounced anti-urban attitude. The perception and image of the city still has predominantly negative connotations: under no circumstances are cities in Switzerland allowed to become too large.

The Decentralized Metropolis

The earliest planning conceptions of an urban Switzerland are found in the 1940s, when Armin Meili—architect, member of parliament, director of the Swiss National Exhibition of 1939, and president of the Swiss Association for National Planning—published sketches for a "largely decentralized metropolis" (Figure 26.1, page 403).[4] One central motivation for Meili's proposal was the fear that small, democratic Switzerland could not tolerate "large, bloated cities." He was concerned about the "increasing anonymity" of our cities and asked: "How long can big cities continue to inundate the open country like a slow-moving flow of lava?" For Meili, the answer was clear: "Stop urban expansion! Create new housing developments separated from the city."[5] His proposal sought to cushion the impact of anticipated urban growth with decentralized satellite towns that were to be distributed throughout the Swiss Plateau.

In the years that followed, others proposed many variations of Meili's idea. Echoes of it are even found in the famous manifesto *Achtung: die Schweiz* (*Attention: Switzerland*) of 1955, in which the urban sociologist Lucius Burckhardt, the writer and architect Max Frisch, and the journalist Markus Kutter sharply criticized the functionalist approach of contemporary urban development and propagated a new societal awakening. They presented the idea of building an exemplary "new town" for 10,000 to 30,000 residents outside the old cities. This manifesto gave the impression of being resolutely modern, but it also aimed to "create decentralized concentrations to cushion the impact of urban growth in the new medium-sized cities" in order to achieve a high degree of economic and political autonomy for the urban communes and to preserve the foundations of federalism in Switzerland.

A working group with the name *Neue Stadt* (New Town) worked out plans for a "prototype city" (*Studienstadt*) in the Furttal region of Zurich. Once again the focus was on decentralized development, and once again there was talk of the "undesirable concentration of population growth in only a few places" and a "crowding of the citizenry resulting from a loss of links to natural communities."[6] Similar ideas also informed the first efforts at regional planning in various urban regions of Switzerland after World War II. Nearly all the regional proposals from that period suggested an "orderly" reduction of the concentration of urban development and encouraging decentralized, regional centers intended to reduce the pressures of development in the large cities. The Zurich study, *Städte, wie wir sie wünschen* (*Cities, as We Would Like Them*), undertaken by the Study Group for National Planning was typical of this trend.[7] It too evoked the danger of anonymity and proclaimed the struggle against urbanization as the most urgent task for planning. Since industry was "not a genuinely urban function," it did not have to be linked to centers and should be moved out, but services, as "a genuinely urban function," could be concentrated in appropriate places, that is, in smaller and medium-sized centers. This idea was essentially based on Walter Christaller's theory of "central places," which at the time was just beginning to be viewed as a forward-looking concept for developmental planning in many Western industrial nations.[8]

As these examples demonstrate, conceptions for an urban Switzerland were consistently based on a specific blend of conservatism and modernism. On the one hand, they called for strong central planning by the state and followed a modern, universalistic conception of space that had gained acceptance in nearly all the Western industrial nations during the postwar period. This conception was based on a Fordist-Keynesian logic and was defined first and foremost by a normative conception of an "equality in space": space was thus seen as isotropic, as uniform. It was thought that a national territory should have a unified organization and that all its regions should have equal access to modern life and be equipped with high quality infrastructure. On the other hand, these conceptions also insisted on preserving what was "characteristically Swiss," and hence on a decentralized model of developments composed of small towns. The notion that there was something "un-Swiss" about a large city, something threatening to our "finely structured and diverse country," became the dominant axiom of Helvetian planning. Switzerland was considered a national unit in which conflicting interests between the various parts of the country, between central and peripheral regions, between city and country had to be reconciled. These proposals and conceptions for regional planning may have been diffused through many official cantonal guidelines at the time, but they were barely implemented and had little impact precisely because of their interventionist strategy. In a Switzerland dominated largely by conservative forces, restrictions on property rights, necessarily involved in such planning, are nearly impossible to push through. The autonomy of the communes stubbornly resists any form of centralized state planning.

As a result, the only major national urbanist project during that period was the construction of the highway system. The highway network, approved by a large majority in a federal referendum in 1958, aimed to provide every small town in Switzerland with access to modern life. Given the political ineffectuality of Switzerland's concepts for developmental planning, the highways became the most important generators of the urbanization process. However, the massively increased accessibility engendered by the construction of the highway system was diametrically opposed to concepts of an "orderly" decentralized development. It reinforced not only the urban sprawl that planners struggled against so vigorously but also the development of large agglomerations.

Decentralized Concentration

The efforts to establish a comprehensive plan for the nation culminated in the reformist mood of the early 1970s. However, even what remains Switzerland's most extensive exercise in planning to date—the *Landesplanerische Leitbilder der Schweiz* (National Planning Models for Switzerland), published by the Swiss Federal Institute of Technology in Zurich—followed the same well-trodden paths.[9] CK-73, the new model for developmental planning, derived from this document by a conference of chief civil servants, promoted a "decentralized concentration" of residential development (Figure 26.2, page 403).[10] As with the earlier conceptions, the goal here was to achieve uniform development for all of Switzerland, to prevent the development of large urban concentrations, and to ensure balanced distribution of centralities across the country.

Beginning around the mid-1970s this proposal was flanked by targeted regional development programs for mountain areas and "economically threatened" regions. The paramount goal was the "reduction of regional disparities," and the primary means was the construction of regional infrastructure, ranging from sewage treatment plants to indoor swimming pools. In consequence, the whole territory of Switzerland is well developed today and the amenities of urban life are accessible almost everywhere. These programs also succeeded in significantly slowing down the kinds of structural transformations in peripheral regions that had been taking place elsewhere in Europe since the 1970s.[11] Nevertheless, they were unable to halt the increase of economic imbalances or the growing concentration of dynamic, innovative and high value-added sectors in the large urban centers.

The planning models were thus squeezed between two negative poles. On the one hand, there was the horror scenario of a polarized Switzerland with large urban centers and peripheral regions; on the other hand, there was the specter of urban sprawl in the countryside. The only escape appeared to be the idea of a planned pursuit of centralization, but in a decentralized way, so that the "pressure to develop" could be absorbed by small and medium-sized centers. Neither goal was realized in practice. Economic restructuring led to considerable territorial polarization, and meanwhile, urbanization followed the preexisting decentralized pattern that was already engrained in the territory.

Urban Network Switzerland

In the 1980s and 1990s, the inexorable trend toward large urban concentrations led to a modest transformation in planning concepts and models. Gradually, people became convinced that the new realities of urban Switzerland had to be accepted. These ideas found programmatic expression in the concept of the "Metropolis Switzerland," first formulated in a report from the Institute for Research on the Built Environment (IREC) at the ETH Lausanne.[12] The report's authors acknowledged that Switzerland as a whole was not a metropolis, but they claimed that it formed a polycentric network of urban regions that, taken together, fulfilled the functions of a metropolis "(Figure 26.3). The idea of a decentralized "Helvetian metropolis," in which the recently inaugurated Rail 2000 program functions as an oversized suburban railway system, has since become a pertinent image of urban Switzerland. Even this concept, however, follows the old blend of modernism with "characteristically Helvetian" features, and ultimately represents nothing other than a reprint of the old decentralized planning approaches.

The concept of Metropolis Switzerland has since entered the debate in a variety of shadings, and has been advanced especially by the Association Metropolis Switzerland, founded in 1994 and including renowned planning specialists among its members. The idea is also behind the two most important current planning conceptions: the *Grundzüge der Raumordnung Schweiz* (Foundations of Spatial Planning for Switzerland) of 1995 and *Agglomerationspolitik des Bundes* (Federal Agglomeration Policy) of 2001. Although they no longer call for "decentralized concentration," they do promote an urban, networked, polycentric space— an "Urban Network Switzerland" (*Vernetztes Städtesystem Schweiz*). This urban system is endorsed as the federalist response to the challenges of increased competition among Europe's urban regions to be chosen as locations for businesses. Although the Swiss centers cannot measure up to the large European metropolises, its urban system—seen as a "city of three million"—has sufficiently attractive metropolitan features to compete with other important cities in Europe. Moreover, the small and medium-sized cities should be positioned to pick up on the development impetus from the large centers and implement it independently. Another goal is to preserve and strengthen peripheral regions by linking them into the network of large, high-growth cities. The advantage of this approach is said to lie above all in the fact that it can prevent large settlement areas from growing together, so that cities can retain manageable dimensions. Finally, there is a renewed call for "relief centers" for the large agglomerations.[13] An all but identical conception of the "urban network Switzerland" is found in *Agglomerationspolitik des Bundes* (Federal Agglomeration Policy) of 2001.[14] In terms of their basic structures, these proposals are nothing but updated copies of previous conceptions for a decentralized Switzerland. They still follow the typically Helvetian system of alliances: everyone should receive something, and every center is to be treated fundamentally in the same way.

The most recent contribution to this debate, *Urbanscape Switzerland* by Avenir Suisse, entails a gradual departure from this position and finally addresses cross-border cooperation in urban regions.[15] The essays in this book do not, however, really get beyond taking stock of current problem areas and planning examples. The bottom line regarding the ineffectuality of the planning concepts proposed thus far shows the profound helplessness that dominates in the present debate:

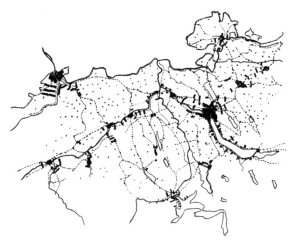

26.1 Example for a national planning of urban and semiurban areas, by Armin Meili (1941)

26.2 Spatial Planning Guideline CK-73. Existing and new main centers, medium-sized centers, and small centers (1973)

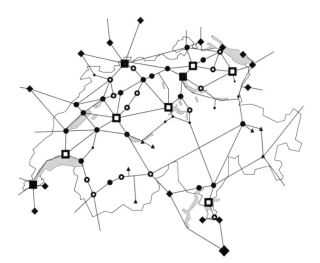

26.3 Urban Network Switzerland. Large, medium-sized, and small urban agglomerations (1996)

According to the Federal Office for Spatial Development, 70 percent of the population now lives in agglomerations (as classified by the Office); there the town and the (surrounding) countryside are manifestly being transcended and transformed into a new, diffuse, aggregate state. The very development that regional policies and planning models sought to prevent has occurred. ... It is not easy to identify the reasons behind this rather unsatisfactory state of affairs.[16]

In light of the fact that the conceptions proposed thus far have been largely ineffectual, there is now a paradigm shift in planning underway: a departure from overall views and ambitious, all-embracing designs in favor of more focus on pragmatic, sometimes openly neoliberal policies.

The Rediscovery of the Urban

In nearly all the pictures of urban Switzerland that have been painted, the city was a negative quantity, a threat, and "un-Swiss." People have only recently begun to realize that cities have specific qualities, and that Switzerland does not have too many urban situations but too few. But even this reorientation starts off with a negative image: the city may no longer be viewed as a threat, but it is still considered a problem.

The social and economic problems plaguing most of the core cities in the late 1980s, ranging from new poverty to the drug question, spurred this reorientation. The city was increasingly seen as a container for the social problems of a globalized society. The scientific model for this view is illustrated by the concept of the "A-City" (*A-Stadt*). The term subsumes a whole series of words that all begin with an A in German: the aged, the poor, singles, single-parents, drug addicts, apprentices, the jobless, foreigners, asylum seekers, dropouts. According to the A-City concept, these groups are concentrated primarily in the inner cities of large centers, creating a kind of vicious circle in which social problems get progressively worse and the associated social costs increase.[17] The negative connotations of this conception are reflected in numerous political efforts that seek to compensate for the social costs of the large cities and to launch a new policy. It is no longer only the peripheral mountain regions that are said to be in need of help, but also the centers, as social focal points, that need state assistance and support. Consequently, specific policies to support the cities have been introduced on various levels, and many cantons, as well as the federal government, have begun to compensate for the burdens of the cities as centers.

At the same time, a new policy toward agglomerations has been implemented nationally as well. It aims primarily at strengthening cooperation and tries to absorb at least some of the grave consequences of communal federalism. Even this policy, however, has not succeeded in breaking free of the idea of a decentralized development. Moreover, it constructs a dubious separation between "urban" and "rural" areas that does more to obscure than to clarify the different sets of problems. In particular, this conception masks the considerable differences and distortions that have emerged in urban regions in recent years.

Switzerland thus reveals a trend that can be observed worldwide: the rediscovery of the urban. The proximity to cultural institutions, a cosmopolitan atmosphere, and not least a trendy image have become important factors in choosing a location, not just for lifestyle-conscious urban professionals but increasingly for companies as well. As a result, in recent years the inner cities, which seemed to be suffering so much, have once again become preferred sites for investment and for wealthy social strata.[18] Yet even today these developments and trends have barely been acknowledged in the Helvetian debate on planning.

The Helvetian Model of Urbanization

Despite differences in point of view and emphasis, these conceptions of urban Switzerland all share certain aspects that are central to understanding the current situation. First, most of these approaches bear the stamp of a strong fixation on a national myth and a corresponding focus on "Switzerland" as a whole. This limits their vision considerably, however, because if the urbanization process covers the whole country and even crosses borders, then Switzerland and its traditional political and territorial borders can no longer be the relevant urban unit.

Second, the failure of planning concepts has not managed to provoke any fundamental reflection on the process of urbanization until very recently. Instead, images of urban Switzerland rotate like a prayer wheel around the negative sides of urbanization—the dissolution of the village community, urban sprawl, destruction of the landscape and environmental problems—without developing an open-minded understanding of the urban and recognizing its potential. This attitude makes it almost impossible to recognize that the doggedly defended autonomy of communes is actually one of the main reasons that the urbanization process in Switzerland has acquired its present form.

Third, the federalism of the communes has consequently never even begun to be questioned. Despite striking differences in scale, communes are still treated like subjects with equal rights that must all be given the same attention and support. Seen in this light, all forms of urban concentration are perceived as fundamentally threatening, as an immediate risk to the system of alliances in Switzerland as a whole. That also goes a long way towards explaining the various types of anti-urban attitude that are expressed in nearly all these conceptions.

Fourth, the urban reality of Switzerland has remained largely hidden in all the planning approaches deployed thus far, preventing them from grasping the great differences in economics, culture, and everyday life that have evolved. Instead, the traditional image of a decentralized and federalist Switzerland with its tripartite territorial structure of federation, cantons, and communes continues to prevail, even in statistical studies.

In order to be able to cope with the new urban realities developing in Switzerland, these old fashioned and outdated spatial representations have to be challenged: the situation today demands a new image of urban Switzerland, a new approach, and a new analysis.

Towards a New Typology of Urbanization: A Methodological Strategy

Our analysis of urban Switzerland is based on Henri Lefebvre's thesis of the complete urbanization of society. All regions in Switzerland should be seen as fundamentally urban. They are all caught up in one form of urbanization or another and have been radically transformed. It no longer makes sense to distinguish between "city" and "countryside," or "agglomerations" and "rural areas": all of Switzerland is urbanized and hence all of its landscapes must be analyzed in terms of urbanization. This does not, however, necessarily mean that all regions are of the same type. In contrast to the widespread fear, that the entire territory is turning into a homogeneous "urban gray zone," distinct urban landscapes have evolved, with very different dynamics and sets of problems, and our goal is to discover and analyze them.

We have therefore developed a typology to help recognize the differences in the nature of the urban. Maps were the most important tools in this analysis. Although maps are usually used to illustrate known facts, here they were employed as tools to *produce* knowledge. Consequently, the research approach differs from other more quantitative approaches: it is transductional and combines procedures from architecture as well as the social sciences. Statistical methods were employed alongside design methods.

One central operation in any cartographic analysis is defining certain areas and demarcating them. There are a variety of methods for doing this. The most common approach for the analysis of urban regions is identifying "agglomerations." In Switzerland, they have been identified and recalculated in every census since 1930. According to the current definition, an agglomeration is a region with at least 20,000 inhabitants and an "urban character." It consists of a core city, plus additional communes that must fulfill three of the following five criteria: a structural connection to the core city, a high population density, strong population growth, a tight network of commuting to the core zone, and a low percentage of the population employed in agriculture. Isolated communes with more than 10,000 inhabitants are also counted as urban areas. According to these criteria, approximately 73 percent of the population in Switzerland was living in urban regions in the year 2000.[19] One central problem with this definition is that it was developed for an earlier, monocentric model of urbanization. It is based on the specific image of core cities surrounded by adjacent, concentric suburban belts. Every 10 years, in other words every time there was another census, agglomerations had absorbed an additional ring of communes. All the regions outside the agglomerations are treated, in essence, as remainders that can only be defined as "rural space." Hence this method just replicates the traditional separation of "urban" and "rural" areas. It ignores not only peripheral forms of urbanization but also the significant differences that exist within areas of agglomeration. Additionally, it is not able to cope with situations in which agglomerations begin overlapping and polycentric urban regions emerge.

More discriminating analyses can be made with the help of typologies that use specific sets of indicators, and often complex statistical methods as well, depending on the question under study. The cartographic result is, in general, an abstract patchwork of different colors that is often comprehensible only to specialists. This patchwork structure also makes it difficult to identify larger contiguous regions.

The approach we have chosen differs in essential points from these methods. The typology developed here is based on qualitative analysis and not on statistical calculations. Although it also operates with statistical data and threshold values, precise statistical demarcation of the various regions was not the intention of this study. The goal was rather to understand and depict urbanization as a complex phenomenon, whose form is constantly changing. Any picture is thus necessarily only a snapshot of a specific moment in time. Moreover, urban reality comprises very different features in overlapping strata. Consequently, lines can be drawn differently depending on one's point of view and on what one wants to know. The maps are therefore designed to represent a wide variety of overlapping features. This kind of cartography seeks to persuade not by means of statistical precision but by way of the imagination.

Our cartographic analysis is based on three theoretical categories: networks, borders and differences.[20] By examining the variations in these three categories, five different urbanization types could be identified in Switzerland: metropolitan regions, urban networks, quiet zones, alpine resorts, and alpine fallow lands (Figure 26.4, next page).

These urbanization types should be understood as ideal types. They are not meant to suggest homogeneity, but rather to illustrate a common set of problems and a common everyday reality. The source material was compiled by approximately 160 architecture students at the ETH Studio Basel. In the course of a total of eight design studios between 1999 and 2003, they "drilled" in all parts of Switzerland. They explored urban situations, collected various materials, took photographs, conducted interviews and prepared maps. The choice of regions to be studied was not based on existing regional units; instead both the maps and the analysis deliberately focused on borders other than the existing regional ones. The knowledge thus obtained was then supplemented with statistical data and additional research, condensed, made more precise and tested in discussions with specialists.

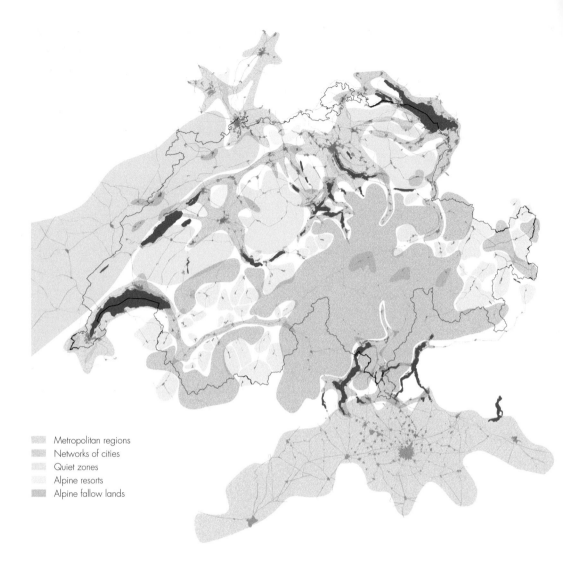

Metropolitan regions
Networks of cities
Quiet zones
Alpine resorts
Alpine fallow lands

26.4 Typology of an urban Switzerland

The mappings, definitions and characterizations of the five urbanization types are presented below. The goal of this typology is to sketch a picture of Switzerland as an urban country. This entails identifying the various forms of urbanization and revealing their corresponding potential. Our urban portrait of Switzerland should be understood as a phenomenological approximation, as an essayistic combination of analysis and design. The picture of urban Switzerland presented here is precise in some areas, imprecise in others and sometimes even speculative.[21]

Metropolitan Regions

Metropolitan regions are areas of urban concentration with a high degree of international networking and reach. They represent nodes within the global network of exchange and communication (Figure 26.5). A metropolitan region is distinguished by a large and varied set of global *networks*: trade and production networks, capital flow, cultural and social networks, and networks of migration as well. Overlapping and linking produce a high degree of economic, social and cultural complexity, which is manifested on the regional level as well. A metropolitan region forms an expansive area that links a wide variety of places to form a highly differentiated, polycentric ensemble. It consists of one or more core cities and incorporates an extensive network of small and medium-sized cities as well as suburban and peri-urban areas.

Metropolitan regions are crisscrossed by a variety of *borders*. Their networks always cross regional borders and sometimes national borders as well. It is characteristic of metropolitan regions that many of the old borders continue to exist but their character has changed fundamentally: they become permeable, fluid and dynamic. For that reason, unlike classic large cities, metropolitan regions have no real form; it is no longer possible to determine their extent with certainty. In metropolitan regions, a wide variety of people, activities and uses collide. Consequently, such regions are distinguished by a large number of *differences*. These differences are dynamic and sometimes explosive. Hence it is crucially important that they not close themselves off from one another but recognize one another, interact, and thereby become creative and fruitful. Atmospheric elements, cosmopolitanism and openness are as much a part of metropolitan regions as debates and conflicts.

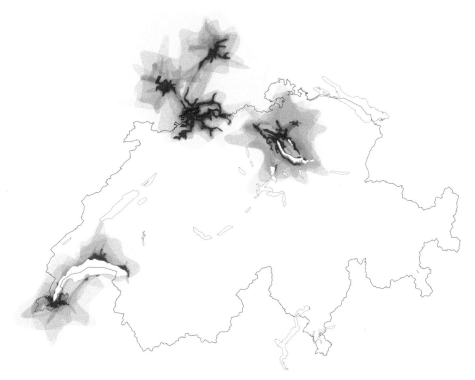

26.5 Metropolitan regions

As a general category, "metropolis" refers to a city with a cosmopolitan culture and worldwide reach. Globalization has given the term a new meaning: metropolises today are to be understood in economic terms as nerve centers of the world economy. The terms "world city" and "global city" have gained currency in the literature on such cities.[22] In general, the processes that led to the creation of world cities or global cities can be understood as "metropolization": the global economy is increasingly organized in the form of overarching networks.[23] At certain nodal points, these networks overlap and consolidate into metropolitan spaces. This consolidation generates specific effects that become highly attractive to companies operating globally. As logistical nodes, metropolitan spaces offer not only easy accessibility but also an opportunity to build heterogeneous chains of activity. This results in the formation of a dense web of overlapping networks that make it possible to combine a wide variety of elements in constantly new ways. The overlapping of diverse cultures thus benefits processes of innovation and learning as well. Sectoral and technological innovations can be achieved in a remote research center, but following up with innovations that result from new and surprising combinations of different elements needs external stimuli. The heterogeneous networks of metropolitan milieus constantly generate such external impulses.

A metropolitan region thus refers to a large, polycentric urban area with global networks. Even today, however, its definition is rather imprecise. The most commonly used criterion is that such a region should have more than a million residents as well as international reach or visibility.[24] Such definitions are problematic, however. First, the number of inhabitants is just one aspect among many, and by itself it says little about the importance of an urban region. The thesis that a metropolis has to have a certain critical mass to remain competitive internationally has yet to be demonstrated empirically. Second, the international importance of an urban region is very difficult to measure. Studies that attempt to do so are usually dominated by an economic bias and frequently do no more than compare the number of headquarters of global companies. Third, a region will also exploit its metropolitan character as a marketing ploy. To improve its international ranking, which provides an advantage in attracting global companies, the metropolitan area is often demarcated generously in order to maximize the statistics for population and economic power.

In short, there are no uniform, unambiguous criteria for determining the extent of a metropolitan region, where various highly distinct urban systems overlap and produce mutual dependencies. In fact, many different criteria can be used to demarcate a metropolitan region, yielding substantial variations in the size of the resulting areas. Approximations of such polycentric and polymorphic regions can be based, for example, on commuter patterns, regional production networks, metropolitan railway systems, consumer and leisure networks, or media systems. The overlapping of such features provides a good approximation of the extent of a metropolitan region. The observation of local processes of transformation also provides important clues: metropolitan regions comprise those areas in which nearly every change can be described as a consequence of or reaction to the development of the overall region.

Although the term "metropolitan region" is problematic in many respects, we have adopted it for our typology. We have, however, proceeded from a more universal, qualitative understanding of the term, which also takes into account a location's social and cultural importance. In this respect, crucial features of metropolitan regions include such things as an open, cosmopolitan culture, the development of dynamic differences, and the innovative potential that results from linking different networks. Social innovations are often the result of unintended and undirected processes and highly dependent on chance discoveries. The more diverse and open a place is, the better its chances for such innovations.

Commensurately with the wide range of definitions, it is possible to identify quite different metropolitan regions in Switzerland, both in terms of size and number. Their identification is guided by a variety of interests and has become a political question.[25] For example, the Federal Office for Statistics has singled out five metropolitan regions: Zurich, Basel, Geneva-Lausanne, Bern, and the Ticino. This definition is not the result of any sophisticated analysis, but merely of an addition of neighboring agglomeration areas based on the study of commuter patterns. Moreover, it still bows to the federalist, decentralized conception that continues to prevail in Switzerland: every part of the country should have its own metropolitan region.

By contrast, a research group from the ETH Zurich identified only two metropolitan regions in Switzerland: the Lake Geneva region and Zurich. It advanced the thesis that there is a "European metropolitan region Zurich" with about four million inhabitants extending from Lake Constance to Basel.[26] This definition is based primarily on the range of the corporate networks of the banking center Zurich. The most important criterion for demarcation is the coherence of the agglomeration areas that can be reached within an hour's drive of Zurich's city center. One consideration is clearly the belief that only regions of this size can compete internationally. But there are still no detailed studies that could provide additional arguments for this thesis.

Our analysis has identified three regions in Switzerland that fulfill the conditions for metropolitan regions, at least in part: Zurich, the bipolar Lake Geneva region, and the trinational region Basel-Mulhouse-Freiburg. There is no debating that these three regions represent the motors of growth in the Swiss economy today. They are all distinguished by a global orientation, but they also contrast relatively strongly in terms of their economies and everyday worlds. Each has a distinct economic specialization and is thus positioned differently within the global hierarchy of metropolitan regions.

Zurich has undergone a fundamental transformation over the last 30 years, evolving from Switzerland's largest industrial city to a global financial center, a global city. Its central position within Switzerland, its strong dependence on national parameters like bank secrecy, the Swiss franc and social stability, as well as its strong control in economic, media and political affairs make Zurich the "Helvetian metropolis." Everyday life in Zurich has also undergone an astonishing transformation alongside these economic changes. A narrow-minded and provincial commune has become a relatively open and cosmopolitan city. This development is the result not only of globalization but also of the urban revolt of the 1980s, in which an urban-oriented generation demanded a "different city," more creativity and freedom for alternative lifestyles. The ensuing change in cultural climate and everyday life have proved extraordinarily productive for Switzerland.

The Zurich region lies in the center of the densely populated Swiss Plateau, and it continues to draw new agglomerations and cities into its catchment area. Although this originally monocentric region has transformed in recent years into a complex, polycentric greater metropolitan area, it has not yet become a political entity because the anti-Zurich reflex is still strong in broad sections of Switzerland. The only political structure that governs this region is the Canton of Zurich.

Switzerland's second financial center, Geneva, is positioned differently and has a different character from Zurich: Geneva is more an international city than a global city, and its past as a city-state is still evident. Geneva's economy is based today on a narrow segment of financial companies, the strong presence of international organizations, and a specialized sector for the production of luxury goods. This specific combination of networks gives Geneva a flavor that is at once cosmopolitan and introverted and explains the ambivalence of its relationship to the metropolitan region that has emerged along Lake Geneva. On the one hand, the Lake Geneva region forms a unified urban landscape with international reach. On the other, this region is bipolar and divided: two clearly separate commuter areas have formed around the international center that is Geneva, and the regional center that is Lausanne.

Basel displays yet another direction and dynamic of development. As late as the 1980s, Basel was still a distinctly industrial city and showed clear symptoms of a crisis. Since then a globalized economy has evolved there as well, focusing primarily on the centralized control functions of global corporations as well as on research and development in the fields of chemistry, pharmaceuticals and biotechnology. Old, established industries and a strong sense of local identity make Basel a relatively homogeneous city in social and cultural terms. On the other hand, Basel is expanding more and more across the French and German borders. In regional terms, therefore, the city is increasingly oriented to the north, toward the upper Rhine. For decades now there have been persistent efforts to build up cross-border co-operation and to create a stronger unity with the neighboring centers behind the Jura Mountains—Mulhouse and Freiburg. This emerging metropolitan region is tripolar and trinational. The borders here clearly manifest their double function as separation and as a source of potential.

The three metropolitan regions of Switzerland have very different economic specializations, and correspondingly distinct positions and characteristics. Although there are many contacts and interconnections between them, strong synergies and complementarities are not evident. The dynamics of evolution in the three regions are different and do not appear to be synchronized. Even the regional constitution of the three areas is quite distinct. The criterion of strong and progressing specialization was another crucial factor in our decision to continue to regard the Zurich and Basel-Mulhouse-Freiburg regions as two separate entities. There are many connections between the two regions, and their commuter areas are increasingly growing together, with their edges starting to overlap. Nevertheless, the differences in culture and in economic and everyday orientation make them two clearly distinct units—even more so than either their topographical separation by the Jura mountain chain or their still pronounced tendency to distinguish between themselves would imply.

Networks of Cities

Networks of cities consist of converging small and medium-sized cities that lie outside metropolitan regions (Figure 26.6). They can take on very different forms and characteristics. The cities have strong economic, cultural and social interconnections based on horizontal relationships. Such *networks* are primarily regional and national, with no significant international dimension. They are of moderate density and moderate heterogeneity. On the one hand, a network of cities exploits complementarities by distributing central tasks

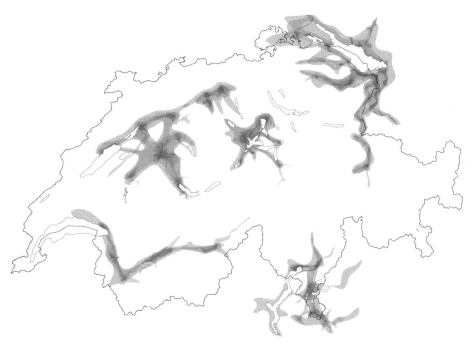

26.6 Networks of cities

in the areas of the economy, culture, education, consumption or administration. On the other, it produces synergies—that is, it has functions and facilities that complement one another and produce economies of scale.

Nearly all networks of cities have a number of *borders* passing through them. As a rule, they combine different regions and in some cases even cross national borders. For that reason, there are also different political jurisdictions and pronounced splits. Their weaker networking dynamic makes these borders more pronounced, despite their great potential. The external borders of networks of cities are often impossible to determine precisely.

The *differences* within the networks of cities can be conspicuous, but as a rule their effect is limited, more passive and tending to the static. Small-town regional milieus within networks of cities tend to show greater social control and hence to cut themselves off. The regional distribution of institutions, infrastructure, and facilities hinders the development of strong differences. Urban potential is distributed and thus partitioned and weakened.

The concept of the network of cities has been in circulation for some time. In practice, it is used only for all kinds of possible cooperative relationships between cities, but frequently also as a label for marketing a particular location or as a way to justify investment in infrastructure. A typical example of this uncritical application of the term is the national concept of an "urban network Switzerland," which is based on the idea that Switzerland comprises a contiguous network of cities. But this concept obscures the great differences that exist between the various Swiss centers. Our analysis shows that it is not possible to identify a contiguous "urban network Switzerland." In fact, the network breaks down into the metropolitan regions and their extended catchment areas, on the one hand, and several regional networks of cities, on the other.

In general, such a network can be defined as a non-hierarchical network of cities of similar size, which is based on a set of horizontal relationships. A central condition that must be met is that of complementarities and synergies between the various cities.[27] Mere proximity is not very significant in itself. The crucial questions are whether the cities complement one another and whether there is close cooperation between them that leads to regional networks based on the division of labor.

In addition to state and private infrastructure, regional systems of production are especially important, and for years now these have been the subject of a broad discussion in regional studies.[28] Regional systems of production are differentiated networks of economic activities that are, on the one hand, distinguished by a specific structure of industrial sectors and are, on the other, embedded in regional milieus that can help promote regional processes of innovation and learning. These networks are based on a large number of firm-independent interconnections and institutions: social and cultural facilities as well as formal and informal channels of communication by means of which the transfer of knowledge is organized. A number of such regional production systems can be identified in Switzerland.[29] In addition to those of Geneva, Basel, and Zurich, and the tourist-based urban system of Lausanne, there are also production systems that coincide entirely or in part with networks of cities: the industrial systems of eastern Switzerland and the Jura region; the tourist, tertiary and industrial system of the Ticino; and the tourist and industrial system of the Valais.

Because of its entrenched federalist structure and decentralized form of industrialization, Switzerland is literally covered with small and medium-sized centers that have a distinct, traditionally small-town structure, and yet have universities of applied sciences, regional hospitals, and cultural and social facilities. There are 26 cantonal capitals alone, with the associated administrative offices. In addition, there are a large number of regional centers that also receive special subsidies. Many of these, especially in the Zurich region, have become dependent on the metropolises and should be seen as part of metropolitan regions.

Nevertheless, large sections of Switzerland—especially in the center of the Swiss Plateau, eastern Switzerland, in the Ticino and in the large alpine valleys—are not directly influenced by large centers. These small and medium-sized cities are too far from metropolitan centers, and are too different in terms of economic structure to profit significantly from the developmental impetus of the metropolitan centers. Many of these small and medium-sized cities have long-established cultural and economic relationships, sometimes quite close ones, particularly in eastern Switzerland, in the Ticino, in central Switzerland and along the southern base of the Jura Mountains. Although these regions have no clearly identifiable, self-contained clusters of urban networks, daily life is interconnected to a certain degree as demonstrated, for example, by commuter patterns.

Within this varied fabric of relationships, there are some clear structures with their own characteristics, such as the urban ring around Bern, the pocket-shaped urban network around Lake Lucerne, or the cross-border network of cities of *rete urbana dei laghi*, which includes the five centers of Bellinzona, Locarno, Lugano, Como and Varese. These three networks of cities, being centered on large cities (Bern, Lucerne and Lugano), have generated star-shaped movement, in contrast to the dispersed, polycentric networks without any real center, which have evolved in the Aarau-Olten region and in eastern Switzerland. Because they are relatively balanced in topological terms, the latter have no dominant direction or striking geometry. Finally, in the industrialized alpine valleys of Valais, there is a linear network of cities.

Even if they do not form clearly definable units, these networks of cities are not just an endless and faceless mishmash of settlements, but reveal structures with unmistakable physiognomies, urban cultures and specific identities. An autonomous urban culture has developed in these areas. It is marked by a specific way of life, which is neither that of a village nor that of a large city, and is even distinct from that of large agglomerations. The countryside is always nearby: all of these networks of cities border on quiet zones and/or alpine fallow lands. Typically, they also transition seamlessly into the metropolitan regions, particularly in the Zurich region.

Most Swiss networks of cities (still) represent the legacy of Switzerland's industrial tradition. A large percentage of industrial production, particularly that of small and medium-sized companies, is located within these networks of cities. That is true in the high-tech sphere as well. Yet these networks of cities have also lost many of their strategic functions. Since many business-oriented services have relocated to the metropolitan regions, they are heavily dependent on the outside world. In most cases, they are not very specialized either and have no clear economic strengths: regional economic clusters that could generate processes of innovation are often poorly developed.

Nearly all the networks of cities are crossed by an elaborate plexus of borders. In several cases, like the Ticino or eastern Switzerland, the networks of cities cross national borders. The urban ring around Bern is split by a linguistic divide, and there is always a confusing jumble of cantonal and regional borders. As a result, separate political jurisdictions and pronounced splits exist as well. Consequently, differences within the networks of cities are only moderately defined and not very effective. A strong aversion to urban concentrations along with the federalist distribution of institutions, infrastructure and facilities means that any potential concentration of differences inevitably meets with opposition. Strong local identities and mutual animosities often lead to an internal homogenization of towns, which reinforces their small-town character.

Even today, the networks of cities have made only cautious attempts to combine into larger political and territorial units. Cooperation between cities has evolved to varying extents, but always arduously. The repulsive forces between the poles are considerable. Typically, they look not to their neighbors but beyond them to the metropolitan centers. Cooperation is often made more difficult by the proximity of, or even intersection with, metropolitan regions.

There are, however, few alternatives to reinforcing regional cooperation. To judge from their economic structure and their perspectives for development, the networks of cities should be seen as the crisis regions of the future. Economically dependent on the metropolitan regions, and holding few economic trump cards, the most important potentials of the networks of cities are their urban structure, their variety, and their attraction as landscapes. By themselves, most of Switzerland's small and medium-sized cites have few prospects. If they combine their everyday worlds, however, they can generate productive differences.

Quiet Zones

Quiet zones are regions of various sizes whose settlement patterns show few signs of urbanization and which have not yet been incorporated into networks of cities or metropolitan regions. The most important feature of the quiet zones is relative distance from larger centers. For the most part, they lack even smaller centers. Hence these areas lack a true core around which they could be structured (Figure 26.7).

The *networks* of the quiet zones are primarily local and are not very intense. The quiet zones do not even have strong internal networks. The most important productive remnants of the agricultural economy and often small and medium-sized industrial companies are located here. Gradually, urban networks are spreading here as well and embedding the quiet zones in a variety of structures.

The *borders* of the quiet zones are not very porous. The traditional borders of village communities and of the historical valley settlements, which often ran along topographic borders, still dominate. Even where the borders are more porous, however, few potentials result, because they combine or separate places of similar type: the quiet zones are isotopic in terms of their internal structure.

As a consequence, *differences* do exist, but their effect is weak. Because of the pull between distinct local character and urban disposition, the quiet zones often remain static and inert. Even while everyday life within them becomes more and more urban, they retain a few particularities: life is slower, steadier, more connected to place and more homogeneous.

26.7 Quiet zones

But relative proximity to urban centers does increase their heterogeneity: urban uses begin to occupy these areas, resulting in overlapping, multiple uses and the attendant conflicts.

Not all of the areas outside the Alps are covered by metropolitan regions or networks of cities. In certain places, the urban fabric frays, gaps appear and a blurred physiognomy results: "green pockets" form in the urban fabric between intensive forms of urbanization. Quiet zones can be viewed from two perspectives: seen from outside, they appear to be bare patches where the urbanization process tapers off. On the other hand, they actively resist urbanization. The communes in the quiet zones still have a certain independence and village culture plays an important role in everyday life.

These areas have no specific designation in official statistics. They are lumped together with most of the alpine areas, as being non-urban, outside the agglomerations, and therefore "rural space."[30] But they lost their rural character long ago. Agriculture may still define the appearance of the landscape, but it is no longer the economic base of these areas. Instead, they increasingly fall within the catchment areas of metropolitan regions and networks of cities. Like waves crashing onshore, they are struck in many ways by the developments of the centers, such as commuters who have settled in old farmhouses, the introduction of leisure facilities, or paved roads: the quiet zones are increasingly becoming peri-urban.

The first studies of peri-urbanization in Switzerland examined Gros-de-Vaud, north of Lausanne.[31] In its broadest sense, the term "peri-urbanization" refers to a connection between the everyday lives of the centers with their "hinterlands." This process happens in both directions: people, often from upper income levels, move further and further from the centers in search of rural communes, while conversely residents of peripheral areas work in the centers, without abandoning their places of residence. The process of peri-urbanization is invisible at first, because in the initial phase neither the settlement pattern nor the landscape changes significantly. In time, however, new zones of detached houses and a variety of infrastructural facilities are built.

There are three substantial contiguous regions in the Swiss Plateau that can be characterized as quiet zones. The *Eastern Quiet Zone* runs along the Prealps from Appenzell by way of Toggenburg to the Zurich Oberland. It is one of the core areas of early industrialization, and even today it is closely interwoven with the network of cities of eastern Switzerland. The *Central Quiet Zone* is situated in the center of the Swiss Plateau, around Napf Mountain, and it combines very different regions, most of which are heavily agricultural and highly introverted: the Emmental, the Oberaargau, the Entlebuch, and the Lucerne Hinterland. A distinct dividing line structures the central quiet zone from north to south: the border between Protestant Bern and Catholic Lucerne. It corresponds to the Brünig-Napf-Reuss line, an older cultural border between eastern and western Switzerland that had a demonstrable ethnographic effect into the mid-twentieth century.[32] The *Central Quiet Zone* is oriented around three networks of cities that are also distinct from one another: the urban ring around Bern, the urban network Aarau-Olten, and the network of cities of central Switzerland. The *Western Quiet Zone* is also intersected by a cantonal and religious border and includes two very different regions: the undulating, agriculturally intensive Gros-de-Vaud and the hilly region of the Fribourg Prealps that is dominated by grassland production. Although the *Western Quiet Zone* lies south of the divide between French-speaking and German-speaking Switzerland; in urbanistic terms it represents a far more important partition that separates the Bern urban ring from the Lake Geneva Basin.

These three quiet zones are thus by no means uniform. Each zone is composed of various regions that form a unit in terms of their structural situation but not in terms of identity and history. All of the quiet zones are crossed by cantonal, cultural and religious borders whose effect is still pronounced. The three quiet zones in the Swiss Plateau are of central significance to the overall picture of urban Switzerland: they interrupt the urbanized axes and belts; they create bars or buffer zones between the densely urbanized areas and thus give the Swiss Plateau a structure. They create a distance between the big centers and divide networks of cities and metropolitan regions. The existence of these quiet zones disproves the frequently asserted notion that the Swiss Plateau form a single city or one urbanized belt from Lake Constance to Lake Geneva.

In addition to these three areas in the Swiss Plateau, the Swiss section of the Jura range also fulfills many of the criteria of the quiet zones. It is relatively far from the large centers, and the look of its landscape is characterized by agriculture. At the same time, however, it reveals clear differences: it has several small to medium-sized cities, and the long industrial tradition that produced considerable wealth is still strongly present. In many places, however, it clearly shows signs of recession and abandonment. The Jura would seem to represent a special case in our typology, one that could perhaps warrant its own urbanization type.

Unlike the Jura, the quiet zones of the Swiss Plateau showed signs of depletion until the 1970s. They felt the effects of heavy emigration to the large centers. Today, this process is being reversed to some extent: parts of the quiet zones have the highest population growth in Switzerland. This is where the urban zones began lapping over into the countryside. The urban character is present in many ways; it imposes a variety of networks on the apparent quietness, thus exploiting the agricultural charms and at the same time transforming them.

The most consequential transformation of the quiet zones is not related to their inner nature but rather to their utterly transformed geography. A mere 50 years ago, the countryside still represented a continuous backdrop against which the urban centers stood out; now, by contrast, the last remains of rural areas are like a patchwork of solitary islands that are starting to resemble parks in an urban topography. Therein lies the potential of the quiet zones: they are the only areas with more or less intact landscapes that lie relatively close to the centers. These green islands should be seen as urban spaces that are extremely important to Switzerland.

Alpine Resorts

Alpine resorts are urban regions in the mountains that belong neither to networks of cities nor to metropolitan regions and whose only economic function is tourism. Alpine resorts are temporary and polycentric spread-out cities of leisure (Figure 26.8). The intensity and character of their *networks* is cyclical. During the brief high season, they are national or even international in scope; in the off-season they are above all local and regional. Essential features include good accessibility, well-developed internal transportation systems of relatively large scope, and an infrastructure of a very high standard nearly identical to that of a city.

The *borders* of alpine resorts are not very permeable. As a rule, the outer borders are defined by topography: because alpine resorts are broken into distinct chambers, their structure is that of an island. Even when the ski areas of different resorts are linked, the only thing it affects is the recreational activity of the guests. When the snow has melted and the ski lifts have stopped running, the topography reemerges as a limiting factor. Hence the resort remains largely a self-contained world, even when it is networked.

The *differences* are also cyclical, because of the specific structure of activities. During the high season the alpine resorts are places where local and global worlds collide. A unique culture has evolved that can be described as an overlapping of alpine culture with urban elements, although the typical separation into locals and visitors limits the effect of this heterogeneity. In fact, restriction to a world of recreation fosters homogeneity. During the off-season, most of the alpine resorts come to resemble the quiet zones.

26.8 Alpine resorts

Tourist zones are an old urban phenomenon. In many respects, the history of tourism in the Alps can be described as one of urban colonization; essential elements of alpine culture have, however, been retained. Urban culture has formed a stratum over alpine culture. The transformation of old tourist locations into modern resorts took place gradually and in parallel with the changing character of tourism. Since the beginnings of alpine tourism in the nineteenth century, various forms of experiencing nature have represented a central motivation for visiting the mountains. Even the mass tourism that began in the Alps from the mid-1950s during the summer season and a decade later during the winter season initially had a strong connection to "nature" and to local alpine culture. Gradually, however, the practices of appropriation changed, and increasingly the practice of tourism was disengaged from unpredictable natural conditions. The mountains became a piece of leisure or sports equipment, as it were, and the distinctive features of the various sites receded into the background. The moment "nature" is no longer experienced as a contrast to "the city," and mountain tourism is no longer a form of compensation, the tourist locations become an integral element of everyday urban life. The alpine resorts reinforce this trend by adapting their infrastructure and programs to meet changing needs. For this reason, the term "resort" is explicitly used here to distinguish from earlier forms of touristic development.

The most important feature of alpine resorts today, the thing that distinguishes them from all other forms of urbanization, is their pronounced seasonal rhythm. Everyday life follows a clearly structured annual calendar: once or twice a year, the alpine resorts swell up for a few weeks into densely populated, almost metropolitan places. For the most part, the summer season attracts domestic and older visitors, while the more important winter season has clearly international traits. It is not just the number of residents, but their increasingly urban lifestyle that gives the alpine resorts a distinctly urban character. At its most extreme, a resort can become a temporary world city, like Davos during the World Economic Forum.

The island-like nature of the small topographic chambers in which the alpine resorts are located makes them look like patchwork on the map. They are not, however, evenly distributed throughout the alpine region. Because they are attractive to tourists, the three large regions in the high mountain zones—eastern Grisons with Klosters-Davos, the Upper Engadine Valley and the southern Valais—have a high density of resorts and complex regional networking patterns.

Alpine tourism in Switzerland not only began earlier than in the neighboring countries, but from the beginning has also been distinctly international in character.[33] It has, however, passed its peak. Since the 1980s, most alpine resorts in Switzerland have seen a slow but steady decline. The number of overnight stays and the number of jobs have been falling nearly everywhere.

The alpine resorts are under pressure from several sides at once. First, they are clearly feeling the consequences of global urbanization. The massive buildup of transportation and the dramatic fall in the price of airplane travel have meant that they now have to compete with remote destinations. The strong Swiss franc and the high prices of Switzerland's domestic market have made vacations in Switzerland a luxury product for international guests. Second, the differentiation of society and the pluralization of lifestyles has made for much greater variety in attitudes toward leisure, affecting where, how, and how long tourists go on vacation. Ski vacations, the main income for most resorts, were once a matter of course for Swiss families, but have lost much of their significance. Third, global climate change has made the amount of snow uncertain for resorts at lower elevations and has led to reductions in revenue. Fourth, in the 1990s, banks began granting loans more selectively. For many smaller destinations, it has become difficult to finance investments in infrastructure for tourism. Consequently, the tourist industry is under a great deal of economic pressure. Many hotels, mountain railways and ski lifts have been suffering a slow decline. The prospect of substantial repairs or renovations can spell the end of a hotel or a small ski area. In that sense, the fate of tourism is similar to that of many other Swiss quality products. Many resorts, especially smaller and more remote resorts, are beginning to resemble old industrial regions in certain respects.

The main response in coping with this insidiously incipient crisis concentrates on particular market segments and on special offers. The current variety of alpine resorts can no longer be adequately described by the facile distinction between chic luxury resorts and simple family resorts. Defining a resort to appeal to a specific target group of tourists—which also entails targeted branding—is capital intensive, however, and hence it accelerates the process of concentration.

The alpine resorts are included as a single category in this typology, but they represent an extremely heterogeneous group of regions. Whereas the top resorts like St. Moritz, Davos, Zermatt, and Grindelwald are developing into specialized global centers in certain respects, regions at the other end of the scale, like Andermatt and Obergoms, already number among the alpine fallow lands.

Alpine Fallow Lands

Alpine fallow lands are zones of decline and gradual recession. Their common feature is steady emigration. They include those areas of the Alps that have no urban networks to connect them to an urban economy and cannot establish a significant tourist industry of their own. The pull effect of the urban networks has produced a negative dynamic in these regions and is increasingly sapping their energy (Figure 26.9).

The orientation of the *networks* in the alpine fallow lands is primarily local. Many of the regions are strongly influenced by local trade and agriculture. The topographical chambers

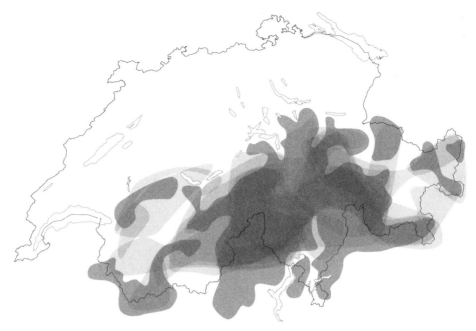

26.9 Alpine fallow lands

prevent or at least hinder the spread of networks, and distances to the nearest centers are often considerable. Even when they have access to the highway system, they remain peripheral: what is lacking is not so much a connection to the urban world as the physical presence of the urban.

The *borders* of the alpine fallow lands are largely determined by topography. They are not very permeable and have only limited potential. As was the case with the quiet zones, they often separate or link areas of a similar type. In addition to the thinly populated regions in the valley bottoms, the area of the alpine fallow areas also extends to the Alpine meadows for summer grazing, the dams and the mountain ranges beyond.

The *differences* are usually poorly developed, and emigration tends to reduce it still further. This is due more to the qualitative than the quantitative aspect of emigration since those who move to the centers are usually from the better educated and innovative sectors of the population. Decreased vocational diversity also contributes to the loss of jobs. As a result, the differences remain small and the spectrum of developmental possibilities limited. The biggest problem in the alpine fallow lands is the limited or even complete lack of perspectives for the future.

Out-migration from the Alps is an old problem. As early as the beginning of the twentieth century, it was causing the decline of villages and alpine pastures. In the European alpine region as a whole, roughly a fifth of all communes experienced a constant decline in population between 1870 and 2000.[34] These alpine emigration areas have therefore been the subject of scientific studies for a long time. The most recent typologies of communes do not paint a uniform picture of Switzerland's mountain regions. On the one hand, they reveal very different patterns of emigration and, on the other, a variety of structural forms and economic problems.[35]

The overlapping and the generalization in the design employed to render our typology nevertheless reveals a startlingly clear picture. Although alpine fallow lands are often called "marginal regions," these areas do not in fact lie on the "edge" of Switzerland, and they are not distributed patchwork-like across the alpine region. They include not only remote side valleys with poor access, but also areas along the important transit axes. Above all, however, there is a large, contiguous fallow area at Switzerland's geographical and mythological center, around St. Gotthard. We call this area the "central fallow land." It extends from the Surselva in the Grisons to the Obergoms in the Valais and from the edges of the metropolitan region around Zurich to the fringes of the metropolitan region around Milan.

The geographic location of this area brings out two essential characteristics of the alpine fallow lands in Switzerland: they are mostly of little attraction to tourists and they lie far from the larger urban centers. Unlike the mountain backdrops of the resorts, the alpine fallow lands have few or no important areas for skiing and the latest sports. They lack the glamour of the Matterhorn or the Jungfrau, even if they do include landscapes of extraordinary beauty. They tend to be accessed by tourists in quiet, traditional ways, usually by hikers or mountaineers. Such tourism is easy on the landscape and environment, but the value added is too small to provide an income for a sufficiently large number of people. The transition between alpine fallow lands and resorts is thus fluid. On the one hand, the resources of the landscape can perhaps be improved for tourist use through new projects. On the other, many alpine resorts risk becoming fallow areas if they are unable to renew their tourist base and evolve.

The second important feature mentioned was the distance to larger centers. The alpine fallow lands are not cut off from the urban world; urban networks have long since penetrated into even the most remote side valleys. But they are still far from the centers and from the attendant range of opportunities in terms of work, consumer goods, and culture. That is why the alpine fallow lands are the only areas in Switzerland that have not been drawn into the vortices and subjected to the pressures of the urbanization process. Along their edges, especially on the sunny sloping terraces of the valley outlets, there are forms of peri-urbanization. From the perspective of the centers, however, the valley areas behind them are at most interesting as places for temporary retreats.

This results in grave economic disadvantages. The alpine fallow lands profit little, if at all, from the developmental impetus of the centers. The increasing concentration of business-oriented services in the large centers—a central resource for more complex production processes—limits the economic structure to value-added-intensive sectors. The decline of classic forms of industry in the larger alpine valleys makes this situation even more critical. The economic activity of the alpine fallow lands is reduced for the most part to agriculture and local trade.

Economic depression is often accompanied by the decline of the local infrastructure. In many areas, stores and schools have been forced to close. It is also increasingly difficult to guarantee medical care. Reciprocal assistance of village communities is increasingly unable to compensate for these deficits. Because of their weak economic base, the alpine fallow lands are largely dependent on a variety of federal and inter-cantonal transfer payments and subsidies. Current debates center primarily on subsidies for mountain agriculture, but they comprise only a tiny portion of the total transfer payments. In addition to contributions to infrastructure, there is also financing for a variety of measures to protect settlements and roads from natural disasters.

For a long time, all of these open and hidden forms of subsidy went uncontested. In comparison to other alpine countries, particularly France and Italy, the funding for mountain regions in Switzerland has been generous since the 1970s. Nevertheless, it has merely slowed the decline of the alpine fallow lands rather than preventing it. With increasing deregulation and intensified pressure to encourage the transparency of costs and profitability, the alpine fallow lands are feeling the pinch. The decision to abandon a uniform blanket policy for agriculture and infrastructure reflects a new national understanding of space: a gradual turn away from the doctrine of a relative "spatial justice." The alpine fallow areas are thus the only region of Switzerland for which the present model of urbanization foresees no developmental perspectives at all. They are the neglected backyards of urban Switzerland.

The provocative choice of the phrase "alpine fallow lands" in this context is intended to signal a problematic situation but also a potential. It seeks to demonstrate that the traditional model of preserving the status quo offers no perspectives for these areas and that the only path forward is an openness to other possible alternative paths of development. This requires new and sophisticated strategies of development. A pure policy of withdrawal and *laissez-faire* could have fatal consequences. If the alpine fallow lands become urban waste dumps, where uses undesirable elsewhere are relocated, their potential for future generations will be lost forever.

Differences as Urban Potential

Our *Urban Portrait* shows that Switzerland is more urban than it thinks. Even if large groups stubbornly continue to defend the myth of a rural Switzerland, and even if the scholarly discourse on planning continues to distinguish between "urban" and "rural" areas, Switzerland today is a thoroughly urbanized space in which economic, cultural and everyday networks have evolved on a number of levels. This space has become a kind of supermarket where those with the resources and mobility are able to pick out the most advantageous offers of places, events and facilities, and build their individual networks for everyday life. This urban space is, however, by no means uniform and homogeneous. On the contrary, it is more diverse than is generally acknowledged. Even if all these areas are caught up in the process of urbanization and are transformed by it, they nevertheless reveal clearly distinct forms, characteristics and sets of problems. Our division of the territory into five urbanization types shows, for all its simplification, several salient aspects of current processes and points to a fundamental set of problems: Switzerland is developing new regional urban spaces that are increasingly drifting apart in everyday, economic and social terms. They have different dynamics and speeds, and their differences tend to be reinforced. Therein lies Switzerland's urban potential.

At the same time, however, countless regional and local interests and debates continue to play a crucial role. Urban space is crisscrossed not only by national, cantonal and communal borders, but also by linguistic, religious and a variety of cultural borders—dividing it into extremely small pieces, right down to its microstructure. The new urban distinctions that have developed in recent years do not, however, follow these traditional divisions and orientations but instead place a new pattern on top of it. A variety of superimpositions and interferences result between these two ordering systems.

This development is diametrically opposed to the idea of a "systematically" networked Switzerland that has been cultivated for decades. The long dominant strategy of equality is breaking down in the face of urban reality. Federalist diversity has many wonderful traits, but it distorts our view of new urban realities. It prevents the recognition of the potential that lies in these differences so that existing elements of an urban Switzerland are not fruitfully exploited. Instead, all energy is still invested in trying to separate, limit, and domesticate differences.

Cartographic depictions are never innocent. They are representations of space that seek to structure and thus influence reality. Like every representation of space, this portrait of urban Switzerland has normative components. It operates on the premise that the urban, and the differences it contains, are a productive factor with positive potential. In that sense, the urban topography expressed in our maps can also be understood as an analysis of urban potentials.

This will enable us to derive an urban strategy that seeks to recognize differences, to strengthen them, and to make them fruitful. Such a strategy would no longer support everything equally everywhere; on the contrary, it would try to reinforce differences rather than smooth them out and to develop different qualities and different urban situations in specific regions. Such a strategy can only be implemented through public debate. That is why our *Urban Portrait* has deliberately foresworn any concrete proposals or packages of measures, which would immediately be ground to dust in political nitpicking. It is a portrait, a potential image of a diverse urban Switzerland. No more and no less.

Notes

1   Roger Diener, Jacques Herzog, Marcel Meili, Pierre de Meuron and Christian Schmid, *Switzerland—An Urban Portrait, Volumes 1–4* (Basel: Birkhäuser, 2006).
2   See Christian Schmid, "Networks, Borders, Differences: Towards a Theory of the Urban," this book, Ch. 4.
3   See Christian Schmid, "The Urbanization of Switzerland," this book, Ch. 18.
4   Armin Meili, *Landesplanung in der Schweiz* (Zurich: Offprint from *Neue Zürcher Zeitung*, 1941); and Armin Meili, *Heute und Morgen: Wille oder Zufall in der Baulichen Gestaltung* (Zurich: Offprint from *Neue Zürcher Zeitung*, 1944).
5   Meili, *Heute und Morgen,* 3.
6   Ernst Egli, Eduard Brühlmann and Werner Aebli, *Die Neue Stadt: Eine Studie für das Furttal, Zurich* (Zurich: Verlag Bauen & Wohnen, 1961) 3.
7   Hans Carol and Max Werner, *Städte, wie wir sie wünschen: Ein Vorschlag zur Gestaltung Schweizerischer Grossstadt-Gebiete, dargestellt am Beispiel von Stadt und Kanton Zürich* (Zurich: Arbeitsgruppe für Landesplanung der Akademischen Studiengruppe Zürich, Regio-Verlag, 1949).
8   Walter Christaller, *Die Zentralen Orte in Süddeutschland* (Jena: Wissenschaftliche Buchgesellschaft, 1949).
9   Neue Regionalpolitik (NRP), *Schlussbericht: Expertenkommission, Überprüfung und Neukonzeption der Regionalpolitik* (Zurich, 2003).
10   Martin Rotach, *Raumplanerisches Leitbild der Schweiz, CK-73: Eine Grundlage für das Gespräch zwischen Bund und Kantonen* (Bern: Eidgenössisches Justiz und Polizeidepartement, 1973).
11   See Martin Schuler, Manfred Perlik and Natacha Pasche, *Nicht-städtisch, rural oder peripher – wo steht der ländliche Raum heute?* (Bern: Bundesamt für Raumentwicklung ARE, 2004) 9.
12   Michael Bassand and Martin Schuler, *La Suisse, une métropole mondiale?* (Lausanne: Institut de Recherche sur l'Environnement Construit [IREC], École Polytechnique Fédérale de Lausanne [EPFL], 1985).
13   Bundesamt für Raumplanung, *Grundzüge der Raumordnung Schweiz* (Bern: Bundesamt für Raumentwicklung, 1995) 38.
14   Schweizerischer Bundesrat 2001, *Agglomerationspolitik des Bundes: Bericht des Schweizerischen Bundesrates* (Bern: Bundesamt für Raumentwicklung, 2001) 11, 33.
15   Angelus Eisinger, "Introduction," *Urbanscape Switzerland*, eds. Angelus Eisinger and Michael Schneider (Zurich/Basel: Avenir Suisse/Birkhäuser, 2003).
16   Ibid., 14.
17   René Frey, *Stadt: Lebens- und Wirtschaftsraum: Eine ökonomische Analyse* (Zurich: vdf, 1996).
18   Christian Schmid and Daniel Weiss, "The New Metropolitan Mainstream," *The Contested Metropolis: Six Cities at the Beginning of the 21st Century*, eds. International Network for Urban Research and Action (INURA) and Raffaele Palosicia (Basel: Birkhäuser, 2004) 252-60.
19   Bundesamt für Statistik, *Pendelverkehr: Neue Definition der Agglomerationen* (Bern: Bundesamt für Statistik, 2003).
20   See Schmid, "Networks, Borders, Differences: Towards a Theory of the Urban," this book, Ch. 4.
21   For a more detailed analysis of these issues, see Roger Diener, Jacques Herzog, Marcel Meili, Pierre de Meuron and Christian Schmid, *Switzerland—An Urban Portrait, Volume 3: Materials for an Urbanistic Project* (Basel: Birkhäuser, 2006).
22   John Friedmann and Goetz Wolff, "World City Formation: An Agenda for Research and Action," *International Journal of Urban and Regional Research* 6, 1 (1982) 309-44; and Saskia Sassen, *The Global City: New York, London, Tokyo* (Princeton: Princeton University Press, 1991)
23   Pierre Veltz, *Mondialisation, villes et territoires: L'économie d'Archipel* (Paris: Presses Universitaires de France, 1996).
24   Hans Blotevogel, "Die Metropolregionen in der Raumordnung-

spolitik Deutschlands: Ein neues strategisches Raumbild?" *Geographica Helvetica* 56, 3 (2001) 157-86; and Michel Bassand, Lena Poschet and Sébastien Wust, "The Leman Metropolis: The Metropolisation of the Leman Crescent," *Urbanscape Switzerland*, eds. Angelus Eisinger and Michael Schneider (Birkhäuser and Zurich: Avenir Suisse, 2003).
25   Jean-Philippe Leresche, Dominique Joye and Michel Bassand, *Métropolisations: Interdépendances mondiales et implications lémaniques* (Geneva: Éditions Georg, 1995).
26   Heiko Behrendt and Christian Kruse, "Die Europäische Metropolregion Zürich: Die Entstehung des subpolitischen Raumes," *Geographica Helvetica* 56, 3 (2001) 202-13; and Alain Thierstein, Christian Kruse, Lars Glanzmann, Simone Gabi and Nathalie Grillon, *Raumentwicklung im Verborgenen: Die Entwicklung der Metropolregion Nordschweiz* (Zurich: Verlag Neue Zürcher Zeitung, 2006).
27   Isabelle Bertrand and Bernard Robert, eds., *En Europe, des villes en réseaux* (Paris: DATAR, 1991).
28   See, for example, Michael Storper, *The Regional World* (New York: Guilford, 1997); and Olivier Crevoisier and Roberto Camagni, eds., *Les milieux urbains: innovation, systèmes de production et encrage* (Neuchâtel: Institut de Recherches Économiques et Régionales, 2000).
29   Olivier Crevoisier, José Corpataux and Alain Thierstein, *Intégration monétaire et régions: des gagnants et des perdants* (Paris: L'Harmattan, 2001).
30   For a more detailed analysis, see Schuler, Perlik and Pasche, *Nicht-städtisch, rural oder peripher.*
31   Philippe Aydalot and Alan Garnier, "Périurbanisation et suburbanisation: des concepts à définir," *DISP* 80/81(1985) 53-55.
32   Richard Weiss, "Die Brünig-Napf-Reuss-Linie als Kulturgrenze zwischen Ost- und Westschweiz auf volkskundlichen Karten," *Geographica Helvetica* 2, 3 (1947) 153-75.
33   Werner Bätzing, *Die Alpen: Geschichte und Zukunft einer europäischen Kulturlandschaft,* Second Edition (Munich: Beck, 2003).
34   Bätzing, *Die Alpen.*
35   Ibid.; and Schuler, Perlik and Pasche, *Nicht-städtisch, rural oder peripher,* 24.

Figure Credits

26.1   Armin Meili, *Landesplanung in der Schweiz* (Zurich: Offprint from *Neue Zürcher Zeitung*, 1941) 10.
26.2   Ueli Roth, *Chronik der Schweizerischen Landesplanung,* Supplement to DISP 56 (1980) 18.
26.3   Schweizerischer Bundesrat, *Bericht über die Grundzüge der Raumordnung Schweiz* (Bern: 1996) 43.
26.4   Roger Diener, Jacques Herzog, Marcel Meili, Pierre de Meuron and Christian Schmid, *Switzerland—An Urban Portrait, Volume 1: Materials for an Urbanistic Project* (Basel: Birkhäuser, 2006) 219.
26.5   Same as above, 203.
26.6   Same as above, 207.
26.7   Same as above, 211.
26.8   Same as above, 215.
26.9   Same as above, 217.

27
IS THE MEDITERRANEAN URBAN?

Neil Brenner and Nikos Katsikis

1

Where do the boundaries of the urban begin and where do they end? This question has long preoccupied urban scholars, and it continues to stimulate considerable debate in the early twenty-first century as urbanization processes intensify and accelerate across the world.

Despite major disagreements regarding basic questions of method, conceptualization and ontology, most twentieth-century urban theorists conceived the urban (or: the city) as a distinctive type of settlement space that could be delineated in contradistinction to suburban or rural spaces. The nature of this space, and the appropriate demarcation of its boundaries, have generated considerable disagreement.[1] However, all major twentieth-century traditions of urban theory have presupposed an underlying vision of the urban as a densely concentrated territorial zone that is both analytically and geographically distinct from the putatively non-urban areas situated "outside" or "beyond" its boundaries.[2]

Such conceptualizations are embodied paradigmatically in Chicago urban sociologist Ernest Burgess' 1925 "dartboard" model of the city, in which diverse population groups are clustered densely together in concentric rings radiating progressively outwards from a dominant central point until the map abruptly ends (Figure 27.1). Beyond the single family dwellings of the suburbs begins a void, a realm disconnected from the urban territory and thus representationally empty.[3]

Jean Gottmann's equally famous 1961 vision of the BosWash Megalopolis complicated the clean, monocentric geometries of Burgess' model and considerably expanded its territorial scale (Figure 27.2, next page).[4] Yet Gottmann's otherwise pioneering approach continued to embrace a notion of the urban as a type of settlement, now upscaled from city to megalopolis, and a vision of settlement space as being divided, fundamentally, among urban and non-urban territorial zones. In Gottmann's provocative map, the territory of megalopolis is vast and its boundaries are jagged, but the zones beyond it are, as in Burgess' visualization of the city, depicted simply as empty spaces.

In contemporary debates on global city formation, the urban/non-urban opposition is reinscribed onto a still larger scale, but the basic geographical imaginary developed in earlier twentieth-century traditions of urban theory is perpetuated. Thus, in John Friedmann's foundational speculations on the emergent world city network, the urban is understood not as a bordered territory, but as a concentrated node for transnational investment and corporate control embedded within a worldwide network of capital flows (Figure 27.3, page 431).[5] Yet, here too, the non-urban zones surrounding the world cities are depicted simply as a void—as a vast empty space that is both functionally and geographically disconnected from the urban condition. Indeed, in the models developed by world city theorists, the

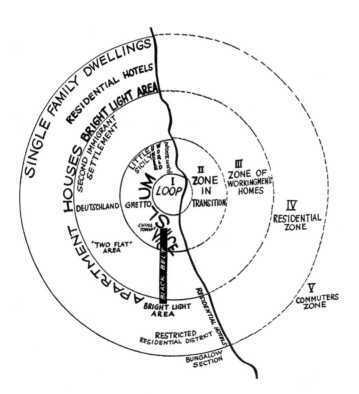

27.1 Burgess' dartboard (1925): the urban as bounded, concentrated settlement space

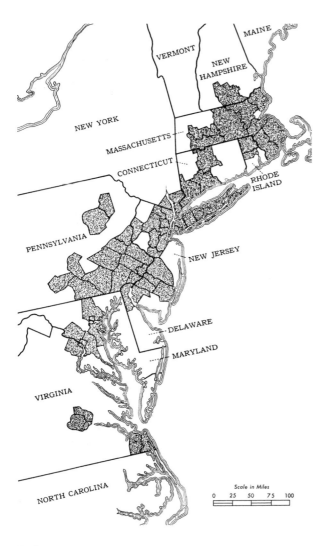

27.2 Gottmann's Megalopolis (1961): the explosion of urban boundaries

space of flows produced under global capitalism appears to have further separated urban zones from their erstwhile territorial hinterlands. Enhanced global connectivity and urban concentration are thus accompanied by new forms of macroterritorial fragmentation that render the non-urban even more distant—socially, economically, institutionally and geographically—from the transnational urban networks that crosscut its unevenly developed landscape.[6]

In the early twenty-first century, urbanization processes are intensifying and accelerating, creating new, multiscalar geographies of urban transformation around the world that are difficult, if not impossible, to decipher on the basis of inherited, settlement-based notions of urbanism and their associated assumption that most of the world's territory can be viewed as a "non-urban" void. Edward Soja and Miguel Kanai describe emergent formations of urbanization as follows:

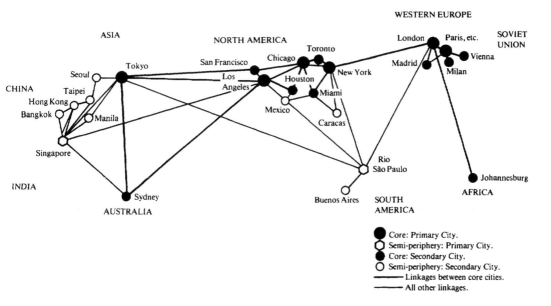

27.3 Friedmann's world city network (1986): urban nodal points in a worldwide system of flows

... urbanism as a way of life, once confined to the historical central city, has been spreading outwards, creating urban densities and new "outer" and "edge" cities in what were formerly suburban fringes and green field or rural sites. In some areas, urbanization has expanded on even larger regional scales, creating giant urban galaxies with population sizes and degrees of polycentricity far beyond anything imagined only a few decades ago ... [I]n some cases city regions are coalescing into even larger agglomerations in a process that can be called "extended regional urbanization."[7]

Can the urban/non-urban distinction be maintained under these conditions? Already in the early 1970s, French sociospatial theorist Henri Lefebvre suggested otherwise. In his classic text, *La révolution urbaine*, Lefebvre proposed a provocative hypothesis that exploded the urban/non-urban binarism on which investigations and visualizations of urban transformations had long been based: "Society has been completely urbanized," he declared, and on this basis he proceeded to develop a radically new understanding of urbanization as a worldwide process of sociospatial reorganization encompassing diverse places, territories and scales, including those situated far beyond the traditional centers of agglomeration, urbanism and metropolitan life.[8] Rather than conceiving the urban as a distinctive type of settlement space, to be contrasted to suburban, rural and other putatively non-urban zones, Lefebvre argued that capitalist urbanization had formed an uneven "mesh" of "varying density, thickness and activity" that was now being stretched across the entire surface of the world.[9]

This situation of complete urbanization, Lefebvre proposed, was creating new, territorially variegated urban landscapes, embodied in huge, polycentric concentrations of infrastructure, investment and population, that radically superseded the local and metropolitan formations of cityness inherited from earlier rounds of capitalist industrialization. Additionally, in Lefebvre's conceptualization, the contemporary urban revolution entailed the "prodigious extension of the urban to the entire planet" through a process of "implosion-explosion" in which inherited models of centrality, territorial organization and scalar hierarchy were being blurred and tendentially superseded.[10] Somewhat polemically, Lefebvre presented this situation using a starkly linear diagram in which urbanization was measured on a 0%-to-100% axis; his claim was that a "critical point" would soon be reached in which "the *urban problematic* becomes a global phenomenon" (Figure 27.4).[11] Under these circumstances, Lefebvre proposed, the urban condition would soon become synonymous with that of planetary capitalism as a whole. Urban transformations would impact all zones of the planet, from the oceans to the earth's atmosphere, and planetary processes, both social and ecological, would in turn shape all dimensions of the urban landscape, at once within and beyond inherited centers of dense agglomeration.

Lefebvre's hypothesis has often been misinterpreted as a vision of planet-wide densification akin to the dystopian science fiction fantasies of writers such as H.G. Wells, J.G. Ballard or Isaac Asimov, in which the entire world is envisioned as a single, seamless skein of built-up, metallic or concrete infrastructure. More recently, however, as illustrated in the other chapters of this book, Lefebvre's notion of an urban revolution has been productively reappropriated by critical urban theorists concerned to decipher some of the patterns and

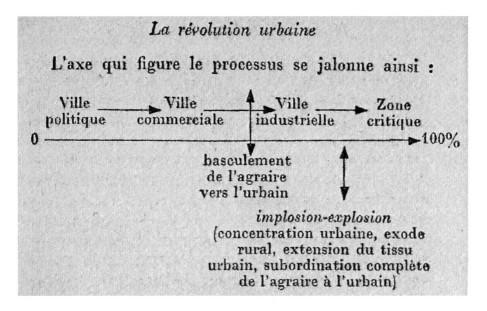

27.4 Lefebvre's (1970) "critical point" of generalized urbanization (1970)

pathways associated with early twenty-first century urbanization processes.[12] For example, building upon several ideas from Lefebvre, geographer Andy Merrifield has interpreted planetary urbanization as a simultaneous instrumentalization and transformation of the erstwhile countryside within an unevenly integrated, thickly urbanized mesh:

> The urbanization of the world is a kind of exteriorization of the inside as well as interiorization of the outside: the urban *unfolds* into the countryside just as the countryside *folds* back into the city. … Yet the fault-lines between these two worlds aren't defined by any simple urban-rural divide, nor by anything North-South; instead, centers and peripheries are *immanent* within the accumulation of capital itself. … Therein centrality creates its own periphery, crisis-ridden on both flanks. The two worlds—center and periphery—exist side-by-side everywhere, cordoned off from one another, everywhere. … Absorbed and obliterated by vaster units, rural places have become an integral part of post-industrial production and financial speculation, swallowed up by an "urban fabric" continually extending its borders, ceaselessly corroding the residue of agrarian life, gobbling up everything and everywhere in order to increase surplus value and accumulate capital.[13]

Within the unevenly woven skein of the planetary-urban condition, the infrastructures of urbanization are no longer localized within dense agglomerations or polycentric metropolitan regions, where they can be counterposed to the "outside" realm of rural existence. Instead, urbanization increasingly crosscuts and supersedes the erstwhile urban/rural divide, stretching across and around the earth's entire surface, as well as into both subterranean and atmospheric zones, which provide "liminal landscapes" for resource extraction, agro-industrial production, energy and information circulation, waste management, and diverse geopolitical strategies.[14] Thus understood, planetary urbanization intensifies interdependence, differentiation *and* polarization across and among places, territories and scales rather than creating the "borderless world" envisioned by globalization boosterists or, for that matter, the globally consolidated "endless city" predicted by some contemporary urban intellectuals.

Such developments pose huge challenges for urbanists and all other scholars concerned to decipher emergent urbanization processes and sociospatial conditions. Insofar as the conceptual grammar of urban theory is inherited from a period of capitalist development and territorial organization that has now been largely superseded, it is essential to experiment with alternative "cognitive maps" that can more effectively grasp the rapidly changing geographies of our planetary-urban existence.[15] In collaboration with Christian Schmid, our own efforts to confront this challenge hinge upon the conceptual distinction between concentrated and extended urbanization, which we consider an essential foundation for theorizing and investigating the geographies of urbanization processes during the last two centuries of world capitalist development.[16]

The concept of *concentrated urbanization* refers to the perpetual formation and crisis-induced restructuring of densely concentrated agglomerations (cities, city-regions, megalopolises, megacity regions and the like). The geographies of concentrated urbanization broadly approximate those of cities, agglomerations, urban regions and metropolitan areas, as traditionally understood and visualized by urban geographers with reference to successive historical formations of urban territorial organization (Figure 27.5).

By contrast, *extended urbanization* denotes the consolidation and continued reorganization of broader operational landscapes   including infrastructures for transportation and communication, food, water and energy production, resource extraction, waste disposal and environmental management—that at once facilitate and result from the dynamics of urban agglomeration. Although it has largely been ignored or "black-boxed" by urban theorists, this realm of drosscapes, *terrains vagues*, in-between cities (*Zwischenstädte*), horizontal urbanization, holey planes, quiet zones, fallow lands and liminal landscapes, has long been integral to the urban process under capitalism, and during the last few decades it has become increasingly strategic in both economic and ecological terms.[17] The visualization of extended urbanization, with its intensely variegated morphologies, its vast territorial scales, its dispersed networks and its apparently all-pervasive voids, poses complex analytical and cartographic challenges. How to understand, and on this basis to represent, the various ways in which agglomerations hinge upon, and continually transform, the operational landscapes associated with such diverse, multiscalar processes as transportation, communication, resource extraction, energy circulation and waste management? A recent visualization of

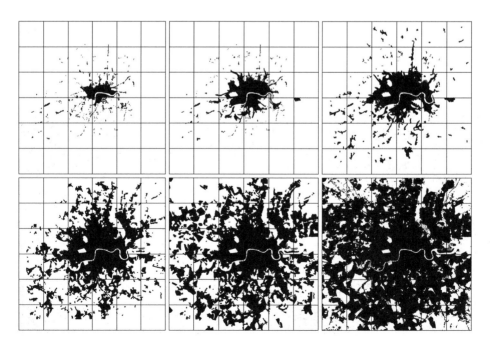

27.5 A window into concentrated urbanization: the expanding scale of agglomeration in London, 1800, 1840, 1880, 1920, 1960, 1980

worldwide transportation infrastructures offers one among many possible strategies for interpreting such connections and their systemic importance to the dynamics of planetary urbanization (Figure 27.6).[18]

We believe that this distinction can provide a powerful analytical and cartographic tool for exploring the question of urban boundaries posed above. It can also offer a basis on which to explore Lefebvre's famous hypothesis of an urban revolution. From the point of view of concentrated urbanization, the urban revolution involves the spatial expansion and increasing strategic centrality of major metropolitan regions, as postulated by global city theorists and other, more recent commentators on the role of cities in economic life.[19] However, consideration of the *problematique* of extended urbanization introduces a more complex, fluid, diffuse and spatially variegated conceptualization of the Lefebvrian notion of an urban revolution, one that we consider essential for investigating and visualizing early twenty-first-century forms of planetary urbanization. From this perspective, the urban revolution entails the consolidation of a new relationship between urban agglomerations and their operational landscapes. The latter no longer serve simply as hinterlands, resource extraction zones, supply depots and waste dumps for city growth—the realms of "un-building" (*Abbau*) and planetary ecological degradation, which Lewis Mumford observed with considerable alarm in the early 1960s.[20] Instead, the operational landscapes of extended urbanization are today increasingly designed, comprehensively managed, logistically coordinated and "creatively destroyed" to serve specific purposes within the broader political-economic and ecological infrastructures of a planetary-urban system. This ongoing instrumentalization, operationalization and logistical coordination of erstwhile hinterlands—their tendential transformation into zones of customized infrastructure designed and managed to fulfill specific production, reproduction and circulatory functions within a worldwide spatial division of labor—represents one of the distinctive tendencies within emergent twenty-first-century formations of planetary urbanization.

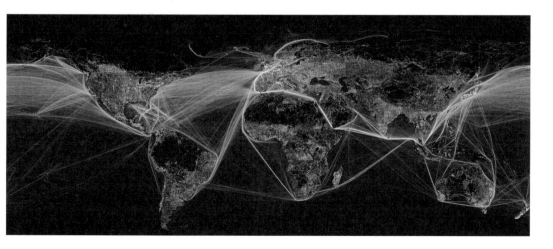

27.6 A window into extended urbanization: the operational landscape of global transportation (a compilation of road, rail and marine transportation networks)

The preceding considerations point towards an ambitious, far-reaching and long-term theoretical, historical and cartographic agenda that we are pursuing with other researchers in the Urban Theory Lab-GSD, as well as with Christian Schmid and his team of collaborators at the ETH-Zürich. In the remainder of this essay, taking the contemporary Mediterranean region as a "test site" for our approach to planetary urbanization, we explore one specific challenge within this massive *problematique*—namely, that of *visualizing* the contemporary urban condition. As Denis Cosgrove has noted, "urban space and cartographic space are intimately related."[21] For this reason, visualizations of the Mediterranean urban fabric may offer some potentially fruitful clues for deciphering the transformed forms, patterns and pathways of early twenty-first-century urbanization both within and beyond this important global region, and in relation to some of the conceptual and epistemological challenges demarcated above.

Since Braudel's classic investigations of the Mediterranean economy and ecology during early modern capitalism, the distinctively urban dimensions of this zone have been widely appreciated.[22] In Braudel's conceptualization, Mediterranean cities represented sites of intense commercial activity within a steadily expanding mercantile capitalist economy. With several major centers, including the city-states of Venice and Genoa, the Mediterranean urban system was visualized primarily with reference to levels of connectivity—especially for communication flows and trade networks—among nodes dispersed within a vast terrestrial and coastal zone (Figure 27.7).

Even though many of the cities examined by Braudel remain vibrant economic centers, the urban fabric of the Mediterranean has of course been transformed dramatically over the last four centuries of capitalist industrial growth, logistical intensification, socioecological reorganization and political-territorial restructuring. Yet, the Mediterranean remains a densely urbanized zone, permeated by thick transportation and communications networks; processes of urbanization and capital accumulation remain as tightly intertwined in the early twenty-first century as they were during the period of Braudel's investigation.

For present purposes, the urban geographies of the contemporary Mediterranean are explored on the basis of an extensive assemblage of recent georeferenced information that have been derived from some of the world's major laboratories for spatial data procurement and analysis.[23] Since the 1970s, the proliferation of new representational techniques associated with geographic information systems (GIS) and other recently established forms of spatial data has radically transformed the cartographic toolkit available to practitioners, policy makers and scholars for mapping the urban landscape. Although many new mapping techniques continue to rely, at least in part, on data collected by state census agencies, most have significantly loosened the hold of state-centric, methodologically territorialist methods in contemporary geospatial analysis. In a methodological maneuver that seriously challenges

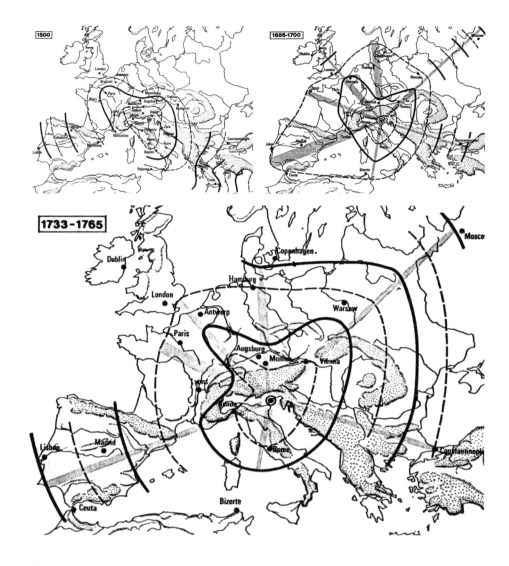

27.7 Braudel's visualization of news travelling to Venice (five-day intervals): 1500, 1686–1700, 1733–1765 AD

the hegemonic embrace of "state-istics" within the social sciences, the development of increasingly sophisticated, remotely sensed imaging techniques has permitted the reaggregation of administratively derived data with reference to coordinates, contours, morphologies and gradients that more directly approximate *de facto* terrestrial conditions across the earth's landscape than has ever previously been possible.[24] The availability of such fine-grained, readily customizable data on diverse spatial conditions thus presents urban theorists with a unique opportunity to interrogate inherited assumptions regarding urban boundaries, and on this basis, to develop new conceptualizations and visualizations.[25]

We confront this challenge using contemporary georeferenced data sets on three key indicators that have been commonly invoked to represent urban territories: (1) population distribution, (2) land cover, and (3) transportation infrastructures.[26] In exploring the visualizations associated with such spatial data, we devote particular attention to their *metageographical* assumptions and implications—that is, to the underlying conceptions of sociospatial order they presuppose or which flow from their technical operations—with specific reference to the analytical and cartographic status of the urban. According to historians Martin Lewis and Kären Wigen, "every global construction of knowledge deploys a metageography, whether acknowledged or not."[27] This proposition certainly applies to the construction of global knowledge on urbanization, including at the smaller scale of the Mediterranean explored here. Figure 27.8 offers a stylized contrast between the two opposing metageographical frameworks—labeled, respectively, the *bounded city* and the *endless urban fabric*—that emerge from the visualizations under discussion here, and that broadly correspond to our own distinction between concentrated and extended urbanization. It is the bounded city metageography that is presupposed in each of the three models from twentieth-century urban theory discussed above (Figures 27.1, 27.2 and 27.3), although Jean Gottmann's concept of megalopolis begins to overturn this vision of territorial organization by extending and interweaving urban borders deeply into the erstwhile hinterlands. The bounded city metageography is still widely taken for granted in

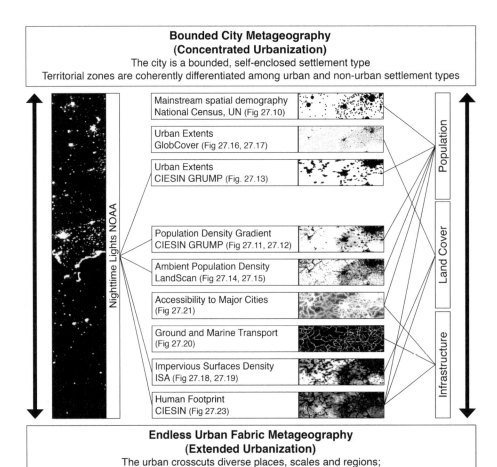

Bounded City Metageography
(Concentrated Urbanization)
The city is a bounded, self-enclosed settlement type
Territorial zones are coherently differentiated among urban and non-urban settlement types

Mainstream spatial demography
National Census, UN (Fig 27.10)

Urban Extents
GlobCover (Fig 27.16, 27.17)

Urban Extents
CIESIN GRUMP (Fig. 27.13)

Population Density Gradient
CIESIN GRUMP (Fig 27.11, 27.12)

Ambient Population Density
LandScan (Fig 27.14, 27.15)

Accessibility to Major Cities
(Fig 27.21)

Ground and Marine Transport
(Fig 27.20)

Impervious Surfaces Density
ISA (Fig 27.18, 27.19)

Human Footprint
CIESIN (Fig 27.23)

Nighttime Lights NOAA

Population

Land Cover

Infrastructure

Endless Urban Fabric Metageography
(Extended Urbanization)
The urban crosscuts diverse places, scales and regions;
it is a spatial fabric stretched unevenly across vast territorial zones

27.8 Geospatial data and the metageographies of urbanization

much of contemporary urban social science, and it is also evident in several of the geospatial models of population and land cover discussed below. However, since the introduction of geospatial data on nighttime lights in the late 1990s, several major approaches to geospatial visualization have begun to advance a more radical, quasi-Lefebvrian vision of an endless urban fabric stretched and woven across place, territory and scale.

In Figure 27.8, the various approaches under discussion in this essay are positioned along an analytical continuum in relation to the two opposed metageographies of urbanization. Those positioned closest to the top of the figure are most tightly connected to a bounded city metageography, whereas those closest to the bottom are most directly oriented towards an endless urban fabric metageography. The figure also differentiates the representations according to which indicator (population, land cover and infrastructure) they attempt to visualize. Finally, the figure shows how several of the approaches build upon the influential nighttime lights data set, which has been connected to a rather broad spectrum of metageographical assumptions. By excavating such metageographies, this analysis is intended to highlight the basic theoretical assumptions that invariably underpin efforts to visualize spatial data on urban questions. In the absence of critical reflexivity regarding such metageographical assumptions, even the most exhaustive, fine-grained forms of spatial data cannot be appropriated effectively to illuminate the urban condition and its restlessly changing geographies.

3

Few images have had a greater impact on contemporary metanarratives of global urbanization than the "nighttime lights of the world" series, one of the oldest and most basic sources of remote-sensed information about urbanization. Although this approach was under development as of the early 1970s, it was only in 1997 that the data set produced by the National Geophysical Data Center (NGDC) in Boulder, Colorado was first used to create an integrated global image showing light sources, including human settlements, thus producing a visually striking, intuitively plausible representation of world urbanization patterns.[28]

According to one prominent team of urban geographers, this paradigmatic image of world urbanization has effectively superseded earlier state-centric, territorialist and Eurocentric models of modernity in favor of a globalized, city-centric model that highlights "flows, linkages, connections and relations; an alternative metageography of networks rather than the mosaic of states."[29] Moreover, as the representation of the Mediterranean in Figure 27.9 (next page) strikingly indicates, such images have also entailed a radical shift in the visualization of urban spaces themselves.

Earlier mappings of an urban landscape configured among distinct, bordered, neatly separated places are here replaced by that of an urbanized *continuum* based upon varying

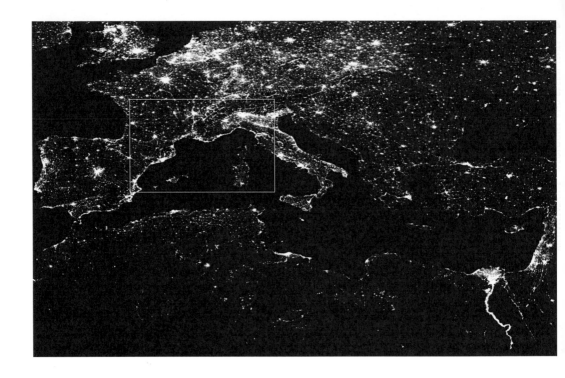

27.9 Nighttime lights around the Mediterranean region (2003 Nighttime Lights of the World data set). The Northwest Mediterranean coast—a focus of several maps below—is demarcated by the white rectangle.

density gradients of settlement and infrastructure ranging from massive, bright metropolitan agglomerations at one extreme to zones of apparent emptiness, darkness and wilderness at the other. Beyond this metageographical influence, the nighttime lights data sets have been among the most ubiquitous sources of spatial information regarding contemporary urban systems; they play an important role in many of the visualizations of spatial data presented below.

The haphazardly intermixed patterns of light depicted in this overview visualization of the Mediterranean lend some initial plausibility to the conceptual distinction between concentrated and extended urbanization introduced above. Traditional zones of urban concentration in the Mediterranean region are readily discernible in the map—for example, Barcelona, Rome, Naples, Athens, Istanbul, Izmir, Beirut, Tel Aviv, Cairo, Tripoli, Tunis, Algiers and Casablanca. But, so too are some much larger scale territories of urbanization whose contours extend well beyond established urban cores, often in uninterrupted bands of high-intensity light emissions stretched along coastal edges. Such large-scale territorial configurations include the lengthy urbanized corridor along the Iberian coastline, the French Riviera conurbation, the Rome-Naples corridor, a northern Adriatic urbanized zone articulated unevenly between Venice and Trieste and an eastern Mediterranean urban corridor stretching almost continuously from Beirut to Gaza. Significant bands of this coastal zone were highlighted for their megalopolitan potentials by Jean Gottmann in the

1970s, and in more recent years scholars have described it variously as the Mediterranean Arc (extending from Barcelona to Marseilles and Genoa), the Mediterranean Sunbelt or as the Latin Arc (including the latter corridor but encompassing a still larger zone stretching from Andalusia to Rome and Naples); others have suggested it also juts inland along Alpine extensions towards Lyon and Milan, among other large cities.[30] Along the north African rim of the Mediterranean, the map reveals impressive complexes of activity bursting westwards along the coastlines of both Tripoli and Algiers, as well as, most strikingly, the thin but intense concentration of light emissions threaded southwards from the Nile river delta along a tightly circumscribed, fluvial band down to the Aswan dam.[31]

Most crucially for our purposes, the nighttime lights map depicts an intricate, transnational complex of settlement patterns and infrastructural grids that crosscut and interpenetrate the major metropolitan zones across the entire Mediterranean region. In stark contrast to the concentric circles of Chicago School urban sociology, the jagged territorial borders of Gottmann's megalopolis or the networked nodal points of world city theory, these urban geographies more closely resemble an uneven latticework that has been woven around and among the major conurbations, metropolitan regions, cities and towns, across an unevenly organized but densely settled transnational territory. This aspect of the nighttime lights image thus provides an initial, impressionistic visualization of the vast, variegated and unevenly developed terrain of extended urbanization in the Mediterranean region as well as across much of northern, central and eastern Europe. Can other visualizations be produced that add more precise analytical content to the metageography of endless urbanization suggested by the nighttime lights image?

4

One obvious indicator for such an endeavor is population, the spatial distribution of which has long been a focal point for visualizations of urban conditions well before the development of remote-sensed, georeferenced data sources. Contemporary georeferenced spatial data permit the visualization of population distribution in several distinct ways corresponding in various gradations to the bounded city or endless urban metageographies.

In the standard demographic approach, whose roots lie in the pioneering research efforts of Kingsley Davis in the post-period after World War II, population distribution is represented with reference to extant municipal units; a numerical threshold is used to delineate urban from non-urban settlement units.[32] Although debates have raged for over five decades regarding the appropriate threshold on which to delineate urban from non-urban populations (100,000? 20,000? 10,000?), this approach still figures crucially in the data classification systems used by the United Nations Population Division (UNPD). For instance, it underpins the widely repeated but hugely problematic proclamation that a global "urban age" has dawned due to the purported fact that over 50 percent of the world's population now lives within urban areas.[33]

Using a population threshold of 10,000, Figure 27.10 illustrates the implications of this approach for the visualization of Mediterranean urbanization. Here, cities are considered to be dimensionless points, positioned according to the terrestrial coordinates of their abstractly defined centers, and weighted according to their population size. Aside from the persistent problem of justifying an appropriate numerical threshold on which to base such visualizations, the resulting representational landscape suggests a purely locational conception of the urban: it is simply a point on the earth's surface, lacking areal articulation or morphological specificity. The operational landscapes of extended urbanization thereby disappear completely from view; cities appear as relatively self-sufficient islands within a vast territorial void. This model thus paradigmatically embodies the bounded city metageography.

Although this approach is still a popular way of representing urban population levels, whether at a world scale or nationally, its core data are not connected to *de facto* settlement patterns, but are derived from extant administrative units. The limits of such procedures are recognized but not resolved through the establishment of larger units for statistical aggregation—agglomerations, standard metropolitan areas, metropolitan regions, and the like—by the United Nations and many national census bureaus. For, as Louis Wirth, Jean Gottmann, Lewis Mumford and other major twentieth-century urbanists recognized, the complex demographic patterns associated with modern urbanization processes persistently leapfrog beyond the boundaries of such administrative units; data which are derived from them are therefore an extremely imprecise basis on which to interpret the geographies of urban processes. In the early twenty-first century, moreover, population settlement patterns are being still further reshuffled in profound ways that undermine even the most reflexive

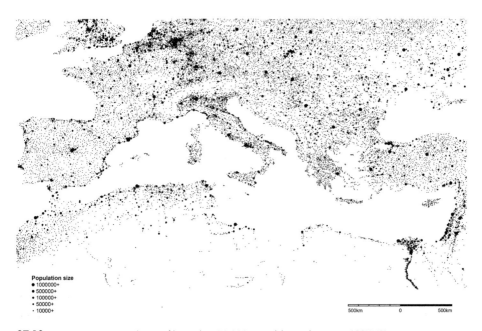

Population size
● 1000000+
● 500000+
● 100000+
• 50000+
· 10000+

500km   0   500km

27.10 Cities containing populations of larger than 10,000 around the Mediterranean (GRUMP)

efforts to develop an appropriate statistical/spatial unit for calculating urban population levels. As Edward Soja notes:

> Once-steep density gradients from the center have begun to level off as peripheral agglomerations multiply and the dominance of the singular central city weakens. What were formerly relatively clear boundaries between city and suburb, the urban and the non-urban, urbanism and suburbanism as ways of life are becoming increasingly blurred as new networks of interaction emerge and the city and the suburb flow into one another in what can best be described as a regional urbanization process.[34]

A second approach to spatial demography, the Global Rural-Urban Mapping Project (GRUMP) developed by a research team at Columbia University's Earth Institute, has attempted to grapple with such issues by plotting population density gradients across broad territorial landscapes around the world. Using a multiparameter algorithm, the GRUMP approach synthesizes three basic types of data in order to estimate and visually distribute population densities: (1) population levels within official administrative zones, (2) the locations of settlement boundaries, and (3) the presence of nighttime lights. Figures 27.11, 27.12 (next page) and 27.13 (page 445) build upon various types of GRUMP spatial data to illustrate some of its implications for the visualization of urban population geographies in the Mediterranean.

At first glance, Figures 27.11 and 27.12 appear to transcend the bounded city metageography of urbanization, offering more nuanced visualizations of population geographies than those associated with standard demographic approaches. These figures illustrate not only the concentrations of high population density in all of the major Mediterranean cities and urban regions mentioned above, but also the outward spread of population clusters across and among the extended metropolitan corridors that are on display in the nighttime lights map in Figure 27.9. These maps of population density gradients appear to reinforce the image of extended urbanization produced through the nighttime lights images, and thus to advance the endless urban fabric metageographical model. Intense light emissions appear to equate seamlessly with high levels of population density, which now occur through the broad networks of interaction mentioned by Soja rather than being confined to traditional city cores.

However, as its acronym suggests, an uninterrogated, methodologically territorialist distinction between urban and non-urban zones underpins the statistical procedures used in the GRUMP approach to visualizing density gradients. Indeed, despite its capacity to map population density gradients across the entire territorial landscape, a key element of the GRUMP approach is to delineate a clear, continuous territorial border around the most densely populated zones. To this end, GRUMP researchers construct what they term an "urban mask" by combining data on the locations of settlements whose populations exceed 5,000 with information on the distribution of continuous-intensity nighttime lights.[35] On this basis, urban areas are represented as clearly bounded territories; other areas are classified as rural, and thus as empty, blank spaces on the map. Whereas Figures 27.11 and 27.12 use GRUMP data to plot the population density gradient across the entire Mediterranean territory, Figure 27.13 illustrates the bounded city metageography that underpins the GRUMP's urban mask technique. As illustrated starkly by the vast, empty spaces scattered across the map, the GRUMP urban mask algorithm generates a

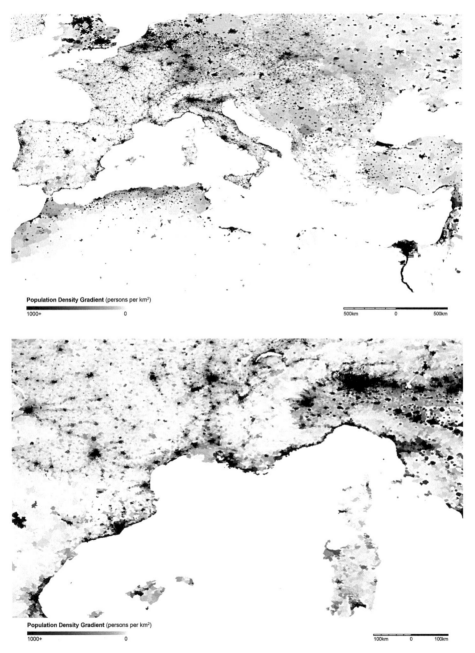

Population Density Gradient (persons per km²)
1000+   0   500km   0   500km

Population Density Gradient (persons per km²)
1000+   0   100km   0   100km

27.11 (top) Population density gradients around the Mediterranean (GRUMP)
27.12 (bottom) Population density gradients on the northwest Mediterranean coast (GRUMP)

visualization of territorial differentiation that, despite its expanded mapping of the urban, is still as untenably binary as the mainstream approach to spatial demography discussed with reference to Figure 27.10.

One further, still more far-reaching approach to spatial demography has been associated with the LandScan data set, which was originally introduced in 1988 at the Oak Ridge National Laboratories (ONL). While its initial purpose was to serve emergency workers responding to disasters, it has subsequently been used to inform investigations of large-scale population distributions. In contrast to the static residential or nighttime population data used by national census bureaus, the LandScan approach uses a complex probability coefficient to capture the fluid movement of populations over a 24-hour period. [36] This "ambient" population is intended more closely to approximate the actual daily distribution of people in space (Figures 27.14 and 27.15, next page).

Although LandScan takes urban agglomerations into account, the database does not impose boundaries upon urban areas, nor does it formally distinguish urban and rural populations. Consequently, even though it does reveal the broad contours of diverse settlement areas, the LandScan approach offers a particularly striking visualization of the vast commuter sheds that undergird and crisscross large territorial zones. Thus, in the enlarged image in Figure 27.15 depicting ambient population around the northwest Mediterranean, major transportation corridors appear highly urbanized. This reveals the intensive daily use of social space, not only road infrastructures, far beyond the core zones of metropolitan areas. In effect, the LandScan database provides a georeferenced foundation for the classic

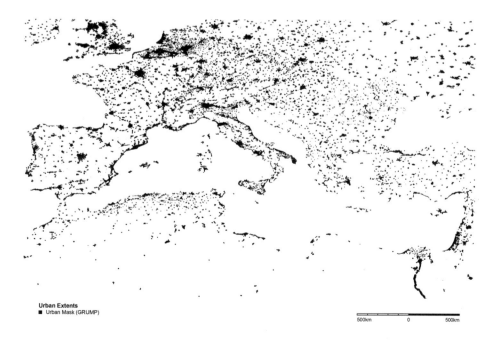

Urban Extents
■ Urban Mask (GRUMP)

500km   0   500km

27.13 Urban extents around the Mediterranean (GRUMP)

concepts of megalopolis, daily urban systems and commuter sheds developed in the 1960s and 1970s by innovative urbanists such as Jean Gottmann, Constantinos Doxiadis and Brian Berry.[37] Much like the LandScan scientists, but lacking such precise geospatial data, each of these theorists was centrally concerned to underscore the fluid movement of populations within and across a large-scale regional or national territory. Mapping this fluidity, the imprint of human mobility within and across territory, is a key contribution of the LandScan approach.

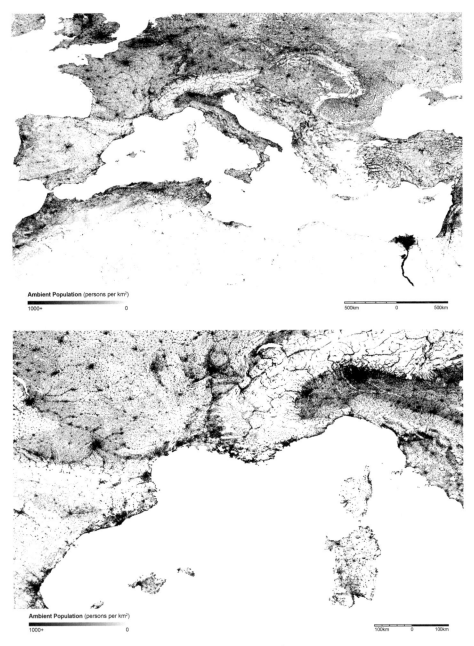

Ambient Population (persons per km²)

1000+   0

500km   0   500km

Ambient Population (persons per km²)

1000+   0

100km   0   100km

27.14 (top) Ambient population density around the Mediterranean (Landscan)
27.15 (bottom) Ambient population density around the northwest Mediterranean coast (Landscan)

Among major geospatial visualizations of population distribution, then, it is the LandScan approach that pushes most forcefully towards an endless urban fabric metageography. Due to its expansive mapping of urban morphologies beyond traditional city cores and its fluid depiction of urban boundaries, the LandScan approach provides a powerful visualization of how population flows produce a landscape of extended urbanization in the Mediterranean.

5

All population-based attempts to bound urban areas in cartographic space, and thus to examine processes of concentrated urbanization, require the specification of some threshold—usually either population size or population density—in terms of which to separate the urban from the non-urban. Mainstream approaches to spatial demography and the GRUMP effort to define the urban mask specify this threshold in different ways, but both undertake a basic statistical operation in order to visualize the presumed areal bounding of urban units from a surrounding non-urban realm. A second approach to the problem of specifying such boundaries focuses not on population distribution or density gradients, but on land cover indicators, with particular reference to the spatial patterns of artificially constructed or built-up areas. Here, too, the delineation of a statistical threshold for the unit of data collection has massive implications for visualization outcomes.

A powerful contemporary method for investigating land cover types is through remote sensing. This technique entails the regular use of satellite sensors to scan the earth's surface, producing gridded data sets in which dominant land cover types are classified and then visualized with reference to quite fine-grained spatial units, ranging in size from one square kilometer to, most recently, 300 square meters. Since the major task of these satellites is environmental monitoring, most of their land cover classifications pertain to types of vegetation or hydrological conditions rather than to human settlement types or infrastructural arrangements. Despite this, however, any number of metageographical assumptions regarding the nature of urban space emerge from georeferenced studies and visualizations of urban land cover. As with the major approaches to geospatial data on population discussed above, contemporary approaches to urban land cover oscillate between metageographies that attempt to circumscribe urban zones and those that emphasize their explosion and differentiation across a vast territorial landscape.

Two of the major approaches to global land cover have been developed by the European Space Agency (the GlobCover data set) and by NASA (the MODIS data set).[38] In the case of GlobCover, the MERIS sensor has been used to scan and classify every gridded cell on the earth's surface among 22 classes, only one of which is used to define urban areas. As in almost all land cover data sets, GlobCover defines the urban condition as a physical feature of the earth's surface, formally analogous to the different types of vegetation or hydrological conditions to which the other 21 land cover categories apply (examples of the latter include: cultivated and managed terrestrial areas, bare areas and artificial water bodies). Within this classificatory scheme, urban areas are those in which built, artificial or non-vegetative surfaces predominate over other land use arrangements. Under the rubric of the technical term "impervious surfaces," such delineations of the urban generally include not only buildings but also roads, pavements, driveways, sidewalks, parking lots and any other surfaces in which artificial forms of land coverage predominate.[39] Crucially, within this database, the threshold for the predominance of any feature within the landscape unit being studied is 50 percent of total land cover. The implications of this approach for visualizing the urban Mediterranean are presented in Figures 27.16 and 27.17, which are derived from the 2006 GlobCover data set.

As Figures 27.16 and 27.17 indicate, the GlobCover data set produces a bounded city metageography in which urban zones are relatively circumscribed and separated representationally from a diversity of other landscape features, which occupy the bulk of the territory. This metageographical orientation stems, first, from the GlobCover's use of a 50 percent threshold as the basis for classifying each landscape unit. Even when a very fine grain of data collection is used, this typological approach to visualization automatically erases all features of land cover that fall beneath the 50 percent threshold within the unit in question. This means, for example, that densely forested or vegetated zones containing moderately dense built environments or populations cannot register on the map as having any urban features. Second, this approach to land cover analysis replaces the urban/rural dualism used in mainstream spatial demography with an equally binary urban/nature divide. Because the GlobCover approach is oriented towards classifying the diversity of ecological landscapes, it envisions the natural environment as extending across the entire earth, thus enabling its features to be investigated systematically and then visually differentiated. This in turn consigns the urban to tightly delineated "bins," in which the 50 percent threshold for artificial surfaces has been crossed. The possibility that putatively "natural" spaces, or those with dense concentrations of particular ecological features (grasslands, water, ice and so forth), may be permeated, crosscut and/or transformed through urbanization processes is thereby excluded from consideration by classificatory fiat.

The Global Impervious Surface (ISA) data set, developed in the early 2000s by the Earth Observation Group in Boulder, Colorado, offers an alternative approach to the *problematique* of urban land cover that begins to map infrastructural geographies beyond city cores and metropolitan regions, and thus to explore the land cover features of extended urbanization. Unlike GlobCover and MODIS, the ISA does not draw upon remotely sensed land cover data; instead, it combines nighttime lights data from NOAA and ambient population information from LandScan (see Figures 27.9 and 27.14). Most crucially, because the ISA is focused on only one general landscape feature, artificially covered or impervious surfaces, it need not deploy a classificatory threshold, 50 percent or otherwise. Instead the ISA creates a 0 percent to 100 percent density gradient for artificial surfaces, leading to a quite differentiated visualization of built land cover densities across vast territorial zones.[40] The visual consequences of this approach are readily evident in Figures 27.18 and 27.19

(page 450), which reveal a thick mosaic of built-up areas and connective infrastructure corridors stretched and threaded unevenly across the Mediterranean zone. For purposes of comparison, the GlobCover urban extents are also depicted in red on these maps, thus offering a striking contrast between an approach to urban land cover oriented towards a bounded city metageography and one that produces an endless urban fabric metageography.

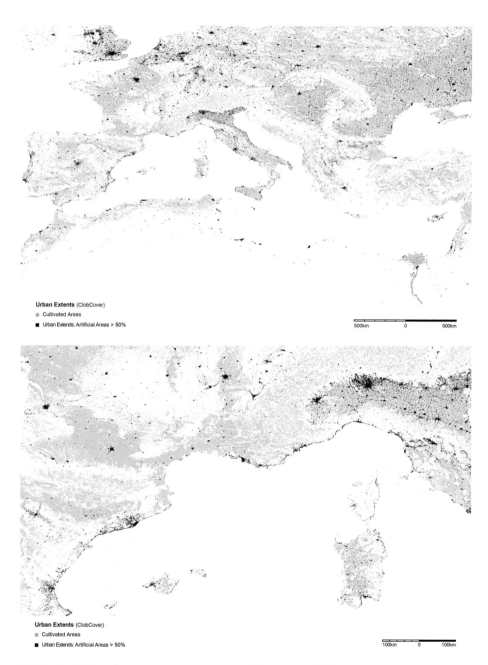

Urban Extents (ClobCover)
▓ Cultivated Areas
■ Urban Extends: Artificial Areas > 50%

500km   0   500km

Urban Extents (ClobCover)
▓ Cultivated Areas
■ Urban Extends: Artificial Areas > 50%

100km   0   100km

27.16 (top) Urban land cover around the Mediterranean (Globcover). The black outline corresponds to urban areas defined as more than 50 percent artificial areas. The background of light gray areas depicts all cultivated areas.
27.17 (bottom) Urban land cover around the northwest Mediterranean coast (Globcover). The black outline corresponds to urban areas defined as more than 50 percent artificial areas. The background of light gray areas depicts all cultivated areas.

While the theoretical significance of impervious surface distribution requires further investigation and clarification, the ISA visualizations underscore the massive extent and variegated distribution of built structures and surfaces across the Mediterranean. According to one team of geospatial scientists, the construction of impervious surfaces is "a universal phenomenon—akin to clothing—and represents one of the primary anthropogenic modifications of the environment."[41] However, rather than viewing the contemporary production and transformation of built surfaces as a universal feature of anthropogenic

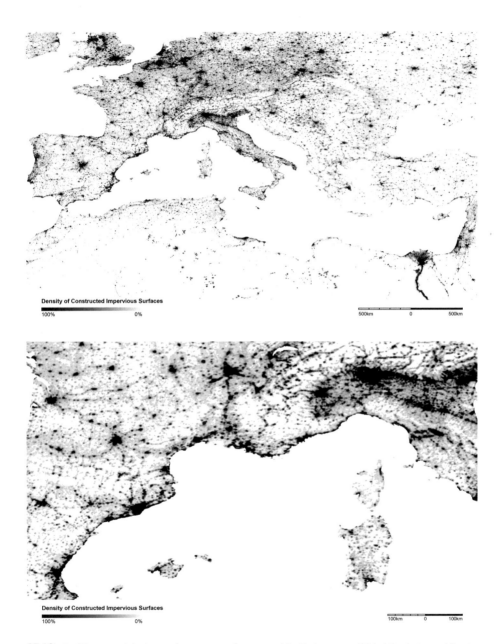

27.18 (top) Density and distribution of impervious surfaces around the Mediterranean (Global Distribution and Density of Constructed Impervious Surfaces data set)

27.19 (bottom) Density and distribution of impervious surfaces around the northwest Mediterranean coast. (Global Distribution and Density of Constructed Impervious Surfaces data set)

activity, we emphasize the historically and geographically specific frameworks of *capitalist* urbanization within which such processes have been occurring, both in the Mediterranean and beyond, since the period of mercantile expansion investigated in Braudel's classic studies. But the metaphor of clothing—or, better, a skein—covering major zones of the earth seems appropriate. In John Friedmann's recent formulation, "as the skein of the urban steadily advances across the earth, its vertical dimensions are layered to produce a new global topography of the urban."[42] The ISA visualization usefully illuminates one strategically important layer of this emergent global-urban topography. While such visualizations do not, in themselves, reveal much regarding the institutions, strategies and struggles through which this skein is produced and transformed, they do offer a more plausible representation of their geographies, than the bounded city model associated with the GlobCover and MODIS approaches.

6

At a very large scale, visualizations of impervious surface gradients reveal the material imprints of infrastructural networks, including those of transportation systems, that extend well beyond city cores and metropolitan centers. These transportation infrastructures— road, rail, marine and air—are obviously essential to both historical and contemporary forms of capitalist urbanization, facilitating the circulation of capital, labor and commodities across large-scale territories and, as David Harvey has famously argued, continuously accelerating both the turnover time of capital accumulation and the "annihilation of space by time."[43] The role of such infrastructures of circulation in the urbanization process has long been recognized. For instance, as discussed above, Braudel's analysis of the urban Mediterranean devoted some attention to the vectors of interconnectivity, for both information and commerce, linking the major ports and economic centers (Figure 27.7). Likewise, despite his territorialist conception of the urban, Jean Gottmann's investigation of Megalopolis included a detailed analysis of internal and external transportation linkages, and presented national-scale visualizations of rail, highway and airplane networks as part of his investigation of commuter flows.[44] In most such approaches, however, the geographies of transportation connectivity are understood as being extrinsic to an urban process that is animated internally, through the powerful socioeconomic and cultural forces unleashed by agglomeration.

Following from the analytical and cartographic explosion of the urban we have been tracking in this discussion, it is no longer plausible to reduce the *problematique* of transport geographies to an adjunct spatial formation, subordinate to the nodal points and bounded urban territories upon which twentieth-century urban theory was focused. Consideration of transportation infrastructures offers a powerful basis on which to visualize the thickening landscapes of extended urbanization. Of course, such a perspective requires continued attention to concentrated urbanization, and to the diverse processes through which centers of socioeconomic activity and population are constructed, reproduced and interconnected. Just as importantly, such an investigation requires an interpretation of transportation networks and their sociomaterial infrastructures as essential elements within an extended fabric of urbanization, regardless of their locational geometries or morphological configurations.[45]

Drawing upon a data set produced by the National Imagery and Mapping Agency (NIMA) of the US Geological Survey (USGS), Figure 27.20 presents such a visualization with reference to the major terrestrial and marine transportation networks around the Mediterranean. This visualization reveals a generalized geography of interconnectivity that stretches across the entire region, from the hyperdense webs along the coastlines and around the major agglomerations, to the latticework of corridors stretched across both marine and terrestrial zones and the sparsely equipped North African desert and mountain hinterlands. It illustrates not only connections among major centers, but also the density and scope of the transportation networks themselves, which are woven thickly across regions, territories and scales, and thus represent important spatial infrastructures for extended urbanization.

A complementary visualization of the operational geographies associated with these transportation infrastructures is presented in Figure 27.21, which is based upon the Global Accessibility Map, a data set that was commissioned in conjunction with the World Bank's World Development Report of 2009. Whereas Figure 27.20 depicts the positionality, shape and density of the various routes, Figure 27.21 uses a cost-distance algorithm to compute the projected travel time to major settlement areas. The resultant "friction-surface" is represented spatially using a color coding system in which brightness denotes high accessibility and darkness indicates low accessibility. The friction surface used to color-code the map is calculated with reference to estimated travel times associated with different types of transport infrastructures, while also taking into account intervening factors such as land cover, slope and political borders.[46] In effect, this approach generalizes Braudel's earlier diagrams of Venetian accessibility (Figure 27.7) to every major destination within the entire Mediterranean territory. Each portion of the zone is assigned a projected travel time to the nearest major city, but as in Braudel's maps, the changing gradient (here, a grayscale coding scheme) represents not a spatial attribute but a time-distance vector. In this way, urbanization is revealed as a relation of access to a broader terrain through networks that link cities, yet expand beyond them via long-distance transport corridors that cumulatively become important landscape attributes.

In different ways, Figures 27.20 and 27.21 provide evidence for the continued centrality of agglomerations as nodal points within medium, and long-distance transport networks. In Figure 27.20, this is due to the obvious presence of cities as endpoints and way-stations within the networks. In the case of Figure 27.21, the calculations that generate the grayscale gradient are tied to the locations of cities containing more than 50,000 people as of the year 2000. Despite this, however, both maps also serve to destabilize the bounded city metageography by illuminating the impressive density and territorial coverage of crisscrossing transportation networks within and around the Mediterranean. For this reason, both maps have been aligned with the endless urban fabric metageography in Figure 27.8. Even if they are not as expansive in their estimation of urban boundaries as the impervious surfaces density (ISA) data set, they do extend them well beyond those associated with GRUMP population density gradients and the LandScan account of ambient population density. More generally, insofar as these maps transpose the territorialist concern with urban boundaries into a more fluid *problematique* of networked infrastructures, interdependencies

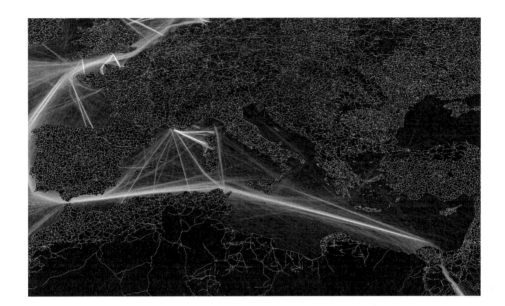

27.20 (top) Major ground and marine transportation routes around the Mediterranean (Compilation of road, rail and marine transportation networks based on VMAP0)

27.21 (bottom) Accessibility map of the Mediterranean region. The gradient is derived from estimations of travel times to major cities with populations over 50,000 in the year 2000.

and connectivities, they offer particularly vivid illustrations of John Friedmann's metaphor of the "skein of the urban."[47]

7

How far can this extended model of Mediterranean urban geographies be stretched? Are there not additional traces, layers and vectors of the urban radiating beyond population density gradients or ambient population densities, the "hardscapes" associated with impervious surfaces and the variegated geographies of transportation accessibility? A particularly expansive visualization of urbanization processes, which almost completely explodes the urban/non-urban distinction, is engendered through the Human Footprint data sets produced by the Wildlife Conservation Society and Columbia's Earth Institute. These approaches are grounded upon a synthetic combination of population, land cover, land use, transportation and energy data, and attempt to grasp the cumulative effects of human transformations on the landscape through a grayscale color-coding system (with darkness signifying high impact, lightness signifying low impact). In Figures 27.22 and 27.23, these putative human impacts on the Mediterranean landscape—arguably a proxy measure for the diverse, historically specific social processes associated with modern capitalist urbanization—are depicted as being nearly co-extensive with the entire region.[48] The non-urban "outside" presupposed in earlier approaches has now been almost totally annihilated; urbanization is represented as an encompassing continuum expressed through a vast assemblage of landscape conditions across the entire territory. This and the previously discussed visualizations of the Mediterranean thus clearly underscore the futility of attempts to demarcate fixed urban boundaries within a territorial landscape that, as Lefebvre recognized over four decades ago, is simultaneously exploding and imploding around, across, among and through inherited city centers.[49]

However, despite their usefulness in illustrating the large-scale areal continuity of the urban fabric and the densely networked interconnections among places and regions across the Mediterranean, one of the most serious limitations of the visualizations discussed here is their static character—their depiction of synchronic conditions and cross-sectional distributions rather than restructuring processes and sociospatial transformations. In the case of geospatial data on population, the visualizations discussed above are purely descriptive; they do not effectively illuminate the unevenly articulated, crisis-prone urbanization processes, with associated moments of explosion and implosion, that underlie and continually transform the variegated patterns of population distribution, growth and decline around the Mediterranean.[50] Similarly, geospatial data on land cover serve mainly to describe the material and morphological configuration of built space around the contemporary Mediterranean, but they explain almost nothing regarding the cyclical, often speculative processes of creative destruction that constantly reshape the latter. Even visualizations that explore the density of impervious surfaces do not effectively illuminate the ways in which such differentiated geographies are mediated through common, large-scale forces of restructuring, such as state planning strategies, tourist infrastructural investment or real estate speculation. Finally, the abstract visualizations of transportation networks presented above are no more than a generic starting point for investigating the interplay between connectivity infrastructures and strategies of urban and regional development at various scales.[51] Indeed, this relationship is left completely indeterminate in Figures 27.20

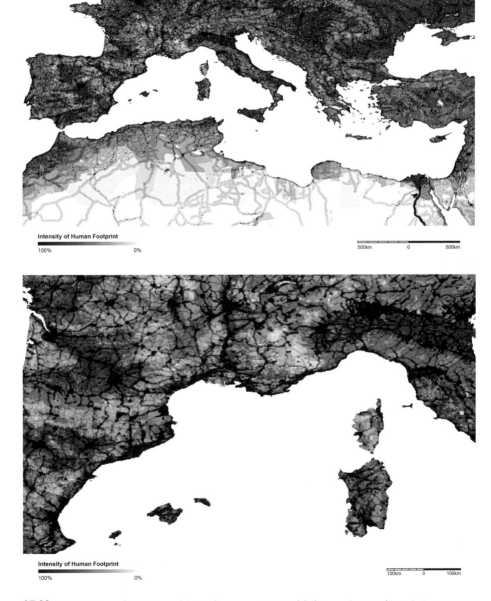

27.22 (top) The human footprint around the Mediterranean (CIESIN Global Human Footprint data set). Human impact is rated on a scale of 0 to 100.

27.23 (bottom) The human footprint around the northwest Mediterranean coast (CIESIN Global Human Footprint data set). Human impact is rated on a scale of 0 to 100.

and 27.21, which do little more than represent real or hypothesized connections among already established population centers.

Such visualizations may also contain profoundly ideological assumptions, which are naturalized through their technoscientific representation as self-evident spatial conditions. For instance, the vision of the bounded city presented in mainstream spatial demography as well as in the GRUMP data on population density is symptomatic of a broader, increasingly hegemonic discourse on the "urban age," which is often used to justify the continued concentration of infrastructure, investment and population within the most economically prosperous cities and metropolitan regions. Such visualizations are thus deeply implicated in the proliferation of urban locational policies that effectively naturalize the shrinkage of redistributive spatial policies and the ongoing state-mediated, publicly funded proliferation of territorial inequalities at all spatial scales, across Europe and beyond.[52] Similarly, the recent roll-out of large-scale, trans-European motorway and sea infrastructures is intended to promote the forms of large-scale spatial integration envisioned in Figure 27.21. However, this visualization is blind to ways in which such initiatives fragment and marginalize some zones precisely as they more tightly interconnect others, thus contributing to a wide-ranging "splintering" of territory.[53] Many other examples of the naturalization of spatial ideology could be excavated from these and other forms of geospatial visualization, not least in relation to the representation of urbanization processes. As powerful and provocative as such representational techniques may appear, therefore, urban scholars must treat them with extreme caution, recognizing their politically inflected, ideologically strategic character, especially in their most technically sophisticated forms.

A fundamental challenge for any attempt to visualize twenty-first-century urbanization is to specify, in substantive theoretical terms, the essential properties and dynamics of this process, at any spatial scale, such that its geographical imprint and effects can be investigated and subjected to representational ordering. Visualization strategies, including those based on geospatial data, can serve as powerful aids in the effort to build such a theorization, but they cannot substitute for the basic analytical work required to invent, refine and operationalize concepts. Indeed, the sources of geospatial data analyzed here deploy relatively simple, mostly descriptive understandings of the urban that may prove useful for information processing and visualization, but do little to clarify the metageographical questions explored above or, for that matter, to illuminate the transformative dynamics that shape and reshape urban landscapes. From our point of view, a new theory of urbanization is today required for deciphering twenty-first-century sociospatial transformations, but its key conceptual elements have yet to be consolidated. This exercise in the visualization of urban boundaries and spaces within the Mediterranean is therefore intended to facilitate reflection and debate regarding the "transformed form" of contemporary urbanization, and thereby, to stimulate further reflection on the "urban question" under twenty-first-century conditions. This is a task to which we and our colleagues in the Urban Theory Lab-GSD are now dedicating considerable energies.

Meanwhile, urban ideologies and associated visualizations persist.[54] The vision of a bounded city, the notion of a worldwide "urban age," the assumption of an urban/non-urban divide and the fantasy of total connectivity continue to pervade scholarly writing, administrative discourse, planning practice and public culture. The production of such ideologies is an important dimension of the urbanization process itself, especially during a conjuncture in which inherited spatial formations are being exploded and reconstituted anew. The visualization of urban space (as bounded or unbounded, for example) and of territorial order (as unified, divided or variegated, for example) may figure crucially in the production and entrenchment of such spatial ideologies. For this reason, even though they are often derived from seemingly technical decisions regarding numerical threshold percentages, measurement instruments, classificatory schemes or unit boundaries, the metageographies associated with geospatial data are never neutral. Such apparently trivial statistical or cartographic manipulations may serve to naturalize, or to unsettle, established assumptions regarding territorial organization, sociospatial interdependence and geopolitical identity. In this sense, our metageographical explorations regarding the visualization of Mediterranean urbanisms may be articulated to some of the broader questions about planetary urbanization and the reinvention of urban epistemologies that are explored throughout this book.

Notes

1   Manuel Castells, *The Urban Question: A Marxist Approach* (Cambridge: MIT Press, 1977); and Peter Saunders, *Social Theory and the Urban Question*, Ssecond Edition (London: Routledge, 1985); and Andy Merrifield, *Metromarxism: A Marxist Tale of the City* (New York: Routledge, 2007).

2   Neil Brenner, "Theses on Urbanization," this book, Ch. 13.

3   Ernest Burgess, "The Growth of the City: An Introduction to a Research Project," *The City*, eds. Robert Park and Ernest Burgess (Chicago: University of Chicago Press, 1967 [1925]) 55.

4   Jean Gottmann, *Megalopolis: The Urbanized Northeastern Seaboard of the United States* (Cambridge: MIT Press, 1961) 20.

5   John Friedmann, "The World City Hypothesis," *Development and Change* 17 (1986) 69-84.

6   Versions of this argument are developed explicitly by Saskia Sassen, *The Global City*, Second Edition (Princeton: Princeton University Press, 2000); and Stephen Graham and Simon Marvin, *Splintering Urbanism* (New York: Routledge, 2005).

7   Edward W. Soja and J. Miguel Kanai, "The Urbanization of the World," this book, Ch. 10, page 146.

8   Henri Lefebvre, *The Urban Revolution*, trans. Robert Bononno (Minneapolis: University of Minnesota Press, 2003 [1970]) 1.

9   Ibid., 4.

10   Ibid., 169.

11   Ibid., 15; italics in original document.

12   See, among other works, Christian Schmid, "Networks, Borders, Differences: Towards a Theory of the Urban," this book, Ch. 4; Andy Merrifield, "The Right to the City and Beyond: Notes on a Lefebvrian Conceptualization," this book, Ch. 31; Edward W. Soja, "Regional Urbanization and the End of the Metropolis Era," this book, Ch. 19; David Madden, "City Becoming World: Nancy, Lefebvre and the Global-Urban Imagination," this book, Ch. 30; Roberto Luís Monte-Mór, "What is the Urban in the Contemporary World?" this book, Ch. 17; and David Wachsmuth, "City as Ideology," this book, Ch. 23.

13   Merrifield, "The Right to the City and Beyond," this book, Ch. 31,

pages 524, 525.

14   The phrase "liminal landscapes" is drawn from Alan Berger, *Drosscape: Wasting Land in Urban America* (Princeton: Princeton Architectural Press, 2006) 29.

15   The concept of cognitive mapping is developed in Frederic Jameson, "Cognitive mapping," *Marxism and the Interpretation of Culture*, eds. Lawrence Grossberg and Cary Nelson (Chicago: University of Illinois Press, 1992) 347-57.

16   This distinction and its implications are developed at length in Neil Brenner and Christian Schmid, *Planetary Urbanization*, manuscript in progress. See also Neil Brenner and Christian Schmid, "The 'Urban Age' in Question," this book, Ch. 21; Neil Brenner and Christian Schmid, "Planetary Urbanization," this book, Ch. 11; and Neil Brenner, "Theses on Urbanization," this book, Ch. 13. We are grateful to Christian Schmid for permission to deploy this conceptual dyad in a preliminary way here.

17   These terms are discussed and elaborated in Roger Diener, Jacques Herzog, Marcel Meili, Pierre de Meuron and Christian Schmid, *Switzerland—An Urban Portrait, Volumes 1–4* (Zürich: Birkhäuser, 2003); as well as, Berger, *Drosscape*.

18   Berger's *Drosscape* represents a particularly sophisticated effort to confront this challenge through a brilliant combination of theoretical analysis, photographic documentation and creative visualization.

19   See, for example, Edward Glaeser, *Triumph of the City* (New York: Trantor, 2011); for a critique, see Brendan Gleeson, "The Urban Age: Paradox and Prospect," *Urban Studies* 49, 5 (2012) 931-43.

20   Lewis Mumford, "Mechanization and Abbau," *The City in History* (New York: Harcourt, Brace, Jovanovich, 1961) 450-2.

21   Denis Cosgrove, "Carto-city," *Geography and Vision: Seeing, Imagining, and Representing the World* (London: I.B. Tauris, 2008) 169.

22   See Fernand Braudel, *The Mediterranean and the Mediterranean World in the Age of Philip II, Volumes 1 and 11*, trans. Siân Reynolds (Berkeley: University of California Press, 1995).

23   These include the Columbia University Center for International

Earth Science Information Network (CIESIN), the Oak Ridge National Laboratory (ORNL), the European Environmental Agency (EEA), the European Space Agency (ESA), the National Geophysical Data Center (NGDC), the National Imagery and Mapping Agency (NIMA), the National Center for Ecological Analysis and Synthesis (NCEAS) and the Joint Research Centre of the European Commission (JRC-EC), among others.

24 On the relation between statistics and "state-istics," see Peter J. Taylor, "A Brief Guide to Quantitative Data Collection at GaWC, 1997-2001," *Globalization and World Cities Research Network*, *Loughborough University*, accessed 30 May 2012, http://www.lboro.ac.uk/gawc/guide.html.

25 Unfortunately, however, this opportunity has yet to be exploited effectively. To date, the dominant approach to the use of spatial data and analytical technologies in urban research has privileged description over theorization or conceptualization. This is a highly problematic tendency, in our view, because the descriptive sophistication and aesthetic complexity of georeferenced data visualizations can easily mask underlying conceptual confusions and a lack of theoretical coherence—in particular, a lack of definitional agreement on basic concepts, such as the "urban." For present purposes, our goal is to appropriate contemporary georeferenced data sets to explore visualizations of the conceptual distinctions introduced above. We shall elsewhere consider the theoretical and epistemological blind-spots of GIS and other new georeferencing technologies in relation to the investigation of planetary urbanization (see Neil Brenner and Nikos Katsikis, *Visualizing an Urban World: A Metageographical Analysis*, Urban Theory Lab-GSD research project, Harvard University).

26 There are other socioecological indicators relevant to this inquiry that cannot be considered here—including, among others, agricultural land use intensity, artificial irrigation infrastructures and human footprints, all of which figure crucially in the operational landscapes of extended urbanization. For present purposes, we have chosen three main indicators and associated forms of spatial data that most readily illustrate the challenges of visualizing the landscapes of extended urbanization.

27 Martin Lewis and Kären Wigen, *The Myth of Continents: A Critique of Metageography* (Berkeley: University of California Press, 1997) ix.

28 Until recently, the only satellite sensor collecting global nighttime lights data was the Operational Linescan System (OLS) developed by the US Air Force Defense Meteorological Satellite Program (DMSP). The program was designed in the 1960s to observe clouds illuminated by moonlight for meteorological purposes. However, it was soon realized that the instrument could also detect light sources present at the earth's surface, including human settlements and transportation networks. Nighttime lights data sets produced by the OLS have been widely used ever since, but they have until recently been dependent upon somewhat outdated technologies that generate a relatively low image resolution. In late 2011, NASA launched the improved National Polar-orbiting Operational Environmental Satellite System Preparatory Project (or Suomi NPP). Suomi is considerably more accurate than the earlier OLS system—it uses a much higher resolution for its images and it is more sensitive to dim lights. For details on the initial DMSP program, see Christopher D. Elvidge, Kimberly E. Baugh, Eric A. Kihn, Herbert W. Kroehl, and Ethan R. Davis, "Mapping City Lights with Nighttime Data from the DMSP Operational Linescan System." *Photogrammetric Engineering and Remote Sensing* 63, 6 (1997) 727-734; for a comparison of the two see Steven D. Miller, Stephen P. Mills, Christopher D. Elvidge, Daniel T. Lindsey, Thomas F. Lee, and Jeffrey D. Hawkins, "Suomi Satellite Brings to Light a Unique Frontier of Nighttime Environmental Sensing Capabilities," *Proceedings of the National Academy of Sciences* 109, 39 (2012) 15706-11.

29 Jon Beaverstock, Richard G. Smith, and Peter J. Taylor, "World City Network: a New Metageography?" *Annals of the Association of American Geographers* 90, 1 (2000) 123.

30 Jean Gottmann, "Megalopolitan Systems Around the World,"

Ekistics 41, 243 (1976) 109-13. For a contemporary discussion of the development of large scale agglomerations across Europe see Gert-Jan Hospers, "Beyond the Blue Banana? Structural Change in Europe's Geo-economy," *42nd European Congress of the Regional Science Association* (2002).

31 For a recent discussion of urbanization around the Mediterranean, see Claude Chaline, "Urbanisation and Town Management in the Mediterranean Countries," *Assessment and Perspectives for Sustainable Urban Development* (Barcelona: Mediterranean Commission on Sustainable Development, 2001).

32 Kingsley Davis, "The Origins and Growth of Urbanization in the World," *American Journal of Sociology* 60, 5 (1955) 429-37; and Kingsley Davis, "The Urbanization of the Human Population," *Scientific American* 213, 3 (1965) 40-53.

33 For an analysis and critique of this proposition—and of the use of urban population thresholds (UPTs) in the study of urbanization—see Brenner and Schmid, "The 'Urban Age' in Question," this book, Ch. 21. Already in the 1930s, the Chicago School sociologist Louis Wirth critiqued the use of UPTs, even though his own theory of urbanism emphasized the importance of population size as an important dimension of urban life. Wirth's critique was echoed in the early 1970s by his neo-Marxist theoretical antagonist Manuel Castells, who likewise emphasized the arbitrariness of the UPTs used in mainstream demography and the persistent need for a theoretical demarcation of "the urban question." See Castells, *The Urban Question.*

34 Edward Soja, "Reflections on the Concept of Global City Regions," *Artefact: Strategies of Resistance* 4 (2005), accessed 3 December 2012, http://artefact.mi2.hr/_a04/lang_en/theory_soja_en.htm.

35 The details of this approach are explained in Deborah Balk, Francesca Pozzi, Gregory Yetman, Uwe Deichmann and Andy Nelson, "The Distribution of People and the Dimension of Place: Methodologies to Improve the Global Estimation of Urban Extents" (paper presented at Urban Remote Sensing Conference, Tempe, Arizona, 2006).

36 The data used in LandScan are produced as follows: "[P]robability coefficients are assigned to every value of each input variable, and a composite probability coefficient is calculated for each LandScan cell. ... The coefficients for all regions are based on the following factors: roads, weighted by distance from major roads; elevation, weighted by favorability of slope categories; and land cover, weighted by type with exclusions for certain types; nighttime lights of the world, weighted by frequency. The resulting coefficients are weighted values, independent of census data, which can then be used to apportion shares of actual population counts within any particular area of interest." See Jerome E. Dobson, Edward A. Bright, Phillip R. Coleman, Richard C. Durfee and Brian A. Worley, "LandScan: a Global Population Database for Estimating Populations at Risk," *Remotely Sensed Cities,* ed. Victor Mesev (London: Taylor & Francis, 2003) 277.

37 Gottmann, *Megalopolis;* Brian J. L. Berry and Quentin Gillard, *The Changing Shape of Metropolitan America: Commuting Patterns, Urban Fields and Decentralization Processes, 1960-1970* (Cambridge: Ballinger Publishing Company, 1977); and Constantinos Doxiadis, *Ekistics: An Introduction to the Science of Human Settlements* (New York: Oxford University Press, 1968).

38 On GlobCover, see Pierre Defourny, Patrice Bicheron, Carsten Brockmann and Marc Leroy. "GLOBCOVER: A 300 m Global Land Cover Product for 2005 Using Envisat MERIS Time Series," (paper presented at ISPRS Commission VII Mid-term Symposium, Remote sensing: From pixels to processes, Enschede, the Netherlands, 2006) 8-11; on MODIS, see Christopher O. Justice, "An Overview of MODIS Land Data Processing and Product Status," *Remote Sensing of Environment* 83, 1 (2002) 3-15.

39 See David Potere, Annemarie Schneider, Shlomo Angel and Daniel L. Civco, "Mapping Urban Areas on a Global Scale: Which of the Eight Maps Now Available is More Accurate?" *International Journal of Remote Sensing* 30, 24 (2009) 6531-6558.

40 See Christopher Elvidge, Benjamin T. Tuttle, Paul C. Sutton,

Kimberly E. Baugh, Ara T. Howard, Cristina Milesi, Budhendra Bhaduri and Ramakrishna Neman, "Global Distribution and Density of Constructed Impervious Surfaces," *Sensors* 7, 9 (2007) 1962-79.

41 Ibid., 1963.

42 John Friedmann, *The Prospect of Cities* (Minneapolis: University of Minnesota Press, 2002) 6.

43 David Harvey, *The Limits to Capital* (Chicago: University of Chicago Press, 1982) chapter 12.

44 Gottmann, *Megalopolis*, chapter 12.

45 Schmid, "Networks, Borders, Differences," this book, Ch. 4, 77-8.

46 Hirotsugu Uchida and Andrew Nelson, "Agglomeration Index: Towards a New Measure of Urban Concentration," (paper for the *World Bank World Development Report 2009*, February 15, 2008), www.worldbank.org.

47 Friedmann, *The Prospect of Cities*, 6.

48 For further details on the Human Footprint data set, see Eric Sanderson, Malanding Jaiteh, Marc A.Levy, Kent H. Redford, Antoinette V. Wannebo and Gillian Woolmer, "The Human Footprint and the Last of the Wild," *BioScience* 52, 10 (2002) 891-904.

49 Lefebvre, *The Urban Revolution*, 14.

50 For a discussion of demographic growth along the Mediterranean rim since the 1950s, see UN Habitat, *State of the World Cities 2008/2009: Harmonious Cities* (Nairobi: UN Habitat, 2008); and for a general recent discussion on contemporary urbanization, Claude Chaline, "Urbanisation and Town Management in the Mediterranean Countries."

51 See, for example, Debra Johnson and Colin Turner, *Trans-European Networks: The political Economy of Integrating Europe's Infrastructure* (London: Macmillan, 1997); and Andreas Faludi, *Making the European spatial development perspective, Volume 2* (London: Routledge, 2002).

52 Neil Brenner, *New State Spaces: Urban Governance and the Rescaling of Statehood* (Oxford: Oxford University Press, 2004).

53 Graham and Marvin, *Splintering Urbanism*.

54 Wachsmuth, "City as Ideology," this book, Ch. 23.

Figure Credits

27.1 Ernest Burgess, "The Growth of the City: An Introduction to a Research Project," *The City*, eds. Robert Park and Ernest Burgess (Chicago: University of Chicago Press, 1967 [1925]) 55.

27.2 Jean Gottmann, *Megalopolis: the Urbanized Northeastern Seaboard of the United States* (Cambridge: MIT Press, 1961) 20.

27.3 John Friedmann, "The World City Hypothesis." *Development and Change* 17, 1 (1986) 74.

27.4 Henri Lefebvre, *La révolution urbaine* (Paris: Gallimard, 1970) 26.

27.5 Based on historical data sets from Shlomo Angel, Jason Parent, Daniel L. Civco, and Alejandro M. Blei, *The Atlas of Urban Expansion* (Cambridge: Lincoln Institute of Land Policy, 2010) http://www. lincolninst. edu/subcenters/atlas-urban-expansion

27.6 Road and rail networks are based on the Vector Map Level 0 (VMap0) data set released by the National Imagery and Mapping Agency (NIMA) in 1997. Marine routes are based on the global commercial activity (shipping) data set compiled by The National Center for Ecological Analysis and Synthesis (NCEAS). http://www.nceas.ucsb.edu/globalmarine

27.7 Fernand Braudel, *The Mediterranean and the Mediterranean World in the Age of Philip II, Volume 1*, trans. Siân Reynolds (Berkeley: University of California Press, 1995) 366-7.

27.8 Created by authors.

27.9 Nighttime Lights of the World data set (2003); National Geophysical Data Center (NGDC) of the National Oceanic and Atmospheric Administration (NOAA). http://sabr.ngdc.

noaa.gov

27.10 Center for International Earth Science Information Network (CIESIN)/Columbia University, International Food Policy Research Institute (IFPRI), The World Bank, and Centro Internacional de Agricultura Tropical (CIAT), 2011. Global Rural-Urban Mapping Project, Version 1 (GRUMPv1): Population Density Grid, Settlement Points, Urban Extents. Palisades, NY: NASA Socioeconomic Data and Applications Center (SEDAC). http://sedac.ciesin.columbia.edu

27.11 Same as above.

27.12 Same as above.

27.13 Same as above.

27.14 LandScan (2009)™ High Resolution global Population Data Set copyrighted by UT-Battelle, LLC, operator of Oak Ridge National Laboratory under Contract No. DE-AC05-00OR22725 with the United States Department of Energy. http://www.ornl.gov/sci/landscan/

27.15 Same as above.

27.16 GlobCover Land Cover v2 2008 database. European Space Agency, European Space Agency GlobCover Project, led by MEDIAS-France. 2008. http://ionia1.esrin.esa.int/index.asp

27.17 Same as above.

27.18 Global Distribution and Density of Constructed Impervious Surfaces data set. National Geophysical Data Center (NGDC) of the National Oceanic and Atmospheric Administration (NOAA). http://sabr.ngdc.noaa.gov and http://ionia1.esrin.esa.int/

27.19 Same as above.

27.20 Same as 27.6.

27.21 Andrew Nelson (2008). Estimated travel time to the nearest city of 50,000 or more people in year 2000. Global Environment Monitoring Unit - Joint Research Centre of the European Commission, Ispra Italy. http://bioval.jrc.ec.europa.eu/products/gam

27.22 Global Human Footprint data set, developed by the Wildlife Conservation Society (WCS), and Center for International Earth Science Information Network (CIESIN)/Columbia University. 2005. Last of the Wild Project, Version 2, 2005 (LWP-2): Global Human Footprint Dataset (Geographic). Palisades, NY: NASA Socioeconomic Data and Applications Center (SEDAC). http://sedac.ciesin.columbia.edu/data/set/wildareas-v2-human-footprint-geographic

27.23 Same as above.

28
VISUALIZING AN URBANIZED PLANET— MATERIALS

Urban Theory Lab–GSD

Any attempt to understand and influence urbanization hinges upon representations of (a) the core spatial units that underpin this process; and (b) the spatial parameters in which its effects are thought to be circumscribed.[1] As other contributions to this book demonstrate, inherited approaches to urbanization demarcate this process with reference to spatial units characterized as "cities"—variously defined with reference to population size or density; land-use features; or nodality within transportation and communications networks. Within such frameworks, the spatial parameters of urbanization are generally represented with reference to two major vectors—inter-city relations (expressed, for instance, in exchange or communications networks); and city-suburban-hinterland relations (expressed, for instance, in flows of labor, food, energy and materials). While many twentieth-century approaches to urbanization conceptualized such parameters primarily within metropolitan, regional or national contexts, a major contribution of more recent, post-1980s studies of globalized urbanization has been to extend them to the world economy as a whole. From this point of view, the geographies of (capitalist) urbanization are necessarily global insofar as (a) cities are connected to one another across the entire world economy; and (b) they consume the resources of widely dispersed territories, which are in turn massively operationalized as their linkages to cities intensify.

Within urban social science, assumptions regarding the spatial units and parameters of urbanization are largely implicit, but have occasionally been articulated in reflexive cartographic forms (see Figures 27.1, 27.2 and 27.3 in Ch. 27). Such cartographies of the urban are of considerable interest and import, because they put into stark relief some of the dominant metageographies—frameworks of assumptions about spatial organization— that inform both research and action on urbanization processes.[2]

One of the major agendas of this book is to supersede city-centric metageographies of urbanization through the development of new conceptualizations of how urbanization processes are imprinted upon the landscapes of capitalism. The pursuit of such an agenda requires us not only to develop new theoretical categories, but also to excavate the ways in which methodologically cityist metageographies have been constructed, disseminated and naturalized through hegemonic strategies of spatial representation. The materials assembled in this chapter represent an initial contribution to such an endeavor, derived from a more comprehensive investigation into the historical and contemporary cartographies of urbanization that is currently being undertaken in the Urban Theory Lab-GSD.

For present purposes, we have selected 14 maps, mostly from the last 60 years, which articulate some of the most prevalent understandings of the spatial units and parameters of urbanization within the social sciences and planning/design disciplines. In curating this selection, we are concerned less with representations of cityness *per se*, than with maps that represent the entire planet as a *space of urbanization*. The majority of these representational strategies reproduce the bounded city metageographies discussed at length in Ch. 27, albeit through a diverse, often quite ingenious range of data, analytical methods and representational techniques. However, several of the maps presented here begin to open up important windows onto the operational landscapes of urbanization, and thus contribute to the construction of countervailing metageographies. As in the various forms of geospatial information on the Mediterranean discussed in Ch. 27, the maps considered here emphasize several core indicators of the urban condition—population (Figures 28.1–28.4); economic activity (28.5–28.7); transportation networks (28.8–28.10); communications infrastructures (28.11, 28.12); and patterns of worldwide land occupation and environmental transformation (28.13, 28.14). These materials also illustrate how, even as new, potentially more sophisticated data sources become available, many of the same basic representational taxonomies remain operative in relation to the classic indicators that have long been used to demarcate urbanization processes.

Urbanization as a Cartography of Population

Figures 28.1, 28.2, 28.3 and 28.4 contain various representations of the spatial distribution of population on a worldwide scale. Figure 28.1 (page 463) is from the *Atlas of Economic Development* produced at the University of Chicago in the early 1960s. Following the population-centric definition of urbanization developed earlier by Kingsley Davis, national territories are shaded according to the percent of their population living in settlements with 20,000 or more people.[3] Insofar as data on settlement sizes are aggregated on a country-by-country basis, the map represents the geography of urbanization as being parceled among distinct national containers. Elsewhere, one of the creators of this map, geographer Brian Berry, famously attempted to explore the links between national urbanization rates and national economic development.[4] Although this correlation proved elusive, the quest to track it embodied the prevailing assumption that the national scale was the privileged level of spatial organization and political intervention.

Despite its pervasive methodological nationalism, however, the map also illustrates the ways in which national units obscure patterns of uneven spatial development. In a striking overlay of data that is superimposed upon the national grid of urbanization rates, the map depicts a population density gradient at three color-coded levels (red, pink and white). In this way, the map productively problematizes its own framing assumption that urbanization within each country could be represented on the basis of a uniform national average, and opens up a cartographic perspective through which to conceptualize patterns of sociospatial inequality at other spatial scales. Of particular interest are the red zones on the map, which reveal the broad contours of the world's most densely settled regions. Here, high population density appears to serve as a proxy for the morphology of subnational urbanization patterns.

Figure 28.2 is a more recent embodiment of this state-centric, population-based cartography of the global urban condition that appeared in *The Guardian* in 2007. In this map, which is based on data compiled by the United Nations (UN), three key indicators are synthesized through the use of bubbles that are scaled and color-coded to express worldwide urban distributions. First, national bubbles are scaled to express absolute urban population levels. Second, the national bubbles are color-coded to express urbanization levels, still understood in Kingsley Davis' classic, mid-century terms as the percentage of the total national population living within urban areas. Third, the map depicts the locations and population sizes of cities containing over 10 million people. While *The Guardian*'s map is intended for journalistic purposes, it embodies each of the core social-scientific maneuvers associated with contemporary "urban age" discourse, as promoted by the UN—the use of nationally specific census definitions, based on arbitrary population thresholds, to define urban areas; the embrace of a rigid urban/rural divide to classify national settlement space; the understanding of urbanization as a property of national territories; and the reduction of urbanization to a simple percentage level.[5] Additionally, through its graphic emphasis on cities with very large populations, the map also advances the popular view of urbanization as a process expressed paradigmatically in the formation of ever larger megacities. In effect, urbanization is understood here as a universal process through which, across national territories, populations are relocated into formally identical, if differentially sized, urban settlement units.

While over four decades old, Figure 28.3 (page 464) offers a strong counterpoint to such assumptions. This map appeared in a 1967 report by the Regional Plan Association, produced as part of the second Regional Plan for the Greater New York region. Here, the urban condition is depicted as a continuous gradient of population density rather than as a rigid percentage level. Instead of plotting population density distributions within the territorial matrix of states, as in Figure 28.1, this map employs the Dymaxion projection scheme developed by R. Buckminster Fuller, in order to represent urbanization as a worldwide process of simultaneous densification and extension.[6] Additional layers

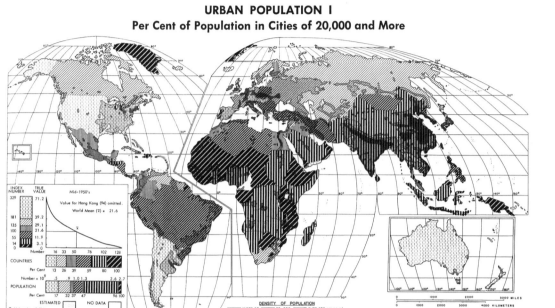

28.1 World urban population as percent of population in cities of 20,000 and larger, 1961

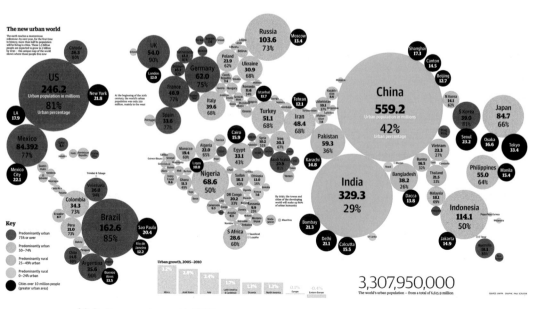

28.2 The new urban world, 2007

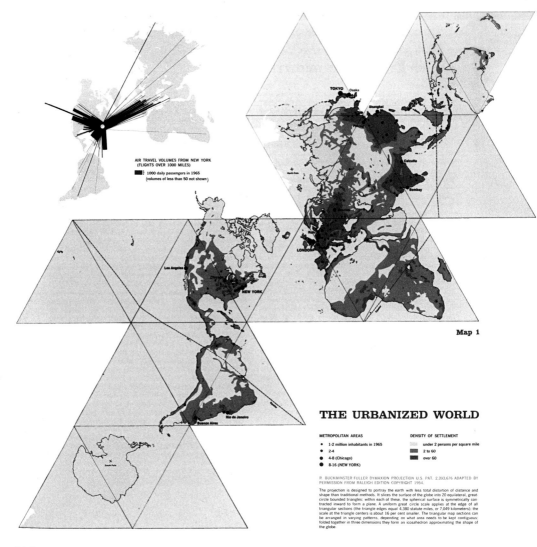

AIR TRAVEL VOLUMES FROM NEW YORK
(FLIGHTS OVER 1000 MILES)

■ 1000 daily passengers in 1965
(volumes of less than 50 not shown)

Map 1

THE URBANIZED WORLD

METROPOLITAN AREAS	DENSITY OF SETTLEMENT
● 1-2 million inhabitants in 1965	under 2 persons per square mile
● 2-4	2 to 60
● 4-8 (Chicago)	over 60
● 8-16 (NEW YORK)	

R. BUCKMINSTER FULLER DYMAXION PROJECTION U.S. PAT. 2,393,676 ADAPTED BY PERMISSION FROM RALEIGH EDITION COPYRIGHT 1954.

The projection is designed to portray the earth with less total distortion of distance and shape than traditional methods. It slices the surface of the globe into 20 equilateral, great-circle bounded triangles; within each of these, the spherical surface is symmetrically contracted inward to form a plane. A uniform great circle scale applies at the edge of all triangular sections (the triangle edges equal 4,380 statute miles, or 7,049 kilometers); the scale at the triangle centers is about 16 per cent smaller. The triangular map sections can be arranged in varying patterns, depending on what area needs to be kept contiguous; folded together in three dimensions they form an icosahedron approximating the shape of the globe.

28.3 The urbanized world, 1967

of information complement this image: dots weighted according to population sizes correspond to the major metropolitan areas; and a smaller diagram shows air connections from New York, suggesting the role of networked linkages among major centers in processes of densification (see also Figures 28.9 and 28.10, pages 469, 470).

The density gradients depicted in Figures 28.1 and 28.3 were based on rough statistical estimations derived from national census data. By contrast, Figure 28.4 introduces a more sophisticated statistical methodology in which census data and satellite imagery are combined to redistribute population variables over a homogeneous terrestrial grid. However, despite its complex quantitative methodology, and the impressive image of worldwide density gradients it produces, the GRUMP approach still hinges upon an underlying taxonomy of planetary space as being rigidly differentiated among urban and

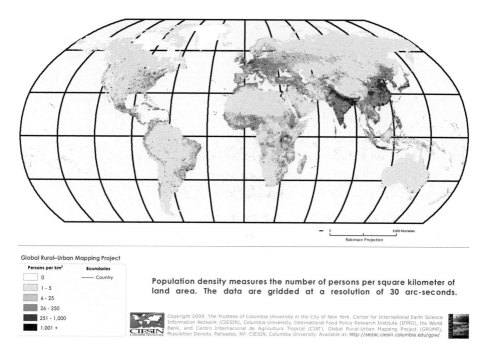

Global Rural–Urban Mapping Project

Persons per km²	Boundaries
0	—— Country
1 - 5	
6 - 25	
26 - 250	
251 - 1,000	
1,001 +	

Population density measures the number of persons per square kilometer of land area. The data are gridded at a resolution of 30 arc-seconds.

28.4 Global population density, 2009

rural zones. As highlighted in our discussion of such data in the preceding chapter (see Figures 27.11, 27.12 and 27.13), the cartography of urbanization extracted via the GRUMP method is premised upon the assumption that settlement space is differentiated coherently among bounded urban regions (statistically defined using a mechanism labeled as an "urban mask") that are in turn surrounded by a vast, worldwide zone of rurality. In this sense, paradoxically, a bounded city metageography underpins a representation that ostensibly depicts a borderless density gradient.

Urbanization and the Geography of Economic Activity

The agglomeration of economic activity is another important indicator of urbanization, and has accordingly figured centrally in influential maps of global urbanization. Figure 28.5 (next page), a map of the San Francisco Port's trade connections in 1922, is a typical example of such a visualization. Produced by the Port of San Francisco as part of a shipping guide, the map was indicative of an era in which water transport was the predominant means of world commerce. Through its use of an original "butterfly" projection scheme, this map illustrates the pattern of flows into and out of a major urban center, in this case via transoceanic shipping, thereby highlighting the port's transnational economic reach. The urban is thus conceived predominantly as a gateway within a global space of commodity flows. The parameters of urbanization are understood with reference to the progressive extension of the city's trade networks—a vast, ultimately worldwide hinterland for resource extraction and commodity exchange.

Figure 28.6 offers a more contemporary depiction of San Francisco's role as an economic agglomeration; it was developed in 2004 by researchers in the Globalization and World Cities (GaWC) research group at Loughborough University. In contrast to the traditional concept of a hinterland mediated through trade among geographically dispersed places, this "cartogram" depicts a "hinterworld" geography defined by networked relations within the

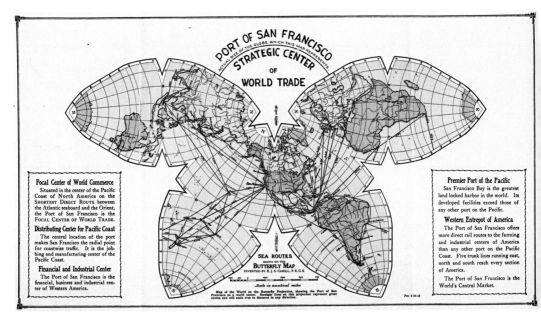

28.5 Port of San Francisco, strategic center of world trade, 1922

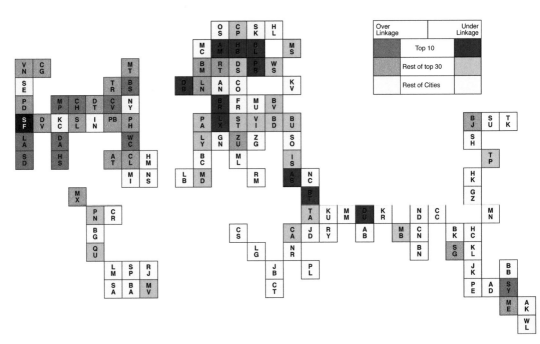

28.6 The hinterworld of San Francisco, 2004

corporate organizational structures of advanced producer services firms. To the degree that such firms are connected to subsidiary offices located elsewhere within the world economy, an inter-firm network emerges based upon differential levels and forms of connectivity to those locations. Represented as a matrix of cells approximating the geographical location of cities, "[a] hinterworld is the pattern of a city's relations with other cities across the world."[7] In effect, this approach treats urban space as a site of corporate agglomeration and the space of urbanization as a zone of intra-firm organizational coordination.

Figure 28.7 offers one further, economically focused visualization of world urbanization based on the apparent "spikes" of economic activity that appear to be clustered together within large, dense urban nodes around the world. Such images of a "spiky world" were popularized in an influential magazine article by urban consultant Richard Florida, and have subsequently been promoted more widely through an online application produced by McKinsey & Company's Global Institute.[8] Figure 28.7 offers a generic, three-dimensional version of this visualization, with the red spikes intended to depict exceptionally intense levels of economic activity, generally measured through a localized aggregation of national GDP levels. Here, urban space is envisioned as a zone in which high value-added forms of economic activity and consumption are clustered together in dense, nodal agglomerations. In this conception, the entire world economy has been effectively disaggregated into an assemblage of cities, surrounded by an apparently unproductive, empty and remote global hinterland. While these maps of cities as economic nodes productively illuminate the centrality of place under contemporary capitalism, they embrace a resolutely city-centric approach that obscures the variegated operational landscapes which support the agglomeration processes being depicted.

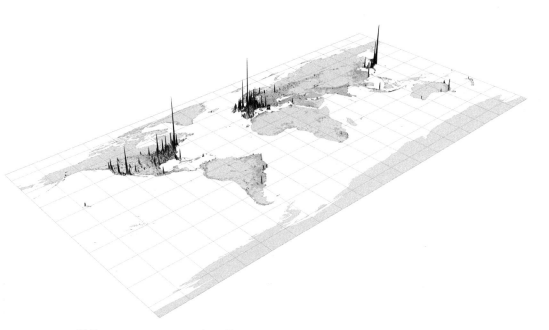

28.7 Economic activity in a spiky world, 2013

World Urbanization and Transportation Infrastructures

In contrast to the densified urban zones and fixed nodal points that prevail in the visualizations of population distributions and economic activity discussed above, the geographies of transportation infrastructures reveal some of the extended corridors of labor, commodity and materials circulation that animate the urbanization process. While Figures 28.8, 28.9 and 28.10 do not explicitly thematize urbanization, their depiction of global transportation networks at various moments in the twentieth century represents a powerful counterpoint to the bounded city metageography that underpins most of the maps discussed previously.

Figure 28.8 is a map of global surface transportation from the 1968 *Pergamon World Atlas*. Rather than representing network operations or flow intensities, it classifies the infrastructural equipment of the planet according to predominant technologies of transportation—from mechanized land-based systems (road and rail) to waterways and pack animals. Large territorial zones are color-coded according to the type of circulatory regime that prevails within them. On this basis, the map depicts various gradients stretching along major connectivity corridors such as waterways or railways, which are intended to illustrate the spatial differentiation of transportation capacities. Additionally, the map depicts the major ports of the world, weighted according to their traffic flows. Most strikingly, this map depicts world transportation space in the complete absence of territorial boundaries. In this sense, the map anticipates the type of accessibility analysis and visualization developed more recently through the World Bank's agglomeration index (see Figure 29.15, page 500).

In Figure 28.9, urban spaces—in this case, airports—are connected to the spaces of urbanization via aerial transport networks. Presented in the 1953 edition of the *World Geographic Atlas*, produced by Bauhaus-educated designer Herbert Bayer under the auspices of the Container Corporation of America, the map uses a polar azimuthal equidistant projection to ensure that air routes are visualized as unbroken spatial trajectories. Although cities are represented mainly as airport terminals within a globally interconnected transportation infrastructure, the map also depicts other land-use conditions, beyond the bounded city, notably the red zones of intense regional industrialization in the United States and the Soviet Union. While building upon updated and expanded data on *de facto* patterns of air transportation, most contemporary work on global intercity networks presupposes an identical metageography of nodes and networks.[9]

Figure 28.10 (page 470), produced by GLOBAIA in 2011, offers a contemporary synthesis of available data on worldwide transportation infrastructures in the context of recent debates on the Anthropocene—a period of the earth's evolution in which human beings are said to have become the most powerful shaping influence on land-use patterns and environmental conditions.[10] Building on geospatial data derived from the Digital Chart

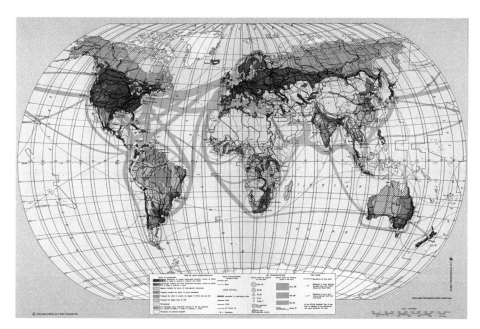

28.8 Modes of surface transportation, 1968

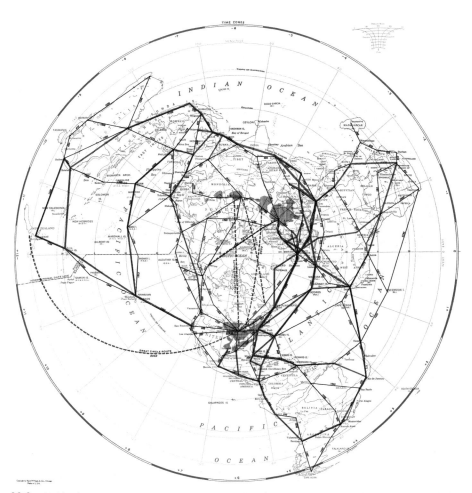

28.9 World airline routes, 1953

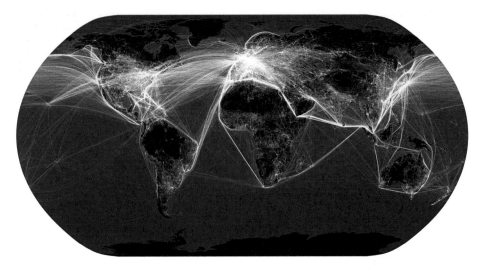

28.10 Global transportation system, 2011

of the World, Figure 28.10 combines depictions of major metropolitan regions with a synthetic visualization of all major surface, marine and air transportation networks. Here, urban agglomerations are depicted in yellow; road networks are coded green, shipping routes blue and air routes white. The map highlights the increasing density and planetary extension of transportation infrastructures, which here appear as a mosaic of operational equipment girding the earth's entire surface, both terrestrial and oceanic. This representation destabilizes the node/network binarism that underpins much work on transport geographies: here, networks have been thickened to such an extent that they are transformed into a dense fabric of connectivity woven across the planet.

Urbanization and Communications Infrastructures

Much like transportation networks, the geographies of communications infrastructures are threaded among major concentration points for population and economic activity, and they similarly extend across places, territories and scales, as well as over terrestrial, oceanic and atmospheric space. Figures 28.11 and 28.12 illustrate such infrastructural geographies at a world scale across the span of a century. Both maps also depict the contours of a "splintered" spatial configuration that promotes high levels of connectivity among some locations while relegating others to relative isolation.[11]

Figure 28.11, published by the International Telegraph Bureau in Bern in 1901, depicts transoceanic and transcontinental telegraph networks, illustrating both their spatial pathways as well as their landing points along the coastlines or in major urban centers. Although the pace, density and reliability of communications through this network are rudimentary by contemporary standards, the map shows how a worldwide infrastructure for information circulation had already been established well over a century ago.

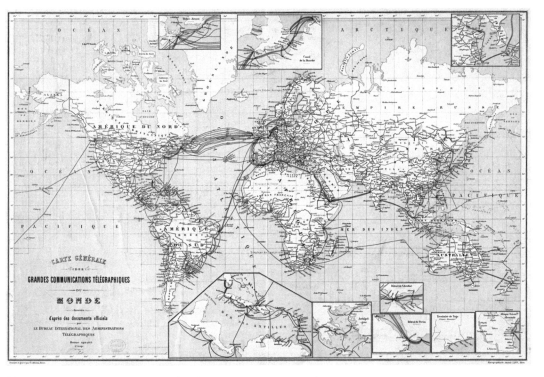

28.11 Major telegraph transmission lines of the world, 1901

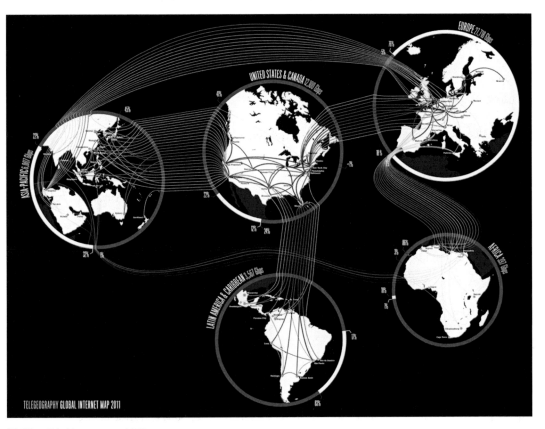

28.12 Global Internet map, 2011

Figure 28.12, published by Telegeography in 2011, illustrates the density and speed of intercontinental internet linkages in the early twenty-first century. Connections among the five main continental regions are colored according to bandwidth capacities, while the circles surrounding the main zones likewise display information regarding internal (gray) and external (white) connectivity levels. Here, too, cities serve as landing points for very large-scale infrastructural networks, operating at once as nodes within the circuits and as major sites in which their capacities are consumed.

Despite their differential historical contexts and technological focal points, both maps illustrate the inescapable duality of large-scale communications infrastructures: even as they contribute to intensifying interspatial connectivity, they also create new vectors of exclusion in which some zones are actively marginalized through the very infrastructural networks that enhance accessibility for others. Such power-geometries must surely be a central concern within any critical cartography of planetary urbanization.[12]

Urbanization as Worldwide Transformation of Land Occupation and Environment

One final cartographic tradition has provocative implications for the project of constructing new metageographies of urbanization: it involves mapping the differentiation of human social activities and land uses across the earth's surface. In most such approaches, urban zones are conceived with reference to the bounded city metageography, and thus appear to occupy only a small portion of the planet's terrestrial surface. However, to the degree that this approach is concerned to grasp the diverse ways in which human social formations have transformed land-use patterns and environmental conditions, it may contain some productive provocations for exploring the operational landscapes of urbanization. Figures 28.13 and 28.14 represent typical examples of such approaches.

Figure 28.13 was produced in 1957 by the University of Chicago geographer Allen K. Philbrick. Much like R.B. Fuller's Dymaxion map (Figure 28.3, page 464), it incorporates an original projection of the planet illustrating the contiguity among continents and the differentiated geographies of human activity that are extended across them. Philbrick's scheme classifies the entire planetary terrain as a space of human "occupance" differentiated among several dominant systems of socioeconomic organization and technological capacity. The zonal typologies on the map demarcate the resultant spatial patterns through a series of areal classifications—urban-industrial zones; various zones of intensive agriculture and resource extraction; zones of shipping and transport infrastructures; and a continuum among various kinds of subsistence economy. Notably, Philbrick viewed the "urban-industrial world core" as a vast territorial field stretching across entire states and even continents (specifically, the United States, Europe and the Soviet Union). In this sense, he forcefully transcended the bounded city metageography that prevailed during his time. More generally, Philbrick's approach began to outline the ways in which industrial urbanization hinges upon, and in turn contributes to, worldwide patterns of land-use reorganization and deepening territorial inequality. His visualizations thus open up some important perspectives for exploring the operational landscapes of extended urbanization.

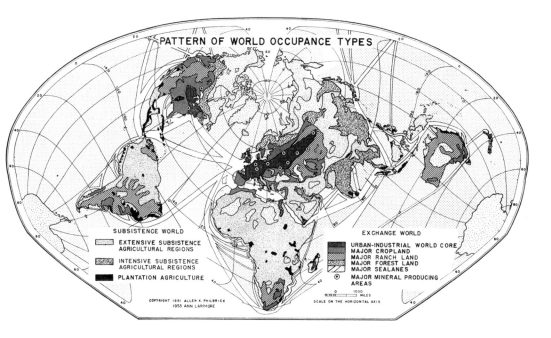

28.13 Pattern of world occupance types, 1957

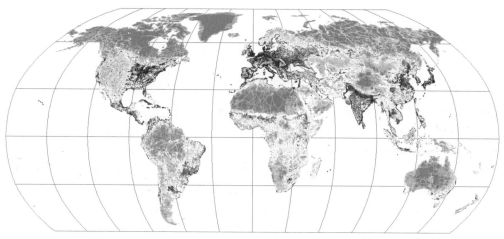

The Human Influence Index

The Human Influence Index (HII) is a measure of direct human influence on terrestrial ecosystems using the best available data sets on human settlement (population density, built-up areas), access (roads, railroads, navigable rivers, coastline), landscape transformation (land use/land cover) and electric power infrastructure (nighttime lights). HII values range from 0 to 64. Zero value represents no human influence and 64 represents maximum human influence possible using all 8 measures of human presence.

Robinson Projection

Human Influence Index

High : 64

Low : 0

28.14 Human influence index, 2008

Map 28.14, developed at Columbia University's Earth Institute in 2008 as part of the Last of the Wild research project, offers a more explicitly environmental perspective on the same set of issues. The Earth Institute's cartographic strategy is derived from a technical procedure that assesses the environmental impact of various human activities as they are articulated across the earth's surface. Drawing upon a range of data sets on human settlements, transportation infrastructures, landscape transformations and energy infrastructures, the map classifies planetary space on a scale from 0 (minimal impact) to 64 (maximum impact). Predictably, urban zones are coded as the highest impact areas, whereas more remote locations are said to be largely "wild," devoid of human influence. The map's representational strategy resonates with Philbrick's concern to differentiate the diverse forms of socio-environmental transformation induced through human activities. However, in contrast to Philbrick, who focused on the organization of socioeconomic activities, the Earth Institute map generates a technoscientific version of the long entrenched society/ nature binarism that is largely divorced from any consideration of worldwide systems of political-economic power or territorial inequality.[13]

To the degree that urbanization processes hinge upon and in turn transform operational landscapes located beyond the most densely settled zones, their classification as largely "natural" areas of low- or zero-influence may require significant reassessment. Perhaps more crucially still, these operational landscapes are inextricably enmeshed within contemporary formations of uneven spatial development, and thus frequently play strategic roles in the reproduction of larger regimes of capital accumulation, political domination and sociopolitical exclusion.[14]

• • •

The conceptual framework under development in this book complicates the task of visualizing urbanization processes, since it destabilizes inherited assumptions regarding both the spatial units and the parameters of the urban condition. It suggests that inherited assumptions regarding such issues are seriously incomplete, because vast terrains of sociospatial relations that have long been relegated to the putatively "non-urban" realm must now be internalized within our understanding of the urban condition. More generally, insofar as urbanization is no longer equated here with the diffusion of a universal settlement type—be it the city, the metropolitan region or the mega-city—it is imperative to develop categories and modes of analysis that permit us to recognize the wide range of sociospatial patterns in and through which such processes unfold. How, then, to map urbanization processes in ways that illuminate the dialectics between agglomerations and their operational landscapes, across places, territories and scales, and over *longue durée* time-periods? These tasks remain to be confronted, but it seems clear that we will be considerably better equipped to do so if we are critically attuned to the metageographical assumptions, visual techniques and spatial ideologies that pervade both historical and contemporary representations of the global urban condition.

Notes

1 This chapter is a collaborative contribution by four members of the Urban Theory Lab-GSD (Neil Brenner, Danika Cooper, Ghazal Jafari and Nikos Katsikis). It is part of a broader project on (geo) spatial ideologies of urbanization that is currently being pursued within our research group.

2 On the question of metageographies, see Neil Brenner and Nikos Katsikis, "Is the Mediterranean Urban?," this book, Ch. 27.

3 See Kingsley Davis, "The origins and growth of urbanization in the world," *American Journal of Sociology* 60, 5 (1955) 429-37. For a critical assessment, see Neil Brenner and Christian Schmid, "The 'Urban Age' in Question," this book, Ch. 21.

4 Brian J. L. Berry, "City size distributions and economic development," *Economic Development and Cultural Change* 9, 4 (1961) 573-88.

5 See Brenner and Schmid, "The 'Urban Age' in Question," this book, Ch. 21.

6 On Fuller's Dymaxion map as a tool for understanding world urbanization: see Nikos Katsikis, "Two approaches to 'World Management': C.A. Doxiadis and R.B. Fuller," this book, Ch. 29.

7 Peter J. Taylor and David Walker, "Urban Hinterworlds Revisited," *Geography* 89, 2 (2004) 145.

8 See Richard Florida, "The World is Spiky: Globalization Has Changed the Economic Playing Field, But Hasn't Leveled It," *Atlantic Monthly* 296, 3 (2005) 48; for McKinsey's analogous visualization and analysis, see: http://www.mckinsey.com/insights/mgi/in_the_news/urban_world_app.

9 See, for example, Ben Derudder and Frank Witlox, "An Appraisal of the Use of Airline Data in Assessing the World City Network," *Urban Studies* 42, 13 (2005) 2371-88.

10 On the Anthropocene, see Paul J. Crutzen, "Geology of Mankind," *Nature*, 415 (2002) 23; and Erle Ellis, "Anthropogenic Transformation of the Terrestrial Biosphere," *Philosophical Transactions of the Royal Society A* 369, 11 (2011) 1010-35.

11 On "splintered" infrastructures, see Stephen Graham and Simon Marvin, *Splintering Urbanism* (New York: Routledge, 2003). As Graham and Marvin emphasize, the project of "rolling out" standardized public infrastructures of communication and transportation at a national scale—which was pursued around the world during much of the twentieth century, up until the 1980s—represents a remarkable exception to the currently resurgent tendency towards splintering.

12 On power-geometries, see Doreen Massey, *Place, Space, Gender* (Minneapolis: University of Minnesota Press, 1994).

13 On such technoscientific legacies in urban theory, see Nikos Katsikis, "Two Approaches to 'World Management'"; and Brendan Gleeson, "What Role for Social Science in the 'Urban Age,'" this book, Ch. 22.

14 This proposition is powerfully illustrated in Stefan Kipfer, "The Fractures of Worldwide Urbanization: Insights from the Literary World," this book, Ch. 20.

Figure Credits

28.1 Norton Ginsburg, Brian Berry and Bert Frank Hoselitz, *Atlas of Economic Development* (Chicago: University of Chicago Press, 1961) 35.

28.2 Graphic by Paul Scruton, from an article by John Vidal, "Burgeoning Cities Face Catastrophe, Says UN," in *The Guardian*, June 27, 2007, www.guardian.co.uk.

28.3 Regional Plan Association, *The Region's Growth: A Report of the Second Regional Plan May, 1967* (New York: Regional Plan Association, 1967) 17.

28.4 Center for International Earth Science Information Network (CIESIN)/Columbia University, International Food Policy Research Institute (IFPRI), The World Bank, and Centro Internacional de Agricultura Tropical (CIAT), 2011; Global Rural-Urban Mapping Project, Version 1 (GRUMPv1): Population Density Grid, Settlement Points, Urban Extents (Palisades, NY: NASA Socioeconomic Data and Applications Center [SEDAC]), http://sedac.ciesin.columbia.edu.

28.5 Board of State Harbor Commissioners, *Port of San Francisco, the gateway of the Pacific: sailing list and shipping guide* (Sacramento: Board of State Harbor Commissioners, 1922).

28.6 Peter J. Taylor and Globalization and World Cities (GaWC) Research Network, as part of the *Atlas of Hinterworlds*, 2004 www.lboro.ac.uk/gawc/visual/hwatlas.html.

28.7 Nikos Katsikis, Urban Theory Lab, Harvard GSD, based on the Gridded Global GDP data set from Center for International Earth Science Information Network (CIESIN), 2002. Country-level GDP and Downscaled Projections based on the A1, A2, B1, and B2 Marker Scenarios, 1990-2100, (digital version). Palisades, NY: CIESIN, Columbia University. www.ciesin.columbia.edu/datasets/downscaled

28.8 Polish Army Topography Service, *Pergamon World Atlas* (Oxford: Pergamon Press, 1968) 57-8.

28.9 Herbert Bayer, *World Geographic Atlas: A Composite of Man's Environment* (Chicago: Container Corporation of America, 1953) 47.

28.10 Globaia: www.globaia.org.

28.11 Carte générale des grandes communications télégraphiques du monde, International Telegraph Bureau (Bern, Switzerland, 1901). Courtesy of the Norman B. Leventhal Map Center, Boston Public Library.

28.12 TeleGeography: www.telegeography.com.

28.13 Allen K. Philbrick, "Principles of areal functional organization in regional human geography," *Economic Geography* 33, 4 (1957) 334.

28.14 Wildlife Conservation Society (WCS); Center for International Earth Science Information Network (CIESIN), Columbia University, 2005, Last of the Wild Project, Version 2, 2005 (LWP-2), Global Human Influence Index (HII) Dataset (Geographic) (Palisades, NY: NASA Socioeconomic Data and Applications Center [SEDAC]), www.sedac.ciesin.columbia.edu/data/set/wildareas-v2-human-influence-index-geographic.

SEVEN
POLITICAL STRATEGIES,
STRUGGLES
AND HORIZONS

How are worldwide urbanization processes, past and present, mediated through political and institutional strategies? What are their operational elements and targets? What are their implications for spatial organization, resource distribution, power relations and political life? What, if any, alternatives to contemporary urbanization patterns have been envisioned, and/or pursued by theorists, designers, policy makers, citizens, inhabitants and activists?

**Nikos Katsikis
David J. Madden
Andy Merrifield
Max Ajl
John Friedmann**

29
TWO APPROACHES TO "WORLD MANAGEMENT": C.A. DOXIADIS AND R.B. FULLER

Nikos Katsikis

First published in 1970, Henri Lefebvre's classic text *La révolution urbaine* famously declared that society was entering a critical zone of complete urbanization in which the urban problematic was becoming global.[1] This hypothesis suggested the need for an expanded understanding of urbanization as a process of sociospatial transformation that transcends the traditional definition of the city and encompasses the entire planet. Six years later, the United Nations (UN) organized the first Habitat Conference, an event that seemed to signal a recognition of this expanded geography of urbanization by thematizing the organization of human life and settlement on a planetary scale.

Against the background of the themes raised in the first UN Habitat Conference in 1976, this chapter considers two approaches to global urbanization developed in the 1960s and previously by Constantinos Doxiadis and R. Buckminster Fuller, which arguably represent important precedents for contemporary efforts to conceptualize, envision and manage the world as a whole. Driven by a belief in scientific rationality and an aspiration for systematic knowledge and control, the agendas of Fuller and Doxiadis were largely aligned, and provided important intellectual foundations for the ideas put forward at the 1976 UN Habitat conference. Working backwards from that event, this discussion surveys the most important elements of these authors' ideas and thus unveils an important yet neglected episode in the long intellectual and political history of the contemporary *problematique* of planetary urbanization.

Doxiadis' and Fuller's engagement with the pressures of population growth, land management, resource consumption, unequal development and environmental degradation represent pioneering forays into the debate on global urbanization. Their attempts to grasp these issues at a global scale, through systematic indexing, diagramming and mapping, highlight the projective power of design in relation to some of the key regulatory and distributive challenges associated with contemporary urbanization. However, Doxiadis' and Fuller's approaches also clearly reveal the limits of technoscientific approaches to reshaping sociospatial structures, which treat fundamentally political questions regarding humanity's future as matters of rational administration. These technoscientific ideologies promoted the universality of managerial approaches to the organization of the world, and were largely indifferent to the social contexts and geopolitical domains in which such strategies were supposed to be mobilized.

Already during the period of Doxiadis' and Fuller's interventions, critical theorists such as Jürgen Habermas, Herbert Marcuse and Henri Lefebvre had criticized the technoscientific determinism of such approaches, underscoring their fundamentally political character and their complex yet often hidden interplay with the power relations, inequalities and contradictions of capitalism.[2] Yet, such critical perspectives on the regulation of worldwide urbanization remain as urgently relevant as ever because technoscientific ideologies continue to be mobilized under early twenty-first-century conditions, albeit in new guises and in relation to contemporary socioenvironmental problems. A critical evaluation of these earlier technoscientific approaches to world urbanization may thus inform and enhance our ability to recognize, deconstruct and counteract more recent incarnations of such approaches both in theory and in practice.

The Institutionalization of the Urbanization Question

In May and June of 1976, the UN organized the first Habitat Conference in Vancouver. Officially titled "Habitat: United Nations Conference on Human Settlements" (later relabeled as Habitat I), the conference marked a historical moment in which the need for an integrated understanding of the interrelationship between urbanization, development and the environment was thematized by one of the most important governance institutions in the world.[3] The concept of human settlements was understood not only with reference to cities and towns, but as the basis for a synthetic framework for considering, under the rubric of urbanization, a series of global concerns that had been discussed in previous UN conferences—the environment (Stockholm, 1972), population (Bucharest, 1974), food (Rome, 1974), and the world economic order (Nairobi, 1976, UNCTAD). The conference discussions explicitly emphasized that the problems of settlements were not only internal to specific places, towns and cities, but reflected the spatial and social organization of entire (national) territories.[4] Moreover, it offered a prescient critique of the urban/rural divide, highlighting the need to "get away from rigid and misleading divisions between rural and urban regions, and to see a country's settlements as part of a continuum of national existence and movement in which the health and viability of the various parts are essential to the vigour and development of the whole."[5]

However, while the 1976 Habitat conference was one of the first prominent public initiatives in the twentieth century to draw attention to the global dimensions of urbanization beyond the traditional definition of cities, its approach was characterized by an unproblematized methodological nationalism. Its main strategy document, the "Vancouver Action Plan," was codified as a set of "Recommendations for National Action" that were to be formulated into development policies by its member states, thus reflecting the national-developmentalist, Keynesian moment in which it was elaborated. Despite its global vision, its policy strategies actually enhanced the role of the nation-state in spatial development and thus implied that the challenges of world urbanization and the inequalities of spatial development could best be resolved on a state-by-state basis. The overall assumption was that:

> there are fundamental relationships among the distribution of population, environment, economic activities, and the pattern of human settlements. National policies for economic and social development can no longer afford to neglect or minimize the role of human settlements.[6]

But how could these "fundamental interrelationships" be analytically decoded and effectively shaped? According to the American anthropologist Margaret Mead, one of the key participants of the conference, even though it had begun to open up an important new agenda for "planetary housekeeping," the bureaucratic and state-centric character of the UN prevented the elaboration of a more rational, systematic approach.[7] What was needed, she believed, was a more comprehensive, transnational and scientific approach to global urbanization that, based on the advancements in general systems theory, would combine an understanding of its constitutive processes with technocratic methods for confronting large-scale social, environmental and institutional problems.[8] Mead's proposal was grounded upon a technoscientific viewpoint that was widespread during her time, reflecting an uncritical faith in technological progress and a corresponding endorsement of scientific rationality as the basis for addressing even the most complex, politically contentious societal problems. Elements of this technoscientific approach to urbanization were, in fact, already being crystallized in the early 1960s through the interdisciplinary efforts of the World Society for Ekistics (WSE), to which Mead herself had actively contributed for many years.

Doxiadis, Fuller and the World Society of Ekistics

From 1963 until 1975, the well-known Greek architect and planner Constantinos Doxiadis organized a series of annual symposia on the Aegean island of Delos, in an attempt to bring together leading figures from different disciplines related to urbanism, including geographers, architects, engineers, technologists, sociologists and historians.[9] His goal was to create a scientific community, labeled the World Society of Ekistics, which would be well equipped to confront the global dimensions of urbanization in a more versatile, interdisciplinary and technically competent way than the earlier *Congrès International d'Architecture Moderne* (CIAM) had been able to do.[10] While the modernist ideas of CIAM were associated closely with postwar national planning policies, Doxiadis highlighted the need for a transnational approach that would be better articulated through international organizations such as the UN. According to architectural historian Panagiota Pyla, the 1976 Habitat Conference was in many respects the culmination of the WSE's intense efforts to highlight the global dimensions of urbanization and to develop common approaches for managing them.[11]

The famous American philosopher, writer, designer, cartographer and inventor R. Buckminster Fuller was likewise a founding figure of and major influence in the WSE, having participated since the first Delos symposium and later serving as the organization's president following Doxiadis' death. Already well known at the time of the UN conference through his versatile practical and theoretical contributions, Fuller had been working for many decades to elaborate the capacity of design to promote what he hoped would be more efficient, universal solutions to a wide range of questions regarding forms of settlement, systems of transportation and methods of energy- and resource-management on a world scale.

Doxiadis and Fuller, brought together through WSE, shared an understanding of the planetary both as a scale of analysis and as a terrain of intervention. In their view, population growth, industrialization and technological development were intensifying human impacts upon the earth, opening up new problems of migration, resource allocation and territorial organization that had to be grasped and confronted at a global scale. Their expectations were grounded upon a simplistic technological determinism according to which the development of communication and transportation technologies would eliminate the friction of distance, making possible the expansion of human interactions at very large scales and producing a "shrinking earth." R.B. Fuller's 1965 diagram (Figure 29.1) illustrates this vision paradigmatically. At the same time, emerging risks of global catastrophe (for

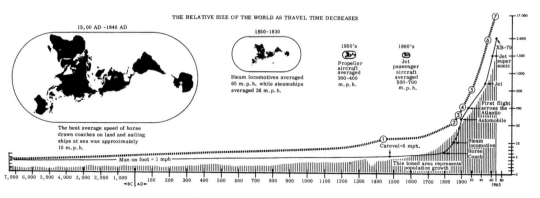

29.1 Diagram of a shrinking earth 500,000 BC–1963

instance, through nuclear war) and new geopolitical struggles over resource allocation (as exemplified in the 1972 oil crisis) were presenting increasingly urgent dilemmas and highlighting the global interdependence of human and environmental problems. As a result, both designers believed that a framework for worldwide management was imperative for human survival.

Although technoscientific and managerial approaches to human development can be traced to the mid-nineteenth-century efforts of the Saint-Simonians for radical social reform, the postwar approaches promoted by Doxiadis and Fuller were characterized by the use of certain new techniques, including cybernetics, general systems theory, linear programming and computer modeling.[12] These methodological tools produced the illusion that problems of immense social complexity and intense political contestation could be addressed effectively simply by being translated into quantifiable, computable variables and codes. In different yet allied ways, both Doxiadis and Fuller mobilized such technoscientific assumptions to analyze the fabric of world urbanization, and on this basis, to propose various interventions for managing its socioenvironmental dislocations.

Doxiadis and Planetary Zoning

Doxiadis developed his theory of "ekistics"—"the science of human settlements"—in order to offer what he believed to be a rational, comprehensive answer to the problems of world urbanization that traditional planning had been unable to address.[13] Ekistics incorporated major developments from urban ecology and the first quantitative revolution in the discipline of geography in the 1950s. During this time, the descriptive, site-based and historically specific approach of regional geography had been superseded by a positivist, nomothetic spatial science that attempted to uncover the supposed "laws" underlying spatial configurations, which were to be quantified and modeled mathematically. Doxiadis' theory of ekistics was derived directly from such approaches; it was an early effort to develop a "scientific" theory of urbanization without presupposing any fixed, historically inherited units of territorial organization, such as city or town, urban or rural. Rather, Doxiadis structured his theory around the more generic interrelation of five key elements:

> Our subject, the whole range of human settlements, is a very complex system of five elements—nature, man, society, shells (that is, buildings), and networks. It is a system of natural, social, and man-made elements, which can be seen in many ways—economic, social, political, technological, and cultural.[14]

Doxiadis' theory was intended to explore and categorize the putatively universal forces of urbanization that were thought to shape the human occupation of the planet as a whole. Figure 29.2 is a characteristic illustration of Doxiadis' effort to codify and diagram the complexities of urbanization with reference to principles he considered to be universally valid. The diagram summarizes how various generic forces corresponding to the five key

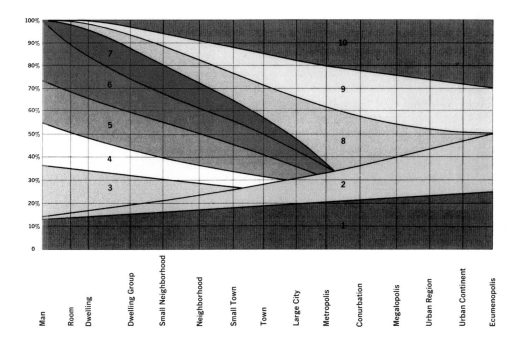

29.2 Synthesis of ekistic forces and their probable relative importance by ekistic unit. (1) Gravity; (2) Geographical; (3) Biological; (4) Physiological; (5) Social; (6) Internal Structure; (7) External Structure; (8) Growth; (9) Movement; (10) Organization

elements (nature, man, society, shells and networks) structure human settlement patterns at various spatial scales, with smaller scales mostly influenced by forces related to humans and society, and larger ones influenced more powerfully by the forces of nature, shells and networks. Based on abstractions such as these, Doxiadis attempted to confront what he viewed as the ultimate question: how most effectively to settle the world as a whole?

Unlike other influential urban thinkers of his time, such as Lewis Mumford, Doxiadis did not believe that explosive population growth and metropolitan expansion could be prevented; he viewed such megatrends as inevitable and thus that they had to be accommodated through planning. Much of Doxiadis' research was thus an effort not to contain, but to manage the growth and dynamic evolution of settlement systems. The flagship project in this effort was a multiyear investigation into the "City of the Future," which Doxiadis launched in 1960 as an experimental attempt to develop projections on the nature, dimensions and distribution of human settlements and to explore a variety of scenarios for the complete urbanization of the world.[15]

Following the pioneering work of Jean Gottmann on the northeast US Megalopolis, Doxiadis had already in the 1960s begun a systematic investigation of the patterns associated with megalopolitan systems around the world.[16] Observing density gradients merging into what was presciently termed "megalopolitan confluence zones," Doxiadis considered megalopolitan formations as intermediate stages in a process of establishing an increasingly continuous pattern of urbanization.[17] The diagrams presented in Figure 29.3 show the flattening out of population densities (and also of incomes) and reveal the transition from a concentrated, nodal form of urbanization to more decentralized, diffuse and regionalized urbanization patterns. At the same time, Doxiadis argued that commuter sheds were also expanding around agglomeration systems, from metropolitan to megalopolitan and subcontinental scales. The diffusion of technological developments in transport and communications, illustrated in Figure 29.1 (page 483), would facilitate the formation of "ecumenic systems of life" that would eventually cover the whole planet. Doxiadis believed that these trends would produce a functionally interconnected, worldwide mesh of continuous urbanization zones of varying densities—a situation that he famously labeled "Ecumenopolis."[18]

The City of the Future project embarked on a detailed investigation of the pattern, shape, structure, density and dimensions of Ecumenopolis. The project exemplified the application

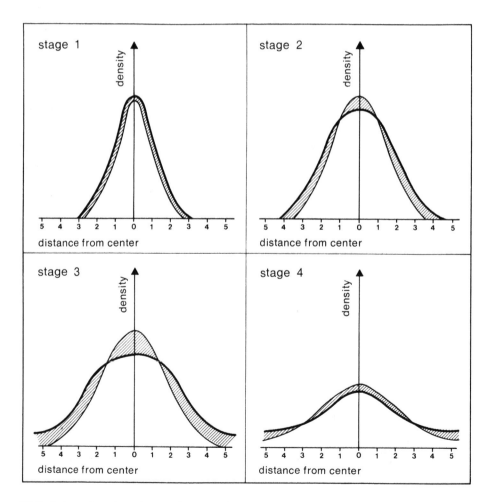

29.3 Evolution of population density and income gradients

of statistical projections, calculations and forecasting in the study of urbanization in relation to social and environmental indicators. Various projections of maximal population levels were constructed based on estimates of future population growth rates, technological development, income patterns and resource availability (including water, energy, food and minerals). These estimates were then projected onto a "habitability envelope" in which the surface of the earth was classified based on its suitability for inhabitation (using environmental criteria such as elevation, climate and the availability of fresh water). On this basis, as illustrated in Figure 29.4, Doxiadis delineated the areas that, in his model, could potentially support extensive urbanization.

Doxiadis abstracted the factors that would shape Ecumenopolis with striking simplicity. They included, he argued, the centripetal forces of existing agglomerations and the population growth rates of regions; and the centrifugal forces of major transportation corridors, economic and industrial clusters, and other landscape features such as coastal areas. Figure 29.5 (next page) illustrates Doxiadis' methodology for defining the structure of Ecumenopolis with specific reference to its probable structure in France. The form of urban expansion around existing agglomerations and along major corridors and coastlines was demarcated and extended based on studies of composite habitability, with projected settlement patterns deformed by major physical obstacles such as mountains, coastlines, deserts and hostile climatic zones.

Doxiadis argued that Ecumenopolis would begin to assume a mature form around the year 2100, at which point it would have achieved a stable state of equilibrium between human settlement systems, processes of resource appropriation and consumption, and terrestrial space. The projected structure of Ecumenopolis was thus characterized by increasing functional interconnectedness between large-scale settlements, which were in

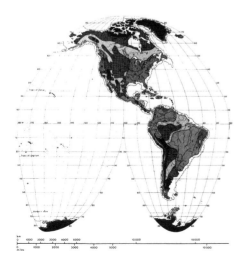 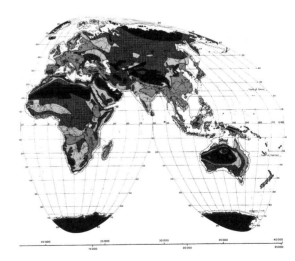

29.4 Composite habitability of the globe, Year 2100

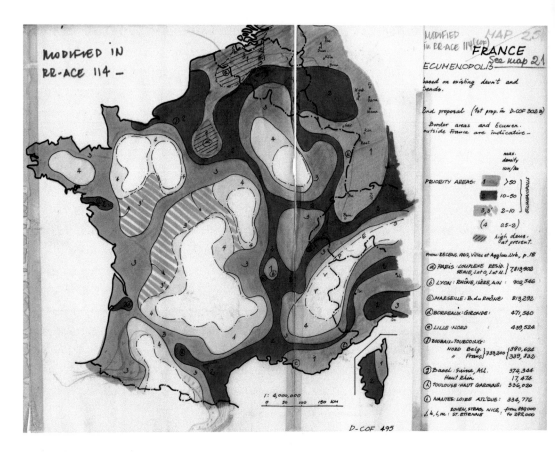

29.5 Preliminary study of Ecumenopolis in France, 1962

turn to be situated along linear development corridors. As Figure 29.6 (page 490) shows, these processes were projected to create a mesh-like settlement pattern covering the major habitable areas of the world.

Doxiadis attributed crucial agency to the plasticity of the expanding "ekistic fabric" of Ecumenopolis. He expected that it would become increasingly sclerotic and difficult to reshape as it was simultaneously extending and densifying around the world. Crucially, however, Doxiadis maintained that the long-term implications of this spatial pattern could indeed be managed through planning and governance techniques. If well planned, he believed, Ecumenopolis could become the successful "real city of man."[19] Thus, developing comprehensive guidelines for the future planning of Ecumenopolis seemed extremely urgent.

Much like earlier approaches to metropolitan growth in the first half of the twentieth century, Doxiadis was centrally concerned with the question of optimal settlement size. Although he believed that the future geography of Ecumenopolis would correspond to the complete spatial organization of the entire human population, Doxiadis insisted that its basic unit should be fixed, small-scale settlements, composing a "unified texture consisting of many cells," nested hierarchically and not scaled up to form larger megalopolitan entities.[20] Based on his research on the size and structure of human communities, he concluded that the physical size of the optimum cell should not be more than 1.3 x 1.3 miles, with a population of no more than 50,000—a size that, he argued, could support all major urban services while offering a level of accessibility and social interaction that promoted a sense of belonging to a whole.

For Doxiadis, then, the question of the social structure of Ecumenopolis involved successfully aggregating the small-cell communities into a larger, coherent formation.[21] Doxiadis responded to this challenge in characteristically technoscientific terms by proposing a system of nested communities organized along an "Ekistic Logarithmic Scale," which extended the central place theory of influential mid-century German geographer Walter Christaller to the entire world. To this end, Doxiadis proposed a comprehensive spatial plan for Ecumenopolis, a grid pattern in which communities would be positioned along large-scale development axes. This model is illustrated through a comparison of the projected configuration of Ecumenopolis in Figure 29.6 with the structure Doxiadis proposed in Figure 29.7 (next page). Within this scheme, the cells served as the building blocks of Ecumenopolis, and the development axes served as its expansion vectors.

As most of the agglomeration zones were organized around the linear development axes, the interior of the mesh was "freed up" and characterized by lower density settlements, vegetation and natural areas. Rather than being conceived as external, non-urban or leftover parts of Ecumenopolis, Doxiadis interpreted this mostly natural pattern as being complementary to the system of agglomerations; it was accordingly labeled "Ecumenokepos," meaning the "global garden." Ecumenokepos was understood not as a non-urban wilderness, but as an indispensible part of the urbanized fabric of the world (Figure 29.8, page 491). Doxiadis' key insight was that urbanization was articulated not only in the hierarchy of agglomerations, but also in the form of an encompassing social and environmental process. This perspective led him to develop a combined vision of Ecumenopolis and Ecumenokepos, an interdependent system that, through appropriate forms of settlement planning, would produce a condition of "Global Ecological Balance."[22] In this way, Doxiadis offered an early perspective on what is today usually envisioned as "sustainable development."

For Doxiadis, an optimal zoning of the earth was needed to promote an appropriate system of world management. Doxiadis thus exploded the concept of land-use zoning from the city and regional scales, complementing it with an environmental dimension, at a planetary scale. Doxiadis believed that a balanced approach to settlement and environment would result from the efficient classification of the entire planetary surface (both land and water), as well as the atmosphere.[23] His proposed categorization included four general types of space—natural areas (*naturareas*); cultivation areas (*cultivareas*), including both on land

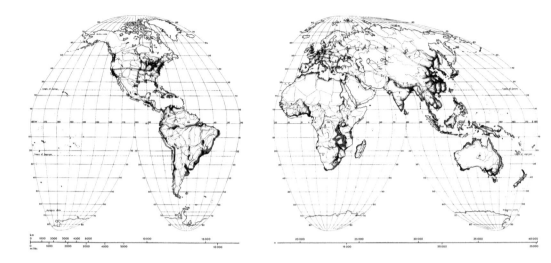

29.6 Probable structure of Ecumenopolis in the year 2100 (population: 15 billion)

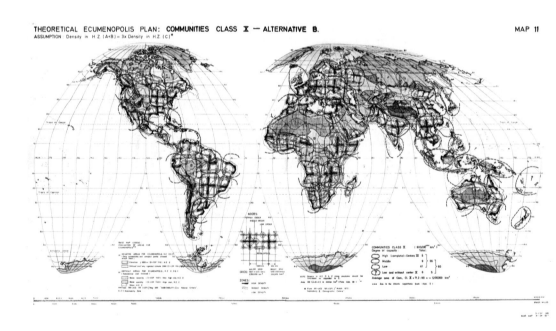

29.7 Theoretical Ecumenopolis plan showing the proposed grid, nodes and structure of communities

(agriculture, cattle) or in water (fishing); human areas (*anthropareas*), including settlement space but also zones of recreation and other infrastructures; and industrial and mining areas (*industrareas*), including resource extraction, industrial production as well as recycling, waste management and so forth. Doxiadis applied these four types of space to land, water and air, which were in turn subdivided into 12 zones each, classified according to degrees of human intervention.

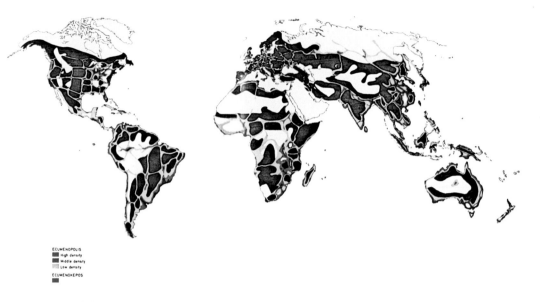

ECUMENOPOLIS
■ High density
■ Middle density
░ Low density
ECUMENOKEPOS
■

29.8 Ecumenopolis and Ecumenokepos

Figure 29.9 (next page) exemplifies this taxonomical approach to the organization of world settlement. With striking precision, the diagram outlines the percentage of global land that would be occupied by each of the twelve zones, as well as the extent of built-up (artificially covered) areas that should correspond to each zone. In Doxiadis' scheme, a regulatory system would be used to define the uses that were compatible with each zone, and their relation to the fabric of both Ecumenopolis and Ecumenokepos. This zoning scheme was the foundation of Doxiadis' framework for managing the world.

Doxiadis' framework exemplified the idea of a planetary city without an "outside," in which a single "ecumenic system of life" encompassed agglomerations and their global hinterlands. Based on systematic investigations of emerging forms of agglomeration and their effects, the thrust of Doxiadis' work was to reject the inherited model of the bounded city, and to focus instead on the variations among population distributions within and among zones of agglomeration across the earth's surface. His emphasis on ecological balance, and his concern to identify optimal proportions of land use and land cover, presciently anticipated the sustainable development agenda that was adopted by the UN in 1996 and that continues to guide contemporary discussions of urbanization.

Fuller and Planetary Resource Utilization

Whereas Doxiadis emphasized the distribution of agglomerations and the structure of land-use patterns across the earth's surface, R. Buckminster Fuller was concerned primarily with the question of flows—of energy, people or other resources (such as food and minerals). During the course of an impressive half-century of work from the late 1920s to the early

1970s, Fuller developed an applied philosophy of design that was focused on questions of energy and material efficiency, as well as on design methodology, and connected to an almost cosmological theoretical apparatus. Fuller managed to develop numerous outlets for his ideas and constructions: he built a series of prototypes (houses, cars and domes); he published a large number of articles, magazines and books; he taught in various universities; he served as science and technology advisor for *Fortune* magazine; and he founded the World Resources Inventory at Southern Illinois University.

For Doxiadis, the worldwide thickening of the urban fabric was a challenge that required new forms of planning; by contrast, Fuller envisioned an almost immaterial world of dense flows of interaction, largely freed from the constraints of political and natural geography. In Fuller's scheme, structures based on politically constructed territorial boundaries, such as nation-states, were the root of global inequality and prevented a more efficient distribution of energy, resources, technologies and knowledge. Like Doxiadis, he believed that the accelerated evolution of transport and communication technologies was eradicating the friction of distance, leading to a "shrinking planet" (Figure 29.1, page 483). Fuller emphasized that surface-based modes of transportation and communication were being superseded by air transport, satellite systems and wireless networks, leading to what he somewhat esoterically termed a vertical "ecological sweep-out" of humanity (Figure 29.10). The three diagrams presented in Figure 29.9 outline the three main stages of the "ecological geometry of man on earth"—a formation of relatively isolated settlements; a terrestrial

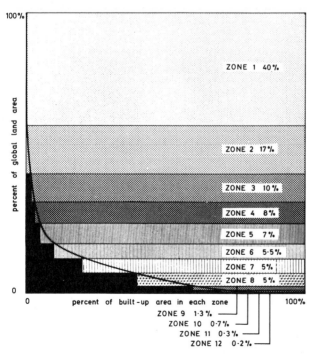

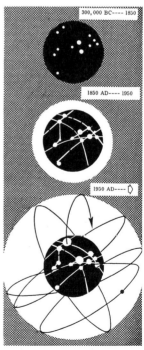

29.9 (left) The twelve global zones of land and their built-up areas
29.10 (right) History of man's Ecological Sweep-Out

mesh of interconnected nodes; and finally, the volumetric expansion of settlement space into the atmosphere and outer space. This technologically deterministic framework led Fuller to envision the future of the world largely without reference to land, territorial boundaries or terrestrial spatial configurations.[24]

Fuller believed that technological progress would not only eradicate the friction of distance but also the significance of climatic differences, thus permitting the settlement of remote or inhabitable places, such as precisely those that had been excluded from Doxiadis' "habitability zones" (Figure 29.4, page 487). Indeed, already in 1927, Fuller had imagined the possibilities that this interconnected system of flows, detached from earthly boundaries, could unveil for a unified "one-town world" (Figure 29.11).[25] This early

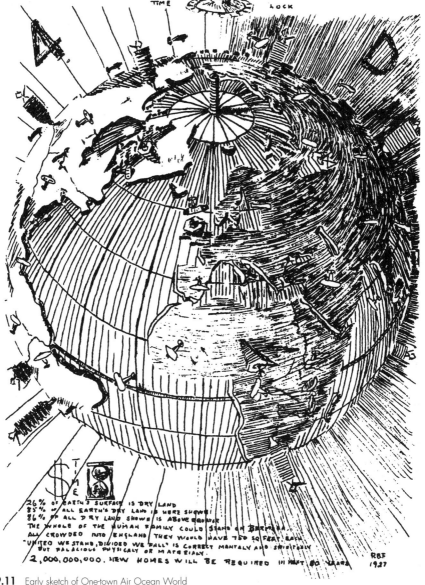

29.11 Early sketch of One-town Air Ocean World

sketch illustrates Fuller's vision of a future world society as an archipelago of earth-bound structures operating merely as "jumping-off points" onto a seamlessly interconnected planetary system of flows, almost entirely detached from earthly boundaries. Lightweight structures such as these, later elaborated in his models of Dymaxion houses and geodesic domes, offered controlled internal environments, and thus could be transported by air and "planted" in inaccessible, climatically unsuitable places such as the Sahara, the Arctic and Siberia.[26]

In Fuller's view, then, material space and physical geography were losing significance; it was the efficient management of global flows, not formal control over land or territory that would lead to the formation of a world society in which humans could peacefully coexist.[27] Much like Doxiadis, however, Fuller proposed to confront the challenges of world management through the mobilization of technoscientific strategies that were detached from political debate or social struggles over resource allocation. In a characteristically blunt statement, Fuller argued that "pure science paces applied science, which paces industry, which paces economics and which eventually paces social political and everyday life."[28] For him, humanity's problems of hunger, housing, poverty and inequality resulted from the inefficient use of resources and energy, not from their scarcity; they could thus be resolved most effectively through the application of scientific rationality and the innovative use of technology. Opposing the influential Malthusian doctrine of overpopulation, Fuller embraced the possibility of unlimited growth and development through the creation of new technological structures, artifacts and systems of production that could, he believed, unleash massive new developmental potentials.[29] Unlike Doxiadis, who expected Ecumenopolis to reach an eventual point of balance due to the constraints associated with the earth's physical size (Figure 29.4, page 487), Fuller believed that the efficient application of design principles could permit the accommodation of "more needs of more people with higher living standards with [the] ever more efficient investment of overall resources per given function."[30] Fuller introduced the notion of "ephemeralization" to describe this process of doing "more and more with less and less until eventually you can do everything with nothing."[31]

In February 1940, Fuller published a study of US industrialization in an issue of *Fortune*. This text synthesized the major elements of his approach. It presented data on resource extraction and industrial processing in the US, and it included a uniquely configured world map depicting the distribution and consumption of global energy resources in relation to population geographies (Figure 29.12). Fuller here introduced the notion of the "energy slave" in order to connect the pace of energy consumption to levels of human productivity to processes of industrial development.[32] This was also one of the first publications of Fuller's now-famous Dymaxion world map, which used an innovative cartographic projection system centered on the north pole, in which the planet was presented as a "one-world island in a one-world ocean, without any visible distortion in the relative size and shape of any of the land masses and without any breaks in the continental contours."[33]

WORLD ENERGY

A Map by R. Buckminster Fuller

○ = 21,250,000 human beings   ● = 368,500,000 inanimate energy slaves

Mechanization, the harnessing of energy, is man's answer to slavery. Man, whose population totals about 2,125,000,000, now possesses the equivalent of some 36,850,000,000 inanimate energy slaves. Their number is estimated by dividing total energy consumed by industrial man from mineral sources and waterpower, by the energy output of one human per year. Each white dot on the map represents 1 per cent of the human population; and the dots are located at centers of population. Each red dot represents 1 per cent of the inanimate slaves, located at focal centers of consumption. Each red dot represents about seventeen times the effective power developed muscularly by a white dot. The U.S. has 54 per cent of the energy slaves, an army of 20,000,000,000.

The faint blue line north of the equator is an isothermic line representing the zone of 32° Fahrenheit mean low. While all of industrial Europe lies to the south of this thermal zone, the heart of U.S. industrialism lies just to the north of it. History has made a clockwise spiral of civilization from East to West and northward.

Executed by Philip Ragan

29.12 Early Dymaxion map of world energy

In this way, through the image of a worldwide "continuous continent," Fuller aimed to highlight the possibility for a global reorganization and coordination of the major issues humanity was facing.

The Dymaxion map illustrated Fuller's emphasis on the importance of conceptual reorientations to the project of promoting global integration. If the world could be *conceived* as a single entity, Fuller believed, it could also be experienced and designed as such. His famous proposal for a global energy grid thus hinged upon the use of a Dymaxion map projection to reveal a potential link between the continental grids of Eurasia and America via the North Pole (Figure 29.13). The proposal was based on the assumption that world energy problems could best be confronted through efficient, reflexive distribution systems that would promote inter-continental infrastructural integration. Fuller accredited crucial agency not only to the Dymaxion map, but also to other newly developed techniques of analysis and representation, including computation. A global scale of operation required new methods, such as indexing and organizational diagramming, that would potentially illuminate key aspects of processes that remained conceptually inaccessible, whether due to their inherent complexity or their long-term temporal scale.

Since Fuller's main concern was with the efficient organization of networks, he highlighted the necessity of mapping the metabolism of the earth's resources. Fuller argued that the invisibility of the processes through which resources were extracted, produced and distributed seriously complicated the prospects for their rational organization. As a result, he engaged in a systematic effort to create an inventory of global energy and resources (such as food and minerals), developing several projects intended to uncover, visualize and redesign their metabolic relation to human development. As part of this effort, in 1961, Fuller launched a ten-year research project with the sociologist John McHale at Southern Illinois University. Their "World Resources Inventory" aimed not only systematically to catalogue, map and analyze the distribution and use of world resources, but also to explore new potentials for design practices in reshaping these sociometabolic systems. Crucially, for Fuller, the project of design was not limited to the configuration of artifacts, but should include the organization of systems of production, distribution, recycling and so forth—

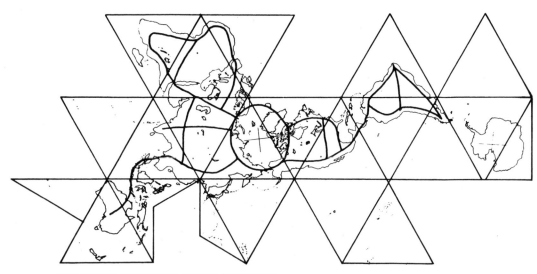

HIGH VOLTAGE TRANSMISSION NETWORK (PROJECTED)

29.13 Proposal for a global energy grid

indeed, it ultimately encompassed the design of the entire world. Much like Doxiadis' proposed "science of human settlements," one of Fuller's major goals was to develop a framework of "anticipatory design science" that would promote this wide-ranging vision of using design in its broader sense to manage world problems.[34]

The project that best synthesized Fuller's ambitions for world management was the "World Game," a hybrid political strategy and gaming program that entailed a large-scale computer simulation of major human, social and environmental problems. The World Game clearly articulated Fuller's vision of rational decision-making, mediated through computational techniques, applied to the management of the world as a whole. It was envisioned as a way to develop design strategies that would confront large-scale challenges of economic and social planning, such as managing global food or energy supplies (Figure 29.14). Based on Fuller's database of world resources, the World Game was also intended to illustrate the potential roles of new satellite technologies in environmental monitoring and remote sensing. As the game unfolded, Fuller proposed, participants would be able to track the impacts of their design decisions on worldwide processes through various kinds of simulations, often depicted through the use of giant Dymaxion maps. Fuller expected that the game's participants would thereby be empowered to adopt more rational design decisions regarding the future of humanity.

In sum, while Doxiadis structured his planning scheme in anticipation of a future equilibrium state of world urbanization, Fuller believed that the world could be managed dynamically, through real-time, information-based and participatory decision-making. Fuller's vision of a kind of cyborg-democracy operating through informational flows exemplified his belief in the ability of "rational man" to manage his environment through the use of quantitative, statistical forms of knowledge. Thus, though Fuller's vision of the future differed from that of Doxiadis in important ways, especially in its emphasis on immaterial flows rather than territorial landscapes, his model likewise endorsed the same underlying technoscientific orientation as the methodological and practical basis for managing the world's problems.

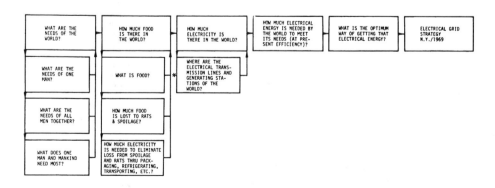

29.14 Steps in a World Game scenario regarding global food supply

The Persistence of Technoscientific Ideologies

Doxiadis and Fuller viewed their approaches as realistic responses to emergent challenges, not as utopian dreams. Fuller proposed the "World Design Science Decade" to the International Union of Architects as a way to transform the curriculum of design schools and to reorient the profession towards his agenda of anticipatory design practice. Doxiadis, meanwhile, organized a series of interventions for the 1976 UN Conference on Human Settlements and prepared several books for release in order to publicize and advance his proposals. However, Doxiadis died in 1975, and thus it was Fuller who eventually presented his "red books" to the plenary session "with an emotional speech, after which the UN's Secretary General referred to Doxiadis as 'the father of human settlements' and suggested that the conference be dedicated to him."[35]

Although both approaches did deal with important questions of global governance, especially in relation to urbanization processes, they were largely driven by a naïve faith in the positive agency and universal knowledge of the "expert." Thus Doxiadis viewed the UN largely as a transnational agent for implementing his proposed solutions for Global Ecological Balance.[36] By contrast, Fuller generally preferred to bypass political institutions entirely; his approach is strikingly summarized in his remark that it would be preferable to invest in "technologically reforming the environment instead of trying politically to reform the people."[37]

Consequently, both Doxiadis' and Fuller's approaches largely ignored the political-economic contexts in which world urbanization was unfolding, and the intense sociopolitical conflicts (for instance, over resource distribution, decision-making authority and public accountability) this process was provoking. It is characteristic, therefore, that state territorial boundaries and systems of economic power were almost completely absent from their analyses of global issues. The proliferation of new information technologies, with their promise of offering ever more fine-grained quantitative descriptions of the world, further entrenched both thinkers' preference for statistical description, quantitative reasoning and calculative modes of argumentation over any form of political-economic or institutional analysis.

Indeed, both Doxiadis and Fuller viewed the realm of politics basically as a disturbance to the scientific procedures of world management. As Lefebvre pointed out in a more general critique of such views in the early 1960s: "the political [*le politique*] was viewed as an obstacle to rationality and scientific procedure, as a perturbation, a kind of irrationality."[38] Lefebvre's harsh critique of such technoscientific approaches in the mid-1970s thus applies with remarkable precision to the two approaches outlined in this chapter:

> In these approaches toward the political and its intervention in urban planning, the postulate of space as objective and neutral was retained. But now it appears

that space is political. Space is not a scientific object removed from ideology or politics; it has always been political and strategic.[39]

Doxiadis and Fuller naively saw their models as rational tools for promoting social and economic modernization. Although driven by a radical reformist optimism, and intellectually pioneering in several important ways, support for their projective models for comprehensive land-use and efficient resource management largely dissolved in the late 1970s with the collapse of the Fordist-Keynesian-national-developmentalist growth regime and the subsequent global turn to neoliberalism in the 1980s.

And yet, even as politico-regulatory struggles and socioenvironmental challenges intensify under the contemporary formation of neoliberalized urbanization, the tendency to neutralize, quantify and objectify planetary space through technoscientific reasoning is being reinvented in a radically new geoeconomic context. Methodologies borrowed from the natural sciences, reinforced through the development of new informational technologies and new forms of geospatial analysis, are now being widely mobilized, especially in relation to debates on sustainability and urban governance. Quantitative, statistical approaches are once again seen as the optimal means for grasping and managing the complexities of large-scale urban transformations, and once again the normative and political dimensions of such processes are being hidden behind a techoscientific veneer. The development of advanced computational and remote sensing techniques, which have dramatically increased the capacity of designers, planners and policy makers to process, analyze and visualize spatial information, appears to offer contemporary "experts" a comforting reassurance— strongly reminiscent of the approaches developed by Doxiadis and Fuller nearly a half-century ago—that the global problems of urbanization can be resolved through the rational deployment of science and technology.

Reflecting this paradigm, efforts to establish universal technoscientific methodologies are becoming increasingly influential within the scientific community as well as within popular media outlets. Influential examples of this renewed, largely unreflexive reliance on natural-scientific paradigms in debates on urban questions include, among many others, studies of urban metabolism through the standardization of material flow analysis (MFA); the physicist Geoffrey West's "general equation" governing city sizes and characteristics; and the popularization of the notion of the Anthropocene to characterize humanity's impact on the transformation of the planet.[40] Whatever their differences of method, data and empirical focus, such approaches share an understanding of urbanization as a politically neutral, almost organic force, and in this sense reintroduce some of the same technoscientific ideologies that were endorsed and popularized among urbanists by Doxiadis and Fuller.[41]

Admist these scholarly trends, influential international institutions are also promoting new forms of research that still further legitimize and entrench the vision of planetary space as politically neutral and fully accessible via quantitative forms of knowledge. A paradigmatic example of this is the World Bank Development Report from 2009, which proposes an alternative representation global urbanization on the basis of a newly constructed "global agglomeration index."[42] This rather striking "heat map" representation of human concentration, derived from data sets on population density and accessibility, closely parallels Doxiadis' earlier scheme (Figure 29.7, page 490) in which a future formation of balanced human development is assumed to follow logically from the establishment of a uniformly accessible urban fabric (Figure 29.15). In the contemporary context, the World Bank's approach privileges the formal clarity of abstract models—a proxy for its vision of seamless worldwide economic integration—over any consideration of the distorting complexities of political institutions, social inequalities, infrastructural misallocations, market failures and ecological crises.[43]

Another characteristic example of this technoscientific vision of planetary space is presented in Figure 29.16, which elaborates upon Fuller's earlier energy grid (Figure 29.13, page 496) as part of a recent World Wildlife Fund report on global energy in collaboration with the research office of Rem Koolhaas' acclaimed firm, the Office for Metropolitan Architecture (OMA).[44] Here, Fuller's vision is updated in technological terms—the representation now includes consideration of the world's potentially renewable energy sources—but once more there is no attempt to consider the geopolitical frameworks and transnational circuits of capitalist control that mediate the appropriation of such resources, much less the territorial conflicts, sociopolitical struggles and socioecological diasters that are often provoked by such processes of extraction. Here, too, then, a global imaginary is produced in which the challenges of contemporary urbanization are understood in narrowly technoscientific terms, simply as a matter of rational management.

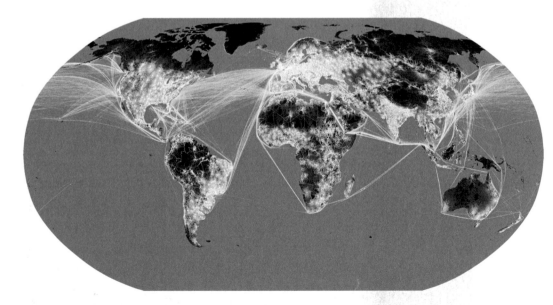

29.15 Global map of accessibility. The accessibility surface corresponds to travel time to major cities with population of 50,000 or more in year 2000. The map is a major component of the Agglomeration Index.

Despite their technoscientific blind-spots, the postwar approaches of Doxiadis and Fuller were connected to broader, reformist visions for the future of human development. Their rationalistic models were still linked to goals that may be viewed as broadly progressive— including, for instance, the redistribution of human resources and assets; the promotion of a more balanced model of settlement space; and the need for ecological sustainability. Such agendas are notably absent from most contemporary approaches to world management, which usually endorse the analytical capacities of technoscience in the interest more

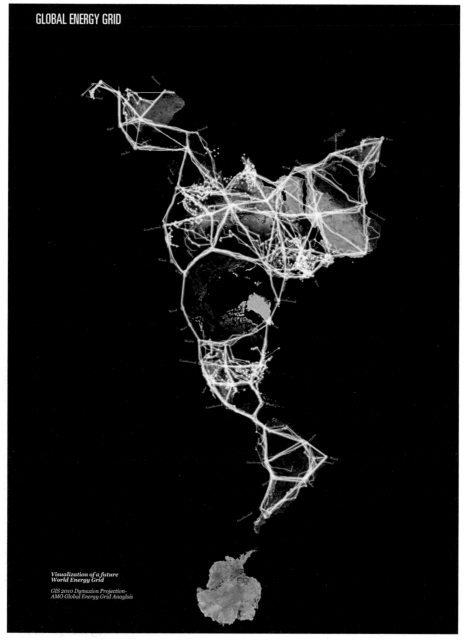

GLOBAL ENERGY GRID

*Visualization of a future
World Energy Grid*

*GIS 2010 Dymaxion Projection-
AMO Global Energy Grid Anaylsis*

29.16   WWF and OMA proposal for a global energy grid

efficiently calibrating existing conditions and trends, without connecting them to an alternative vision for a more balanced, socially just or democratic future for global human society. For this reason, such models fail to grapple with, much less to challenge, the destructive, polarizing consequences of the still-dominant neoliberal model of promoting seamless global market integration.

Clearly, any attempt to analyze and shape contemporary urbanization patterns can build productively upon the accumulation of quantitative knowledge and data processing capacities that has been accomplished over the past decades. However, such an endeavor will be most productive if it does not equate information and data gathering with substantive understanding. Indeed, there is today a quite urgent need for conceptual leaps and representational innovations, perhaps akin to those offered by Doxiadis' metaphors of planet-wide zoning or Fuller's Dymaxion map, in order to uncover the qualitative transformations of political-economic and ecological space that are currently under way around the world. Without the conceptual perspective, analytic insight and representational imagination that such experiments can promote, the massive technoscientific apparatus we now have at our disposal will serve to do little more than process data, and thus to recycle inherited assumptions and understandings that may have become obsolete. From this point of view, although ideologically quite divergent from Lefebvre, the approaches developed by Doxiadis and Fuller may actually offer some productive intellectual resources for considering some of the forms in which his "virtual object" of complete urbanization might eventually be materialized on a planetary scale. Perhaps more importantly still, these designers also offered some preliminary sketches and visions of the potential global society that could emerge—through coordination, negotiation and struggle—beyond the critical point of the urban revolution.

Notes

1   Henri Lefebvre, *La révolution urbaine* (Paris: Gallimard, 1970).

2   See Jurgen Habermas, "Technology and Science as Ideology," *Toward a Rational Society: Student Protest, Science, and Politics*, trans. Jeremy J. Shapiro (Boston: Beacon Press, 1970); Herbert Marcuse, *One-dimensional Man: Studies in the Ideology of Advanced Industrial Society* (Boston: Beacon Press, 1964); and Henri Lefebvre, "Reflections on the Politics of Space," *State, Space, World: Selected Essays*, eds. Neil Brenner and Stuart Elden, trans. Gerald Moore, Neil Brenner and Stuart Elden (Minneapolis: University of Minnesota, 2009).

3   The conference took place in Vancouver, Canada from May 31 June 11, 1976. It led to the creation of the United Nations Centre on Human Settlements (UN-Habitat) two years later in 1978. Since then, the interplay of development and environment has been a central focus for UN strategies. The next UN Conference on Human Settlements (Habitat II) was held 20 years later in Istanbul (1996) and emphasized the notion of sustainable development. For an extensive review of the first Habitat conference see *Ekistics* 252 (1976).

4   United Nations, *The Vancouver Declaration*, Habitat: United Nations Conference on Human Settlements, Vancouver, Canada, 31 May - 11 June 1976, published in *Ekistics* 252 (1976) 252-66.

5   Ibid., 268.

6   Ibid., 253.

7   In a postconference report she noted: "The UN and its agencies, fragmented as they remain today, continue to exemplify separate headings which reflect ancient bureaucratic arrangements—and these unfortunately have been replicated in the bureaucratic arrangements of the new nations." Margaret Mead, "Habitat: Building a Global Constituency," *Habitat International* 3, 3-4 (1976) 284.

8   Ibid., 283-6.

9   The World Society for Ekistics (WSE) was conceived at the 1965 Delos Symposium. The Society was inaugurated in 1967, and its founding members included Doxiadis and Fuller, as well as Jean Gottmann and Margaret Mead. Every year, the proceedings of the Delos symposia were presented in the journal *Ekistics*, published by Doxiadis' Athens Center for Ekistics.

10 For a review of CIAM debates on planning and radical social reform see Eric Mumford, *The CIAM Discourse on Urbanism, 1928-1960* (Cambridge: MIT Press, 2002).

11 See Panagiota Pyla, "Planetary Home and Garden: Ekistics and Environmental-Developmental Politics," *Grey Room* 36 (2005) 6-35.

12 Antoine Picon, *Les Saint-Simoniens: Raison, Imaginaire et Utopie* (Paris: Belin, 2002); and Antoine Picon, "Fuller's Avatars: A View From the Present," *Buckminster Fuller: Starting With the Universe*, eds.

Michael Hays and Dana Miller (New Haven: Yale University Press, 2008).

13 Constantinos Doxiadis, *Ekistics: an Introduction to the Science of Human Settlements* (London: Hutchinson, 1968).

14 Ibid., 393.

15 The "City of the Future" was one of three projects that Doxiadis' office, the Athens Center of Ekistics, initiated in 1960 and pursued for over 15 years. The findings of the project were presented in condensed form in several issues of the journal *Ekistics*, and eventually in Constantinos Doxiadis and John Papaioannou, *Ecumenopolis: The Inevitable City of the Future* (New York: Norton, 1974).

16 Jean Gottmann, *Megalopolis: The Urbanized Northeastern Seaboard of the United States* (Cambridge: MIT Press, 1964). For a systematic investigation of megalopolitan formations around the world as part of the City of the Future project see John Papaioannou, *Megalopolises: A First Definition* (Athens: Athens Technological Organization / Athens Center of Ekistics, 1967).

17 Doxiadis developed his approach to Megalopolitan Confluence zones based on the findings of a report that he commissioned to geographer Brian Berry in the context of the City of the Future project. See Brian J. L. Berry, *Megalopolitan Confluence Zones: New Growth Centers in the United States* (Athens: Athens Technological Organization / Athens Center of Ekistics, 1971). See also Edward Soja, "Regional Urbanization and the End of the Metropolis Era," Ch. 19, this book.

18 Ecumenopolis is terminologically based on the Greek word *Ecoumeni* which refers to the whole world as an entity. First coined in 1961, Doxiadis defined Ecumenopolis as "the coming city that, together with the corresponding open land which is indispensable for man, will cover the entire earth as a continuous system forming a universal settlement." See Doxiadis and Papaioannou, *Ecumenopolis*, 436.

19 Doxiadis envisioned that Ecumenopolis would help humanity overcome regional differences and disparities. See Constantinos Doxiadis, "Ecumenopolis: Tomorrow's City," paper prepared for *Britannica, Book of the Year 1968*, C.A. Doxiadis Archives, Athens, Folder 2924.

20 Ibid., 21.

21 Ibid., 20.

22 Constantinos Doxiadis, *Ecology and Ekistics*, ed. Gerald Dix (Boulder: Westview Press, 1977) 28.

23 Constantinos Doxiadis, *Building Entopia* (Athens: Athens Publishing Center, 1975); Doxiadis, "The Ecological Types of Space That We Need," *Environmental Conservation* 2 (1975) 3-13; and Doxiadis, *Ecology and Ekistics*.

24 Buckminster Fuller and Robert Marks, *The Dymaxion World of Buckminster Fuller* (New York: Reinhold, 1973) 153.

25 Fuller's concept of the One-Town World first appeared in the 1927 sketch above. For Fuller's supra-national vision of an integrated world society, see Buckminster Fuller, "Preparing for a Small One Town World," Congressional Record at US Senate May 15, 1975, published in Buckminster Fuller, *Humans in Universe* (Berlin: Walter de Gruyter, 1983) 207-14.

26 Fuller and Marks, *The Dymaxion World of Buckminster Fuller*.

27 Buckminster Fuller, *Operating Manual for Spaceship Earth* (Carbondale: Southern Illinois University Press, 1969); and Fuller, *Synergetics* (New York: Macmillan, 1975).

28 Fuller and Marks, *The Dymaxion World of Buckminster Fuller*, 152.

29 In 1966 the British economist Barbara Ward, a key member of the World Society of Ekistics and one of the organizers of the 1976 UN conference, published an influential book on the concept. See Barbara Ward, *Spaceship Earth* (New York: Columbia University Press, 1966).

30 Buckminster Fuller, "The World Game," *Ekistics* 28, 167 (1969) 286-92.

31 Buckminster Fuller, *Nine Chains to the Moon* (New York: Anchor Books, 1971) 252.

32 Buckminster Fuller, "U.S. Industrialization," *Fortune* 21, 2 (1940) 50-7.

33 Buckminster Fuller, "Humanity's Critical Path: From Weaponry To Livingry," *Proteus* 1 (1983) 3.

34 Buckminster Fuller and John McHale, *World Design Science Decade, Document 4* (Carbondale: World Resources Inventory, 1965).

35 Pyla, "Planetary Home and Garden," 28.

36 Doxiadis presented an incremental plan structured around the 1976 UN conference, which he hoped would adopt his scheme for Global Ecological Balance. See Constantinos Doxiadis, "Global Ecological Balance: the Human Settlement that We Need," Paper prepared for the *Tyler Ecology Award*, September 1974, C.A. Doxiadis Archives, Athens, Folder 6287.

37 Fuller, "Humanity's Critical Path: From Weaponry To Livingry," 2.

38 Lefebvre "Reflections on the Politics of Space," 170.

39 Ibid.

40 For an application of material flow analysis to the study of planetary metabolism, see Peter Baccini and Paul H. Brunner, *Metabolism of the Anthroposphere: Analysis, Evaluation, Design* (Cambridge: MIT Press, 2012); and Fridolin Krausmann and Marina Fischer-Kowalski, "The Global Sociometabolic Transition," *Journal of Industrial Ecology* 12 (2008) 637-56. For Geoffrey West's "Science of Cities," see Luis Bettencourt and Geoffrey West, "A Unified Theory of Urban Living," *Nature* 467 (2010) 912-13. On the "Anthropocene" see, among other works, Paul Crutzen, "The Geology of Mankind," *Nature* 415 (2002) 22-3.

41 For a critique of such views, see Brendan Gleeson, "What Role for Social Science in the 'Urban Age'?" this book, Ch. 22. For a critique of technoscientific approaches to urban metabolism, see Nik Heynen, Maria Kaika and Erik Swyngedouw eds., *In the Nature of Cities: Urban Political Ecology and The Politics of Urban Metabolism* (London: Routledge, 2006); and Timothy Luke "At the End of Nature: Cyborgs, 'Humachines,' and Environments in Postmodernity," *Environment and Planning A 29, 8* (1997) 1367-80.

42 Hirotsugu Uchida and Andrew Nelson, *Agglomeration Index: Towards a New Measure of Urban Concentration*. Background paper for the *World Bank World Development Report 2009*, February (2008). www.worldbank.org; published in *World Institute for Development Economics Research*, 29 (2010) www.hdl.handle.net/10419/54112.

43 For a critique of 2009 World Bank Development Report see David Harvey, "Reshaping Economic Geography: The World Development Report 2009," *Development and Change* 40 (2009) 1269-77.

44 World Wildlife Fund, Ecofys and Office for Metropolitan Architecture, *The Energy Report: 100% Renewable Energy by 2050* (Gland: World Wildlife Fund, 2011). www.wwf.panda.org

Figure Credits

29.1 Courtesy of the Estate of R. Buckminster Fuller. Buckminster Fuller and John McHale, *World Design Science Decade (WDSD), Document 4* (Carbondale: World Resources Inventory, 1965) 111.

29.2 Courtesy of Constantinos and Emma Doxiadis Foundation. Constantinos Doxiadis, *The Future of Human Settlements*, Paper prepared for the Nobel Foundation symposium on "The Place of Value in a World of Facts," Stockholm, 19 September 1969. Constantinos A. Doxiadis Archives, Athens. Folder 6006.

29.3 Courtesy of Constantinos and Emma Doxiadis Foundation. Constantinos Doxiadis and John Papaioanou, *Ecumenopolis: the Inevitable City of the Future* (New York: Norton, 1974), 128.

29.4 Courtesy of Constantinos and Emma Doxiadis Foundation. Constantinos Doxiadis and John Papaioanou, *Ecumenopolis: the Inevitable City of the Future* (New York: Norton, 1974), 192-3.

29.5 Courtesy of Constantinos and Emma Doxiadis Foundation. Constantinos A. Doxiadis Archives, Athens. Folder 35982.

29.6   Courtesy of Constantinos and Emma Doxiadis Foundation. Constantinos Doxiadis and John Papaioanou, *Ecumenopolis: the Inevitable City of The Future* (New York: Norton, 1974), 368-9.

29.7   Courtesy of Constantinos and Emma Doxiadis Foundation. Constantinos A. Doxiadis Archives, Athens. Folder 26409.

29.8   Courtesy of Constantinos and Emma Doxiadis Foundation. *Ekistics* 47, 282 (1980), cover.

29.9   Courtesy of Constantinos A. Doxiadis Archives. Constantinos Doxiadis, *Ecology and Eekistics*, ed. Gerald Dix (Boulder: Westview Press, 1977) 28.

29.10 Courtesy of the Estate of R. Buckminster Fuller. Buckminster Fuller and Robert Marks, *The Dymaxion World of Buckminster Fuller* (New York: Reinhold, 1973), 153.

29.11 Courtesy of the Estate of R. Buckminster Fuller. Buckminster Fuller and Robert Marks, *The Dymaxion World of Buckminster Fuller* (New York: Reinhold, 1973) 141-2.

29.12 Courtesy of the Estate of R. Buckminster Fuller. Buckminster Fuller, "World energy map," *Fortune* 21, 2 (1940) 57.

29.13 Courtesy of the Estate of R. Buckminster Fuller. Buckminster Fuller, *The World Game: Integrative Resource Utilization Planning Tool.* (Carbondale: Southern Illinois University Press, 1971) 100.

29.14 Courtesy of the Estate of R. Buckminster Fuller. Buckminster Fuller, *The World Game: Integrative Resource Utilization Planning Tool.* (Carbondale: Southern Illinois University Press, 1971) 122-3.

29.15 Andrew Nelson, *Estimated travel time to the nearest city of 50,000 or more people in year 2000*. (Ispra Italy: Global Environment Monitoring Unit - Joint Research Centre of the European Commission, 2008). http://bioval.jrc.ec.europa.eu/products/gam.

29.16 World Wildlife Fund, Ecofys and Office for Metropolitan Architecture, *The Energy Report: 100% Renewable Energy by 2050* (Gland: World Wildlife Fund, 2011) 53.

30
CITY BECOMING WORLD: NANCY, LEFEBVRE AND THE GLOBAL-URBAN IMAGINATION

David J. Madden

Introduction: A Vast Urban Hive

> Will the city disappear or will the whole planet turn into a vast urban hive?—
> which would be another mode of disappearance.
>
> —Louis Mumford[1]

The twenty-first century is coming to be known as the moment when the planet became urban. For a growing number of analysts, boosters, critics and political actors, this is the era of megacities and urban hyper-development, an epoch marked by the demise of rural autonomy and the unprecedented permeation of the world by urban society. It is becoming part of the common sense of mainstream public discourse that the contemporary age is a "new urbanized era."[2] The United Nations and the World Bank seek to manage the "global urban expansion."[3] Think tanks mull the arrival of the "urban future."[4] Geologists debate the emergence of an "anthropocenic" epoch when human action transforms the planet and "Urbanisation totally dominates the huge metalogistical systems. ... that make up the contemporary world."[5] Geographers, planners, philosophers, economists and environmental historians all propose, from a wide range of perspectives, the idea that we are witnessing a "transition to a predominantly urban world."[6]

For much of the twentieth century, the urban globe was still what Henri Lefebvre considered to be a "possible object," an "illuminating virtuality."[7] Today, however, Lefebvre's virtual object seems to have become real. According to Soja and Kanai:

> More than ever before, it can be said that the Earth's entire surface is urbanized to some degree, from the Siberian tundra to the Brazilian rainforest to the icecap of Antarctica, perhaps even to the world's oceans and the atmosphere that we breathe. Of course, this does not mean that there are dense agglomerations everywhere, but the major features of urbanism as a way of life—from the play of market forces and the effects of administrative regulations, to popular cultural practices and practical geopolitics—are becoming ubiquitous. To a degree not seen before, no one on Earth is outside the sphere of influence of urban industrial capitalism.[8]

Soja and Kanai make clear that to speak of an urban planet is not to imagine that highways and skyscrapers cover the entire earth. Nor do theorists of the global-urban necessarily posit a "radical break" in the development of urban space, so much as numerous processes of sociospatial transformation.[9] What most statements of the global-urban imaginary do tend to share, despite their differences, is the notion that the planet no longer hosts discrete urban islands. Instead, there is a sprawling worldwide urbia, massively uneven and unequal and ranging across radically different social spaces, which has covered the globe and brought "the most remote parts of the world into its orbit and woven diverse areas, peoples, and activities into a cosmos."[10]

Planetary urbanization raises huge questions about politics, space and social knowledge. How can we understand the politics of the global-urban imagination? What counts as valid knowledge in urban studies for a world dominated by cities? Is what Mendieta calls "our conceptual gestalt of the planet" adequate to account for our planetary practices?[11] David Harvey has written, "acceptance of the globalization language is disempowering for all anti-capitalist and even moderately social democratic movements."[12] If that is the case, how can we even begin to formulate critical conceptions of the globe "without always already having accepted the discursive framework that makes it possible to talk about globalization"?[13] In our "global urban condition," can the city still function as normative ideal?[14] As Amin asks, "What remains of the urban as *demos* in these circumstances?"[15] In other words, what constitutes the urban globe and how can we reason about it politically?

This chapter attempts to address some of these questions through readings of key works by Jean-Luc Nancy and Henri Lefebvre. In contrast to many approaches to contemporary global urbanization that blanket and mystify the political questions at stake, these two thinkers offer critical theories of globalized urban society. Both Nancy and Lefebvre understand globalization as a fundamentally violent and unequal process that unfolds, at least in part, through the expansion of a particular sort of urban space. They both strive to articulate a critical stance towards this process by opposing to globalization the idea of *mondialisation* or world-forming, although their respective notions are rooted in different political impulses. As I shall argue, neither of their accounts fully resolves all of the theoretical quandaries surrounding the global-urban. But they both provide indispensable critical tools for conceptualizing the urban planet and its political possibilities.

While today's globe is the product of recent conditions, the emergence of an urban planet has been anticipated for more than one hundred years. Lefebvre notes, "Globalization and the planetary nature of the urban phenomenon. … appeared in science fiction novels before they were revealed to our understanding."[16] Indeed: at the dawn of the twentieth century, H. G. Wells predicted the "probable diffusion of great cities" which would usher in a future when "the city will diffuse itself until it has taken up considerable area and many of the characteristics … of what is now country … The old antithesis will indeed cease, the boundary lines will altogether disappear."[17] Not only science fiction writers and utopian socialists like Wells but also conservative intellectuals like Oswald Spengler imagined the coming of a future "World-City."[18] Patrick Geddes saw "conurbations" as representative of either unlivable "Kakotopia" or pleasant "Eutopia," both of which signified urbanism beyond city limits.[19] Functionalist sociologists and demographers like Kingsley Davis anticipated "complete world urbanization," the not-too-distant time when "rurality" will "have disappeared, leaving only a new kind of urban existence."[20] Futurists and planners such as K. A. Doxiadis imagined the coming of a worldwide "Ecumenopolis" when "the unified settlement of Anthropos will cover the entire globe," a form of life that will require the authoritarian rule of a technocratic "global leader."[21] As these brief examples demonstrate, the urban planet has been posited from a wide range of political and methodological perspectives.

Nancy and Lefebvre can be seen as critical voices in this larger tradition of imagining an urban globe. Their positions are particularly important today, when global economic conditions seem to foreclose the field of political possibility. Many narratives of globalization—such as Thomas Friedman's well-known vision of a flat world characterized, among other things, by mass rural-to-urban migration and global competition—use the specter of an interconnected planet in order to make neoliberal policies appear inevitable.[22] Proceeding from the image of an omnicompetitive, interlinked urban world, management consultants and business analysts compile intricate quantitative hierarchies of global cities that have the effect of steering politicians and planners further towards neoliberal urban policies.[23] Movements in urban design associated with "new urbanism" and the "creative city" draw upon a similar global-urban imaginary to promote the desirability and necessity of "returning" to relocalized urban space. And other contemporary voices, such as that of Edward Glaeser, promote reinvestment in urbanism on the grounds of economic efficiency. In all of these cases, market-centric political claims are bolstered by particular global-urban imaginaries.[24]

As critics of these ideas have pointed out, each of these new urbanisms can be seen as compatible with an unequal urban order, if not generative of new forms of inequality.[25] And as these examples show, many usages of concepts such as globalism, cosmopolitanism, community and urbanity are unable to articulate critical perspectives on today's city or world. In contrast, both Nancy and Lefebvre provide critical global-urban imaginaries. I will not attempt here to provide comprehensive overviews of their social thought, nor do I intend to affirm one over the other. Rather, by exploring the ways in which they imagine the global-urban, I want to show how both Lefebvre and Nancy point towards new theory and new political possibilities for an urban planet.

Urbs et orbis

> These days, it seems like the world is being stolen from the world, at the very moment it's becoming "worldwide," at the very moment of globalization.
> —Jean-Luc Nancy[26]

In *The Creation of the World or Globalization*, Jean-Luc Nancy asks, "can what is called 'globalization' give rise to a world, or to its contrary?"[27] This question at first seems to be nonsense. But Nancy's "critical way of thinking the world," drawing from Hegel, Marx, Derrida and especially Heidegger, is built upon a number of important contrasts, and one of the most central is the distinction between different meanings of "the world."[28] Nancy argues that two senses of "the world" are generally conflated: "world as the givenness of what exists" and "world as a globality of sense."[29] The former sense of "world" is merely the sum total of things in existence, as in the phrase "everything in the world." In contrast, the latter is "a totality of meaning. If [for example] I speak of 'Debussy's world' … one grasps immediately that one is speaking of a totality, to which a certain meaningful content or a certain value system properly belongs."[30] A world in this latter sense means a meaningful, shared context. Worldhood here implies "an ethos, a *habitus* and an inhabiting."[31] A group that holds anything in common—living in proximity, or sharing vulnerability to disease, say—can be said to exist in the same world in the first sense. But in order to qualify as sharing a world in the second sense, they need to be able to form this bare world into something more sensible or inhabitable—to be able to communicate dialogically, for example, or to cooperatively transform the conditions of their coexistence.

This contrast underpins another distinction that Nancy deploys, between globalization and *mondialisation*. The former refers to the integration of world in the first sense. It has "up to this point been limited to economic and technological matters."[32] Globalization links together the world, but its links are purely formal. As I shall explain, globalization, as "enclosure in the undifferentiated sphere of a unitotality," has something threatening and overwhelming about it.[33] The qualities of enclosure, finality and totalistic lack of differentiation are central to it. *Mondialisation*, in contrast, stands for incompleteness, becoming, openness, natality. The term refers to becoming-worldwide, or "worldwide becoming," "world-forming" or the "creation of the world." It could be put as "worldization," or perhaps as "worlding."[34] It refers to the emergence of a world in the second sense of a shared context or dwelling. Nancy is not the only theorist to make use of the globalization/*mondialisation* distinction.[35] Jacques Derrida, one of Nancy's mentors and inspirations, used these same terms in a number of interviews in the late 1990s, a few years before *The Creation of the World* was originally published.[36] But Nancy is probably this distinction's most systematic and creative user.

Considering that "*mondialisation*" is the French equivalent to "globalization" in English, there is obviously some potential for confusion. Indeed, the terms present perennial problems for translators.[37] But Nancy would insist that this confusion is actually a symptom. He casts the English language as something like the official dialect of neoliberal economic integration. The English word "globalization" thus names precisely a process where the distinctiveness of the world is drowned by something becoming ubiquitous. Whereas *mondialisation* suggests something else: the emergence of a world that is open-ended and creative, a way of social existence that is necessarily shared and inherently unique. That is why Nancy insists that "*mondialisation* preserves something untranslatable while *globalization* has already translated everything."[38]

Globalization, for Nancy, has unfolded over centuries. It is the process whereby "the West has come to encompass the world," where scientific modernity colonizes the planet and severs all connection to an otherworld.[39] Globalization is constituted by a long process of secularization and disenchantment. Nancy sees "the modern enigma" as "the end of the world," in the sense of loss of order and orientation.[40] "There is no longer any world: no longer a *mundus*, a *cosmos*, a composed and complete order (from) within which one might find a place, a dwelling, and the elements of an orientation."[41] There is now only *this* world, with no constitutive outside or next-world—neither a transcendent god nor external nature—from which to provide limit or meaning. The process of becoming-global—so far it has been only technological and economic—removed the beyond-world that had been the source of our "sense of the world," which now must be formulated, by us, from within this world.[42]

This centuries-long process of globalization has entered a new stage with the increased integration of the planet into a social and spatial system dominated by the world market of neoliberal techno-capitalism. Nancy's critique is that with this phase of globalization, "the world has lost its capacity to 'form a world' (*faire monde*)."[43] Not only is globalization the creation of a whole (in the first sense) that is not a world (in the second sense), it is the *opposite* of world-forming, in that it means "the suppression of all world-forming of the world."[44] In fact Nancy identifies globalization with "that capacity of proliferating the unworld"—*immonde*, which also means unclean, vile or sinful.[45] Globalization here is the proliferation of something uninhabitable, something deadly. Indeed, for Nancy, global experience today originates in the concrete possibility of planetary destruction. "The fact that the world is destroying itself is ... the fact from which any thinking of the world follows."[46] If anything today is global or universal, it is the threat of catastrophe, insecurity and terror, a worldwide "death drive," which is increasingly experienced by all—and which thus raises planetary being as a question.[47]

There are many different ways of forming a planetary whole. Everything on Earth could become linked together. But if this whole only brings with it a common danger rather than shared agency, it is not the dawn of some new global society, not the creation of a world in Nancy's second sense, but instead just a "piling up," the accumulation of junk, "an unprecedented geopolitical, economic, and ecological catastrophe."[48] It is one of Nancy's main goals to highlight the distinction between these two forms of totality, a distinction not captured by the usual narratives about globalization.

Central to Nancy's stance here is that globalization entails the homogenization of sense and a flattening of meaning. Perhaps in response to this, Nancy's discussion includes a number of puns and translinguistic epithets. He writes that, as colonized by globalization, the Earth, which would be (in Latin) *globus*, the sphere of the world, is actually just a ball, *glomus*, which he links to the word "agglomeration," a piling-up that is often associated with conurbation. "The agglomeration invades and erodes what used to be thought of as *globe* and which is nothing more now than its double, *glomus*."[49] Nancy names the "globality" of *glomus* as "*glomicity*," a horrific blob-world marked by "indefinite growth of techno-science, of a correlative exponential growth of populations, of a worsening of inequalities of all sorts" and "the circulation of everything in the form of commodity."[50] Despite this lexical cheekiness, the simultaneous covering and stripping bare of the globe—its glomalization, as it were—is a deadly serious matter characterized by inequality, death and suffering. As he has it, the *glomus* of globalization "is not a 'world': it is a 'globe' or a 'glome,' it is a 'land of exile' and a 'vale of tears.'"[51]

This is where Nancy's account of globalization reconnects with urban questions. The language of *glomus* brings Nancy's critique of globalization into contact with the tradition of literary social criticism that imagines an urban planet as an anarchic, polluted dystopia. One of the hallmarks of globalization, and a sign of its unworldliness, is the planetary diffusion of a certain kind of debased urban space. The urban is not some "local" antithesis to the global; here globalization unfolds through urbanization. With globalization, "it is no longer possible to identify either the city or the orb of the world in general."[52] The same process of agglomeration that erodes the spacing of the world also erases the order of the city.

> The city spreads and extends all the way to the point where, while it tends to cover the entire orb of the planet, it loses its properties as a city, and, of course with them, those properties that would allow it to be distinguished from a "country." That which extends in this way is no longer properly "urban"—either from the perspective of urbanism or from that of urbanity—but megapolitical,

metropolitan, or co-urbational, or else caught in the loose net of what is called the "urban network."[53]

Nancy criticizes this "urban network" on the grounds that it is deracinated, starkly violent and unequal, a space marked by "inequality and apartheid" rather than the "dwelling, comfort and culture" that he identifies with the properly "urban milieu."[54] For Nancy, agglomeration disperses the city such that it is no longer city at all, but a distended spatial network.

He casts the urban network as a kind of bare cityhood that "on the one hand, simply concentrates (in a few neighborhoods, in a few houses, sometimes in a few protected mini-cities) the well-being that used to be urban or civil, while on the other hand, proliferates what bears the quite simple and unmerciful name of misery."[55] The figure of the city here represents a lost compass or lost order, and Nancy associates it with a lost religious ordering of the city and world. "*Urbi et orbi*: this formulation drawn from papal benediction has come to mean 'everywhere and anywhere' in ordinary language. Rather than a mere shift in meaning, this is a genuine disintegration."[56] Instead of an *urbs* emplaced in an *orbis*, Nancy argues, there is just a conurbation, and this "network cast upon the planet—and already around it, in the orbital band of satellites along with their debris—deforms the *orbis* as much as the *urbs*."[57] He might have been more straightforward here regarding the sources of global misery, which are far likelier to be found in the political economy of social space than in its dispersal and loss of ordering *per se*. But in arguing that the centrifugal disbandment of the city forecloses its potential as place of common being, he raises genuine questions about urban imaginaries and the spatial organization of power in a global age.

It is important to place this discussion in the larger context of Nancy's thought. Without it, the multiple narratives of loss—loss of meaning, loss of order, loss of certainty, loss of cityhood—might suggest a nostalgic yearning for communal wholeness. But these readings should be rejected, as Nancy is no communitarian. When he writes of community, it is "community without communion."[58] For Nancy, all existence is coexistence; "being singular plural" (Nancy, 2000) is the basic moment of the social. Otherness is originary, and "one appears to oneself insofar as one is already an other for oneself."[59] His larger political-philosophical project is to rethink community, identity and the social from a post-foundationalism that specifically denies immanent wholeness or atomistic individualism.[60]

For Nancy, the product of globalization is a compressed, conurbated planet, and it is not a nice place. It results from knitting together the planet into a sort of whole, but a whole without proper spacing, a totality that does not, in his view, provide an opening or a place for dwelling. What is this notion of *mondialisation* that he considers an alternative? Though he is clearly skeptical of the idea of complete emancipation or liberation, Nancy can be read to offer, if not a "way out," then at least a critical response to the global-urban experience.

When Nancy affirms *mondialisation*, he means struggle "*to create the world*: immediately, without delay, reopening each possible struggle for a world."[61] A true world is "precisely that in which there is room for everyone: but a genuine place, one in which things can genuinely take place (in this world). Otherwise it is not a 'world.'"[62] This is a politics of plurality and difference. World-forming means "sharing singularity (always plural)."[63] As he puts it, "A world is a multiplicity of worlds," and so being worldly requires egalitarian, communicative practices of "sharing out" and "mutual exposure."[64] But this should not be confused with garden-variety multiculturalism, liberal pluralism or cosmopolitan consumerism—Nancy is pushing at something more radical. He blends together ideas from Spinoza, Marx, and Lacan and argues that world-forming would be the "shared appropriation … of what cannot be accumulated" based upon a human "excess of enjoyment" beyond the realm of necessity.[65]

Mondialisation is never one movement or project but "a thousand revolts, a thousand rages, a thousand creations."[66] He invokes the spirit of struggle. It is definitely not the classical Marxian narrative of class struggle, an idea that "seems insufficient—precisely because it is a 'figure,' an organizing scheme, and because 'struggle' still refers to classical combat, force against force."[67] But Nancy argues, "Marx's demand is not obsolete."[68] He is not aiming to repudiate the anti-capitalist imagination but to reformulate the perspective from which that tradition can be articulated.[69] *Mondialisation* is "a matter of creating the meaning" of this demand anew. Central to this ethic of struggle is the constant movement of the horizon of politics itself. "New forms of struggle or resistance are now being invented, or at least should be."[70]

Nancy sees *mondialisation* as a struggle for justice—"straightaway and definitively a matter of concrete equality and actual justice."[71] But it is, as he puts it elsewhere, "'justice' without foundation or end," the meaning of which comes precisely from its permanent incompleteness, from the challenge of creating shared justice in a world without foundations.[72] He offers a never-ending struggle to define justice as the true infinite and thus the counterpoint to the bad infinity of capitalist accumulation. Ultimately, *mondialisation* means "struggle precisely in the name of the fact that this *world* is coming out of nothing, that there is nothing before it and that it is without models, without principle and without given end, and that is precisely *what* forms the justice and the meaning of a world."[73] As some commentators have noted, Nancy can appear to offer only a critical, negative politics.[74] It is true that for all of his emphasis on creation, his language surrounding *mondialisation* is permeated by negativity. But this refusal to foreclose is his central ethical and political gesture.

I would argue that Nancy makes an important critical contribution to the discourse of the global-urban. He invents a new language through which to interpret global agglomeration. The distinction between globalization and *mondialisation* makes possible a position from which one can critique at once techno-utopianism, nostalgic communitarianism and market fundamentalism. Globalization is usually seen as a unidirectional process, the progressive expansion of economic reason and techniques across the planet. Nancy opens a complicating dimension: there are in fact dueling processes of world-erasing and world-forming. By calling our attention to these competing, antagonistic forms of being global, he reminds us that real globality involves creation, possibility, and equality.

But at the same time, it does not reduce the critical power of Nancy's arguments to suggest that he might ultimately be more interested in city and world as philosophical figures rather than as geographical or sociological ones. By seeing the problem of political community foremost as an existential dilemma—about how to exist with others in a world without pre-given sense—some crucial questions are never satisfactorily resolved and some important distinctions are elided. How can we think through spatial and social difference in the agglomerated world that Nancy describes? By understanding questions about the world as questions about existence *per se*, it becomes difficult to account for the inequalities and differential miseries that glomal denizens experience. The distinction between world and unworld may be too stark. Does globalization promote any new strategic sites or political opportunities? From his perspective, what are we to make of informal, peri-urban housing, which, as represented in global "slum" studies, constitutes precisely a struggle for inhabitation in the midst of apparently uninhabitable agglomeration?[75] The creation of worlds from within unworld suggest that globalism may be more ambivalent and contradictory than these seemingly absolute categories would allow.

Connected to this, the language of world and unworld misses those practices that proliferate both. It is one thing to make the argument that a world is not a world if it is not shared and does not have room for everyone. But it is easy to think of examples where one project for well-being, dwelling and coexistence functions to block or destroy other competing projects—and it is difficult to see how an ethic of worldhood and inhabitation could help adjudicate between them. Contemporary political reason rarely faces an absolute choice between world or unworld. What is needed is more subtle language that attends to the complexity and mutability of concrete global-urban spaces.

Finally, is there anything about cityhood specifically that might encourage the sort of struggles that Nancy affirms? By connecting the violence of globalization to the loss of urban coherence and order, he leaves us with the suggestion that some sort of re-urbanization could be part of the *mondialisation* of the world. But this seems to invoke an order of the city that is now impossible and, from Nancy's own position, undesirable. If the classical connection between urbanism and *polis* is now decisively occluded by the urbanization of the world, can there be a new connection between urbanity and world-forming? Nancy suggests that this might be the case, but the point remains unclear.

Urban Society and Urban Revolution

> Will you try to find a crack for freedom to slip through, silently filling up the empty spaces, sliding through the interstices? Good old freedom, you know it well. It needs a "world," neither a completely empty nor a completely full one.
>
> —Henri Lefebvre[76]

Compared to Nancy, Henri Lefebvre anchors his account of globalization much more firmly in a story about the development of urban space itself. "I'll begin with the following hypothesis: Society has been completely urbanized.... An *urban society* is a society that results from a process of complete urbanization. This urbanization is virtual today but it will become real in the future."[77] These lines open *The Urban Revolution*, one of many works where Lefebvre provides a picture of urban modernity in upheaval, transgressing older bounds in a process of global colonization. In *The Right to the City*, originally from 1967; *The Urban Revolution*, originally from 1970; in some of his 1970s-era texts recently published as *State, Space, World*; and elsewhere, Lefebvre envisions the urbanization of society and the formation of planetary social space.[78] Like Nancy, Lefebvre distinguishes between worldly inhabiting and global agglomeration, and attempts to think the former as an antidote to the injustices of the latter.

Lefebvre introduces a distinction between "the city" and "the urban," where "the city" represents bounded, traditional cityhood, in contrast to "the urban" or urban society, which is much more diffuse and attenuated. Lefebvre argues that there has been a shift "from the city to urban society," a shift that coincides with the most recent phase of globalization and which necessitates a rethinking of social space in general.[79] On more than one occasion, he proposes a hypothetical scale, from zero to maximum urbanization.[80] At the zero point, he posits "'pure nature,' the earth abandoned to the elements," or what he later calls "absolute space."[81] Moving outwards from the zero point, Lefebvre places the "political city," the "commercial city," and the "industrial city," respectively, the details of which do not concern us here. What does concern us is where Lefebvre placed (then-) contemporary society: near the maximum limit, in what he calls the "critical zone." This is a place of crisis where the industrial city is being dismantled and something new is emerging: "complete urbanization."[82] In this condition, urbanization is not a by-product of industrialization or political authority but itself "becomes a productive force."[83] This process of the urban-becoming-global, of "generalized urbanization" is partly what Lefebvre means by the phrase "urban revolution."[84] Just as the Industrial Revolution marked the emergence of a new form of transformative, worldwide industry, so too, the urban revolution marks the onset of a new phase of transformative, planetary urbanism.

In this process, the morphologies of industrial urbanism do not disappear. Quite the opposite: the forms of traditional urbanism persist, but they are transformed and integrated with one another in a new way. "The 'urban-rural' relation does not disappear" but instead "intensifies itself down to the most industrialized countries"; likewise, "urban cores do not disappear" but instead "survive by transforming themselves."[85] Neither downtown nor "nature" disappears. What Lefebvre sees happening is the "implosion-explosion" of the city, whereby urban society spreads across the entire globe in a process of continual, tumultuous uneven development.[86]

Complete urbanization, it is clear, is not "complete" in the sense of reaching an end-stage or final destination. Urbanization links the world together, but it continues to change and develop. A continuum between zero and completeness implies quite strongly that Lefebvre sees global-urbanization as a linear process. But this might be a misleading simplification on his part. Throughout his urban writings he describes a discontinuous history rather than the growth of a stable and scalable object. Urbanization moves, haltingly, in the direction of greater complexity, but nowhere does he mention any complete end-state, and such an idea is not a necessary part of his thought.

In order to represent the integration-fragmentation of the world becoming global, Lefebvre uses a series of metaphors of human-made webs: networks, patchworks and fibers. He describes an "urban fabric" that "grows, extends its borders" and weaves together diverse corners of the globe.[87] "More than a fabric thrown over a territory, these words designate a kind of biological proliferation of a net of uneven mesh, allowing more or less extended sectors to escape."[88] As with similar motifs in Nancy, for Lefebvre the fabric imagery captures a number of important qualities of the global-urban. Through countless separate connectors, a network weaves together a decentered multitude of points. A patchwork is constitutively uneven; the "thickness" of the urban fabric varies greatly. The idea of a fabric or blanket problematizes the relationship between whole and part. It is *not* that the global is "the big" in contrast to something else, such as the local, that is "the small." Rather, like a textile or cloth, urban society is that form of social life where all points in a totality are potentially interactive with one another, albeit unevenly. It is not a matter of size but of relationships and qualities. The ubiquitous contemporary network-speak can be traced partly to mid-twentieth century urbanism to which Lefebvre is responding.[89] But rather than affirming networked-being as a form of technical efficiency or an ideal of anti-essentialist freedom, Lefebvre uses the language of networks to capture the contradictory character of a type of social space that is at once "homogenizing," "fragmenting," and "hierarchizing."[90]

The urbanization of society is more than just a spatial process—it also involves forms of knowledge and frames for action. For Lefebvre, "The urban problematic, urbanism as ideology and institution, urbanization as a worldwide trend, are global facts."[91] The concept of the *problématique* was in wider circulation in 1960s French Marxist thought, especially associated with Louis Althusser. For Lefebvre to say that the urban problematic becomes global is not to make a claim about the totalization of any particular urban form. Rather, it is to say that what becomes planetary is the urban as a question, as a theoretical framework, as a conceptual object of struggle. "Urban questions and movements … emerge, they appear and disappear pretty much everywhere in the world. The problems posed by the modern city…are worldwide problems."[92] By "urban problems" we can understand not crime or congestion but the question of producing social space in the world-as-city.

As with Nancy, Lefebvre's conception of the urban planet focuses on the unequal, and dominating nature of social and economic life therein. Urban life threatens to destroy the planet in an act of "terricide."[93] Quoting René Thom, Lefebvre refers to planetary space as a "space of catastrophe," distinguished by a number of dangers: exploitation, inequality and class domination; environmental degradation; stultification and oppression in the form of state-socialist and state-capitalist planning; the quotidian "terrorism" of the "bureaucratic society of controlled consumption."[94] Planetary urban space is, above all else, a space of "violence," where "a formidable force of homogenization exerts itself on a worldwide scale, producing a space whose every part is interchangeable (quantified, without qualities)."[95] Lefebvre's urban planet is a manifestly unequal globe dominated by brutal political and economic instrumentalities.

To a large extent, then, Lefebvre and Nancy present very similar criticisms of the global-urban. Lefebvre writes, "Mounting a critique of the confusions surrounding the term 'world' may be increasingly a key issue for reflective thought."[96] Like Nancy, and drawing on their shared Heideggerian influence, Lefebvre sees the creation of the world as a technological product as the loss of the world that can only be rectified through political praxis.[97] But Lefebvre does not conceptualize the violence of globalization through the category of "unworld," and as a result, compared to Nancy, his account is much more contradiction-laden and paradoxical. Precisely because global urbanism universalizes, socializes and totalizes society, it lays the foundation for its own critical resistance. To some extent, for Lefebvre, the problematic of worldhood activates older associations with political agency in new ways. "The *world* revolution—through which the world will become a 'world'—is happening, in ways that are stranger, richer and more unexpected than were ever imagined a century ago."[98] But he emphasizes that social conditions have changed since nineteenth-century *laissez-faire* industrial capitalism and so too must the radical imagination. In the early 1960s, channeling Rimbaud, Lefebvre wrote, "Revolution must be reinvented, but first we must recognize—*recognize*—it!"[99] By the late 1960s, he was arguing that revolution, through which the world could become worldly, should be rethought as *urban revolution*.

Despite his scathing criticisms of the global-urban fabric, in "urban life" Lefebvre still sees an irreducible opening or opportunity, what he calls the "*non-closing* of the circuit."[100] Whereas Nancy conceives of something similar as an opening onto the sharing of singular-plurality, Lefebvre offers the more concrete project of a reactivation of the political possibilities of urbanism itself. A reconceived, transformed and transformative urbanism—which was an uneasy suggestion for Nancy—is at the center of Lefebvre's notion of the urban world. Another meaning of the phrase "urban revolution" thus emerges. It can be understood not only as a way to describe radically-changed social relations, but can also be used in a more intentional sense—as a transformation that is actively sought, rather than only experienced. Lefebvre's position is that with the shift from industrial society to urban society, the politics of resistance and emancipation can no longer be located within the industrial experience and instead must be found within the urban experience. The emergence of the global-urban makes possible, but does not guarantee, urbanism as a new kind of transformational politics.

Elsewhere, Lefebvre invokes "the ghost of revolution," and here there is a similar sense of postmortem return.[101] The condition of possibility for the right to the city is the death of the city. He writes that the "city historically constructed is no longer lived and is no longer understood practically. It is only an object of cultural consumption for tourists, for aestheticism, avid for spectacles and the picturesque." But despite the end of the city, "the *urban* remains in a state of dispersed and alienated actuality, as kernel and virtuality."[102] In other words, beneath the spectacular but cruel global cityscape, there remains some hard core of critical potentiality within urbanism itself. The eternal return of radical urban movements across the world would seem to be a manifestation of this idea. Hence Lefebvre declares: "Urban life has yet to begin."[103] This paradoxical claim—that the city is over but some new, truer urbanism has in fact not yet even begun—is the center of Lefebvre's critical stance.

I would argue that it is in fact only in this context that one can properly understand Lefebvre's notion of the "right to the city." It is often glossed as the "right to urban life" or the right to inhabit, and discussed as a desired but not yet established claim to centrality, place, equality, public space, participation and citizenship.[104] But the right to the city must be more than a demand for the good life. It is arguably only against the backdrop of the *end* of the city, and its replacement by urban society, that the concept of the right to the city can be seen in its fully ironic originality. Lefebvre is not urging some sort of return to the existing city. He is challenging urban inhabitants to develop *new* spaces, institutional forms and political frames.

What does this mean for Lefebvre in essence to replace a narrative of politics rooted in the contradictions of industrial capitalism with one rooted in the contradictions of global urbanism? It means that resistance will not primarily come from industrial contexts and conflicts—it will come from urban conflicts, in all of their complexity. His picture of urban revolution is, like the idea of *mondialisation*, a political ethic that affirms, in an abstract way, local struggles in their singularity as prime examples of worlding. Lefebvre's urban revolution would "gather the interests (overcoming the immediate and the superficial) of the whole society and firstly of all those who *inhabit*."[105] A movement of this sort would agitate for social capacities of urban inhabitation—not only a question of housing but of the capacity to collectively produce urban space more generally.

Lefebvre wants an urbanism that breaks down unequal "segregation" and strengthens pluralistic and egalitarian "difference."[106] And he proposes a radical program of "urban reforms" to change urban capitalism and urban institutional structures as far as possible, a reformism that he thinks can become "revolutionary" if pushed far enough.[107] He wants radical urbanism to make a space for audacious, utopian, unrealistic "planning projects" that might help urbanites to rethink what is possible or desirable, as part of a larger effort to radically transform urban planning.[108] In other words, Lefebvre envisions an urban social movement that will address itself towards all of those practices that produce urban space in global conditions. His line here is not necessarily consistent. By the original 1974 publication of *Production of Space,* he seems to have jettisoned the phrase, if not the notion, of the right to the city.[109] But even in that work there is the sense that as a politics of space, as a spatial problematic, urbanism still holds critical potential.

As Peter Marcuse has recently pointed out, the notion of the "right to the city" only makes sense if Lefebvre is arguing for a revolutionary transformation of economy and politics.[110] If "the city" is understood to be any actually existing city, then Lefebvre is imagining a movement that is, by his own reasoning, impossible both logically and practically. If the city has ended, then the right to the city is the right to nothing. The city that Lefebvre imagines, then, must be a future version of the urban world, one that has yet to come into existence. This might be utopianism, but it is utopianism based upon a critique of the urban world as it exists. He sees globalization-urbanization as that process which produces planetary urban space, and thus imagines that a radical urban politics is not only still possible, but the only possibility. Whatever specific form this takes—radical environmentalism, some kind of regionalist anarchism or municipal socialism are all plausible applications—a faithful understanding of Lefebvre's conception of urban society must always emphasize his insistence on urban *revolution* that transforms the global urbia rather than merely reveling in it.

Lefebvre's position here raises a number of problems, many of which stem from the fact that his critical-utopianism can be easily misunderstood, misconstrued or forgotten. Without an insistence upon political-economic transformation, the affirmation of urbanism can easily degrade into cheerleading for conspicuous neighborhood consumption, "smart" technocracy or renewal-as-gentrification—the sort of policies that a segment of planners, politicians and real estate developers pursue everywhere in the name of "livability" and the "creative" city. Today, precisely when older critical perspectives have been abandoned, discourses about dwelling, inhabitation, the right to the city, indeed urbanism itself, always threaten, as if by radioactive decay, to lose their critical content and sink back into a neoliberal lifestyle politics. Lefebvre's critical urban theory clearly provides the conceptual resources with which to resist such a reading. But that particular understanding of the concepts of dwelling and inhabitation is an ever-present possibility in today's political scene.

Even if the right to the city is not mistaken for neoliberal urbanism, there are some other questions to be raised. There is still no fully developed theory here about the mechanics of how planetary urban space will contribute to its own transformation—there is mostly the suggestion that it can and should. There is no real account here of how, say, public space, critical planning or the urban process more generally might encourage a transformative urban politics, and no theory about how to handle clashes of interests between different urban inhabitants. Indeed, there is still little here about the specificity of the urban itself, and Lefebvre often appears to be urging a more general politics of inhabitation. This would not, in itself, be a problem, but it raises the question once more about the persistence of the urban in his urban revolution.

And while we can accept his point about the centrality of urban conflicts in contemporary struggles, we should be careful in distinguishing between the urban and the industrial. In a world filled with mass-produced commodities, the notion of the end of industrialism is highly questionable, and Lefebvre would be the first to stress that industrial conflicts do not disappear. We can accept his arguments that urban politics are not reducible to industrial politics and become relatively more central, the more that the urban fabric thickens across the globe. But we still need to clarify the complex relationships between industrial and urban struggles.

Ultimately, however, I do not think that these questions undermine Lefebvre's more basic goal. It is clear from the tone of his urban writings that his aim is less to provide a complete political sociology of urban society than it is to open a conceptual space within which a transformation of the urban globe can be imagined. Certainly, important theoretical questions remain. But he clearly succeeds at the important task of crafting a new critical vocabulary for global-urban society.

Conclusion: The World as an Opening

> *Globalization* names a process which universalizes technology, economy, politics, and even civilization and culture. But it remains somewhat empty. The world as an *opening* is missing … The thing that is called *globalization* is a kind of *mondialisation* without the world.
>
> –Kostas Alexos[111]

The global-urban imagination is becoming central to the present age. One recent event where the political connotations of the urban age discourse were particularly striking was the 2010 World Expo in Shanghai, which had the theme of "A Better City, A Better Life." It is typical of world's fairs to combine nation-branding and technological demonstrations with a "culture of heroic consumption."[112] But this event was perhaps unique in the extent to which it linked the themes of urbanization and planetary existence with the promotion of a supposedly benign urban techno-utopia. In pavilions named City Being,

Urban Footprint, Urban Future, Urban Planet and Urbanian, a series of exhibits offered a vivid journey across our planet, taking as its starting point the inevitability of technocratic statecraft, universal urbanization and manageable climate change. Videos, models and dioramas displayed planning techniques, corporate accomplishments, lifestyle innovations, engineering schemes and scientific achievements from around the world that will solve the logistical and environmental problems of the present and future. In an exhibit on "utopias" and "ideal cities," columns were decorated to resemble piles of giant-sized editions of key books in urban studies, including *Spaces of Hope*, *Invisible Cities*, *The City in History*, *The New Atlantis* and *The Urban Revolution*. The room suggested that the cities of the future will be supported by the utopias of the past. But only the books' spines were visible. And in all of the materials on city planning and urban design, nowhere was anything mentioned that resembled democracy or participatory politics.

The specifics of contemporary Chinese capitalism and politics notwithstanding, Expo 2010 presented one of the most common uses of the motif of an urban planet. Through text, graphics and architecture, the Expo communicated the message that technology and density will carry humanity forward to a harmonious future, to a world that will be interconnected even as it will continue to be structured by walls and barriers. It suggested that the horizon of politics lies in the development of progressively smarter solutions by an alliance of business, science and authoritarian state and city governments. The global-urban problematic, from this perspective, is above all a question of efficiency and proper management, where political contentiousness, like pollution, is one more problem to be solved.

Notes

1   Lewis Mumford, *The City in History: Its Origin, its Transformations, and its Prospects* (New York: Harvest Books, 1989 [1961]) 3.

2   Parag Khanna, "Beyond City Limits," *Foreign Policy* 181 (2010) 122.

3   Shlomo Angel, Stephen C. Sheppard and Daniel L. Civco, "The Dynamics of Global Urban Expansion," Transportation and Urban Development Department, The World Bank (2005); Department of Economic and Social Affairs (UN-DESA), *World Urbanization Prospects, 2007 Revision*, United Nations (2008); and UN Development Programme (UN-DP), *A Home in the City: Improving the Lives of Slum Dwellers* (New York: United Nations, 2005).

4   Worldwatch Institute, *State of the World: Our Urban Future* (Washington: Worldwatch Institute, 2007).

5   Jan Zalasiewicz, Mark Williams, Alan Smith and others, "Are We Now Living in the Anthropoocene?" *GSA Today* 18, 2 (2008) 4-8; Paul J. Crutzen, "The Geology of Mankind," *Nature* 415, 23 (3 Jan 2002); and Mike Hodson and Simon Marvin, "Urbanism in the Anthropocene: Ecological Urbanism or Premium Ecological Enclaves?" *City* 14, 3 (2010) 300.

6   See, among other works, Edward W. Soja and J. Miguel Kanai, "The Urbanization of the World," this book, Ch. 10; Christian Schmid, "Networks, Borders, Differences," this book, Ch. 4; Tony Champion and Graeme Hugo, eds., *New Forms of Urbanization: Beyond the Urban-Rural Dichotomy* (Burlington: Ashgate, 2004); Edward W. Soja, *Postmetropolis: Critical Studies of Cities and Regions* (Malden: Wiley Blackwell, 2000); David Clark, "Interdependent Urbanization in an Urban World: An Historical Overview," *The Geographical Journal* 164, 1 (1998) 85-95; Thomas Sieverts, *Cities*

Without Cities: an Interpretation of the Zwischenstadt (New York: Spon Press, 2003); David Cunningham, "The Concept of the Metropolis: Philosophy and Urban Form," *Radical Philosophy* 133 (2005) 13-25; Alastair S. Gunn, "Rethinking Communities: Environmental Ethics in an Urbanized World," *Environmental Ethics* 20 (1998) 341-60; Mark R. Montgomery, "The Urban Transformation of the Developing World," *Science* 319 (2008) 761-4; J. R. McNeill, *Something New Under the Sun: an Environmental History of the Twentieth-century World*, (New York: Norton, 2000) 269-95; and David Satterthwaite, "The Transition to a Predominantly Urban World and its Underpinnings," *Human Settlement Discussion Paper, Series 4, International Institute for Environment and Development* 3 (2007).

7   Henri Lefebvre, *The Urban Revolution*, trans. Robert Bonnono (Minneapolis: University of Minnesota, 2003 [1970]) 5, 17.

8   Edward W. Soja and J. Miguel Kanai, "The Urbanization of the World," this book, Ch. 10, page 150.

9   Robert A. Beauregard, "The Radical Break in Late Twentieth-century Urbanization," *Area* 38, 2 (2006) 218-20.

10   Louis Wirth, "Urbanism as a Way of Life," *American Journal of Sociology* 44, 1 (1938) 2.

11   Eduardo Mendieta, "Invisible Cities: a Phenomenology of Globalization from *Below*," *City* 5, 1 (2001) 7.

12   David Harvey, *Justice, Nature and the Geography of Difference* (Malden: Blackwell, 1996) 429.

13   Urs Stäheli, "The Outside of the Global," *The New Centennial Review* 3, 2 (2003) 6.

14   Neil Brenner, David J. Madden and David Wachsmuth, "Assemblage

521

Urbanism and the Challenges of Critical Urban Theory," *City* 15, 2 (2011) 226; and Iris Young, "City Life and Differnce," *Justice and the Politics of Difference* (Princeton: Princeton University, 1990).

15 Ash Amin, "The Good City," *Urban Studies* 43, 5/6 (2006) 1011.

16 Henri Lefebvre, *Writings on Cities*, eds. and trans. Eleonore Kofman and Elizabeth Lebas (Cambridge: Blackwell, 1996) 113.

17 H. G. Wells, *Anticipations of the Reaction of Mechanical and Scientific Progress upon Human Life and Thought* (New York: Harper & Brothers, 1901) 70.

18 Oswald Spengler, *The Decline of the West* (New York: Oxford University Press, 1991 [1932]).

19 Patrick Geddes, *Cities in Evolution* (London: Williams & Norgate, 1949 [1925]).

20 Kingsely Davis, "The Origin and Growth of Urbanization in the World," *American Journal of Sociology* 60, 5 (1955) 437.

21 Konstantinos Doxiadis and J. G. Papaioannou, *Ecumenopolis: The Inevitable City of the Future* (New York: W. W. Norton, 1974) 343, 382. See also Nikos Katsikis, "Two Approaches to 'World Management': C.A. Doxiadis and R.B. Fuller," this book, Ch. 29.

22 Thomas Friedman, *The World is Flat: A Brief History of the Twenty-first Century* (New York: Farrar, Straus, and Giroux, 2005).

23 For example, Richard Dobbs, Sven Smit, Jaana Remes, James Manyika, Charles Roxburgh and Alejandra Restrepo, "Urban Mapping: Mapping the Economic Power of Cities," McKinsey Global Institute (2011).

24 Edward Glaeser, *Triumph of the City: How Our Greatest Invention Makes Us Richer, Smarter, Greener, Healthier, and Happier* (New York: Penguin, 2011).

25 For example, Jennifer Robinson, *Ordinary Cities: Between Modernity and Development* (New York: Routledge, 2006); Jamie Peck, "Struggling with the Creative Class," *International Journal of Urban and Regional Research* 29, 4 (2005) 740-50; Neil Brenner and Nik Theodore, eds., *Spaces of Neoliberalism: Urban Restructuring in North America and Western Europe* (Malden: Blackwell, 2002); and Ute Angelika Lehrer and Richard Milgrom, "New (Sub)Urbanism: Countersprawl or Repackaging the Product," *Capitalism, Nature, Socialism* 7, 26 (1996) 49-64.

26 Jean-Luc Nancy, "Nothing but the World: An Interview with *Vacarme*," *Rethinking Marxism* 19, 4 (2007), 530.

27 Jean-Luc Nancy, *The Creation of the World* or *Globalization*, trans. François Raffoul and David Pettigrew (Albany: SUNY Press, 2007) 29.

28 Pieter Meurs, Nicole Note and Diederik Aerts, "This World Without Another: On Jean-Luc Nancy and *la mondialisation*," *Journal of Critical Globalization* 1 (2009) 43.

29 Nancy, "Nothing but the World," 532.

30 Nancy, *The Creation of the World* or *Globalization*, 41.

31 Ibid., 42.

32 Ibid., 29.

33 Ibid., 28.

34 But see Ananya Roy, "Urbanisms, Worlding Practices, and the Theory of Planning," *Planning Theory* 10, 1 (2011) 6-15; and AbdouMaliq Simone, "On the Worlding of African Cities," *African Studies Review* 44, 2 (2001) 15-41.

35 See Henri Lefebvre, *State, Space, World: Selected Essays*, eds. Neil Brenner and Stuart Elden, trans. Gerald Moore, Neil Brenner, and Stuart Elden (Minneapolis: University of Minnesota, 2009); Stuart Elden, "*Mondialisation* before Globalization: Lefebvre and Axelos," *Space, Difference, and Everyday Life: Reading Henri Lefebvre*, eds. Kanishka Goonewardena, Stafan Kipfer, Richard Milgrom and Christian Schmid (New York: Routledge, 2008); Victor Li, "Elliptical Interruptions or, Why Derrida Perfers *Mondialisation* to Globalization," *The New Centenial Review* 7, 2 (2007) 141-54; Kostas Axelos, "*Mondialisation* without the World: Interviewed by Stuart Elden," *Radical Philosophy* 130 (2005) 25-8; and Stäheli, "The Outside of the Global."

36 See, for example Jacques Derrida, *Paper Machine*, trans. Rachel

Bowlby (Stanford: Stanford University Press, 2005) 112-20.

37 See Rachel Bowlby, "Translator's Note," *Paper Machine*, Jacques Derrida (Stanford: Stanford University Press, 2005) ix; Neil Brenner and Stuart Elden, "Introduction," *State, Space, World: Selected Essays*, eds. Neil Brenner and Stuart Elden (Minneapolis: University of Minnesota Press, 2009) 22; and François Raffoul and David Pettigrew, "Translators' Introduction," *The Creation of the World* or *Globalization*, Jean-Luc Nancy (Albany: SUNY Press, 2007) 1.

38 Nancy, *The Creation of the World* or *Globalization*, 28.

39 Ibid., 35.

40 Ibid., 50.

41 Jean-Luc Nancy, *The Sense of the World*, trans. Jeffrey S. Librett (Minneapolis: University of Minnesota, 1997) 4.

42 It should be noted that neither Nancy nor Lefebvre considers the idea—perhaps best represented by Carl Sagan's "cosmic perspective"—that science itself could be a form of *mondialisation*. They both see science almost exclusively as part of technocracy and an agent of disenchantment. But a democratized science could potentially contribute to world-forming as well. See Carl Sagan, *Pale Blue Dot: A Vision of the Human Future in Space* (New York: Random House, 1994).

43 Nancy, *The Creation of the World* or *Globaliztion*, 34.

44 Ibid., 50.

45 Ibid., 34.

46 Ibid., 35.

47 Ibid., 34.

48 Ibid., 33, 50.

49 Ibid., 33-34.

50 Ibid., 33-34, 37.

51 Ibid., 42.

52 Ibid., 33.

53 Ibid.

54 Ibid.

55 Ibid.

56 Ibid.

57 Ibid.

58 Jean-Luc Nancy, *The Inoperative Community*, trans. Peter Connor (Minneapolis: University of Minnesota, 1986) 144.

59 Jean-Luc Nancy, *Being Singular Plural*, trans. Robert D. Richardson and Anne E. O'Byrne (Stanford: Stanford University Press, 2000) 67.

60 See Benjamin C. Hutchens, *Jean-Luc Nancy and the Future of Philosophy* (Chesham: Acumen, 2005); Ian James, *The Fragmentary Demand: An Introduction to the Philosophy of Jean-Luc Nancy* (Stanford: Stanford University Press, 2006); Catherine Kellogg, "Love and Communism: Jean-Luc Nancy's Shattered Community," *Law and Critique* 16 (2005) 339-55; Andrew Norris, "Jean-Luc Nancy and the Myth of the Common," *Constellations* 7, 2 (2000) 272-95; John Schwarzmantel, "Community as Communication: Jean-Luc Nancy and 'Being-in-Common,'" *Political Studies* 55 (2007) 459-76; and Richard V. Welch and Ruth Panelli, "Questioning Community as a Collective Antidote to Fear: Jean-Luc Nancy's 'Singularity' and 'Being Singular Plural,'" *Area* 39, 3 (2007) 349-56.

61 Nancy, *The Creation of the World* or *Globalization*, 54.

62 Ibid., 42.

63 Ibid., 46.

64 Ibid., 109.

65 Ibid., 46.

66 Ibid., 53-54.

67 Nancy, "Nothing but the World," 533.

68 Nancy, *The Creation of the World* or *Globalization*, 53.

69 See Jean-Luc Nancy, "*La Comparution* / The Compearance: From the Existence of 'Communism' to the Community of 'Existence,'" trans. Tracy B. Strong, *Political Theory* 20, 3 (1992) 371-98.

70 Nancy, "Nothing but the World," 533.

71 Nancy, *The Creation of the World* or *Globalization*, 53.

72 Nancy, "Nothing but the World," 533.

73 Nancy, *The Creation of the World* or *Globalization*, 54-5.

74 James Gilbert-Walsh, "Broken Imperatives: The Ethical Dimension of Nancy's Thought," *Philosophy & Social Criticism* 20, 2 (2000) 29-50; and Andreas Wagner, "Jean-Luc Nancy: A Negative Politics?" *Philosophy & Social Criticism* 32, 1 (2006) 89-109.

75 Mike Davis, *Planet of Slums* (New York: Verso, 2007); and Robert Neuwirth, *Shadow Cities: A Billion Sqatters, a New Urban World* (New York: Routledge, 2005).

76 Henri Lefebvre, "Notes on the New Town," *Introduction to Modernity: Twelve Preludes*, trans. John Moore (New York: Verso, 1995 [1960]) 124.

77 Lefebvre, *The Urban Revolution*, 1.

78 Lefebvre, "The Right to the City," *Writings on Cities*, eds. Eleonore Kofman and Elizabeth Lebas (Malden: Blackwell, 1996) 61-181; Lefebvre, *The Urban Revolution*; and Lefebvre, *State, Space, World*.

79 Lefebvre, *The Urban Revolution*, 1-22.

80 Lefebvre, "The Right to the City," 123; and Lefebvre, *The Urban Revolution*, 15.

81 Lefebvre, *The Urban Revolution*, 7.

82 Ibid., 4.

83 Ibid., 15.

84 Ibid., 17.

85 Lefebvre, "The Right to the City," 72-3.

86 Ibid., 71.

87 Lefebvre, *The Urban Revolution*, 3.

88 Lefebvre, "The Right to the City," 71.

89 Mark Wigley, "Network Fever," *Grey Room* 4 (2001) 82-122.

90 Lefebvre, *State, Space, World*, 212-6; and see Neil Brenner, "Global, Fragmented, Hierarchical: Henri Lefebvre's Geographies of Globalization," *Public Culture* 10, 1 (1997) 135-67.

91 Lefebvre, *The Urban Revolution*, 113.

92 Lefebvre, *State, Space, World,* 282.

93 Ibid., 278.

94 Ibid., 246; Lefebvre, *The Urban Revolution*, 4; and Henri Lefebvre, *Everyday Life in the Modern World* (New Brunswick: Transaction, 1984).

95 Lefebvre, *State, Space, World,* 204.

96 Lefebvre, *Everyday Life in the Modern World*, 254.

97 See Neil Turnbull, "The Ontological Consequences of Copernicus: Global Being in the Planetary World," *Theory, Culture, & Society* 23, 1 (2006) 125-9.

98 Lefebvre, *Introduction to Modernity*, 250.

99 Ibid., 238.

100 Lefebvre, *Everyday Life in the Modern World*, 188.

101 Lefebvre, *Introduction to Modernity*, 237.

102 Lefebvre, "The Right to the City," 148.

103 Ibid., 150.

104 Ibid., 158; see David Harvey, "The Right to the City," *New Left Review* 53 (2008) 23-40; Don Mitchell, *The Right to the City: Social Justice and the Fight for Public Space* (New York: Guilford Press, 2003; and Mark Purcell, "Citizenship and the Right to the Global City: Reimagining the Capitalist World Order," *International Journal of Urban and Regional Research* 27, 3 (2003) 564-90.

105 Lefebvre, "The Right to the City," 158.

106 Lefebvre, *The Urban Revolution*, 133.

107 Ibid., 154.

108 Lefebvre, "The Right to the City," 155.

109 Henri Lefebvre, *The Production of Space*, trans. Donald Nicholson-Smith (Malden: Blackwell, 1991).

110 Peter Marcuse, "Whose Right(s) to What City?" *Cities for People, Not for Profit: Critical Urban Theory and the Right to the City*, eds. Neil Brenner, Peter Marcuse, and Margit Mayer (New York: Routledge, 2012) 24-41.

111 Axelos, "*Mondialisation* Without the World," 27.

112 David Ley and Kris Olds, "Landscape as Spectacle: World's Fairs and the Culture of Heroic Consumption," *Environment and Planning D: Society and Space* 6, 2 (1988) 191-212.

31
THE RIGHT TO THE CITY AND BEYOND: NOTES ON A LEFEBVRIAN RECONCEPTUALIZATION

Andy Merrifield

One of Henri Lefebvre's last essays, "Dissolving City, Planetary Metamorphosis" (*Quand la ville se perd dans une métamorphose planétaire*), originally published in *Le Monde Diplomatique* in 1989, is by far one of his most enigmatic.[1] The title alone says bundles; an atypically downbeat Lefebvre is on show, two years before death, dying like his cherished traditional city: when the city loses its way, he says, when it goes astray, in a planetary metamorphosis …

Nobody can ever write as whimsically and gaily about the city, Lefebvre laments, nor with the same lyricism as Apollinaire once wrote about Paris. Now, the situation is more sobering, more depressing; and somehow the octogenarian author of *Le droit à la ville* mirrors this depressing state of affairs. The more the city grows, Lefebvre says, develops, extends itself, spreads its tentacles everywhere, the more social relations get degraded, the more sociability is torn apart at the seams.

As it extends, as the city urbanizes hitherto un-urbanized worlds, as it urbanizes rural worlds, strange things equally happen to labor markets: they, too, Lefebvre says, seem to get obliterated. Traditional forms of work, secure forms of salaried and decent paying jobs, seem to melt into air as fast as "urban forms" settle everywhere, establish connections everywhere. People the world over migrate to the city looking for work only to discover that there's no more work—at least no more dignified "formal" work, one paying a living wage. Once, they came for steady jobs, for steady factory jobs, but those industries have now gone belly-up or cleared out to someplace cheaper, to somewhere more exploitable and expendable. Thus cities have lost their manufacturing bases, and, says Lefebvre, in consequence have lost their "popularly" productive centers.[2]

Millions of peasants and smallholders across the globe are each year thrown off their rural land by big agribusiness, by corporate export farming, by the "rational" dynamics of the neoliberal world market; these people lose the means to feed themselves as well as the means to make a little money. So they come to an alien habitat they can little afford or understand, a habitat which is now strangely neither meaningfully urban nor exclusively rural, but a blurring of both realities, a new reality the result of a push-pull effect, a vicious process of dispossession, sucking people into the city while spitting others out of the gentrifying center, forcing poor urban old-timers and vulnerable newcomers to embrace each other out on the periphery, out on assorted zones of social marginalization, out on the global *banlieue*. The urbanization of the world is a kind of exteriorization of the inside as well as interiorization of the outside. The urban *unfolds* into the countryside just as the countryside *folds* back into the city.

All of which, Lefebvre suggests, has now begotten a "specific dialectic," a paradox in which "centers and peripheries oppose one another." Yet the fault lines between these two worlds aren't defined by any simple urban-rural divide, nor by anything North-South; instead, centers and peripheries are *immanent* within the accumulation of capital itself, *immanent* within its "secondary circuit of capital." Banks, finance institutions, big property companies and realtors spearhead the formation of this secondary circuit. If ground rents and property prices are rising and offer better rates of return than other industrial sectors, capital sloshes into assorted "portfolios" of property speculation. From capital's point of view, as a class, this makes perfect bottom-line sense: the landscape gets flagged out as a pure exchange value, and activities on land conform to the "highest," if not necessarily the "best," land-uses.

Profitable locations get pillaged as secondary circuit flows become torrential, just as other sectors and places are asphyxiated through disinvestment. Therein centrality creates its own periphery, crisis-ridden on both flanks. The two worlds—center and periphery—exist side-by-side everywhere, cordoned off from one other, everywhere. The "menace," Lefebvre says, is that this amorphous monster we call "the city" becomes a planetary metamorphosis that is totally out of control.[3]

Urban society is born of industrialization, a force that shattered the internal intimacy of the traditional city, a force that gave rise to the giant industrial city which Friedrich Engels documented, yet which has now superseded itself, been killed off by its own progeny. Industrialization has, in a word, negated itself, bitten off its own tail, Lefebvre says, advanced quantitatively to such a point that qualitatively it has bequeathed something new, something pathological, something economically and politically *necessary*: planetary urbanization. Absorbed and obliterated by vaster units, rural places have become an integral part of postindustrial production and financial speculation, swallowed up by an "urban fabric" continually extending its borders, ceaselessly corroding the residue of agrarian life, gobbling up everything and everywhere in order to increase surplus value and accumulate capital.

Citizen and city-dweller have been dissociated; what has historically been a core ideal, a core unity, of modern political life has, Lefebvre says, perhaps for the first time, perhaps forever, been wrenched apart, prized open. City-dwellers now live with a terrible intimacy, a tragic intimacy of proximity without sociability, of presence without representation, of encounter without real meeting. The tragedy of the urban-dweller is a tragedy of having hoped excessively, and of having these hopes serially dashed.

Lefebvre's tonality throughout his essay is Céline-like in its journey to the end of the night; yet he can't quite resist a few Whitmanesque flourishes, throwing out one final thought about what a new democratic vista might look like: it will surely necessitate a reformulation of the notion of *citizenship*, he says, one in which city-dweller and citizen somehow embrace one another again. Indeed, "the right to the city," he concludes, as a proverbial "cry and demand," now "implies nothing less than a new revolutionary conception of citizenship."[4]

· · ·

As ever with Lefebvre, the latter proposition raises as many questions as it provides answers. Right to *what* city? If urbanization is planetary, if the urban—or urban society—is everywhere, is this right to the city the right to the metropolitan region, right to the whole urban agglomeration? Or does it just mean the right to a certain neighborhood, to the city's downtown, the right to centrality? And if there are centers everywhere, just as there are multiple peripheries, does that mean the right of these peripheries to occupy, take back, the centers?

A major motif of Lefebvre's right to the city is, of course, the "the right to centrality"; not a simple visiting right, he says, no tourist trip down memory lane, gawking at a gentrified old town, enjoying for the day a city you've been displaced from, but a right to participate in life at the core, to be in the heat of the action. Yet in a lot of US urbanism this is precisely what many urban dwellers already have: the right to centrality. Needless to say, it's a right not worth very much, given that those with power and wealth have long suburbanized themselves, long ago fled the center in favor of the periphery, leaving to the dispossessed the task of reassembling of motley shards of downtown centrality. Power's own centrality, meanwhile, is now somehow a decentered centrality, a multinodal superiority, global in its polycentric potency, rendering hopelessly archaic Lefebvre's singular demand. (Don't people create their own centers anyway, the centers of their own universes, wherever they find themselves? Isn't the right to centrality something internally generated, something existential, and not only geographical? Doesn't the idea of the right to centrality, too, especially when voiced by an elite intellectual, merely reflect a power yearning, a yearning to dominate, to tower over, to master conceptually? It's an impulse, perhaps, very few "ordinary" people actually have.)

Now, one could justifiably ask: does it still make any sense to talk about right to *the* city, to the city that's monocentric and clear-cut about what's inside and what's outside? Moreover, is there any political purchase in defining citizenship through something "urban," especially when urban territoriality is so formless and expansive, so global in its reach? Is the right to the city an empty political signifier? Never before—even more than in Lefebvre's day—has the urban process been so bound up with finance capital and with the caprices of the world's financial markets. The global urbanization boom, with its seemingly insatiable flows into the secondary circuit of capital, has depended on the creation of new mechanisms to wheel and deal fictitious capital and credit money, on new deregulated devices for legalized looting and finagling, for asset stripping and absorbing surplus capital into the built environment.

Crucial here is a marked penchant for what David Harvey labels "accumulation by dispossession," which upgrades Marx's theory of "primitive accumulation," mobilizing it in a twenty-first-century neoliberal context.[5] In *Capital*, Marx said the history of primitive accumulation is always epoch-making, always acting as a lever for the capitalist class in the course of its own formation (and re-formation).[6] The process is simple enough: "the divorcing of the producer from the means of production."[7] As written in the annals of capitalism, primitive accumulation, Marx thought, took many forms; though in these annals the ink still seems wet:

> when great masses of men are suddenly and forcibly torn from their means of subsistence, and hurled onto the labor-market free, unprotected and rightless. The expropriation of the agricultural producer, of the peasant, from the soil is the basis of the whole process.[8]

But, in our times, as Harvey makes clear, accumulation by dispossession signals other terrains for speculation and market expansion: asset-stripping through mergers and acquisitions, raiding of pension funds, privatization of hitherto common assets, like water and other public utilities, and the general pillaging of hitherto publicly-owned property.[9]

Baron Haussmann tore into central Paris, into its old neighborhoods and poor populations, dispatching the latter to the periphery while speculating on the center; the built urban form became simultaneously a property machine and a means to divide and rule; today, neo-Haussmannization, in a similar process that integrates financial, corporate and state interests, tears into the globe, sequesters land through forcible slum clearance and eminent domain, valorizing it while banishing former residents to the global hinterlands of post-industrial malaise.

Hence the issue: the urban process is now global because it is energized by finance capital; ergo, democratization has to be global. However, at the same time, according to right to the city theorists like Lefebvre, we have to separate out the urban realm, give it some political specificity, some political priority in struggles against neoliberalism, even some priority with respect to global citizenship. So, on the one hand, the city needs to be considered globally because urbanization is global, masterminded by transnational finance capital. On the other hand, in this global struggle the city somehow holds the key, though only if it's considered in the broadest sense of the term, at its broadest territorial scale. The specificity of the city seems to be that there's no longer any specificity; the right to the city is a global struggle for citizenship that needs to be grounded in the city. Perhaps it's just me, but isn't this logic rather tautological? Aren't we left going around in circles?

The problem emerges when we (correctly) identify the dominant role finance capital plays in global neoliberalism, only to then, in the same breath, voice some looser political invocation that "the urban" must now be the principle site of any contestation of this project. The shift from one to the other doesn't quite stack up; in fact, it strikes as a *political and theoretical non sequitur*. Indeed, even if we accept the "urban" as a specific terrain for political struggle, one might wonder: what would the right to the city actually look like?

Would it resemble the Paris Commune, a great festival of merriment, of people storming into the center of town, when there was a center, occupying it, tearing down significant statues, abolishing rents for a while? If so, how would this deal with the problem Marx identified? How would it deal with the central banks and all those flows of capital and commodities? And why should taking over "the city" necessarily prevent these transactions, this trade, anyway? Even if people reappropriated downtown HQs of the big corporate and financial institutions, or squatted Wall Street, how would this really destabilize "the system"? (Even a so spectacular act of urban dismantling—the downing of the World Trade Center—barely stopped world trading for a day.[10])

What's more, if we look at twentieth century revolutionary history, it's clear that wrestling control over urban areas has often been the icing on the revolutionary cake: by then, the social movement has already been built, the bonds already forged; taking control of the city announces the culmination of victory, the storming of the Winter Palace, the demolition of the Berlin wall, the last battle in a dogged war of position, the social movement's final, joyous fling. In many ways, too, revolutionary juices of modern times haven't had their source in the city at all, but have flowed *from* the countryside onto the urban streets.[11] It's almost like what Régis Debray said in *Revolution in the Revolution*: that the city has been the "empty head," largely impotent, deaf to the plight of those who feel accumulation by dispossession the most; that it's the rural hinterlands, mountain jungles, and abandoned *banlieues* that is the "armed fist" of rebellion.[12] "The city, for the guerilla movement," Debray wrote, "was a symbol, *the purpose of which was to create the conditions for* a coup d'état in the capital."[13] Mao, Che, Castro, Ortega (in Nicaragua) all knew this, and with Subcomandante

Marcos they'd doubtless concur: the city doesn't so much radicalize as *neutralize* popular elements.[14]

The city, from this standpoint, isn't so much a Lefebvrian dialectical *œuvre* as a Sartrean *practico-inert*, the prison-house of past actions, the *formless* form of a passive totality, of inert bricks and mortar that gnaw away, that inhibit *active praxis*. The practico-inert, Sartre insists, opposes active activity because its anti-dialectic announces that dead labor dominates over living labor, that praxis has been absorbed into an objective alien form, into the city itself.[15] And while in *Métaphilosophie* Lefebvre was critical of Sartre's formulation of the urban as practico-inert, this understanding nonetheless explains the relative conformity of urban populations today, the majority of whom are ex-peasants and people with rural roots, a million-fold mass such as never existed before, a flow of dynamic people who soon become passive vagrants, unemployed, subemployed and multiemployed attendants, trapped in shantytowns, cut off from the past yet somehow excluded from the future, too, from the trappings of "modern" urban life; instead, they're deadened by the daily grind of hustling a living.[16]

Such a collision of urban and rural worlds, and the complex mix, the entangled loyalties and schizophrenia that ensues, forms the basis of John Berger's novel *Lilac and Flag*, his "old wives' tale of the city," a fictionalized rendering of the problematic but one which reveals a few facts.[17] Berger's narrator, an aged peasant woman who remains in the village after everybody has left, is leery of the city. For her, when push comes to shove, there are really only two types of people: peasants and those who feed off peasants. Her tale is of Zsuzsa and Sucus, a.k.a. Lilac and Flag, two lovers who are trying to tread their slippery way through the spectral metropolis of Troy, a paradigmatic po-mo city of expressways and concrete blocks, of money values and deceit, of immense freedom and brutal imprisonment.

Sucus lives with his mother and father on the 14th floor of an anonymous high-rise on the city's periphery; Clement, Sucus' Papa, came from the village as a teenager and worked all his life opening oysters. One day Clement has a freak accident, gets badly burned, and slips away in hospital. He's always wondered whether his son could find a job. "There are no jobs," Sucus tells Papa on his deathbed, "except the ones we invent. No jobs. No jobs." "Go back to the village, that's what I'd like to do," says Clement to his son. "See the mountains for the last time."[18] Half the men in the ward, he says, remember either their village or their mothers; that's all they think about. Sucus' generation, of course, doesn't know the village, so can never go back anywhere; and yet it can't quite find itself in the alien city either, even in the city in which this generation was born. Sucus' generation can go neither backwards nor forwards: it has nostalgia for neither the past nor the future. And yet, they're not prepared to take the same shit their parents did. Their expectations are different. But their prospects are non-existent.

Berger's *Lilac and Flag* delves into a generation of men and women, a generation of urban dwellers for whom "the right to the city" serves no purpose—either as a working concept or as a political program. It remains at a too high level of abstraction to be anything that is *existentially meaningful in everyday life*. Put a little differently: the right to the city politicizes something that is *too vast and at the same time too narrow*, too restrictive and unfulfilling, too empty a signifier to inspire collective retribution, to provoke Sucus and his generation to get itself together, to act as a collectivity as a fused group.

The right to the city quite simply isn't the *right* right that needs articulating. It's too vast because the scale of the city is out of reach for most people living at street level; and it's too narrow because when people do protest, when they do take to the streets en masse, their existential desires frequently reach out beyond the scale of the city, and revolve around a common and collective humanity, a pure democratic yearning. Berger's Sucus is a latent political subject waiting in the wings, perhaps even hoping against hope; yet he's waiting for something closer to home, something trivial—something he can touch and smell and feel—*and* for something larger than life, something that's also world-historical. He's waiting, that is, for a praxis that can somehow conjoin both realms at once, square the lived with the historical, two sides of praxis "that go badly together."[19]

•   •   •

If the right to the city won't do, what else might? Are other aspects of Lefebvre's political arsenal more politically fruitful, more empowering for radical politics today? Maybe his idea of the *encounter* can spawn a different way of conceiving the urbanization of the world, and of straddling the dialectic between the lived and the world-historical. Lefebvre, remember, says that the city is the supreme site of encounters, often chance encounters, especially chance political encounters; but why be so discriminatory?[20] Why not posit the power of encounters as the stuff of radical politics, the stuff that percolates *through the whole social fabric*, through the entire zone of possible militant praxis? The notion of "encounter," after all, is a tale of how people come together as *human beings*, of why collectivities are formed and how solidarity somehow takes hold, takes shape, shapes up.

The politics of the encounter, too, is something that can mediate between the lived and the historical, between an individual life and dynamic group fusion. It can overcome the inertia of apparent mass powerlessness. When striving individuals encounter one another, when people express their collective power of acting because their *conatus* (in Spinoza's understanding) inspires a desire to exist democratically, a social movement is in the making, a historically significant social movement. Common notions bond people, bond their bodies and minds, and diverse peoples will now likely intersect and intermingle in real and virtual space, in a blurry liminal and subliminal zone in which it makes no theoretical or political sense to differentiate between what's city and what's countryside, between what's urban and what's global.

A meaningful politics of the encounter will replace *passive* affects with *active* ones; it must and will recognize that a "singular essence" applies to us all, especially to all humiliated and exploited people the world over, who might and can encounter one another not always directly, but intuitively through a mode of relating to the world, through unwritten and unstated common agreement, through solidarity. It has happened before and it will continue to happen in the future, especially in a future where global communications both integrate and separate everybody. Indeed, as soon as people find one another, touch one another ideationally, emotionally and maybe experientially, as soon as *we* begin to reach into ourselves as human beings, we start to piece together certain concepts about *our* lives: we universalize, make more coherent what seems, on the face of it, only specific experience—vague, lived experience. And yet, what appears particular is in fact general; what seems just our plight is actually the plight of many people, the plight of a multitude of different people.

A politics of the encounter is potentially more empowering because it is politically and geographically more *inclusive*. Let's forget about asking for our rights, for the rights of man, the right to the city, human rights. A politics of the encounter utters no rights, voices no claims. It doesn't even speak: rather, it just does, just acts, affirms, takes, takes back. It doesn't ask, doesn't plead for anything abstract. It has little expectation of any rights, and doesn't want any rights granted, because it doesn't agree upon any accepted rules, isn't in the mood for acceptance by anyone in power. If it says anything, the politics of the encounter talks a language that the group has only just collectively invented.

When people encounter one another they often do so by virtue of an *affinity* taking hold, congealing at a felicitous moment; only those elements that are susceptible to interlocking will somehow interlock. Needless to say, things have usually been gurgling within the bowels of society: undercurrents, clandestine organization, politicking, subversion, growing dissatisfaction; though when things explode, when they really erupt, when the proverbial shit does hit the fan, it's invariably by *surprise*.

Here affinity becomes the cement that bonds, perhaps only for a moment, but a moment that's enough, a moment that lingers, a lasting encounter, a bonding of people across frontiers and barriers. In desiring another reality, in inventing it, in willing it up, people find their kindred souls, perhaps nearby, perhaps faraway; and in finding one another they struggle together for the realization of common hopes. People create a group commonality because of a taking hold of bodies and minds in a space, on the street, face-to-face through "strong-tie" offline activism, and online through virtual "weak-tie" association. The two flanks strengthen one another and give a new dimension to the idea of taking hold: *speed*, the speed at which crowds assemble, the speed at which demos take place, the speed at which people today encounter other people.

One of the curious things about the recent street demos in Tunisia and in Egypt was that although they occurred in the streets of Tunis and Cairo, in capital cities, the stake wasn't really about the city, but about *democracy*, about something simpler and vaster than urbanism as we once knew it. A lot of the activism and organizing was done deterritorially, *posturban*, if you will, through Facebook and Twitter, and was essentially leaderless, a sort of series of radical *moments*, Lefebvrian moments that intersected and overlapped. The politics of the encounter is when a "constellation of moments" (Lefebvre's term) assumes galactic proportions. Here each moment contains the presence of the future, the beginnings of the end of one kind of rule, and the commencement of another. The moment lurks between the lines, Lefebvre says, lurks in a certain context, disrupts linear duration, punctuates it, drags time off in a different, contingent direction, towards another, as-yet-unknown staging post. The moment is a political opportunity to be seized and invented, something metaphorical and practical, palpable and impalpable, something intense but fleeting, too, the delirious sense of pure feeling, of pure immediacy, of being there and only there, like the moment of festival, or of revolution.

Just as alienation reflects an *absence*, an inert, dead moment bereft of critical and dynamic content, the Lefebvrian moment signifies a *presence*, "a modality of presence," Lefebvre call it, a fullness, a connection, a social connection of like-minded people.[21] As Lefebvre conceives it, the moment implies a certain notion of liberty, as well as risky game of chance. There are moments of play and struggle, he says, and of rest and poetry, always with a "certain specific duration." The moment "wants to endure," he says. "It cannot endure (at least, not for very long). Yet this inner contradiction gives it its intensity, which reaches crisis point when the inevitably of its own demise becomes apparent."[22] For a moment,

> the instant of greatest importance is the instant of failure. The drama is situated within that instant of failure: it is the emergence from the everyday or collapse on failing to emerge, it is a caricature or a tragedy, a successful festival or a dubious ceremony.[23]

Therein lies the problem: one moment leads to other moments, and a politics of encounter explodes when moments collide, collide on the street. Yet how to sustain the intensity of the encounter, how to harmonize it with a continuous political evolution, with an authentic politics of transformation? How to ensure that this moment in everyday life—this spontaneous lived moment—assumes a mutation of world-historical significance?

Nobody can answer the question in advance; nor are there preconceived formulas for success. What's evident, though, is how any moment of encounter will likely be a kind of process without a subject, spreading rapidly, a moment in which crowds will become speedy *ensembles of bodies*, created via spontaneous online and offline ordering; participants here will simultaneously act and react, both affect and get affected; a human kaleidoscope will result in which joy and celebration, violence and wildness, tenderness and abandon find structuring, somehow get defined. Participants will congeal not only as a singularity sharing their passions and affirming their hopes, but as a force that creates its own historical space.

For in any politics of encounter, it's not in space that people act: *people become space by acting*. Nothing is scenic anymore, nothing is necessarily urban; nothing is frill or redundant, alienating or thing-like; all action, all human connectivity, each body, if it really connects, literally fills the space; action breathes, and participants' own bodies become the major scenic element, the spatial form as well as the spatial content. To that degree, the politics of the encounter will always be an encounter *somewhere*, a spatial meeting place. It will always be an illicit rendezvous of human bonding and solidarity, a virtual, emotional and material topography in which something takes hold, something disrupts and intervenes in the parallelism, in the paralysis.

This, in the end, seems a better way to rework and reframe Lefebvre's right to the city: to negate it by moving beyond it, moving through it as Lefebvre implied we should. If a concept didn't fit, somehow didn't work, Lefebvre insists that we should always ditch that concept, abandon it, give it up to the enemy. Indeed, for Lefebvre the whole political utility of a concept isn't that it should tally with reality, but that it enables us *to experiment with reality*, that it helps us glimpse another reality, a virtual reality that's there, somewhere, waiting to be born, inside us. A politics of encounter forces us to encounter ourselves, concretely, alongside others; it doesn't make a facile, abstract claim for something that's all around us and which is already ours.

Notes

1 Henri Lefebvre, "Dissolving City, Planetary Metamorphosis," this book, Ch. 34.
2 Ibid., 16.
3 Ibid.
4 Ibid.
5 David Harvey, *The New Imperialism* (New York: Oxford University Press, 2003).
6 Karl Marx, *Capital, Volume 1* (Harmondsworth: Penguin, 1976).
7 Ibid., 875.
8 Ibid., 876.
9 Harvey, *The New Imperialism.*
10 At the United Nations-organized World Urban Forum in Rio in March 2010, the UN and the World Bank both adopted the right to the city in its charter for addressing the global urban poverty trap. Across the street in Rio, at the Urban Social Forum, a people's popular alternative was being staged. Activists there were appalled by the ruling class's reappropriation of a hallowed grassroots ideal. David Harvey, who spoke at both events, said when he declared at the World Urban Forum that "the concept of the right to the city cannot work within a capitalist system," his fellow panelists fell embarrassingly silent (see http://usf2010.wordpress.com/). Perhaps it's unsurprising that Harvey's comment should turn off the mainstream; what's more interesting is what it means for leftists: does it imply the right to the city is a right that can only be expressed in a postcapitalist reality?
11 Lefebvre himself knew this well. Remember how much of his thinking about radical urban politics sprang from rural everyday life, especially from seasonal festivals and raucous, Rablaisian blowout feasts (*ripaille*). Lefebvre's own disposition was a strange urban-rural mix. When describing his physiognomy in *La somme et le reste*, he spoke of his long angular urban face—his head of Don Quixote; yet his stocky body was peasant-like (*trapu*), he said, resembling Sancho Panza's. See Henri Lefebvre, *La somme et le reste*

—*tome 1* (Paris: La nef de Paris, 1959) 242. Lefebvre was proud of this curious combination. He lamented the destruction of the countryside almost as much as he lamented the destruction of the traditional city, even though he knew that in both instances there was no going back.
12 Régis Debray, *Revolution in the Revolution? Armed Struggle and Political Struggle in Latin America* (New York: Grove Press, 1967).
13 Ibid., 77, emphasis added.
14 Ibid., 76-7.
15 Jean-Paul Sartre, *Critique of Dialectical Reason, Volume 1* (London: Verso, 1976).
16 Henri Lefebvre, *Métaphilosophie* (Paris: Éditions de minuit, 1965) 85.
17 John Berger, *Lilac and Flag: An Old Wives' Tale of the City* (London: Granta Books, 1990).
18 Ibid., 47.
19 Lefebvre *Métaphilosophie*, 77.
20 Henri Lefebvre, *Le droit à la ville* (Paris: Éditions du seuil, 1974).
21 Henri Lefebvre, *Critique of Everyday Life, Volume 2* (London: Verso, 2002) 345.
22 Ibid.
23 Ibid., 351

32
THE HYPERTROPHIC CITY VERSUS THE PLANET OF FIELDS

Max Ajl

In a crisp vignette, the urban planner and social critic Lewis Mumford asked, "What is a City?" He answered: the city is a "Geographic plexus, an economic organization, an institutional process, a theater of social action, and an aesthetic symbol of collective unity … It fosters art and is art; the city creates the theater and *is* the theater."[1] For Mumford, as for the slightly younger Paul Goodman and the slightly older Patrick Geddes, the city could encourage social complexity and be an incubator for human culture.[2] But they also knew that the urban form could grow wildly: "Megalopolis is fast becoming a universal form," Mumford wrote, with humanity moving fast towards a future "mechanized, standardized, effectively dehumanized, as the final goal of urban evolution."[3]

Mumford and his contemporaries had cuttingly diagnosed the late twentieth-century urban form. They would have been chagrined, but probably not shocked, to find that the future had not merely borne out their diagnosis, but that those charged with arresting the problem were still in denial about it. The hydrocephalic city remains the goal of most planners. Shared goals do not always mean shared means, but in this case, lying underneath that goal is a seldom acknowledged but universally shared underside: the end of the countryside and the relocation of its peoples. Nearly the entire policy spectrum and the dominant ensemble of cultural critics and development practitioners reject outright the notion that "cities grow on the planet of plants."[4] Instead, the ruling idea is that plants and the planet are there for cities. With most of the world's population drawn into the cash nexus, and the percentage of people on the planet living in cities (purportedly) rising constantly, technocrats have focused debate on the urban age, and in turn swiftly dismiss both rural people and the production of food. If they even raise the still-lingering agrarian question, it is only to quickly dash it to the ground. The primary resort is to either tacitly or explicitly assert a double-helix modernization teleology: one ascending spiral, intensive rural-to-urban migration, and the second, the development of capital intense and labor light agriculture in the countryside.[5]

In this way, those advocating a future of megacities sidestep critiques of contemporary agricultural and metropolitan forms. Such analyses have devastatingly anatomized the ecological dislocations and entropic modes of energy use linked to industrial agriculture, and tied such dissections to alternative models of food production—with strong implications for future development and planning regimes.[6]

But such stances are now on the margins, even in circles concerned with development.[7] Outside the peasant international Via Campesina and its associated intellectuals, few discussions are about the relative weight of city and country, or indeed whether these categories are of any use. Instead, cities are seen as fixed and modular units, without any substantive relationship to the flows which constitute them and the effects those flows have beyond municipal borders.[8] In turn, debates hinge on the technicalities of how to pack the people of the countryside into the cities. In the process, a modernization narrative becomes the background in front of which planners and politicians numbly discuss substantively identical trajectories. Indeed, from the Right, it is not even a background; it is the plan. Bevies of experts, oblivious to the fallout from their forebears' fetishization of capital-intense agriculture and high-density, high-population urban living, shrugging at the ashes and ruins that lay behind the juggernaut of the development project (which, given the anti-rural bias of such policies, must also be viewed as an *urbanization* project), now peddle a second Green Revolution in agriculture, hoping to structure the sowing of the fields of Africa and Asia on a fully scientific and rational basis: capital-intensive, labor-light, and petroleum-fueled.

Yet this line of thinking is not just the province of devotees of industrial agriculture, or semireformed apologists for the system such as Jeffrey Sachs and Joseph Stieglitz. It is one that has captured the imagination of a broad sweep of analysts—from the boosters of capitalism, to myriad reformist tinkerers, and even on to its most prominent Cassandras.

Indeed, from the Left, it is often much the same as on the Right, only with the modernization process criticized for its effects, yet simultaneously framed as unavoidable and thus as inevitable. For example, in a recent essay entitled, "Building the Ark," urban theorist Mike Davis argues that the cities of the future and the cities of the South, the centers of both human population increase and carbon emissions, will become the arks in which the culture of twenty-first-century human civilization will ride out the floods and tempests of the ecological devastation wrought by twentieth-century carbon civilization.[9] With sufficient care to safeguard public space, to make public the city's private riches, Davis argues, the metropolis might be transformed from one of the major causes of climate change into the Great Ark. For others, the question of agricultural production in the global North is transformed into a problem of massive technological advance braided with socialist revolution. One proponent argues for "solar arrays, green fuels, new food sources and vertical farms necessary to feed billions of people in an ecologically sustainable fashion," suggesting that such infrastructures would entail a "wholesale technological transformation of existing agriculture."[10] Through this resort to agro-Prometheanism, lessons from the global South are made irrelevant.

In short, from Left to Right, the contemporary agrarian question is dominated by a solid wall of modernization narratives that dismiss lightly capitalized agricultural systems and embrace a nearly surreal 1950s-style, progressivist-developmentalist narrative. They refuse to discuss the appropriate size for human communities, and assume that humanity can simply invent its way out of ecological crisis. It is a tableau riddled with problematic assumptions—most fundamentally, that existing patterns of rural-to-urban migration are both sustainable and desirable; and relatedly, that very large cities are the appropriate spatial units for future human development.

In what follows, I begin by explicating the concept of the energy regime in order to show how the widespread view of the Euro-American pattern of industrialization as a global ideal type rests upon a naturalization of large-scale fossil fuel consumption. I then clarify that the concentration of populations in large-scale metropolitan regions in the global North has hinged upon global ecological plunder. On this basis, I discuss the implications of further urbanization in the global South and its probable effects on agriculture, as well as on the planet as a whole. I argue that this process is linked both to an acceleration of entropic modes of living as well as to unsustainable forms of agriculture. I conclude with a counter-proposal focusing on the centrality of agriculture to the creation of a sustainable form of urbanization.

Fossil Capitalism and Energy Regimes

First, consider forms of energy, which we can interpret using the concept of the energy regime.[11] In the earliest regime, that of hunter-gatherers, the human population took what it needed from foraging in the surrounding environs, with living standards corresponding to what Marshall Sahlins describes as stone-age affluence.[12] That regime was extremely low-impact. It also could not support more than a tiny population.[13] Whatever the abstract merits of such societies—large amounts of leisure among them—they offer nothing to the massive populations inundating the cities and countrysides of the contemporary global South.

The second historical regime is a society based on non-fossil-input-based farming, in which people skim off a surplus from the biome while managing it so as to increase the quantity of primary production usable by human beings in the form of cereals or other kinds of caloric or non-caloric goods. Agriculture is a *sine qua non* for urbanization, because to concentrate a population into cities one needs to produce an excess to supply non-farmers with food.[14] Ecologically speaking, farming represents a massive intrusion into biological cycles, as natural cycles of succession, in which increasingly dense and big forms of flora replace simpler ones, are continuously interrupted by human ingenuity and intervention.

And then there is a third energy regime, the one in which basically the entire global North and large swathes of the global South live, work and die. This is the industrial energy regime, which relies on the subterranean forests that previous generations have left us, and which has used them up at an astonishingly fast rate. This regime increasingly relies on industrial forms of agriculture, substituting dead biotic energy in the form of fossil fuels for human and living biotic energy that has been displaced from the countryside.[15] Such forms of agriculture go hand-in-hand both historically and practically with high industrial civilization—the making of modern cities, modern slums and the factories and workshops within which the working classes labor.

Capitalism is conceptually distinct from the types of energy that power it. It is also distinct from industrialization, an entropic mode of material production that takes in concentrated materials from far-flung places, processes them using machines and non-human energy, and produces finished products and waste. For that reason, it abrades the rest of the ecology: "Industry does not have environmentally good and bad forms. Industry just is inherently disruptive, and ignorant of its own effects."[16] Capitalism is also conceptually distinct from urbanization, "a process of continual sociospatial transformation, a relentless 'churning' of settlement types and morphologies that encompasses entire territories and not just isolated 'points' or 'zones' within them."[17] Nevertheless, historically, each of these processes has been tightly intertwined. This intersection was particularly stark in eighteenth- and nineteenth-century Britain, where industrialization, urbanization and capitalism developed in a synergistic whirl, generating social and ecological changes on increasingly large scales.

Ecological Imperialism and the Limits to Limitless Growth

As Kenneth Pomeranz has pointed out, British industrial development came to rely on extra-territorial supplies of land to overcome the land squeeze and the equilibrium trap it would have entailed, and fortuitously located coal supplies to overcome the timber squeeze.[18] The cotton that fueled it was grown by slave labor in the American South. The slaves who worked that land were stolen from West Africa, whose land and resources England and the US planter class effectively pillaged in the form of the human bodies, which that land and resources had nurtured to adulthood.[19] Although hydrocarbons did not set capitalism in motion, they did enable it to increase its size and scope by temporarily allowing the material processes that capitalists order and reorder to increase substantially in size, drawing on ancient energy from the sun as well as that lying beyond the immediate geographical confines of England—and later, Europe.[20] If capitalism is a system premised on the growth and differential accumulation of capital, it also tends to rely on the growth of the material structure of production and consumption which that social hierarchy restlessly shapes and molds.[21] And such growth leads to geographical expansion, at least when the choice is between that and increasing domestic consumption.[22]

Oil only aggravated this dynamic, contributing to "the new conception of the economy as an object that could grow without limit in several ways."[23] Oil initially declined in price for the entire 1920–1970 period of national developmentalism, making it so that "the cost of energy did not appear to represent a limit to economic growth."[24] This in turn allowed the new discipline of economics, which would soon spawn the step-child discipline of development economics, to "conceive of long-run growth as something unrestrained by the availability of energy."[25] Furthermore, both the European and American periods of pronounced national development, from 1945 to 1970, were periods when oil profits were modulated as part of a planning regime that—in its American form—locked together several disparate social practices and physical infrastructures into a very particular kind of modernity. Suburbs, cheap food, massive employment, continuous GDP growth, the spread of the interstate highway system, the universalization of the automobile—these parts were all linked into a spectacularly energy-intense regime of accumulation, which, in turn, activated the final destruction of the American countryside.[26] Those processes and institutions encouraged a presentist morality, one that was locked into a tight affinity with corporate institutions that privileged a short time-horizon, foreshortened constantly by capital flows calibrated to quarterly profit reports.[27] So for the North, there has been enough, at least for some, but only because its dominant accumulation regime has been grounded upon the theft of resources, both spatially and temporally, from the present inhabitants of the Third World and from the future inhabitants of the whole world.

William Rees and Mathis Wackernagel, who have formalized the notion of the ecological footprint to capture the spatial aspect of this dynamic, point out that:

> material flows in trade thus represent a form of thermodynamic imperialism. The low cost energy represented by commodity imports is required to sustain growth and maintain the internal order of the so-called "advanced economies" of the urban North.[28]

As they go on to write, the "toys and tools" of industrial man, the "human-made 'capital' of economists," should be characterized as the "exosomatic equivalent of organs."[29] And much like organs, they require circulatory flows in the form of continuous inputs of energy to keep them functioning. However, it is impossible to put any reasonable price on those inputs when they come from fossil fuels that are not renewable on human time scales—the temporal theft, in this case from the future.[30] Since the energy stocks condensed in carbon fuels cannot currently be replaced, and since there is no viable technology for scrubbing carbon dioxide from the atmosphere on human time scales, the market is incapable of accurately pricing hydrocarbons and most metals. The corollary of the market's failure in this domain is that consumption patterns and social institutions should be organized such that future inheritors of the earth will have as much ability to use carbon and metallic ores as the inhabitants of the industrial epoch have had. As I will show, this proposition has strong implications for planning patterns, and for the question of when, how and where necessarily scarce and difficult-to-process metals and dense and compact energy sources should be used.

The question of sustainable planning is thrown into even sharper relief with the dawn of the Anthropocene, and amidst increasing public clarity, if not yet consensus, on the unsustainability of fossil capitalism.[31] Still, the question is not, *pace* the peak-oilers, whether the planet will run out of oil. The question is not even one of whether burning that oil will emit so much carbon dioxide as to destabilize entire continents. By now, such destabilization is a foregone conclusion. Rather, the most urgent question is how societies will deal with the socioecological chaos such transformations will induce, a situation that is transforming the question of development into one of "managing the future," and of the terms on which that future will be managed.[32] To put it differently, the world's future inhabitants will have to deal with a "full planet" in ways that the world's past and current inhabitants have not.[33] This fact, too, has unavoidable implications for development planning. Institutions are interlaced with the physical material which they arrange. That being so, sustainable social institutions and their physical infrastructures will have to be made of renewable materials. Much that is currently constructed out of petroleum and metal will soon have to be procured and fabricated in other ways. That means that the massive metal-and-glass cities of today are not likely to be the cities of tomorrow.

End of the World's Smallholders?

The notion that there are no glass and metal megacities on offer for the future denizens of the global South may sound anti-developmentalist. In fact, it undercuts one of the ideologies that has long justified faith in the development project: the chimera of inclusion. Pushing for the remainder of the world's peasants to flood the already-massive cities of the South means forced migrations, whether as drawn out and excruciating as the British enclosure of the commons, or as rapid as the modern-day sales of state land in Africa.[34] The growth of megacities is not a natural phenomenon. It is the result of a plan, one whose human-made outlines are concealed by naturalistic metaphors that turn the topology constructed by political and economic forces into preexisting contours of the social landscape.[35] Moreover, it is a plan for catastrophe. Poor countries simply lack adequate resources to construct these planners' dream cities—neither vertical farms nor capital-intense hydroponics are feasible in the medium-run for developing countries, nor are well-constructed eco-towers or stunning, sprawling, and comprehensive subterranean public transportation systems. On the social horizon of megacity schemes is not an urban utopia but rather the total denuding of the countryside of people, and their increasingly dense enclosure into the *favelas,* barrios and shantytowns of Rio de Janeiro, Caracas, Mumbai, Shanghai, Lagos and Dakar.[36] There is no planet of cities on offer. Only a planet of slums.[37]

In concert with such postdevelopmentalist planning, others argue for eliminating the last remaining vestiges of small-scale agriculture—or, at least, roughly incorporating them into large-scale international commodity markets—on the assumption that urban productivity increases are what will necessarily lead to "development." For example, as Collier and Dercon argue, "there are good reasons to suspect that larger farmers have an important role to play in experimenting and pushing the technological frontier in agriculture," since they are the ones with enough spare capital to invest in modern production technology.[38] Rural-urban migration is thereby turned into a natural law, deflecting the question of where former smallholders will live, never mind how they will find work, in the African and Latin American cities that are now either deindustrializing or which never industrialized to begin with. Just as importantly, in such arguments, the question of why peasants should relocate to cities instead of cities being built around peasants is never raised—an astounding omission that uncritically reflects the agro-export agenda lurking behind such models. In any case, the assumptions supporting a large-farm and agro-export-centered development schema dissolve for being breathed upon, not least the contention that such processes can promote developmental take-off in the cities of the global South. Such models miss or ignore the silent violence of throwing millions of peasants off their land, and they are based upon naïve and inaccurate assumptions regarding the degree to which, under a global neoliberal regime, agro-export-based accumulation strategies can finance internal growth, much less social reproduction.[39]

Furthermore, even putative success in this project would amount to failure, for projected productivity increases cannot compensate for both the loss of the situated knowledge in contemporary smallholders' hands and minds, as well as their by now well-established advantages in productivity per unit-of-land.[40] If, with enough innovation and investment, it should actually come to pass that those ushering in the new pattern of rural development could somehow conjure up Collier and Dercon's "technological frontier in agriculture," it would be a hollow victory, for with it would come the permanent disappearance of the remainder of the rural smallholders, overwhelmingly women, who still produce 70 percent of the planet's food—most food is not traded on international markets.[41] Indeed, the role of smallholders in overall world food production is overwhelmingly unknown, perhaps because of whose hands are actually carrying out such production.

Megacity formation in the global South presents other social problems, too. As consumers move into cities, they produce less of their own food, and increasingly have to buy food produced under conditions in which profits accrue to multinationals. Urban eaters "shift from sorghum, millet, maize and root crops to rice and wheat (often processed into bread)."[42] Rice and wheat are traded on international commodity markets. Roots and cassava are not. The urban poor become subject to price variations in the global market.[43] The rural poor retain a thick protective buffer. Moreover, that rural-based buffer is one that can extend to inhabitants of cities, since the families of first-generation migrants often retain small plots in the countryside even as younger generations flood metropolitan areas in search of work. With the right policy incentives, such a buffer could become denser yet, especially given the increasing efflorescence of urban and peri-urban agriculture. Cuba is the widely cited posterchild of these projects, yet such production patterns are common across Africa as well.[44] But given urban agriculture's centrality in feeding the people of countries like Senegal and Ghana, it is unclear why there is such a thrust to impose the social dislocation that drives peasants into cities in the first place. Is it better to farm in a cityside slum than in the countryside?

Given the multiple roles even minifundia play in warding off total subjection to the market, it is no surprise that the project of land alienation continues to encounter vigorous resistance.[45] Indeed, some who otherwise argue for eliminating small-scale agriculture accept the role of subsistence farming in fending off food crises.[46] Across Asia and Latin America, the defense of subsistence agriculture is not a dying echo of populist thought. It is an active anti-systemic struggle.[47]

Furthermore, those who argue for more capital-intense, commercialized agro-exports on the Brazilian model—and the accompanying rural-urban migration—seldom consider the ecological costs of shifting large quantities of food production to the entropic regime of industrial agriculture while also constructing the input-intensive cities required for such a massive population shift.[48] Concerning the industrialization of agricultural production, the energetic basis for the ideal-typical modernization process, the Vandermeer Report notes,

> We have moved from an "ecosystem function" of energy generation to one based on fossil fuels, thus converting an agricultural system whose main purpose was to *provide* energy to human beings, to a system that is a *net consumer* of energy. Paraphrasing Richard Lewontin, it was a change from "using sun and water to grow peanuts" to "using petroleum to manufacture peanut butter." As a consequence, it has been estimated that this industrial food system expends 10–15 energy calories to produce 1 calorie of food, thereby effectively reversing the reason for the invention of agriculture in the first place.[49]

Instead of paying attention to these facts, those peddling a new urban age seem to consider cities a kind of black box into which one can dump the human population and worry later. Not so. Cities come in all shapes and sizes, but they all consume a great deal of resources. And resource consumption inevitably raises the question of recycling. The knot of the problem is that modern cities are basically black holes, drawing in massive amounts of energy and matter, and then excreting degraded waste into the biosphere.[50] Of course, all organisms do this. The vice of modern megacities is their size. Being so big, rather than having a smooth metabolism with their peripheries, they disrupt them radically. In the past, agriculture mediated waste processing, thereby not only making efficient use of wastes but also doubling as an early-warning signal for the excessive build-up of toxic effluent. But under the megacity/agro-export regime, such processing becomes impossible, as raw or manufactured materials are imported from elsewhere, and the waste products thereupon are subsequently dumped in highly concentrated form, elsewhere. To construct cities on such a huge scale has meant making much of the global South and the global North peripheries—or, to draw on a more familiar parlance, colonies. Imperialism has always had an ecological component.

The troubles of mass urbanization and the universalization of industrial agriculture appear not just with respect to recycling, but also in relation to resource consumption. Here, the limits are Malthusian—there is not enough world. Turning the global South's remaining two billion peasants into city dwellers on the model of affluent global North urban nodes means massive population shifts. Such shifts may cause their consumption patterns decreasingly to resemble those of people living in organic economies reliant on biomass, and to be transformed into those particular to mineral economies, reliant on the buried forests of the past which time and pressure have turned into coal, oil and gas.[51] An early foretaste of this catastrophic scenario is the doubling and redoubling of meat consumption amongst the massively growing Chinese middle class over the last two decades. If the 70 percent of the world's population currently stuck in poverty—most of them rural, and most of those in China, India and Africa—were to adopt resource-use patterns replicating those of the affluent, urban and peri-urban and suburban global North, humanity would require between 20 to 30 times the amount of annual US energy use—about equal to the potential net primary production of all of Earth's terrestrial biota.[52] That will never work, because it would not leave anything for the rest of the living species with which we share the planet, never mind what would happen to the atmosphere if we cut down all the trees. Meanwhile, if the fuel came from coal, the world would swiftly turn to Venus, one reason why more "progressive" environmentalists such as James Lovelock are having a late-stage love affair with nuclear power.[53]

Why Centralize Agriculture?

If the space in the atmosphere for the waste products of this particular sort of industrial civilization is shrinking, and will soon disappear, then one way or another, a regime based on sustainable forms of farming and a considerably less-entropic mode of production more generally must come to the fore, what environmental historian Colin Duncan refers to as the centrality of agriculture.[54] As he writes, future forms of agriculture will have to provide much of the "materials and energy that we are now in the habit of procuring almost exclusively in the industrial style, from petroleum especially."[55] Much of what is now fabricated hinges upon the use of non-renewable methods and non-renewable resources—especially metals and hydrocarbons. Eventually, these resources will become untenably expensive to extract, and their ecological costs will become unbearable. At that point, human societies will have to revert to direct photosynthetic processes of energy concentration to produce the raw materials upon which civilization rests.

The question, then, is one of turning agriculture into a means for producing the raw materials for satisfying human needs, especially food, in a sustainable manner, and interlacing it with urban systems built according to plans that constrain, not end, the reliance upon materials acquired through disruptive forms of extraction. This means that skylines of skyscrapers should not be set up as the normative goal for architects and planners, nor should human society be made needlessly expensive from an energetic perspective.[56] That means thinking about scale. For example, smaller cities could return waste to their agricultural hinterlands instead of relying on treatment plants that consume tremendous amounts of energy to do what nature can do for free. Existing cities could be carefully perforated with urban agricultures that would also help recycle wastes, and would also cool off buildings and cut down transport costs for the commodities grown on such plots.

The question of land and agriculture is, ultimately, at the core of such a model. In the industrial energy system, oil is almost literally transformed into corn, turning nature's logic on its head. In contrast, in a sustainable agricultural system, land use must yield a positive energy balance. The amount of energy put into agricultural production by human and animal traction must be less than the amount of energy that is withdrawn from it in the form of consumable harvest. Without hallucinating a prelapsarian idyll—agricultural civilizations have been capable of tremendous harm to their environments—societies centered on agriculture are capable of relative long-run sustainability and could take relatively good care of the people who live in them, given democratic control over both planning and the means of production.[57] They also secure, rather than diminish, the amount of space available within the world for human culture. It is an ahistorical anthropocentrism to think that the environment must always contain a large place within it for human beings, summed up in the conceit of man's supposedly increasing dominance of nature. Nature always calls the shots.[58] At the moment, the environment is arranged in such a manner as to facilitate large human populations and easy living. That could change very quickly.[59]

To forestall misreading, this is not a polemic against civilization, or against cities or indeed against industrialization. As Mumford recognized, all human cultures contained within them warring tendencies. Hypertrophic cities and the civilizations within which they were embedded rested on complex, hierarchical technologies. Mumford laid out the pathways of such megatechnics, contrasting them with democratic, organic, simple, and egalitarian technologies.[60] Both have existed in all human societies. The former allowed for incredible population densities, miraculous feats of engineering, and most importantly, an enormous accumulation of wealth. The latter had a different merit: they survived. This insight allows us to think of technology as the use of human knowledge for human ends. But technology cannot tell us anything about those ends. In and of itself, it is socially and ecologically neutral. That also means it is not limited to metabolically entropic modes: industry. Agriculture is also a technology—as Braudel noted, perhaps the first technology, certainly for millennia the most widespread—and done properly, is the apotheosis of the democratic, resilient, and human-scale technologies which Mumford praised.[61]

But nor is this a call for the world to return to isolated subsistence farming as a universal form, and still less for a reversion to hunting and gathering. Early twentieth-century social critics, from Mumford to Peter Kropotkin to Ebenezer Howard, were not primitivists. They did not attack cities; they attacked their size, as part of a holistic vision of the appropriate scale for human communities—Howard's notions of garden cities were one example of this tendency.[62] They proposed urban forms that could incubate human creativity, interweave fields and factories, and in the process heal the metabolic rift which twentieth-century capitalism was constantly stretching.[63]

How to Centralize Agriculture

Putting such theory into practice means moving beyond postdevelopmentalist abstractions, which seek to replicate the American model of laborless agriculture, endless highways and petroleum use, and, of course, megalopolis, and impose it on the rest of the planet. There is no reason to set up skylines of skyscrapers as the normative horizon for cities. Those that are already built should remain—there is nothing else to do with them. But there seems little justification for building more of them. They are also expensive, and need immense expenditures of energy for their steel, concrete, and infrastructure. Finally, their super-abundance contributes to the kind of urbanization marked by too dense and too big core cities and the neglect of medium-size or small cities.[64] This was, of course, a theme which Mumford and his contemporaries raised insistently over five decades ago. For them, there could be no rootless and restless dreaming about an abstract urban form. Urbanization and human communal density produced culture. But too much density was damaging. As Mumford wrote, "the mere mechanical massing of the population creates difficulties which can be overcome only by an undue expenditure of capital and income on the means of existence: that is to say, on measures which, though they produce no good in themselves, are necessary in order to overcome the defects of congestion," such as highways, the need to tap increasingly distant sources of water, and expensive mass-transit systems.[65]

This refocusing on agriculture has slightly different implications for the cities of the South and the cities of the North. In the latter, to tackle the largest task, it means fundamentally rejigging American patterns of urban and spatial planning. In the short- to medium-run, making agriculture central means massive state support for urban farming initiatives, as well as agro-ecological training for those working on such plots. While this tendency is frequently ridiculed as a form of *haute couture* green capitalism or localism-gone-mad, many hollowed-out urban areas have a high potential for achieving food sovereignty, matching up unemployable labor with Keynesian policies that could also lead to a relatively more socially embedded capitalism with increased backwards-and-forwards linkages, as well as healing the metabolic rift by enabling waste recycling and reducing the production of the carbon dioxide wastes for which the food production system is responsible.[66] This does not mean sidestepping the question of social power. Counter cyclical policies will not be on the table without social pressure. Here the Cuban example is entirely appropriate—Havana derives a huge proportion of its produce from low-input urban gardens. Some object that this kind of occupational and spatial transition is impossible. This claim seems odd. Do people prefer working at McDonalds to receiving retraining to work in small-scale and locally controlled agriculture? The question should at least be posed in the form of progressive social policy. And if current energy prices make such a transition unfeasible by subsidizing unsustainable rates of hydrocarbon use, once again, the answer is using political tools to change such prices: massive gasoline taxes, which could then be used for all sorts of socially determined processes, not least paying sufficient salaries to newly trained urban and peri-urban gardeners to make their work pay a living wage.

Another short-run planning policy is to ditch entirely the notion of building or expanding existing suburbs and ex-urbs. Such sprawl is not sustainable, and new patterns are necessary. That may indeed eventually mean resettling the American countryside. John Friedmann's agropolitan districts are one example of how to conceptualize such a shift: areas of between 20,000 and 100,000 people, largely self-sufficient and capable of self-governance.[67] This is precisely the size of the ideal cities that Howard and Kropotkin, as well as modern radical ecologists like Kirkpatrick Sale, have proposed.[68] Such a transition would mean decentralizing cultural and educational institutions, and in turn drenching the new spaces in such institutions. If such districts are to be urban—that is, if they are to have high population densities and a high proportion of their populations engaged in non-farm labor—then they could be organically and symbiotically tied into the surrounding countryside on the basis of reciprocal exchange.

Here some object that purposive planning patterns and any such control of population flows require a sort of authoritarian technocracy. But such objections are nothing more than a deification of the processes of "the market" and the social arrangements that those processes produce.[69] There is no reason why green Keynesianism policies could not set these shifts in motion, thereby beginning the important process of relocalizing continental or ocean-length commodity chains, and also putting people to work. Others object that commodities produced through agro-ecological methods are too expensive for those without adequate purchasing power. The answer is to guarantee incomes high enough to make such goods affordable—which then immediately revives the issue of social power by putting into question how and to what ends it is used. A third objection is that "socialism" should mean a world without labor. Putting aside the oddly anti-humanist misanthropy of such a formulation, in countries with massive and structural unemployment like the United

States and the southern European countries, there is nothing wrong with medium-run programs that would put that manpower to work in return for adequate reward. This is to say nothing of silvicultures that do not require a great deal of labor, but that do require immense amounts of long-term planning, or the elaborate forms of gardening exemplified by the rice farming methods in Fukuoka's *The One Straw Revolution*, which require minimal, but well-timed, labor.[70]

In the global South, a sustainable model of urbanization means, perhaps counterintuitively, an immediate end to state support for policies, often enough coming from the World Bank or other transnational institutions, which provoke rural-urban migration.[71] In a world of unaffordable capital and unemployed—indeed, unemployable—labor, why worsen the situation by packing people into cities, especially when labor is needed in the field? Instead, the countries of the South should be deploying policies removing them from global commodity production loops, most importantly, through food sovereignty strategies based on heavy investment in small-holder agriculture—again, a demand that entails a massive reorganization of social power and property relations, as powerfully expressed in the ongoing struggle for local control of land use systems and redistributive agrarian reform by groups like the Landless Workers' Movement (MST) in Brazil.[72] For such currents, smallholder agriculture is far from an antiquarian curio. It is a fight for survival. A sustainable urbanism, woven into a global urban fabric, must defend that fight, rather than undermine it. Crucially, then, a wholesale shift in the form of urbanization in the global South requires revolutionary change in property relations in the countryside.

Elsewhere, if urbanization is taking place *in situ*, then there is all the more reason to focus on the qualitative aspects of germinating sustainable urban forms. This raises the question of planning, to support the growth of smaller cities linked tightly and organically to agricultural production. Indeed, shifts in occupation are inevitable as the implicit subsidy of atmospheric space for carbon wastes slowly disappears and the costs of burning so much cheap energy catch up with the planet. The question is whether they will also be calamitous.[73] Since urbanization in much of the global South consists of cities swelling over and enveloping agricultural hinterlands, the question there would be one of constructing those cities in ways that respect preexisting agricultural forms. This does not mean envelopment of agricultural plots within cities. Urban agriculture is a stop-gap measure, in the global North and South alike; it should not be raised to the level of principle. Cities are cities because they are dense. What this means is constructing cities so that they do not swell onto their hinterlands. If in India, for example, governments can subsidize special economic development zones for IT, they can as easily secure peasant property rights and divert development into resources that people, rather than corporations, need. The latter include, for example, electrification, healthcare and sanitation, all of which have a historical rather than necessary association with industrialization and a fossil-fuel based model of urbanization.[74] As in the global North, that should also mean distributing cultural institutions in spots of relative density.

There is, finally, a question of populations perhaps choosing to return to the countryside.[75] Ghana experienced repeasantization during the 1970–1984 period as its economy tumbled into disaster, a situation enabled by recent rural-urban migrants, extensive knowledge of farming practices.[76] The Cuban government has carried out a program of repeasantization during the Special Period.[77] Some Landless Workers' Movement (MST) settlements are made up of former slum-dwellers from Brazil's cities, as are some of the residents of Venezuela's new agrarian settlements. There is no reason to rue these facts. Agriculture need not be an afterthought or an awkward adjunct to development. It could be, as Duncan writes, the framework for a sustainable socialism nested in bioregions.[78] The question is not one of plopping the populations of New York and London into fields with pitchforks in their hands. It is, rather, a matter of designing social and planning policy so that the populations currently on the land are not so eager to leave it, and working forward from there.

In such a vision, megacities can hardly serve as ecological arks, and the bigness fetish of high modernism must be abandoned as a relic of industrial excess.[79] Immense human population concentrations are not a value in and of themselves. Cities should be built to accommodate people, not the other way around. That includes accommodating the pre-existing social fabric of their lives. Just as the countryside's people can be brought to the cities, that which is crucial about cities—for instance, hospitals, universities, museums, art collectives, a profusion of social interaction—can be easily brought to the countryside.

Conclusion

The notion that in a free society, some work will still have to be done and some of it will be hard, and that is okay so long as it is evenly distributed; the view of modernization and development as having often had destructive consequences; the idea that modern society need not fetishize industry; and the assumption that cities ought respond to the needs of the countryside, which they in any case rely on, ecologically and economically, for survival—all these are commonly cast aside as a vague and retrograde populism. As arguments, they run against the grain of over 100 years of development thinking, Marxist and mainstream alike.

Yet these claims are not new. Nearly a century ago, as the Soviet Union was beginning its heavy industrial lock-in, Ivan Kremnev penned a story about a time-traveler who woke up in 1980 after having been adrift for decades after the Bolshevik Revolution. Rather than the violent concentration of the peasantry in cities amid forced collectivization, peasant forces had captured the state. They rebuilt the entire country, abolishing towns of more than 20,000 people, dispersing the massive Moscow metropolis, creating local centers at railroad junctions, perfecting the communications network, and saturating the local centers in culture—theaters, museums, peoples' universities, sport activities, choral societies, all the classical accoutrements of city life that, he understood, did not require the dense, unsustainable conglomerations of people that inhabited Moscow.[80] The text's English translation is introduced dismissively by another Soviet writer: "The forms of the peasant economy … are retrograde even compared with capitalist forms of agriculture"; the "peasantry generally follows the proletariat, its politically more advanced and better organized fellow," while the former struggles to preserve its "essentially reactionary ideals."[81] Even then, on a planet of peasants, the prevailing assumption was that farmers' struggles were anti-modern, and destructive of the ideal of human progress.

It is, though, an odd concession to the modern-day religion of progress to think that only industrialized society can secure healthy lives for people. As Halperin makes clear, it was not industrialization in and of itself that delivered social development to the North.[82] Indeed, industrialization has seldom closed the North/South divergence in living standards, which continue to widen.[83] Furthermore, as Duncan points out, "It is striking that those recognized elements of a 'good life' that are most strongly cross-cultural—good food and drink, nice garments, fine music and conversation, and comfortable housing—in no way require industry."[84] Advanced medical care, as he points out, is a separate issue, but the Cuban example shows clearly that a healthcare system capable of achieving excellent quality-of-life indicators need not be dependent on either extensive energy use or a society based on heavy industrialization and hyper-dense, large-scale urbanization. Networks of thousands of small and medium cities, linked by high-speed trains, is one such vision, and a more productive use of limited resources than concentrating them in unlivable cities, where daily commutes along desperately overcrowded and under-serviced arterial roads can exceed three hours in the global South's megacities.

So is this a Luddite fantasy, a reincarnation of the Romantic penchant for the countryside? That is the perspective of the neoliberal clergy. Collier writes of "the middle- and upper-class love affair with peasant agriculture … With the near-total urbanization of these classes in both the United States and Europe, rural simplicity has acquired a strange allure. Peasant life is prized as organic in both its literal and its metaphoric sense."[85] And indeed, this is the same criticism those holding out the promise of perpetual growth and industrial development as a route to universal prosperity have been putting forward for over a century. But top-down industrialization has simply failed to deliver what it has promised. Chants for bread animate the revolts of the new millennium as surely as they did 100 years ago. The idea of progress has promised so much and come through with so little, and that for so few. It must be acknowledged that people have neither wanted nor asked for industrial societies of the sort which have been relentlessly imposed upon them. Perhaps it is now time to listen to the victims of our visions.[86]

Notes

1   Lewis Mumford, "What is a City," *Architectural Record* 82 (1937) 59-62, 60.

2   Percival Goodman and Paul Goodman, *Communitas* (New York: Columbia University Press, 1990).

3   Mumford, "What is a City," 62, 61.

4   André Torre and Lise Bourdeau-Lepage, "When Agriculture Meets the City… a Desire for Nature or an Economic Necessity?" *Metropolitiques* 10 (2013). http.//www.metropolitiques.eu/When-agriculture-meets-the-city.html.

5   For a representative example, see Hiroaki Suzuki, Arish Dastur, Sebastian Moffatt, Nanae Yabuki and Hinako Maruyama, *Eco2 Cities: Ecological Cities As Economic Cities* (World Bank Publications, 2010).

6   On agro-ecology, see Eric Holt-Giménez and Miguel A. Altieri, "Agroecology, Food Sovereignty, and the New Green Revolution," *Agroecology and Sustainable Food Systems* 37, 1 (2013) 90-102.

7   For a representative dismissal, see Tom Brass, "Moral Economists, Subalterns, New Social Movements, and the (re-) Emergence of a (post-) Modernized (middle) Peasant," *Journal of Peasant Studies* 18, 2 (1991) 173-205.

8   See Neil Brenner, "Theses on Urbanization," this book, Ch. 13. It would be intriguing to develop a comparison between the historical development of this concept of the city as an analytical category immured from the flows which constitute it and the development of the concept of the economy as a free-standing sphere of life walled off from the wider world within which it is necessarily although not conceptually embedded, especially since cities can no more exist without their hinterlands than can "economies" without the world in which their so-called "externalities" are dumped. On this see Timothy Mitchell, "The Properties of Markets," *Do Economists Make Markets?*, eds. Donald A. MacKenzie, Fabian Muniesa, and Lucia Siu (New Jersey: Princeton University Press, 2007) 244-75.

9   Mike Davis, "Who Will Build the Ark?" *New Left Review* 61 (2010) 29-46.

10 Greg Sharzer, "A Critique of Localist Political Economy and Urban Agriculture," *Historical Materialism* 20, 4 (2012) 75-114, 105.

11 Rolf Peter Sieferle, *The Subterranean Forest* (Cambridge: White Horse Press, 2010). See also Helmut Haberl "The Energetic Metabolism of Societies," *Journal of Industrial Ecology* 5, 2 (2002) 71-88.

12 Marshall Sahlins, *Stone Age Economics* (London: Routledge, 2012).

13 See William Cronon, *Changes in the Land* (London: Macmillan, 2011), for a discussion of the merits and demerits of such societies as they occurred in America.

14 James Scott develops an intriguing argument linking forms of low-intensity agriculture to attempts to escape incorporation into cities. See James Scott, *The Art of Not Being Governed* (New Haven: Yale University Press, 2009).

15 Joan Martinez-Alier, "The EROI of Agriculture and Its Use by the Via Campesina," *Journal of Peasant Studies* 38, 1 (2011) 145-60.

16 Colin A. M. Duncan, "On Identifying a Sound Environmental Ethic in History: Prolegomena to Any Future Environmental History," *Environmental History Review* (1991) 15.

17 Neil Brenner and Christian Schmid, "The 'Urban Age' in Question," this book, Ch. 21.

18 Kenneth Pomeranz, "Political Economy and Ecology on the Eve of Industrialization: Europe, China, and the Global Conjuncture," *The American Historical Review* 107, 2 (2002) 425-46.

19 Walter Rodney, *How Europe Underdeveloped Africa* (Baltimore: Black Classic Press, 2011).

20 As Moore insightfully argues, the expansion of the timber frontier to the Baltic region was part of this process. For example see, Jason W. Moore, "'Amsterdam Is Standing on Norway' Part II: The Global North Atlantic in the Ecological Revolution of the Long Seventeenth Century," *Journal of Agrarian Change* 10, 2 (2010) 188-227, 196-211.

21 Jonathan Nitzan and Shimshon Bichler, *Capital as Power: A Study of Order and Creorder* (Milton Park, Abingdon, Oxon: Routledge, 2009).

22 In three critically important works of comparative historical sociology, Sandra Halperin makes clear that human or social development in Europe was not the result of any "organic" process built into modernity but was, rather, the result of massive popular mobilizations coinciding with preparations for war. See Sandra Halperin, *Re-Envisioning Global Development* (London: Routledge, 2013); and Sandra Halperin, *In the Mirror of the Third World: Capitalist Development in Modern Europe* (New York: Cornell University Press, 1997); Sandra Halperin, *War and Social Change in Modern Europe* (Cambridge: Cambridge University Press, 2004).

23 Timothy Mitchell, *Carbon Democracy: Political Power in the Age of Oil* (London: Verso, 2011) 139.

24 Ibid.

25 Ibid.; Farshad Araghi, "Food Regimes and the Production of Value: Some Methodological Issues," *Journal of Peasant Studies* 30 (2003) 41-70.

26 Matt Huber, "The Use of Gasoline: Value, Oil, and the 'American Way of Life,'" *Antipode* 41, 3 (2009) 465-486; Matt Huber, "Fueling Capitalism: Oil, the Regulation Approach, and the Ecology of Capital," *Economic Geography* 89, 2 (2013) 171-94. On oil prices in this era, see John R. Blair, *The Control of Oil* (New York: Pantheon Books, 1976).

27 Duncan, "On Identifying a Sound Environmental Ethic in History," 16-22.

28 William E. Rees and Mathis Wackernagel, "Urban Ecological Footprints: Why Cities Cannot be Sustainable and Why They are a Key to Sustainability," *Environmental Impact Assessment Review*, 16 (1996) 223-48, 239.

29 Ibid., 225.

30 Nicholas Georgescu-Roegen, "Myths About Energy and Matter," *Growth & Change* 10, 1 (1979) 16; Herman E. Daly, "Myths About Energy and Matter: Comment," *Growth & Change* 10, 1 (1979) 24.

31 Larry Lohmann, "Capital and Climate Change," *Development and Change* 42, 2 (2011) 649-68.

32 Philip McMichael, *Development and Social Change* (Thousand Oaks: Sage Press, 2011) xiv.

33 Joshua Farley and Herman Daly, "The Failure of the Free-Market on a Full Planet," *Vortragsskript für ISEE/RC* (2001). http://www.utopia.uzh.ch/research/Farley_Daly_paper.pdf, 26.

34 See, among many critical studies of this phenomenon, Lorenzo Cotula, *Land Deals in Africa: What is in the Contracts?* (London: International Institute for Environment, 2011).

35 From a far more critical angle that claims to be skeptical of the "grand narrative of power and people-decentered architecture that dominate the iconic mega cities of today," one still reads of how "Asia and Africa in particular are experiencing rapid rural to urban migration." See Wendy Harcourt, "Editorial: Designing Urban Living," *Development* 54, 3 (2011) 291-2, 292, 291. Such accounts bracket the nature of the "push" factors that were creating that rural-to-urban migration in the first place.

36 One might object that much of the critical literature does in fact note that massive rural-urban migration is an effect of structural adjustment policies that make the countryside unlivable. But such an objection does not hold. First, the push-pull factors that produced massive and unsustainable urbanization preceded the structural adjustment policies, and were instead rooted in other kinds of unsustainable urban-biased policies—although those same structural adjustment policies are indeed intensifying and accelerating previous processes. Second, much of the literature accepts and arguably naturalizes the flow of population from country to city, since they accept the demographic projections which presuppose the continuance of such flows—an odd ontology that removes from consideration a range of possible scenarios that would arrest or alleviate such flows.

37 The instant-classic reference is Mike Davis, *Planet Of Slums* (London: Verso, 2006). I take issue with this important landmark due to its normalization of existing rural-urban migration tendencies, and due to its downplaying of the role of rural organizing in the world's anti-systemic movements.

38 Paul Collier and Stefan Dercon, "African Agriculture in 50 Years: Smallholders in a Rapidly Changing World?" *Expert Meeting on How to Feed the World In* (2009) 24-26. http://iis-db.stanford.edu/evnts/7365/Collier_Dercon_Africa_2013_world_development.pdf.

39 Under very different circumstances, agro-export financed substantial industrialization in late nineteenth-century Russia and early nineteenth-century Egypt. On the latter, see Jean Batou, "Nineteenth-Century Attempted Escapes from the Periphery: the Cases of Egypt and Paraguay," *Review (Fernand Braudel Center)* 16, 3 (1993) 279-318. But price volatility for agricultural commodities makes creating a development model around them chancy at best.

40 Miguel A. Altieri, "Applying Agroecology to Enhance the Productivity of Peasant Farming Systems in Latin America," *Environment, Development and Sustainability* 1, 3-4 (1999) 197-217.

41 Jack Ralph Kloppenburg, *First the Seed: The Political Economy of Plant Biotechnology* (Madison: University of Wisconsin Press, 2005). The point about 70 percent of the planet's food is a commonplace in the critical literature. As one report notes, the "ETC Group notes that there are 1.5 billion small farmers on 380 million farms; 800 million more growing urban gardens; 410 million gathering the hidden harvest of our forests and savannas; 190 million pastoralists and well over 100 million peasant fishers. At least 370 million of these are also indigenous peoples. Together these farmers make up almost half the world's peoples and grow at least 70 percent of the world's food" (footnote no. 8 in Fairtrade Foundation, *Powering up Smallholder Farmers to Make Food Fair* (Fairtrade Foundation, 2013) 44); Nick Minot, "Transmission of World Food Price Changes to Markets in Sub-Saharan Africa," *Washington, IFPRI* 34 (2011); and Jacques Morisset, "Unfair Trade? The Increasing Gap Between World and Domestic Prices in Commodity Markets During the Past 25 Years," *The World Bank Economic Review* 12, 3 (1998) 503-26.

42 Marc J. Cohen and James L. Garrett, *The Food Price Crisis and Urban Food (in)Security* (London: IIED and UNFPA, 2009) 6.

43 Joseph Baines argues that these prices are also the product of politically instituted markets, engineered to concentrate profits in some hands and not others. See Joseph Baines, "Food Price Inflation as Redistribution: Towards a New Analysis of Corporate Power in the World Food System," *New Political Economy* (2013) 1-34.

44 David Satterthwaite, Gordon McGranahan and Cecilia Tacoli, "Urbanization and Its Implications for Food and Farming," *Philosophical Transactions of the Royal Society B: Biological Sciences* 365 (2010) 2809-20.

45 Tom Lavers, "'Land Grab' as Development Strategy? The Political Economy of Agricultural Investment in Ethiopia," *Journal of Peasant Studies* 39, 1 (2012) 105-32; and Silvia Federici, "The Debt Crisis, Africa and the New Enclosures," *Midnight Notes* 10 (1992) 10-17.

46 Alain de Janvry and Elisabeth Sadoulet, "Subsistence Farming as a Safety Net for Food-price Shocks," *Development in Practice* 21, 4-5 (2011) 472-80. In Latin America, for example, the remaining rural population is living amidst the aftermath of centuries of colonial land concentration and a mid-century interlude of capitalist agrarian reforms, and rural semi-proletarianization and functional dualism in agriculture remain the dominant modes of production and social reproduction. But the question of what follows from the social organization of production is an inherently political question. On semiproletarianization, see Cristóbal Kay, "Rural Poverty and Development Strategies in Latin America," *Journal of Agrarian Change* 6, 4 (2006) 455-508; and on functional dualism, Alain de Janvry, *The Agrarian Question and Reformism in Latin America* (Baltimore: Johns Hopkins University Press, 1981).

47 María Elena Martínez-Torres and Peter M. Rosset, "La Vía Campesina: The Birth and Evolution of a Transnational Social Movement," *Journal of Peasant Studies* 37 (2010) 149-75; and Wendy Wolford, *This Land Is Ours Now: Social Mobilization and the Meanings of Land in Brazil* (Durham: Duke University Press, 2010).

48 Collier and Dercon, "African Agriculture in 50 Years."

49 John Vandermeer, Gerald Smith, Ivette Perfecto, Eileen Quintero, Rachel Bezner-Kerr, Daniel Griffith, Stuart Ketcham, Steve Latta, Brenda Lin, Phil McMichael, Krista McGuire, Ron Nigh, Diana Rocheleau and John Soluri, *Effects of Industrial Agriculture on Global Warming and the Potential of Small-scale Agroecological Techniques to Reverse Those Effects.* www.viacampesina.net/downloads/DOC/ViaNWAEG-10-20-09.doc.

50 Rees and Wackernagel, "Urban Ecological Footprints," 237.

51 Sieferle, *The Subterranean Forest.*

52 Helmut Haberl, Fridolin Krausmann and Simone Gingrich, "Ecological Embeddedness of the Economy: A Socioecological Perspective on Humanity's Economic Activities 1700-2000," *Economic and Political Weekly* 41, 47 (2006) 4896, 4903.

53 James Lovelock, "Nuclear Power is the Only Green Solution," *The Independent* (2004). http://www.independent.co.uk/voices/commentators/james-lovelock-nuclear-power-is-the-only-green-solution-6169341.html

54 Colin A. Duncan, *The Centrality of Agriculture: Between Humankind and the Rest of Nature* (Montreal: McGill Queens University Press, 1996).

55 Ibid., 47.

56 Duncan makes this point with reference to the example of wooden versus metal furniture, writing, "Perfectly cheap and profitable projects are refused a hearing in our type of modern economy if they are very long-term. This explains why along the shores of Lake Ontario you see nuclear electric power plants instead of oak forests. Oak forests have quite negligible start-up costs but are extremely slow at growing. The commitments we make in these fields are pervasive and include expensive feed-back loops. For instance, schools and universities in Ontario have hardly any more oak furniture. Instead they have mostly steel furniture. Steel production facilities are enormous consumers of electric power, as Ontario citizens were recently reminded (December, 1989) when the electric power authorities shut various factories down for a period. Inattention to long-term projects, makes our lives now, and later, simply more expensive than they need be." Duncan, "On Identifying a Sound Environmental Ethic in History," 21.

57 David R. Montgomery, *Dirt: The Erosion of Civilizations* (Berkeley: University of California Press, 2012).

58 The debate about whether or not nature is a useful term is rich and contentious, and makes specific citation here useless. I use "nature" and "the environment," interchangeably to refer to non-human material world around us, which includes both the ecology as well as the human built environment. For that reason, I think it is a reasonable claim to say that the environment can be arranged in such a way as to allow different maximal human populations.

59 Duncan, "On Identifying a Sound Environmental Ethic in History," 9.

60 Mumford, *The City in History.*

61 Fernand Braudel, *The Structures of Everyday Life* (Berkeley: University of California Press, 1981), 430-31; and Stephen A. Marglin, "Farmers, Seedsmen, and Scientists: Systems of Agriculture and Systems of Knowledge," *Decolonizing Knowledge,* eds. Frédérique Apffel-Marglin and Stephen A. Marglin (Oxford: Oxford University Press, 1996) 185-248.

62 Peter Kropotkin and George Woodcock, *Fields, Factories, and Workshops* (Montreal: Black Rose Books, 1993 [1898]); and Ebenezer Howard, *Garden Cities of To-Morrow* (London: Routledge, 2013 [1898]).

63 Mindi Schneider and Philip McMichael, "Deepening, and Repairing, the Metabolic Rift," *Journal of Peasant Studies* 37 (2010) 461-84.

64 New York City, for example, needs a massive hinterland to supply its eight million people with food. In the long run, such imbalances ought to be fixed through collective processes of decision-making and society-wide planning.

65 Lewis Mumford, "Garden Cities and the Metropolis: a Reply," *The Journal of Land & Public Utility Economics* 22, 1 (1946) 67.

66 Sharanbir S. Grewal and Parwinder S. Grewal, "Can Cities Become Self-reliant in Food?," *Cities* 29, 1 (2012) 1-11.

67 John Friedmann, "Basic Needs, Agropolitan Development, and Planning from Below," *World Development* 7, 6 (1979) 607-13.

68 Kirkpatrick Sale, *Human Scale* (New Catalyst Books, 2007).

69 Stephen Marglin, "Development as Poison: Rethinking the Western Model of Modernity," *Harvard International Review* 25, 1 (2003) 70-75, 73.

70 Masanobu Fukuoka, *The One-Straw Revolution: An Introduction to Natural Farming* (New York: New York Review Books Classics, 2009). This example is taken from Duncan's *The Centrality of Agriculture*.

71 Davis, *Planet of Slums*, 1-19, 55-61.

72 There is an important debate within circles concerned with rural development between land reforms, which are redistributive and involve minimal or no compensation for large landholders, and "market-friendly" land reform, which involves compensation for land-holders at market rates. See Saturnino M. Borras, *Pro-poor Land Reform: a Critique* (Ottawa: University of Ottawa Press, 2007).

73 Jörg Friedrichs, "Global Energy Crunch: How Different Parts of the World Would React to a Peak Oil Scenario," *Energy Policy* 38, 8 (2010) 4562-69.

74 Michael Levien, "The Land Question: Special Economic Zones and the Political Economy of Dispossession in India," *Journal of Peasant Studies* 39, 3-4 (2012) 933-69. See also John Friedmann, "Becoming Urban: On Whose Terms?" this book, Ch. 33.

75 I do not mean to sidestep the question of people being forced to stay in the countryside or being pushed there and dying as a result. For example, see Ben Kiernan, "The Demography of Genocide in Southeast Asia: the Death Tolls in Cambodia, 1975-79; and East Timor, 1975-80," *Critical Asian Studies* 35, 4 (2003) 585-97. However, there is a sharp difference between inclusive, democratic modes of planning and authoritarian ones, and it was obviously the latter—not the return to the countryside as such—that produced mass death in the Cambodian context.

76 Jacob Songsore, *The Urban Transition in Ghana* (IIED, 2009). http://pubs.iied.org/pdfs/G02540.pdf.

77 Carmen Diana Deere, Niurka Pérez, and Ernel Gonzales, "The View from Below: Cuban Agriculture in the 'Special Period in Peacetime,'" *The Journal of Peasant Studies* 21, 2 (1994) 194-234.

78 Kirkpatrick Sale, *Dwellers in the Land* (Athens: University of Georgia Press, 2000).

79 James C. Scott, *Seeing Like a State* (New Haven: Yale University Press, 1999).

80 Ivan Kremnev, "The Journey of My Brother Alexei to the Land of Peasant Utopia," *The Journal of Peasant Studies* 4, 1 (1976) 63-108.

81 P. Orlovskii, "Foreword," *The Journal of Peasant Studies* 4, 1 (1976) 69, 70.

82 Industrialization worsened human welfare indicators in England and elsewhere. See John Komlos, "Shrinking in a Growing Economy? The Mystery of Physical Stature During the Industrial Revolution," *Journal of Economic History* 58 (1998) 779-802.

83 Giovanni Arrighi, Beverly J. Silver and Benjamin D. Brewer, "Industrial Convergence, Globalization, and the Persistence of the North-South Divide," *Studies in Comparative International Development* 38, 1 (2003) 3-31.

84 Duncan, *The Centrality of Agriculture*, 182.

85 Paul Collier, "The Politics of Hunger: How Illusion and Greed Fan the Food Crisis," *Foreign Affairs* 87, 6 (2008) 67-79, 69, 70.

86 I borrow the phrase "Victims of Our Visions," from Piero Gleijeses's review of Richard Drinnon's "Facing West," *Washington Post* (Washington) 28 September 1980.

33
BECOMING URBAN: ON WHOSE TERMS?

John Friedmann

In this chapter, I address three questions: first, the language of urban research, or more precisely, when we speak of the urban, what do we mean? Second, when we do research, especially in Asia, why should peri-urban zones command our attention? And third, whose imaginary of the city counts? I conclude with some reflections on urban research in Asia by Western and indigenous Asian scholars.

The Language of Urban Research

It is said that we live in an urban age: the phrase has become a cliché, but what does it mean? In a recent article, Neil Brenner and Christian Schmid launch a blistering attack on the rural/urban dichotomy.[1] Counting heads, population densities, and the lit-up globe at night all suggest some form of urbanity that has burst through territorial limits. And yet, while putting dots on a map, we still cling to outdated notions of "the city." But, according to Brenner and Schmid, what we still refer to as "city" is an untheorized phenomenon constructed by statisticians (whom they call "state-isticians"); according to the authors, it is a "chaotic" concept. I would agree. What they are after is a new and theoretically grounded language of "the urban" on a planetary scale.

What does this "new urban" look like? Here are some numbers produced by statisticians. Without being too precise—the data are posted on official websites and arbitrarily bounded—the scale is, by any definition, huge: a Lagos of 8 million, a Cairo 10 million, an Istanbul of 15 million, a Mumbai of 20 million, a Chongqing of 30 million, a Tokyo of 35 million. And all of them still growing at top rates! These places are no longer "cities" in any conventional sense but vast assemblages of human settlement that are the demographic size of some mid-sized countries: metropolitan Lagos is larger than Scotland, Tokyo larger than all of Canada. But of course, counting only heads, these numbers don't even begin to tell us how these monster places are to be understood as "urban" and indeed as places, and how they can be managed, never mind "rationally planned."

In one aspect of their conceptualization, Brenner and Schmid encourage us to think of certain "essential" characteristics that we generally associate with the term urban, and also that they configure the urban in some quantifiable way. But let's be clear about one thing: even if we could dispense with boundaries as we attempt to quantify the urban—and every boundary (we recall) is drawn in our heads more than on the ground—the urban is an inherently spatial concept, part of the earth's human geography. We therefore have to deal not only with defining what we mean by the urban, but also deal with the urban's counter-concept, the spaces that lie beyond it, and which by common consent are called "rural." But the rural is, of course, an equally "chaotic" concept.

So let us begin to think of some (measurable) criteria that would allow us to pinpoint whatever we think of as the "inherently urban" in twenty-first-century local jurisdictions.[2] Let me throw out a few terms for consideration: year-round accessibility (time-distance *thresholds* to critical urban services, jobs, and administrative centers); a given proportion of income derived from production in the secondary, tertiary, and quaternary sectors; reliable year-round electric power; the number of computers/TV receivers per 1,000 households; high levels of education (for women and men); invested capital per unit area; and similar criteria on which most of us could (hopefully) agree as representing today's urban. Preferably, the number of criteria should be kept small, but they must be sufficient to allow us to differentiate among *degrees* of the urban continuum. Such a list suggests to me that we might want to think of "the urban" not so much as a settlement space or some form of the built environment, but as varied *assemblages* of certain measurable characteristics.[3]

Suppose then that we could map these indicators. The result would be a map showing *degrees of urbanity* distributed over space. There is a well-known saying that a woman can't be a little bit pregnant: either she is, or she isn't. But as regards the urban, one can indeed be a little bit urban, all the way to being fully urban, depending on the number of characteristics (or the intensity) of the urban that combine to produce the assemblage at particular localities. In some parts of the world, a few of these assemblages might even be called "super-organisms," a term I borrow from biology, which are densely settled urban clusters such as we find in the Pearl River Delta outlined by Guangzhou, Shenzhen, Hong Kong, and Macao with over seventy million people, and which are largely on auto-pilot.

With such a map in hand, you could draw boundaries over this global *skein of the urban* (Teilhard de Chardin called it the noösphere, which stands for the sphere of the human mind) to define specific governmentalities, regions, and zones for whatever analytical purposes you have in mind. But your map would clearly reveal forms of urban intensification (which we conventionally call towns, cities, metro-regions or by similar designations), and of spatially extended urban phenomena that are linked to each other through lines of electronic communication and high-speed transport, thus producing ever larger and more complex urban networks or systems. What I think we would see on such a map is that in most parts of the world, there are very few areas today that are not already touched in some ways by the urban. Or to put it otherwise: the rural, increasingly capitalized and inevitably drawn into the urban sphere through means of communication, thus comes to be gradually metamorphosed into the urban.[4]

Let me now take this line of reasoning a step further. Neil Brenner has suggested that the urban, however we choose to define it, constitutes a "force field" that could be further divided according to certain salient forces, such as the complex contours of economic, political, and cultural variables.[5] It seems to me that force fields such as these would have proportionately *inverse* effects on ecology and the environment, so that we can say that "the more intensively urban an assemblage at a given location, the greater will be its negative impact on air, water, land and global resources—in short, on the planet's natural environment." Additionally, as a powerful and networked force field, intensively urban areas tend to attract both population and capital which, once converted into political and administrative power, seek to penetrate and colonize areas both near and far and their less articulated force fields because it requires them to strengthen and consolidate its power.[6]

But enough for now of the urban and its theorization. What I want to focus on in this chapter is precisely these contoured spaces of penetration and colonization that surround major urban concentrations, and which we call the peri-urban. As "zones of encounter," the peri-urban can fall entirely within the realm of one or more administrative urban regimes or else show an admixture of urban and rural regimes of governmentality as defined by local conventions.

Peri-urban Zones of Encounter

Let me be geographically more specific: I will focus here on East, Southeast, and South Asian regions that are, first, undergoing an accelerated process of becoming more intensively urban; and second, displaying relatively high population densities, especially along sea coasts and major river basins—densities of occupance that are equal to, if not higher than typical North American suburbs.[7] The boundaries that define these peri-urban zones are themselves dynamic and imprecise. On the near side, they shade off into local suburbias, on the far side, into areas whose penetration by the urban is still relatively weak though increasing over time. For simplicity's sake, I refer to the high-intensity urban core as "the city," but this designation is intended as merely a symbolic expression for a space that has a very high overall intensity of agreed-upon assemblages of urban characteristics.

Cities in Asia are now expanding at breath-taking rates in both population and land coverage. Millions of migrants are moving in from the countryside propelled by a search for a better life, which they perceive to be "urban." As the city thus expands into the peri-urban, it comes into conflict with already densely occupied spaces in villages, towns and secondary intensifications of the urban, such as urban satellites. The peri-urban zone is thus inevitably a zone of conflict and struggle, ostensibly over land but at a deeper level also over people's subsistence and livelihood. It would be false, however, to cast this as just another moral tale, with a hegemonic city "colonizing" the living fabric of the peri-urban. Generally speaking, villagers and townspeople on the city's periphery want to share in what they perceive as the promise of life in the urban centre and its margins, where they can sell what they produce, find jobs, and where their children hope, in a not too distant future, to become full-fledged urbanites themselves. Yet at the same time, they also resist colonization and displacement from lands which give them a measure of security.

Meanwhile, and despite local resistance, the urban force field of the city extends its reach ever outward into the peri-urban, particularly along major access roads. The city needs to safeguard its water supply, needs land to dump its solid wastes, needs additional land for ports, airports, and warehousing, all of which are space-extensive. Harried middle-class urbanites dream of recreation areas in the remaining pristine hills and forests surrounding the city. Special Economic Zones for export production are projected into the peri-urban along with middle-class real estate ventures and luxury resorts, all of which require vast tracts of land. Some cities, such as Manila and Beijing, have banned noxious industries from their center, which now have no other choice than to find new locations in the peri-urban. And not least, many of the migrant workers who are drawn, as if by a magnet, to the city, are settling on *terrains vagues* of varied ownership claims, putting up self-built housing where they can, because there is no other place that will have them.

The peri-urban zones, then, are not a *tabula rasa* nor *terra nullius,* a no-one's land. In Asia, they are already densely inhabited spaces, the land cultivated and productive, sustaining the livelihood of multitudes: there are no extensive, unclaimed tracts of open unclaimed space in the peri-urban for the city to move into and consolidate its existence. Each new urban land claim encounters prior claims to land by squatters, peasant farmers, shanty dwellers, townsfolk whose livelihood is now at stake, and already existing smaller concentrations of the urban. Their titles to the land are often murky, but there is no question regarding their actual use-claims on the land and the utilitarian values these claims have for them as spaces of production and social reproduction. The question then is: on whose terms will the resulting conflict of this encounter be resolved? And are there alternate forms of becoming urban to the ones I've sketched? Whose vision of the future city will prevail? To answer these questions, let us consider several stories, the first from Istanbul, the second a more complex story from Rajasthan, India. Both deal with dispossession.

Whose Imaginary of the Future City?

A recent article by Asu Aksoy explains how this city of 15 million is being utterly changed according to an imaginary of the urban that has swept the world in a single-minded attempt to attract investments, promote globalized economic development and so "become modern."[8] Supported by successive mayors of Istanbul and now also by the central government, the aim of this imaginary is to wipe away the old and replace it with the look of a particular form of glossy Western modernity to which the middle class and its ruling elites aspire as, indeed, they have done for over a century. "Every part of the city is exposed to radical change," he writes, "as more and more land is being pulled into the market sphere, catapulting the whole of Istanbul into an irreversible process of large-scale urban development." He continues:

> In hegemonic circles, there is now a shared aspiration and vision of Istanbul as a globalized and gentrified city, with monitored and orderly public spaces and residential zones, with an attractive public image, world-class services and with a cleaned-up heritage. The spatial politics of the city are governed by the needs of the new economy of consumption, tourism, recreation, and high-end services.... As Istanbul now becomes fragmented into an archipelago of gated communities, residential complexes, recreational zones and tourist areas, it ceases to be a real city and becomes simply an immense agglomeration of disparate zones and construction.[9]

Of course, there is resistance as old neighborhoods are torn down and replaced by condominiums, malls, and sleek office towers many of them designed by foreign architects. But, Aksoy continues:

> maybe the most challenging of all ... is the complexity and diversity of dispositions among social actors and citizens of Istanbul. This may well be the Achilles heel of the civic-democratic movement. Simply put, the growth paradigm promising increased urban rent is undermining the effective coalition....[G]rowth rhetoric has become part of the political [imperative] to make Istanbul a global powerhouse.[10]

This story brings to mind Schumpeter's famous phrase that, inexorably, capitalism is inherently propelled forward by wave after wave of "creative destruction." Innovation, competition and ruthless entrepreneurial energy are central to this obsession with a form of economic growth that celebrates whatever is new, no matter its human and environmental costs, costs that tend to be treated as "collateral damage," regrettable but unavoidable.

History is bunk, declared Henry Ford a century ago. It has been melted down into the coin of profit.

In this latter-day view, capitalism seeks to trans-value all values but one: the virtues of continuous accumulation. The global capitalist class of the super-rich has therefore been raised to dizzying heights to which we are expected to bow down. Give me land, demand the global financiers, and land is given them, along with the people who live on it and work the land. And to accomplish this expeditiously, the state has entered into a partnership with global capital, for reasons, one presumes, of mutual benefit.[11]

My next story comes from Rajasthan in India. India is still predominantly a country of small farmers. Two-thirds of its people live off the land, supplementing their meager earnings with mostly unskilled non-farm work, and—as Michael Levien tells it—"significant sections of that peasantry remain, for various reasons, uninterested in selling it." Following the economic historian Karl Polanyi, he argues that:

> Land is a "fictitious" commodity, not only because it is a non-produceable [sic] asset with location-specific qualities but also because it is valued in multiple ways (for example, as a habitation and a long-term source of security) that are not readily reducible to exchange value. Even where farmers would, in principle, like to exit agriculture, they are often reluctant to surrender land where non-farm opportunities appear unpromising ...[12]

To facilitate this process of dispossession, the government has stepped in to expropriate the land for what it declares to be a "public purpose" and then to lease it back to private developers of Special Economic Zones (SEZ), for instance, to build luxury housing, golf courses, hotels and shopping malls. As Levien tells it, "SEZs thus complete the transition to a land-broker state in which the chief economic function of state governments [in India] is to acquire land for unrestricted private capital accumulation."[13]

Levien's case study is based on field work in the grandly named Mahindra World City, a multipurpose "integrated industrial city" in the peri-urban zone of Rajasthan's capital, Jaipur, which is slated to become the largest IT Special Economic Zone in the country. In the early part of the millennium, the Jaipur Development Authority acting as an agent of the state, acquired nine villages and 3,000 acres of land, of which 2000 acres were privately owned farm land and 1,000 acres were common grazing land nominally owned by the government.[14] The private properties were compensated at a price set by the Authority, but no compensation was paid for the grazing land, which until then had sustained a livestock economy in the surrounding villages. Such cattle as there were had to be sold off at whatever price they could fetch.

In the villages studied by Levien, land ownership varied according to caste, grouped into four broad categories: General castes (mostly Brahmin), Jat (a traditional land-cultivating caste), Otherwise Backward Castes (OBC), and Scheduled Castes/Tribes (SC/ST) at the bottom. The starting position in average size of family landholdings was then as follows (all figures expressed in hectares): 4.6 (General), 7.3 (Jat), 3.0 (OBC), and 2.2 (SC/ST). Although the scheduled castes and tribals made up 35 percent of the sample population, they owned only 15 percent of the land. They were also the least educated and economically most vulnerable part of the population: 15 percent of them were landless. By contrast, Jat caste families, comprising 17 percent of all households, owned about a third of all village lands.

Official compensation maintained this initial position of economic inequality. Land-holding households received a basic compensation, according to the amount of land they owned. In addition, however, they also received back a quarter of the land they had given up (in quantity, though not necessarily land they had previously cultivated) to do with as they saw fit. In the land rush that ensued—speculative buyers converged upon the nine villages from distant locations to buy up these parcels of land conveniently located on the edge of the SEZ. Those households that had the greatest need for cash—the scheduled castes and tribes—were the first to sell their land at the lowest prices on offer, while those with greater ability to hold off sales as the Special Economic Zone came to be built out, were able to benefit from the ever escalating prices, that surged from $16,000 per hectare in 2003 to $280,000 in some areas some five years later.

Existing economic inequalities were thus not merely reproduced, they were actually increased as those with better networks and more education (the higher castes) put their money to work in a variety of activities, from paying off debts, constructing housing, digging wells, buying up properties in more distant places, or starting small business ventures (a form of agrarian involution, according to Levien). Also notable is the number of households who now had less food on the table. Seventy-five percent of the lowest, most numerous caste, the vast majority of whom had already sold their compensation plot at the time of Levien's survey, claimed that they now had "less food" to eat. In short, they had been reduced to penury and now went hungry. By contrast, among the Jat who at the time of research still held on to 75 percent of their compensation plots, only 25 percent reported having less food.[15] Still, hunger is hunger. And half the dispossessed peasantry claimed to have less food to eat now that they no longer farmed their own lands or had cattle to graze.

I have stylized this story somewhat to show what "creative destruction" looks like when it sweeps over farming communities in peri-urban India. With appropriate variations, it is a story that could be multiplied the length and breadth of the Indian federation with its 1.2 billion people of whom roughly two-thirds are still tied to the land. The destruction is clear in terms of human lives. Its effects on the environment are also devastating. Both, however, are typically treated as "collateral damage" of global accumulation in a race for "worlding" Asia's cities.[16] I am not saying that all peasant farmers are "victims," and that they have no means of creatively responding to the circumstances that confront them. But the old ways of life and livelihood are being sacrificed for the glittering promise of the new.

So what, if anything, is to be done? To move what are now considered regrettable if unavoidable side effects of economic growth into the center of attention would dramatically change the perspective. No longer would we then automatically buy into the capitalist utopia of cumulative growth forever, no longer accept the erasure of history and place, no longer embrace competition as if cooperation were not also vital to the human enterprise and perhaps the more important part, and finally get rid of the bizarre notion that, at the end of the day, the only values that matter are those to which a dollar sign can be attached.

All this is easy enough to say, but to what practical effect? Those of us who are Westerners— even though we might imagine ourselves as "global citizens"—hold no sway over India's government, or China's or Turkey's. We also know that the ideology and rhetoric of capitalism in its extreme neoliberal version is essentially an Anglo-American invention that also strikes close to home. We—Canadians, Americans and Europeans—have been its victims much as the peasantry on the outskirts of Mahindra World City or the migrant workers and modest citizens of globalizing Istanbul, for whom there is no place in the city's official imaginary.[17] My argument is therefore that the struggle for another city, a city that is inclusive and ecologically sustainable must, in the first instance, become our own struggle to be waged primarily at home.

And if the urban imaginary in much of Asia today is borrowed from the West even though it is destructive of human lives and history and place, then changing that imaginary in the heavily urbanized West, where it all started, pointing to the possibilities of other ways of becoming urban, may inspire civic movements in Asia that stress endogenous values of what it might mean to be urban and modern in this century. There are some signs that this may already be happening. Pankaj Mishra, closes his new book, *From the Ruins of Empire*, with these words:

> The hope that fuels the pursuit of endless economic growth—that billions of consumers in India and China will one day enjoy the lifestyles of Europeans and Americans—is as absurd and dangerous a fantasy as anything dreamed of by al-Quaeda. It condemns the global environment to early destruction and looks to create reservoirs of nihilistic rage and disappointment among hundreds of millions of have-nots—the bitter outcome of Western modernity, which turns the revenge of the East into something darkly ambiguous and all its victories truly Pyrrhic.[18]

These words, I take it, are aimed directly at us.

• • •

To conclude, I would like to share some reflections on these stories and what I think they imply for our research as Western scholars. I ended on what some might think a nihilistic mode, expressing skepticism concerning our ability as political outsiders to suggest ways of how to confront "becoming urban" in the countries of Asia where these processes are currently rampant. Let me summarize my thoughts.

First, although I have argued that Western scholars are powerless to change what happens in regions of the world where we conduct our research, the work we do is nonetheless important, I believe, because we act as public witnesses to processes that unless they are checked will continue to cause human pain and suffering. Although outsiders, our voices matter. They are the voices of record. On the other hand, scholars indigenous to countries in Asia, whether schooled abroad or not, are perforce insiders claiming a legitimate right as citizens, indeed an obligation to participate in local debates on policy in the countries of their birth.

Second, the authorial self and how we position ourselves *vis-à-vis* the phenomena observed matters. The old belief in the possibilities of a value-free, objective social science was clearly in error. To present the stark reality of things: we are either with the few who command power or with the many who are powerless and whose rights as human beings are being violated by the juggernaut of the capitalist city. By exposing social wrongs, we declare ourselves in solidarity with those who are wronged. In public displays of solidarity; we strengthen those who are resisting.

Third, as public witnesses, the observed differences of time and place matter. Becoming urban may be the general descriptive term, but what is ultimately important resides in the detailed stories: the specific actors and institutional settings involved, the hows and whys of converging or diverging processes of the phenomena examined. All these help to evoke and explain reality. To avoid the phrase from becoming a cliché, it is their specificities that bring historical phenomena to life.

Fourth, comparative research is important because it is in the context of multiple comparisons that specific differences of similar processes can be identified and reliable interpretations can be made. Similar results may have different causes, while similar causes may have diverging outcomes. None of this becomes evident so long as we focus on only single case studies, neglecting to draw comparisons.

Fifth and finally, as urban scholars, we need to have a clear understanding of the urban in its multiple meanings, spatial configurations, and forms of governance. *The urban is no longer simply a specific place—though it is that as well—but a global meta-process of continual change.* As the context of specific stories of "becoming urban," this meta-process is itself a theoretical construct concerning the larger operative forces that frame the phenomena we undertake to study.

Notes

1   Neil Brenner and Christian Schmid, "The 'Urban Age' in Question," this book, Ch. 21. From a planning approach, see also Shlomo Angel, *Planet of Cities* (Cambridge: Lincoln Institute of Land Policy, 2012). And for a neo-Marxist view, Andy Merrifield, "The Urban Question Under Planetary Urbanization," this book, Ch. 12.

2   As an aside, the time period chosen for this exercise is important. What used to be "essentially urban" in the past, thinking from Babylon on up to our own times, has varied enormously. See Joyce Marcus and Jeremy Sabloff, eds., *The Ancient City: New Perspectives on Urbanism in the Old and New World* (Santa Fe: School for Advanced Research Press, 2008).

3   Ignacio Farías, "The Politics of Urban Assemblages" *City* 15, 3-4 (2011) 365-74 and the literature cited therein.

4   Edward Soja, "Regional Urbanization and the End of the Metropolis Era," this book, Ch. 19.

5   Neil Brenner, email correspondence with author, April 2013.

6   See Alan Berger, *Drosscape: Wasting Land in Urban America* (New York: Princeton Architectural Press, 2006).

7   The peri-urban in North America is very different, because in most parts of the country, there are plenty of open spaces into which the urban can expand unless it meets the force field of another expanding city. You might consider the urban density of Los Angeles' sprawling suburban areas whose average density is about 7,000 per square mile. This and more is brilliantly on display in Berger, *Drosscape*.

8   Asu Aksoy, "Riding the Storm: 'New Istanbul,'" *City*, 16, 1-2 (2012) 93-111.

9   Ibid., 99 and 108.

10 Ibid., 109.

11 For the US, see www.nytimes.com/interactive/2012/12/01/us/government-incentives.html. Local governments give away $80.3 billion a year, with Texas in the lead.

12 Michael Levien, "The Land Question: Special Economic Zones and the Political Economy of Dispossession in India," *Journal of Peasant Studies* 39, 3-4 (2012) 933-69.

13 Ibid., 945.

14 Ibid., 946.

15 Ibid., 958, Table 3 .

16 For China, see Elizabeth C. Economy, *The River Runs Black: The Environmental Challenge to China's Future* (Ithaca, Cornell University Press, 2004). On "worlding," see Ananya Roy and Aiwah Oi, *Worlding Cities: Asian Experiments and the Art of Being Global* (Malden: Wiley-Blackwell, 2011).

17 For some telling details, see Hedrick Smith, *Who Stole the American Dream?* (New York: Random House, 2012).

18 Pankaj Mishra, *From the Ruins of Empire* (New York: Farrar, Straus and Giroux, 2012) 309-310.

CODA

If the traditional city is dissolving, and urbanization is being generalized across the planet, can new forms of citizenship be constructed that empower people collectively to appropriate, transform and reshape the common space of the world?

Henri Lefebvre

34
DISSOLVING CITY, PLANETARY METAMORPHOSIS

Henri Lefebvre

Several decades ago, the urban—viewed as the sum of productive practices and historical experiences—was seen as the vehicle for new values and an alternative civilization. Such hopes are fading concurrently with the last illusions of modernity. Today, it is impossible to write with the lyricism and modernist ecstasy embraced by Apollinaire:

> Paris nights are drunk with gin
> And blaze with electricity
> Green fires, flashing along their spines
> Tramways up and down their rails
> Shed tunes of mechanical folly.[1]

Eventually, the critique of the modern city dovetails with the critique of everyday life in the contemporary world. And yet, this conclusion leads immediately to several paradoxes. The first is that the more the city is extended, the more its social relations deteriorate. Since the end of the nineteenth century, cities in most developed countries experienced an extraordinary growth, kindling considerable hopes. But, in reality, city life did not produce entirely new social relations.

Everything occurs as if the expansion of older cities and the establishment of new ones served to preserve and protect relations of dependence, domination, exclusion and exploitation. In short, the framework of everydayness was slightly modified, but its contents were not transformed. And due to the expansion of urban forms on the one hand and the explosion of traditional forms of productive labor on the other, it is plausible to claim that the condition of city-dwellers (*citadins*) was degraded even further. These consequences are intertwined. The appearance of new technologies leads simultaneously to new ways of organizing production and to new ways of organizing urban space. The latter interact in ways that are mutually detrimental rather than beneficial.

There was a time when city centers were active and productive, and thus belonged to the workers (*populaire*). In this epoch, moreover, the City (*cité*) operated primarily through its center. The dislocation of this urban form began in the late nineteenth century, resulting in the deportation of all that the population considered active and productive into suburbs (*banlieues*), which were being located ever further away. The ruling class can be blamed for this, but it was simply making skillful use of an urban trend and a requirement of the relations of production. Could factories and polluting industries be maintained in the urban cores?

Nevertheless, the political benefit for the dominant classes is clear: the gentrification (*embourgeoisement*) of city centers, the replacement of the earlier productive centrality with a center for decision-making and services. The urban center is not only transformed into a site of consumption; it also becomes an object of consumption, and is valued as such. The producers, who had earlier been exported—or more accurately deported—to the suburbs (*banlieues*), now return as tourists to the center from which they had been dispossessed and expropriated. Peripheral populations are today reclaiming urban centers as places of leisure, of empty and unscheduled time. In this way, the urban phenomenon is profoundly transformed. The historic center has disappeared as such. All that remains are, on the one hand, centers for power and decision-making and, on the other, fake and artificial spaces. It is true, of course, that the city endures, but only as museum and as spectacle. The urban, conceived and lived as a social practice, is in the process of deteriorating and perhaps disappearing.

All this produces a specific dialecticization of social relations, revealing a second paradox: centers and peripheries presuppose and oppose one another. This phenomenon, which has deep roots and infamous historical precedents, is currently intensifying to such a degree that it encompasses the entire planet—as illustrated for example in North-South relations. Hence emerges a crucial question that exceeds that of the urban. Are new forms arising in the entire world and imposing themselves upon the city? Or, on the contrary, is an urban model gradually expanding to the worldwide scale? A third hypothesis suggests that we are currently in a transitory period of mutations in which the urban and the global crosscut and reciprocally disrupt each other.

Let us continue this critical assessment. Towards the end of the nineteenth century, scientific knowledge began to address the city. Urban sociology, understood as a scientific discipline, was inaugurated in Germany by, among others, Max Weber. But this science of the city has not kept its promises. It brought forth what we today term "urbanism" (*l'urbanisme*), which amounts to extremely rigid guidelines for architectural design and extremely vague information for the authorities and bureaucrats. Despite a few meritorious efforts, urbanism has not attained the status of a theory (*pensée*) of the city. What is worse, it has gradually shrunk to become a kind of gospel for technocrats.

How and why have so many investigations and evaluations failed to produce a living and livable City (*cité*)? It is easy to blame capitalism and the pursuit of profitability and social control. This response seems all the more inadequate since the socialist world has encountered the same difficulties and the same failures in that domain. Shouldn't we therefore interrogate and call into question the Western mode of thought? After so many centuries, our way of thinking still hinges upon its earthbound (*terriennes*) origins. It has not yet become completely urbane (*citadine*) and has only been able to produce a strictly instrumental conception of the urban (*l'urbain*). This conception has prevailed since the Greeks and grounded their thinking. For them, the City (*cité*) is an instrument of political and military organization. It becomes a religious environment in the Middle Ages before subsequently, with the arrival of the industrial bourgeoisie, acquiring the status of an instrument for the reproduction of labor power. Until this time, only poets have understood the city as the dwelling-place (*demeure*) of humans. It is here that an astonishing fact may be explained: the socialist world has only slowly and belatedly become aware of the immensity of urban questions and of their decisive nature for building a new society. This represents a third paradox.

Yet, serious dangers weigh upon the city in general and upon each city in particular. These dangers are aggravated daily. Cities are made doubly dependent upon technocracy and bureaucracy, in a word, upon institutions. Indeed, the institutional is the enemy of urban life (*la vie urbaine*), whose fate it freezes. In the new towns, the signs of technocracy are all too evident, indelible stains that illustrate the impotence of all efforts to promote urban stimulation, be it through architectural innovation, information, cultural initiatives or associational life. Everyone can see that the municipalities are subsumed under a statist framework (*le modéle étatique*); they reproduce at a small scale the customs of management and domination associated with the State's bureaucratic hierarchy. City dwellers (*citadins*) see their formal rights as citizens (*citoyen*) reduced, along with the opportunity to exercise such rights. There is much talk about decisions and the powers of decision-making, but in fact these powers remain in the authorities' hands. There is even more talk about information and information technologies at the municipal scale.

But if such technologies, such as computer cabling and communication networks, provide a new right to consume information, they fail to grant a right to produce the latter. At most, this happens only through the contemptible charade of communication that is labeled "interactivity." The consumer of information does not produce any information, and the citizen is separated from the producer. Yet again, the forms of communication have been changed in the urban milieu, but not its contents.

Another threat: the planetarization of the urban. It will span all of space during the third millennium if nothing manages to control its movement. This worldwide expansion entails the major risk that space will be homogenized and that diversities will be annihilated. But homogenization is accompanied by fragmentation. Space is divided into plots that can be bought and sold. Their prices depend on a hierarchy. In this way, even as it is homogenized, social space is also fragmented among spaces of work, leisure, material production and diverse services. During this process of differentiation, a further paradox appears: social classes are hierarchized as they are inscribed into space—this tendency is increasing rather than, as if often claimed, diminishing. Soon, only islands of agricultural production and concrete deserts will remain at the Earth's surface. Hence the importance of ecological questions: it is correct to assert that the milieu of life and the quality of the environment have acquired an urgent, politically central status. Inasmuch as one accepts such an analysis, the prospects for action are profoundly transformed. Several well-known but somewhat neglected forms—such as associative life or grassroots democracy (*autogestion*)—must be reinstated as key priorities; they assume new meanings when applied to the urban. The question then is to know if social and political action can be formulated and rearticulated in relation to specific problems that, even if they are concrete, concern all dimensions of everyday life.

At first glance, everydayness appears quite simple. It is strongly imprinted by the repetitive. The analyst of everydayness quickly discovers its complexity and its multiple dimensions: physiological, biological, psychic, ethical, social, aesthetic, sexual, etc. None of these dimensions is fixed once and for all, and each of them can become the object of multiple claims insofar as everyday life represents the busiest crossroads (*le lieu le plus traversé*) for the contradictions of social practice. These contradictions are themselves revealed only incrementally. For example, those between play and gravity, use and exchange, the commodity and the commons, the local and the worldwide, and so forth. In the city, notably, play and gravity are at once opposed and merged; dwelling, going down the street, communicating and talking—they are both serious and fun.

The citizen (*citoyen*) and the city-dweller (*citadin*) have been dissociated. Being a citizen used to mean remaining for a long period of time in a territory. But in the modern city, the city-dweller is in perpetual movement—constantly circulating and settling again, eventually being extricated from place entirely, or seeking to do so. Moreover, in the large modern city, social relations tend to become international, not only due to migration processes but also, and especially, due to the multiplicity of communication technologies, not to mention the becoming worldwide (*mondialisation*) of knowledge. Given such trends, isn't it necessary to reformulate the framework for citizenship (*la citoyenneté*)? The city-dweller and the citizen must be linked but not conflated. The right to the city implies nothing less than a revolutionary concept of citizenship.

Translated by Laurent Corroyer, Marianne Potvin and Neil Brenner

Notes

1   Guillaume Apollinaire, "The Song of the Poorly Loved," *Alcools*, trans. Anne Hyde Greet (Berkeley and Los Angeles: University of California Press, 1965) 37.

CONTRIBUTORS

NEIL BRENNER, editor, is Professor of Urban Theory and Director of the Urban Theory Lab (UTL) at the Graduate School of Design, Harvard University. His research focuses on urbanization and territorial regulation under contemporary capitalism, as well as on questions of concept formation, method, spatial representation and critique in urban studies.

Max Ajl is doing doctoral work in development sociology at Cornell University. He is an editor at *Jacobin and Jadaliyya*.

Hillary Angelo a PhD candidate in Sociology at New York University. Her research focuses on urbanization and conceptions of nature in Germany and the United States.

Álvaro Sevilla-Buitrago is Associate Professor of Architecture, Universidad Politécnica de Madrid. Blending radical history and critical sociospatial theory, his research is focused on the social history of planning and the capitalist reterritorialization of subaltern social reproduction. He is editor in chief of the Spanish journal *Urban*.

Danika Cooper is a Master of Landscape Architecture and Master of Design Studies candidate at the Graduate School of Design, Harvard University. Her research focuses on the intersection between landscape architecture, social policy and urbanization.

John Friedmann is Professor Emeritus in the Luskin School of Public Affairs at UCLA. Since 2001, he has served as Honorary Professor in the School of Community and Regional Planning at the University of British Columbia, Vancouver. His most recent book is *Insurgencies: Essays in Planning Theory* (Routledge 2011).

Matthew Gandy is Professor of Geography at University College London and was Director of the UCL Urban Laboratory from 2005 to 2011. He has published widely on urban, cultural and environmental issues, and has been a visiting professor at several universities including Columbia University; Technical University, Berlin; Humboldt University, Berlin; Newcastle University; and UCLA.

Brendan Gleeson is Professor of Urban Policy Studies at the University of Melbourne. His research interests include urbanization, planning, social policy and environmental change. He Is a Fellow of the Australian Academy of Social Sciences.

Kanishka Goonewardena was trained as an architect in Sri Lanka and now teaches urban design and critical theory at the University of Toronto. He co-edited *Space, Difference, Everyday Life: Reading Henri Lefebvre* and writes on space, ideology and capital.

David Harvey is Distinguished Professor of Anthropology and Geography and Director of the Center for Place, Culture and Politics at the Graduate Center of the City University of New York (CUNY). His most recent books are *The Enigma of Capital and the Crises of Capitalism* (2010) and *Rebel Cities* (2012). His earlier books—*Social Justice and the City* (1973), *The Limits to Capital* (1982), *The Urbanization of Capital* (1985) and *The Urban Experience* (1989)—continue to inspire generations of critical urban thinkers and activists around the world.

Ghazal Jafari is a Master of Design Studies candidate at the Graduate School of Design, Harvard University. Her current work is concerned with the intersection of information technology, digital media and the operational landscape of urbanization. She is cofounder of Op.N, a research and design office based in Cambridge and Toronto. www.op-n.net.

J. Miguel Kanai is Assistant Professor of Geography at the University of Miami where he has also been affiliated with the Urban Studies Program since 2008. He has published extensively on the urbanization of the world, particularly with reference to the Amazon Rainforest. Additionally, he is conducting research on the new cultural and neighborhood politics associated with the neoliberal worlding of Buenos Aires since the 1990s.

Nikos Katsikis is an architect and urbanist, and a Doctor of Design Candidate (DDesS) at the Graduate School of Design (GSD), Harvard University. His research seeks to contribute to an expanded understanding of the relation between cities and hinterlands building upon the notion of the hinterworld. He is co-editor of the forthcoming *New Geographies 06: Grounding Metabolism*.

Stefan Kipfer teaches in the Faculty of Environmental Studies at York University, Toronto. He is curious about politics, urbanization and social theory in comparative context.

Henri Lefebvre (1901-1991) was a Marxist philosopher, sociologist and urbanist whose work on space, urbanization, the state, everyday life, politics and struggle remains paradigmatic for Left theory and practice around the world. Among his major urban works are *The Right to the City* (1968; English translation 2006) and *The Urban Revolution* (1970; English translation 2003).

Other landmark works are *The Production of Space* (1974; English translation 1991) and a four-volume contribution to state theory, *De l'Etat* (1976-78; partially translated into English in 2009 under the title *State, Space, World*).

Garth Lenz's images of threatened wilderness and industrial impacts have been published and exhibited worldwide, and have anchored some of the largest and most successful conservation campaigns for over 20 years. He is a Senior Fellow in the International League of Conservation Photographers. Further details of his work can be found at www.garthlenz.com.

David Madden is Assistant Professor in the Department of Sociology at the London School of Economics, where he also teaches in the Cities Programme. His research and teaching interests include urban sociology, social theory, housing and public space.

Terry G. McGee is Professor Emeritus of Geography and former Director of the Institute of Asian Research at the University of British Columbia. His books include *The Urbanization Process in the Third World* (1971) and *Theatres of Accumulation* (1985) as well as the co-edited volume *The Extended Metropolis* (1991). In 2000, he was awarded the Award for Scholarly Distinction in Geography by the Canadian Association of Geographers (CAG).

Marcel Meili is an architect in Zurich. In 1987, he established his own firm in Zurich, together with Markus Peter. He has been Professor at the Faculty of Architecture of ETH Zurich since 1999, where he established and runs the ETH Studio Basel/Contemporary City Institute, together with Jacques Herzog, Pierre de Meuron, Roger Diener and

Christian Schmid. He co-authored the book, *Switzerland— An Urban Portrait*, as well as several other books and chapters on the urbanization of the territory.

Andy Merrifield is a writer, social theorist and urban geographer, author of numerous books, including *Metromarxism* (2002), *Dialectical Urbanism* (2002), *Magical Marxism* (2011) and *The Politics of the Encounter* (2013). His latest book, *The New Urban Question*, is forthcoming with Pluto Press in 2014.

Roberto Luis Monte-Mór is a Brazilian architect and planner, who teaches in the Graduate Programs in Economics and in Architecture, at the Federal University of Minas Gerais, Brazil. He has researched and published extensively on urbanization theory, urban and regional planning, and about the Brazilian Amazonia.

Christian Schmid is a geographer and urban researcher. He is Professor of Sociology in the Department of Architecture of ETH Zurich and is part of ETH Studio Basel/Contemporary City Institute. His scholarly work is on planetary urbanization in international comparison, and on theories of urbanization and of space. He is a founding member of the International Network for Urban Research and Action (INURA).

Edward W. Soja is Distinguished Professor Emeritus of Urban Planning at UCLA and Centennial Professor in the Cities Programme at the London School of Economics. He is among the most influential theorists of the contemporary global urban condition, and his works are widely read across the social sciences, humanities and planning/ design disciplines. His major books include *Postmodern Geographies* (1989), *Thirdspace* (1996), *Postmetropolis* (2000) and *Seeking Spatial Justice* (2010).

David Wachsmuth is a PhD candidate in sociology at New York University, researching urban political-economic restructuring in the United States. He was trained as an urban planner at the University of Toronto.

SOURCES

Ch. 1   Original contribution.

Ch. 2   Excerpted from Henri Lefebvre, *The Urban Revolution*, trans. Robert Bononno (Minneapolis: University of Minnesota Press, 2003) 1-7, 11-18, 165-80, slightly abridged from original.

Ch. 3   From *City* 1, 1 (1996) 38-61.

Ch. 4   From *Switzerland: An Urban Portrait, Book 1: Introduction*, eds. Roger Diener, Jacques Herzog, Marcel Meili, Pierre de Meuron and Christian Schmid (Zurich: Birkhäuser, 2006) 164-73.

Ch. 5   From *Architectural Design* 82, 1 (2012) 128-32.

Ch. 6   From *Landscript 1: Landscape, Vision, Motion*, eds. Christophe Girot and Fred Truniger (Berlin: Jovis, 2012) 138-55.

Ch. 7   From *Switzerland—An Urban Portrait, Book 3: Materials*, eds. Roger Diener, Jacques Herzog, Marcel Meili, Pierre de Meuron and Christian Schmid (Zurich: Birkhäuser, 2006) 919-27.

Ch. 8   From *Territorio, Globalização e Fragmentação*, eds. Milton Santos, Maria Adélia Aparecida de Souza and Maria Laura Silveira (São Paulo: Hucitec, 1994) 169-81.

Ch. 9   From *The Endless City*, eds. Ricky Burdett and Deyan Sudjic (London: Phaidon, 2007) 54-69.

Ch. 10 From *Urban Constellations*, ed. Matthew Gandy (Berlin: Jovis, 2011) 10-13.

Ch. 11 From *International Journal of Urban and Regional Research* 37, 3 (2013) 909-22.

Ch. 12 From *Public Culture* 25, 1 (2013) 85-114.

Ch. 13 From *Globalization of Urbanity*, eds. Josep Acebillo, Jacques Lévy, and Christian Schmid (Barcelona: Actar + Università della Svizzera Italiana, 2012) 51-77.

Ch. 14 Original contribution.

Ch. 15 Original contribution.

Ch. 16 From *Cadernos de Saúde Pública* 21, 3 (2005) 942-48.

Ch. 17 From *Switzerland—An Urban Portrait, Book 1: Introduction*, eds. Roger Diener, Jacques Herzog, Marcel Meili, Pierre de Meuron and Christian Schmid (Zurich: Birkhäuser, 2006) 175-85.

Ch. 18 From *The New Blackwell Companion to the City*, eds. Gary Bridge and Sophia Watson (Oxford: Blackwell, 2011) 679-89.

Ch. 19 Original contribution.

Ch. 20 From *City* 13, 2–3 (2009) 198-207.

Ch. 21 Original contribution.

Ch. 22 From *International Journal of Urban and Regional Research* (2013), in press.

Ch. 23 From *International Journal of Urban and Regional Research* (2013), in press.

Ch. 24 From *Environment and Planning D: Society and Space* (2013), in press.

Ch. 25 From *International Journal of Urban and Regional Research* (2013), in press.

Ch. 26   Slightly abridged and expanded from *Switzerland—An Urban Portrait, Book 1: Introduction*, eds. Roger Diener, Jacques Herzog, Marcel Meili, Pierre de Meuron and Christian Schmid (Zurich: Birkhäuser, 2006) 186-219.

Ch. 27   From *New Geographies 5: The Mediterranean* (Cambridge: Harvard Graduate School of Design, 2013) 215-34.

Ch. 28   Original contribution.

Ch. 29   Original contribution.

Ch. 30   From *Environment and Planning D: Society and Space* 30, 5 (2012) 772-87.

Ch. 31   From *City* 15, 3–4 (2011) 468-76.

Ch. 32   Original contribution.

Ch. 33   Original contribution.

Ch. 34   Originally published as "Quand la ville se perd dans une métamorphose planétaire," *Le monde diplomatique* (May 1989); republished in *Manière de voir* 114, *Le monde diplomatique* (December 2010/January 2011) 20-23.